D0890855

Violence and the Body

Violence and the Body

Race, Gender, and the State

EDITED BY **ARTURO J. ALDAMA**

FOREWORD BY ALFRED ARTEAGA

INDIANA
University Press

Bloomington & Indianapolis

This book is a publication of
Indiana University Press

601 North Morton Street
Bloomington, IN 47404-3797 USA

http://iupress.indiana.edu

Telephone orders   800-842-6796
Fax orders   812-855-7931
Orders by e-mail   iuporder@indiana.edu

© 2003 by Indiana University Press

All rights reserved

No part of this book may be reproduced or utilized in any form or by any
means, electronic or mechanical, including
photocopying and recording, or by any information storage
and retrieval system, without permission in writing from the
publisher. The Association of American University Presses'
Resolution on Permissions constitutes the only exception
to this prohibition.

The paper used in this publication meets the minimum
requirements of American National Standard for Information
Sciences—Permanence of Paper for Printed Library
Materials, ANSI Z39.48-1984.

Manufactured in the United States of America

Library of Congress Cataloging-in-Publication Data

Violence and the body : race, gender, and the state / edited by
  Arturo J. Aldama.
    p.   cm.
  Includes bibliographical references and index.
  ISBN 0-253-34171-X (alk. paper) — ISBN 0-253-21559-5 (pbk.
: alk. paper)
    1. Violence.   2. Social control.   3. Feminist theory.   4. Body,
Human—Political aspects.   5. Body, Human—Social aspects.
6. Race relations—Political aspects.   7. Sexism.   8. Marginality,
Social.   I. Aldama, Arturo J., date
HM1116.V557   2003
303.6—dc21   2002011358

1   2   3   4   5   08   07   06   05   04   03

H M
1116
.V557
2003

CONTENTS

Part 1. Global Crossings:
Racialized and Sexualized Conflicts

Part 2. Coloniality and the
Consumption of the Other

Part 3. Performing Race, Gender, and Sexuality

Part 4. Understanding "Trauma": The Psychic Effects of Material Violence

FOREWORD

The Red and the Black

ALFRED ARTEAGA

The violent act, the violent event, is a bodily occurrence. It is the sharp flash against flesh, and it is the blood-colored response. The red act is a rape, the tearing of genitals and the bruising of forced arms and choked neck. The red event is a head aflame in a state-sanctioned execution. The spilling of human blood is the fact of violence, and in those instances where it is not spilled, it nevertheless remains as the flow of life barely kept from the blows or beating by the thinness of human skin. Because our lives are metered in the flow of blood at every moment, its appearance, its color, accompany attacks on our lives. Violence, act and event, is red.

In the painful act of violence, in the stab and gunshot, and in the terrible event, in the massacre of bound prisoners of war, the flash of human red is more than a sign of violence; it is, in fact, violence incarnate. This is to say that the slash, the chokehold, and the beating with police batons are enacted in the disruption of the life flow. Violence is not apart from blood, but rather the hot articulation of it. It is a blood act; it is a red event. It is the red of death and the push toward death.

In the essays on violence—as in its epithets as well—we call on language to invoke the memory and image of the blood act and red event. For it is by use of signs that we conjure up violence after the fact. For the survivors of bloodletting, words can evoke the memories, almost like echoes, reverberating still in the tremble of the flesh. For others who are not the victims, language can call images of blood to the mind. Whether by analog memory or metaphor image, the linguistic act and event brings red to the fore.

To do so, we employ black: black graphemes on the otherwise blank. Through black alphabet and black typeface, we call to mind the attacks on the body. Black serves to articulate the memory and image of unspeakable acts and events. The disruption of blood is enacted in the black analog of ink and the digital black metaphor of pixel. It is by the absence of light and color that we denote violence. On the fields of all color, the white of page and screen, absence-shaped graphemes spell out pain, torture, killing.

For human gray matter, black is the link to red. It is true that the grapheme of absence is the means to recall act and event after the fact, that language transfers violence to us, but what of violence actually transfers? Does the violent impulse transfer, does its echo, does the shudder of split flesh? In other words, is the transfer a vital one, one by which the heat of act and event is conducted after the fact? Or is the transfer an image that recreates the body's red experience? Or is the transfer a creation anew?

The red of the body is real. Real bloodletting is real life spilled. And perhaps the black text is mimesis, absent of violence, or perhaps itself a violence. After the red fact of life cut into, language cuts consciousness by its absence, by its severance from blood and red. The linguistic act and event bring violence to mind in a manner that makes one question violence's presence in the mind, question the violence of thought after the fact. Absent text ascribes meaning to the shedding of red, but perhaps it is a meaning not linked to act, just as, conversely, perhaps the red act just occurs, devoid of meaning.

Are the words presented before you violent? Do the sentences evoke killing, rape? Literally, they do not. And yet while the red moments of electrocution may pass in little real time, its memory and story and meaning last as long as articulated from the black graphemes. After the fact, facts are remembered, recounted, and rendered meaningful.

For the Aztecs and Mexican natives, red and black were both the colors of writing and of existence itself. One vision held that human life was merely played out in the writing of the gods, that we were so much the absent grapheme if without divine articulation. The red and the black signified knowledge, for it is through writing that we know the awful truths of being human.

Violence and the Body

VIOLENCE, BODIES, AND THE COLOR OF FEAR
An Introduction

> On the eve of the twenty-first century, hatreds explode in such places as sarajevo, argentina, chechnya, rwanda, los angeles, and oklahoma city. The hatred embodies a complex set of fears about difference and otherness. It reveals what some people fear in themselves, their own "differences." Hatred forms around the unknown, the difference of "others." . . . Because people grow othered by their racialized, sexualized and engendered bodies, bodies are important to the writing of hatred on history.
>
> —Zillah Eisenstein, *Hatreds* (1996)

When bodies feel sudden fear, the adrenaline curve in the nervous system spikes in the first few milliseconds, provoking a fight-or-flight response with varying intensities in the physiology of individual subjects. Unlike the spontaneity of an individual lashing out, pushing off or running away fast, or the collective adrenaline surges of crowds in protests (e.g., the WTO protests in Seattle and the G-8 demonstrations in Italy), the sustained proliferation and normalization of fear in the "nervous system" of the body politic has different effects. The propagation and internalization of fear in the social body attempts to keep people docile, numb, silent, and afraid to challenge the status quo of racist, sexist, and global capitalist hegemonic ordering and orders in the United States and other Euro-Western nation-states.

Fear of unconformity, fear of race, fear of disease, fear of touch, fear of blood, fear of nonstraight sex, fear of workers, fear of desire, fear of women, fear of subaltern rage, fear of color, fear of desire, fear of crime, fear of "illegals," and the fear of uprising: Fear is both the metanarrative that drives the disciplinary apparatus of the nation-state (police, Immigration and Naturalization Service [INS], military, schools) and the intended effects on the body politic. Fear drives the repression, containment, coopting, torture, and annihilation of "unruly" subjects whose class, race, sex, and ideology identity differences, and indigenous land claims (for example) are threats to bourgeois, capitalist, patriarchal, and neocolonial orders. Fear drives the militarization of borders, antigay violence, abortion clinic bombers, the CIA, the NSA, xenophobia, the denial of imperial guilt, enslavement, lynchings, police, the Christian right, John McCain's and Pat Buchanan's *Death of the West* (2001), anti–affirmative action policies, Proposition 187, racial profiling, and *migra* shootings, to name of few.

DESIRE AND THE EROTICS OF FEAR

In patriarchal family systems that mimic the bourgeois or are bourgeois, young women are taught to fear their desire and feel shame at their bodies while at the same time seeking the "validating" gaze of "appropriate" young men. Men are taught to be fearless in their pursuit of desire. The rescue of desire by those seen as objects of desire invokes a desire that does not have to colonize and subjugate bodies to controllable fantasies of seduction, redemption, and disavowal. In the emerging nation-state of the Taliban pre–September 11, the fear of women and the control of sexuality in the guise of religious orthodoxy translates into an absolute obliteration of women and girls from participation in work, schools, and other aspects of public life. The disturbing image in the December 31, 2001, *New York Times* article by Dexter Filkins on women in the Taliban shows widows who are forced to beg because they are not permitted to work (A1, col. 4). These widows are clad in all-enveloping coarse burlap *burqas* with sewed-in mesh face plates that barely allow them to breathe in the stifling heat. This Kafkaesque image of institutionalized patriarchal control is made more disturbing by the fact that it is not fully anachronistic to premodern Muslim culture, but seems to belong to the cusp of the twenty-first century.

In the horrific spectacles of racial lynching, castrated limp bodies of black/brown men evidence the "blood erotics" of racial fear—the eugenic purity of the inheritors of America must be protected at all costs. As the antimiscegenation laws of colonial America attest, children produced through rape of women of color result in an increase in slave stock, a profitable investment. The fear that African, indigenous, and Mexican women have at being raped and violated with impunity and without any recourse does not count: it was irrelevant to the operation of white patriarchal power in colonial America. In the case of the colonial genocide of native peoples, in *Mixblood Messages*, Louis Owens comments (1998) on "the erotic nature of Euroamerica's desire to simultaneously possess and destroy the Indian" and argues that it "is nothing less than the indigenous relationship with place, with the invaded and stolen earth, that the colonizer desires" (124).

FEAR, THE STATE, AND RACE

In thinking about "state" violence toward "others" on the cusp of the twenty-first century—police shootings and beatings of suspected "illegals," gangbangers, an African American woman asleep in her car, or Mario Paz, a Mexican grandfather asleep and gunned down in his home—"officers of the law" justify their actions with fear. In arrest reports where lethal violence is used, it is common to see the following cited: "I thought the suspect had a gun." "I saw him reach in his pocket/her purse." "He/she ran away." In these scenarios, the "sudden movements" that fear in the "suspects" produces (an understandable physiological response) are justifications for the exterminating fear of the "officers." When officers prove fear of bodily harm on their persons by a suspect, usually validated only by word of mouth and with the corroboration of other officers who fear the consequences of challenging the blue wall of silence, then they have a clean shoot—another justified homicide.

The Scriptural Economy by Michel de Certeau reminds us that "there is no law that is not inscribed on bodies. Every law has a hold on the body" (139). For de Certeau, in "order for the law to be written on bodies, an apparatus is required" whose tools or instruments of inscription "range from the policeman's billyclub to handcuffs and the box reserved for the accused in the courtroom" (141). So for those who are criminalized and racialized by dominant bourgeois discourses, their bullet-ridden, handcuffed, kicked, stun-gunned, and baton-beaten bodies become semiotic generators of fear for subaltern communities in the United States. At the same time, these desecrated bodies serve to appease middle-class panic about the surging color of crime.

In the U.S.-backed death squads of Guatemala and El Salvador, officers are trained in the torture science of counterinsurgency at the School of the Americas in Fort Benning, Georgia. Torturers are trained to recognize the smell of fear in the subjects that they beat and mutilate as evidence that they are on the verge of being broken. The raped and mutilated bodies of suspected guerrillas are always tossed in shantytowns and busy streets as warnings to spread fear.

The intended effects of these fear-driven desecrations of subaltern bodies by the military state in the late twentieth century echo the flayed and torched bodies of women, Jews, and other heretics of Holy Inquisitions; the decapitated heads of "criminals" presented to the queen and king in medieval Europe; the severed heads of revolutionary leaders of Mexican independence from Spain in 1810; and the pickling of Joaquin Murieta's head during the California Gold Rush of 1850 for daring to confront the growing racial hegemony. These spectacles of hegemonic terror of previous centuries put into practice a psychic campaign whose purpose is to spread fear of insurgency to enslaved and oppressed communities: *"How dare you. . . . Look at the consequences. . . . This could be you."*

However, in the late 1990s and 2001, these spectacles of terror, where "real criminals get what they deserve," are now televised in such reality programs as *COPS* and *LAPD: Life on the Beat* and *America's Most Wanted*, further creating a voyeuristic approval between the use of technologically sophisticated disciplinatory violence, race, and class. Sloppy pan shots of the run-down white trash trailer parks, Spanish-speaking families in overcrowded one-bedroom apartments, single-mother welfare families in the projects, unkempt children, the beeping out of profanities, and a general visual tone of squalor are meant to cement the semiologic seal between poverty, race, and crime. Close-up shots of tattoos on the hands, arms, legs, necks, and backs of Chicanas/os who are hog-tied and laid facedown on the pavement give officers on *COPS* the opportunity to narrate directly to camera: "Just as I suspected. . . . another gang member." These "signs" of the criminality of subjects already criminalized as thugs and *cholas/os* further provoke the significatory practices of the Law and its multiphase violating apparatus. On the cusp of the twenty-first century, the paranoia of the racialized panoptic regime in the United States is directed inward at the "domestic" terrorists of inner cities (gangbangers) and at the edges of the United States–México border—to survey and contain what Pat Buchanan calls "the invading Mexican hordes"—and now to all those suspected as being terrorists.

As we begin this new millennium, Western nation-states attempt to seduce subject citizens into believing that we live in a borderless cyber "utopia," a cosmopolitan free market of e-commerce and anonymity. The cyber consumers and fantasists in the "fearless" cyber world continue the false magic of global capitalism, further marking the distance between elite consumers and hyperexploited producers of goods. The simulacrum of e-commerce masks the multidirectional movements of "free market" manifest destiny and depends on the learned fetishes for material commodities. You add to your "shopping cart" the latest and best commodity fetish— DVDs, digital zoomcams, and $49.99 Gap khakis. However, I ask: Who makes them and under what conditions? What happens to the ecosystems that are strip-mined, clear-cut, and irradiated by toxic waste? What happens to worker's children who drink water contaminated by unregulated industrial waste by the *maquiladoras* on the U.S.–México border? What happens to the young women in El Salvador, Honduras, and the Philippines who are fired, beaten, raped, and disappeared for protesting the horrific work conditions of "free trade" zone factories such as the Gap, Old Navy, and Nike? What happens to the software-producing ghettoes of south India? And what happens to social responsibility to hyperexploitation of subaltern workers, mainly women and children? Do they disappear with a click of a mouse? The "fearlessness" of cyber wealth is the fruition of the phantasmagoria of the "free market" whose violence of predatory capitalism is deadly.

The global proliferation of neocolonial predatory capitalism and its accompanying panoptic regime requires one to be politically creative and self-reflexive in our privileges, margins, and differences (race, nationalities, class, gender, and sexuality), cultural assumptions, and epistemologies. To resist the violence of predatory capitalism, we must learn to forge transnational and transethnic opposition coalitions that are fluid, multilevel, and sustained without becoming autocratic. Confronting "our" fear that alienation and neocolonialism produce will allow us to create new collective alliances of local and global political resistance.

VIOLENCE AND THE BODY: A SPACE OF RESISTANCE

It is in this spirit of coalitions of resistance that this volume, *Violence and the Body*, seeks to create a dialogic space (to use Bakhtin's term) to explore the relationships between discursive violence—that is, fear-based discourses of otherization and pathologization of subjects whose positions are at the margins and borders of dominant political and cultural apparatuses—and the materiality of violence on these otherized bodies. In doing so, *Violence and the Body* provides an alternative political and theoretical space where feminist work on the social constructions of the body (Judith Butler, Elizabeth Grosz, and Zillah Eisenstein) with women of color theories of the multiplicity of oppression and resistance (Norma Alarcón, Chandra Mohanty, Chela Sandoval, bell hooks, Angela Davis, Elaine Kim, Pat Hilden, and M. A. Jaimes Guerrero) can intersect to discern the materiality of physical and representational violence on the "otherized" body.

In trying to ground the "performance" of identity to the materiality of violence as both terminal and regenerative acts, *Violence and the Body* seeks to understand how physical and material violence forms and reinforces the structures of oppression that drive the interanimation of political and symbolic economies that are predicated on abject/subject subjugations and privileges. What Judith Butler's *Bodies That Matter* discusses as the "exclusionary matrix by which subjects are formed thus requires the simultaneous production of a domain of abject beings, those who are not yet 'subjects,' but who form the constitutive outside to the domain of the subject" (3).

In doing so, the purpose of this volume is to create a dialogue with and within the communities that comprise what Frantz Fanon's classic study poetically termed the *Wretched of the Earth*, whose colonial conditions of abjection, subalternity, and "slavery" (Bales)—especially for young women and children—are in some cases more extreme and oblique under the "new" social orders of the global economy. By discussing the operations, consequences, and strategies of resistance of communities and subjects designated as abjects, the analytic threads that tie the essays of this volume together are in keeping with Butler's important 1993 observation:

> The abject designates here precisely those "unlivable" and "uninhabitable" zones of social life which are nevertheless densely populated by those who do not enjoy the status of the subject, but whose living under the sign of the "unlivable" is required to circumscribe the domain of the subject. (3)

In tandem with this inquiry into how subjects whose positions are at the margins and borders of dominant cultural apparatuses and whose status of otherization, subalternity, and abjection are reinforced, regulated, and regenerated by physical violence, the major interest of this volume is to consider how discursive and physical violence on the body affects, injures, and traumatizes the interior psychic formation of subjects. Part of the inquiry that this volume proposes is to consider how the materiality of violence attempts to script and determine interior psychic space through the conduits of the body to reinforce the social structures that predicate privilege and access in the political and cultural economy. What Elaine Scarry's groundbreaking earlier study of torture and war, *The Body in Pain: The Making and Unmaking of the World,* discusses as the "dream" of a nation-state is to script the absolute interpellation, regulation, and control of its "unruly" subjects through pain and wounding of the body:

> The dream of an absolute, one-directional capacity to injure those outside one's territorial boundaries, whether dreamed by a nation-state that is in its interior a democracy or a tyranny, may begin to approach the torturer's dream of absolute nonreciprocity, the dream that one will be oneself exempt from the condition of being embodied while one's opponent will be kept in a state of radical embodiment by its awareness that it is at any moment deeply woundable. (80)

Part of what *Violence and the Body* asks is this: Is the goal of racial, sexual, and colonial violence to discipline and regulate otherized bodies and to traumatize interior psychic space—to mirror and map social colonialist rubrics of race, class, gender, and sexuality hierarchies? If so, how do these issues of trauma and injury[1] affect the ways in which subalternity and identity are understood and the ways in which subjects who negotiate the violence and trauma of racism, sexism, and heterosexism enact the agency of resistance and survival?

This edited volume, grounded in U.S.–México border and Latin American cultural studies, seeks to intersect discussions of subalternity, violence, and discourses of the body in a transethnic, feminist, and global cultural studies context. In Part 1, "Global Crossings: Racialized and Sexualized Conflicts," the essays engage with racial, sexual, neocolonial and antiémigré violence and its representation in Eastern Europe, France, Pacific Islander, and Filipina/o and among Latina/o, Asian American, and African American subjects. These essays provide a global mapping of contemporary modes and acts of physical and representational violence and point to how discourses of otherization are reinforced and interanimated through violence on what Elizabeth Grosz, in *Volatile Bodies,* refers to as the "intensities" and "flows" of the body. For example, my essay on borders and violence attempts to ground the rise of border theory and discourses of the "abject" (to use Kristeva's term) to the materiality of state violence on the bodies of Mexican border crossers and Chicana and Chicano youth.

Anikó Imre's "Hungarian Poetic Nationalism or National Pornography? Eastern Europe and Feminism—With a Difference" examines the propensity of sexual violence, the proliferation of survival sex economies, and the normalization of pornography in Eastern Europe as exalted forms of femininity that all women should embrace. Imre attempts to ground a feminist and postcolonial theory with the understanding of the materiality of physical and discursive violence against present-day Eastern European women in general, and Hungarian women in particular. Imre calls into question how the male-defined nationalist aesthetics of the contemporary cinematic and literary culture construct a narrative of womanhood and gender socialization, especially for subaltern Romani or Gypsy women, as objects of colonialist-like fetish and possession.

Yamuna Sangarasivam's "Militarizing the Feminine Body: Women's Participation in the Tamil Nationalist Struggle" explicates a subaltern feminist politics as an "insider" to the grassroots anticolonialist movement by the Liberation Tigers of Tamil Eelam to reclaim its material and cultural sovereignty in present-day Sri Lanka. Through interviews with woman cadres and an analysis of Tamil women cadre recruitment posters, she is able to discuss how Tamil women engage in an agency of empowerment in conditions of extreme state-sponsored "antiterrorist" violence. Her interest is to understand how the revolutionary fighters, such as women in Central America, redefine their roles as women and assert a newfound ownership and control over their bodies where patriarchal and sexual violence is exacerbated by daily military conflict.

The extreme to which women went in transforming the subjection and disciplining of their incarcerated bodies is clearly analyzed in Leila Neti's essay, "Blood and Dirt: Politics of Women's Protest in Armagh Prison, Northern Ireland." Neti analyzes how Northern Ireland's women prisoners' political protest utilizes a new symbolic weapon of protest, menstrual blood. They purposefully turned the "infliction of filth" by the guards as a form of punishment "into a means of protest by seizing control of the filth in order to in turn inflict it on the visual and sensory space of the guards."

Catherine Raissiguier's "Bodily Metaphors, Material Exclusions: The Sexual and Racial Politics of Domestic Partnership in France" provides a look into the unfulfilled promise of universal inclusion and integration in present-day France. She analyzes how the "deployment of anti-immigrant and antigay politics in the late 1990s have intersected to produce political and popular discourses that represent postcolonial immigrants and queers as threats to the national body." Specifically, the essay analyzes the conflu-ence of nativist and homophobic discourse in a completely irrational and ahistoric logic that circulates in the slogans of the popular French culture that state "Islam equals AIDS."

Rolando B. Tolentino's essay, "Mattering National Bodies and Sexuali-ties: Corporeal Contest in Marcos and Brocka," explores how the symbolic economy of the Marcoses' military regime actively constructed a represen-tation and spectacle of the presidential couple's bodies based on excess, costume, and virility. They flaunted an unlimited acquisition potential and performed almost allegorical extremes of masculinity and femininity. These spectacles of the presidential bodies of the first couple juxtapose the conditions of "national bodies" of the Filipino population (many of whom are engaged in the sex economy as a means of survival). During the Marcos regime (1965–1986), the majority of the Filipinas/os lived in conditions of extreme poverty, with alarming rates of malnutrition and preventable diseases.

The final essay of Part 1, Elizabeth Grosz's "The Time of Violence: Deconstruction and Value," returns us to the violence of language and epistemology and revisits Derrida's theory of the signifying process and deconstruction. She argues, "Contrary to this prevailing representation of Derrida's politics as a politics of negativism, nihilism, or anarchism . . . , he offers a profound, if unsettling, reconfiguration of political activity that centers on the question of violence." This section, which focuses on the materiality of physical and representational violence of the state in a trans-national lens, ends by considering the violence of how epistemology and the significatory processes of thought and language can engender and ma-terialize the violence that marks, otherizes, shames, and desecrates both the social and material bodies. This essay invites the readers of this volume to engage in a self-reflexive analysis of their own epistemic, analytic, and linguistic processes and their complicity with violence.

In considering these complex intersections of discursive violence and corporal resistance, Part 2, "Coloniality and the Consumption of the Other," connects the analysis of violence to the violence of European colo-nial expansion. The concern of this section is the violent construction of non-Western subjects in pathological and inferior terms. These construc-tions of colonized subjects through colonial discourse mitigate, deny, and displace the violence of the colonial regimes on lands, resources, and bod-ies consumed and recycled by what Robert Young, in his 1995 book *Colo-nial Desire,* calls the colonialist "desiring machine" that has predicated social relations since the sixteenth century. For example, Mike Hayes, in

"Consuming Cannibalism: The Body in Australia's Pacific Archive," considers "Australian and Aotearoa/New Zealand texts on cannibalism in the Pacific" from the eighteenth to the twentieth centuries to explicate the simultaneous fascination with and the need for subjugation of the diverse Pacific Islander communities. Hayes's argument centers on the realization that the "cannibal" is an invented simulacrum produced and consumed by colonialism. He states, "While decrying cannibalism as barbaric and representative of 'primitive' cultures, the Western authority consumes the body of the cannibal and trades the flesh as trophies of the success of Western religion, science, or entertainment."

M. A. Jaimes Guerrero's "Global Genocide and Biocolonialism: On the Effect of the Human Genome Diversity Project on Targeted Indigenous Peoples/Ecocultures as 'Isolates of Historic Interest'" analyzes how the biomedical industry and the Human Genome Project itself take the legacies of colonial violence on indigenous peoples across the globe to new extremes of "consumption" on the global market. Guerrero analyzes the bioprospecting agendas of the pharmaceutical megacorporations that seek to patent raw genetic materials and knowledge systems from the full-blooded bodies of indigenous peoples for biomedical research, with the tacit assumption that these peoples will soon die out. Guerrero's timely analysis links the eugenically based biocolonial agendas of genetic and biomedical industries to the genocide, ethnocide, and ecocide that affect the current physical and cultural survival of more than seven hundred indigenous groups, scientifically labeled as "isolates of historic interest."

Dennis Childs's "Angola, Convict Leasing, and the Annulment of Freedom: The Vectors of Architectural and Discursive Violence in the U.S. 'Slavery of Prison'" continues the analysis of how the brutality of U.S. plantation slavery has reconstituted itself in the Angola prison in Louisiana. Angola Prison, called "The Farm," has moved from being a slave plantation to a convict lease space to a state penitentiary that houses a disproportionate number of African American men. Childs considers how the normalization of racial violence during slavery intersects with a type of architectural violence to create what he terms the "structural terror" of the prison cell, which shares an alarming similarity in both space dimensions and design to the ship compartments that brought the abjected bodies of Africans across the Atlantic.

Jonathan Markovitz's "Bernhard Goetz and the Politics of Fear" looks at white rage and white panic as a way to justify and mitigate vigilante-like violence by considering Bernhard Goetz's subway "self-defense" shooting of African American teenagers. Markovitz astutely points out how the media and public opinion polls quickly cast Goetz as a victim and hero, showing how acts of violence—the finality of a bullet shot—can be literally constructed and "read" depending on the subject position of the perpetrator and victim. The reception of Goetz ties into larger historical patterns of acceptance and denial of justifiable and nonjustifiable violence that undergirds the legally bound fabric of colonially formed race relations in the United States.

Margarita Saona's "Pierced Tongues: Language and Violence in Carmen Boullosa's Dystopia" examines how Carmen Boullosa's 1997 novel *Cielos de la Tierra* engages with how native Mexican Indian bodies negotiate their agency and resistance in the colonial dystopia of the Americas. Saona considers how colonized subjects use language as a means to articulate one's body and pleasure and how the reclamation of the "mother tongue" is necessary to reconstruct one's symbolic and material body fractured by regimes of male-centered colonial and neocolonial violence.

Part 3, "Performing Race, Gender, and Sexuality," reinserts issues of agency on subjects affected by violence and engages with how identity is performed by subjects at the margins of nation-states and of cultural and patriarchal cultural economies. Several of the essays complicate discussions of violence on bodies away from explicit acts of state apparatus violations (police, military, INS prisons), hate crimes, domestic violence, rape, and abuse. These essays deal with a type of representational politics where subaltern subjects give consent and seek to have external features of their ethnic and gender identity manipulated and removed to match the interiority of their desired identities with their surgically manipulated "body space."[2] For example, William Anthony Nericcio's (Guillermo Nericcio García's) "When Electrolysis Proxies for the Existential: A Somewhat Sordid Meditation on What Might Occur if Frantz Fanon, Rosario Castellanos, Jacques Derrida, Gayatri Chakravorty Spivak, and Sandra Cisneros Asked Rita Hayworth Her Name" considers how the famous transborder Hollywood figure, Rita Hayworth, born Margarita Cansino, crosses the border from Tijuana, México, to Hollywood. To transform from Cansino to Hayworth, Rita allowed her body to be literally de-ethnicized through permanent cosmetic adjustments to her hairline and hair color to assume and then radiate Anglocentric norms of femininity and beauty. Rita thus engages in a type of reverse ethnic and feminine minstrelsy, converting her visage and body type to a form of "passing" into the U.S. mainstream with the use of racialized cosmetic surgery.

Heidi Rimke's "Constituting Transgressive Interiorities: Nineteenth-Century Psychiatric Readings of Morally Mad Bodies" opens Part 3 by considering how nineteenth-century psychiatry constructed deviant, transgressive, and morally mad "interiorities" based on a subject's markings of physiological difference from a bourgeois eurocentric norm. Rimke eloquently argues that "the scientization of corporeal difference came to be inscribed as biological and physiological registers of pathological interiorities. As an exterior representation of abnormal, inferior, dangerous, or deranged interiorities, bodies provided a way in which to evaluate psychical constitution that, inter alia, was deduced from corporeal 'natures.'"

Sel J. Wahng's "Double Cross: Transmasculinity and Asian American Gendering in *Trappings of Transhood*" considers the transgender and biracial performance of identity by video artist Christopher Lee. Lee, an FTM (female to male transsexual), literally "disidentifies" (Muñoz) and reconfigures gender and ethnicity to perform a transgendered and ethnic space of masculinity that challenges how Asian American men have been symbolically castrated by the U.S. dominant culture, in keeping with war propaganda. In Wahng's reading, Lee redefines the physiological and psychic hierarchies that exist between female and male subjectivities, creating a third space that confronts the violence of gender and racial formation.

Elaine H. Kim's "Teumsae-eso: Korean American Women between Feminism and Nationalism" expands the discussion of how Korean American women construct and defend their subjectivities in the masculinist, gendered, and racialist violence of both nation-states: Korea and the United States. Her essay contributes to an understanding of the transnationality of violence that travels through several loci of social power in each nation-state. Kim argues that on one hand, Korean American women must defend themselves "against the material violence occasioned by racial and sexual discrimination and political and economic inequality in the United States and the psychic violence of both abjection and homogenization into conceptual invisibility by the U.S. racialized state." On the other hand, Kim points out that Korean American women are berated in Korea for not being submissive enough, being too concerned with the equality of gender rights and the restoration of social dignity to comfort women (women forced into prostitution and shunned), and selling out to the West.

The essay "Mapuche Shamanic Bodies and the Chilean State: Polemic Gendered Representations and Indigenous Responses," by Ana Mariella Bacigalupo, a Chilean feminist anthropologist, contributes to the understanding of performance of indigenous identity in the matrix of patriarchal and neocolonial violence of the Chilean nation-state. Bacigalupo discusses how the machis, traditional Mapuche healers who have withstood more than five hundred years of physical and cultural genocide, defend their precolonial-based nonbinary articulations of gender and cast into crisis the accepted and fixed notions of masculinity and femininity. Even though the machi healers are still pathologized and infantilized (and, in the case of anatomic males, the subject of homophobic ridicule and rage) and their practices relegated to the status of "primitive" *brujería* superstitious witchcraft, they are crucial to the healing and maintaining of the Mapuche social fabric. According to Bacigalupo, the machi's agency lies in their ability to juggle diverse systems of knowledge, including gender roles. Her interactions with two machis, Maria and Sergio, show how the machi chart spaces of resistance to the colonialist heteronormativity of the Chilean nation-state to perform gendered rituals of healing that syncretize, subvert, and decolonize in the name of restoring balance to the diseased body.

Part 4, "Understanding 'Trauma': The Psychic Effects of Material Violence," seeks to add new directions in scholarship that consider the issues of trauma and injury and that query the relationship between the physical and discursive acts of violence and their effects on the interiority of a subject. Part of what this section seeks to accomplish is a discussion of the relationship between the exteriority of a subject manifested in the physicality of the body, and the type, interpretation, and effects of violence that are registered according to a subject's position in the loci of race, class, gender, and sexuality hierarchies. As *Raising the Dead: Readings of Death and (Black) Subjectivity,* by Sharon P. Holland, reminds us, "Bodies are still marked—by sex and/or pigmentation—so they are not subjected to discourse so much as discourse is constructed around certain bodies so that others may survive, thrive, and evolve. *Power is literally felt and realized differently depending on the loci of race, class, sex, and sexuality*" (32; emphasis added).

Yvette Flores-Ortiz, a Chicana/o Studies professor and practicing clinical psychologist, in "Re/membering the Body: Latina Testimonies of Social and Family Violence," provides an important analysis of the multiple sustained traumatic effects of physical and sexual abuse on Latinas who already negotiate the violence of racism and sexism in the United States. In the discussion of "how social and familial injustice is encoded in the body, resulting in what Western psychology labels depression, dissociation, and anxiety," Flores-Ortiz considers how abuse victims practice a range of self-destructive practices and suffer from the effects of posttraumatic stress disorder. She interestingly ties both the victimization of Latinas and internalization of this trauma in terms of self-blame to the larger sexist patterns of seeing women as intrinsically traitorous and blameworthy. In the case of México and among Chicanas/os in the United States, the colonialist trope of La Malinche (Hernán Cortés's translator), who is still blamed for the conquest of México, continues today as a way to label women and those perceived as cultural sell-outs.

In similar terms, Sunita Peacock's "Sita's War and the Body Politic: Violence and Abuse in the Lives of South Asian Women" continues the discussion of familial and domestic violence among South Asian women immigrants who internalize "blame" for their own abuse, coupled with the language, cultural, and legal barriers they negotiate as non-European immigrants in the United States and Canada. Unaware of their rights, fearful of deportation, and fearful of being shunned by their extended families and friends in a country that is alien to them, these women are afraid to report abuse and to seek proactive solutions outside of the family structure. Peacock illustrates how already sexist cultural and religious structures assume new forms of oppression and violence in the immigrant communities that enslave and isolate women in the domestic sphere.

The analysis of patriarchal violence is continued in David William Foster's "Arturo Ripstein's *El lugar sin límites* and the Hell of Heteronormativity," in which Foster examines how homophobic violence is tied to the contradictions of hypermasculinity in his reading of *El lugar sin límites*, a disturbing and important film by avant-garde Mexican filmmaker Arturo Ripstein. *El Lugar* tells the story of "La Manuela, a transvestite prostitute killed by one of her preferred customers for having gone too far in insinuating a questioning of his masculinity as regards his preference for men cross-dressed as women over supposedly real women." Foster queries the contradictory logics of a machismo that promotes an intense homosociality and homoeroticism among men, whose heterosexuality is defined by hanging with the men, and whose heterosexism, the sexual dominance of women and violence against gays, is performed for the benefit and approval of other men. In his reading, Foster illustrates how the death of La Manuela, as the abject/object of male desire, is necessary to "cleanse" and "purify" (Girard) the institution of patriarchal power that sustains itself through the violent enforcement of its heteronormativity.

Lessie Jo Frazier's "Medicalizing Human Rights and Domesticating Violence in Postdictatorship Market-States" considers how the authoritarian regimes of state terror in Chile and Argentina have shifted from military to civilian rule. However, Frazier argues that the postdictatorship societies continue to carry spaces of death that violently enforce bourgeois patriarchal structures of social and legal power predicated on an amnesia of its own violence. Frazier points out that the discourse of healing, reconciliation, and democracy in civil society does nothing to promote the rights of women, children, gay and lesbians, the elderly, and those in extreme poverty. The irony for the patients who continue to seek mental health counseling for the trauma they negotiate as a result of surviving a brutal military dictatorship is that they are diagnosed as suffering from individualized personality disorders.

The 1999 volume *Between Woman and Nation,* edited by noted feminist scholars Caren Kaplan, Norma Alarcón, and Minoo Moallem, makes the following important observation that attests to the collective agency of women subordinated by the nation-state:

> Modern nation-states participate in the institutionalization of women's subordination by means of regulatory processes, the discursive formations that construct and discipline citizen-subjects. Yet, the quotidian practices that regulate women, nation and state can be subverted by local community networks and relations out of which emerge a civil arena to counter masculinist nationalist agendas. (12)

In keeping with this observation, the final essay by Cynthia L. Bejarano, "Las Super Madres de Latino America: Transforming Motherhood and Houseskirts by Challenging Violence in Juárez, México, Argentina, and El Salvador," looks at the disappearances, killings, and sexual mutilations of young women, mainly *maquiladora* workers, in Juárez, México, in the 1990s. She considers how working-class Mexican women organized themselves into a group called Voces Sin Echo (Voices without Echo) to protest how the local authorities and media cast the *desaparecidas* (disappeared) as prostitutes and "loose" women. Bejarano compares how the Juárez group Voces Sin Echo, like the CoMadres of El Salvador and the Madres de la Plaza de Mayo in Argentina, create forms of protest and opposition that attempt to hold the state accountable for the violence and its unwillingness to prosecute the violators. In doing so, these grassroots groups of subaltern women transform the items and symbols of domesticity (pots, pans, shawls, brooms, and altars) into vehicles of protest and solidarity for all victims of violence.

Finally, I want to thank the more than four hundred fifty scholars from all over the globe who submitted their proposals and essays for this volume. It is truly heartening to see how scholars are touched to the nerve by how racial, sexual, and discursive violence plays itself out on the bodies of those made subaltern by that violence. I dedicate this volume to those bodies that have been violated by the violence of history, and to all those who continue, like the mothers of the disappeared, to organize and put their bodies on the line to bring social justice to the bodies oppressed, mutilated, and disappeared by the terror of violence. Also, I dedicate this volume to Balbir Singh Sodi, a Sikh man from the Punjab in India, who was shot a few miles from my house in Mesa, Arizona, because he looked like an Arab terrorist. This volume is also dedicated to all victims of hate crimes like Matthew Shepard, Teena Brandon, and James Byrd Jr.; to all those in Rwanda, Bosnia, Germany, and the Américas decimated by a genocide based on a pathologized "otherness."

NOTES

1. For a psychoanalytic discussion of trauma as a way to understand the psychoanalytic effects on witnessing and surviving the Nazi Holocaust, see Shoshana Felman and Dori Laub, *Testimony*. Also consider Carl Gutierrez-Jones, *Critical Race Narratives*, which seeks to expand the notion of "racial injury" as a way to discuss institutional racism, the racialization of crime, and the normalization of punitive violence toward people of color in the United States.

2. For an important discussion of the rise of "aesthetic" surgery and how it fulfills racial and gender scripts, see Sander Gilman's *Making the Body Beautiful*, 85–119.

RECOMMENDED READINGS

Bales, Kevin. 2000. *Disposable People: New Slavery in the Global Economy*. Berkeley: University of California Press, 2000.

Bouson, J. Brooks. *Quiet as It's Kept: Shame, Trauma, and Race in the Novels of Toni Morrison.* Albany: State University of New York Press, 2000.

Butler, Judith. *Bodies That Matter: On the Discursive Limits of Sex.* New York: Routledge, 1993.

de Certeau, Michel. *The Practice of Everyday Life.* Berkeley: University of California Press, 1988.

Eisenstein, Zillah. *Hatreds: Racialized and Sexualized Conflicts in the Twenty-First Century.* New York: Routledge, 1996.

Fanon, Frantz. *The Wretched of the Earth.* Translated and edited by Constance Farrington. New York: Grove Press, 1986.

Felman, Shoshana, and Dori Laub. *Testimony: Crises of Witnessing in Literature, Psychoanalysis and History.* New York: Routledge, 1992.

Foster, Gwendolyn A. *Captive Bodies: Postcolonial Subjectivity in Cinema.* New York: State University of New York Press, 1999.

Gilman, Sander L. *Making the Body Beautiful: A Cultural History of Aesthetic Surgery.* Princeton, N.J.: Princeton University Press, 1999.

Girard, Rene. *Violence and the Sacred.* Translated by Patrick Gregory. Baltimore, Md.: John Hopkins University Press, 1979.

Grosz, Elizabeth. *Volatile Bodies: Toward a Corporeal Feminism.* Bloomington: Indiana University Press, 1994.

Gutierrez-Jones, Carl. *Critical Race Narratives: A Study of Race, Rhetoric, and Injury.* New York: New York University Press, 2001.

Hartman, Saidiya V. *Scenes of Subjection: Terror, Slavery, and Self-Making in Nineteenth Century America.* New York: Oxford University Press, 1997.

Holland, Sharon P. *Raising the Dead: Readings of Death and (Black) Subjectivity.* Durham, N.C.: Duke University Press, 2000.

Kaplan, Caren, Norma Alarcón, and Minoo Moallem, eds. *Between Woman and Nation: Nationalisms, Transnational Feminisms and the State.* Durham, N.C.: Duke University Press, 1999.

Muñoz, José. *Disidentifications: Queers of Color and the Performance of Politics.* Minneapolis: University of Minnesota Press, 1999.

Price, Janet, and Margrit Shildrick, eds. *Feminist Theory and Body.* New York: Routledge, 1999.

Scarry, Elaine. *The Body in Pain: The Making and Unmaking of the World.* New York: Oxford University Press, 1985.

Slattery, Dennis P. *The Wounded Body: Remembering the Markings of Flesh.* Albany: State University of New York Press, 2000.

Terry, Jennifer, and Jacqueline Urla, eds. *Deviant Bodies.* Bloomington: Indiana University Press, 1995.

Young, Robert J. C. *Colonial Desire: Hybridity in Theory, Culture, and Race.* New York: Routledge, 1995.

Part 1. Global Crossings: Racialized and Sexualized Conflicts

Chapter 1

Borders, Violence, and the Struggle for Chicana and Chicano Subjectivity

ARTURO J. ALDAMA

> The events of 1836 brought forth charges of Mexican depravity and violence, a theme which became pervasive once Anglos made closer contact with the state's Hispanic population following the war. In the crisis of the moment, firebrands spoke alarmingly of savage, degenerate, half-civilized, and barbarous Mexicans committing massacres and atrocities at Goliad and the Alamo.
> —Arnoldo de León, *They Called Them Greasers: Anglo Attitudes toward Mexicans in Texas, 1821–1900* (1983)

> We were thrown out of just about everywhere, but what really made me feel bad was when we tried to go into a restaurant or a restroom downtown, and we were told, "No you can't use it." The police would always come and say, "This is a public place, you have to get out, you're not allowed here."
> —Maria Elena Lucas, *Forged under the Sun/Forjada bajo el Sol* (1993)

Chicana/o border studies, devoted to understanding the complex dialectics of racialized, subaltern, feminist, and diasporic identities and the aesthetic politics of hybrid mestiza/o cultural production, is at the vanguard of historical, anthropological, literary, cultural, artistic, and theoretical inquiry. This essay is an invitation to situate the diverse practices of critical U.S.-Mexican borderland inquiry in the historical moment of a new millennium, with all the promises and anxieties that these times produce. For our inquiry, one of the most important of these anxieties is the unkept promise that ensued from the signing of the Treaty of Guadalupe Hidalgo more than 150 years ago. This treaty signed at the end of the U.S.-Mexican war resulted in the formation of the U.S.–México border and the forced purchase of northern México for $15 million (California, New Mexico, Texas, Arizona, Nevada, Utah, and parts of Colorado, Oklahoma, and Kansas), as well as the supposed protection of property and civil, cultural, and religious rights of Chicanos and Mexican peoples.[1] Disturbed and outraged by the continued prevalence of historical patterns of criminalization, marginalization, dispossession, civil rights violations, and torture in Chicana/o and other subaltern communities, my essay seeks to contribute to the field of critical border studies by exploring the relationship between discourses of otherization crystallized by the U.S.-México border (racial, sexual, ideological) and state-enforced acts of violence (Immigration and Naturalization Service [INS], paramilitary, and police) on the bodies of Mexicana/o and Latina/o immigrants and Chicana/o youth.

"Shifting Borders, Free Trade, and Frontier Narratives," by Pamela María Smorkaloff, summarizes the movement of critical border studies as it responds to specific geopolitical locations. Smorkaloff considers the ways in which theorists, writers, and performance artists map transfrontier social space challenging monologic sociopolitical forces that maintain national borders: "Transfrontier writers and theorists are developing a kind of syncretism of the first and third worlds in their writing that captures not only the complex reality of the border zone, but also a more profound understanding of the contemporary US and the Latin America living within" (97).

In similar terms, *Border Writing* by D. Emily Hicks examines the dialectics of transfrontier identity and border writing. Hicks uses the concept of border crossings as a metaphor and a tool to analyze the heterogeneity of identity in Latin American writing. Even though the bulk of the text focuses on two major Argentinean writers, Julio Cortázar and Luisa Valenzuela, Hicks begins the study by discussing the U.S.–México border region and concludes it by returning to Chicano and Mexicano writing in the U.S.–México border regions.

Hicks argues that border writing "emphasizes the differences in reference codes between two or more cultures" (xxv), expressing the "bilingual, bi-cultural, bi-conceptual reality" of border crossers. However, Hicks is emphatic in positing that border writing is about crossing cultural borders and not physical borders. This leads to her disturbing characterization of the U.S.–México border as a theater of "metaphors" where "actors"— *pollos* (undocumented border crossers), *la migra* (INS), and *coyotes* (contractors who bring undocumented people over the border)—act their daily "dramas." Hicks creates a universalizing model that moves beyond concrete historical understandings of subaltern Latina/o "border crossers" as "real people" responding to "real" geopolitical social realities and understands their experiences as a type of carnivalesque and postmodern theater. In doing so, Hicks deracinates the individuality of people—their/our specific histories, and family and community ties—who negotiate the often violent border crossing for such reasons as poverty, hunger, political persecution, as well as the desire to reunite with loved ones, or a simple curiosity to see life *al otro lado* (on the other side).[2]

The foundational anthology *Criticism in the Borderlands*, edited by José David Saldívar and Héctor Calderón, grounds the discussion of transfrontier ideology in a concrete geopolitical zone. This anthology challenges the exclusionary practices of the American literary academy and the formation of the canon by recovering "neglected authors and texts" in the "Southwest and the American West." The work also provides a forum for diverse theoretical perspectives: "Chicano/a theory and theorists in our global borderlands: from ethnographic to post-modernist, Marxist to feminist" (6). What renders the anthology even more significant to the growth of critical border studies is the argument by its contributors that Chicano theoretical analyses can move from a regional understanding of relations of power to a global one without denying the historical specificities of each geopolitical locale.

In an earlier essay, "Limits of Cultural Studies," Saldívar articulates the cultural and border studies imperative in more detail, arguing that cultural studies must be both regional and global: "Finally, cultural studies, a border zone of conjunctures, must aspire to be regionally focused, and broadly comparative, a form of living and of travel in our global borderlands" (264). In this essay, Saldívar critiques the subjectifying forces that inferiorize and homogenize non-Western peoples in the social relations of power, and he discusses how scholarly practices replicate these forces. Saldívar shares in the British cultural studies understanding of culture as a dynamic and heterogeneous site where tensions of domination and resistance compete, linking these principles to forge a greater understanding of borders, resistance, and mestizaje. By studying the "subordinate and dominant cultures like public schoolchildren in Great Britain or low riders and *cholos* in East Los Angeles," Saldívar argues that cultural studies is committed to "transforming any social order which exploits people on the grounds of race, class, and gender." Cultural studies and border theory challenge "the authority of canon theory and emergent practice" and the relations of power which sustain this authority (252). After setting up his critique of monologic tendencies in anthropological practices, Saldívar surveys several key border writers, "native informants" Rolando Hinojosa, Gloria Anzaldúa, Guillermo Gómez Peña, and Renato Rosaldo. Saldívar argues that these writers offer counternarratives to the master narratives of nations that attempt to normalize identity and totalize cultural heterogeneity. Saldívar summarizes their writings as "cultural work" that "challenges the authority and even the future identity of monocultural America" (264).

Saldívar's *Border Matters*, a dazzling and impressive study of border writers, artists, musicians, theorists, and scholars, dramatically builds on this critique of the master narratives that author the hegemonization of "monocultural America." Saldívar argues that

> U.S.-Mexico border writers and activist intellectuals have begun the work of exploring the terrains of border crossing and diaspora amid the debris of what El Vez calls our "national scar" of manifest destiny and the cultures

of the U.S. imperialism. . . . The history of migration, forced dispersal in the Américas as represented in the vernacular border cultures, challenges us to delve into the specific calculus of the U.S.-Mexico border crossing condition. (197)

In similar terms, "Beasts and Jagged Strokes of Color," by literary scholar and Chicano poet Alfred Arteaga, addresses the multidimensional intersection of real and discursive forces along the U.S.–México border— the border patrol and Tex-Mex *caló*, for example—by discussing the formation of the Chicana/o subject in relation to tensions produced by the border. With reference to Chicano poet Juan Felipe Herrera's "Literary Asylums," a heteroglossia of voices subjectified by and resistant to competing discourses of the nation-state, Arteaga states:

> "Literary Asylums" and other Chicano poems play in a poetics of hybridization that calls to mind the quotidian cultural politics of hybridization in the material space of the frontier. What is at play is the formation of a Chicano subject coming to be amid the competing discourses of nation. (91)

Arteaga continues his discussion of Chicano poetics of hybridization or dialogic poetics by grounding the discussion in the material border. Arteaga considers the purpose of the border as intended by the nations at stake—the United States and México:

> Consider the border: in the imagining of nation, it is the infinitely thin line that truly differentiates the US from México. The absolute certainty of its discrimination instills confidence in national definition, for it clearly marks the unequivocal edge of the nation. Its perceived thinness and keenness of edge are necessary for the predication of national subjectivity, which defines itself as occurring inside its border and not occurring outside. (92)

Arteaga observes how "the thin borderline cleaves two national narratives, two national monologues of ideal and finalized selves" (92). Central to Arteaga's argument is the tension between the monologic tendencies of national narrative and the dialogic, interlingual, and hybridizing impulses of Chicana/o subjects and their literary expression. Arteaga locates the border zone as a site that is lived and expressed by those marginalized by nationalizing forces and who reside in the physical/discursive interstices and margins generated by the border.

The border for Arteaga is a site of power that selectively privileges and marginalizes, reinforcing social hierarchies along axes of race, class, nationality, and sexuality. He compares the experience of elite Mexican bourgeois Octavio Paz—who knows himself to be fully Mexican when crossing the border, a line that reinforces his imagined singular self—with that of Chicana-Tejana lesbian theorist and writer Gloria Anzaldúa, who argues that "borders are set up to define the places that are safe and unsafe, to distinguish us from them. The prohibited and the forbidden are its inhabitants" (94).[3]

However, to consider the experience of Mexican immigrants or émigrés crossing the border from the south, I assert a series of propositions that add to Arteaga's discussion of the multivalent nature of the U.S.–México border. At the outset, I need to clarify that these assertions on the effects of the border for Mexicans traveling north reflect the socioeconomic conditions of peoples who do not enjoy the privilege of such national subjects as Paz and other bourgeois elite who can demonstrate to the visa-granting embassy in México City, Ciudad Juárez, or Tijuana that they have sufficient economic ties to México—bank accounts, businesses, and high-status occupations. As border performance artist and poet Gerardo Navarro states in his reference to the "apartheid" of the border, the Tortilla Curtain (as many refer to the U.S.–México border) operates like "a valve that is closed or opened by the invisible hands of the market in accord with the fluctuations in Wall Street and in the global market" (4). My propositions are as follows:

1. The border serves as a "free zone" for U.S. citizens and U.S. corporations (U.S. border crossers). The free zone applies, among others, to weekend tourists crowding the bars, drinking cheap beer, and seeking male and female prostitutes, and to U.S. companies exploiting "cheap" labor and lax environmental regulation controls.[4]
2. Contrary to the free zone where all Euro-American taboos drop, the border is also a free zone of violence, a barrier to those trying to cross from the south—as evidenced by the Border Patrol, weekend vigilantism, bandits, and *coyotes* who, after collecting their fees, rob, rape, and denounce border crossers.
3. Even though the border is selectively open to those whose class positions confirm their tourist and student status, it forces a discourse of inferiorization on Mexicans and other Latinos, especially those whose class position, ethnicity, and skin color emerge from the *campesina/o* and urban proletariat groups.
4. Finally, once crossed, the border is infinitely elastic and can serve as a barrier and zone of violence for the Mexican or Latina/o who is confronted by racialist and gendered obstacles—material and discursive—anywhere he or she goes in the United States. This means that the immigrant continually faces crossing the border even if he or she is in Chicago (or wherever in the United States)—a continual shifting from margin to margin.

In no way do these propositions give breadth to the infinite variety of experiences and struggles for Mexicans and other Latin American immigrants moving across and through this infinitely elastic border to the

United States. The immediate questions that the border poses are these: How can we chart the multiple vectors of forced liminalities produced by the U.S.–México border? Is it enough to say that "no matter where a Mexican travels or lives in the United States, he or she always inhabits an economic, racial and discursive status that is automatically secondary and perpetually liminal?"[5]

In *Shadowed Lives,* an important study of contemporary Mexican immigration, Leo R. Chávez understands liminality as a state of living in the shadows. Chávez illustrates the liminality in concrete terms with the following description of a family trying to visit Disneyland from San Diego: "Undocumented immigrants frequently told me that because of their illegal status they were not free to enjoy life, often citing as an example the fact that they were unable to take their children to Disneyland because of the immigration checkpoint at San Clemente" (14).

On February 1, 1997, the Rocky Mountain regional conference of the National Association of Chicana and Chicano Studies took place in downtown Phoenix, Arizona. The event was an inspirational gathering of scholars from a wide variety of disciplines, Chicana/o studies department chairs, community leaders and activists, cultural workers and students dedicated to promoting the interdisciplinary and multifaceted field of Chicana/o studies, as well as to reigniting further consciousness regarding the marginalized and uneven status of the Chicana/o communities. My participation in this rich *encuentro* of scholarly and political knowledge made me question further the roles of critics and scholars dedicated to Chicana/o studies as we begin the new millennium.

Specifically, I balance the wonderful gains that the field of Chicana/o studies has witnessed—a proliferation of interdisciplinary scholarship, an increased focus on issues of gender and sexuality, the recent establishment of the Chicana/o Studies Department at Arizona State University, an increased enrollment of Chicana/o students at all levels, and further support for Chicana/o graduate students—with the realization and recognition that there are still negative constants facing the Chicana/o community.[6] Examples of these constants are: (1) continued economic marginalization, (2) substandard housing, schooling, and general public services, (3) extremely high incarceration rates,[7] and (4) an increase in the sophistication and deployment of violence, especially toward Chicana/o youth and Mexicana/o immigrants, including those residents and citizens of Mexican descent unfortunate enough to get caught in immigration or *migra* sweeps. Regarding Chicana/o youth, their style of dress, music, and art is categorically demonized and criminalized by the dominant culture, thus continuing hegemonic patterns of demonization and the concomitant violation of youth seen most dramatically during the "Zoot Suit Riots" (1940s) and the repression of Chicana/o youth believed to be associated with the Brown Berets (1970s), and in the treatment of the youth suspected of being involved in gangs (1940s to the present), who are now called "urban and domestic terrorists."[8]

Also, there is a continuing increase in the sophistication of methods of surveillance, weaponry, capture, and detainment in the Chicana/o communities by such state and federal agencies as the INS and state and county police and sheriffs. Growing technological sophistication, coupled with a continuance of brute force and strategies of deception, are evidenced by the use of infrared technologies, video surveillance, bulletproof vests, assault rifles, and laser tracking devices, as well as such vulgar ruses as informing alleged "illegals" that they need to show up at a warehouse to claim their televisions and cars—prizes that they supposedly won by lottery—only to be captured, detained, and deported.[9]

I ask these unsettling questions: What does it mean for me to write as a Chicano on the cusp of the new millennium, more than 500 years after the full-scale invasion of the Américas—the usurpation of lands, the wholesale rape and slaughter of indigenous peoples, the forced importation and brutal enslavement of African peoples, and the institutionalized criminalization and marginalization of the Chicana/o community? What is my responsibility to the past, to the present, and to the future, as well as to the practice of representation? What does it mean for me to enter into the practice of methodologies that empower peoples who have not only been physically colonized—the "Other," the "marginal," the "subaltern"—but also intellectually colonized by apparatuses of representation that reify their status as savage with all of the connotations of barbarism, inferiority, and childlike innocence that accompany such an identification?[10]

We celebrate the epistemological shifts that feminist, multiethnic, postmodernist, and postcolonial discourse provides us scholars, writers, activists, and theorists.[11] We rally together with freedom to discuss and analyze the social formations of the subject and the hybridity of forces that impinge on and constitute the subject.[12] The epistemological shifts in the politics and practice of ethnography, literary criticism, and cultural studies free us up to discuss the micro- and macropolitics of how subjects are formed, positioned, and represented in both social and discursive economies. We challenge each other to implement interdisciplinary methods that embrace the heterogeneous nature of social reality.

As critics, writers, and theorists of communities and histories that are our own, we, as insiders and outsiders, call for the questioning of borders and an end to neocolonialism, to racism, to sexism, and to homophobia, as well as to the devastation of ecosystems through agribusiness and mining, and the timber industry. At the same time, however, in even the seconds, minutes, hours, and days that I write and think about this project and about ways to discuss subaltern peoples in liberating terms, funds are being transferred electronically. The funds pass into the "borderless" global free trade market, legalized by such international accords as the

General Agreement on Tariffs and Trade (GATT) and the North American Free Trade Agreement (NAFTA); yet travel for subaltern peoples— Mexicanos and other Latinos, for example—is highly restricted by militaristic border patrol agents. If the travelers and refugees cannot prove sufficient economic ties to their home country, they have to run like *pollos* (a slang term which literally means "chickens" and refers to border crossers)—hungry, stressed, and avoiding robbery, assaults, and rape by a variety of predatory groups, and human rights abuses by the INS—to cross the border into *el Norte,* or *el otro lado,* where they will live in fear of deportation and racial harassment, and suffer extreme exploitation. Put simply, money travels; people can't (well, at least some people).[13] For example, consider the following depiction of the potential hazards of crossing the U.S.– México border in *Across the Wire* by Luis Alberto Urrea:

> Now say that you are lucky enough to evade all these dangers on your journey. Hazards still await you and your family. You might meet white racists, complimenting themselves with the tag "Aryan." They "patrol" the scrub in combat gear, carrying high-powered flashlights, rifles, and bats. . . . And of course there is the Border Patrol (*la migra*). (17)

Labor-intensive sweat factories, *maquiladoras,* are built in the "free-trade zones" of México, Central America, and Southeast Asia to take advantage of extreme inequities in global pay scales. Mexican, Salvadoran, and Filipino women and children are hired not only because they are the most exploitable in local economies, but also because they are perceived to have nimble fingers and rapid hand–eye coordination. Thankful to have some job in a crippling economic crisis, they race to meet their production quotas in fourteen-hour days, with two strictly enforced bathroom breaks of ten minutes each, so that U.S., Arab, Japanese, and European consumers, as well as the bourgeois consumers of each producing country, can buy Gap clothes and Nike shoes at ever-greater discounts, and in a greater variety of styles.[14]

In trying to understand the larger patterns of race, class, and gender oppression, as well as movements of capital on the global stage that inform a given historical moment and contextualize a given literary, cultural, and social text, the importance of specific peoples and individuals affected by these plays of power is easily overlooked. To do this, discourses and movements of oppression and resistance need to be analyzed at the level of the body and personhood to illustrate how they have "real" consequences for "real" people. I say this aware that statements on the "real," the "individual," and the "person" could imply that I am recapitulating notions of the fixed, stable autonomous subject—a concrete, knowable, a priori subject—so idealized by Western metaphysics. To do this would disregard or repress what poststructural, postcolonial, and feminist thought has taught us regarding the social construction of subjects.[15]

However, I ask: How is the diverse play of heterogeneous discourses that constitute human subjectivity (re)understood when subjects are shot at, chased, detained, raped, and incarcerated because they are of a certain ethnic group, sexuality, and gender; or, with respect to Mayan, Kenyan, and Mexican workers, for example, because they are demanding some kind of union protection for their labor; or, in the case of Chicana/o youth, because they are walking home from school and get caught in an INS sweep? Perhaps the dialectic that drives discursive practices of inferiorization and materialist practices of repression is precisely that: the "play" of human subjectivity is handcuffed, imprisoned, deported, and violated in acts of containment and repression by monologues of dominance and denial which state and enforce: "You are Other . . . You are Alien . . . You are Messican . . . You have no rights . . . You are unnatural . . . You are a beast." In *Borderlands/La Frontera*, Gloria Anzaldúa eloquently speaks to the violent otherization of Chicana/os and other peoples marginal to the dominant Euro-American culture:

> Gringos in the U.S. Southwest consider the inhabitants of the borderlands transgressors, aliens—whether they possess documents or not, whether they're Chicanos, Indians or Blacks. Do not enter, trespassers will be raped, maimed, gassed, shot. The only "legitimate" inhabitants are those in power, the whites and those who align themselves with whites. Tensions grip the inhabitants of the borderlands like a virus. Ambivalence and unrest reside there and death is no stranger. (4)

A dramatic example of how anti-Mexican immigrant discourses of otherization and dehumanization translate into acts of state-enforced physical violence was the brutal April 2, 1996, Riverside County, California, sheriff beatings of Mexican immigrants, called by many "another Rodney King beating" because of the extreme and brutal nature of the physical batterings. To recount the dramatic footage, a truck full of Mexicanas/os and Latinas/os, allegedly "undocumented" subjects, is being vigorously pursued, first by Border Patrol agents, then by Riverside County sheriffs through "parts of Riverside, San Bernardino and Los Angeles counties before ending on Pomona Freeway about 20 miles east of Los Angeles" (*CNN Interactive*, Web post 11:05 A.M., April 2, 1996). The truck is so old and worn that it literally starts deconstructing. At the height of the pursuit, pieces of the fenders and siding start to fly off onto the freeway; the truck motor is shaking and the suspension is pushed to its ultimate limits. A large group of people grip what is left of the shell on the back. After the truck veers to the side, those who can escape flee into the nearby brush, but the situation is much different for those left in the cab. Video footage clearly shows how one sheriff swings his baton at least six times with full force on the male driver, who offers absolutely no resistance, and more dramatically, both sheriffs repeatedly strike a woman on the passenger seat with their batons, even though Alicia Sotero-Vásquez offers no physical resistance and goes limp as a rag doll. One of the sheriffs viciously "pulls her to the ground by the hair" (*CNN Interactive*). This disturbing event illustrates the absolute unambiguity in the violation of the civil and human rights of these suspected "illegals" and asks the following question: Does having the status of "illegal alien" ascribed to you because of your physical and linguistic characteristics and your appearance legalize violence against your person and community?[16] I ask: Will these actions, which speak so directly to the impunity with which state-enforced violence occurs and which nakedly reflect the brutality of the relationship between the United States and Mexican and Latina/o immigrants, be the ones that propel us into the new century?[17]

In the case of police, paramilitary, and INS bullets shooting "Others" (as well as fatal violence from other coercive agents of the dominant culture, such as neo-Nazi vigilante groups or thugs hired by *finca* owners), the historicity and vitality of subaltern subjects are stopped and driven into annihilation by the monologism of the state. Persons whose bodies are violated and nullified—and who are characterized in such abject terms as "greaser," "drunken Indian," "black gangbanger," "Jap stealer of jobs," or "Castro-loving *indio*"—are remembered only in the collective consciousness of each person's family and community. The impunity with which these deaths and violence occur only reinforces the subaltern and abject status of these subjects and communities.

Powers of Horror, by the prolific psychoanalytic feminist scholar Julia Kristeva, argues that abjection, the most extreme form of otherization, is the process that expulses, then mutilates, defiles, and desecrates anything that is deemed alien and opposed to the "I" of the Self: "Abjection, on the other hand, is immoral, sinister, scheming and shady: a terror that dissembles, a hatred that smiles, a passion that uses the body for barter instead of inflaming it, a debtor who sells you up, a friend who stabs you." To illustrate the politics of abjection further, Kristeva reflects on her visit to the halls of the Auschwitz museum where she observes "a heap of children's shoes" and "dolls" under a "Christmas tree." Kristeva eloquently observes: "The abjection of Nazi crime reaches its apex when death, which, in any case, kills me, interferes with what, in my living universe, is supposed to save me from death: childhood, science, among other things" (4).

Bodies that are marked as "Other" because of race, class, gender, sexuality, ethnicity, religion, and political affiliation become sites where power brands subjects, turning them into social abjects: invisible, subversive (un-. . .), libidinal, and violent, and in the case of slavery, branded objects to be bartered, sold, and literally worked to death. An example in classic American literature comes to mind: Nathaniel Hawthorne's *The Scarlet Letter,* where the letter "A," cut from crimson cloth, "brands" Hester Prynne, marking her body as Other for transgressing the sexual taboos and cultural mores of puritan society. Another instance where power literally brands subjects—turning them into social abjects—is the yellow cloth stars and serial numbers worn by and tattooed on the arms of Jewish peoples in Germany and Europe during World War II. These violently engraved "signs" of otherization and abjection compare to the literal hot-iron branding of the skin of African and indigenous slaves in the Américas (and other areas of colonial conquest) that marked their bodies not only as Others, but also as property or commodities of the colonial overlords.[18]

The Conquest of America, by Bulgarian linguist and critic Tzvetan Todorov, is a landmark study of the ideological justifications and methods of the conquest of the Américas which resulted in the horrific genocide of more than 90 percent of the indigenous populations: More than seventy million people died between 1500 and 1650 due to direct murder and warfare, slavery, and work cónditions, as well as the "microbe shock" of diseases unknown in the Américas—smallpox, syphilis, and cholera (133–37). Todorov recalls Vasco de Quiroga's description of the slave traffic and the practice of branding indigenous peoples, first by the royal seal of Spain, then by the individual brands of the Spanish *encomenderos* or royally appointed overlords in the so-called New World.

During the first years after the conquest, the slave traffic flourished, and slaves often changed masters: "They are marked with brands on the face and in their flesh are imprinted the initials of the names of those who are successfully their owners; they pass from hand to hand, and some have three or four names, so that the faces of these men who were created in God's image have been, by our sins, transformed into paper" (137). Todorov analyzes further the physical consequences of enslavement and observes the horrific effects of the Spanish abjection and desecration of the indigenous Other to a literal "trunk" of "flesh":

> Enslavement, in this sense of the word, reduces the other to the status of an object, which is especially manifested in conduct that treats the Indians as less than men: their flesh is used to feed the surviving Indians or even the dogs, they are killed in order to be boiled for grease . . . all their extremities are cut off, nose, hands, breasts, tongue, sexual organs, thereby transforming them into shapeless trunks. (175)

Nez Percé historian and cultural studies critic Patricia Penn-Hilden calls the Anglocentric cultural hegemony, among others imposed by the colonizing forces in the Américas, the "overculture" or the *überculture*. This term resonates directly with the fascist culture of dominance in wartime Germany. I can't help but recall that at the height of the Nazi genocide of Jews, gays, and Romanian Gypsies, officers of the Third Reich loved to show off the lamps made from stretched Jewish skin.[19] In trying to understand how Euro-American, Spanish, and even Mexican *übercultures* (as with all nation-states) operate in multidimensional ways—power circulates and dis-

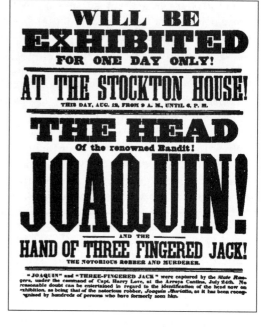

FIGURE 1.1.
The first known poster
advertising the exhibition,
in Stockton, California,
August 12, 1853, of the
bandits' remains.

perses on multiple fronts, layers, and vectors—I argue that the trajectories
of an overculture end, only to then regenerate themselves in the complete
abjection and desecration of the Other. To illustrate this process of abjection, desecration, and regeneration in the history of the U.S.–México borderlands, one needs only to examine the consequences of figures who were
perceived as threats to the race- and gender-coded social order of the
United States. One example is the case of the renowned social bandit of
the 1850 California Gold Rush, Joaquín Murieta, who after being perse-
cuted, ambushed, and executed, was decapitated, after which his head was
pickled and put on a traveling display; or the case of the shrunken head of
Mexican revolutionary leader Pancho Villa, a prized collector's item among
prominent Western capitalists.[20] Consider the reprint of an 1853 poster
advertising the traveling exhibition of the "The Head of the Renowned
Bandit! Joaquin!" (Figure 1.1).[21]

According to *The Life and Adventures of Joaquin Murieta, the Celebrated
California Bandit* (1854) by Yellow Bird (or John Rollin Ridge, a Cherokee-
Anglo crossblood), Captain Love, the commissioned California ranger who
captured Joaquín Murieta, was paid much more than the "sum of one
thousand dollars," the reward money posted for the capture of the "bandit, dead or alive" by the governor of California: "And subsequently, on

the fifteenth day of May 1854, the legislature of California, considering that his truly valuable services in ridding the country of so great a terror—were not sufficiently rewarded, passed an act granting him an additional sum of five thousand dollars" (158).

In addition, perhaps the starkest example of legalized vigilante violence in the California Gold Rush years aimed at the Mexicana/o community in general, and women in particular, is the barbaric lynching of Josefa Vasquez, a pregnant woman from Sonora, México. In 1851, Vasquez, popularly known as Juanita de Downieville, in an attempt to defend herself against vile verbal abuse and rape in her own home, stabbed and killed Fred Cannon, a well-liked Anglo-American miner. By four o'clock that afternoon, when a kangaroo trial "proved" that Juanita was an "antisocial prostitute" and Cannon was a "peaceful" and "honest" man, Vasquez was lynched. *Occupied America*, by Rodolfo Acuña, a Chicano historian, evokes this tragic and brutal moment:

> Senator John B. Weller was in town but he did nothing to stop the hanging. Weller was an ambitious politician who was later to become governor, and one voteless Mexican made no difference. Over 2000 men lined the river to watch Josefa hang at the bridge. After this, lynching became commonplace and Mexicans came to know Anglo-American democracy as "Linchocracia." (119)

I mentioned the conquest of the Américas and the violent aftermath of the U.S.–México war for the Mexicana/o community in the United States, as well as the violence of state repression and the violence of hyperexploitation, in order to ground the discussion of identity in the "real" world of contemporary social relations where, I argue, the lives of the "Others"—Chicanas/os, Latinas/os, Mayan women, Salvadoran campesinas, Turks, Tunisians, Asians, and gays and lesbians, to name a few—still have little meaning within cultures of dominance (the *übercultures*). In the case of the Américas, the torture of individuals—inquisitions of the late twentieth century—is now called interrogation or intelligence gathering. To induce a confession, CIA-refined science uses techniques of pain dating back to the Spanish Inquisition, developed by the infamous fifteenth-century inquisitor Tomás de Torquemada, as well as the most advanced surgical, electrical, and video technologies. The modus operandi includes electrocutions and incisions, which are extremely painful but show little on the skin, and violent beatings. In addition to these practices, people are subjected to audiovisual recreations or simulations of loved ones and comrades being tortured or confessing to their crimes against the state, with the goal of inducing and intimidating the insurgent "subjects" into admitting to whichever crime or crimes the state has decided that they committed. These "scientific" techniques, along with other methods of repression, are taught by U.S. military advisors to the members of a given military regime who are fighting, in the words of both groups, "the communist terrorists" (in, e.g., El Salvador, Nicaragua, or Guatemala), or they are taught in a more systematic way to officers of a given military regime in Latin America "lucky" enough to attend the "School of the Americas," whose campus is at Fort Benning, Georgia.[22] The scrivener's pen of the Inquisition is now replaced by ready-to-sign typewritten forms and the video cameras that film the subject's "confession." These victims of torture are dressed in clean shirts and heavily made up with powder to cover bruises and swollen faces.[23] Videotapes of torture are prized commodities on the underground market that circulates "snuff films," child pornography, and materials about bestiality and necrophilia.

In cases of imperial conquests, counterinsurgency, repression, and torture, the body is literally broken apart and reconstituted: people are imprisoned, starved, and beaten; bones are broken; muscles are ripped; skin is flayed and burned; body hair is ripped out by the roots or shaved with a rusty razor; women and men are raped and sodomized; and in more extreme cases, bodies are dismembered and decapitated. The following questions are crucial in engaging these realities: What is the relationship between the body and the subject? Can subjects, enveloped by conditions of intense physical domination by the state, maintain a sense of their own subjectivity while the body is being repressed and tortured? Or is torture and repression precisely the point at which subjectivity is reconstituted via the channels of the body? The Other, the insurgent subject, is obliterated, used to obliterate others, or made into a model citizen, obedient to the laws and morals of the state.[24] I ask: What does resistance mean within these conditions?

In the contemporary urban context of the United States, I ask: How do we theorize about or respond to such acts of power on the body, which are an all-too-familiar sight in poor neighborhoods in the United States, where Chicanas/os, Latinas/os, African Americans, Native Americans, Southeast Asians, and the homeless—the Others of Anglo-American society—are bent over with their cuffed hands pulled back or are lying facedown with arms spread, each like a fallen crucifix? As a visual semiotic, what is the "language" of an arrest scenario? When an officer has somebody cuffed, bent over, or facedown in order to search for drugs or weapons, the way in which that officer intervenes into the body of a "suspect" betrays a violent posture of invasion. In the case of male officers collapsing the body of male suspects, there is a homoerotic possibly in denial of itself that underpins heterosexist and patriarchal culture.[25] What do the bodies of both the officer and "suspect" become in these situations? Are they "texts" where the micro- and macrophysics of power can be read? Are the police and military the agents of master narratives whose discourse and practice suppress the Other as a countertext?

Furthermore, what does "resistance" (in the cultural studies sense of the word) mean in these situations where people are severely beaten or killed because, in the words of an officer, they "resisted arrest"? In fact, as I wrote these words, a young Chicano from Oakland, California, was lying in the hospital in a coma because he had resisted arrest. The story that circulated on the local Spanish-speaking stations recounted that officers, at the request of the victim's family, came to arrest him because he was drunk. When he staggered because of his intoxication, his body was interpreted as resisting arrest. Police threw the young man down with such force that he received a severe concussion, putting him in a coma.

In the United States, a rise of theories, testimonials, and histories is empowering the marginal, the Other, the people of color, the poor, and it is mounting political challenges to create a fair and just multicultural society. All of this, however, is tempered by the implementation of cuts in federal aid for education, welfare for single mothers, and job training; the end of affirmative action; increasing prison, police, and border patrol budgets; and the enforcement of laws against sodomy and other "unnatural" sexual relationships. For people of color in general, and for Chicanas/os in particular, more police translates into more harassment, more beatings, and more unexplained deaths.[26] More prisons, more police, fewer educational opportunities, and no job training means that more disenfranchised youth—*cholas/os* and "homeys"—will act out the rage of racism, alienation, and poverty by shooting and raping each other for their *clicas,* their sets, their streets, and their colors—red or blue.[27] Meanwhile, "Middle America" retreats farther into fortified suburban ethnic enclaves, buying guns, locking the doors to their houses and cars, fearing robbery, assault, and carjacking. At the same time, people glue themselves to their TV sets to watch the "heroic regulators" of postmodern society confirm their worst fears of the Other in such prime-time hits as the filmed-on-location *COPS* or *LAPD,* further denigrating subaltern peoples, especially African Americans and Spanish-speaking Latinas/os, and normalizing police brutality. As we enter a new millennium, to be a witness, a victim, and a participant requires from us a state of alarm—that we write, teach, resist, and act with urgency.

Linguistic violence—the creation of the Other—interanimates violence on the body. However, the present chapter engenders further questioning. For example, taking into account the scenarios mentioned above, how do we theorize on the social text of violence? Is it a language of social relations? If so, what is the *langue* and *parole* of violence? Is violence both the fringe and the center of social relations, as well as the enforcer of the social order in a given historical and cultural context? How does the consideration of physical violence affect conceptions of race, class, ethnicity, gender, and sexuality? In general, future analyses need to focus directly on the interrelationship of discourse, violence, resistance, and the body. Specifically, they must aim to understand further how Chicana/o bodies are "raced," "sexed," and "Othered" by discourses and practices of abjection, as well as how Chicanas/os reclaim our bodies, enunciate our subjectivities, and articulate a resistance of the spirit and the flesh.

I end this essay by considering the death of Julio Valerio, a 16-year-old Chicano teenager from Phoenix, Arizona, whose violent and brutal killing provoked an emotional and focused panel at the National Association of Chicana and Chicano Studies, as well as other acts of community support around issues of police violence and racism. According to the *Arizona Republic*, "Six officers fired a total of 25 rounds—20 from 9mm handguns, five from shotguns" (November 17, 1996). Six fully armed, non-Hispanic officers with bulletproof vests and extensive training in arrest procedures—and whose collective physical weight was easily over a thousand pounds—were not able to subdue the slim and distressed youth without the use of lethal force. When the Phoenix police force faced public outcry, Mike Pechtel, president of the Phoenix Law Enforcement Association, responded as follows: "'For their efforts, these officers are being vilified by opportunist politicians, whose support for a dope selling, dope smoking gang member is disgusting," drawing on the rhetoric of the War on Drugs as a way to validate the appalling use of violence on youth (*Arizona Republic*, November 26, 1996). Thus, the vicious police execution of this Chicano teenager, gainfully employed at a furniture factory and with dreams of owning his own home and taking care of his family, was justified because he was perceived as a "drug-crazed, knife-wielding gangbanger." However, the knife Valerio carried was in all probability so dull that it could have been a butter knife.

NOTES

This essay first appeared in *Decolonial Voices: Chicana and Chicano Cultural Studies in the 21st Century* (Indiana University Press, 2002). José Saldívar, Vicki Ruiz, Sonya Saldívar-Hull, Ramon Gutiérrez, Teresa McKenna, Norma Alarcón, Alfred Arteaga, Gloria Anzaldúa, Rolando Romero, Homi Bhabha, and James Clifford have made substantial contributions to critical border studies. I am especially indebted to Dr. Vicki Ruiz and Dr. Manuel de Jesus Hernández-Gutierrez at Arizona State University for their insightful comments on this essay.

1. This border was established after the defeat of General Santa Anna through the Treaty of Guadalupe Hidalgo in 1848. This border is literally a straight line more than 2,300 miles long that has no respect for natural ecosystem formations or tribal territories. Yet this arbitrary and intentionally rigid line has immense consequences for both nations. See Gutiérrez.

2. For a critique of Hicks's often-cited work, see Bruce-Novoa and Cordoba.

3. See Gloria Anzaldúa's *Borderlands/La Frontera*, which catalyzed the rise of border theory and discourse in the late 1980s.

4. For a discussion of how border cultures resist and subvert these tendencies,

see Guillermo Gómez-Peña's consideration of hybridity and carnival along the border in "Border Culture" and *Warrior for Gringostroika.*

5. As a term, the word "immigrant" is problematic in understanding Mexican people. What is the status for Mexicans who lived in Mexican territories before they were annexed by the Treaty of Guadalupe Hildalgo in 1848? For a discussion of identity for recent immigrants, see Rouse and see Rosaldo, both of whom discuss cultural invisibility for undocumented workers in the United States.

6. See Maciel, ed.

7. See Vicki Ruiz, "And Miles to Go . . . ," which charts systematically low wage earnings of Chicanas. For a discussion of the criminalization of the Chicano community and the resultant incarceration rates, see López, ed.

8. For discussion of the systemic and historic criminalization of the Chicana/o community from the Treaty of Guadalupe Hidalgo to the present, see Mirandé, and see Trujillo. For studies that attempt to understand Chicana/o youth cultural expression on its own terms, see Bright and Bakewell, eds., and see Martinez.

9. The deceptive tactic of the INS was brought up in a talk by Dr. Lisa Magaña on the dual roles of the INS, given at Arizona State University in spring 1997.

10. For discussion of the savage in European colonial imagination, see Hanke; and see White; for how the idea of the savage was used to justify the colonization of non-European peoples in general, see Robert C. Young, *Colonial Desire,* 1–29; and for the savagization of Chicanas/os in specific, see Mirandé; and De León.

11. My use of "we" is a strategically essentialist act (Spivak) of imagining a community (Anderson) of cultural studies scholars, writers, and activists who are concerned with challenging racism, homophobia, sexism, and colonialism in our scholarly and theoretical work and the larger academic and nonacademic communities.

12. For good summaries of the social construction of the subject from a wide range of critical trajectories, see Paul Smith; and Alcoff. For discussion of the postcolonial hybrid subject, see Bhabha; Young. For discussion of social constructivism in feminist thought, see Fuss.

13. See Sassen.

14. See the National Labor Committee Education Fund in Support of Worker and Human Rights in Central America, investigation updates of the Gap clothing company in El Salvador, October 1995; also see their video, *Zoned for Slavery: The Child behind the Label.*

15. See the following: Firdous Azim, *The Colonial Rise of the Novel,* 1–34; Sidonie Smith, *Subjectivity, Identity and the Body,* 3–14; and Caren Kaplan.

16. To appreciate further this act of racially coded nation-state violence reenacted in the form of a video clip, visit the following Web site: <http://cnn.com/US/9806/12/immigrant.beating/index.html>. Accessed June 5, 2002.

17. Although Alicia Sotero-Vásquez and Enrique Funes Flores, hospitalized for the vicious beatings by Riverside County Deputy Tracy Watson and Deputy Kurtis Franklin, will share a $740,000 settlement provided by the Riverside County, California, Sheriffs Department, these officers will not face any indictments for civil rights violations. See <http://cnn.com/US/9806/12/immigrant.beating/index.html>. Accessed June 5, 2002.

18. See Takaki; Forbes.

19. See Goldhagen.

20. See Vanderwood and Samponaro, *Border Fury,* which in general details how the Mexican Revolution became a spectator sport for Euro-Americans who would sit on bleachers next to the Rio Grande; in particular, it shows how any memorabilia of General Pancho Villa became highly sought-after collector's items after his death.

21. Downloaded from <http://www.calweb.com/~rbbusman/outlaws/mur-head.gif>. Accessed October 30, 2001.

22. See the documentary *School of the Americas, School of Assassins* (Maryknoll World Productions, VHS, 1994).

23. Much of my commentary is informed by the following testimonies: María Teresa Tula, *Hear My Testimony*, and Rigoberta Menchú, *I, Rigoberta Menchú*.

24. See Scarry.

25. A most poignant example of this type of violence is the case of the Haitian immigrant Abner Louima, who was viciously tortured and sodomized with a toilet plunger by officers Schwarz, Volpe, Bruder, and Weise of the New York Police Department, August 9, 1997. See the following CNN Web site: <http://cnn.com/US/9709/08/police.torture/index.html>.

26. Examples of this are two police killings of "dubious" circumstances that come straight to mind. See "The Mendocino Murders," *San Francisco Bay Guardian,* June 7, 1995, 15–18, which recounts how Leonard Davis, a tribal person from the Round Valley Reservation, was "mistakenly" shot dead by an M-16-toting sheriff's deputy. Also, I think of Aaron Williams, a local African American who died as a result of police brutality. See "12 S.F. Cops Accused by Chief of Lying," *San Francisco Chronicle,* November, 27 1995, A-1, which discusses how seven officers are accused of covering up their brutality, which unjustifiably killed Aaron Williams.

27. Chicano/Latino gangs in San Francisco are split by *Norte* (north), symbolized by the color red, and *Sur* (south), symbolized by the color blue, paralleling splits in the African American gangs: the Bloods (red) and the Crips (blue). However, I refer to an event that has troubled many activists who work with Chicano/Latino youth in the Mission area of San Francisco, where two adolescent girls were abducted, gang raped, and sodomized by the opposing gang (North: Red).

REFERENCES

Acuña, Rodolfo. *Occupied America: A History of Chicanos.* 3rd ed. New York: Harper and Row, 1988.

Alcoff, Linda. "Cultural Feminism versus Post-Structuralism: The Identity Crisis in Feminist Theory." *Signs* 13 (1988): 405–36.

Anderson, Benedict. 1983. *Imagined Communities: Reflections on the Origin and Spread of Nationalism.* London: Verso, 1987.

Anzaldúa, Gloria. *Borderlands/La Frontera: The New Mestiza.* San Francisco: Spinsters/Aunt Lute, 1987.

Arteaga, Alfred. "Beasts and Jagged Strokes of Color." In *Chicano Poetics: Heterotexts and Hybridities,* 91–100. Cambridge: Cambridge University Press, 1997.

Azim, Firdous. *The Colonial Rise of the Novel.* London: Routledge, 1993.

Bhabha, Homi K. *The Location of Culture.* London: Routledge, 1994.

Bright, Brenda Jo, and Liza Bakewell, eds. *Looking High and Low: Art and Cultural Identity.* Tucson: University of Arizona Press, 1995.

Bruce-Novoa, Juan, and María Cordoba. "Remapping the Border Subject." *Discourse* 1–2 (fall–winter 1995–1996): 32–54, 146–69.

Chávez, Leo R. *Shadowed Lives: Undocumented Immigrants in American Society.* Fort Worth, Tex.: Harcourt, 1992.

Clifford, J., and G. Marcus, eds. *Writing Culture: The Poetics and Politics of Ethnography.* Berkeley: University of California Press, 1986.

De León, Arnoldo. *They Called Them Greasers: Anglo Attitudes towards Minorities in Texas, 1821–1900.* Auston, Tex.: University of Texas Press, 1983.

Forbes, Jack. *Columbus and Other Cannibals.* New York: Automedia, 1992.

Fuss, Diana. *Essentially Speaking: Feminism, Nature and Difference.* New York: Routledge, 1989.

Galeano, Eduardo. *Memory of Fire I: Genesis.* Translated by Cedric Belfrage. New York: Pantheon Books, 1985.

Goldhagen, Daniel. *Hitler's Willing Executioners: Ordinary Germans and the Holocaust.* New York: Knopf, 1996.

Gómez-Peña, Guillermo. "Border Culture: A Process of Negotiation towards Utopia." In *The Broken Line/La Linea Quebrada* 1, no. 1 (May 1986). San Diego/Tijuana: A Border Arts Publication, 1986.

———. *Warrior for Gringostroika: Essays, Performance Texts, and Poetry.* St. Paul, Minn.: Graywolf Press, 1993.

Gutiérrez, David. *Walls and Mirrors: Mexican Americans, Mexican Immigrants, and the Politics of Ethnicity.* Berkeley: University of California Press, 1995.

Hanke, Lewis. *Aristotle and the American Indians: A Study in Race Prejudice in the Modern World.* New York: H. Regnery, 1959.

Hicks, D. Emily. *Border Writing: The Multidimensional Text.* Minneapolis: University of Minnesota Press, 1991.

Jonas, Susanne. *The Battle for Guatemala: Rebels, Death Squads, and U.S. Power.* Boulder, Colo.: Westview Press, 1991.

Kaplan, Caren. "Resisting Autobiography: Out-law Genres and Transnational Feminist Subjects." In *De/colonizing the Subject,* edited by Sidonie Smith and Julia Watson, 115–39. Minneapolis: University of Minnesota Press, 1991.

Kristeva, Julia. *Powers of Horror: An Essay on Abjection.* Translated by Leon S. Roudiez. New York: Columbia University Press, 1982.

Lopez, Antoinette Sedillo, ed. *Criminal Justice and Latino Communities.* New York: Garland Press, 1995.

Maciel, David, and Isidro D. Ortiz, eds. *Chicanas/Chicanos at the Crossroads.* Tucson: University of Arizona Press, 1996.

Martinez, Rubén. *The Other Side: Notes from the New L.A., México City, and Beyond.* Los Angeles: Vintage Books, 1993.

Menchú, Rigoberta. *I, Rigoberta Menchú: An Indian Woman in Guatemala.* Edited by Elizabeth Burgos-Debray. Translated by Ann Wright. London: Verso, 1993.

Mirandé, Alfred. *Gringo Justice.* Notre Dame, Ind.: University of Notre Dame Press, 1987.

Navarro, Gerardo. From a live performance, Mission Cultural Center, San Francisco, Calif., October 30, 1994.

Penn-Hilden, Patricia. "Ritchie Valens is Dead: E Pluribus Unum." In *As We Are Now: Mixblood Essays on Race and Identity,* edited by William S. Penn, 219–52. Berkeley: University of California Press, 1997.

Rosaldo, Renato. "Ideology, Place, People without Culture." *Cultural Anthropology* 3, no. 1 (1988): 77–87.

Rouse, Roger. "Mexican Migration and the Social Space of Postmodernism." *Diaspora* 1 (1991): 8–23.

Ruiz, Vicki. "'And Miles to Go . . . ': Mexicans and Work, 1930–1985." In *Western Women, Their Land, Their Lives,* edited by Vicki Ruiz, Janice Monk, and Lillian Schlissel. Albuquerque: University of New Mexico Press, 1988.

Saldívar, José David. *Border Matters: Remapping American Cultural Studies.* Berkeley: University of California Press, 1997.

———. "Limits of Cultural Studies." *American Literary History* 2, no. 2 (1990): 251–66.

Saldívar, José David, and Héctor Calderón, eds. *Criticism in the Borderlands: Studies in Chicano Literature and Ideology.* Durham, N.C.: Duke University Press, 1991.

Sassen, Saskia. "Why Migration?" *Report on the Americas* 26, no. 1 (1992): 14–48.

Scarry, Elaine. *The Body in Pain: The Making and Unmaking of the World.* Oxford: Oxford University Press, 1985.

Slotkin, Richard. *Regeneration through Violence: The Mythology of the American Frontier, 1600–1860.* Middletown, Conn.: Wesleyan University Press, 1973.

Smith, Paul. *Discerning the Subject.* Minneapolis: University of Minnesota Press, 1988.

Smith, Sidonie. *Subjectivity, Identity, and the Body.* Bloomington: Indiana University Press, 1993.

Smorkaloff, Pamela María. "Shifting Borders, Free Trade, and Frontier Narratives: U.S., Canada, and México." *American Literary History* 6, no. 1 (1994): 88–102.

Spivak, Gayatri Chakravorty. *In Other Words: Essays in Cultural Politics.* New York: Routledge, 1988.

Takaki, Ronald. *Iron Cages: Race and Culture in the Nineteenth Century.* Oxford: Oxford University Press, 1990.

Todorov, Tzvetan. *The Conquest of America: The Question of the Other.* Translated by Richard Howard. New York: Harper and Row, 1984.

Trujillo, Larry. "La Evolución del 'Bandido' al 'Pachuco': A Critical Examination and Evaluation of Criminological Literature on Chicanos." *Issues in Criminology* 9 (1974): 43–67.

Tula, María Teresa. *Hear My Testimony: María Teresa Tula, Human Rights Activist of El Salvador.* Translated and edited by Lynn Stephen. Boston: South End Press, 1994.

Urrea, Luis Alberto. *Across the Wire: Life and Hard Times on the Mexican Border.* New York: Anchor Books, 1993.

Vanderwood, Paul J., and Frank N. Samponaro. *Border Fury: A Picture Postcard Record of Mexico's Revolution and U.S. War Preparedness, 1910–1917.* Albuquerque: University of New Mexico Press, 1988.

White, Hayden. *Tropics of Discourse: Essays in Cultural Criticism.* Baltimore: Johns Hopkins University Press, 1978.

Yellow Bird [John Rollin Ridge]. *The Life and Adventures of Joaquin Murieta, the Celebrated California Bandit.* 1854. Reprint, Norman: University of Oklahoma Press, 1955.

Young, Robert C. *Colonial Desire: Hybridity in the Theory, Culture and Race.* London: Routledge, 1995.

Chapter 2

Hungarian Poetic Nationalism
or National Pornography?

Eastern Europe and Feminism—With a Difference

ANIKÓ IMRE

There is something frivolous about arguing for feminist theory in Eastern Europe in the shadow of the crimes recently committed against Yugoslavian women.[1] Textuality does not help explain the killing in Bosnia, states Susan Rubin Suleiman succinctly in her essay, "The Politics of Postmodernism after the Wall (Or, What Do We Do When the 'Ethnic Cleansing' Starts?)" (53). The Croatian writer Slavenka Drakulić rightly and poignantly mocks the "critical theory approach" of Western feminists, whose "cold, artificial, slippery" questions about "the position of East European women" do not touch her reality. She writes, on the eve of war, in an imaginary response to a white feminist scholar from the United States:

> Dear B . . . we live surrounded by newly opened porno shops, porno magazines, peepshows, stripteases, unemployment, and galloping poverty. In the press they call Budapest "the city of love, the Bangkok of Eastern Europe." Romanian women are prostituting themselves for a single dollar in towns on the Romanian–Yugoslav border. In the midst of all this, our antichoice nationalist governments are threatening our right to abortion and telling us to multiply, to give birth to more Poles, Hungarians, Czechs, Croats, Slovaks. We are unprepared, confused, without organization or movement yet. Perhaps we are even afraid to call ourselves feminists. Many women here see the movement as a "world without men," a world of lesbians, that they cannot understand and cannot accept. And we definitely don't have answers for you. A Critical Theory approach? Maybe in ten years. (*How We Survived*, 132)

Yet despite realizing that intellectual discourse can accomplish little "when the shooting starts," Suleiman suggests that postmodernist intellectuals are obliged to continue translating and interpreting across traditions, in order to prevent situations in which it comes down to "blows versus words" (62–63). "Since the public rhetorics of certainty, whether of the historicist or the universalist variety, don't seem to have worked at all well in preventing war, genocide, and other forms of political murder in the past two thousand years, why not try a public rhetoric of doubt?" (60). Even Drakulić asks the question, "But if [the Western feminist] doesn't understand us, who will?" (*How We Survived,* 128).

In Hungary, just north of the former Yugoslavia, the postcommunist transition has not led to civil war. On the contrary, President Clinton expressed the sentiments of many proud Hungarians—eager to distance themselves from the "barbarism" of the Balkans—when he welcomed Hungarian president Árpád Göncz during Göncz's 1999 visit to the White House: "Now, Hungary is one of the fastest-growing economies in Europe . . . [It] has acted to protect the rights of its own minority groups, and worked for the rights of ethnic Hungarians in other nations. Hungary has stood with the United States as a NATO ally against ethnic cleansing in Kosovo, and for a more positive future for all the peoples of Central and Eastern Europe. Hungary is leading the way toward what people dreamed of throughout the long Cold War." In his response, President Göncz evoked the "indivisible future" of Hungary and Europe, and talked about Hungarians' "natural Western orientation," which, he said, was the main reason for Hungary's spectacular post–cold war economic development ("Remarks").

At the same time, as in other postcommunist East European countries, in Hungary, "there is a singular absence of discussion of gender as part of the revitalized notion of democracy and democratic theory, as well as a singular absence of women in new democracies" (Eisenstein, "Eastern European Male Democracies," 310). The velvet revolutions that Western observers have enthusiastically celebrated have brought, "at best, male-dominated democracies; at worst, examples of ex-communist paternalist opportunism" (Eisenstein, *Hatreds,* 45). What Zillah Eisenstein has called "new–old nationalism"—a resurgence of nationalized panic in reaction to the transnational and global economy—has played out in racial and sexual terms. Most obviously, and yet most invisibly, it has evoked various forms of violence against women: Hungary is a new center of sexual trade in female bodies (IREX). Pornography is generally accepted as a necessary aspect of freedom of expression (see Molnár; Arpad; Eisenstein, *Hatreds,* 112–14; Mihancsik). Most well-paying jobs unabashedly target men. The parliament has only token female representation, and even the few female politicians are eager to emphasize their primary roles as mothers and women (Békefy; Goven). Rape is not considered a serious crime; domestic violence is a private, "family" matter. The examples would fill volumes.

Since 1989, many well-intentioned volumes of feminist writing have, in fact, been published about the horrors and inequalities of East European— predominantly Russian—women.[2] However, the majority of this literature is wrapped in the language of what Gayatri Chakravorty Spivak has called "hegemonic feminist theory" ("Rani of Sirmu," 147),[3] which—as Drakulić objects above—is incomprehensible for East European women. I do believe that—ten years after Drakulić's rhetorical prophecy—the time has arrived for a feminist intervention in East European cultures. The current, transitional blend of political systems and ideologies exposes the struggle for ideological domination among various groups, which undermines the efforts of patriarchal-national elites to solidify their power in the "new" democracies. Eastern Europe today is an "uncharted territory" for theory, which "should hold out the possibility for dislodging the patriarchal foundation of male gender privilege of *both* capitalism (and with it liberalism) and socialism" (Eisenstein, "Eastern European Male Democracies," 304). However, feminist intervention needs to be flexible enough to address the particularity of postcommunist and East European, national, sexualized, and racialized representations, and the ways in which those representations are affected by global corporate power. Even more important, it needs tools to access those more private elements of East European lives that reveal which identities are centered in nationalist discourses and which are marginalized or regarded as irrelevant by both native and Western observers (Kennedy, 26).

Therefore, moving beyond the egalitarian concerns of liberal feminism[4] and the traditional "ethnic" and "political" approaches to East European nationalisms in the social sciences (Kennedy, 4), I will focus on one of the least acknowledged—but all the more influential—sites of violence against women: cinematic and literary discourses of the "transition" that reveal an intense thematic concern with female sexuality and the racialized female body. Beautiful women—often of Gypsy origin, ravenously sexual but at the same time submissive and nurturing, victimized, and idealized—proliferate in Hungarian film and literature of the last twenty years as protagonists, and, even more interesting, often as alter egos of male intellectuals. These texts, most frequently categorized as "postmodern" or "postromantic," share a peculiarly East Central European aesthetic mixture of romantic lyricism and postmodern irony.[5] Poetry and irony function to distance these ideal femininities from actual women and to silence the gender politics of representation.

My first goal is to "depoeticize" these texts, in order to politicize them from a feminist perspective. I argue that these texts idealize and naturalize certain femininities that are indispensable to the task of shaping national identities. They appropriate women's voices in the service of national allegory, which inherently serves the interests of male elites. In order to argue that these textual femininities constitute violence against women, I will show the continuity of these postmodern texts with concurrent antifeminist and pornographic discourses. My second goal is to politicize the potentially subversive aspects of a postmodernist aesthetic that puts female bodies on pornographic display. Rather than simply condemning the patriarchal blend of poetry and pornography, I want to call attention to the excess of gendered pleasures that it liberates and generates. Women can appropriate these pleasures to challenge the hegemony of male national allegory. Processes of the transition from socialism to postsocialism have already greatly undermined this hegemony. Setting up an analogy between postsocialism and postcoloniality, one can argue that communist oppression and post-communist inferiority to the desired West have registered in the sexual identity of Eastern and Central European men as emasculation. The fact that male artists choose to represent themselves in feminine bodies and voices can be read as a symptom of symbolic feminization. As in other postcolonial national situations, it is precisely this crisis of masculinity that has provoked a compensatory violence against women and other minorities.

I propose a postcolonial feminist approach to East European cultures that draws on the often-overlapping work of poststructural theorists of coloniality, feminists of color, and (post)–third worldist feminists. My ultimate intention is to propose an antiessentialist, feminist, postcolonial approach to Hungarian, and by extension East European, representations of gender and sexuality that is able to address women who are socialized, from the cradle, to love and cherish their nation through loving and cherishing its poetry and poetic culture, who are unanimously prejudiced against feminism and Marxist-socialist politics, and for whom the terms "colonized" and "third world" conjure up images of poverty and the fear of racial contamination. It appears to be a utopian task, and it may turn out to be one. Hungarian—and most East European—women's gender and sexual identities are so thoroughly saturated with nationalism that it would take a difficult, gradual transformation for them to realize that their interests may not coincide with those of male, national elites. However, any approach that does not take these factors into consideration is doomed to be ineffectual.

POETIC MASTERS AND THEIR WOMEN: IN TRANSITION

The prototype of Hungarian postmodernist literary texts in which "men write in the feminine" is Sándor Weöres's long poem *Psyché* ("Psyche"), written in segments throughout the 1970s. *Psyché*, the lyrical autobiography of a fictional nineteenth-century Hungarian poet, Erzsébet Lónyai—alias Psyché—is a combination of memoir, diary, lyric poems, translations, and letters, accompanied by a "biographical study" by one of Psyché's imaginary contemporaries, and by a real critic's review. It is written in untranslatable, artificial, archaic Hungarian. Psyché herself is the adopted daughter of a Hungarian count and the natural daughter of a Gypsy woman. Her Gypsy ancestry explains, in the Hungarian critical accounts, her propensity to "extremes," "adventure," and "amours," defying the convent education she received as a result of her more distinguished paternal heritage (Vajdo, 18). This description of Psyché's extremisms is euphemistic. In the narrative, she appears simply, biologically, promiscuous. She makes contact with outstanding Hungarian and European male artists of the age— Goethe, Hölderlin, Beethoven—but this intellectual "elevation" of her character only slightly counterbalances her inability to resist sex and her almost predatory seductiveness.

Miklós Vajdo, a Hungarian literary critic, comments on how Weöres's *Psyché* "goes beyond the display of Weöres's empathy and love of games and turns into a feat of psychological transvestism as well. We experience the lives, loves, maturation into a woman and later mother, the happiness and sufferings of a real woman" (20). Going even further, Vajdo writes that *Psyché*

> is the virtual creation of a life-style and a new possibility for life. The dream of a late rococo, early *biedermeier* literature in an independent and free Hungary, where poets are not burdened by the need to express the crucial problems of society and the nation but are free to devote themselves to the common manifestations of love, joy, and sorrow: this is the dream of a Hungarian literature, European in character, one that could afford the luxury of being Hungarian in language and not necessarily in subject. (20)

This interpretation is typical of the way in which national allegory erases gender and sexuality as valid categories of politics and criticism. The transcendence of female experience is not understood as problematic in the national imaginary because it is made clear that Psyché is not a real woman. She is an allegory of the Hungarian, oppositional intellectual, castrated and feminized by political oppression under communism.[6] The intellectual is the real object of identification for similarly oppressed and "castrated" male citizen-viewers, who have had ample practice in reading texts through the allegorical double talk. On the one hand, the alleged absence of sexual difference—which characterizes national allegory and lyric poetry alike— appears to grant female readers an "androgynous" ground of identification. On the other hand, this strategy deprives the female character of her bodily, sexual reality and prevents the examination of the connections between representational violence against her and real violence against actual women.

Such connections have been at the center of feminist analyses of postcolonial texts. In her readings of postcolonial allegorical novels, Monique Y. Tschofen wishes to "undermine and unravel the typology that makes it possible for this mode of allegorical signification to challenge and resist colonial power structures and yet reinforce patriarchal power relations" (503–4). Tschofen shows, for instance, that the literal and symbolic levels are inseparable in the Sudanese author Taleb Salih's novel *Season of Migration to the North* (1966), and there is a constant slippage between the two. The English women who are violated by the colonized protagonist, who yearns for mastery, are supposed to be metonymical: "The personal is steeped with political meaning, sexual relations become a way of waging war, and the woman's body is a battle field: a territory to be scouted, fought over, and possessed, a fertile semiotic field upon which layers of meaning can be projected" (506). In a similar vein, Tschofen shows, the Canadian Dany Lafarrière's novel *Comment faire l'amour avec un Negre sans se fatiguer* (1985) also "uses representations of rape in order to create a textual allegory of resistance" (511). But although Salih's novel asks the reader to overlook the literal by reading violation metaphorically, Lafarrière's is a playful, ironic text, which creates a contract with the reader to forget or ignore the trope of rape altogether, "even though it is on every page of the book" (513).

There is a similar allegorical contract at work between *Psyché* and its readers. Yet this contract is also specific to the conditions of decaying state socialism. On the one hand, it issues the "hermeneutical imperative" of national allegory, that "crucial aspect of the liberating and resisting imperative of postcolonial writing" (Tschofen, 501). On the other hand, it is also understood that *Psyché*'s fickle, ironic lyricism is a rightful resistance to the expectation of naive representational realism prescribed by socialist realist aesthetics. This resistance justifies a degree of hermeneutic nihilism. The paradoxical duality of these liberties—the right to speak allegorically on behalf of the nation and the denial of straightforward meanings—provides unlimited political freedom over the female body. The male artist's "natural" entitlement to representation, and his simultaneous release from the responsibility of representation present serious obstacles to a feminist critique.

Such a critique is prevented, in the first place, by the fact that Psyché is the author's invention. She is removed from the contemporary and the familiar to a mythic past, which is, at the same time, a nostalgically evoked part of national history, embedded in a desirable European cultural context. This era is represented in a language at once real and fictional. Psyché's Gypsy blood, which in the biological essentialism of the national imagination is solely responsible for her excesses, is not the blood of real Gypsies, but of exotic, free, art-loving creatures—products of the eurocentric, orientalizing fantasy that the Hungarian artist mimics. She is worlds apart from real, contemporary Gypsies, who are blatantly marginalized throughout Eastern Europe. Significantly, Psyché is half-Gypsy, half "poet-nobleman"—a perfect allegory of the feminized, but beautiful and rebellious, "noble" artist whose masculinity is clearly tied to her intellect, which in turn easily transcends his fictional femininity.[7] Psyché is a woman forged out of the two man-made stereotypes that have been endlessly employed in European arts to contain the threatening, castrating aspects of women's sexuality: she is a promiscuous whore and a creative mother—with a mind—in one; she is for and about men with maternal productive talent in a politically prostituted, feminized world.

But even if male intellectuals are supposed to emerge from this risky play with the female persona untainted with femininity, women's identifications with an androgynous image like this must contain an element of subversion. It is true that women in nationalistic East European cultures are conditioned to identify with men's points of view and read "their" cultures through the filter of national allegory. Yet the poem's beautiful, brave, and sophisticated Psyché may open up a possibility of agency—or at least a form of empowerment—for female audiences.

The issue of women's identifications with such images is even more relevant to the film version of Weöres's poem, Gábor Bódy's *Nárcisz és Psyché* (*Narcissus and Psyche*, 1980). Despite that fact that the film adaptation pays homage to the self-reflective literariness of the original poem through visual metaphors and intertextual references,[8] Psyché, embodied by the exotic and seductive Patricia Adriani, is more immediate and visible than she is in the poem. Although the film has been hailed as the product of the postmodernist male artist's heroic "search for self-expression" (Forgách, 5) and Bódy's own "secret artist-autobiography" (6), such a romantic mission is undermined by the realism with which Psyché's frequent sexual encounters are depicted. Of course, the erotic lure of the exotically racialized and frequently unclothed protagonist is aimed primarily at male spectators—even if it must also provide women furtive visual pleasure. The significance of a half-Gypsy woman representing the "artist" remains unexplored in the Hungarian critical reviews.

The subversive ambiguities of representation that are inherent in this kind of "poetic androgyny" became increasingly noticeable toward the end of the 1980s. The gender politics that was still more or less successfully silenced in *Psyché*'s supposedly ideology-free postmodern universe became momentarily exposed in the case of a literary venture that was admittedly inspired by *Psyché*. In 1987, an autobiographical novel appeared by Lili Csokonai, in serialized form, in the literary journal *Élet és Irodalom*.[9] The novel, *Tizenhét hattyúk* (*Seventeen Swans*), was written in archaic Hungarian and told the contemporary love story of a brilliant and beautiful young half-Gypsy woman, Lili, who falls fatally in love and lust with a married journalist, Márton Kéri. Their relationship consists of a series of furtive sexual encounters. In the process, Lili also conceives and aborts a child. The romance ends when Kéri's careless driving leads to a near-fatal accident. As a result, Lili remains crippled and disfigured, and Kéri abandons her. The text is written from the wheelchair. The last recorded act is Lili's desperate and pitiful attempt at revenge: she shoots Kéri with his own gun.

The first reactions of the literary public were mixed: the enjoyment of semipornographic details mingled with castration anxiety over the fact that a *woman* published these details. This threat was so overwhelming that many were ready to overlook the literary merit of the work and simply labeled the "newly discovered" poet a whore (Tamás, 16). Others suspected, however, that Lili Csokonai was a pseudonym and that the female persona hid Péter Esterházy, a prominent and widely translated postmodernist writer. Esterházy soon admitted the truth. The novel was published in book form in 1988 and was later adapted into a film by a male director.

The film version, *Érzékek iskolája* (*School of Sensuality*), directed by András Sólyom, was completed in 1996, seven years after the "fall" of socialism. It reflects intellectuals' changed positions and the new expectations that filmmakers have had to face on a capitalist, global market. Similar to other Hungarian and East Central European films of the 1990s, it tries to appeal not only to national but also to international audiences—a concern that filmmakers had had to consider to a much smaller extent during the period of state-funded filmmaking (Cornell, 43–44). At the same time, it also engages in and continues the national poetic tradition. The director has acknowledged his debt to Esterházy's poetic work in several interviews (Tamás; Varga) and expressed his intention to employ the more accessible means of cinematic language to entice young audiences to read highbrow literature. His visual style evidently attempts to be faithful to the "high postmodernist" style of the original: the narrative structure is nonlinear; there are frequent black-and-white segments; and Lili's fantastic drawings occasionally interrupt the narrative flow.

However, the moral mission that had still managed to glue films of the early 1980s into more or less coherent allegorical universes had slipped away by 1996. The erotic display of women's bodies became the principal means of achieving commercial success. Lili's literary ambitions, foregrounded in the stylized, poetic prose of Esterházy's novel, are downplayed in the film, and the emphasis falls on the romantic-melodramatic plot. Lili's (the actress Dorka Gryllus's) exoticized, dark-skinned beauty is complemented by contemporary commercial Gypsy music, which the successful Romani band Ando Drom provides. A brief "lesbian" episode enhances the erotic lure of the film: an attractive female friend tries to seduce Lili, who is not to be detained from her heterosexual conquest.

The transition from national allegory to "global" aesthetics has been seamlessly achieved in other Hungarian films of the 1990s as well. Female bodies have provided essential vehicles for this shift. Catherine Portuges writes that the exhibitional fetishization of youthful bodies in recent East European films has shocked Western observers. Hungarian filmmakers have responded to demands of liberalization by repudiating "the repressive sexuality of Stalinism" and by "embracing the more commercially viable trajectory of the eroticized spectacle" ("Lovers and Workers," 287). Of course, the eroticized spectacle was already a feature of late 1970s and 1980s Hungarian culture: literature and, especially, films of the period—deprived of the possibility of meaningful political action—have rebelled against the communist stifling of public communication by the liberation of the private. Sexual rebellion, ostensibly against the prudishness of the regime, served as an allegorical weapon against political oppression. At the same time, the allegorical substitution of the sexual for the political, the private for the public, kept the terms of those oppositions separate by the logic of analogy. This is obvious in films such as *Egészséges erotika* (*Healthy Eroticism*, directed by Péter Tímár, 1985) and *Falfúró* (*The Wall-Driller*, directed by György Szomjas, 1985). In these films, what one could call "(anti)communist pornography"—represented by naked women in repeated heterosexual intercourses in typical socialist settings, such as the factory and a block of flats—carries an explicit political critique of the socialist regime in comic form. The erotic aspects of films of the 1980s anticipated the imminent transition to commercially oriented, audience-centered filmmaking.[10]

The uncontrolled outburst of pornography in Eastern Europe and Russia, which several Western feminists have recently addressed (Dolby; Goscilo; Occhipinti), was well prepared by the "soft-porn" spectacles of poetic-erotic and comic-erotic film and literature in Hungary—where "Stalinist aesthetics" had become greatly undermined by the 1980s, together with official censorship. While the erotic texts of the 1980s masqueraded as allegorical critiques of the system, large-scale, post-1989 pornography has been justified as the demand of the free market—an essential component of the uncriticized notion of liberal democracy. The liberal democratic nation-state, eager to participate in its own recolonization, has taken over from the totalitarian state the task of surveilling and selling women's bodies. The patriarchal-national continuity has prevailed under the surface, simultaneously erasing and inadvertently foregrounding the fact that the proliferation of pornography is an exercise in "phallic freedom," "which merely exchanges one form of political enslavement for another" (Goscilo, 165).

The privileges of the national artist and the political justification for the poetic eroticism of postmodernist texts became difficult to maintain after 1989 (see Tötösy, 97). Poetic eroticism has shifted into a pornographic eroticism. This shift is clearly illustrated by comparing Péter Esterházy's two novels, both preoccupied with pornography: the pre-1989 *Kis magyar pornográfia* (*A Little Hungarian Pornography*), and the post-1989 *Egy nö* (*She Loves Me*): The former, an ironic set of anecdotes in which the political and the personal/sexual inseparably interweave, relies on women and the feminine to convey a collective, gender-neutral powerlessness. Esterházy introduces the book this way:

> This is the author's most East-European book, and his most helpless, too. It was written in 1982–83, in the overripe period of the Kádár era, under small, Hungarian, pornographic circumstances where pornography should be understood as meaning lies, the lies of the body, the lies of the soul, our lies. Let us imagine, if we can, a country where everything is a lie, where the

lack of democracy is called socialist democracy, economic chaos socialist economy, revolution anti-revolution, and so on. . . . Such a total, all-encompassing lie, when from history through green-pea soup, when from our father's eyebrows and our lover's lap everything is a lie, not to mention this theoretical yet very tangible presence of threat, all this makes for a highly poetic situation. (v–vi)

Although according to this the national "we" is being corrupted by communist oppression, in the book, only the prostitution of *women's* bodies is represented as "natural" and morally reprehensible. Men's "prostitution" by other men always appears in invisible quotation marks. It is metaphorical, tragic, temporary, and it ennobles through the suffering imposed. It seems as if women's "natural," "bad" prostitution were necessary precisely to protect the boundaries of the male body and male poetic soul from contamination with the dangerous performativity of the feminine. If the sexual is the allegory of the political, then it is clear that women's real prostitution and the (forbidden) performativity of gender[11] stands for "lies," whereas men's allegorical prostitution hides the "truth" of democracy, inseparable from maleness. The imp*lie*d audience of Esterházy's preface is a masculine, collective political subject, who is familiar with the "absolute" meaning of "democracy."

In contrast to *A Little Hungarian Pornography,* Esterházy's postcommunist novel, *Egy nö (A Woman,* 1995)—translated into English under the title *She Loves Me* (1997)—appeared without a preface to clarify the author's politics. The cover features the naked ass—any euphemism would falsify the effect—of an otherwise clothed woman, part of an unspecified Egon Schiele painting. The image is the perfect visual commentary on the book's intention, which is to celebrate the freedom of calling everything by its name. The text wallows in destroying taboos. Although there is still the resonance of something vaguely political about this triumph over the shadow of censorship, the actual taboos the book tackles are related to women's bodies and female sexuality.

The text is structured as a succession of ninety-seven short, numbered segments, each one of which is entitled "A Woman." The majority of these pieces describe, in explicit detail, sexual adventures of the male speaking subject—an invisible Don Quixote—with various anonymous women. As in actual pornography, the women's identities are reduced to objectified and isolated body parts. The central subject is present predominantly as an intellectual source, the origin of sophisticated, humorous, ironic, and erotic descriptions. He has the power to describe even the most secret parts of female bodies in a language that mixes the obscene with the aesthetically refined. Even though national allegory has ceased to be the exclusive mode of public communication, the right to undifferentiated representation does not disappear altogether in Esterházy's work in the historical and aesthetic transition between *A Little Hungarian Pornography* and *She Loves Me.* In the latter, pornographic descriptions continue to mix with political references to life under communism and postcommunism, as in this chapter:

> There is this woman. She loves me. (I have decided you love me, I said to her once, a very long time ago, although I mention this only in passing.) She has it in for the commies. As much as she loves me, that's how much she hates the commies. More to the point, she loves me as much as she hates them. When her hatred subsides, her love cools, and when she is boiling over with hatred of them, she is burning with love for me. This is socially unjust, but when it comes down to it (to me), what do I care about justice? For instance, during the first freely elected gentlemen's government, our relationship was nothing to write home about. Nothing irremediable happened, it's just that . . . in short, we limited our discussions to the household chores and sending the children off to school, and she never broke into tears when she looked at me, she didn't flee, screaming, from me in her underwear, jumping over tables and chairs, she didn't open the bathroom door on me when I was inside. Not so after the elections![12] Ah! So you're back, are you!, and those cute little starry eyes of hers flashed like the very devil. They lay sprawling over this country for forty years. And these assholes went and voted for them! I keep mum. I'd rather not say that these assholes are us, the country. I didn't vote for them, and don't you go saying it, even as a joke, and if you voted for them in secret, I'm going to kill you. What a sweetheart. I don't even try to calm her down, I wouldn't dream of it: memories of Tuscany. Why, they can't even speak the language properly, she screeches. Inside me, everything is stretched tight as a bow, that's how close I feel to her. They robbed us blind, and now they're playing Mr Clean! They crippled this nation, and now they're shooting their mouths off. I turn white, my hands tremble, I hear the beating of my heart. Trade union lobbyists!, and she squeezes my balls, but with so much feeling, passion and oomph, it would suffice to rebuild the nation. (157–58)

Esterházy reaffirms his right to analyze the political transition through indispensable references to the feminine. The "us" versus "them" binary opposition is rendered trivial by its very projection into everyday sexual situations. Yet the text also reveals Esterházy's eagerness to continue the allegorical game because it is as safe and pleasurable as women's bodies are—unlike the inscrutable rules of postcommunist politics and globalization.

In his collection of journal articles, *Az elefántcsonttoronyból* (*From the Ivory Tower*, 1991), Esterházy talks about a recently published literary collection. He, "as a temporary woman writer," "objects to the fact that women are missing from the anthology" (40). In other words, he will not only continue to do the talking for women, but will even represent an allegedly feminist cause on their behalf. He later describes his intention to liberate his writing from the burden of politics: "I will allow politics as little weight in my writing as, for instance, the weight of a light female shoulder" (72). The fact that the female and the feminine provide the imagery for the author's apolitical stance is a telling symptom of the absence of public discussion about the politics of sexuality.

Furthermore, Esterházy dismisses the earlier, allegorical politics of the "we" in sarcastic terms: "Perhaps the most egotistic society in history built itself here on constant reference to this virtual we" (144). At the same time, similar to other prominent writers, his entitlement to a position outside of the "we" remains unquestionable even after the transition. As in his novels, he asserts his "natural" place in the family of male Hungarian poets and writers, thereby justifying his birthright to a politically neutral status.[13] "I am an indebted and grateful son and product of Hungarian literature, and, at the same time, I am someone who is indifferent to some of the important traditions of this literature; for instance, that fact that it makes the collective its central value. I am not attracted by the heroism that follows from this. Then I would rather be a woman writer than a real man" (77).[14]

WHERE ARE THE REAL WOMEN?

Although such an erasure or metaphorization of actual female bodies is certainly an act of violence, the fact that Esterházy dresses his ambivalence toward the nation in female images could be used by feminists productively to point to women's ambivalent position within the nation. This is why the crisis of nationally privileged, traditional masculinities has recently provoked defensive attempts throughout Eastern Europe to coerce women into remaining faithful resources for the nation state. The "antifeminist backlash"[15] in Hungary has blamed women for the emasculation of men and the abandonment of family priorities. The demonization of "monstrous" women had already begun in the 1980s, condemning women who had supposedly made an alliance with the communist state against men in exchange for protectionist policies.[16] Spokespersons for the campaign—among them leading dissidents intellectuals—accused women of destroying the nation by neglecting their "natural" duty of bearing and nurturing children, by abandoning their husbands, and by following their own insatiable sexual appetites (Goven, 224–35). The analogy with women's situation in postcolonial nations is impossible to miss. Amina Mama claims that in emerging nations of Africa, the masculinity of nationalist discourses is a source of male bias. Although nationalisms always call on "the new woman," postcolonial leaders are unable to view women beyond reproductive and nurturing roles (Mama, 54–55).[17]

This hostile atmosphere partly explains why East European women have been so cautious to associate themselves with feminism. Their choices are extremely limited, unless they are willing to face utter alienation from their environment. Most women, especially in positions of relative empowerment, opt to perform a masquerade. They identify—or pretend to identify—with the dominant masculine viewpoint, they conform to the sexual roles approved by the national imagination, and they never address gender as a political matter (Mihancsik). Thus, in the Hungarian antifeminist campaign, politically active and publicly present women such as Kata Beke and Magda Gubi joined the woman-bashing chorus, implicitly distinguishing themselves from "bad" women (Goven).

This does not mean that women's creative voices have been absent in Eastern Europe. Female filmmakers have been an especially significant part of East Central European film cultures of the last few decades (see Quart, "A Few Short Takes" and *Women Directors*). In itself, however, this is hardly a reason for optimism. In Hungary, female directors have been able to pass as the "ideologically neutral and androgynous" national artist, on the condition that they renounce their female-ness and specifically feminine concerns and radically distance themselves from the politicization of gender that feminism represents.[18] In reality, women have been entitled to a narrower range of representable femininities than men have. Esterházy and other male artists have unproblematically appropriated female voices and bodies, and in Károly Makk's film *Egymásra nézve* (*Another Way*, 1981), even lesbian protagonists were accepted as vehicles of national allegory. By contrast, women have entirely avoided addressing the question of lesbianism, or they have disguised it as innocent female friendship.

The need to masquerade often makes woman filmmakers emphasize the antifeminist features of their films. Krisztina Deák's recent *Jadviga párnája* (*Jadviga's Pillow,* 1999) turns the far more complex female protagonist of the literary original—Pál Závada's popular postmodernist novel of the same title (1997)—into another insatiable, immoral *Psyché*.[19] Deák's Jadviga, devoid of Psyché's freedom of allegorical performance—the prerogative of the male artist—remains a monstrous female who ruins her family for a deceitful lover. Many recent films made by women continue the pornographic objectification of the female body, evoking the hard-won freedom of expression as justification. For instance, Ildikó Szabó intends her film *Csajok* (*Bitches,* 1995), which relies heavily on attractive nude women for commercial appeal, to be a true picture of "*our* relationships" (emphasis added) "in the twentieth century, today, in Hungary, in Eastern Europe" (Szabó, 5).

An even more alarming way of mimicking men's strategies is women's appropriation of voices that are racially determined to be the margins of the national collective. Júlia Szederkényi's film, *Paramicha,* winner of the 1994 Hungarian film festival, features a poor old Gypsy man as the "artist's" alter ego. Szederkényi says in an interview, "I consider it a delightful thing that I can be an eighty-year-old Gypsy man just as much as a four-year-old Zulu boy from South Africa; all the same, not to mention girls.

And we will not understand each other less just because we don't speak each other's language, since we don't understand each other even when we do speak the same language" (Csáky, 16). This declaration sums up Hungarian female artists' general approach to "freedom of expression": instead of strategic essentialism, a consciously chosen reconnection with a political community, they assume a free-floating, postmodern multiidentity without political responsibility. As men put on the mask of the inferior gender, Szederkényi puts on that of the inferior race, without any hint of awareness that the act involves aggression.

How can feminism make a meaningful intervention in a situation where women have gone from communist-nationalist colonization straight to postcommunist, nationalist demonization? Transnational feminist alliances are the obvious goal for women to work toward, in order to undermine the patriarchal alliances among transnational corporations, nation-states, and local cultural elites. As a first step, however, it should be possible to separate "woman" from the sexual essentialisms in which it is firmly grounded and from the allegorical, nationalistic discourses that daily confirm this grounding. One strategy for translating the missing concept of "gender" into East European languages is to read through the inadvertent and intentional ruptures of reifying national discourses.

An effective feminist approach to East European texts should draw on the work of theorists of postcoloniality, women of color, and (post)–third worldist feminists, who have successfully de-essentialized the nation to show that it is "an evolving, imaginary construct rather than an originary essence" (Shohat, 190). In a similar vein, Judith Butler suggests that feminists should read pornographic texts "against themselves"—not as constitutive of or representative of what women really are, but as allegories of "masculine wilfulness and feminine submission," as expressions of a desire that "repeatedly and anxiously rehearses its own unrealizability" (68). Spivak defines a deconstructive critique as one in which someone says "no" to a structure he or she intimately inhabits. Accordingly, she says, feminism and postcoloniality both operate from a "deconstructive stance" ("Making of Americans," 794–95).

In order to practice deconstructive reading, however, it is first necessary to read the discourses of the East European nationalist-patriarchal transition in their own languages. Suleiman writes that politics does not reside in texts themselves, but in the ways they are read. They are what they do for a community at a particular place and time (53). From this deconstructive theoretical position, the apparently disconnected phenomena of Hungarian postmodern art's aesthetic (ab)use of the feminine, the current antifeminist backlash, and the invasion of pornography can be read—and critiqued—as analogical processes. Recent East European, "feminized," (post)communist, (post)modernist texts provide many opportunities for critiques that would counter the "plural text" with an analysis of the "political status of the plural self" (Suleiman, 53). In the texts I have looked at, male authors take a considerable risk when they put on female masks. The postcommunist cultural "opening" has exposed patriarchal and national prejudice even more blatantly in many recent cases.[20]

Textuality might not help explain the killing in Bosnia, but it might make visible increased violence of other kinds against nationally marginalized groups. Textual rape of women is one of the most common and least recognized forms of these practices. Following up on Jenny Sharpe's feminist work on allegory and postcolonial violence, Tschofen argues that—even though the trope of rape is not identical with literal rape—the two are situated along a continuum. Rape encompasses a spectrum of represented sexual relations that signify violence, violation, and domination. Rape can occur even when the dominated woman is supposedly willing and desiring (Tschofen, 503–5). In perhaps the most telling case of textual rape, Hungarian literary scholars recently organized a "deconstructionist" conference dedicated exclusively to Esterházy's novel *Fuharosok* (1983), a text that centers on the rape of a virgin. The novel is postmodern in its intertextuality, written in a highly poetic, symbolic language, refusing to take an explicit moral-political stand. Yet if it were an Anglo-American text or part of a postcolonial context, it would still be unimaginable for feminist critics to ignore the gendered significance of rape as a representational vehicle. Fourteen leading "progressive" literary scholars, whose essays on *Fuharosok* were collected in the conference's proceedings, managed to do just that. They invariably addressed rape as a symbolic (mythical, ritual) act without any reference whatsoever to its gendered and sexualized politics.[21]

Fuharosok appropriates the female body on behalf of the nation in order to eroticize women's victimization. It unites the two ways in which nationalistic fears and desires become projected onto female bodies—"a territory to be scouted, fought over, and possessed, a fertile semiotic field upon which layers of meaning can be projected" (Tschofen, 506): Women are idolized, revered, and eroticized in the name of "proper" national love. But they are also brutalized, tortured, raped, and often killed in the name of hatred of "improper" nationalism, as happened in the course of planting Serbian seed in Bosnian women (Eisenstein, *Hatreds,* 56)—two sides of the same coin. Although the latter is made more horrifying by virtue of its literariness, it is also a figurative act, an act of representation, in which women's bodies are used to shape national identities.

Although East European women are currently suffering the consequences of nationalist backlash, they also have much to gain. This transitional moment provides an opportunity to foreground the discursive tools of oppression, which national political and intellectual elites inadvertently expose in their increased effort to maintain the status quo. Their violence can only be opposed by another kind of violence, the "violent shattering of the unitary sense of self, as the skill which allows a mobile identity to form takes hold" (Sandoval, 23).

NOTES

1. Eisenstein gives an excellent feminist analysis of the rape of Bosnian women in her *Hatreds,* especially chapter 2, "Writing Bodies on the Nation," 43–61. See also Drakulić's *Café Europa.*

2. See, for instance, the majority of the articles in the collections *Postcommunism and the Body Politic,* edited by Ellen E. Berry; *Gender Politics and Post-Communism,* ed. Nanette Funk and Magda Mueller; *Women in the Face of Change,* edited by Shirin Rai et al.; and *Women in Central and Eastern Europe* (a special issue of *Canadian Woman Studies*), edited by Brenda Cranney.

3. See also Sandoval's "U.S. Third World Feminism," 1–10, for a detailed discussion of the concept.

4. I agree with Eisenstein that Western liberal feminist theory is limited because, similar to East European "state socialist feminisms," its concern with sexual equality is reduced to the economic and the legal. It does not recognize the biological reality and the gendered and racialized meaning of the sexed body ("Eastern European Male Democracies," 306–8).

5. See Töttössy; Szegedy-Maszák; and Aczél.

6. Václav Havel writes that communist oppression rendered East European cultures "castrated" and "morally impotent" (quoted in Eisenstein, "Eastern European Male Democracies," 314).

7. Rachel Blau DuPlessis's words aptly describe the mechanism when she claims that the postmodern poet remains the "third term" of modernist poetry, "mediating between the polarized sexes," in the spiritual realm where men and women are equal in the spirit of "psychic and intellectual androgyny" (*Writing beyond the Ending,* 74). The voluntary revelation of the fractured basis of his work provides him with a degree of "femininity," but this femininity is strictly metaphorical, easily contained: "It is a strong position to be both male oneself and masculine/feminine in one's own writing, but avoiding the three dangerous places of writing practice: the 'male but stupid,' the feminist, and the effeminate" ("Corpses of Poesy," 75).

8. The film has become something of a national cult item in the last twenty years, retrospectively immortalized by Bódy's tragic suicide at a young age, in 1985. The film has become one of the founding documents of Hungarian postmodernist cinema, which has also been described as "neoromantic" or "neosentimental" (Forgách; Varga). Bódy himself has been identified as the "archetype of the romantic artist of the 1980s" (Forgách, 4).

9. Esterházy, *Tizenhét hattyúk.*

10. This trend started well before 1989, in the international collaborations of the best-known, most successful directors, such as Miklós Jancsó, Márta Mészáros, and István Szabó. See Zsugán.

11. In Hungarian, as in most other East European languages, there is no expression for "gender." This makes it difficult not only to translate feminist theories

into Hungarian, but also to conceptualize nonessentialized sexualities. See also Arpad; Kürti.

12. In 1994, when the reform communists won against the right-wing Hungarian Democratic Forum.

13. In the foreword to his 1985 novel *A szív segédigéi* (*Helping Verbs of the Heart*, published in English in 1991), Esterházy acknowledges his intertextual indebtedness to forty-three predominantly Hungarian and European male writers. Two of his recurring, often-acknowledged role models are Dezső Kosztolányi and Gyula Krúdy, turn-of-the century modernist writers, whose self-referential, poetic universes abundantly drew on representations of the female and feminine.

14. Tötösy makes similar observations about the work of Endre Kukorelly, another Hungarian postmodernist writer. Kukorelly's poetic texts circle "around and about relationships with women," interweaving the national and the political contexts in the personal (Tötösy, 98). Although Kukorelly's reliance on the female and the feminine is "profoundly patriarchal" and male-oriented, he himself calls himself a "feminist" (97).

15. Although the term is widely used, "antifeminist" is, of course, incorrect where there is no feminism to attack. On the East European antiwomen and antifeminist propaganda, see Occhipinti; Mihancsik; Goven; Eisenstein, "Eastern European Male Democracies"; and Dolby.

16. On East European communist states' protectionist legislation, see, e.g., Eisenstein's "East European Male Democracies." On the Hungarian situation, see Corrin.

17. Eisenstein levels a similar charge against Václav Havel and Mikhail Gorbachev ("East European Male Democracies," 312–14).

18. See Mihancsik; Holland; Iordanova; Portuges, "Gendering Cinema"; and Szabó.

19. In a private conversation in May 2000, the director acknowledged her artistic debt to Bódy's *Psyché.*

20. For instance, some demonstration of public intellectual engagement with feminist and postcolonial theories has become unavoidable—both dangerous "deconstructive cases" in a culture of national and gender essentialisms. The Hungarian journal *Helikon* devoted a special issue to "postcolonial theory" (1996: 4), carefully avoiding the naming of the obvious analogy between postcoloniality and postcommunism. This would be a meaningful silence for a deconstructive reading to address. Other examples could be the special section that *Filmvilág*, the prominent Hungarian film journal, published on "feminist film theory" (1999), or the special issue of the literary journal *Ex-Symposion* on pornography (1992). All the articles in both are written by men. *Filmvilág* approaches feminism with ignorance, hostility, and condescension. One author calls feminism "the proof of human stupidity" (Nánay, 28); another equates feminist film theory with cultural studies (Hirsch, 25). Arguments erupt into irrational outbursts of anger and anxiety over sensitive issues, revealing striking contradictions of reasoning: One piece attacks what it calls Hollywood's "woman-protecting censorship," which allows the representation of rape but forbids that of the nice, "innocent" slap on the (female) buttocks (Hirsch, 26). Another bemoans the disappearance of "real women" from Hungarian films and from Hungarian life and associates this phenomenon with the demise of "real Hungarian men" (Galambos). These texts *invite* deconstructive, feminist, postcolonial readings. Even more promising places for such readings are the attempts that deliberately seem to question the parareligious admiration of the national and try to politicize gender. Films by women, and—less frequently—by

men occasionally contain the promise of such antinational subversion. Ildikó Enyedi's *Az én huszadik századom* (*My Twentieth Century*, 1989); Ibolya Fekete's *Bolshe Vita* (1995), and István Szabó's *Drága Emma, Édes Böbe* (*Dear Emma, Sweet Böbe*, 1992) are outstanding examples.

21. The critical collection is *Fuharosok,* edited by Müllner and Odorics.

REFERENCES

Aczél, Richard. "'Modernism' and 'Postmodernism' in Contemporary Hungarian Fiction." *Studies in Cultural Interaction in Europe, East and West* 3 (1993): 37–45.

Arpad, Susan S. "On Teaching Women's Studies in Hungary." *Women's Studies International Forum* 17 (1994): 485–97.

Békefy, Anett. "Nök a politikában." *Délmagyarország,* January 15, 2000, 3–4.

Berry, Ellen E., ed. *Postcommunism and the Body Politic.* New York: New York University Press, 1995.

Butler, Judith. *Excitable Speech: A Politics of the Performative.* New York: Routledge, 1997.

Cornell, Katharine F. "After the Wall: Eastern European Cinema since 1989." *Cinéaste* 19 (1993): 43–46.

Corrin, Chris. "Gendered Identities: Women's Experience of Change in Hungary." In *Women in the Face of Change: The Soviet Union, Eastern Europe, and China,* edited by Shirin Rai, Hilary Pilkington, and Annie Phizacklea, 167–85. New York: Routledge, 1992.

Cranney, Brenda, et al., eds. *Women in Central and Eastern Europe. Canadian Woman Studies/Les Cahiers de la femme* 16, no. 1 (1991) (special issue).

Csàky M., Caliban. "Van." *Filmvilág* 37, no. 9 (1994): 15–17.

Dolby, Laura M. "Pornography in Hungary: Ambiguity of the Female Image in a Time of Change." *Journal of Popular Culture* 29, no. 2 (1995): 119–27.

Drakulić, Slavenka. *Café Europa: Life after Communism.* New York: Norton, 1996.

———. *How We Survived Communism and Even Laughed.* New York: Harper Perennial, 1993.

DuPlessis, Rachel Blau. "'Corpses of Poesy': Some Modern Poets and Some Gender Ideologies of Lyric." In *Feminist Measures: Soundings in Theory and Poetry,* edited by Lynn Keller and Cristanne Miller, 69–95. Ann Arbor: University of Michigan Press, 1994.

———. *Writing beyond the Ending.* Bloomington: Indiana University Press, 1985.

Eisenstein, Zillah. "Eastern European Male Democracies: A Problem of Unequal Equality." In *Gender Politics and Post-Communism: Reflections from Eastern Europe,* edited by Nanette Funk and Magda Mueller, 303–30. New York: Routledge, 1993.

———. *Hatreds: Racialized and Sexualized Conflicts in the Twenty-First Century.* New York: Routledge, 1996.

Esterházy, Péter. *Az elefántcsonttoronyból.* Budapest: Magvetö, 1991.

———. *Fuharosok.* Budapest: Magvetö, 1983.

———. *Helping Verbs of the Heart* (*A sziv segédigéi*). Translated by Judith Sollosy. New York: Grove Weidenfeld, 1991.

———. *A Little Hungarian Pornography* (*Kis magyar pornografia*). Translated by Judith Sollosy. New York: Quartet Books, 1995.

———. *She Loves Me* (*Egy nö*). Translated by Judith Sollosy. Evanston, Ill.: Northwestern University Press, 1997.

————. *Tizenhét hattyúk.* Budapest: Magvetö, 1987.
Forgách, András. "A késöromantika elöérzete." *Filmvilág* 39, no. 2 (1996): 4–7.
Funk, Nanette, and Magda Mueller, eds. *Gender Politics and Post-Communism: Reflections from Eastern Europe.* London: Verso, 1993.
Galambos, Attila K. "Nöi vonalak." *Filmvilág* 42, no. 7 (1999): 22–23.
Goscilo, Helena. "New Members and Organs: The Politics of Porn." In *Postcommunism and the Body Politic,* edited by Ellen E. Berry, 164–94. New York: New York University Press, 1995.
Goven, Joanna. "Gender Politics in Hungary: Autonomy and Antifeminism." In *Gender Politics and Post-Communism: Reflections from Eastern Europe,* ed. Nanette Funk and Magda Mueller, 224–40. New York: Routledge, 1993.
Hirsch, Tibor. "Pörén, buján, pajkosan: Erotika és öncenzúra az ezredfordulón." *Filmvilág* 47, no. 7 (1999): 24–27.
Holland, Agnieszka. "Másképp filmezek." *Magyar Lettre Internationale* 24, no. 1 (1997): 51–52.
Iordanova, Dina. *"Screen Memories:* The Hungarian Cinema of Márta Mészairos" (book review). *Canadian Women Studies* 16, no. 1 (1995): 110–111.
IREX. "Putting an End to the Trafficking in the NIS and CEE." Proceedings of a policy forum held on August 16, 2000. Available at: <http://www.irex.org/publications/policy-papers/trafficking_women.pdf>. Accessed September 2000.
Kennedy, Michael D. "An Introduction to East European Ideology and Identity in Transformation." In *Envisioning Eastern Europe: Postcommunist Cultural Studies,* edited by Michael D. Kennedy, 1–45. Ann Arbor: University of Michigan Press, 1994.
Kürti, Laszlo. "The Wingless Eros of Socialism: Nationalism and Sexuality in Hungary." In *The Curtain Rises: Rethinking Culture, Ideology, and the State in Eastern Europe,* edited by Hermine G. De Soto and David G. Anderson, 266–88. Atlantic Highlands, N.J.: Humanities Press, 1993.
Mama, Amina. "Sheroes and Villains: Conceptualizing Colonial and Contemporary Violence against Women in Africa." In *Feminist Genealogies, Colonial Legacies, Democratic Futures,* edited by M. Jacqui Alexander and Chandra T. Mohanty, 46–62. New York: Routledge, 1997.
Mihancsik, Zsófia. "A láthatatlan nem: Magyar nök filmen." *Filmvilág* 47, no. 7 (1999): 16–21.
Molnár, Dániel. "Minden szörfös 'azt' akarja." *Filmvilág* 41, no. 6 (1998): 31–33.
Morgan, Thaïs E., ed. *Men Writing the Feminine.* New York: State University of New York Press, 1994.
Müllner, András, and Ferenc Odorics, eds. *Fuharosok.* Szeged: Ictus, 1999.
Nánay, Bence. "Himnen, nönem: Feminist Filmelmélet." *Filmvilág* 42, no. 7 (1999): 28–29.
Occhipinti, Laurie. "Two Steps Back? Anti-Feminism in Eastern Europe." *Anthropology Today* 12, no. 6 (1996): 13–18.
Portuges, Catherine. "Gendering Cinema in Postcommunist Hungary." In *Postcommunism and the Body Politic,* edited by Ellen E. Berry, 297–313. New York: New York University Press, 1995.
————. "Lovers and Workers: Screening the Body in Post-Communist Hungarian Cinema." In *Nationalisms and Sexualities,* ed. Andrew Parker et al., 285–96. New York: Routledge, 1992.
Quart, Barbara. "A Few Short Takes on Eastern European Film." *Cinéaste* 19, no. 4 (1993): 63–64.
————. *Women Directors: The Emergence of a New Cinema.* New York: Routledge, 1988.
Rai, Shirin, Hilary Pilkington, and Annie Phizacklea, eds. *Women in the Face of Change: The Soviet Union, Eastern Europe, and China.* New York: Routledge, 1992.

"Remarks by President Clinton and President Arpad Goncz of Hungary at Arrival Ceremony." U.S. White House Press Office, June 8, 1999. Available at: <http://whitehouse.gov/WH/New/html/19990608.html>. Accessed June 8, 1999.

Sandoval, Chela. "U.S. Third World Feminism: The Theory and Method of Oppositional Consciousness in the Postmodern World." Genders 10 (1991): 1–25.

Sharpe, Jenny. Allegories of Empire: The Figure of the Woman in the Colonial Text. Minneapolis: University of Minnesota Press, 1993.

Shohat, Ella, and Robert Stam, eds. Unthinking Eurocentrism: Multiculturalism and the Media. New York: Routledge, 1994.

Spivak, Gayatri Chakravorty. "The Making of Americans, the Teaching of English, and the Future of Culture Studies." New Literary History 21, no. 4 (1990): 781–98.

———. "The Rani of Sirmu." In Europe and Its Others, edited by Francis Barker, 146–58. Colchester: University of Essex Press, 1985.

Suleiman, Susan Rubin. "The Politics of Postmodernism after the Wall (Or, What Do We Do When the 'Ethnic Cleansing' Starts?)." In International Postmodernism: Theory and Practice, edited by Hans Bertens and Douwe Fokkema, 50–64. Philadelphia: John Benjamins, 1997.

Szabó, Ildikó. "Csajok: Forgatókönyv-részletek." Filmkultúra 30, no. 7 (1994): 4–7.

Szegedy-Maszák, Mihály. "Postmodernism in Hungarian Literature." In International Postmodernisms: Theory and Literary Practice, edited by Hans Bertens and Douwe Fokkema. Philadelphia: John Benjamins, 1997.

Tamás, Amaryllis. "Érzékek iskolája." Filmvilág 39, no. 2 (1996): 16–19.

Tötösy de Zepetnek, Steven. "Configurations of Postcoloniality and National Identity: Inbetween Peripherality and Narratives of Change." Comparatist 23 (1999): 89–110.

Töttössy, Beatrice. "Hungarian Postmodernity and Postcoloniality: The Epistemology of a Literature." Canadian Review of Comparative Literature 22, no. 3–4 (1994): 881–91.

Tschofen, Monique Y. "Post-Colonial Allegory and the Empire of Rape." Canadian Review of Comparative Literature 22 (1995): 501–5.

Vajdo, Miklós. Introduction to Eternal Moment, by Sándor Weöres. London: Anvil Press, 1988.

Varga, Balázs. "Két ugrással a szakadék felett." Filmkultúra 34, no. 2 (1998). Available at: <http://www.filmkultura.iif.hu:8080/articles/films/erzekek.hu.html>.

Zsugán, István. "A hetedik szoba." Filmvilág 28, no. 10 (1995): 18–21.

Chapter 3

Militarizing the Feminine Body

Women's Participation in the Tamil Nationalist Struggle

YAMUNA SANGARASIVAM

Since 1984, Tamil women have joined the Liberation Tigers of Tamil Eelam (LTTE) and undergone the rigors of arms training. As prepared combatants, the initial participation of women cadres in battle was during the LTTE's major offensive against the Sri Lankan government's military forces in the northern coastal town of Mannar in October 1986 (Ann, iii). This essay examines women's self-representations of political agency and militarization as participants in the Tamil nationalist movement.[1] In an attempt to understand the choices that Tamil women are making to militarize their bodies and become active agents in the violence of war, I argue that there is a need to examine the material reality and historical experiences of Tamil communities in resistance to the violence and oppression of the Sri Lankan state (and previously, against the forces of the Indian military).[2] Confronted with the images of a militarized feminine identity, I suggest that we suspend the popular impulse to regard women cadres as "fodder for the masculine machinery of war"[3] because to do so would be to deny their sense of agency amidst the immediate crises of war; to deny their everyday lived experiences of violence that war engenders; and to give way to the popular stereotypes of women as predisposed to motherhood and nurturing, and therefore coded as nonviolent and peaceful in contrast to men, who are coded as aggressive and violent. While engaging feminist critiques of nationalism and militarism, my intent is to reconsider women's place in "civil society" and urge the reader to be willing to understand women's choices to transform themselves, their bodies, their identities, and their networks of social relations in response to state violence and war.[4]

My analysis emerges out of my transnational experiences as a Tamil woman from Jaffna living in the United States, with friends and relations that have joined the LTTE's struggle for national liberation. I am acutely aware of the challenges of studying a movement that is largely marginalized by the international community as a "terrorist organization"[5] and excluded from the spaces of social and political legitimacy. As such, my work is largely motivated by the need to understand the subject positions of Tamils who are pushed to the margins by the constructions of a violent, terrorist

Other. Toward this objective, I present the self-representations of LTTE women cadres who are agents in creating their destinies: they freely make the choice to militarize their bodies and transform their identities. I focus my analysis on a set of posters that were produced by women cadres in the LTTE's Women's Front. Incorporating excerpts of interviews conducted during my fieldwork in Jaffna between 1994 and 1995, I present the perspectives of Tamil women who are within and outside the movement.[6]

LTTE women cadres are the most visible agents of social change in redefining the gendered spaces of feminine identity. Given the everyday violence of war in Sri Lanka, Tamil women are making radical choices in the struggle for survival. People living in these extreme conditions realize that survival in war is not fully congruent with the notions of survival in peace. In the context of peace, it is difficult to understand that to survive and live with dignity amidst the crisis of war may require one's participation in the very same violence that destroyed one's sense of dignity and integrity.

Why and how are people making the choice to join the movement? This is a principal question that motivates my study of nationalism and violence. When I posed this question to Kala, a 23-year-old woman cadre, she said,

> When we see our sisters and mothers raped by the army, when we see our brothers taken away, beaten, and killed, when we watch our homes burn up in flames in the aftermath of aerial bombardments, what are we to do? Where do we go to hide, to live? I decided that I was not going to let that happen to me. I was not going to be raped and killed in the hands of the army. I saw the courage of other girls who were joining the movement and decided that this was really the only way to survive.

According to Kala, violence was a means of survival as well as a means of communicating resistance and the integrity of a struggle for self-determination to the Sri Lankan army. There is little movement in her body, in her face, when Kala responds. Her delivery, her choice of words are matter-of-fact. There are no nervous jitters of the hands, no shifting of the body or shuffling of the feet as she describes and makes sense of why she and others like her made the decision to join the movement. I recognized this kind of discipline of the body in most of the LTTE cadres. An underlying pragmatism flows through Kala's words, and an ideological awareness disciplines her demeanor. The cadres that I spoke with (both women and men) were not anxious or disturbed by my questions; rather, they were genuinely interested in my understanding the reality of coming face-to-face with state violence as a path to understanding why or how they chose to join the movement.

MATERIALITIES OF STATE VIOLENCE AGAINST THE
TAMIL OTHER: A BRIEF HISTORICAL CONTEXT

Throughout the postcolonial history of Sri Lanka, the state has responded with systematic violence to the democratic participation and nonviolent protests of Tamils seeking a parity of status with the Sinhalese and equal access to civil liberties and freedoms.[7] After the initial waves of colonization led by the Portuguese (1505–1621) and Dutch (1621–1796), the British ruled the island they named Ceylon until 1948, when the nation-state gained independence. Ceylon inherited the parliamentary system of government from the British and maintained the unitary system of rule over the Tamil and Sinhalese regions of the island.[8] At the time of independence, constitutional safeguards (instated by the Soulbury Constitution of 1947) were put into place to protect the rights of minority ethnic groups. After independence, however, the fundamentalist fervor of the Buddhist *Sanga* (Sri Lanka's formal Buddhist religious organization) shaped the nationalist sentiment of the 75 percent Sinhalese majority.[9] Reflecting the social and cultural interests of this majority at the parliamentary level, a series of breaks in the constitutional safeguards for a plural, multiethnic society led to a complete dissolution of the civil rights that were once assured to the Tamil people of northern and eastern Sri Lanka.

For example, the Ceylon Citizenship Act of 1948 denied citizenship to all Indian Tamils (the category of Tamil people who were brought to the island from the southern region of India in the nineteenth century as indentured servants to work in the tea estates that the British occupied). In this single constitutional legislation, approximately 1 million Tamils of Indian origin were declared stateless. In 1949, the Ceylon Parliamentary Elections Amendment Act denied franchise to all Indian Tamils without citizenship. This effectively disabled the Ceylon Indian Congress, thus denying Indian Tamils the right to political participation and representation. In 1956, the "Sinhala-Only" Official Language Act was introduced to declare Sinhala as the only national language, thus denying national status for the Tamil and English languages. Consequently, Tamil government employees were denied promotions and dismissed from their jobs. The Standardization Act of 1973 prohibited Tamil students from entering universities by requiring Tamil students to score higher than Sinhalese students in the national university entrance exams. This led to the economic marginalization of Tamil youth, who were denied access to higher learning and professional development.

Faced with the history of discriminatory constitutional legislation, political parties, such as the Tamil Federal Party, the Tamil Congress, and Tamil United Liberation Front (TULF) have sought to engage in parliamentary democratic processes to protect the lives and livelihoods of their communities. After numerous failed attempts to secure the fundamental rights of citizenship, language, education, and autonomy from the military rule of the state (which was allowed by the ongoing Powers of Emergency), in 1976, the TULF declared the rights to national self-determination. By winning a sweeping Tamil majority in the 1977 general elections and emerging as the principal opposition in parliament, the TULF called for the separation of the northern and eastern provinces from the nation-state of Sri Lanka. The Sinhalese United National Party, led by then president J. R. Jayawardene, responded with state-sponsored violence to the TULF victory at the general election and the Tamil demand for a separation. Riots were organized by the government and executed throughout the island, where large mobs of Sinhalese people, aided by the Sinhalese-dominated police and military forces, systematically attacked Tamil homes, businesses, schools, and neighborhoods in the capital city of Colombo and in other parts of the island.[10] In 1979, the Prevention of Terrorism Act allowed for the indiscriminate arrests, disappearances, and death of Tamil youth and the establishment of military rule over the Tamil communities of the north and east. The draconian measures of the Prevention of Terrorism Act were also a state response to the growing sentiments of Tamil nationalism and the grassroots efforts of social movements that began to organize into what would eventually take the form of approximately thirty-six Tamil nationalist movements that emerged in the north between 1983 and 1985.

E. Valentine Daniel; Valli Kanapathipillai; Satchi Ponnambalam; A. Sivanandan; Stanley J. Tambiah (*Sri Lanka;* "Ethnic Fratricide in Sri Lanka"; *Buddhism Betrayed*), and Rajan Hoole et al., among others, have documented the brutality of the July 1983 anti-Tamil riots. More than three thousand Tamils lost their lives during these riots, and thousands more were displaced as refugees in India, England, Canada, and Australia. Many of those who were displaced have witnessed the burning of their family members, homes, and businesses in Colombo; they returned to Jaffna to begin their lives again in the villages of their birth and suburban communities. The July 1983 riots marked a turning point in the postcolonial history of Sri Lanka, giving way to the rise of the leading Tamil nationalist movement, the LTTE, and the escalation of war that continues today.

WOMEN'S LIBERATION AND THE NATION

The cultural and physical landscape of war provides amongst the most felicitous spaces for the rise of resistance and struggle. The LTTE women's liberation struggle is embedded in such a landscape of war. The transformation of women's identities is connected to the violent transformations of neighborhoods, schools, temples, households, and everyday social relations that once constituted the spaces of home in terms of family and community. Rather than constructing a prescriptive or predictive answer to the question of what happens to women's liberation after achieving nation-

hood, I am interested in understanding how LTTE women cadres are articulating their experiences of liberation in dialogue with state oppression
and the patriarchy of the LTTE.

As feminists have argued, in the study of nationalism, it is important to
understand that the constructions of gender and gendered power are central to the process of a nationalist struggle as well to the process of nation-
state building (Enloe, "Feminism, Nationalism and Militarism"; Jayawardena; Lorentzen and Turpin; McClintock; Yuval-Davis and Anthias). This
is not to say that these kinds of struggles for the transformation of gendered roles, gendered mobility, and gendered power are simply "by-
products" of nationalist struggles that are based on patriarchal power (Mc-
Clintock). To conform with a notion that women's liberation struggles
were and are simply by-products of patriarchal nationalist struggles would
potentially erase women's histories and women's experiences and displace
women from any history of everyday, organized resistance to patriarchal
authority.

Arguably, the women's suffrage movements in Europe and the United
States were part of the historical trajectories of nationalist movements.
Within the parameters of a nationalism centered on patriarchal power,
women were demanding participation equal to that of men in the construction of the nation-state. To dismiss the histories and experiences of women
and their participation in suffrage movements as by-products of male-
centered nationalisms would effectively erase the radical transformations
in women's identities and women's identification with the nation-state. In
line with feminist concerns, Uta Klein is observant of Israeli women's military participation as lacking an effect on access to political power and equal
status for women in society. In her analysis of how "national duties are
gendered in times of conflict and war" (148), Klein concludes that Israel's
incorporation of women in their military forces allows women "to be militarized but not to be empowered" (153). The likelihood of Tamil women
encountering similar limitations in the context of the LTTE masculine,
hierarchical structure is very real. Yet the question of how and why women
are feeling empowered in the context of resistance and struggle against
state oppression remains unanswered. Are they simply duped into military
service without any sense of empowerment?

It is important to acknowledge women's participation in the LTTE,
rather than dismissing the women as shaped by false consciousness while
they attempt to forward a women's liberation movement within a nationalist struggle. With this acknowledgment, the challenges remain for the
LTTE and other nationalist movements to come up with ways in which the
agenda for women's liberation will not be deferred at the moment of national liberation. In the meantime, the process of nationalist struggle underscores and calls up the subject position of "the not-yet" in terms of
being unable to claim an internationally recognized place of citizenship

for both men and women. I am particularly interested in understanding the ways that women are constructing or reconstructing gendered identities within this process.

MILITARIZATION OF THE FEMININE BODY

Feminists have examined the cultural constructions of the category "woman" by observing the female body as a site of struggle and contestation (Butler, *Bodies That Matter* and *Gender Trouble*). Recently, the body, as a "space where gender differences seem [to be] materially inscribed," has become a focus of interdisciplinary theoretical inquiry into the ideological and discursive practices that shape the representation of feminine and masculine identities (Conboy et al., 8).

In examining the expressions of violence in the contests between the military powers of the state and resistant nationalist movements, feminists such as Cynthia Enloe are urging us to look into the processes of militarism, "a distinctive set of beliefs and structures" and militarization, "a particular societal process entrenching these beliefs and structures" ("Feminism, Nationalism and Militarism," 25–26). With the emergence of women's participation in the postcolonial movements and armed struggles of the Sandinista National Liberation Front in Nicaragua, the Farabundo Marti Front for National Liberation in El Salvador, the Eritrean People's Liberation Front, and the Palestinian Liberation Organization, for example, there has been an increasing need to understand the choices that women were making toward the militarization of the feminine body. Representing the immediacy of women's transformations in the Farabundo Marti Front for National Liberation's struggle in El Salvador during the mid-1980s, Shelley Saywell records the words of Ileana, a woman cadre:

> I believe now that armed confrontation is the only way for El Salvador, even if it is the most painful way, because all the political expressions of the people have been suppressed, all the peaceful means of protest have been attacked. What other way is there to change things? The only way left is to pick up our guns and fight for a better life. (283)

Feminists have argued against militarism and militarization as sociopolitical processes that signify the quintessential expression of masculine aggression and violence. In particular, Cynthia Enloe (*Does Khaki Become You?*; *Bananas, Beaches, and Bases*) has consistently argued for a vigilant feminist perspective on the patriarchal constructions of post–cold war 1990s nationalism. As Enloe urges us to rethink nationalism in the context of militarized patriarchy, she acknowledges that the militarization of men and women and their participation in armed struggle is "not a process greased with natural inclinations and easy choices," and that "because it is a process riddled with gendered contradictions, the militarization of any nationalist movement is usually a contested process" (Enloe, "Feminism, Nationalism and Militarism," 27–28).

It is within these contested spaces and gendered contradictions that women in the Tamil communities of the north and east are making the choice to transform their identities, militarize their bodies, and participate in the front lines of battle. Their choices are not easy. When they join the movement and enter into arms training, they must discipline their minds and their bodies in preparation for war. They are resolved to the understanding that their most intimate and loving relationships with their parents, siblings, and extended families are forever transformed: that they will not have access to them, that the likelihood of death is more real than that of survival in war, and that their experiences of femininity are forever radically transformed in their own eyes and in the eyes of their community. To this extent, there is little evidence of a duped mind or a false consciousness in the choices that they make to join the armed struggle.

In their fatigues, holding their AK-47s, LTTE women cadres stand in stark contrast to the traditional village woman and the suburban, educated woman. In contrast to LTTE women cadres, these women are socially and culturally prepared for the quintessential expression of feminine auspiciousness through the process of arranged marriage, which, in Jaffna society, is still regarded as a marriage of integrity, in comparison to taboos of "love marriages." The traditional, Jaffna, Tamil woman is circumscribed by the social expectations and cultural conventions of *addaccam* (modesty and silence) and *odduccam* (poise and restraint). Her physical mobility is monitored and limited in public spaces by the social construction of "proper girls" who are discouraged from wearing trousers or moving about on the streets and lanes other than for the explicit purpose of traveling to work and school, for example.

How are women cadres constructing and mobilizing radical changes in feminine identities while simultaneously calling for community participation in the Tamil nationalist struggle? What are the responses of women, in general, to the radical changes in a militarized, Tamil, feminine identity that LTTE women cadres represent?

"Could we have ever imagined that our girls would take up arms and fight? Now they are all over the streets on bicycles, on motorbikes, we've even seen them driving trucks on KKS road! Ten years ago, we would never have thought of this as something possible." One of my aunts in Jaffna made this observation. As a woman in her late forties, she has witnessed the changes in the lives of women since the escalation of the war between the LTTE and the Sri Lankan state between 1984 and 1994. Her words indicate two principal areas of radical transformation in the feminine body and, as a result, in emergent women's identities: first, the militarization of the feminine body, and second, the greater mobility of women in Jaffna society. Confronted with the image or the live person of an LTTE woman

FIGURE 3.1. "Seventh Year Commemoration of Malathi"

cadre, these two areas of transformation are the most striking and engaging in this emergent feminine identity.

CULTURAL PRODUCTIONS OF FEMINISM, NATIONALISM, AND MILITARISM

Posters produced by women cadres in the LTTE's Women's Front speak to the questions of self-representation I pose above. Mobility and militarization of the feminine body are two important themes that emerge in the posters and songs of the Women's Front of the Liberation Tigers (Figure 3.1). The poetic text beneath the illustration of a fallen woman cadre on the poster reads,

> In becoming the first Woman-Tiger, you wrote the opening passages
> *(of our struggle).*
> *Tiger! With your life's sacrifice in battle, the narratives of thousands follow.*
> *History will relate the story of a fallen Tiger.*
> Raise your weapon, as you endure the fall—
> *hands will extend anew.*

Malathi, the woman cadre represented at the upper right corner and as the fallen cadre in this poster (Figure 3.1), is remembered as among the first documented women cadres to die in battle on October 10, 1987. In commemorating the death of Malathi, the principal message here is that her death was not a meaningless "sacrifice." Rather, Malathi's death signifies the "sacrifice" for liberation (for woman and nation) and the choice of a young woman who broke from traditional feminine roles to inscribe, with her life, the passages of a new history in Tamil society. The message suggests that there will be others who will reach out to pick up her weapon to continue on the path that she and others like her have carved out to redefine the place of women in the making of a nation-state.

In representing the feminine body of the woman cadre, the LTTE's Women's Front is explicit in rendering a new feminine identity that simultaneously finds continuity with and breaks from the past. Malathi's physical body, represented in her photograph at the top right corner of the poster, is transformed from her life experiences as an individual into a representative of a larger women's struggle in a movement toward social and political change. The visual narrative implies that the fallen figure is Malathi, but the physical representation of the body is a generic one, replicated in many of the posters produced by the LTTE (Figures 3.2 and 3.3). In this sense, the feminine body is divorced from the individual self, from personal history with its connection and ties to family, immediate kin, and community, and becomes symbolic of nation.

In the process of divorcing the body from the individual toward the integration of the body in struggle for nation, representations of the feminine body are not fully desexualized. For example, in all three posters (Figures 3.1, 3.2, and 3.3) the subtle distinctions of femininity—the rounded face, the fuller lips, the smaller and slighter frame—are artistic choices made by LTTE women cadres in the portrayal of themselves. Radical changes in women's identities are signified by adding details of strong, muscularly defined arms and legs taking strides, bearing the weight of AK-47s as well as grenades and other explosives strapped to her breasts (represented in Figures 3.1 and 3.3 in particular). Also, the neatly plaited, long black hair, a quintessential feature of feminine beauty in Tamil aesthetics, remains a key marker of distinction between representations of male and female cadres. This representation contradicts the reality of many women, who crop their hair after joining the movement.

The militarization of the female body does not necessarily translate into the self-perceived desexualization of that body. In some instances, this reconfigured female body is sexually empowered with an authority vested on women who bear weapons. This sense of empowerment is evidenced by a qualitative shift in the extent of women's mobility and women's presence in public spaces after the emergence of women cadres. Dharsini, a 26-year-old woman cadre, said,

FIGURE 3.2.
"Sixth Year Commemoration
of Malathi"

When women first came out on the streets in fatigues and bearing arms,
riding bicycles and driving trucks and motorcycles on the road, people were
extremely uncomfortable. They stared, pointed, talked in low whispers—
they didn't know what to think or how to respond to us. There has been
nothing like this in the history of our community. Now, we are a part of
everyday life. People don't stare or gape at us. But there's a difference between us women cadres and the everyday woman on the street. Boys will
not approach us in any way, will not dare to harass us in the way that girls
still get harassed when they step out of the house, when they walk to school
or work, when they wait for the bus. They can't touch us. (With a laugh) I
guess it's pretty clear that we are trained and armed. If at all there is a need
to interact with us, it is in the most official and respectful way.

Dharsini's words indicate an understanding of her self in a way that demonstrates a greater sense of personal, individual agency in the expression of
the female body in public life.

VIOLENCE, SACRIFICE, AND MORTALITY

The public display of sacrifice and mortality as a direct result of women's
choice to participate in the violence of armed struggle is another theme

FIGURE 3.3.
"International Women's Day,
March 8, 1994"

that emerges in an earlier poster of commemoration for Malathi. In Figure 3.2, the visual narrative reflects the radical transformation of Jaffna's landscape with the emergence of large memorial parks, *mahaveerer thuyilum illum* (place of rest for the great heroes), which serve to honor those who committed their lives to the nationalist struggle and died in battle.

The physical geography of war memorials has served as a means of claiming space and as an assertion of territorial rights that are intimately connected to national identity.[11] In the Tamil nationalist context, memorial grounds also signify the radical change in the reconstruction of gendered spaces. The placing of bodies (whether it is the full or cremated remains of the body) and the building of tombstones mark the landscape and inscribe the presence of the honored dead into the land. Their physical substance coalesces with the soil of the land to create a culturally circumscribed sacred space for those who have sacrificed their lives in battle. Implicit in creating these official sites of commemoration is the signification of a moral ground. This respect for the dead was destroyed by the Sri Lankan military forces upon their occupation of the north in October 1995, when they bulldozed these war memorials, unearthing the dead and leveling the tombstones.

With their construction of war memorial grounds, the LTTE effected a significant change in the social construction of gendered spaces. In the context of Jaffna's predominantly Hindu society where the dead are cremated and the cremation ground is culturally constructed as sacred yet polluted—in comparison to the sacred and pure space of the temple complex—there is a significant cultural shift in the attitudes of people toward the spaces where the dead retire. Gendered spaces are marked by the assignment of purity and pollution to the landscape of local communities and to the space of the body. Traditionally, Hindu women are prohibited from entering into, or even approaching, the cremation grounds. One important cultural explanation for this is that women's bodies as a site of auspiciousness and purity will be contaminated by entering into the "polluted" space of the cremation or burial ground.[12]

By forging a political and social culture of commemoration, the LTTE have successfully broken the taboos of "pollution" by transforming burial grounds into the "pure" and sacred spaces of war memorial parks. In doing so, the movement has also managed to reconfigure the "pure" sites of feminine bodies by introducing women into the grounds of war memorials to commemorate the lives of their family members who have died in battle.

It is within this larger context of social change where gendered spaces are reconfigured that this poster finds its visual and textual significance. The poetic text at the bottom of the poster (Figure 3.2) proclaims that

> *Just as Tigers are borne of this soil,*
> *stand firm in the knowledge that ever new roots,*
> *ever new foundations of life will emerge.*
> *As these roots spread and grow into the sacred tree of liberation, stand determined*
> *that the (aerial) roots of freedom will reach skyward in success.*

The poster not only recognizes the presence of women in the now reconfigured spaces of memorial grounds, but it calls for the celebration of that implicit moral ground by stating that more courageous souls and bodies of women will emerge from the soil of this newly defined sacred ground. Both the visual and textual narratives call for the reader to stand firm and assured in the knowledge that as surely as these new bodies emerge from the sacred soil of sacrifice, the new nation of Tamil Eelam will emerge also! The subtext of the narrative points toward the contradictions of armed struggle as a form of violence that is also regenerative: this message indicates that this kind of death, this kind of violence is not in vain because new generations will emerge to continue the struggle. It is not a senseless death, but rather one endowed with purpose, with vision, with integrity, and with the determination that liberation and freedom in the territories of the Tamil homeland will be realized.

The visual and textual narratives suggest that by the coalescing of Malathi's body with the soil of Tamil Eelam, new women Tigers will be born of this same soil—divorced from family, from maternal and paternal kinship, no longer originating from the womb of mother, but from the womb of mother Earth. As such, the narrative representations of the soil—which has sustained violence—serve as a regenerative and commemorative metaphor for kinship, community, and nation. The significance of muscular arms rising in a demonstration of strength and victory is employed as an intertextual device that references the multiple levels of empowerment in the uprising of women and nation.

In the context of these posters, the transformation of the physical landscape with the emergence of memorial grounds to bury the dead underscores the transformations of the feminine body and of feminine identity. The social power of these visual assertions is found in the reality that more and more young women continue to make a choice for armed struggle by participating in the LTTE's nationalist movement. These narratives also acknowledge Tamil women's struggle as part of a larger international women's struggle for liberation and freedom. Constructed to precisely carry this message, the poster aims to find solidarity with international women's experiences in armed struggle (Figure 3.3). The heading of the poster reads "International Women's Day, March 8, 1994." Here, the militarized feminine body is dynamic, in motion, in contrast to the static, restrained body of the traditional woman, who is represented by a faceless body, chained by her bangles within the barred walls of the home, the traditional space and place of a proper Tamil girl. Placed on the diagonal line of the poster frame, the body of the woman cadre is virtually soaring toward the sun as it directs its power of enlightenment to enflame the torch of freedom for woman and nation. The poetic text reveals the path to liberation:

> Your life transforms to ignite the flame.
> Your body is the fuel that sustains the fire.
> For your community, for your nation
> Woman, you light the flames of liberation!
> We are calling upon you.
> Pick up the torch of liberation and struggle
> for with each heartbeat, our nation is taking form—Tamil Eelam!
> Experience the dawning of Womankind!

The visual and textual narratives make clear the choice between the political agency of militarization and the passivity of a gendered victim of war. Also, here, the sustaining of the "flames of liberation" in the LTTE's nationalist project is represented as a dialogical process between the militarized woman cadre and her comrade, who is encumbered by the enclosed, moldering, cobwebbed home space of the traditional Tamil woman. What is seen in these posters as acts of commemoration and transformation of the feminine body and feminine identities, though, are simultaneously acts of mobilization. At first glance, posters like these can be immediately marked as part of the LTTE's propaganda to enlist young people in their nationalist project. With a close contextual examination of the material realities of war, these self-representations of LTTE women cadres are a testimony to their empowerment and agency.

CONCLUSION

My intent here is not to romanticize the militarization of the feminine body or valorize women's sacrifice. Rather, I am suggesting that we need to understand the self-representations of women in the LTTE, how they choose to become active agents in the violence of war, and how they choose to participate in a movement that is committed to the violence of armed struggle. The material reality of everyday violence is one that thousands of Tamils face each day in Sri Lanka, particularly in the north and east. The Sri Lankan military's searches and "clearing" operations to weed out the insurgent presence of the LTTE continue to result in the disappearances and deaths of Tamil women and men.

In this context, women are making the choice to transform themselves, their bodies, and their identities from the norms of traditional civil society to the norms of violence and war. Confronted with images of a militarized feminine body, our challenge is to move beyond the cognitive dissonance that may consume our visions and our perspectives on who these women are and what they have become. Popular assumptions about the brainwashing and conscription of women to act as fodder for the LTTE's masculine machinery of war not only reveal a bias that is partially shaped by gendered stereotypes, but also reveal a gap in understanding the choices that Tamil women are making. Through their authorship in the visual and textual narratives of political posters, LTTE women cadres have articulated their experiences of empowerment and agency. As the violence of state oppression and military aggression invites the responses of militarized nationalist movements in Sri Lanka and in other international stages of conflict, there is a critical need to recognize the experiences of empowerment and agency of women soldiers. In order to forward a more nuanced understanding of the intersections of violence and the subaltern body, we need to fearlessly engage in conversations with those who are working toward social justice and peace as combatants in the environment of violence that war engenders.

NOTES

1. Women have long been involved in the Tamil nationalist struggle. For example, in 1961, "A selection of woman volunteers perform[ed] satyagraha in front

of Jaffna's secretariat building" staging a sit-down protest (Balasingham, 19). For detailed discussions of women's participation in the LTTE, see Schalk; and Ann. For a critique of the militarization of Tamil women and the LTTE, see Coomaraswamy.

2. In July 1987, the Indian state intervened militarily and politically by enforcing the Indo-Lanka Accord. After a series of diplomatic debacles, the Indian state found itself in direct combat with the LTTE between 1987 and 1990. With the subversive support of the Sri Lankan state, the LTTE was successful in ousting the Indian military occupation of the Tamil communities in the northern and eastern regions of Sri Lanka. For a detailed analysis of India's military occupation and the Indo-Lanka Accord, see Bose; Gunaratna, *War and Peace* and *Indian Intervention*; and Wilson.

3. This was a phrase pronounced by a woman academic and researcher at the International Center for Ethnic Studies, the leading research institute in Colombo, during our conversation on women's participation in the LTTE's nationalist struggle. With a similar sentiment, representing the voices of feminist antimilitarists, Uta Klein claims that "the 'business' of war and conflict is an exclusively male one" as she dismisses the possibility of empowerment experienced by women participating in armed struggle (153).

4. The experiences of the Karum Pulikhal (Black Tigers), the LTTE's elite squadron of male and female cadres who have deployed their bodies as missiles in the theater of war, are an expression of the most extreme form of militarizing the body. I will not include an analysis of what has been popularly misrepresented as the phenomenon of "LTTE suicide bombers" here. The language of "suicide" is not present in the everyday speech and representation of Tamils in, within, or outside the movement. This representation is largely put forward only by the politicized media representations of the Sri Lankan state; it is also uncritically incorporated into the language of the international media. For example, in reporting an incident of violent confrontation between the LTTE and Sri Lankan military forces on March 10, 2000, the British Broadcasting Corporation states, "At least 21 people have been killed and more than 50 wounded in a *suicide bombing* and ensuing gun battle in the Sri Lankan capital, Colombo. . . . Previous attacks in the capital have been blamed on the LTTE, who are fighting for independence in the north-east of the island. The group has been accused of several *suicide attacks* against politicians and the military" (emphasis added).

5. On October 8, 1997, with pressure from the Sri Lankan government, the United States has listed the LTTE among thirty other "terrorist organizations." For example, Jansz reports that Sri Lankan Foreign Minister "Lakshman Kadirgamar in his address at the 52nd General Assembly of the United Nations called on the international community to declare the Liberation Tigers of Tamil Eelam (LTTE) a terrorist group and close their doors to the Tigers fund raising campaigns on foreign soil" (19).

6. All interviews were conducted in the Tamil language. I have translated both the interviews and the Tamil texts that are found in the poster analyses below.

7. The Sinhalese (the Buddhist, Sinhala-speaking) people were designated by British colonists as the majority ethnic population of the island. Consequently, the Hindu, Tamil-speaking people were designated as the largest ethnic minority population, along with other so-called minorities, such as the Tamil-speaking Muslim and Christian populations, the Indian Tamils, and the population of peoples with local and colonial heritage called Burghers.

8. Historically, the people of Kalinga state (the Sinhalese) and Tamil Nadu (the Tamils) of India migrated to the island and built their respective kingdoms in

74 / Yamuna Sangarasivam

maintenance of their territorial integrity. From approximately the third century B.C. to the early sixteenth century, the territorial integrity of the north and east was recognized as a separate, sovereign geographical entity ruled by Tamil kings, while the southwestern and central regions of the island were recognized as areas of Sinhalese rule (Ponnambalam). The early histories of Sinhala and Tamil migration remain a highly contested space of competing nationalist accounts in the claim for territorial integrity of the two nations of people. During the Portuguese and Dutch occupations of the island, the geographical and sovereign distinctions between the north and east and the central and southwestern regions of the island were maintained. When the Dutch ceded the island to British colonial rule, the British crown glimpsed an opportunity to consolidate its political and administrative power. In 1833, the island was fully absorbed as the British crown colony of Ceylon. For the first time in recorded history, the distinct territories of the Tamil and Sinhalese kingdoms were unified and brought under a single, unified political power: that of Britain (Ponnambalam; Wilson).

9. For a detailed discussion of Buddhist fundamentalism and nationalism in Sri Lanka, see Bartholomeusz and de Silva; and Tambiah, "Ethnic Fratricide in Sri Lanka." For a broader, comparative analysis of fundamentalism and nationalism, see Marty and Appleby.

10. Since 1956, every decade has been marked with the violence of state-sponsored riots against members of Tamil communities. Tamils, distinguished by their national identification cards, were detained; as a means of identification and humiliation, they were asked to recite passages from the Buddhist religious doctrine, the *Mahavamsa*. Unable to concede and perform this requirement of membership to the circumscribed Sinhala-Buddhist national identity, Tamils were beaten to death, dismembered, and burned alive in gunnysacks; they were doused with kerosene and gasoline and set on fire on the streets; and school buses transporting Tamil children were stopped and burned on the road.

11. The design and meaning of war memorials have attracted considerable interest. For example, see the study of World War I memorials of McCannell; and of Sturken; and see Hass on the Vietnam war memorial in the United States.

12. Also important to note here is that the physical labor of cremation is performed by specific lower-caste men, who are themselves culturally signified as bearers of inauspiciousness and pollution. Children are also prohibited from entering cremation sites. Hinduism's stratified structures of castes also serve to mark the spaces of purity and pollution in society. As such, only men are permitted to enter into the "polluted" cremation or burial space to conduct the required ritual duties. Upon their return, men will bathe outside the house, usually at a private or communal well site, before entering the "pure" spaces of the household.

REFERENCES

Ann, Adele. *Women Fighters of Liberation Tigers.* Jaffna, Sri Lanka: LTTE Publications, 1993.

Balasingham, Anton. *Liberation Tigers and Tamil Eelam Freedom Struggle.* Madras: Political Committee, Liberation Tigers of Tamil Eelam, 1983.

Bartholomeusz, Tessa J., and Chandra R. de Silva, eds. *Buddhist Fundamentalism and Minority Identities in Sri Lanka.* Albany: State University of New York Press, 1998.

Bose, Sumantra. *States, Nations, Sovereignty: Sri Lanka, India and the Tamil Eelam Movement.* New Delhi: Sage, 1994.

British Broadcasting Corporation. "Rebel attack in Sri Lanka." BBC News: World: South Asia. 10 March 2000. Available at: <http://news6.thdo.bbc.co.uk/hi/ english/world/south_asia/newsid_672000/6 72957.stm>. Accessed March 10, 2002.

Butler, Judith. *Bodies That Matter: On the Discursive Limits of "Sex."* New York: Routledge, 1993.

———. *Gender Trouble: Feminism and the Subversion of Identity.* New York: Routledge, 1990.

Conboy, Katie, Nadia Medina, and Sara Stanbury, eds. *Writing on the Body: Female Embodiment and Feminist Theory.* New York: Columbia University Press, 1997.

Coomaraswamy, Radhika. "Tiger Women and the Question of Women's Emancipation." *Tamil Times* 15, no. 12 (1996): 20–23.

Daniel, E. Valentine. *Charred Lullabies: Chapters in an Anthropography of Violence.* Princeton, N.J.: Princeton University Press, 1996.

Enloe, Cynthia. *Bananas, Beaches, and Bases: Making Feminist Sense of International Politics.* Berkeley: University of California Press, 1989.

———. *Does Khaki Become You? The Militarization of Women's Lives.* London: Pandora, 1983.

———. "Feminism, Nationalism and Militarism: Wariness without Paralysis?" In *Feminism, Nationalism and Militarism,* edited by Constance R. Sutton, 13–32. New York: Association for Feminist Anthropology/American Anthropological Association, 1995.

Gunaratna, Rohan. *Indian Intervention in Sri Lanka: The Role of India's Intelligence Agencies.* Colombo: South Asian Network on Conflict Research, 1993.

———. *War and Peace in Sri Lanka.* Kandy: Sri Lanka Institute of Fundamental Studies, 1987.

Hass, Kristin Ann. *Carried to the Wall: American Memory and the Vietnam Veterans Memorial.* Berkeley: University of California Press, 1998.

Hoole, Rajan, Daya Somasundaram, K. Sritharan, and Rajani Thirangama. *The Broken Palmyra: The Tamil Crisis in Sri Lanka—An Inside Account.* Claremont: Sri Lanka Studies Institute, 1988.

Jansz, Frederica. "The Worsening Human Rights Situation." *Tamil Times* 16, no. 10 (1997): 19–21.

Jayawardena, Kumari. *Feminism and Nationalism in the Third World.* London: Zed Books, 1986.

Kanapathipillai, Valli. "July 1983: The Survivor's Experience." In *Mirrors of Violence: Communities, Riots and Survivors in South Asia,* edited by Veena Das, 321–44. Delhi: Oxford University Press, 1990.

Klein, Uta. "War and Gender: What Do We Learn from Israel?" In *The Women and War Reader,* edited by Lois Ann Lorentzen and Jennifer Turpin, 148–54. New York: New York University Press, 1998.

Lorentzen, Lois Ann, and Jennifer Turpin, eds. *The Women and War Reader.* New York: New York University Press, 1998.

Marty, Martin E., and Scott R. Appleby, eds. *Fundamentalisms and the State: Remaking Polities, Economies, and Militance.* Chicago: University of Chicago Press, 1993.

McCannell, Dean. *Empty Meeting Grounds: The Tourist Papers.* London: Routledge, 1992.

McClintock, Anne. *Imperial Leather: Race, Gender and Sexuality in the Colonial Contest.* New York: Routledge, 1995.

———. "'No Longer a Future in Heaven': Gender, Race, Nationalism." In *Dangerous Liaisons: Gender, Nation and Postcolonial Perspectives,* edited by Anne McClintock, Aamir Mufti, and Ella Shohat, 89–112. Minneapolis: University of Minnesota Press, 1997.

Ponnambalam, Satchi. *Sri Lanka: The National Question and the Tamil Liberation Struggle.* London: Zed Books, 1983.

Saywell, Shelley. *Women in War: First-Hand Accounts from World War II to El Salvador.* Wellingborough, UK: Grapevine, 1985.

Schalk, Peter. "Birds of Independence: On the Participation of Tamil Women in Armed Struggle." *Lanka,* no. 7 (1992): 45–142.

Sivanandan, A., ed. "Sri Lanka Racism and the Authoritarian State." Special Issue, *Race and Class: A Journal for Black and Third World Liberation* 26, no. 1 (1984).

Sturken, Marita. *Tangled Memories: The Vietnam War, the AIDS Epidemic, and the Politics of Remembering.* Berkeley: University of California Press, 1997.

Tambiah, Stanley J. *Buddhism Betrayed: Religion, Politics and Violence in Sri Lanka.* Chicago: University of Chicago Press, 1992.

———. "Buddhism, Politics, and Violence in Sri Lanka." In *Fundamentalisms and the State: Remaking Polities, Economies, and Militance,* edited by Martin E. Marty and Scott R. Appleby. Chicago: University of Chicago Press, 1993.

———. "Ethnic Fratricide in Sri Lanka: An Update." In *Ethnicities and Nations: Processes of Interethnic Relations in Latin America, Southeast Asia and the Pacific,* edited by Remo Guidieri, Francesco Pellizzim, and Stanley J. Tambiah, 293–319. Austin: University of Texas Press, 1988.

———. *Sri Lanka: Ethnic Fratricide and the Dismantling of Democracy.* Chicago: University of Chicago Press, 1986.

Walby, Sylvia. "Woman and Nation." In *Mapping the Nation,* edited by Gopal Balakrishnan, 235–54. London: Verso, 1995.

Wilson, A. Jeyaratnam. *Sri Lankan Tamil Nationalism: Its Origins and Development in the Nineteenth and Twentieth Centuries.* London: Hurst, 2000.

Yuval-Davis, Nira, and Floya Anthias, eds. *Woman-Nation-State.* New York: Macmillan, 1989.

Chapter 4
Blood and Dirt

*Politics of Women's Protest in Armagh Prison,
Northern Ireland*

LEILA NETI

In February 1980, the Republican women prisoners of Armagh Prison in Northern Ireland went on a no-wash protest. For nearly one year, the women lived in cells surrounded by bodily filth. Because a similar no-wash protest was already under way in Long Kesh men's prison (also in Northern Ireland), it can be argued that the women's protest was anticipated, and perhaps even instigated by, the British prison authorities.[1] According to one of the prisoners, the no-wash protest was "forced on them, after prison staff locked up the landing toilets, the wash basins and the baths, and locked the women into their cells. She says that when some of the toilets were later opened, the women then decided to continue on the no-wash as a protest" (Magill, 13). While the British prison authorities perhaps initiated the infliction of filth on the prisoners, they did not anticipate that the women would effectively turn their punishment into a means of protest by seizing control of the filth in order to in turn inflict it on the visual and sensory space of the guards. Following the lead of the men's dirty protest at Long Kesh, the women began smearing their excrement on the walls of their prison cells in order to graphically draw attention to the physical conditions of their existence. While urine and feces had already been used in the men's protest, the addition of menstrual blood in the women's prison had several important effects on the ramifications of the protest.

It is my aim to show that the women's dirty protest added a new dimension to the men's protest because it introduced a series of reversals. Blood as an emblem of pain and violence, I will argue, was appropriated by the women in Armagh as a weapon against the British penal institution. The women used the blood as a signifier of violence that was not available to the men of Long Kesh and were thus able to encode a counterinstitutional agency within the menstrual blood. The menstrual blood, in this sense, was no longer merely a marginal and filthy substance that must be hidden. Rather, it became central to the politics of a building discourse of protest. I would further suggest that the use of menstrual blood as a weapon of protest was, and must be, antagonistic to the modern British penal system, the Catholic Church, and the Irish Republican Army (IRA), all of which played important roles in the governing of nationalist women.

My attempt here is not to speak for the women involved in the protest. Nor is it my wish to unconditionally valorize the women's positions within the IRA. As a non-Irish woman, my goal in this chapter is to provide an analysis, and one way of reading, the specific events that occurred during the women's dirty protest.[2] My hope is that my reading of the women's roles in the Irish context here can ultimately add to and resonate with other locations of feminist and anticolonial struggle.[3]

In order to investigate the consequences of the women's protest, it is necessary to at least briefly situate the protest within the historicopolitical climate of Northern Ireland.[4] The women's dirty protest in Armagh Prison in Northern Ireland began on February 7, 1980. Before this, male Republican prisoners in Long Kesh had already commenced their dirty protest by smearing urine and feces on their cell walls. A complex chain of events worked together to bring about this particular form of protest. In 1976, "special category" status for IRA prisoners was revoked by the British penal system. This new categorization meant that Republican prisoners were now to be classified as ordinary criminals, stripped of the special privileges granted to political prisoners (Coogan, 115). IRA prisoners would now be required to wear prison uniforms and to work on prison projects, and they were subject to normal prison visitation rules (NCCL, 2). Most importantly, however, the new classification refused to acknowledge the political and insurrectionary motivations of the prisoners' acts. In response to the denial of "special category" status, the prisoners of Long Kesh refused to wear prison uniforms and in protest donned only blankets. For these "blanket-men," as they were termed, using the prison toilets became a violent and humiliating confrontation with prison authorities. The prisoners' bodies were routinely searched, prodded, and beaten by prison guards when the prisoners attempted to use prison toilets. As a means of evading such confrontations, the prisoners began to refuse to leave their cells (Feldman, 171–74). In the early stages of the protest, prisoners emptied their chamber pots through windows and under cell doors. In response to the prison guards' continued violence, the prisoners began to smear their excrement on cell walls; the men's dirty protest began in earnest on March 18, 1978 (Feldman, 173).

The loss of "special category" status was also the impetus for the women's dirty protest. On February 7, 1980, the prisoners of Armagh were summoned from their cells to eat a surprisingly good lunch consisting of chicken and of apple pie. The women soon found out, however, that the meal was a pretext to draw them out of their cells. Mairead Farrell, one of the prisoners whose narrative of the inception of the protest was smuggled out of Armagh, describes having "a funny feeling something wasn't right" when prison officials, who were "tradesmen [who] do painting etc. in the gaol" surrounded her wing.[5] Then, she goes on to say, "next minute I looked onto B1 where fourty [*sic*] to fifty male screws [prison guards] came out of a corridor between B and A wing and they surrounded all of our ones at the hot plate" (Farrell, 1).[6] The women were then taken forcibly by about sixty male and female warders, "and they were all locked up in the wings' two association cells. Their own cells were searched, and according to the girls' version, 'wrecked'" (Coogan, 116). After the cell searches, the women prisoners were searched bodily, beaten, and assigned punishments for their resistance to the searches. Farrell describes "the male screws beating the hell out of some of the girls, just picking them up and throwing them," and further claims "it was obvious they were after our black uniforms [which denoted IRA affiliation] and by the look of things our blood as well" (Farrell, 1–2). In this process, Farrell says,

> We weren't allowed to use the toilets and the male screws took over the running of the wing although the females remained. We didn't get any exercise or food and they told us to use our pots 'cause we wouldn't be getting to the toilet, never mind wash, when our pots were full they wouldn't let us empty them. (3)

While the women's dirty protest began in response to a particular violent conflict, it escalated to become an organized revolt against the authority of the prison system. It is important that the women attempted, in the beginning, to avoid contact with the filth, but their refusal to use the toilets even after they were opened would seem to be a specific attempt to convert their punishment into a means of protest. Over time, the walls of Armagh were not only smeared with feces and urine, but also with menstrual blood. It is the blood, and the associations of violence and rejuvenation that it carries with it, that I wish to draw particular attention to here. As Begoña Aretxaga, one of the few scholars to deal critically with the women's protest, notes, the addition of menstrual blood to the existing tableau of urine and feces added a new, and not entirely intended, realm to the dirty protest. As menstruating women, the bodies of the prisoners in Armagh became unconditionally gendered and sexualized (Aretxaga, "Dirty Protest," 139).

In the course of this chapter, I aim to argue that the dirty protest in Armagh arose in reaction to the modernizing and normalizing efforts of the British penal system. With Britain's refusal to acknowledge the IRA's use of modern weaponry as a means for political struggle, instead deeming them ordinary criminals, the prisoners resorted to their own bodies in order to politicize their existence in prison. The IRA women were placed in prison because they had attempted to use modern weapons in an organized revolt against the state. However, that attempt was not viewed by the government as "political." In effect, to subvert the authority of the modern prison apparatus, the prisoners espoused the primitivism and dirtiness that has been used by the British to racialize the Irish. The specific importance of viewing the dirty protest as a countermodern struggle, then, arises in the prisoners' appropriation and self-conscious dramatization of this stereotypical dirtiness that characterized the popular British conception of the Irish (Aretxaga, *Shattering Silence,* 90–93). Here I use the term "countermodern" because I see the protest in direct contest with the modern prison system. However, the dirty protest also plays on the historical British position that Irish "dirtiness" and "primitivism" betrays an inherent incapacity for self-governance.[7] For example, Charles Kingsley offered the following comments during his visit to Sligo, Ireland, in 1860:

> I am haunted by the human chimpanzees I saw along that hundred miles of horrible country. I don't believe they are our fault. I believe . . . that they are happier, better, more comfortably fed and lodged under our rule than they ever were. (Kingsley, 111)

Here the Irish, as a race, are animalized and presented as incapable of governing and caring for themselves with the degree of human decorum acceptable to their British colonizers.

While Kingsley's commentary predates the dirty protest by more than a century, similar sentiments were echoed in the European Commission on Human Rights' ruling on the prisoners' demand for political status. The commission report stated that the Long Kesh prisoners' "strategy [in the dirty protest] involved self-inflicted debasement and humiliation to an almost subhuman degree" (Bowyer Bell, 594). The same commission then used this report as grounds to absolve the British penal system of its responsibility for what it perceived as the inmates' self-determined conditions. At this point, it seemed as though the dirty protest was a failure for the Irish prisoners. In fact, the men's protest worked to garner global support for British rule.

The addition of menstrual blood to the protest, though, added an entirely new dimension to the political ramifications of the protest. The menstrual blood on the walls of Armagh was perceived as taboo not only because it was dirty, but also because it was explicitly sexualized. The sexual aspect of the blood, then, carried with it connotations of both pain and suffering, as well as birth potential. For this reason, the British condemnation of the protest could no longer be seen as strictly a reaction against dirt and filth. With the addition of menstrual blood, the British now appeared to be condemning the sexualized bodies of Irish women. The women's dirty protest, I suggest, can be read as an attempt to locate and define a subjective mode of resistance that, unlike the men's protest, could not be contained and explained within the dominant British rationality.

Before proceeding further, I feel it is necessary to bring attention to the fact that, to date, very little has been written on the struggle in Armagh. While the men's dirty protest is comparatively well documented, the women of Armagh are virtually left out from the chronology of the Troubles. Here I would like to offer an incident that I believe exemplifies well the exclusion of the dirty protest at Armagh from the history of Northern Ireland. In my search for source materials for this chapter, I consulted *Web of Punishment*, Carol Coulter's excellent investigation into women's experiences as the family members of prisoners in Northern Ireland. When I checked the index for Armagh Prison, I was directed to page 10. When I turned to that page, however, I found it blank. Although this particular episode is no doubt the result of a printing error, it is emblematic of the Armagh women's struggle as a whole. My attempt here is to make a contribution to the filling of the empty page. Borrowing from Aretxaga, "subjectivity is always grounded in history—a history that includes the scars left by forgotten episodes and hidden discourses as much as conscious narratives" (Aretxaga, "Dirty Protest," 125). To deal critically with the women's dirty protest, then, is to lend credence to the "forgotten episodes and hidden discourses" that are a necessary counterpart to the "conscious narratives" that comprise the history of the Troubles in Northern Ireland. Within the larger framework of Northern Irish prison history, these "forgotten episodes and hidden discourses" can be seen as the women's dirty protest in relation to the "conscious narrative" of the dirty protest as a whole. In a more narrow context, the "forgotten episodes and hidden discourses" may represent the menstrual blood, while the "conscious narratives" are characterized by the excrement smeared on the walls of both Armagh and Long Kesh Prisons.

In the aftermath of the dirty protest, bodily filth seemed to be divided into two categories. It was acceptable to discuss feces (evidenced by the numerous books and essays on the men's protest), but menstrual blood did not receive much public attention. Granted, this is partly because the majority of prisoners on the dirty protest were men, and smearing feces on the wall was something that both male and female prisoners took part in. Yet the social taboo of discussing women's bodily functions seems to play a role in silencing the women's struggle. While the leaders of the IRA, and even the women prisoners, tended to view the blood as shameful and taboo, I would suggest, following Aretxaga, that it brought to the fore issues of feminism, violence, and protest that may have otherwise remained hidden. Although this line of analysis is possible in retrospect, during the dirty protest, many private acts became public performances, and menstruation in prison came to be seen, by the prisoners and those who looked upon them, as a process deeply embedded with feelings of shame. An inquiry into the practice of strip searching in Armagh conducted by the National Council for Civil Liberties noted the following:

> Many people to whom we spoke stressed the moral strictness which pervades the homes and schools of Protestants and Catholics alike. Youngsters

are imbued with a sense of embarrassment about their bodies, sex and
bodily functions. . . . A number of the prisoners we met expressed their
feelings of horror and shame in very much these terms. (29)

As the members of the inquiry board suggest, the shame these women felt
was a product of their socialization into strict codes of religion. The Virgin
Mary, as a social and religious symbol of Catholicism, is certainly feminized,
but arguably not at all "womanized." As a virgin mother, the figure of
Mary is disassociated from the processes of ovulation and menstruation as
biological requisites and precursors to a successful pregnancy. Yet the ideal
role for Irish women, put forward by the Catholic Church and the education system, is that of mother. Indeed, it has been argued that the authority
of the church has been reinforced by the state through the education system creating "an adhesive effect between church, state, women and morality" (McWilliams, 82). Through religion and education, women are taught
that the ideal to which they should aspire is that of the Virgin Mary. This
is in direct opposition to encouraging political activism, for "not only were
Catholic girls to model themselves on the Virgin Mary by maintaining their
chastity and purity, but equally were they called upon to adopt the mother's passive, unquestioning role" (McWilliams, 83).[8] Here it is interesting
that the ideology of motherhood is very much present, yet the biology of
the woman's body is noticeably absent. Motherhood, then, becomes a state
that can be valorized without actually conflating the ideal of Mary with the
bodies of real women. Marina Warner argues that "by making the virginity
of Christ's mother an article of faith, the Catholic Church has quite consciously separated sex from motherhood" (in McWilliams, 83). The state
and the church become complicit in demarcating this division, and it has
been argued "that by passing this philosophy on through the Catholic education system, it has taught women to hate their bodies" (McWilliams, 83).

Arguably, as part of this division between the ideal (which transcends
sex) and the real (which is bound to the functions of the body), Irish Catholic women are socialized to believe that "menstrual blood is considered
impure and the bodies of menstruating women [are] dirty. Traces of menstrual blood, like pads or tampons, are hidden and quickly thrown out,
especially if there are men in the household" (Aretxaga, *Shattering Silence,*
139). For the women prisoners, then, menstruation would no doubt have
been a bodily function that caused embarrassment and that they would
have preferred to have kept hidden. To overcome this shame and participate in the dirty protest, therefore, was to deny the totalizing power of
socially enforced rituals of cleanliness. To shirk the authority of modern
societal and religious edicts was to invent an alternative civilization that was
in some ways radically antimodern.[9]

The feelings of "horror and shame" (NCCL, 29) that the women experienced were grounded in a highly developed (i.e., modern) system of so-

cial rules and mores. The prisoners' refusal to accept the shame and indignity imposed by these conventions on a woman's body systematically dismantled the presumed authority of modern dictates for personal hygiene and decorum. In this sense, the prisoners were able to subvert the sterilizing goals of modernity through the use of nonmodern weaponry and methods of protest. The woman's body, then, was both the means of organized resistance and the subject of repulsion and condemnation. This embodied paradox is expressed in Tim Pat Coogan's reaction on confronting the women in Armagh Prison. Regarding the women's clothes, Coogan, who has chronicled the dirty protest in *On the Blanket: The H Block Story,* says, "as they had them on for a week . . . they were beginning to smell a bit. In fact I found the smell in the girls' cell far worse than that at Long Kesh, and several times found myself having to control feelings of nausea" (Coogan, 216). Citing the same passage, Aretxaga asks, "What can make 30 dirty women more revolting than 400 dirty men if not the exposure of menstrual blood—an element that cannot contribute much to the fetid odors of urine and feces but can turn the stomach" (Aretxaga, "Dirty Protest," 138). It is significant here that while admitting his revulsion, Coogan defers its reference to the women's clothing rather than locating its cause in the actual presence of menstrual blood. Coogan's hesitance to deal with the subject of menstruation is further demonstrated in his refusal to acknowledge the prisoners as women. Instead, he consistently refers to them as "girls." Coogan's effort, and failure, to sublate the issue of menstrual blood emblematizes a larger degree of embarrassment felt by Irish nationalists when confronted with the taboo subject of menstruation. It is precisely this sort of forced coming to terms with shame and embarrassment, as Aretxaga argues, that has opened a dialogue of feminist politics surrounding the issue of Armagh.[10]

In her work, Aretxaga brings to the fore the significance of menstrual blood as a symbol for the real bodies of IRA women:

> [The menstrual blood] objectified a difference that women had carefully obliterated in other dimensions of their political life. That is, while their political identity as members of the IRA entailed at one level a cultural desexualization, and the dirty protest a personal defeminization, at a deeper level the exposure of menstrual blood subverted this process by radically transforming the asexual bodies of "girls" into the sexualized bodies of women. In so doing, the menstrual blood became a symbol through which gender identity was reflected upon, bringing to the surface what had been otherwise erased. (139)

The women's presence in prison as "sexualized bodies" allowed for a feminist politics to arise out of their struggle. Feminist journalist Nell McCafferty, for example, seized on the menstrual blood as a gender marker and a marker of the women's bodies when she wrote, "there is menstrual blood *in* the walls of Armagh Prison in Northern Ireland" (in Aretxaga, "Dirty Protest," 142, emphasis added). Implicitly, by objectifying the women as their menstrual blood, McCafferty's statement forces a reckoning with the extent to which the woman's body has traditionally been excluded from her political activities and value. The women who are in prison are emblematized, she implies, as much by their blood as by their political activities.

The menstrual blood in the prison context can be seen as representing both a physical and dialogic lack. The physical process of menstruation enacts a loss, that of blood, birth potential, and self. But the ability to menstruate and to repeat the cycle is, on a very simple level, an affirmation of life-giving potential and of existence. The sustained visible presence of menstrual blood is a constant testimony to the women's capacity to reproduce and, specifically, to reproduce resistance. The addressing of the above loss/lack through continued menstruation is therefore the beginning of its fulfillment. The blood is lost episodically, yet its birth potential is deflected from the literal physical realm to the discursive realm. By smearing the blood on the walls, the women were, to an extent, bringing about both a dialogue concerning their physical conditions and a dialogue concerning their bodies as women. The women's bodies were no longer ungendered, and therefore gender was forced into recognition and visibility by the prison authorities and by the Republican men and women. The application of menstrual blood to the walls of a disciplinary institution (particularly in a colonized culture) serves as an utterance against the hegemonic structure of the British prison system. With collective episodic repetition, each woman's menstrual period contributes to a building discourse.

As Allen Feldman documents in his *Formations of Violence,* the male prisoners of Long Kesh imprinted their prison cells with "scatological writing" as the excrement on the walls was turned into a performance piece and narrative. Often the prisoners combined feces with urine and used this mixture to paint political slogans on the walls (Feldman, 165–74). These narratives were a powerful form of resistance, both in their material composition and in their linguistic signification. Whether or not such actual writing existed on the walls of Armagh, I would suggest that the presence of blood in the women's prison added a necessary counterpart to the existing narrative that began in Long Kesh. During the men's protest, dirt and filth became the primary focus. In the women's protest, however, menstrual blood encapsulated notions of pain and rejuvenation.[11] In this capacity, the women's blood served as a catalyst to bring forth a feminist politics of continued existence amid torture and pain. The relevance of this discourse turns on the choice of a "primitive" symbol used to destabilize modern procedures of discipline.

In *Purity and Danger,* Mary Douglas examines the significance of modern society's desire to keep dirt contained and ordered. Conversely, she also discusses the power that lies in society's margins, particularly with reference to what she terms primitive societies. In Douglas's framework, however, implications of modernity and primitivism are double and contradictory. On the one hand, modern societies rigidly uphold order against chaos. On the other hand, primitive societies are characterized for Douglas by an extreme fear of pollution. The seemingly opposing terms "primitive" and "modern" thus betray a similar concern for purity, albeit with different motivations. Douglas distinguishes between grounds for hygiene in primitive and modern societies as follows:

> The difference between us [primitive and modern societies] is not that our behaviour is grounded on science and theirs on symbolism. Our behaviour also carries symbolic meaning. The real difference is that we do not bring forward from one context to the next the same set of ever more powerful symbols: our experience is fragmented. Our rituals create a lot of little sub-worlds, unrelated. Their rituals create one single, symbolically consistent universe. (70)

Creating a consistent discourse of resistance through the use of filth, then, would for Douglas place the dirty protest in the realm of the primitive. Each defecation or menstrual period is not significant in and of itself, but rather builds a narrative through repetition and the continuity of its display. The addition of menstrual blood to the dirty protest engenders discourse and ensures that it is continuous.

Operating within Douglas's construct, the dirty protest functions by using a primitive symbol of pollution to bring about in a modern system of discipline a primitivistic fear of contamination. The antimodern struggle of the women in Armagh, then, plays on modernity's emphasis on order (organized and yet fragmentary) to reveal what Mary Douglas conceptualizes as a landmark of primitive societies, the fear of pollution. In Douglas's analysis, filth is produced by offending against order within a particular social context. Douglas claims that

> As we know it, dirt is essentially disorder. There is no such thing as absolute dirt: it exists in the eye of the beholder. If we shun dirt, it is not because of craven fear, still less dread of holy terror. Nor do our ideas about disease account for the range of our behaviour in cleaning or avoiding dirt. Dirt offends against order. Eliminating it is not a negative moment, but a positive effort to organise the environment. (2)

This effort is positive, of course, insofar as the subjects at stake subscribe to a belief in the same structures of order. Borrowing from Douglas, though, I would suggest that the dirty protest created an alternative conception of filth that offended against the order of the prison system. The prison staff were frightened not because the filth threatened their bodies, but because it threatened the structures of order that kept them in possession of power.

The women's protest in Armagh thus turns the tables on modernity by forcing one of its key markers—the prison system—into a submissive state of primitivistic fear. Confined within structures of order, the prisoners used disorder to enact a threat against the ordered and hegemonic structure of the prison. Again, Mary Douglas proves useful in locating danger in disorder:

> Granted that disorder spoils pattern, it also provides the material of pattern. Order implies restriction; from all possible materials, a limited selection has been made and from all possible relations a limited set has been used. So disorder by implication is unlimited, no pattern has been realised in it, but its potential for patterning is indefinite. . . . [Disorder] symbolises both danger and power. (95)

The danger of disorder in Armagh threatened the power structures that, if they were functioning as intended, would have prevented the dirty protest at its inception. The protesters' success at causing and harnessing disorder toward their own goals brought to light the prison system's fallibility. The guards depended on the unified workings of the system to keep them out of danger. Breakdowns in discipline, such as the dirty protest, thus signify a potential threat to the safety of the guards. At the inception of the protest, Farrell, for example, documented being surrounded by "fourty [*sic*] to fifty male screws" (Farrell, 1). As the protest continued, however, Farrell says, "the male screws aren't about so much now" (Farrell, 3).[12] It follows then, if complete control could not be asserted over the bodies of the prisoners at all times, there could possibly arise a new threat of resistance at every level of discipline. In this manner, the fear of primitive symbols of disorder translated into a corresponding fear regarding the efficacy of the modern British prison.[13] On a fundamental level, the prisoners forced the British penal system into a state of powerlessness.

I would stipulate here that the physical presence of blood on the walls was a crucial element necessary to incite such fear. Blood, as a register of pain and violence, provoked in the prison authorities a sense of intimate fear. Aretxaga notes that "prison officers felt defiled coming into contact with the prisoners. As the women looked increasingly dirty, the guards tried to counteract defilement by increasing their care in making themselves up and having their hair done" (Aretxaga, "Dirty Protest," 136). This reaction to an implicit perception of danger was undoubtedly heightened by the guards' own use of blood to induce fear among prisoners. Feldman describes an apparently common practice in Long Kesh in which blood is used as a visual referent to pain, torture, and violence:

> The PIRA [Provisional Irish Republican Army] captives move from the parade of mutilation and mob violence [interrogation and examination] with its attendant scenes of weeping and anger to the showers, where supposedly

any violence enacted against them can be masked by the washing away of blood with water. . . . Red paint masquerading as blood is thrown around the shower stall before the arrival of the prisoners. (122)

On the walls of Armagh, however, the blood was real, and the dirty protest refused to let fade the scars of pain, violence, and resistance. The blood in Armagh, belonging to and within the control of the prisoners, was consciously inflicted on the visual and sensory space of the guards. Reversing the techniques of punishment, the protesters in Armagh were able to counteremploy the tools of modern discipline they sought to displace.

Elaine Scarry elucidates the notion of the weapon as a visual tool of agency in her description of the power play of torture. Although my use of Scarry's analysis here is clearly not within her intended context, I believe her work provides an interesting point of comparison to what I am exploring. The crucial difference between her realm of investigation and mine is that while Scarry deals with torture within a hegemonic system, my application here of her insights is to a counterhegemonic struggle. Acknowledging this central difference, I aim to reinvest agency and authority in the wielders of these particular weapons of revolt. For Scarry, "what assists the conversion of absolute pain into the fiction of absolute power is an obsessive, self-conscious display of agency" (Scarry, 27). The prison mechanism, and that of torture, depends on its ability to induce a stupor of fear. But the use of menstrual blood on the walls as a weapon of protest articulates a powerful reversal. In Armagh, the prisoner's body was both the target of torture and, alternatively, the weapon with which she could inflict a torture of her own. Thus, in their ability to claim agency for themselves through the display of blood, the prisoners defied the authority of the prison system. Scarry continues,

> On the simplest level, the agent displayed is the weapon. Testimony given by torture victims from many different countries almost inevitably includes descriptions of being made to stare at the weapon with which they were about to be hurt. (27)

This point is made more significant in light of McCafferty's earlier noted characterization of the prisoners in terms of their blood. McCafferty says "there is menstrual blood *in* the walls of Armagh Prison in Northern Ireland" rather than "on" the walls. The prisoner is embodied in her menstrual blood, which in turn becomes the agent capable of inflicting torture. The use of blood as a weapon, then, to an extent deflects pain from the body of the menstruating woman onto the consciousness of the prison guard. Here I do not mean to absolve of responsibility, or undermine, the prison system's ability to inflict real torture and pain. Rather, I wish to create a separate space in which the women prisoners' acts can realize their separate locus of empowerment. Within this scope, the prisoners' uprising was able to render defunct the prison's capacity to punish.

For Foucault, discipline and punishment are intricately joined. But how must a modern prison punish a group of prisoners who elude discipline? To effectively realize the goals of incarceration, Foucault stipulates that the prison system must uphold a series of conditions. Arguably, the entire project of effective imprisonment hinges upon two such conditions. First, the imprisoned subject must be constantly visible. Second, he or she must be trainable (Foucault, 191, 188). The Armagh revolt successfully subverted both grounds of control by deflecting visibility away from the prisoners onto the blood and by resisting the training that mandates the use of the chamber pots. In the words of a former prison officer, "you could see the dirty protest as virtually resistance to toilet training" (Feldman, 192). In this basic rejection of training, the prisoners also called into question the prison's capacity to govern them by refusing to adhere to the shame that would typically characterize their bodies' uncontrollability. Elizabeth Grosz, in her far-ranging analysis *Volatile Bodies,* reads Julia Kristeva's discussion of the relationship between menstrual blood and excrement. Both menstrual blood and excrement, Grosz suggests, are socially constructed to denote shame if not controlled:

> The clean and proper body's development is directly linked to the child's negotiations with the demands of toilet training and the regulation of body fluids. Within this cultural constellation it is not surprising, then, that women's menstrual flow is regarded not only with shame and embarrassment but with disgust and the powers of contaminating.[14] (206)

Again, as I have argued earlier, it is this overcoming of shame and disgust that threatened the penal institution's power to order and control the women's bodies. The prisoners' refusal to conform to basic socially prescribed rules of decorum and hygiene suggests a fundamental negation of the prison's disciplinary powers. Further, as a result of the prisoners' resistance to the second condition for discipline (trainability), the first condition (visibility) is also called into question.

The prisoners' bodies became weapons that they used in order to disrupt the gaze of modern surveillance imposed by the British state through the penal institution. During the protest, spyholes and windows were routinely kept closed in order to prevent the prisoners from using them to eliminate waste from their cells. No longer subject to constant surveillance, the women were able to reappropriate their time in order to further a self-determined politics. A narrative smuggled out from Armagh describes the prisoners' activities on a routine day as follows:

> The evening passes swiftly. The singing has started. Different ones called for a song. The supper arrives. A pancake each. Big deal. We're locked in

for the night. We listen to the male prisoners cleaning the wing. Soon they will be off and all will be quiet. Then our entertainment begins. Every night at 9.00 p.m. we have the Rosary in Irish. One shouts it out the door and the rest respond. Afterwards we have our Irish class shouted out the doors. Our voices are good and strong now from persistent shouting. Then perhaps bingo from our own made cards. It's good crack. Anne-Marie next door persists in cheating but is always found out. Then at eleven the ghost story is continued from the night before as most lie in their beds under the covers to keep warm as they listen to the story. At midnight all noise ceases—an order from our own staff. I get into my bed under the blanket—no sheets or pillowcases. Those too were taken by screws and think another day over as Sinéad voices my thoughts "perhaps it'll be cornflakes tomorrow." Yes maybe tomorrow will be our lucky day. (Coogan, 125–30)

Such practices, clearly reflecting a nationalist Catholic bent, would undoubtedly have been viewed as refractory by prison authorities. Notably, the prisoners were not resistant to all forms of discipline, for they had a "staff" from which a leader was chosen. Rather, they were hostile to a system of discipline that sought to efface the women's ability to exist as self-determining subjects. It is such episodes of self-government within the confines of the prison system that resulted as empowering by-products of the protest. With continued, sustained resistance, the women were able to systematically reduce the enforcement of control over their time, space, and bodies.

It is significant, I believe, that such alternative practices manifested as a result of an antimodern means of protest. The success of a modern prison is contingent on both the prisoners' and the guards' willingness and desire to participate in systems of order. While the technology of a modern prison system is equipped to quell and/or prevent a modern revolt, it has little means of arresting the prisoners' countermodern tactics. Guns, knives, and bombs can easily be detected mechanically, but what technological advancement can prevent a prisoner from smearing blood and excrement on the walls of her own cell? It is precisely this element of ungovernability that was seized on by the prisoners. In this context, the women in Armagh Prison were able to convert their bodily refuse into a psychosocial weapon of protest.

The dirty protest, which lasted for thirteen months, did not ultimately succeed in restoring political status to prisoners, nor did it radically alter the workings of the British prison system. It certainly did not free Northern Ireland from colonial oppression. The protest's real triumph, I believe, lies in its success in creating a viable space for resistance in a prison culture obsessed with control. The goals realized by the protest were to at least momentarily invert the structures of power and to paralyze the gaze of modern surveillance. But equally powerful, and no less remarkable for its lack of intention, the women's dirty protest launched a discussion that ultimately moved toward the subjectification of women's bodies. The dialectics of pain and perseverance surrounded, and were encoded in, the presence of menstrual blood as a signification for the experience of real women within the prison. In the context of the protest, what was considered filthy was reappropriated by the women and made integral to the performance of struggle. Socially constructed filth was thus reconfigured as a politically necessary weapon of protest. The inversion of power relations between the prisoners and the guards ultimately is rooted in the fundamental transformation of bodily waste products—specifically, menstrual blood—into tools for social change, thus making available alternative, and potentially countermodern, methods of protest.

NOTES

I would like to thank several people whose help in writing this essay has been invaluable. First, I am indebted to Niall Farrell for inviting me into his home, sharing personal memories, and providing important documents about his sister Mairead's role in the dirty protest. I also thank Lionel Pilkington for putting me in touch with Niall so that we were able to meet in Galway. David Lloyd provided the original inspiration for this essay by first drawing my attention to the dirty protest, and Fredric Jameson added by supplying ideas for new directions of analysis. Finally, I thank Mrinalini Chakravorty for reading and editing this essay.

1. Long Kesh is also known as the Maze Prison. Political prisoners were kept in the H Block section after the removal of special category status. Political prisoners formerly received special rights, including the right to wear their own clothes and the right to refuse to perform prison labor.

2. Of course, reading the women's actions in terms of their bodily functions risks placing my analysis within the tradition of patriarchal discourse that has objectified women solely in terms of the biology of their bodies. However, my intent here is to look at a particular aspect of the dirty protest, which, in the scope of this chapter, confines me to emphasizing the physicality of the women's struggle. Needless to say, it would be productive to also study the important social and intellectual contributions that the women have also made to the Republican movement.

3. To this end, I would mark alliances between the dirty protest and other feminist and/or anticolonial struggles (such as the Telangana women's protest in South India or the Zapatista uprising in Chiapas). This is not to erase specificity or difference, but rather to engender a dialogue that is vigilant of both the possibilities of collectivities and the limitations of universalisms. For a discussion of these issues, see Mohanty et al.

4. This chapter is focused on providing a reading of a specific event in the history of Northern Ireland and is not a broad historical study of the colonial presence in Ireland or a history of the Troubles. For more detailed historical studies, see, e.g., Page; and Bowyer Bell. For a history of the hunger strikes and other prison protests in Northern Ireland, see O'Malley. O'Malley provides a detailed history not only of the Long Kesh hunger strikes of 1980–1981, but also a good analysis of the "legacy" that the protests had on future politics in Northern Ireland. See also

Coogan. For a compilation of narratives from the men's dirty protest, see *Nor Meekly Serve My Time,* compiled by Brian Campbell.

5. Mairead Farrell was one of three IRA Volunteers shot down in Gibraltar by the British Special Air Services on March 6, 1988. The British government initially claimed that the three Volunteers were suspected of having plans to carry out a bomb attack. The Volunteers, however, were unarmed at the time of the shooting. On September 27, 1995, the British government was found guilty by the European Court of Human Rights of violating the right to life of Mairead Farrell, Dan Mc-Cann, and Sean Savage.

6. This information is taken from a comm (communicado) written by Mairead Farrell on toilet paper during the time of the protest. The comm, which was addressed to Niall Farrell, Mairead's brother, describes the inception of the protest at length:

> During the whole thing [search and adjudication] the girls were held spread-eagled in the air with shoes removed then they were thrown into empty cells, there were some cuts and bruises after that crowd! After that we weren't allowed to use the toilets the male screws took over the running of the wing although the females remained. We didn't get any exercise or food and they told us to use our pots 'cause we wouldn't be getting to the toilet, never mind wash, when our pots were full they wouldn't let us empty them so we'd no alternative but to throw it out the spyholes but the male screws nailed those shut although we managed to break them off using our chairs. Last Wed. they moved us to this wing, took all our belongings off us and we were brought over here with nothing. On Friday they supplied us with pens and paper, they gave us a few photos and that's it. We have sent everything out all our clothes etc. and are now on a no-wash protest. Our cells are leaping not to mention ourselves but morale is brilliant. (3)

7. When I invoke the term "countermodern," I mean to suggest that the protest works against the modern and postmodern penal institution. Yet on a more fundamental level, I would also like to think of the protest as against the model of history that would view colonial subjects as lagging developmentally behind their colonizers. In this sense, although the protest is in some ways classically postmodern as well as premodern, it ultimately resists classification within the developmental schema of historical "progress." For an excellent discussion of alternative conceptions of history and resistance, see Lisa Lowe and David Lloyd's introduction to *The Politics of Culture in the Shadow of Capital.* I see this essay as complicit with their theoretical project, which is "interested in another understanding of the temporality of the breakup of modernity, taking into account the antagonisms to modernity that take place in a variety of locations and that emerge simultaneously with and in relation to modernity itself" (4).

8. In September 1980, Father Raymond Murray, the Catholic chaplain for Armagh Prison, made the following speech at the International Permanent Commission of Catholic Chaplains in Lucerne, Switzerland:

> I feel that the Church has a special duty in the case of women prisoners for whom jail, even in reasonably relaxed and enlightened conditions, is a burden altogether unsuitable for them to bear even for a short period. I feel that the Church should campaign for the recognition of a policy that women who offend against the laws of society would be kept in hospital-type institutions rather than be sent to prison cells. The Church has been challenged much of late in regard to its attitude to women. . . . It must recognize that

the longing for friendship and companionship makes women particularly unsuited for life in harsh prison conditions. (74–75)

Although Father Murray's intention here is no doubt to aid the women, his plea to treat as ill those women who act against the state simply reveals the degree to which the Catholic Church is entrenched in patriarchal ideology. To claim that the women should be hospitalized instead of penalized works to desubjectify the women and make them frail in order to remove from them the capacity to choose a course of action, willfully, that will result in their imprisonment.

9. The prisoners were themselves products of the socialization process that condemned the filthy conditions that they produced and continued to live in. Yet I would suggest that the need to sustain these conditions was met by an attempt to distance themselves ideologically from those who condemned them. In this vein, the prison guards, or screws, were delineated by the prisoners as wholly ideologically opposite to the beliefs of the prisoners. This ideological power play was necessary, I think, for the prisoners to embrace the conditions in which they existed. To an extent, though, the prisoners' resentment of the guards obscured the fact that the guards were at the mercy of the prison apparatus as well. Margaretta D'Arcy's account does, however, take note of some acts of kindness on the part of the guards.

10. For an interesting, if somewhat bizarre, account of the dirty protest, see D'Arcy's *Tell Them Everything.* D'Arcy, a feminist theater actress from the Republic of Ireland, purposefully has herself imprisoned during the dirty protest in order to serve time in Armagh. Although she gives an important firsthand account of conditions during the dirty protest, it must be remembered that her story is not that of a Republican political prisoner. Her actions leading to her imprisonment (refusing to pay a fine) on the one hand reveal how little it takes to find oneself imprisoned in Northern Ireland. On the other hand, however, they also can be seen as trivializing the real political activism undertaken by her fellow women prisoners.

11. Elizabeth Grosz links the sight of menstrual blood not only to pain, but also to powerlessness and infancy:

> for the girl, menstruation, associated as it is with blood, with injury and the wound, with a mess that does not dry invisibly, that leaks uncontrollably . . . indicates the beginning of an out-of-control status that she was led to believe ends with childhood. The idea of soiling oneself, of dirt, of the very dirt produced by the body itself, staining the subject, is a "normal" condition of infancy, but in the case of the maturing woman it is a mark or stain of her future status, the impulsion into a future of a past that she thought she had left behind. (205)

Although my reading of the blood here focuses on its empowering effect, it is also important to keep in mind the analysis Grosz offers here. Grosz's interpretation of the blood should, I think, be seen as a concurrent counterpart to the power which I suggest the blood holds as a weapon.

12. The reduction in the number of male guards is also evidence of the increasingly gendered politics of the protest. The prison seems to have responded to the sexual dynamic of the protest on an official level through the placement of personnel.

13. The guards' fear was, however, also precipitated by real events. D'Arcy reports that "an 'execution' of female screws took place in the early summer of 1979, (two months after our first demo on 8 March), when the INLA shot four screws in the road in front of the jail, killing one" (64).

14. For a discussion of polluting and nonpolluting bodily fluids and their conditions of abjection, see Julia Kristeva's *Powers of Horror.* In the chapter entitled

"From Filth to Defilement," Kristeva reads bodily pollution in association with the incest taboo.

REFERENCES

Aretxaga, Begoña. "Dirty Protest: Symbolic Overdetermination and Gender in Northern Ireland Ethnic Violence." *Ethos* 23, no. 2 (1995): 123–48.
———. *Shattering Silence: Women, Nationalism, and Political Subjectivity in Northern Ireland.* Princeton, N.J.: Princeton University Press, 1997.
Bowyer Bell, J. *The Irish Troubles: A Generation of Violence 1967–1992.* New York: St. Martin's Press, 1993.
Campbell, Brian, ed. *Nor Meekly Serve My Time: The H Block Struggle 1976–1981.* Belfast: Beyond the Pale Publications, 1994.
Coogan, Tim Pat. *On the Blanket: The H Block Story.* Dublin: Ward River Press, 1980.
Coulter, Carol. *Web of Punishment: An Investigation.* Dublin: Attic Press, 1991.
D'Arcy, Margaretta. *Tell Them Everything: A Sojourn in the Prison of Her Majesty Queen Elizabeth II at Ard Macha (Armagh).* London: Pluto Press, 1981.
Douglas, Mary. *Purity and Danger: An Analysis of Pollution and Taboo.* 1966. London: Ark, 1984.
Farrell, Mairead. Unpublished personal correspondence with Niall Farrell.
Feldman, Allen. *Formations of Violence: The Narrative of the Body and Political Terror in Northern Ireland.* Chicago: University of Chicago Press, 1991.
Foucault, Michel. *The Foucault Reader.* Edited by Paul Rabinow. New York: Pantheon, 1984.
Grosz, Elizabeth. *Volatile Bodies: Toward a Corporeal Feminism.* Bloomington: Indiana University Press, 1994.
Kingsley, Frances E., ed. *Charles Kingsley: His Letters and Memories of His Life.* Vol. 3. London: Macmillan, 1901.
Kristeva, Julia. *Powers of Horror: An Essay on Abjection.* Translated by Leon Roudiez. New York: Columbia University Press, 1982.
Lowe, Lisa, and David Lloyd. Introduction to *The Politics of Culture in the Shadow of Capital,* 1–32. Durham, N.C.: Duke University Press, 1997.
McWilliams, Monica. "The Church, the State and the Women's Movement in Northern Ireland." In *Irish Women's Studies Reader,* edited by Ailbhe Smyth, 79–99. Dublin: Attic Press, 1993.
Magill. *Ireland's Current Affairs Monthly,* October (1986): 8–18.
Mohanty, Chandra Talpade, Ann Russo, and Lourdes Torres, eds. *Third World Women and the Politics of Feminism.* Bloomington: Indiana University Press, 1991.
Murray, Raymond. *Hard Time: Armagh Gaol 1971–1986.* Cork: Mercier Press, 1998.
National Council for Civil Liberties [NCCL]. "Strip Searching: An Inquiry into the Strip Searching of Women Remand Prisoners of Armagh Prison between 1982 and 1985." London: NCCL, 1986.
O'Malley, Padraig. *Biting at the Grave: The Irish Hunger Strikes and the Politics of Despair.* Boston: Beacon Press, 1990.
Page, Michael von Tangen. "Northern Ireland, 1969–97." In *Prisons, Peace and Terrorism: Penal Policy in the Reduction of Political Violence in Northern Ireland, Italy and the Spanish Basque Country, 1968–97.* Basingstoke: Macmillan, 1998.
Scarry, Elaine. *The Body in Pain: The Making and Unmaking of the World.* New York: Oxford University Press, 1985.

Chapter 5

Bodily Metaphors, Material Exclusions

The Sexual and Racial Politics of
Domestic Partnership in France

CATHERINE RAISSIGUIER

> The articulation of the struggle against homophobia with the
> struggle against racism is an urgent priority, and yet our under-
> standing about the connection between homophobia and racism
> within specific political contexts is insufficient.
> —Anna Marie Smith, "The Centering of Right-Wing
> Extremism through the Construction of an 'Inclusionary'
> Homophobia and Racism"

I open this essay with a quote from Anna Marie Smith as a way of foregrounding the theoretical and political impetus of this chapter. Recent
historical, feminist, and postcolonial scholarship has mounted ample evidence of the deep and ongoing connections between racial, sexual, and
national thinking within the context of Europe's colonial project (Bhabha;
Gilman; McClintock, *Imperial Leather;* Stoler). However, we still lack empirical and theoretical discussions of the ways in which these connections articulate and shape current political struggles within postcolonial[1] settings. In
this essay, I begin to fill this gap by showing that current homophobic and
racist discourses in France borrow from each other and use similar metaphors. Through this analysis, I hope to uncover how the deployment of
anti-immigrant and antigay politics in the late 1990s have intersected to
produce political and popular discourses that represent postcolonial immigrants and queers as threats to the national body.

Such discursive crossings can certainly be analyzed as traces of France's
colonial project. Indeed, this dual and linked focus on queer and postcolonial subjects at this particular historical juncture echoes a colonial past
where discourses of sexuality, racial thinking, and nationalist rhetoric intersected in the construction of the bourgeois/national subject and its others
(Gilman; McClintock, *Imperial Leather;* Stoler). Here, however, I choose to
focus on something else. I analyze these discursive intersections and bor-
rowings as part of an ongoing process of subjectification that articulates

different hierarchies of power and locates individuals and collectivities in contradictory relations to the French State and its republican promise of universal inclusion and integration.

First and foremost, it must be noted that these discourses do have the potential of creating subaltern subjects/classes by establishing hierarchies of bodies, sexual practices, and cultures/religions. Once discursively located on the margins of the French citizenry, postcolonial immigrants and queers are "entitled" to different treatments and opportunities, uneven access to rights and civil protections, and unequal claims to social benefits. The demonization of queer and postcolonial subjects lays the ideological foundations for the development of new forms of discrimination that can rob entire segments of French society of the basic civil rights protection to which they are entitled by the constitutional texts of the republic. Needless to say, discursive practices that construct certain subjects/collectivities as outsiders and threats to the national order also have the potential of legitimating and spurring individual, collective, and state violence against these subjects and collectivities.

With this analysis, however, I hope to disrupt the naive notion that homophobia, racism, and their complex intersections with other axes of domination generate one-dimensional or simply additive forms of exclusion. Rather, I argue that although based on imagined fears, these discourses create "real" but different threats for postcolonial immigrants and queers in France. Most endangered are queer postcolonial immigrants who— located at the crossroads of several discourses and practices of exclusion— find themselves particularly vulnerable to the complex processes that ultimately construct them as third-class citizens and usher them to the precarious realm of ongoing structural inequality.[2] In the context of patriarchal relations in their countries of origin as well as in their "host" country, postcolonial immigrant lesbians—who are by and large erased from public discourse—encounter yet another layer of discriminatory practices that have yet to be fully understood.

The nation, in Western political parlance, is often associated with an imagined ideal human body. This idealized body "has been cast implicitly in the image of the robust, European, heterosexual gentleman, an ideal defined by its contradistinction to a potpourri of 'deviant' types" (Terry and Urla, 4). Nations are also imagined through the trope of the reproductive heterosexual family. Indeed, as McClintock argues, "despite their myriad differences, nations are symbolically figured as domestic genealogies" (*Imperial Leather*, 357).

The construction of the nation around bodily and familial metaphors suggests its ongoing reliance on and reinforcement of a gender hierarchy, which itself depends on a "natural" (but ironically, strictly enforced) division of labor between the sexes. Women's bodies then are not simply used to embody the nation; they also often figure at the heart (even when invisible) of many national debates and struggles. Indeed, questions of female sexuality, reproductive rights, and respectability have been central to the ongoing process of nation building and the centering of the male body/ citizen within that process (Mosse; McClintock, *Imperial Leather;* Mohanram). Women thus appear within the discourse of the nation as static symbols that uphold and reproduce the active male body/citizen described above by Terry and Urla (Mosse; Yuval-Davis and Anthias; McClintock, *Imperial Leather;* Yuval-Davis; Mohanram).

Within recent political debates in France, this virile body, however, is imagined as being assailed by a series of threats from foreign forces that, if not controlled, can weaken and ultimately destroy it. Current dominant representations of the national body therefore depend on the othering of a number of human bodies, including most prominently, postcolonials, women, and homosexuals.

*   *   *

In summer 1997, Parisian walls are littered with the slogan "Islam equals AIDS" ("Islam = SIDA").[3] The slogan, in its violent simplicity, captures the political climate of the moment. In the French collective imagination, Islam has been equated with a disease (a viral infection, which can spread and weaken—even destroy—the national body).[4]

By a series of metonymic shifts, we can see the larger implications of the slogan: "Islam" is used here to represent a whole set of undesirable immigrants who will not/cannot be integrated into French society. These postcolonial immigrants are those from sub-Saharan Africa and the Maghreb. They, like their religion (assumed to be Islam and equated with radical fundamentalism) and their culture (reduced to a monolithic backward and dangerous whole), are invading and polluting the national space constructed in contrast as white and Christian.

AIDS, like Islam, is equated with a group of people—the homosexual community. And homosexuals, in particular white homosexual men, are persistently connected—and dangerously so—with the spread of AIDS within Europe and North America. AIDS, interestingly enough, has also been connected with Africans and people of the African Diaspora. Cindy Patton, for instance, reminds us that a "scientist of the stature of Luc Montaigne has persistently maintained, despite contrary epidemiologic data, that 'AIDS' started in 'Africa.' His claim is based on the genetic similarity of a simian immunodeficiency virus found in monkeys" (137, n. 6). The racist implications of such a claim are obvious and noted by Patton. The rhetorical device in the slogan, which uses Islam to stand for the whole of Africa and African immigrants, rearticulates Montaigne's problematic claim. It suggests that immigrants from Africa are bringing the disease into France, wherein it is rapidly disseminated by (white) homosexuals. The final discursive link is made: immigrants, homosexuals, and especially the subjects who embody both types of "deviance" are in collusion, and together, they represent an acute danger to the stability and well-being of the French Republic.[5]

Islam and AIDS can also be said to have generated a great deal of "dis/ease" among French nationals in that they produced the kind of discomfort that both incites and legitimizes national/sex panics. The "dis/ease" here is both cause and effect of such panics, and it allows the body (individual, collective, national) imagined heretofore as "under threat" to think in terms of self-protection, border controls, and insularity. Needless to say, all these reactions pave the way for the emergence (or rather the rearticulation) of nationalist and racist narratives and practices that promise to contain and soothe such "dis/ease." The escalation of racist and homophobic violence in such contexts is one of the symptoms and releases of the dis/ease.

Pointing out the multiple connections between the fears generated by postcolonial immigration and homosexuality, Barbara Browning, in *Infectious Rhythms,* argues that "HIV emerged as a pathogen simultaneously with new anxieties over the risks of these other [migrational, spiritual, cultural] 'contagions.' And while it may seem clear that one pandemic is painfully literal, the others figurative, they were quickly associated with one another." Browning further reminds us that "in fact, economic exploitation, cultural exchange, and disease are interrelated—but Africanness is hardly the deadly pathogen" (7).

"Islam = AIDS," then, is a condensed political narrative that ironically borrows from the ACT UP slogan "Silence = Death" to conjure up the notion of a national body "at risk" and penetrated by infected foreign populations and sexual minorities. So the logic goes: immigrants from sub-Saharan Africa and the Maghreb, like/with homosexuals, are a threat to France's culture and values—they represent a danger to the national body that should not tolerate them within its boundaries. This, of course, is a matter of life and death for the French nation and the French people—who are imagined as racially pure and strictly heterosexual.

The opposition of the national body as healthy, but open to infections, and of all foreign bodies as bearers of these infections creates a dichotomy between health and pathology that is linked with notions of national security and social danger. The displacement of social conflicts (immigration and sexual politics in this case) onto the body has been analyzed as part of a discursive tradition that can be traced to the nineteenth century and that focuses on the "somatic territorializing of deviance." "In this late-twentieth-century form," Jennifer Terry and Jacqueline Urla argue,

> the idea that deviance is a matter of somatic essence—having passed through a period of disrepute following the "excesses" of the Third Reich—has arrived again, through the back door facilitated by moral dis-

courses concerning addiction as well as techniques of genetic engineering, neuroanatomical imaging and virology. In an age of "compulsive behavior," killer viruses, and dangerous genes, methods for finding a host of socially and scientifically menacing pathogens inside certain bodies are contributing to the construction of new, biologically demonized under-classes. (1–2)

This reemergence of the body and biological determinism is somewhat obscured, however, by an ongoing and parallel effort to explain difference and deviancy in terms of culture and religion. The juxtaposition of these two explanatory models of "difference" sheds some light on the continued racist practice of *contrôles au faciés* (identity check based on appearance)[6] and the recurring cultural explanations of the inability of certain immigrants to assimilate and melt into the French melting pot.

What you have here, in a nutshell, is the political platform and the imaginary lexicon of the National Front and its outspoken leader, Jean-Marie LePen. Disturbingly, however, this extremist message has become normalized and part of a hegemonic discourse about France and the "problem" of immigration. Etienne Balibar links this phenomenon to the emergence of what he sees as a form of neoracism. Against the backdrop of a globalizing economy, the formation of the European Community, and the continuing pressures of international migrations, France—like many other European countries—is undergoing a deep national identity crisis. Within such a context, social anxieties about race, class, gender, and sexuality intersect to feed and transform the formation of this neoracism.

Speaking of the United Kingdom, Anna Marie Smith defines the contours of the neoracism invoked by Balibar:

New racist immigration discourse never took the simple form of the defense of geographically fixed borders that protected one biologically defined group from the invasion by another biologically defined group, for it constructed white-Christian-Englishness as an imaginary cultural space. In addition to its simplistic invasion logic, it organized the immigration crisis around the highly mobile metaphors of leeching, contamination, and subversion. In this manner, the very logic of the new racism prepared the way for the redeployment of its immigration discourse to other sites of contestation around the boundaries of "normal" white Britishness. (120)

In France, one such site of contestation can be found around the public and political discussions of the Pacte Civil de Solidarité (PaCS)—a national form of domestic partnership open to heterosexual as well as homosexual couples—voted into law on November 10, 1999. The PaCS is a contract that two adults (of the same sex or of different sexes) sign in order to organize their communal life. The PaCS cannot be contracted between parents and children or siblings. The PaCS needs to be recorded in court (the Tribunal d'Instance) and consists of a mutual declaration stipulating the nature of the contract. The PaCS grants basic social benefits, such as the ability to file a joint tax form (after three years) and health care coverage, and is considered to be one of the elements attesting to a "personal link" with a French national in relation to the acquisition of entry and residency permits for nonnationals. The duties of the partners who have signed a PaCS are "mutual material aid," which is codified more specifically in each contract; the parties are jointly responsible and accountable for common-living debts. The PaCS is ended when one partner dies or marries. It can be annulled by a simple declaration by one or both of the partners. If the rupture is a unilateral one, one party needs to "signify" the rupture to the other, after which the PaCS is annulled within three months. Individuals joined in a PaCS are not considered a "family" and are not given rights to adoption or medically assisted procreation.

The empirical focus of this chapter will be an analysis of the national discussions that have surrounded the passage and promulgation of the French PaCS law. In particular, I will focus on the National Assembly debates and the unique contribution of representative Christine Boutin (L'Union Démocratique Française, or UDF), who challenged the PaCS on twelve counts of unconstitutionality. Her thorough and time-consuming efforts (her presentation to the National Assembly lasted more than five hours) failed, but they give us a condensed summary of the conservative/religious anti-PaCS/antigay sentiment in France.[7]

In the next section, I identify two themes around which this national debate can be organized: homosexuality/PaCS as a threat to the family (and by extension as contributing to the "fall" [*décadence*] of France), and homosexuality/PaCS as an open door to illegal immigration. Both themes, I will show, deploy, albeit in different ways, basic tropes of French anti-immigrant feelings. I conclude the chapter by pointing out some of the limitations of the new PaCS law, as well as the emergence of new kinds of citizenship suggested by activists' organizing efforts that have emerged around the discussions and the voting of the PaCS law. These new forms of citizenship are bound to further transform the political space of the French republic.

ANALYSIS OF THE NATIONAL ASSEMBLY DEBATES

The PaCS law proposal was first introduced in the French National Assembly on October 13, 1998.[8] After two round trips between the Assembly and the Senate, several amendments, and tumultuous debates, the law was finally promulgated on November 10, 1999. The discussion of the text generated a wave of homophobic statements and reactions within the conservative ranks of the French Parliament. Similar reactions emerged from within the French religious right and its grassroots organizations.[9]

The bulk of the right's criticism of the PaCS proposal resides in its opposition to the codification of homosexuality into French law. In particular, conservative deputies underscored the ways in which such codification would eventually destroy both heterosexual marriage and the procreative family. Such criticism must be understood against the backdrop of what some observers have described as a French national identity crisis. For the past forty years, France has experienced deep structural changes brought about by the overall processes of decolonization and globalization, as well as France's gradual inclusion in the supranational body of the European Community. These profound changes have generated deep anxieties about the meanings of all things French. The ability to maintain and protect a core identity has become a central theme within national debates. Reimagined around blood and filial metaphors, this national identity, needless to say, is dependent on the existence and maintenance of the "French family."

HOMOSEXUALITY/PACS AS A THREAT TO THE FAMILY

Two mommies or two daddies: we're heading toward disaster![10]
[*Deux mamans ou deux papas: bonjour les dégats!*]
—Anti-PaCS demonstration in Paris, January 31, 1999

As illustrated by this slogan from an anti-PaCS demonstration, a recurring criticism leveled against the PaCS is that the new law would destroy the heteronormative bourgeois family. Needless to say, this family depends on a strict division of labor between the sexes and on a "natural" order where the head of the family is male and his "helpmate" female. It is not surprising, then, to see that Boutin—one of the leaders of the anti-PaCS movement and a conservative Catholic—is also the president of the anti-abortion association Alliance pour les Droits de la Vie.[11] The complex connections between respectable bourgeois sexuality, racism, homophobia, and patriarchal forms of domination that run through these debates are dangerously reminiscent of those underscored by George Mosse in his important 1985 study of the construction of German national identity in modern Europe.

Throughout the PaCS parliamentary debates, conservative politicians argued that homosexual unions and parenting would destabilize the traditional family. As a result, first children, then the whole country would suffer. These politicians claimed that in spite of its false universal appeal (the PaCS is open to both homosexual and heterosexual couples), the basic and hidden goal of the text is to grant homosexual couples rights and duties heretofore only extended to heterosexual couples within the boundaries of civil matrimony:

I formally oppose this vision, which negates the role of the biological principle of reproduction and of the natural male–female relation in the legal definition of the couple. . . . We must privilege the marital model and its corollary, the family. (Jacques Kossowski, Rassemblement pour la Republique [RPR], November 7, 1998)

Jacques Kossowski and his colleagues stressed the naturalness (equated here with its procreative capacity) and therefore superiority of the heterosexual "marital model," which they then linked to the very foundations of society. Boutin's comments are enlightening:

It is not within our power here to modify a reality that has existed since the beginning of time, namely the natural relation between man and woman that forms the basis of society and sustains it. With this evidence in mind, societies have always tried to protect this natural and vital relation from what could distort or weaken it. Hence we can explain the rejection of homosexual proselytism and its condemnation to varying degrees that we encounter in all civilizations. . . . [Homosexuality] is not written within the frame of non-written laws that establish life within societies. . . . Not fecund by nature, it cannot meet the demographic and educational criteria that would entitle it to state protection. (Boutin, 3 November 1998)

Homosexuality, then, is not natural because it is nonprocreative and therefore unworthy of state recognition and protection. In this contractual vision of the state's duties toward its citizens—the state only needs to protect the couples that produce its children and provide them with basic educational and socialization skills—homosexual couples are left out. The perverse logic of the French (religious) right does not stop here. Not only are homosexual couples not able to "breed" and parent—and therefore they are not protected under the law—but it is crucial to ensure that they can never do either. It is therefore the very possibility of homosexual procreation and parenting inscribed in the PaCS that needs to be stamped out. Indeed, conservative deputies argued that the PaCS must be opposed because it would eventually open the door to homosexual marriages, homosexual adoptions, and homosexual parenting (whether via artificial insemination, medically assisted procreation, or adoption).

Boutin recalled the current legal barriers to homosexual adoption and artificial insemination[12] and warned the National Assembly that the PaCS "would inevitably lead to [homosexual] parenting [*filiation*] and adoption" (November 3, 1998). Citing statements made by several gay and lesbian organizations in favor of homoparenting, she warned again, "If we adopt today this 'infra-marriage,' the republican institution of marriage will be profoundly upset or destroyed" (November 3, 1998). Commenting on the new law, Dominique Dord suggested that doing away with civil marriage as the legal basis of the family and opening parenting to homosexuals would endanger the well-being and the lawful protection of children:

We would sacrifice then the right of the child to the right to a child, as if we did not measure every day the damage generated among many pre- and post-adolescents, by the absence of a father's image or by the breakup of families. In a century where everything is possible, even the most unreasonable choices, let's not play the apprentice sorcerer; let's not destabilize the fundamental principles of social development and the most powerful symbols of our civilization. ("PaCS: Un mauvais projet," *Le Figaro*, October 9, 1998)

Dord here starts with the fear of homosexual parenting and its potentially damaging effects on children and then moves to an apocalyptic level where legalized homosexual parenting would lead to the general and global destruction of French society. Such fears are shared by Eric Doligé:

Why would [the legislative body] weaken the relationship between man and woman, the origin of society and of its renewal? Can we imagine a society composed of male and female couples? Can someone explain to me how children will be conceived then! [laughter on the left] (Eric Doligé, RPR, November 7, 1998)

Doligé's commentary is interesting because it captures the fantastic quality of the fears generated by the lawful presence of homosexuals within the nation. The French deputy here imagines a French society where homosexuals have taken over and where, deprived of its good reproductive heterosexuals, France is now unable to renew and sustain itself.[13] Homosexuality, then, like immigration, is presented not as something that is dangerous by itself, but rather by its capacity to infiltrate/invade and eventually to undo the very fibers of France's societal order:

Homosexuality is not a fact that we need to combat, but its propagation and its publicity are. (RPR, November 7, 1998)

This fear, as I have shown at the beginning of the chapter, is similar to the fear of immigrants "invading" France and diluting the "French stock" of the nation. In a shocking moment of homophobic lack of restraint, Emmanuel Hamel (RPR, Rhône) clearly associated the PaCS with the notion of AIDS contamination. He renamed the PaCS "the Practice of AIDS Contamination" (*pratique de la contamination sidaïque*). The metaphor of contamination runs through these debates. It opens up a discursive space for the linkage of homosexuality and immigration.

Moreover, whether addressing homosexuality or immigration, the question of who can constitute an acceptable family and who is allowed to reproduce is of course at the core of this discussion. Boutin helps us see the connection between homophobic and anti-immigrant feelings in this particular construction of the French family:

Who will prevent cultural communities on the margins of the republic from claiming a special contract that would make licit in France habits and customs that are contrary to our tradition? . . . Is M. Jospin ready to accept polygamy in France? (Boutin, UDF, November 3, 1998)

Boutin's point here is that once the legal definition of "family" is opened up to include homosexual couples and other duos, the ability is lost to preserve and protect the ideal of a French marital and heterosexual bourgeois family. The gate is open to even more dangerous and alien forms of families, such as the polygamous families that the French connect with immigrant communities from sub-Saharan Africa and whose numbers are often blown out of proportion. The connection between the deviant homosexual family and the deviant postcolonial immigrant family is reiterated when Boutin and her allies claim that the PaCS, which can be annulled unilaterally by one member of a couple, introduces the principle of repudiation within French law and practices:

The PaCS should be called indeed the Open Repudiation Union Contract. (Thierry Mariani, RPR, December 8, 1998)

You are legalizing repudiation. (Christian Estrossi, RPR, November 7, 1998)

As an infra-marriage, the PaCS will be undone via an infra-divorce. By authorizing a unilateral rupture [of the contract], the PaCS consecrates the institutionalization of an infra-marriage that can be annulled by repudiation—an idea that, however, *horrifies* us. (Boutin, UDF, November 3, 1998; emphasis added)

Here the idea of "repudiation," which again is associated with Islamic family law, "horrifies us." (Who is this "us" that Boutin claims to be speaking for?) Boutin, in a clever (and perverse) appropriation of feminist critiques of unilateral annulment of matrimonial bonds that traditionally favor men, inserts a common theme used to discredit the ability of certain immigrant families to "assimilate" within the French melting pot.

By waving the red flags of polygyny and repudiation within France, Boutin clearly and cleverly creates a semantic link between homosexuality, the PaCS, postcolonial immigrants, and the basic threat they pose to the very structure of French society. Having created such a link, there is no need any longer to insert an obvious referent—the dual threat, we now know, is subtly and dangerously established and silently (but powerfully) haunts the discourse of our conservative politicians:

The PaCS defends the interest of a minority and risks destabilizing society as a whole. (Jacques Masdeu-Arus, RPR, November 7, 1998)

This text is dangerous for society. (Thierry Mariani, RPR, November 7, 1998)

> The model you propose is based on consumerism and violence. . . . It is the sign of a will to destroy the bases of society. . . . Your new PaCS is simply a return to barbarism. You follow the steps of those who, in order to destroy society, began with the destruction of the family. You are about to do violence to the most established law of our old civilization! You are playing with the very foundations of society! . . . The opposition will do all it can to prevent you from demolishing society, the family, and France! (Philippe Le Jolis de Villiers de Saintignon, Mouvement pour la France [MPF], November 7, 1998)

> The cycle is irreversible and it is one that leads to decadence. (Philippe Houillon, November 7, 1998)

In the above quotations, the ideas of "minority," "danger," "violence," and "decadence" function—without "homosexuality" or "immigration" ever being mentioned—as a refrain that continues to imprint and reassert the connections more clearly delineated by Boutin. Renamed as "Pact of Social Destruction" (*pacte de destructuration sociale*) by Bernard Accoyer (RPR, December 8, 1998), the PaCS can now be imagined as an evil and dangerous pact between homosexuals, immigrants, and leftist intellectuals who together work toward the subversion of a traditional French society.

The linkage between homosexuality, PaCS, postcolonial immigrants, and the dangers they represent for France is even more clearly established when French deputies begin to discuss article 6 of the law.[14] This article stipulates that the signing of a PaCS between two individuals "constitutes one of the elements in the appreciation of the personal links" used to establish eligibility for legal entry and sojourn into France. I next highlight the disturbing ways in which the PaCS was often opposed on the grounds that it would create an open gateway to all kinds of fraudulent immigration.

HOMOSEXUALITY/PACS AS AN OPEN DOOR TO ILLEGAL IMMIGRATION

> The PaCS will be considered as a "personal reason" to obtain the right to sojourn: this is equivalent to completely opening our borders to immigration. (Boutin, UDF, November 3, 1998)

> The PaCS represents a new blow to the containment of migratory fluxes. (Jacques Masdeu-Arus, RPR, November 7, 1998)

> This text is dangerous; I will not come back to article 6, which as far as foreigners are concerned will open up the possibility for all kinds of abuses. (Thierry Mariani, RPR, December 8, 1998)

Boutin and her colleagues, after having symbolically linked homosexuality/PaCS and immigration, are now establishing some real material connections between the two. Since the 1970s, French politicians have maintained—at least in theory—the principle that France needs to contain immigration fluxes. In the context of rising unemployment rates and over-all economic stress (and with the nationalist right having successfully linked unemployment and immigration in the minds of French people), this has been a "commonsense" and widely popular principle.

By underscoring the threat of uncontrollable immigration, Boutin per-versely uses commonplace anti-immigrant feelings to discredit a law that would in fact benefit only a very small number of immigrants: heterosexual and homosexual partners of French nationals. These have been denied legal entry and residency rights because they do not meet the marital re-quirement that currently qualifies immigrants for legal entry and long-term residency papers in France. In Boutin's imagination, immigrants and queers would combine efforts and would generate massive fraud:

> There will be a black market of fake [*blanc*] PaCS. (Boutin, December 1–2, 1998)

Here Boutin is directly tapping into the common process of the crimi-nalization of immigrants in France (and in Europe). Immigrants from France's former colonies, as well as those from Eastern Europe, are com-monly constructed as potential criminals—always prepared to "work the system," cheat their way into undue benefits, and engage in actual criminal activities. Within such imagined constructions, the existence of the PaCS opens a new legal space within which immigrants can develop their never-ending fraudulent activities:

> This text is dangerous for society. It will lead to multiple forms of fraud. (Thierry Mariani, RPR, November 7, 1998)

> Our country cannot afford to make any mistake here. If [the PaCS] gives the impression that the gates are open, it will generate, beyond the Mediter-ranean, hopes that will be exploited by unscrupulous individuals, who know our laws very well and usher foreigners into our territory under the condi-tions that you well know. . . . Instead of having fake marriages [*mariages blancs*] we'll have fake PaCS: and it will be so much easier! (Claude Goas-guen, December 1–2, 1998)

Goasguen's main focus is somewhat hidden behind his concern for the potential exploitation of immigrants by others. But a closer reading of his comment clearly demonstrates how Goasguen is simply elaborating on Boutin's fears and persistent stereotypes. The danger is imminent and po-tentially destructive; "no mistake" is permissible here! Goasguen is also very clear about the geographic location of the danger. It simply lies "be-yond the Mediterranean." By invoking the hopeful masses just waiting to flood the gates, the fear of foreign invasion is rearticulated. Moreover, criminality is again associated with immigration by conjuring up notions of traffickers, fraudulent bundles, and black markets. The porous and weak borders of the French nation are now even further weakened by the presence of a law that is presented as a proxy for the open legalization of all forms of immigration within France:

> [We] remain absolutely hostile to the legalization of illegal immigration through the [PaCS]. (Dominique Dord, UDF, November 7, 1998)

> Nothing will prevent a French national to contract three successive PaCS in a year and help legalize three illegal immigrants [*clandestins*]. (Thierry Mariani, RPR, November 7, 1998)

The number of amendments generated to suppress or weaken article 6 of the PaCS law reveals the clear connection that is perceived between homosexuality/PaCS and immigration.[15] This imagined connection has produced deep anxieties in the minds of conservative French politicians. These anxieties include, as Mariani's comment above indicates, the fear that activists and intellectuals on the left will engage in collective acts of disobedience (such as those that we have seen around the *sans-papiers* struggle[16]) and will help undocumented immigrants by allowing them to repeatedly form PaCSs with successive partners.

CONCLUDING REMARKS/BACK TO THE POLITICAL

By and large, lesbian and gay groups in France have welcomed the passage of the PaCS law. They see it as a definite victory in the overall struggle toward equality between homosexual and heterosexual couples in that the text does recognize the existence of nonheterosexual couples and grants them some basic social rights. However, to varying degrees, they deplore the limitations of the new law and the symbolic message attached to it. The law still denies marriage and parenting to homosexual couples. Few PaCS supporters challenged the racist and anti-immigrant rhetoric used by conservative politicians to fight the passage of the law. Quite rare also were critiques that pointed out the multiple types of discrimination written into the law. The PaCS Observatory (Observatoire du PaCS),[17] which defines itself as a "collective of associations of future users of the PaCS," does offer such a multifaceted critique, denouncing the following limitations of the law:

- The PaCS does not write into French law equality among all couples—civil marriage is still unavailable to homosexuals.
- The PaCS is registered in court and not at City Hall (like civil marriages).
- The PaCS, unlike marriage, does not grant immediate fiscal benefits. A three-year time period is required before these rights are open. This sug-

gests that certain couples are less legitimate and automatically under suspicion. They need to go through a probationary period before acquiring certain rights that are automatically granted to married people.

- When you sign a PaCS, you immediately lose certain social benefits. These social benefits are particularly important for the poor future users of the PaCS. The observatory demands the individualization of these minimal social benefits (*minima sociaux*).[18]

- The PaCS does not grant immediate access to legal residency and in turn access to French nationality. Under the terms of the current text, the immigration administration is free to determine the personal links and to take or not take a PaCS into consideration (an administrative memorandum gives specific directives on how to handle this particular issue[19]).

- Partnerships formed through the PaCS are not considered families, and therefore the PaCS does not provide homosexual couples with access to adoption or medically assisted procreation.

What's interesting about the observatory is its coalitional basis. It involves queer groups as well as feminist groups, immigrant groups, and organizations working on basic social welfare issues. All of them are interested in broadening the definitions of couple, marriage, and family. All of them are interested in broadening social coverage and rethinking the bases on which these benefits are granted. All of them are interested in extending citizenship rights to formally excluded individuals and groups.

Whether the passage of the PaCS law and the new forms of activism and coalitional politics that it has generated are perceived as additional threats or as welcomed revitalizing forces to traditional forms of citizenry is of course a matter of ideological positioning. As it stands now, French public opinion is equally divided on the issue. As of November 1999, 48% of the French were opposed to the PaCS and 46% in favor. The plural left coalition (*la gauche plurielle*) that forms the majority and includes socialists, communists, and other left-wing and green parties, managed to get the PaCS voted into law. What happens after the passage of the law should be of great interest to many lesbian, gay, bi, and transgendered (LGBT) groups in France and internationally. Particular attention needs to be paid to continuing linkages between homophobia and racism. A lack of attention to these connections would be dangerous to the future of antihomophobia and antiracist struggles that are bound to emerge in the context of the making of a fortress Europe and the reemergence of moralist/religious forms of nationalist thinking.

As I sent off this essay for review, one of the perverse effects of the implementation of the new PaCS law was recorded in the French press. On March 9, 2000, an Algerian lawyer, Nadir, who had been denied territorial asylum[20] and who had contracted a PaCS (in October 1999) with a French citizen, Pierre, was under threat of deportation. The French court in charge of this case applied the law strictly. It considered the PaCS established between Nadir and Pierre as too recent (Nadir and Pierre met in 1997) to count as a valid "personal link" in France and to justify the granting of legal sojourn and residency papers for Nadir. Ironically, Nadir and Pierre had been featured in the French press a few months earlier when a story in *Le Progrès* reported that they were the first couple to contract a PaCS in Lyon. Without papers (*sans-papiers*) but rather privileged through his class, gender, and educational status (Nadir was enrolled at the law school in Lyon), Nadir was able to garner quite a bit of powerful support from his professors and from local political actors and organizations, and he was able to avoid immediate deportation. Stories such as that of Nadir and Pierre are likely to multiply. Many queer immigrants who have contracted PaCSs with French citizens will not be able to leverage the kind of support that Nadir was able to generate in his favor. These stories should serve as cautionary tales to those who have acclaimed the passage of the PaCS as a major victory for French democracy and its republican tradition. They should warn LGBT activists (and their allies) in France that the passage of the PaCS law must certainly be welcomed as a step in the right direction, but at the same time, it should be critiqued for its many flaws and the differential forms of exclusion they are bound to engender.

NOTES

This article is based on a paper first presented at the 2000 Annual International Studies Association Meeting in Los Angeles, California. Partial funds for travel were generously provided by the University of Cincinnati Taft Memorial Fund and the Center for Women's Studies. A slightly different version of this article also appeared under the title "The Sexual and Racial Politics of Civil Unions in France," in *Radical History Review* 83 (spring 2002, 73–93).

1. Although a full critical engagement with the term "postcolonial" is beyond the scope of this chapter—others have done it quite eloquently before me (Shohat; McClintock, "Angel of Progress"; Frankenberg and Mani; Kaplan et al.)—I wish to qualify my own usage of the term in this essay. "Postcolonial" in the French context signifies that France has now lost most of its former colonies with which it has maintained strong neocolonial links. The breakup of the French colonial world and the emergence of global capitalism have created the conditions for the massive immigration into France of people from France's former colonies. Postcolonialism also signals that France is now a locale where a host of postcolonial subjects (including many women) have come to occupy vulnerable positions within the French social order. The presence, settlement, and precarious status of these postcolonial subjects within French metropolitan borders are posing serious challenges to France's republican foundational promise of universal inclusion and equality.

2. For interesting Web sites on these issues and immigrant organizing in France, see the following: <http://www.hivnet.ch/migrants>, <http://www.chex.com/ardhis/liens.htm>, <http://www.geocities.com/WestHollywood/Heights/728/liens_Fr.htm>, and <http://www.bok.net/pajol>. Accessed April 12, 2002.

3. This analysis of the "Islam = SIDA" slogan was first developed in my article "Women from the Maghreb and Sub-Saharan Africa in France." In this chapter, I use a slightly different and expanded version of the analysis. Here, I introduce the importance of bodily metaphors in the parliamentary discussions of the PaCS, and I locate these discussions within a larger discursive context where layered and complex constructions of race and sexuality articulate and deploy specific forms of differences and exclusions.

4. Mosse has documented, especially in the German context, how the racist imaginary often revolves around tropes of disease, infection, and contagion: "Racism branded the outsider, making him inevitably a member of the inferior race, whenever this was possible, readily recognized as a carrier of infection, threatening the health of society and the nation" (134).

5. Mosse argues that from its inception, the concept of racism was associated with (deviant) sexuality. In the context of German nationalism and anti-Semitism, Mosse shows that both Jews and homosexuals were seen as "decadents" who weakened the nation and deprived it of "healthy sons and daughters" (109).

6. The focus on looks and visible characteristics of these *contrôle au faciés* (you can actually tell an "illegal immigrant" when you see him or her) clearly inscribes current anti-immigrant politics in France within the logic of a long racist tradition that relies on visual clues to infer the character and status of individuals and entire communities.

7. Boutin, a representative from the Yvelines, was one of the strongest opponents to the PaCS in the National Assembly debates. Although she had been asked to intervene on the PaCS by her party, L'Union Démocratique Française, on November 3, 1998, she was then criticized within the party for the extremity of her homophobic comments. Her speech generated a wide range of protest across the political spectrum.

8. An earlier text, introduced on October 9, 1998, had been rejected by the National Assembly because several Socialist deputies were absent.

9. Générations Famille and Jeunesse Action Chrétienté are two representatives of this movement. Organized in a collective "for marriage and against PaCS," these groups have organized educational campaigns and demonstrations and have lobbied President Jacques Chirac to call for further discussion of the text, when it had already been voted into law and approved by the Conseil Constitutionnel—a constitutional right of the president.

10. All translations from the French are mine.

11. Mosse also suggested a clear connection between "the persecution of homosexuals and the effort to maintain the sexual division of labor" in his study of nationalism in Nazi Germany (164).

12. Although single adults have been allowed by French law to adopt children since 1966, the Conseil d'Etat on October 9, 1996, stipulated that the right to adoption is not extended to homosexuals. Similarly, artificial insemination and medically assisted procreation are exclusively granted to married couples and common-law heterosexual couples who have lived together for a period of at least two years.

13. This hallucinatory scenario taps into an old French anxiety about the country's demographic weakness: "While our society is undergoing a demographic crisis without precedent, you choose to grant official status to couples who cannot procreate" (Jacques Kossowski, RPR, November 8, 1998).

14. Article 12 in the final version of the PaCS. The one-year time period that was included in the initial text has also disappeared from the final text.

15. Accoyer introduced amendment 434, which would forbid aliens illegally

residing in France from contracting a PaCS. Boutin introduced an amendment that would make the PaCS available to French citizens only (rejected). Mariani introduced several amendments aiming at the exclusion of the *sans-papiers* (amendments 200 and 300—both rejected) and amendment 301, which would forbid a foreigner who had entered France illegally from being able to contract a PaCS. Goasguen's amendment 220 demanded the removal of article 6 (rejected). Mariani introduced amendment 322, which would forbid the contracting of a PaCS outside of France (rejected); amendment 329, demanding that one of the persons signing a PaCS must be a French citizen (same as amendment 717—both rejected); amendment 323, demanding a five-year time limit before it opens rights to legal sojourn; amendment 324, three-year time limit; amendments 325 and 908, two-year time limit; and amendment 907, one-year time limit (all rejected).

16. In spring 1996, postcolonial immigrants launched a resistance movement that has redrawn the boundaries of grassroots immigrant politics in France. The *sans-papiers*—literally, "without papers"—are undocumented immigrants and refugees sometimes under threat of deportation. The *sans-papiers* and their allies organized early as collectives and demanded that the French state legalize their status. The movement gained national and international attention when, in August 1996, the police forcibly removed 300 *sans-papiers* from the Saint-Bernard church, in Paris, which they had been occupying for two months.

17. L'observatoire du PaCS includes the following organizations: Agir Ensemble Contre le Chômage (AC!), ACT UP-Paris, Aides Fédération Nationale, Aides Paris–Ile de France, Association des Parents et Futurs Parents Gais et Lesbiens, Association pour la Reconnaissance des Droits des Personnes Homosexuelles et Transexuelles à l'Immigration et au Séjour, Centre Gai & Lesbien, Pro-Choix-Paris, and SOS Homophobie.

18. These benefits are the API (Allocation for Isolated Parents); ASS (Specific Solidarity Allocation); RMI (Minimum Insertion Revenue); and AAH (Handicapped Adult Allocation).

19. The administrative memorandum of December 10, 1999, specifies that the person seeking legal sojourn and residency papers must prove—regardless of the date of the PaCS—three years of common life with a French citizen.

20. "Nadir, pacsé bientôt expulsé" in *Libération,* available at: <http://altern.org/ardhis/nadirlibe.html>; "Malgré le pacs, la menace" in *Lyon Capitale,* available at: <http://www.lyoncapitale.fr/anciens/une-271-3.html>; accessed April 12, 2002. Nadir, who had fled Algeria after receiving death threats from a Moslem fundamentalist group (he was the defense attorney for a woman who had survived a violent attack perpetrated by the group), appealed the decision. His case is still pending. It is worth noting that Nadir cannot seek asylum on the basis of the persecutions of homosexuals in his country. Unlike Great Britain and the Netherlands, France does not recognize this kind of persecution as valid grounds for granting someone territorial asylum.

REFERENCES

Bhabha, Homi. "The Other Question." *Screen* 24, no. 6 (1983): 18–36. Reprinted in *Contemporary Postcolonial Theory,* 37–54. London: Arnold, 1996.

Browning, Barbara. *Infectious Rhythms: Metaphors of Contagion and the Spread of African Culture.* New York: Routledge, 1998.

Compte Rendus Intégral, Séance du 3 Novembre 1998. Available at: <http://www.assemblee-nat.fr/2/cri/19990057.htm>. Accessed April 12, 2002.

Compte Rendu Analytique Officiel, Sommaire des Comptes Rendus du 3 Novembre 1998. Available at: <http://www.assemblee-nationale.fr/2/dossiers/pacs/981103.htm>. Accessed April 12, 2002.

Compte Rendu Analytique Officiel des Comptes Rendus du 7 Novembre 1998. Available at: <http://www.assemblee-nationale.fr/2/dossiers/pacs/981107.htm>. Accessed April 12, 2002.

Compte Rendu Analytique Officiel, Sommaire des Comptes Rendus du 8 Novembre 1998. <http://www.assemblee-nationale.fr/2/dossiers/pacs/981108.htm>. Accessed April 12, 2002.

Compte Rendu Analytique Officiel du 9 Decembre 1998. Available at: <http://www.assemblee-nationale.fr/2/dossiers/pacs/981209.htm>. Accessed April 12, 2002.

Décision du Conseil Constitutionnel. Available at: <http://www.conseil.constitutionel.fr/decision/1999/99419/9941dc.htm>. Accessed April 12, 2002.

Extraits des Séances du Mardi 3, Samedi 7, et Dimanche 8 Novembre 1998 sur le sujet des Etrangers. Available at: <http://altern.org.ardhis/etrangers.htm>. Accessed April 12, 2002.

Frankenberg, Ruth, and Lata Mani. "Crosscurrents, Crosstalk: Race, 'Postcoloniality' and the Politics of Location." *Cultural Studies* 7, no. 2 (May 1993): 292–310. Reprinted in *Contemporary Postcolonial Theory: A Reader,* edited by Padmini Mongia, 347–64. London: Arnold, 1996.

Gilman, Sander. "Black Bodies, White Bodies: Toward an Iconography of Female Sexuality in Late Nineteenth-Century Art, Medicine, and Literature." In *Race, Writing and Difference,* edited by Henry Louis Gates Jr., 223–61. Chicago: University of Chicago Press, 1985.

Kaplan, Caren, Norma Alarcón, and Minoo Moallem, eds. *Between Woman and Nation: Nationalisms, Transnational Feminisms, and the State.* Durham, N.C.: Duke University Press, 1999.

McClintock, Anne. "The Angel of Progress: Pitfalls of the Term 'Post-colonialism.'" In *Colonial Discourse and Post-Colonial Theory: A Reader,* edited by Patrick Williams and Laura Chrisman, 291–304. New York: Columbia University Press, 1994.

———. *Imperial Leather: Race, Gender and Sexuality in the Colonial Context.* New York: Routledge, 1995.

Mohanram, Radhika. *Women, Colonialism, and Space.* Minneapolis: University of Minnesota Press, 1999.

Mosse, George. *Nationalism and Sexuality: Respectability and Abnormal Sexuality in Modern Europe.* New York: Howard Fertig, 1985.

Patton, Cindy. "From Nation to Family: Containing African AIDS." In *The Lesbian and Gay Studies Reader,* edited by Henri Abelove, Michele Aina Barale, and David Halperin, 127–38. New York: Routledge, 1993.

Proposition de Loi No 1118 Relative au Pacte Civil de Solidarité. Available at: <http://www.assemblee-nationale.fr/2/dossiers/pacs1118.htm>. Accessed April 12, 2002.

Raissiguier, Catherine. "Women from the Maghreb and Sub-Saharan Africa in France: Fighting for Health and Basic Human Rights." In *Women and Africa and the African Diaspora,* edited by Obiama Nnaemeka (forthcoming).

Shohat, Ella. "Notes on the 'Post-Colonial.'" *Social Text* 31/32 (1992): 99–113. Reprinted in *Contemporary Postcolonial Theory: A Reader,* edited by Padmini Mongia, 321–34. London: Arnold, 1996.

Smith, Anna Marie. "The Centering of Right-Wing Extremism through the Construction of an 'Inclusionary' Homophobia and Racism." In *Playing with Fire: Queer Politics, Queer Theories,* edited by Shane Phelan, 113–38. New York: Routledge, 1997.

Sommaire des Comptes Rendus du 8 Decembre 1998. Available at: <http://www.assemblee-nationale.fr/2/dossiers/pacs/981208.htm>. Accessed April 12, 2002.

Stoler, Ann Laura. *Race and the Education of Desire: Foucault's History of Sexuality and the Colonial Order of Things.* Durham, N.C.: Duke University Press, 1995.

Terry, Jennifer, and Jacqueline Urla, eds. *Deviant Bodies: Critical Perspectives on Difference in Science and Popular Culture.* Bloomington: Indiana University Press, 1995.

Yuval-Davis, Nira. *Gender and Nation.* London: Sage Publications, 1997.

Yuval-Davis, Nira, and Floya Anthias, eds. *Woman-Nation-State.* London: Macmillan, 1989.

Chapter 6

Mattering National Bodies and Sexualities

Corporeal Contest in Marcos and Brocka

ROLANDO B. TOLENTINO

In this essay, I discuss the performative materiality of national bodies and sexualities in the Philippines during the more than twenty years of the Marcos regime (1965–1986). My interest is to consider how the spectacle of power was generated by and about the "first couple," Ferdinand and Imelda Marcos, and as a counternarrative, I address the subversive critiques of power in Lino Brocka's films about sex workers in the Philippines. The presidential bodies of the first couple are differentiated through a regime of power signifiers made distant and inaccessible to subordinated bodies. Although devoid of such signifiers, the subordinated bodies of the poverty-ridden and repressed populace attempt to "mimic" the leaders' hypermasculinized and hyperfeminized bodies. The site of hegemonic construction of national bodies and sexualities, however, becomes the site of locating reiterative performances of its subversion.

The "performance" of Ferdinand Marcos's presidential body as the model to emulate is both prolific and distant to national bodies. Although the cultural landscape is dominated by images of the president bearing markers of power, these same markers are also inaccessible to most "otherized" bodies. His physique, clothing, voice, and gestures evoke signifiers of hegemonic power privileged in the healthy maintenance of the presidential body. Furthermore, the first lady, Imelda Marcos, becomes the presidential body's pivotal supplement, the marriage of "primordial strength with eternal beauty" (Rafael, 283). Whereas Marcos's body interiorized power through its centralization in the presidency, Imelda as first lady exteriorized its play, donning excessive embellishment in a quizzical display of power. The gender-related use of national power complements the conjugal aspect of the dictatorship, which can be further read as the Marcoses' positioning themselves as "the origin of circulation [of power] itself in the country" (Rafael, 282). What I am trying to arrive at in the couple's manufacture of national power through their bodies are the various spheres and negotiations in which these are represented. Within the margins, a further peripheralization occurs that reifies and rejects the national power play. In this sphere, national bodies are mass produced through its reiteration of the spectacle of power. Within the insular plane as enmeshed in multinational operation, the specific effect is produced on women's bodies as they perform "homework outside the home."

THE PRESIDENTIAL BODY

Sometime in 1983, soon after the assassination of political rival Benigno Aquino in August, President Marcos called for a press conference in his private office to quell speculations about his ill health. A photograph taken during the conference foregrounds the relationship between discourse and the presidential body. The photograph, taken by photojournalist Sonny Yabao, shows a dual image of constructing the presidential body.[1] Marcos—appearing harassed, with a bloated face, visible lines of tension on his forehead, and shrunken eyes—points to an almost life-size photograph of himself in swimming trunks, smiling, in robust health, with firm breasts and arms, his eyes hidden by sunglasses. The "real" Marcos is covered to the neck by a white *barong*, his other hand on the table, supporting his compact body. He points his finger to the crotch area of the "doubly photographable" Marcos, carried by an aide whose face is hidden by the picture and whose body is equally dressed in a long-sleeved *barong tagalog*. Later accounts hypothesized that Marcos was actually indisposed when Imelda and chief of staff Fabian Ver were plotting the Aquino assassination. He was supposedly recuperating from a kidney transplant, making himself conspicuously absent from the national scene. Consequently, when he came back to the limelight, his body constantly shifted from a normal to grotesquely bloated figure; its expansion was caused by the drugs he took to prevent the body's rejection of the transplanted organ.

The real Marcos signifies decay, death, and struggle for power, whereas the photographed Marcos signifies health, vigor, and self-assured power. The former reassures the people of his idealized image, however parodic in its attempt to foster unity between the real and the photograph. The scene poses the question, who is the original and who is the copy? The former is the regulatory ideal, showing immediate distinction between the physical attributes of the modern leader and its nonexistence in subordinated bodies. In pointing to the phallic locus in the photograph, Marcos himself points to the ideal locus of power maintenance. The robust image of the presidential body is not only proof of the president's health, but more, it is targeted to be an analog of the health of the presidency and its hold on national power. A Marcos supporter, faceless and nameless, symbolically carries the analog, donned in the same formal wear. Its naming and contouring of national bodies, subordinated in poverty and therefore lacking in middle- and upper-class signifiers, supports Marcos's body.

The picture of Marcos in swimming trunks was taken in an exterior area, his body teeming with available space like the direction of the radiant rays in the image of the Sacred Heart of Jesus. In the exterior shot, there are no other figures except him. The real Marcos, on the other hand, is surrounded by cluttered interior spaces—bodies of supporters on the left; papers, documents, pens, and two pairs of eyeglasses are in the foreground on the table; and a pulley, probably used to hoist the flag, is at the center. In choosing to be photographed in his private office, he was exposing the interior operations of the presidency in a current state of crisis. The interior space presents the notion of self-reflexivity in the presidency; the operations are laid bare and are therefore susceptible to interrogation.

This section of the chapter interrogates the construction of the presidential body along the dialectics of vigor and decay, high media profile and high maintenance, democratization and authoritarianism, popularization and imposition of "high" standards, and organic and fragmented bodily representations. The height of the national economic and political crisis in 1983 coincided with the decline in Marcos's health. After investing his body with signifiers of national power, his age and declining health "conspired," so to speak, to foreground and intensify the national crisis. His long absence from media attention to recuperate from the kidney transplant did not go unnoticed. Ironically, this absence was made obvious by his previous efforts to proliferate his presence in the media. At the height of the crisis, the operations of the dialectics were more pronounced, producing contradictory images of the presidential body he had sought earlier to homogenize as the ideal national body.

Marcos was so fascinated by his youthful prime that he concocted a presidential apotheosis based on the vitality of his youthful body: his alleged guerrilla leadership during the Japanese Occupation, and the twenty-eight medals he earned for this experience; the exemplar of the all-around athlete in his college days; the young turk in his various political party affiliations; the young senator who swept a beauty queen off her feet during eleven days of courtship; and presidential material. Although these stories have remained questionable privately, the wholesale public approach Marcos made of his presidential body somehow cemented his grasp of national power. The pristine, youthful body permitted Marcos to forcefully remain in power, allowing for a potent political rhetoric to be tied to a brute pacification drive in the founding and implementation of the New Society and the New Republic. In the polemic of modernizing the nation on all fronts, Marcos's vision of Philippine society is as equally represented as youthful and innovative as it remains caught up in traditional values and institutions.

His youthful body politic reverberated in the fierceness of his political speeches, all delivered extemporaneously; the wide gesticulations; the Malakas painting; the decisiveness of his presidency; the affair with American movie starlet Dovie Beams, among others. The fetish for the youthful body also projected Marcos's fantasy to remain in power. His control of the media allowed him to maneuver his body as the image of national fetish. The day martial law was declared, all television shows were canceled. What remained was the static frequency, waiting for his singular presence to give an "important announcement to the nation." In awaiting and partaking of the national figure in this televisual event, national bodies were going to be defined in ways that would continue to contour their present form and location. For even after this event, Marcos's image continued to haunt the everyday lives of national bodies. The image of the leader is made prolific, yet unreachable to its citizens.

In the latter part of his regime, the contradictions were made more pronounced by the nostalgia for the youthful body. During his recuperation from the kidney transplant, Marcos's body moved between normal and grotesque. He would maximize his "normal" state by staging scenes of the "healthy" use of the presidential body. In this period, he would be photographed golfing one day, swimming the next, or he would lift his shirt to dispel rumors of a surgical operation. The president's health became front-page material that directed to how other lingering national news was covered. Marcos's aging and disfigured body became a trope for articulating the discourse of crisis in the political, economic, and moral arenas. Like the state of the presidential body, by the time the 9th Philippine Business Conference came about, its theme had metamorphosed from "National Recovery to National Survival" (Maglipon, "Confetti Power," 9).

The physical body had obviously aged, but the ideal regulatory body remained in its robust shape, widely circulated in official national discourse. Like the paranoia of the deposed dictator in Gabriel Garcia Marquez's famous novel *Autumn of the Patriarch,* Marcos's doubly imaged body has lost touch with reality. Holding on to dear power, "spying and intrigues had escalated" (Burton, 265). The social crisis has no use for either a presidential body in decay or its utopian ideal. In the ensuing so-called February 1986 Revolution, the presidential body was detached from the fast-changing national reality. Its abrupt loss of currency was noticeable precisely because the loss stemmed from an earlier drive toward its wide circulation. I will trace the circulation and loss of currency of the presidential body along two junctures—the president's clothing, and the president's voice and gestures. Although the president's clothing addresses the historical positioning of local elites in Philippine society, the president's voice and gestures mark Marcos's specific use of body substitutes ("body doubles") to invoke a body politic in the larger sphere of national politics.[2]

However, in media discourse, whether garbed in formal or informal wear, the presidential body is always at work. A trip to the airport to welcome his children taking their breaks from schools abroad becomes a media event. The presidential body's personal and family activities are translated into official business. In proliferating the presidential body, media's role has also extended its official bodily life. This means that the presidential body has gone beyond the legalities of the constitution limiting the presidential term, and to a large extent, it even defied the natural impediments of aging and sickness. So long as it is deemed working for certain national ideals, the presidential body remains centrally positioned. Like its semblance of sustained national prominence, the presidential body's central positioning creates a semblance of national unity.

The semblance becomes the contradictory trace in the narrative of the presidential body. It results from a motivation to engulf all others into the rubric of the "presidential body." The national bodies are constructed in official discourse to be beholden and accepting of the presidential body's benevolence. Drawing on themes of national unity, the presidential body becomes the substance that flattens internal differences and catalyzes the nation into a semblance of organic being. However, such a unifying function of the presidential body only presents its further disappearance, fragmentation, depreciation, and obsolescence. Filmmaker Lino Brocka's constant use of presidential portraits disseminated to local offices and households calls attention to both their material and imagined dominance in the political landscape. Like the proliferation of religious icons, the images of the presidential body are simultaneously naturalizing and alienating of personal and social experiences. As the presidential body is profusely circulated by its unlimited access to media, what remains is the simulacrum of the body made more and more devoid of presidential authority.

The kinetic drive to unify the nation for modernization ironically rests on the fragmentation of the presidential body. The body could not possibly be everywhere every time. Thus, the presidential body metonymically functions through its parts—to simultaneously be in one place and elsewhere. For Marcos, his voice and gestures substituted for the organic body. Media proliferated these body parts—radio disseminated the voice, newspapers the active gestures, and film and television both. Marcos's baritone voice is characterized by its deep enunciation of perfect English, Tagalog, and Ilokano. His extemporaneous speeches were marked by their forceful delivery. He knew the rhetoric of getting people's attention. His gestures reiterated authority. Regardless of the size of the audience, Marcos's gestures were wide and animated, similar to actions performed when speaking to a huge crowd.

These parts then amount to a "quasicorporeal body," a body whose unity has been lost in the efficacy of the parts to represent the entity.[3] On the one level, these parts have produced "afterimages" of the organic presidential body, resuscitating whatever is left of its unifying substance. On the other level, their proliferation calls attention to their dispersion and the impossibility of coherency. Thus, the organic component of these bodily parts will fail the test of time—Marcos begins to stutter more frequently, he becomes more incoherent; his gestures have become frail, even comic. Still widely disseminated, the ailing body parts no longer produce the same resonance they had in the past, further calling attention to the breakdown of the entity that is the presidential body.

Marcos's sick body was further aggravated by its association to dead and healthy bodies of other prominent national figures. On the one hand, his sick body did not equal the torment of Aquino's assassinated body, which lay in state, retaining the bruises and bloodstains, in the aftermath of his brutal death. In Aquino's formal laying-out, which was designed to expose the atrocity of the assassination, the body was laid in an open casket; hundreds of thousands of mourners walked through and paid their respects. So potent is the image of the assassinated body that even when finally sealed for burial, an estimated 2 million people witnessed and participated in the funeral march. Marcos's sick body further suffered in contrast to the enduring health and energies of the national women (Imelda and Corazon Aquino, president of the Philippines from 1986 to 1992). Imelda did most of the campaigning for Marcos's presidential bid in the snap polls. A van equipped with a dialysis machine was on standby for Marcos's unreliable health. Corazon Aquino remained tireless as she recounted Ninoy's story and her torment in all the campaign venues.

What is ironic in Marcos's encroachment of power through television in 1972 is its disruption through the same media in 1986. While griping to the whole nation about the insurrection led by Defense Chief Juan Ponce Enrile and General Fidel Ramos, Marcos's image was zapped by a television dot; static replaced both image and sound. Addressing a national broadcast in the company of his complete family, including small children running around the makeshift news area in the palace, his image was ended by the insurrection's control of the television station. The televisual display of a cohesive presidential family was not enough to unify the nation. He tried to use the same forceful voice and gestures that characterized his fiery 1972 televised declaration of martial rule, but failed. A newer image of the presidential body was beginning to form, one whose "housemaker's" body has maximized the political mileage of an assassinated husband. Corazon Aquino's body would be constantly draped in yellow, her favorite color, which, in the snap election campaigns, Imelda referred to as reminding her of "jaundice, or a lemon" (quoted in Ellison, 235). It would also be initially constructed as a maternal body, whose newness comes from being the silver lining in a dark period of the nation's history. Ramos thereafter surrounded himself with phallic symbols to remasculinize the presidential body. A cigar in his mouth and the thumbs-up symbol of his medium-term vision of an industrialized Philippines in the year 2000 were phallic reinvestments in the premier body of the nation.

One result of the proliferation of the image of the presidential body is the continuing discourse built on Marcos even after his absence and death. When the first couple departed Malacañang Palace, people flooded the parameters and inner sanctum of the presidential home, stomping on presidential portraits, tearing documents, uprooting plants, and performing acts that would otherwise have been deemed illegal. His body was returned to the country after being kept in a refrigerated mausoleum in Hawai'i, only to be kept in the same state in the museum in his hometown. Together with his dead mother, their bodies are both regularly retouched and disinfected, open to public viewing. Scrupulously, a Sacred Heart image stands beside Marcos's body, Marcos's face inscribed in Jesus' place. A "postmortem" remnant of the presidential body's legacy emphasizes Butler's notion of the deed without the doer. So naturalized is the effect of power that subjectivity is preceded and succeeded by this power; one speaks and is spoken for only in relation to power. For if the presidential body is hegemonized to be the model of national bodies, then one can speak of other identities only in relation to his hegemony.

POLITICIZING NATIONAL BODIES

Whereas the presidential body is constructed on the basis of a "legacy of excess on display," national bodies are represented through their internalized lack (Rafael, 282).[4] National bodies participate in the display, only to remain invisible thereafter. The institution of this dialectics of excess and lack, display and invisibility was undertaken through the politicization of national bodies. The spectacle is the paradigm utilized by the Marcoses to construct difference on the basis of a hierarchy of power-knowledge. Involving a clear demarcation of positions, the spectacle becomes a ritual for reaffirming privileged and marginal positions in national politics. During Gerald Ford's trip to Manila in 1975, the first by a U.S. president after the declaration of martial rule, the couple pulled out all stops:

> Imelda Marcos forcibly moved squatters, and on arrival day the seven-mile route from the airport to Malacañang was lined with at least 1 million Filipinos, cheering, waving flags, and tossing flower petals at the motorcade. Some 10,000 Filipinos, attired in native costumes, from loincloths to butterfly dresses, performed in the streets—elaborate dances, banging on steel drums, blowing on flutes. It was all "elaborately stage managed" and "carefully contrived," with most of the participants obliged to be present, the [U.S.] embassy reported. As the motorcade moved slowly through the gathering dusk and sporadic drizzle, two trucks mounted with huge floodlights directed their beams on the two presidents, who stood through the sunroof to wave at the crowd. (Bonner, 154)

In the staging of spectacle, the leaders' bodies bask in the foreground while the amassed national bodies constitute the background. The singularity of bodies of leaders in the empty highway is juxtaposed with the masses of national bodies along the sidewalks. In other words, national bodies matter only in the sheer mass they are able to constitute, rendering appropriate the deep presidential voice and wide gestures. The consignment of bodies in terms of their ability to populate space for the staging of national spectacles is symptomatic of how family planning and population control have become equally charged issues, connoting a disciplinary function. The subordinated bodies are made to perform a nation beholden to the presidential body, staging the landscape of the nation for another foreign body that mattered. This foreign body represented Marcos's ideal of being considered as equal to his U.S. presidential counterpart. The televised event marks a macrospectacle that has a transnational predicament, linking the nation with the desire for international capital.

Spectacles have been staged by the elite to set the parameters that distinguished them from the rest of the local population.[5] The Marcoses were building from the tradition of local elites. In staging elaborate spectacles, the local elite not only competed among themselves, but also marked the stark income gaps between the few rich and the majority poor. In so doing, the elites are able to maintain the distance and are beheld by the poor, whose poverty accepts its subordination. The historical advantage of landed holdings has produced a feudal body whose access, even in present-day politics and economics, remains undisputed. Eighty-three percent of representatives during Marcos's time came from these elite families, whereas 67 percent came from traditional political clans.

The dictatorship similarly constructed the national bodies based on difference. While the presidential body projected health and strength, the national bodies projected emaciation and disease. Difference is constructed through the institutionalization of "invisible" poverty and the display of excess wealth. By "invisible" poverty, I refer to the official discourse of nation building that renders the issue either as natural or eyesore, to be ignored, covered up, or effaced. A gaze toward poverty is institutionalized, constructing the poverty scene as an absent presence. The Lacanian formulation of subjectivity—I am where I am not; I am not where I am—is similarly invoked. Poverty can be likened to the primal scene where national identity can be deciphered. Just like the Marcoses' cover-up of their meager origins through their construction of apotheoses, poverty needs to be disavowed for the trajectory of national identity to be articulated in modernity. The rationale of development and modernization is the elimination of poverty. The project of nation building, however, already foregrounds poverty as the structuring absence.

On the other hand, poverty among those who continue to wallow in its institutionalization has opted for three related maneuvers. The first two present the hegemonic bind; the third breaks away from the bind. The first is to make do with their conditions; the second is to dream of social mobility through the attainment of higher-class signifiers; the third is the group's mobilization as a social movement called the "urban poor." The mattering of national bodies involves the politicization of bodies for hegemonic use. It entails the institutionalization of conditions where poverty remains widespread, yet silent. With this condition, the form of the metropolitan body in recent modernization and national development begins to take shape. By 1975, for example, 48 percent of the population could not meet the minimum requirements for food, clothing, and shelter.[6] The number of "poorly fed"—those unable to meet the minimum food threshold—was estimated in 1975 to be anywhere from 69.9 percent to 84.3 percent of households.[7]

The national body also wallows in disease and disability. Some 17 million people, or 32.4 percent of the population, suffer from tuberculosis; twenty percent of public school teachers are infected by this respiratory disease. Seventeen million people suffered from a correctable form of eye defect in 1983; 97 percent of Filipinos in 1982 had tooth decay. The Philippines has the third largest number of blind people in the world. Of 780 Filipinos who died every day in 1974, some 330 deaths were the result of preventable diseases. The infant mortality rate is one of the highest in Asia; 24.3 percent of infants die for every thousand live births, mainly from preventable causes such as pneumonia and other respiratory conditions. And for every 1,000 live births, one mother dies. About 10 percent of adolescents suffer from mental handicap due to poor nutrition. Malnutrition makes national bodies more susceptible to disease.[8]

The formation of subordinated national bodies begins at an early age. Infants and children are most affected in the institutionalization of poverty. In a report on youth and underdevelopment, the following information provides a bleak picture of the effects on children of widespread poverty: 720,0000 infants are born with low intelligence due to iodine deficiency; 1,227 children die from pneumonia every day; 56.4 percent of 7.8 million schoolchildren are malnourished and underweight; 1.5 million children live on the streets; 120,000 children are affected by the insurgency every year; seventeen children become blind every day due to vitamin A deficiency, and twelve die in the process; there are about 777,000 children workers aged 10 to 14, and 1.4 million aged between 15 and 17; even with free primary and secondary schooling, 1.4 million children aged seven to twelve dropped out of school in 1993 as a result of their parents' inability to meet daily school expenses.[9] What becomes obvious with this image of the emaciated national body is its readiness to yield to politicization for the national culture, bearing the promise of basic access to goods and services, and to social mobility.

However, the only way to figure out the insensitivity to these statistics on the nation's health is to imagine a process of detachment. In the delusion and confusion of nation building, the local elites effaced everything that negated the vision of enforced health. Marcos built "designer" hospitals that specialized in body organs—kidney, heart, and lung. Prime Minister Cesar Virtua even went so far as to suggest that "Filipinos may have to give up one meal a day." His wife complained "about the difficulty of finding Butter Ball brand turkeys in the Philippines" (Manapat, 9).

Marcos, on the other hand, was health conscious. He flaunted the body produced by an austere and regimented diet. Before declaring martial rule, Marcos prepared his body like he was preparing for a bout.[10] Marcos disciplined his body in ways that represented his administration of the nation—regimented, enclosed, and forceful. As austerity and authoritarianism began to foreground national development, freedom became a luxury. Marcos shunned meat, for example, preferring vegetables and fruits, thus depriving the nation of this class of food. In his diary, he mentions that meat is analogous to freedom: "so I conclude that freedom is not always good. There may be periods in a country's life when it is like meat. For the time being it must be curtailed or denied" (Rempel, 154). Through the drama of a fit body, Marcos defied its corporeal limits. He projected its healthy image as the image of the health of the presidency. He was able to incorporate foreign ways of maintaining this body. Like clothing, food intake, diet, and exercise are also informed by the local elites' ability to move between national and international spaces in contouring the shape of bodies and power.

However, the image of the virile body is punctured by its own contradictions. Marcos's midsection had always been the area of his ill health. The exercise of power produces its toll on the body. Although he maintained a health regimen before installing his own regime to the nation, Marcos also suffered from stomach pains: "My tummy shows some hyperacidity so I take something every two or three hours. It is most probably due to the tension arising out of the plans for the proclamation of martial law" (Rempel, 125). An earlier account of presidential sickness is a report on the inflammation of his gallbladder (De Manila, 81–88). His eventual bout with kidney and lupus problems called attention to the breakdown of the filtering system of bodily fluids. Marcos's body, no longer able to cleanse its own system, first shifted from normal to grotesque, then eventually broke down. Like the national crisis it signifies, the sick state of the presidential body is not able to get a grip on itself. It poisons its own system until the political network produces a new presidential body from the bodies of disenfranchised oligarchs.

Furthermore, the presidential body indulged in high-maintenance sports and a lifestyle few would be able to emulate. Accounts of his golfing placed peripheral bodies in complicity on his regular attainment of decent scores: "Marcos' handicap was kept low by caddies, who altered the number on his scorecard, and solicitous security men, who, upon arriving at balls before Marcos, nudged them into better lies" (Bonner, 47). What struck some U.S. diplomats in a round of golf with the president was "the scene in the locker room afterward: Marcos' aides would sit the president on a locker room bench, remove his golf spikes, loosen his belt, remove his golfing shorts, slip on a fresh pair of trousers, then tighten his belt" (Bonner, 47). The scene presents an analog to the way subordinated bodies have maintained the image of the presidential body. Most national bodies did not have the economic resources to reproduce the signifiers of the presidential body and therefore would rearticulate these in terms of renegotiations of power. The middle class would slowly lose access in the duration of the regime. Only a favored body from the middle class became privileged during the regime; others were shut out, choosing to go into exile. Some of those who stayed on were of the traditional rich, beyond the machinations of the nouveau riche lifestyle of Marcos's hold on national power. Thus, the choice to pursue the presidential body lies only with certain privileged class formations. Those without the choice are inculcated into the hegemony of the presidential body, resonating the culture in negotiated ways: enforced with the dominance of the presidential body, national bodies would translate the culture into their own class- and gender-specific terms.

POLICING BODIES AND SEXUALITIES FOR NATIONAL DEVELOPMENT

Imelda Marcos's 3,000 pairs of shoes are the iconography of feminine display of excessive power. Ferdinand Marcos first staged the spectacle on his body, made to serve as an analog of the material transformation of the nation-state. This effort allowed Imelda the currency to do the same, transforming, however, in the spiritual domain. What then results is a body politic signifying abuse of national power that directly translates in Ferdinand Marcos's use of power (e.g., human rights violation and economic crisis) and indirectly in Imelda's "misuse" (e.g., "edifice complex," moral crisis).

IMELDIFIC BODY AND SEXUALITY

Whereas Ferdinand Marcos interiorized material power, Imelda Marcos exteriorized spiritual power. On the one hand, she evoked feminine excess, assuming the traditional role of woman as nurturer of the nation's inner sanctum. According to her, the ideal woman is "gentle [and] does not challenge a man, but . . . keeps her criticisms to herself and teaches her husband only in the bedroom" (quoted in Ellison, 235). On the other hand, she equipped herself with multinational skills, becoming Marcos's ambassador of goodwill to foreign missions abroad, his Human Settlements minister, and his Metro Manila governor. More than transcending women's traditional position, the first lady affirmed women's role in the fast-changing capitalist economy of Marcos's New Society and New Republic.

In this sense, she complemented the modernization of the nation through her efforts to emulate its model of the "new woman."

Rafael has traced Imelda's ascent to power in relation to the "new images of female ambition and subjugation [that] emerged in film and politics" (238). He sees her "cultural projects" as a "logical extension of Ferdinand's attempts to leave traces of his power everywhere" (295). So whereas Ferdinand Marcos involved the rhetoric of nationalism in modernization and development, Imelda complemented this rhetoric by invoking the spiritual role of women in a kind of partnership for nation building.[11] Imelda's work reveals the dual task of women in the modern nation: while maintaining their traditional role in the home, women are also to be integrated in nation building. Her own position reveals the specific terrain where she envisions women: "to remake Philippine culture into the totality of the marks of the regime's patronage" (Rafael, 295).

Imelda Marcos's various commissioned portraits were painted to emphasize an overpowering Filipina body—slimmer than usual, made taller by her hair in a bun, her body fully covered by formal wear, sometimes bearing her parasol. Her body is distinguished by her difference from other women's bodies, which are unable to have the same signifiers of feminine national power. Her portraits do not gaze at the viewer—although in her excessively feminine way, she knows she is being gazed at. The uncunning seductress plays on transference of excess desire in the very impossibility of identifying with her. Although disavowal is also an alternative, it remains equally distant as the image concurs the material basis of the partnership in national power. The viewer can neither completely ignore nor identify with her image.

It almost seems natural that Imelda's spectacles were in tune with the equal spectacularization of her body. Projects were intended to be spectacles in two ways: in their abnormal expanse in the landscape of Philippine poverty, and in their ability to cohere in Imelda's body rather than with anyone else's. The term "imeldific" connotes grandiosity, campiness, and excess. Her body, like Ferdinand Marcos's virile regulatory ideal, is prolific, yet inaccessible to other national bodies. Like Marcos, it is also a body working; however, it works in the realm of "cultural projects" intended for high visibility in the local and global scenes. She was able to initiate her own sphere of operation by complementing Marcos's rhetoric and projects of national development, "turning state power into a series of such spectacles as cultural centers, film festivals, landscaped parks, five-star hotels, and glitzy conferences which seemed to be present everywhere yet whose source was infinitely distant from those who viewed them" (Rafael, 295).

Like her husband's body, Imelda's body was also high maintenance; as such, the stress from creating spectacles also took its toll. Her entourage grew bigger, her social obligations grew longer. She complained of insomnia, low blood pressure, kidney trouble, bad teeth, even fainting spells and miscarriages. Unofficial biographer Carmen Navarro Pedrosa writes, "what the photographs did not show was the battle that raged within the beautiful body. The resplendently gowned and bejeweled figure was under a strict regimen of anti-aging tablet and anti-biotics to cope with a recurring internal infection" (*Rise and Fall,* 177). Nonetheless, the imeldific body embodied the two standards imposed on women in the modern state. Imelda was always dressed in conservative wear, maintaining allegiance to her boss and husband. However, most of her ventures were initiatives sanctioned by Marcos. The first lady's body grapples with the feminine aspect of national power by maintaining her traditional role as wife and mother, and by seeking out her owns turf parallel to Marcos's dispensation of power. In so doing, Imelda was mapping out a traditional and modern role for the first lady as invoked in notions of conjugal dictatorship and partnership.

Thus, the concept of the "new woman" comes at a historical juncture when foreign capital was being induced to the national space, calling into focus the greater range of roles women could perform in its service. The "sweetie" roles portrayed by teen megastar Sharon Cuneta, a daughter of a city mayor aligned with Marcos, typifies the roles attuned to the "new woman." Her films, rags-to-riches narratives, proved to be regular box-office draws. With perseverance, patience, and luck, anyone can make it big. This actress validates Imelda's own story, which "inspire[s] hundreds of thousands of Filipinos by reckoning her past as a proof that the poor need not despair" (Navarro Pedrosa, *Untold Story,* 231). Similarly, the signifiers of middle- and upper-class lifestyles have been prolific in Cuneta's films— fancy clothes, jewelry, majestic homes, and cosmetics, as well as a certain aura that comes with wealth. Imelda's own clothing and accessories also come with a certain campiness that implied multicultural fashion—huge bottles of perfume from France, hundreds of Italian shoes, fake paintings, "native" yet excessively ornate formal wear, etc. What this "new woman" signified is a mobility and flow of bodies and wealth bestowed as gifts by the system. Without a strong middle-class base, the image of the "new woman" remains attractive and distant to national bodies. This logic affirms what Imelda has done with national culture, "construed as a gift from above that circulated to those below" (Rafael, 295).

Any discussion of the metropolitan body bearing the mark of spectacle and invisibility needs to make a brief detour to the declaration of martial rule in 1972 to foreground issues of prohibition and display of the body and sexuality. One thing noticeable immediately after the declaration of martial rule was that everything seemed to work. Garbage was collected promptly, people crossed the streets in designated pedestrian lanes, and even traffic seemed to flow more quickly. The price tag in experiencing flow and mobility involved the quelling of opposition and of media and business control. The New Society's slogan, *"sa ikauunlad ng bayan disiplina ang kailangan"* (discipline is needed for the nation to progress), was borrowed from the experience of the newly industrialized countries in Asia that imposed authoritarian rule to allow the national economy to take off.[12] Martial rule echoed the need and acceptance of discipline for the price of national development.

One effect of martial rule was the construction of ideal body types. Long hair was considered part of the youth and drug subcultures and therefore prohibited. Also banned were miniskirts, which invoked the promiscuity of the sexual revolution of the 1960s; miniskirts were also deemed antithetical to the feminine ideals of the New Society. Those caught with long hair were given instant haircuts, performed by the police in front of the public. Other petty violations, including jaywalking and violations of the curfew hours, were punishable with the visible and embarrassing chore of cleaning Manila's leading highway. The violating bodies are displayed in the highway's center aisle performing menial tasks, such as pulling grass or picking up litter, a deterrent to all others witnessing the spectacle. The site of enforced work is also a "free" space to shout invectives and jokes to these violators. By cleaning up the highway, the excessive ways of these violators are also poised for some form of cleansing. The violating body cleans and is cleaned through menial work. The crimes of trespassing incur a return of the violating body to its working ideal, to be disciplined by work.

This simple maneuver effectively reinforced the construction of martial rule. Marcos sought to interiorize all material power to his body, as only the presidential and complementing first lady's bodies can trespass and be excessive. All other excess of the body was to be prohibited by being placed in a site with greater visibility. This making visible of bare bodies has its affinity in surveillance and punishment. The working body becomes the model for national bodies. There is an asexual impediment to the national body. As primarily male and female working bodies define nation building, sexuality is left behind in the domain of the prohibition. In being placed in the private domain, sexuality presents both possibilities and limits of transgression during the Marcos period. Even Imelda's relationship with the aging Marcos was embellished with love and devotion, while at the same time she was escorted and surrounded by male personalities. Ferdinand Marcos's dismal liaison with Dovie Beams remained the first and only news of an extramarital affair.

The first couple's asexual impediment to the national body is inversely poised against the themes of overtly sexual bodies of the masses. Although popular representations of both the first couple and the people have used sexual themes to distinguish their positions, they have done so for divergent interests. For the first couple, sexuality was mobilized to socialize the people to the rudiments of citizenry needed for national development. For the people, sexuality became a form of subversion that bogged down the first couple's project of nation building, which included population control, censorship, family code, and others.

PERIPHERALIZATION OF THE MARGINS

Two of Brocka's films on prostitution invoke a cultural rereading of national power through its translation in the margins. *Macho Dancer* (1989) and *White Slavery* (1985) tackle the sexual trade in the underbelly of national power. Along this sphere, national power is recoded through a multinational redefinition of the residual feudal family and en masse display of subordinated bodies. In *White Slavery,* prostitution is enforced on women recruited from the provinces, tricked into working in the sex trade rather than the promised jobs of being waitresses and house help in the city; in *Macho Dancer,* it becomes a survival tactic, using youthful virility to financially survive.

Given these grids in which prostitution takes place in the city, national power is translated into a similar conspiracy among individuals and microinstitutions involved in the sex ring. Police are either directly involved in this ring—extorting "protection" money from gay club managers, as drug dealers, and contacts to foreign pornographers—or indirectly by remaining oblivious to the oppression. Club and *casa* (whorehouse) owners are equally oppressive in the iron-willed ways their spaces are managed. Both national power and its translation in the margins govern the sex worker. Poverty remains the naturalizing force of microinterpretations of power. Because the sex trade involves a hand-to-mouth existence, the sex worker is busied with the struggle of earning a living and surviving. Like the presidential body, the sex worker is forced to work regularly. Even outside their "official" line of work, their spare time involves more work—distributing drugs, performing in a pornographic movie, and finding odd jobs to make ends meet. In a hilarious scene in *Macho Dancer,* the gay manager introduces the young male character to the club's sideline business, a cottage industry where boys, during quiet periods in the club, work on a quota basis making exportable flower crafts and lighted ornaments.

All other acts outside sexual work translate into additional costs or burden. The brother who looks for an only sister forced into prostitution in *Macho Dancer* risks losing his regular income and eventually, his own life. In the underbelly of the sex-trade world, morality is lost, only to be recovered through the further disenfranchisement of other subordinated bodies or the functioning of hegemonic institutions of its "public safety" task. Self-reliance becomes the only recourse to social entrapment. The brother dies in freeing an only sister enslaved in the sex trade. His friend avenges his death vigilante-style, shooting the police-syndicate chief in the forehead. The tabloid headline reiterates the official recourse to social chaos, blaming the shooting on communist insurgents. In using the insurgency tactic of eliminating "undesirable" elements of the state, the main character is able to escape prosecution. However, he suffers from a moral failure in his inability to save his prostitute girlfriend, who preferred maintaining her work than facing starvation by taking a chance with a "decent" profession.

The residual family hovers to define relationships in the margins. The *casa*, the Spanish word for "home," and club become the organizing principle of this feudal family. Forced into sexual work, the young men and women are positioned as siblings under the care of oppressive mother figures—the club's gay manager assaults and shouts curses at squabbling dancers, and the "mama san" in the *casa* orders the lives of the confined women. At night, the *casa*'s living room space is transformed into a display window. All the women are originally positioned in this public domestic space before they are chosen and sent to their rooms to perform sex work. A sibling relation is reconstituted through a similar value system among the sex workers. In *White Slavery*, three women initiated in the trade at the same time construct sisterly bonds. In *Macho Dancer*, brotherly love and homoerotic tension are experienced between the more experienced and neophyte workers sharing the same living quarters.

In another set-up, the women are already positioned in their individual cubicles, each with the basic equipment for sexual work—electric fan, bed, and basin of water. The male customers are escorted to these rooms; doors are opened, and available women are exposed for viewing before their selection for work. In the gay club, the male workers perform on stage as "macho dancers" before their selection by customers. They stage virility in their writhing snake dance, yet they are campily costumed in underwear and ornaments.

The pointing finger hails the chosen sex worker. Capital speaks for the body who speaks through parts. Like Marcos's voice and gesture in national politics, the customer's finger initiates the ordering and delivery of sexual bodies. The sex workers are hailed through their presence in the erotics of a public domestic space, then paid to do private sex work for the customer's leisure. What is then analogous in this location is the related mode in which national power is staged. Through the spectacle, en masse, bodies are interpellated for sexual work. The public domestic space becomes a site of surveillance. Their lack of agency is exposed in the bodies' use as display. They are emptied of middle-class signifiers; cash flows into their body, constructing their identity as sex workers. Their bodies mark the division of labor in the sex trade. Like labor value, their performances of sex work translate to surplus value for the layers of business and institutions to generate profit. The sex worker's body is made to bear the weight of the sedimented layers of micropower operations, forming other levels from which to negotiate with national power.

The worker's body becomes the location of citizenship, the heralding of the individual's subordination to larger national constructs. For if the national leadership has not prioritized the basic delivery of social services, then people in the margins make do with this lack in their lives. In most instances, resistance does not take an overtly political mode. Their enforced daily survival is the cornerstone that allows the dictatorship to be focused on its own amassment of excess. Their subjectivation under these conditions becomes the precursor of their citizenship. In being abjected, the national bodies are forced to be self-reliant by and integral to the national design. In doing what they do where they do the act of self-reliance, the national bodies are consequently poised as subordinate to the complex arena of national politics. The extreme form takes place in the margin's reification of national power play, leading to its further peripheralization. By creating further hierarchies, national politics hopes to further the distance between extreme income poles, thereby further perverting the possibilities of reversal and transgression. In creating citizens out of "denizens," the national leadership politicizes subordinated bodies for the project of nation building.

There is an another trope to understand the politicization of national bodies. The materialization of national bodies through poverty and national politics explains the acceptance of subordination. The notion of patronage, however, explains a materiality only in relation to its mythification through the collective unconscious.[13] Although it finds visible presence in the translation of national cultural politics, patronage also has a structural bent to its operation, providing both an ahistorical and automatic transliteration of traditional issues. Patronage, like the issue of subordination through poverty, can be materially reworked to invoke both the social construction of its own mythification and the negotiations taking place from "below." In so doing, agency in the margins is relationally poised, thereby shifting the notion from its "top-down" approach in the writing of cultural politics.

Sexualities and bodies are sites of contestation for meaning. Although national development policies of the Marcosian state sought to mobilize the people for citizenry, Brocka's filmic representations of sexualities and bodies sought to challenge such a hegemonic position. It is through the ensuing contest that sexualities and bodies are mattered, as both hegemonic and subcultural efforts remain neither thoroughly dominant nor subservient. Just as the discussion of sex work in Brocka's films informs us, state strategy for control and subcultural tactics for subversion necessarily go hand in hand to fill in the lack of actual national development. Such sex work is both negated in the espousal of a puritan dictatorial democracy and covertly valorized in the name of national development. The mantle on which national development rests, after all, is vested in sexual work that results in the sexual global division of labor—from women in multinational factories, to men in feminized overseas contract work, to the feminized position of the Philippines in the newer global division of capital and labor. In other words, bodies and sexualities are subjectivized for both national and multinational development.

N O T E S

1. A copy of Sonny Yabao's photograph of the "two Marcoses" is reprinted in Jo-Ann Maglipon's "Reprise 1983," 8.

2. In formal gatherings, the presidential body has always been clothed either by traditional wear or Western-style fashion. The president's clothing evokes the privileged positioning of local elites, allowing them to shift between a nationalist and an internationalist position. In other countries, nationalist policies would find affinity in some form of adherence to an outside mode of production. In India, for example, Gandhi's advocacy for self-reliance in the household level has been incorporated in Nehru's socialist planning of the national economy. China's acceptance of multinational business has found justification in the state's "democratization" of its socialist economy. While calling on an indigenous rhetoric of self-reliance, Philippine local elites have historically relied on international assistance: that national development can only be achieved through foreign borrowing and aid. Their ability to physically and intellectually move through national spaces has culturally positioned them differently. For most Filipinos, the effect of this international engagement translates either to the proliferation of American goods and ideals in the national sphere or immigration to the United States.

These two types of formal wear already foreground the elites' hold on a local base and national stature, and access to Western-style education, to foreign travel, and to Western ideals. Marcos reified both the elites' privileged position and the social stratification. Seeing himself as a maverick, along the lines of Kennedy's effect on U.S. politics, he introduced casual wear and sportswear in informal gatherings. In his campaign contact with the people, Marcos dressed casually, mostly in a short-sleeve white polo shirt that bore the presidential insignia. He donned sportswear to further construct an active presidential body attuned to the fast-changing developments in the local and global scenes. These two other types of presidential clothing rested on a body politic based on Marcos's youth. Anchored in youthful vitality and the drive to lead the nation into modernization, the president is perennially depicted in kinetic motion, busily working in an infinite number of official activities.

3. "Quasicorporeality" is a term used by Brian Massumi and Kenneth Dean to denote Reagan's body *without* an image: it "has social prestige, not for its inherent qualities or the superior symbolizations and ideations but simply because its kinetic geography is more far-reaching" (166–67). See Massumi and Dean, "Postmortem on the Presidential Body."

4. Rafael uses the phrase to characterize Aquino's government efforts to transform the presidential palace into a museum housing the Marcoses' collection, composed mainly of items left behind in their hasty flight to the United States.

5. Ricardo Manapat cites at least three examples of social circles flaunting their wares:

The Moncomunidad Pampangueña, a social circle composed of wealthy families from Central Luzon, held parties and social gatherings expressly to parade the latest in fashion. The parties were carefully engineered so that the national dailies could publicize in detail the apparel worn by the society matrons. . . . As recorded in the newspapers of this period, the price of these dresses were between $2500 and $5000. What did these amounts mean in the late 1940's and the 1950's? In the Philippines, it meant that the laborer from the Central Luzon plantations of these families had to work an equivalent of more than 12 years to be able to earn enough to buy one of these gowns. . . .

The Ilongo families from the sugar-producing provinces of the Visayas region had their own social gatherings. They had the Kahirup, a social circle largely composed of the wealthy Negrense families from the sugar-rich island of Negros. . . . They engaged in a form of social competition with the elites of other provinces, and ribbed the Pampangueños from Central Luzon for having wealth but not knowing enough flaunting it.

The situation was again not different in the 1960s and in period right before Marcos imposed martial law in 1972. The advent of the jet plane gave members of the elite a way to alleviate their boredom. One practice of the very rich at this time was to take quick plane trips to Hong Kong, arrive in time for lunch, shop for a few hours, and then go back to Manila on the same day. (71–72)

6. I cull from statistics reported in Manapat, 6–9, and in de Guzman, 3–7.

7. The statistics are drawn from de Guzman and Manapat's research: The Food and Agriculture Organization lists the country in 1974 as among the top five countries with the worst malnutrition rates. In 1976, 76 percent of preschool children experienced varying degrees of malnutrition. A survey by the Philippine Nutrition Program of the Food and Nutrition Council said that among the effects of malnutrition were the following: permanent damage to brain cells, stunted physical growth, impaired eyesight, and extremely poor condition of the teeth. According to de Guzman, such deficiency in food intake echoed that in 1984, when consumption provided only 91 percent of the energy intake, 43 percent of proteins and minerals, and 54 percent of the level of regulating food required for good health. This made the Philippines second only to Bangladesh as Asia's poorest-fed nation. Malnutrition in turn affects development and education: of a hundred students who enter grade 1, only four will complete high school, largely as a result of malnutrition and poverty (3–7).

8. The following information is also culled from de Guzman's and from Manapat's research: It was reported that 80 percent of those who suffer from communicable diseases are preventable. Forty-three percent of all deaths in the country would have been prevented if the patients were provided with basic medical care. Sixty-two of every hundred deaths did not even receive medical attention. The situation is made worse with the institutionalized policy of migrant labor. Eighty percent of nurses and 68 percent of doctors practice their professions abroad. In central Mindanao, there is only one doctor for every 207,177 patients.

9. See Danilo Arao-Araña, "Of Youth and Underdevelopment," 3.

10. Marcos "launched a regimen of exercise and diet intended to bring him to the very peak of fitness. His simple diet sometimes consisted of little more than sardines and vegetables. He drank water and fruit juices. He was particularly interested in a recently introduced Ukrainian vegetable 'guaranteed to stop the aging process and to lower blood pressure.' He lifted weights, jogged, played a form of handball, and golf" (Rempel, 165–66).

11. Imelda R. Marcos writes,

Indeed the Filipina, like her Oriental sisters, knows by instinct and by tradition that as the bearer of life she has the duty, and yes, the right to nourish it thereafter, and to cherish it, and that to cherish is to love. . . . I trust we would remember and keep in mind the Oriental woman and her mystique, her concept of sharing and participating, her understanding that a woman does not only have an equal status but must play an equal role which should not seek to divide and to antagonize but to unify. In such a partnership, we achieve our full humanity.

Thus we must explore further the participation of women in ensuring international peace, in the elimination of racism and racial discrimination, and in the integration of women in the processes of development. That is surely a measure of the role that we must play, and are entitled to play, in the future human race. (83–84)

12. A return to the Marcosian discipline and punishment has been echoed through Aquino's and Ramos's administrations. Ramos's men continue to argue for a "soft authoritarianism and martial rule tactics to stop crime." What these retro calls are citing is the perceived strong base of East Asian states that paves the way for sustained industrialization. Jose T. Almonte, a Ramos cabinet member, states that in Japan, Korea, and Taiwan, the state is "strong, bureaucratic and authoritarian" (108). Such mythification of the strong state flattens culturally specific differences and produces the tendency for greater and tighter political control of the citizenry.

13. Rafael invokes a nostalgia for the patron–client relationship in the proliferation of images of the Marcoses: "Patronage implies not simply the possession of resources but, more important, the means with which to instigate the desire for and the circulation of such resources. In a political context ruled by actional rather than class-based opposition, patronage becomes the most important means for projecting power. . . . Patronage thus mystifies inequality to the point that makes it seem not only historically inevitable but also morally desirable, as it recasts power in familiar and familial terms. As such, the display of patronage is meant to drain the potential for conflict from social hierarchy. Conflict is ideally thought to occur among factions . . . not between patrons and their clients" (296).

REFERENCES

Almonte, Jose T. "The Politics of Development in the Philippines." *Kasarinlan: A Philippine Quarterly of Third World Studies* 9, no. 2–3 (1993–1994).
Arao-Araña, Danilo. "Of Youth and Underdevelopment." *Ibon Facts and Figures* 17, no. 24 (1994): 3.
Bonner, Raymond. *Waltzing with a Dictator: The Marcoses and the Making of American Policy.* Manila: National Bookstore, 1987.
Burton, Sandra. *Impossible Dream: The Marcoses, the Aquinos, and the Unfinished Revolution.* New York: Warner Books, 1989.
Butler, Judith. *Bodies That Matter: On the Discursive Limits of "Sex."* New York: Routledge, 1993.
———. *Gender Trouble: Feminism and the Subversion of Identity.* New York: Routledge, 1990.

de Guzman, Ros-B. "Where Is the Human in Development?" *Ibon Facts and Figures* 17, no. 16 (1994): 3–7.

De Manila, Quijano. *Reportage on the Marcoses 1964–1970.* Manila: National Book Store, 1981.

Ellison, Katherine. *Imelda: Steel Butterfly of the Philippines.* New York: McGraw-Hill, 1988.

Maglipon, Jo-Ann. "Confetti Power." In *Primed Reportage on an Archipelago.* Manila: Anvil, 1993.

———. "Reprise 1983." In *Primed Reportage on an Archipelago.* Manila: Anvil, 1993.

Manapat, Ricardo. *Some Are Smarter than Others: The History of Marcos' Crony Capitalism.* New York: Aletheia Publications, 1991.

Marcos, Imelda R. "The Mystique of the Oriental Woman." In *The Compassionate Society,* 83–84. Manila: National Media Production Center, 1976.

Massumi, Brian, and Kenneth Dean. "Postmortem on the Presidential Body, or Where the Rest of Him Went." In *Body Politics: Disease, Desire and the Family,* edited by Michael Ryan and Avery Gordon. Boulder, Colo.: Westview Press, 1994.

Navarro Pedrosa, Carmen. *The Untold Story of Imelda Marcos.* Manila: Navarro Pedrosa, 1969.

———. *The Rise and Fall of Imelda Marcos.* Manila: Navarro Pedrosa, 1987.

Rafael, Vicente L. "Patronage and Pornography: Ideology and Spectatorship in the Early Marcos Years." *Comparative Studies in Society and History* 32, no. 2 (April 1990): 282–304.

Rempel, William C. *Delusions of a Dictator: The Mind of Marcos as Revealed in His Secret Diaries.* Boston: Little Brown, 1993.

Chapter 7
The Time of Violence
Deconstruction and Value

ELIZABETH GROSZ

1

My interest in this essay is to explore the ways in which we may see violence both as a positivity and as an unspoken condition of a certain fantasy of the sustainability of its various others or opposites, peace, love, and so on. Rather than simply condemning or deploring violence, as we tend to do regarding the evils of war and suffering and the everyday horrors we believe we can ameliorate, I am interested in raising the question of violence not simply where it is most obvious and manifest—in the streets, in relations between races, classes, sexes, political oppositions (although I hope what it will raise does not avoid these issues)—but also where it is less obvious, and rarely called by this name, in the domain of knowledges, reflection, thinking, and writing. Not simply to condemn it, but to explore its constitutive role in the establishment of politics, of thought, of knowledge. For this reason: that, as intellectuals or philosophers (they are not always, or are only rarely, the same thing), we play a part in various structures of violence, whether we choose to or not, not only in our daily but also in our professional and intellectual lives, but it is rare that we have the intellectual resources by which to think the level of our investment in the very violence that constitutes our relations to work. I want to use some of the rather sensitive and self-conscious resources provided by Jacques Derrida to look at the very violence of writing, of thought, and of knowing as the conditions of possibility and of existence of our own immersion in disciplinarity.

Although it has been commonplace to claim that Derrida, and along with him the whole of postmodernism, represents a mode of depoliticization and transformation of feminist, class, and postcolonial discourses,[1] Derrida has never written on anything other than politics and violence, even if it is also true that he does not write *only* on politics and violence. I would argue that his are among the most intensely political texts of the late twentieth century, although the language he uses is not one he shares in common with political theory. He is commonly accused of blurring or immobilizing politics, of refusing to provide answers or the conditions of answers to political problems, and of reducing political to theoretical problems. In this vein, Thomas McCarthy's reading of Derrida's politics is representative: McCarthy argues that in the long run, Derrida produces "wholesale subversion, with no suggestion of remedies or alternatives" (McCarthy, 157)—in short, that while critical and perhaps in that sense useful, it remains ironic, parodic, skeptical, negative. Deconstructive, perhaps, but never adequately constructive. Able to criticize politics, but never able to positively contribute to it.

I would like to argue, contrary to this prevailing representation of Derrida's politics as a politics of negativism, nihilism, or anarchism, that he offers a profound, if unsettling, reconfiguration of political activity that centers on the question of violence. It is true that he refuses to offer political advice, to provide remedies or solutions to answer to the pressing needs of today. But it is the very idea that we can find a solution to the questions of these questions, and to the question of violence that is put under political interrogation itself. Derrida refuses the kinds of question that McCarthy, Nancy Fraser, and others use to define the political—which does not mean Derrida abandons or refuses politics, but that he engages in different ways and in different questions.[2]

The nature of the violence he both articulates and mobilizes is discernible only through a careful reading of a number of texts in which he appears to be talking of other matters. The question of violence is never very far from these matters. Whenever he talks of force ("Force of Law"), of discord ("Différance"), of the trace (*Of Grammatology*), of dislocation ("Eating Well"), of fraying ("Freud and the Scene of Writing"), as well as in texts more explicitly devoted to the question of violence ("Violence and Metaphysics," "Violence of the Letter"), it is with the politics of violence that Derrida deals. And moreover, while accused of either political indifference or nihilism, Derrida has addressed the more manifest and concrete political issues of violence—in relation to race and apartheid, in his writings for Nelson Mandela, in his writings on feminist questions, in his discussions of the rhetoric of drugs, and so on—in a much more explicit and direct manner than virtually any other contemporary philosopher one can think of. That his works are seen as apolitical, as lacking a mode of political address, is surely the result of a certain freezing up of politics and an attempt to constrain it to well-known or predetermined forms, the very forms whose naturalness or stability is contestable through deconstruction.[3]

From the very earliest conceptions of *différance* he develops an understanding of the "worlding of the world," the marking of the earth, as a mode of cutting. *Différance* is understood as the inscriptive, dispersing dissonance at the impossible "origin" of any self-presence. As he described it, "*Différance* is the name we might give to the 'active' moving discord of different forces" ("Différance," 18). As "active" moving discord of forces, or differential forces, one that precedes the opposition between active and passive or moving and stationary, *différance* is the originary tearing of that which, unknowable and unspeakable as it is, was always amenable to inscription, was never "full" enough to retain its self-presence in the face of this active movement of tearing, cutting, breaking apart. This movement is also a bringing together, a folding or reorganizing, and the very possibility of time and becoming.

In *Of Grammatology*, Derrida asks the crucial question, which in a sense I want to adopt as my own: "What links writing to violence? And what must violence be in order for something in it to be equivalent to the operation of the trace?" (112). Note that he does not ask the more obvious, and manifestly Derridean, question: "What must *writing* be in order for something in it to be equivalent to violence," but rather, seeks into the modes of divergence, ambiguity, impossibility, the aporetic status of violence itself, a status that it shares in common with the trace, and thus with writing, inscription, or difference. This is in many senses a more interesting and complicated question, for it asks: in what ways is violence bound up with the structures of equivocation, of *différance*, of undecidability that so radically structure and unhinge all discourse and all representation, all modes of self-presence? If violence is no longer so simply identifiable and denounceable, if it is not readily delimited in its spheres of operation, if it becomes ambiguous where the divide between violence and its others can be drawn, then violence is a form, possibly the only form, that writing, arche-writing, or the trace can take. Derrida does not ask how violence is like writing, but rather, what is it *in* violence, what operative element in violence, that is equivalent to the trace. Violence is not containable itself as an identity of the trace: it is its own particularity and excessiveness over and above any conceptual schema, deconstruction notwithstanding. Derrida is inquiring into the allegiance of something in violence with writing—indeed, with the very operations of deconstruction itself, which can be considered a writing of the violence of writing, and thus a self-consciously violent writing of writing as violence (and production, of violating production).

What makes Derrida's work at once intensely political and ethical, while he remains acutely aware of the problems involved in any straightforward avowal of one's commitments to political and ethical values, is his readiness to accept that no protocol, no rhetorical or intellectual ploy is simply innocent, motivated by reason, knowledge, or truth alone, but carries with it an inherent undecidability and repeatability that recontextualizes it and frees it from any origin or end. His politics is not the espousal of a position, but rather an openness to a force, the force of *différance*. He lives up to the simultaneous necessity and impossibility of ethics, of politics, and of knowledge, the paradoxical binding of that which we must move beyond with how we move beyond.

Derrida outlines his earliest linkage of violence with the structure of writing or difference in his discussion of Lévi-Strauss in a section in *Of Grammatology* called "The Violence of Writing." There, he argues that the structure of violence is itself marked by the very structure of the trace or writing: a three-pronged process in which concrete or vulgar, everyday writing, or violence, is the reduced and constrained derivative of a more primary and constitutive arche-writing or arche-violence that is the very condition of both writing/violence and its opposite, speech/peace: "In the beginning," there is an arche-writing, a primordial or constitutive violence that inscribes "the unique," the originary, the thing itself in its absolute self-proximity, into a system of differentiation, into the systems of ordering or classification that constitute language (or representation more generally). This violence is the containment and ordering of the thing to give up its thingness and to submit itself to the leveling of representation, a mythical and impossible leveling that assumes a self-identity the thing itself never possessed:

> To think the unique *within* the system, to inscribe it there, such is the gesture of the arche-writing: arche-violence, loss of the proper, of absolute proximity, of self-presence, in truth the loss of what has never taken place, of a self-presence which has never been given but only dreamed of and always already split, repeated, incapable of appearing to itself except in its own disappearance. ("Violence of Writing," 112)

Primordial inscription, the ontological equivocation of *différance*, is the rendering of an originary self-presence as impossible: it is the "production" of presence through the structure of the trace, the binding up of the real in writing or marking. This arche-writing, the writing or violence, inscription or trace brings about the system of terms, differences between which oppositions, structures are made possible. It requires a second, "reparatory" or compensatory violence, the violence whose function it is to erase the traces of this primordial violence, a kind of counterviolence whose violence consists in the denial of violence. This is a malignant inscription that hides its inscriptive character, that dematerializes and deidealizes itself, that refuses to face up to its own dependence on and enmeshment in the more primordial structure. This is a violence that describes and designates itself as the moral counter of violence. This is the violence that we sometimes name the law, right, or reason.

There is, moreover, a third-order violence, one that we can understand in the more mundane and viscerally horrifying, and thus ordinary, sense of the word:

> It is on this tertiary level that of the empirical consciousness, that the common conception of violence (the system whose possibility remains yet of the moral law and of transgression) unthought, should no doubt be situated. . . .

> This last violence is all the more complex in its structure because it refers at the same time to the two inferior levels of arche-violence and of law. In effect, it reveals the first nomination which was already an expropriation, but it denudes also that which since then functioned as the proper, the so-called proper, substitute of the deferred proper, *perceived* by the *social* and *moral consciousness* as the proper, the reassuring seal of self-identity, the secret. ("Violence of Writing," 112)

This is a dense and difficult discussion worth careful investigation. Derrida is suggesting that empirical violence, or "war in the colloquial sense" (112) rests upon, indeed is made possible by, the logically prior two senses of violence. The violence of nomination, of language or writing, is an expropriation, covered over and concealed by the violence that names itself as the space of nonviolence, the field of the law (which in its very constitution structures itself as lawful, and thus beyond or above violence, that which judges violence). Empirical violence, war, participates in both these modes of violence (violence as inscription, violence as the containment of inscription, the containment of violence). Mundane or empirical violence reveals by effraction the originary violence, whose energy and form it iterates and repeats; yet it "denudes" the latent or submerged violence of the law, whose transgression it affirms, while thus affirming the very force and necessity of the law.

If Derrida refuses to locate the "mundane" violence of "evil, war, indiscretion, rape" (112) as originary, as the eruption of an unheralded violence upon an otherwise benign or peaceful scene (this is how he locates Lévi-Strauss's Rousseauism), he manages to show that everyday violence, the violence we strive to condemn in its racist, sexist, classist, and individualist terms, is itself the violent consequence of an entire order whose very foundation is inscriptive, differential, and thus violent. It is thus no longer clear how something like a moral condemnation of violence is possible—or at least how it remains possible without considerable self-irony. The very position from which a condemnation of (tertiary) violence is articulated is itself only made possible because the violence of the morally condemnatory position must remain unarticulated. Which is of course not to say that moral condemnation is untenable or impossible, but rather that its own protocols are implicated in the very thing it aims to condemn. Which means that the very origins of values, ethics, morality, and law, "all things noble in culture" (as Nietzsche says) lie in the trace, in the dissimulating self-presence that never existed and whose tracks must be obliterated as they are revealed. Force, violence, writing not only "originate" but also disseminate and transform even that violence which cannot be called as such:

> The arche-writing is the origin of morality as of immorality. The nonethical opening of ethics. A violent opening. As in the case of the vulgar concept

of writing, the ethical instance of violence must be rigorously suspended in order to repeat the genealogy of morals. ("Violence of Writing," 140)

2

Although his work has strayed very far from many of his initial concerns, Derrida returns to a remarkably similar problematic in more recent works, a number of which are clearly linked to the question of violence and its founding role in the constitution of systems of ethics, morality, law, and justice, in the operation of modes of gift and hospitality, in the structure of relations to the other, notions of singularity, heterogeneity, the movement of double affirmation, not to mention in his earlier preoccupations with iteration, trace, and undecidability. He gives the name "violence" a number of catachrestical formulations: force, discord, dislocation, anthropophagy, among their more recent incarnations. These terms are not without ambivalence for him insofar as they are both "uncomfortable" and "indispensable" ("Force of Law," 929), paradoxically necessary and impossible: they must be thought, but the terms by which they are thought are complex and overdetermined, and they bind one to what one seeks to overcome or remove.[4]

Derrida poses the question, one of the crucial political questions of our age, "How are we to distinguish between this force of the law . . . and the violence that one always deems unjust? What difference is there between, on the one hand, the force that can be just or in any case deemed legitimate, not only as an instrument in the service of law but the practice and even the realization, the essence, of *droit,* and on the other hand the violence that one always deems unjust? What is a just force or a non-violent force?" (927). As his ostensible object of investigation, he takes Walter Benjamin's formative essay "The Critique of Violence" (1978). He asks, following and problematizing Benjamin, where we can draw the dividing line between legitimized or justified force and the forces that are either prior to, excessive of, or not obedient to law, legitimation, right, or the proper. Can there be a distinction between a constitutive and inscriptive violence and a gratuitous, excessive violence, between a founding violence and the violence of conservation, that is not warranted or justified? And what provides the force of justification that legitimizes one form and not another? Is it legitimated, if it functions as legitimating?

Derrida suggests, contrary to the characterization of deconstruction as apolitical, as neutral, self-preoccupied, or merely formalist and representational in its orientation, that this question of violence and its relation to the law inheres in, is, the very project of deconstruction. It is not a peripheral concern, something that deconstruction could choose to interrogate or not, but is the heart of a deconstructive endeavor: the violence of writing, the violence of founding, of in-stating, of producing, of judging or knowing is a violence that both manifests and dissimulates itself. A space of necessary equivocation. The spaces between this manifestation and dissimulation are the very spaces that make deconstruction both possible and necessary and impossible and fraught, the spaces that deconstruction must utilize, not to move outside the law or outside violence (to judge them from outside—which is impossible), but to locate its own investments in both law and violence.[5] Justice, law, right are those systems, intimately bound up with writing; the law is writing par excellence, and the history of legal institutions is the history of the reading and rewriting of law, not just because the law is written, and must be to have its force, but also because law, and justice (we will conflate them for only a moment) serve to order, to divide, to cut: "Justice, as law, is never exercised without a decision that *cuts, that divides*" (963). This indeed is the very paradox of the law: that while it orders and regulates, while it binds and harmonizes, it must do so only through a cut, a hurt that is no longer, if ever, calculable as violence or a cut. Deconstruction is not the denunciation of the violence of the law, but rather a mode of engagement with, a participant in, this violence: for it exerts its own modes of judgment, its own cuts on its deconstructive objects, including the law, ethics, morality. And is in turn subject to other deconstructive and iterative maneuvers. That which makes the law both a part of and that which is inherently foreign to violence is what introduces the structure of *undecidability* into the law and thus into deconstruction itself:

> The Undecidable remains caught, lodged, at least as a ghost—but an essential ghost—in every decision, in every event of decision. Its ghostliness deconstructs from within any assurance of presence, any certitude or any supposed criteriology that would assure us of the justice of a decision, in truth of the very event of a decision. ("Violence and Writing," 965)

The undecidable is not a thing, a substance or self-presence that inhabits any situation of judgment, any decision or action; rather, it is the very openness and uncertainty, the fragility and force of and in the act of judgment itself: it is the very equivocation of judgment itself, the limit (as Drucilla Cornell puts it) of the law's legitimacy or intelligibility, that is the object of deconstructive interrogation. Deconstruction exploits this undecidability as its own milieu, the fertile internal ground on which it sows disseminating germs and uncertainties. It is not simply critique (as Benjamin conceives it), nor is it prophylactic: there is no "remedy" or cure (or at least no cure that isn't also *pharmakon*) for undecidability. My point is that what is marked, or unmarked, through this equivocation is always the field of violence within and through which the trace weaves its dissimulating web. Undecidability is the hinge that renders Benjamin's clear-cut distinctions between a founding or constitutive and regulative or conserving justice, between mythic and divine justice, no longer tenable and on the continual verge of exchanging places and identities with each other:

> the very violence of the foundation or position of law . . . must envelop the violence of conservation . . . and cannot break with it. It belongs to the structure of fundamental violence that it calls for the repetition of itself and founds what ought to be conserved, conservable, promised to heritage and tradition to be shared. . . . Thus there can be no rigorous opposition between positioning and conservation, only what I will call (and Benjamin does not name it) a *différantialle* contamination between the two, with all the paradoxes that this may lead to. ("Violence and Writing," 997)

It is no longer clear (if it ever was) that one can distinguish between a "good" and a "bad" violence, a violence that is necessary and one that is wanton, excessive, and capable of, in principle, elimination—one that is justified by virtue of its constructive force while the other is condemned as destructive, negative. Which is not at all to say that there is no difference between different forms of violence or that we must abandon the right to judge force and violence, whatever force and violence such judgments involve; quite the contrary: it means that we must hone our intellectual resources much more carefully, making many more distinctions, subtleties, and nuances in our understanding than any binarized or dialectically structured model will allow. And refuse the knee-jerk reactions of straightforward or outright condemnation before we understand the structure and history of that modality of violence, its modes of strategic functioning, its vulnerabilities and values.

I do not believe that Derrida abandons the moral and ethical dilemmas raised by very concrete and disturbing explosions of violence in the "real world," and indeed, much of his work is occasioned by or is an indirect response to the question: what is an academic to do? His work sometimes disturbs those concerned by these concrete issues of violence (e.g., LaCapra articulates a common fear that in abandoning the right to provide a pure judgment about violence, violence is simply equated with justice and the right to judge, and deconstruction abandons all violences to their own devices), especially because he does not attempt to provide solutions, definite responses or unequivocal judgments. Is this the abandonment of political judgments, or simply its complexification?

What is it that undecidability changes in our conceptions of law, politics, ethics, and epistemology? Why has this concept exercised such terrifying implications for those concerned with moral and political values? It is not the claim that political or conceptual events are *ambiguous,* and thus difficult to judge, or that they are so complex as to render judgments simplistic or irrelevant (although these may be true as well). Undecidability is probably another name for iteration, for *différance,* for the openness of destination of any articulation, any object or any event, the propulsion of any "thing" (whether avowedly self-present or not) to a future context or scene where its current meaning, value, and status are reread, rewritten, transmuted. Undecidability is precisely the endless iterability of any articulation, the possibility of endless quotation, endless recontextualization where the most crushing defeat is made into the most complex accomplishment, and maybe returned again to defeat. Undecidability dictates that the signification and effect of events or representations can never be self-present insofar as they always remain open to what befalls them, always places them elsewhere: in other words, it dictates that it is only futurity, itself endlessly extended to infinity that gives any event its signification, force, or effect. Which has terrifying consequences for those who would like to correct situations or contexts here and now, and once and for all. What the principle of undecidability implies is that the control over either the reception or the effect of events is out of our hands, beyond a certain agentic control. This is what an openness to futurity entails: that things are never given in their finality, whatever those "things" might be. That whatever is made or found, whether it be nature or artifact, must be remade and refound endlessly to have any value:

> What threatens the rigor of the distinction between the two types of violence is at bottom the paradox of iterability. Iterability requires the origin to repeat itself so as to have the value of origin, that is, to conserve itself. Right away there are police and the police legislate, not content to enforce a law that would have had no force before the police. The iterability inscribes conservation in the essential structure of foundation. This law or this general necessity is not a modern phenomenon, it has an *a priori* worth. . . . Rigorously speaking, iterability precludes the possibility of pure and general founders, initiators, lawmakers. ("Violence and Writing," 1007–9)

Iterability, *différance*, undecidability mean that no founding violence can be contained within the moment of foundation but must endlessly repeat itself to have had any force in the first place; and that any moment of conservation must rely on the repetition of this founding violence to have any force or effect of its own, for it rides on the waves of force that *différance* initiates. In other words, an origin never could infect an end unless it wasn't simply or even an origin, and an end is always implicated in the origin that it ends. Violence and force—indeed, law and right, this means—function only in the yet-to-come, the *à-venir*. Which is the unforeseeable, the yet-to-come that diverges from the what is present. This is what futurity is, and the way in which the implosive effects of the to-come generate both the possibility and the undoing of force. Derrida understands the *avenir* as the domain of the new and of surprise, the very condition of iteration and context:

> Paradoxically, it is because of this overflowing of the performative, because of this always excessive haste of interpretation getting ahead of itself, be-

cause of this structural urgency and precipitation of justice that the latter has no horizon of expectation (regulative or messianic). But for this very reason, it *may* have an *avenir*, a "to-come," which I rigorously distinguish from the future that can always reproduce the present. Justice remains, is yet, to come, *à venir*, it has an, it is *à venir*, the very dimension of events irreducibly to come. It will always have it, this *à venir*, and always has. ("Violence and Writing," 969)

There is, in short, no way to decide in advance, through principle or by dint of position, authority, or knowledge, the standard by which to judge violence. As Cornell argues, "there can be no projected standards by which to judge *in advance* the acceptability of violent acts" (167). This indeed is the very heart of the deconstructive endeavor: that the status and value of violence—given especially the role of violence in the foundation and maintenance of status and value—is only ever open to a future, and a very particular position within futurity, to decide, which itself is endlessly open to its own modes of futurity, its own disseminating flight to either oblivion (insofar as its force is spent) or its own endless production (insofar as its force remains virulent and mobilized).

3

What is the counter to violence? What is the other of violence? If it can no longer be seen that the law is the barrier that divides violence from civilization, partitioning the violent, the excessive as either before or outside the law, and thus subject to its judgment, and positing the law as the space of a regulated violence that refuses to see itself as such or call itself by that name, then is there any cultural or natural space outside its ambit or other than its economy of forces? While it is not clear that there is a space before or free of this economy of the cut, the tearing separations of the structures of nomination, Derrida, following Levinas,[6] seems to suggest an alternative economy, which exceeds the very notion of economy. It too, like violence, inscription, or writing, goes by many names in Derrida's writings. Among the more resonant of these is the Other, which he also describes, through readings of Mauss and Benveniste, in terms of the gift, hospitality, donation, generosity, or ethics (these themes are developed in "Plato's Pharmacy," *Glas*, *The Post-Card*, *Psyché*, and *Given Time*).

The gift is both a part of and in some sense always beyond the economy of exchange. It is an impossible (yet imperative) relation in which what is given cannot be what it is: the gift can only function in not being a gift. For the moment an economy of reciprocity or exchange is set up (one gift for another), the gift ceased to be a gift and becomes an object in a system of barter or exchange. To function as gift, it must be given without return, without obligation, without expectation, given "freely"; and moreover, it must be taken without debt, without the need to return or repay, a pure excess, without accumulation. The gift thus cannot be anything that presents itself as gift, anything that is sent or received with a debt or a structure of return. The gift cannot be received as such, for if it is it is marked by debt: but nor can the gift be refused. For the gift is both superfluity and poison.[7] It must be given, but not in excess (for to give in excess is to reinstate the structure of reciprocity), nor in the hope of return or obligation. The gift in this sense is outside the law, beyond calculation. But not outside of them altogether. For the gift must not only be given and received while its objectness is annulled, it must also be given *responsibly,* according to a logic of temporization, of timeliness.[8]

The gift, as Derrida says, gives time. It does not give itself, an object, the given, to be possessed or consumed: it gives temporality, delay, a calculation of timeliness. This is the very time needed for the time of judgment: the gift gives a possible future, a temporality in excess of the present and never contained within its horizon, the temporality of endless iteration:

> The gift is not a gift, the gift only gives to the extent it *gives time.* The difference between a gift and every other operation of pure and simple exchange is that the gift gives time. *Where there is gift, there is time.* What it gives, the gift, is time, but this gift of time is also a domain of time. The thing must not be restituted *immediately and right away.* There must be time, it must last, there must be waiting—without forgetting. It demands time, the thing, but it demands a delimited time, neither an instant nor an infinite time, but time determined by a term, in other words, a rhythm, a rhythm that does not befall a homogeneous time but that structures it originarily. (*Given Time,* 41)

The gift gives time, not because it is placed in a structure of preexisting temporization, the rhythms and cadences of economic exchange; rather, it is the object, *the given* that carries with it a force, an impetus of donation, pure expenditure:

> the requirement of circulatory différance is *inscribed in the thing itself* that is given or exchanged. Before it is a contract, an intentional gesture of individual or collective subjects, the movement of gift/countergift is a *force* (a "virtue of the thing given," says Mauss), a property immanent of the thing or in any way apprehended as such by the donors and donees. Moved by a mysterious force, the thing itself demands gift *and* restitution, it requires therefore "time," "term," "delay," "interval" of temporisation, the becoming-temporalization of temporalization, the animation of a neutral and homogeneous time by the desire of the gift and the restitution. Différance which (is) nothing, is (in) the thing itself. It is (given) in the thing itself. It is (given) in the thing itself. It (is) the thing itself. It, différance, the thing (itself). It, without, anything other. Itself, nothing. (*Given Time,* 40)

The thing, like the other, is pure exteriority, with its own order, priority, time, and rhythm. Our encounters with it are in part their force or impetus upon us, and in part the force of our inscriptions of them. The problem is that it is undecidable which is which, where one crosses the other and feeds off from it. The thing, whether it is the gift of language, the gift of law, or an object, is given as such: the gift to be received must be accepted in its singularity and specificity before it is codified, submitted to economic value and integrated in the circuits of exchange. It gives itself up to be in some sense returned as itself. Is it then that justice, a justice beyond the legalism and formalism of the law, moves beyond the field of violence to the structure, the noneconomy, the pure excess of the gift? Does the idea or ideal of justice, a justice not given in full presence from God or derived from the Law, provide an other "logic," "order," or "system" outside that of calculation, economy, derivation? Is this another way of asking: is there, beyond violence, a way to love, to give without fear of expending and to take without fear of vulnerability? The deconstruction of all presumption of a determinant certitude of a present justice itself operates on the basis of an "infinite justice," infinite because it is irreducible, irreducible because it is owed to the other, before any contract, because it has come, the other's coming as the singularity that is always other. This "idea of justice" seems to me to be irreducible in its affirmative character, in its domain of gift without exchange, without circulation, without recognition or gratitude, without economic circularity, without calculation and without rules, without reason and without rationality. And so we can recognize in it, indeed accuse, identify a madness. "And deconstruction is mad about this kind of justice. Mad about this desire for justice. This kind of justice that isn't law, is the very movement of deconstruction at work in law and the history of law, in political history and history itself, before it even presents itself as the discourse that the academy or modern culture labels 'deconstructionism'" ("Force of Law," 965).

The gift is not outside the economy and expenditure that is regulated law, but rather it operates entwined with and sometimes indistinguishable from it. In this sense, law can only be given and received as gift. But beyond law, where there is "ideal justice," the structure of the gift can function in a different way, not other than or in a different sphere from violence. Rather, violence, force, disseminates itself into the futurity of the gift, of given time, as its mode of excessive production. It is time itself, only the future, the time to come, *avenir*, that the gift gives, that makes judgment possible (if always provisional), and that converts force into production. The what-is-to-come disseminates with its own force what the gift is. This is a double gift, a double affirmation.

NOTES

1. This is the position adopted by Benhabib, Fraser, and Nicholson, among many feminist theorists, or the followers of the Frankfurt school, or post-Althusserian marxists. See Fraser for a clear example.

2. McCarthy in effect accuses Derrida because Derrida's questions are not Mc-Carthy's, or the critical tradition he represents. Yet this is already the refusal to engage with Derridean questions, a mode of refusal of the possibility of a Derridean politics: "Although he explicitly eschews any idea of a radical break, the politics of friendship gestures toward a transformation so radical that we can say nothing (positive) about what lies beyond it. I have found nothing in Derrida's writings to persuade me that his quasi-apocalyptic, near-prophetic mode of discourse about politics should displace the more prosaic modes available or constructible in our tradition" (162).

3. On this question, see Bennington and Derrida.

4. As Derrida makes clear, "For me, it is always a question of differential force, of difference as difference of force, of forces as *différance* (*différance* is a force *différée-différante*), of the relation between force and form, force and signification, performative force, illocutionary or perlocutionary force, of persuasive or rhetorical force, of affirmation by signature, but also and especially of all the paradoxical situations in which the greatest force and the greatest weakness strangely enough exchange places. And that is the whole history" ("Force of Law," 929).

5. Derrida locates violence, law, transgression as the field of deconstructive play: "Deconstruction is justice. It is perhaps because law (which I will consistently try to distinguish from justice) is constructible, in a sense that goes beyond the opposition between convention and nature, it is perhaps insofar as it goes beyond this opposition that it is constructible and so deconstructible" ("Force of Law," 929). Derrida, though, is even stronger in his claim: law, force, and violence are the "proper place" of deconstruction, if this phrase has any meaning: "it was normal, foreseeable, desirable that studies of deconstructive style should culminate in the problematic of law (*droit*), of law and justice. (I have elsewhere tried to show that the essence of law is not prohibitive but affirmative.) It is even the most proper place for them, if such a thing exists" (929).

6. As already outlined in "Violence and Metaphysics," Derrida wants to suggest that the encounter with the other is somehow outside an economy of the logos—or at the least that Levinas's understanding of the ethical relation sets up a "logic" or "structure" other than the Greek conception of the relation between self and other: "What, then, is the encounter with the absolutely-other? Neither representation nor limitation, nor conceptual relation to the same. The ego and the other do not permit themselves to be dominated or made into totalities by the concept of relationship . . . there is no was to conceptualize the encounter; it is made possible by the other, the unforeseeable and 'resistant to all categories.' Concepts suppose an anticipation, a horizon within which alterity is amortized as soon as it is annulled precisely because it has let itself be foreseen. The infinitely-other cannot be bound by a concept, cannot be thought on the basis of a horizon; for a horizon is always a horizon of the same" ("Violence and Metaphysics," 95).

7. Cf. Derrida's footnote in "Plato's Pharmacy": "We are asked why we do not examine the etymology of *gift*, translation of the Latin *dosis*, itself a transcription of the Greek *dosis*, dose, dose of poison" (131).

8. Derrida writes in *Given Time:*

One must—*il faut*—opt *for* the gift, for generosity, for noble expenditure, for a practice and a morality of the gift ("*il faut donner*," one must give). One cannot be content to speak of the gift and to describe the gift without giving and without saying *one must* give, without giving by saying one must give . . . to do more than call upon one to give in the proper sense of the word, but to give beyond the call, beyond the mere word.
But—because with the gift there is always a "but"—the contrary is also nec-

essary: It is necessary [*il faut*] to limit the excess of the gift and also generosity, to limit them by economy, profitability, work, exchange. And first of all by reason or by the principle of reason: it is *also* necessary to render any account, it is also necessary to give consciously and conscientiously. It is necessary to *answer for* [*répondre*] the gift, the given, and the call to giving. It is necessary to answer to it and answer for it. One must be *responsible* for what one gives and what one receives. (63)

REFERENCES

Benhabib, Seyla. "Feminism and Postmodernism." In *Feminist Contentions: A Philosophical Exchange,* edited by Seyla Benhabib, Judith Butler, Drucilla Cornell, and Nancy Fraser, 17–34. New York: Routledge, 1995.

Benjamin, Walter. "The Critique of Violence." In *Reflections: Essays, Aphorisms, Autobiographical Writings,* edited by Peter Dements and translated by Edmund Jephcott, 277–300. New York: Harcourt Brace Jovanovich, 1978.

Bennington, Geoffrey, and Jacques Derrida. *Jacques Derrida.* Translated by Geoffrey Bennington. Chicago: University of Chicago Press, 1993.

Cornell, Drucilla. *The Philosophy of the Limit.* New York: Routledge, 1992.

Derrida, Jacques. "Différance." In *Margins of Philosophy.* Chicago: University of Chicago Press, 1982.

———. "Force of Law: The 'Mystical Foundations of Authority.'" *Cardozo Law Review* 11, nos. 5–6 (1990): 919–1046.

———. *Given Time: 1. Counterfeit Money.* Chicago: University of Chicago Press, 1992.

———. *Glas.* Translated by John Leevey. Lincoln: University of Nebraska Press, 1986.

———. "Plato's Pharmacy." In *Disseminations,* translated by Barbara Johnson, 63–171. Chicago: University of Chicago Press.

———. *The Post-Card from Socrates to Freud and Beyond.* Translated by Alan Bass. Chicago: University of Chicago Press, 1987.

———. *Of Grammatology.* Translated by Gayatri Chakravorty Spivak. Baltimore, Md.: Johns Hopkins University Press, 1976.

———. "Violence and Metaphysics." In *Writing and Difference,* 79–154. London: Routledge and Kegan-Paul, 1978.

———. "The Violence of the Letter: From Lévi-Strauss to Rousseau in *Of Grammatology.*" Baltimore: Johns Hopkins University Press, 1974.

Fraser, Nancy. "The French Derrideans: Politicizing Deconstruction or Deconstructing Politics." *New German Critique* 33 (1984): 127–54.

LaCapra, Dominick. "Violence, Justice and the Force of Law." *Cardozo Law Review* 11, nos. 5–6 (1990): 701–14.

McCarthy, Thomas. "The Politics of the Ineffable: Derrida's Deconstructionism." *Philosophical Forum* 21, nos. 1–2 (fall–winter 1989–1990): 146–67.

Nicholson, Linda J., ed. *Feminism/Postmodernism.* New York: Routledge, 1990.

Part 2. Coloniality and the Consumption of the Other

Chapter 8

Consuming Cannibalism

The Body in Australia's Pacific Archive

MIKE HAYES

The survivors of the Andes plane crash eating dead passengers; the Noble Prize–winning study of Kurukuru and ritualized cannibalism in Papua New Guinea; Captain Cook's description of Maori cannibal feasts; missionaries trapped in the large cooking pots of African cannibals—from a variety of sources, popular images of cannibalism are in narratives of horror, myth, fascination, investigation, and adventure. The interest in cannibalism has marked numerous academic and literary studies for centuries. My intention in this chapter is not to prove or disprove cannibalism; undoubtedly humans have eaten portions of other humans for a variety of reasons. However, I wish to examine one specific aspect of this topic—how cannibalism operates within Western systems of knowledge to justify a number of Western philosophical, economic, and cultural beliefs, and, importantly, to justify colonialism itself. Primarily, I want to describe how anthropological texts from the eighteenth to the early twentieth centuries used cannibalism to validate the study of what were considered "primitive" cultures. What these literary connections demonstrate is the fundamental and interdependent relationship between the study of anthropology and the entertainment of horror and adventure stories, as there are many similarities between these two genres.

I draw on a significant body of contemporary critical analysis on cannibalism.[1] However, I address specifically Australian and Aotearoa/New Zealand texts on cannibalism in the Pacific and contextualize the study with surrounding colonial politics. The representation of a society as "primitive" has political ramifications in the colonial intervention, jurisprudence, and study of the colonized society. From these statements and studies can be traced a genealogy of myths about cannibalism still present today. What is paradoxical about the circulation of such myths is the hypocritical participation in cannibalism by the "investigators" or authorities on a level of representational consumption. For it is this definition of cannibalism: a symbolic exchange registered through consumption, one that is not permitted to be read into the practices of non-Western cultures by the Western authorities. While decrying cannibalism as barbaric and representative of "primitive" cultures, the Western authority consumes the body of the cannibal and trades the flesh as trophies of the success of Western religion, science, or entertainment.

An anonymous short verse from the June 23, 1894, edition of the Australian magazine the *Bulletin* entitled "The Cannibal's Convert" describes the complexities of such colonial representations of cannibalism and underscores the West's participation in the acts of cannibalism it vehemently opposes. In its response to cannibalism, this verse displays the colonial racism that represented male Pacific Islanders to a popular white Australian audience in the 1890s:

> The poor, untutored savage,
>   Who no collection pays,
> Knows human nature's dual,
>   Conversion cuts both ways.
>
> When Reverend Howler sought to save
>   A South Sea Island Sinner,
> Whose *soul* polite attention gave
>   And *body* yearned for dinner.
>
> He was not—nigger wary!—
>   Converted in belief,
> But the reckless missionary
>   Was converted into beef. (18)

This piece demonstrates how cannibalism fits into discourses of colonialism within the specific context of the Pacific Islands. Its doggerel verse exemplifies the widespread popularity and the supposed simplicity of cannibal narratives. What I find particularly interesting about this poem, and much colonial literature about cannibalism, is the concept enunciated here of *cutting both ways*. The poem describes a conflict of consumption within a Christian economy. The Reverend is consumed by the Islander while attempting to convert him; the missionary falls prey to "savage" practices of consumption. However, the Pacific Islander's actions are resisting consumption by Christianity—for the Pacific Islander is a potential commodity for consumption by the missionary; his conversion is marketed to church groups and sold through church collections in colonizing countries such as Australia. In this sense, indigenous conversion and colonial consumption are equivalent: they cut both ways, as if the missionary were the cannibal. But operating to distinguish the two systems is not the frequently articulated European myth that cannibalism is an original sin such as incest, used as a fundamental structure of most critical studies of representations of cannibalism, but instead the distinction between soul and body. The bodily urges or the hunger of the cannibal, according to the poet, oppose the polite soul and drive the Islander to eat the missionary. The attribution of bodily functions to the Islander is a typical strategy in colonial narratives: it positions the mind, and hence reason and rationalism, in the colonizer. Thus, while this poem on one level deconstructs the privileging of Western forms of consumption by equating them with cannibal consumption, indigenous resistance is managed by corporealizing, by making it irrational.

The dissemination of this colonialist stereotype will be investigated here through the interchanging concepts of cannibalism and consumption, for the two systems exemplified in this poem are hierarchized so that Western forms of commerce are privileged and valorized through representing indigenous consumption as cannibalistic. In this relationship of consumption and corporeality, I want to map the operation of cannibalism in Australian colonial texts to examine the investment of various Australian institutions in representing Pacific Islanders and the epistemic conditions circulating in Australian culture that produce these stereotypes as objects of knowledge.

The Pacific Islanders are consumed by academic narratives on a representational level because they are conscripted into an economy in which their popular representation as the cannibal is used as, to take a term from Rey Chow, "raw material" (109)[2] to profit and reproduce academic intervention. They invigorate and add energy to the colonial formation. However, first I want to consider an indigenous response to cannibalism. There are a few archival traces of indigenous accounts of cannibalism to rupture the simplistic and horrific picture by the West or outline the colonial and historical context that was unseen by the Western observers. The saturation of Western texts with representations of cannibalism, compared with their virtual absence in Pacific Islander texts, demonstrates the prestige the archive is given in each society, but more, it spells out the relative interest— and perhaps importance—each culture has made of this practice. More often, it is the legacy of stereotypes such as cannibalism that inscribes the Pacific Islander's history as "savage" or "barbarous." The Papua New Guinean Bernard Narokobi, in *Life and Leadership in Melanesia,* in arguing for the importance of the "Melanesian way" in national identity, states, "Since the impact [of colonialism], many people hold the view that the only history worth recording and remembering is the history of Western and Eastern peoples. They maintain that our own past history is so inferior, negative, and uncivilized that it is best forgotten" (22). The move to devalue the history of Pacific Islanders is particularly insidious because the very production of that "inferior" history is managed and articulated by colonial discourse.

I want to briefly look at accounts by Maretu (*Cannibals and Converts*), a London Missionary Society (LMS) native missionary, whose discussion of cannibalism problematizes the observational objectivity of the colonial interlocutor.[3] Maretu recorded his notes on cannibalism for his missionary teacher, Rev. Dr. William Wyatt Gill, a graduate of London University, who gained his doctorate through his ethnographic work. This work was circulated in Australian academia through publications such as the *Journal of Polynesian Society*.[4] The origin of cannibalism is situated by Maretu in a Rarotongan history about two feuding cousins whose conflict and pursuit led them to Rarotonga. Although Maretu, in *Savage*, gives numerous accounts of cannibalism, the "deed" from which "generation after generation seeks revenge" through cannibalism is when one group became "bereft of reason and went like animals to an opposing tribe" (*Cannibals and Converts*, 52).[5] They were kept like slaves for some time until they were killed and eaten. This example appears to have particular resonance for a society facing colonialism where some groups, against the wishes of others, put their allegiance behind the colonial or Christian mission, and, if this metaphor is extended, were "consumed" by the colonial power. Indeed, the conditions that are necessary for cannibalism, according to Maretu, correlate directly to colonial intervention. Cannibalism is the result of an act of revenge, mainly through warfare, and is committed by the warriors. The chiefs do not consume human flesh, and no one is consumed in times of peace, according to Maretu (33).

Maretu detailed an account of cannibalism when Captain Goodenough visited Rarotonga in 1814 on a private Sydney-financed venture for sandalwood. Four Europeans were killed because they had desecrated a sacred *Marae*[6] and had stolen coconuts. Because their bodies were the victim of war, according to Maretu, they were eaten, an action the Rarotongans were forced to carry out. In this example, the intervention of the colonial sandalwood market demands initiated the interventions—indeed, it produced the final result of their consumption. In an act of cutting both ways, the European bodies are victims to their own economy since their intervention and desecration, not the Rarotongan's hunger, addiction, or desire for human flesh (three common reasons for cannibalism in colonial representations), forced this action. Further, in Maretu's account, what exactly was eaten, how much, and the level of symbolism associated with the consumption are not stated. William Wyatt Gill, who records Maretu's story, ignores the possibility of cannibalism as figurative or as exaggerated. Gill discusses the killing and eating of children in another translation of Maretu's notes, republished by Gill in a Christian storybook for children; the purpose of these "horror" stories is blatant.[7] Gill was both audience and translator of Maretu's confessions.

The role of the interlocutor Gill, who may have suggested that Maretu describe these acts and who embellished many of these stories for his other work, cannot be ignored. The suggestion to write about cannibalism is similar to Captain Cook's sensationalist attempt, recounted by Obeyesekere, to prove the Maoris were cannibals by giving them a piece of broiled human flesh and recording for the "general reader" their obvious "relish" at eating this ("British Cannibals," 653).[8] On Cook's first voyage to Aote-aroa/New Zealand, Joseph Banks writes of the crew's insistence on discussing, whenever possible, occurrences of cannibalism:

> we have never faild [*sic*] wherever we went ashore and often when we conversed with [Maori] canoes to ask the question; we have without one exception been answered in the affirmative. . . . They however as [*sic*] universally agree that they eat none but the bodies of their enemies who are killd [*sic*] in war. (Salmond, 228)[9]

These acts can be described as eighteenth-century anthropological "verbals" attempting to implicate the indigenous subject in the activity, verbals that underlie the basis of cannibalism: it is the product of colonial intervention, a clash of systems and struggle for power in which the forces of European rationalism attempt to construct an emotional and mindless non-Western other as an observable and transmissible commodity, a process that disguises the violence of imperial consumption of non-Western culture. And it is a clash in which the Pacific Islanders, perhaps to appear powerful and threatening, pass themselves as cannibals to play with and scare the Europeans with their bloodthirsty dramatics.

CANNIBALISM AND EROTICISM AS WHITE MYTHOLOGY

To approach the problem of consumption in these stereotypes, Jacques Derrida's essay "White Mythologies" is pertinent. In this essay, Derrida problematizes the notion of metaphor, suggesting philosophy is both a theory of metaphor and metaphor for theory (254). A principal focus of Derrida's deconstruction is the supposed link metaphor enables between words and ideas, as if metaphor were a process of making present a transcendent idea. The "ideal of every language, and in particular of metaphor, [is] . . . to bring to knowledge the thing itself, the turn of speech will be better if it brings us closer to the thing's essential or proper truth" (247). The theory of metaphor thus is located in a philosophy of metaphysics. Derrida concentrates on deconstructing the status of mastery or dominance of particular metaphors central to Western mythology: "What other is to be found if not the metaphor of *domination,* heightened by its power of dissimulation which permits it to escape mastery: God or the Sun?" (266). Metaphor presumes an idea beyond language, an idealism that is not subject to the "forced" or "abusive" inscription of language (255). There are points in Derrida's deconstruction of metaphor that can be ably applied to an investigation of stereotypes in this context, for stereotypes similarly attempt to make "present" an essential truth. A deconstruction of metaphor is not a process of reducing everything to words, as if this will eradicate the metaphysical, but a reading of the stratification of metaphors and metaphysics and a criticism of the reasons why some metaphors gain dominance.[10] The metaphor of the "Tahitian Venus" as a dominant metaphor of Pacific Island women (strictly Polynesian women), for example, springs from an idealism that the transcendent, proper truth of the Pacific for the Western observer is the aesthetics of the sexualized, "heavenly," body. Thus, the privileging of this metaphor, its domination, reinforces the politics of colonial "penetration." By bringing Tahitian culture to order through its feminization by the active, intrusive white mythology, the metaphor asserts its mastery in the patriarchal rape, the "penetration," which is first enacted figuratively to make possible the literal.

The descriptions of the Pacific Islander women's beauty or the Pacific Islander men's barbarity are exemplary of the white mythology of Derrida's essay. Derrida quite specifically critiques in metaphor a politics of language that situates reason and meaning in the "illuminated" West and the loss of meaning through metaphor, or figurative language, in the "East" (268–69).[11] As Derrida points out, metaphysics, or what he calls the white mythology, "reassembles and reflects the culture of the West: the white man takes his own mythology, Indo-European mythology, his own *logos*, that is, the *myths* of his idiom, for the universal form of that he must still wish to call Reason" (213). Thus, the figurative language of the East is a reassemblage of the West's own metaphysical mythology, a metaphorical visitation by the language of the West in a "specular circle, a return to itself without loss of meaning, without irreversible expenditure" (268), a maneuver consolidating Reason as the property of the West.

The task here on one level is to identify the politics of the projection and locate in it the functions of colonial discourse. That is, what relationships of power do cannibalizing Pacific Islanders produce? A second task is to investigate the circulation of consumption as an Australian commercial venture in these representations. How does the evaluation of these representations, and their circulation in Australia, benefit colonialism? Of particular interest is the incorporation of an economy in this system. In using the term "*usure,*" defined as the effacing of the marks of value from a coin, to describe metaphor, Derrida suggests there is in the theory of metaphor a contradiction between an "acquisition of too much interest," or "linguistic surplus," and a degradation or "deterioration through usage" (209 n. 2, 211). Defacing a coin can both deface the specific value of the coin and overinvest value by suggesting its value is now universal. Metaphor is a distancing, a traveling away, of words or language from the idea, and thus a degradation of the original, transcendent meaning. Simultaneously, metaphor is an addition, an investment or expansion on the meaning, in which figures of speech accumulate and supplement the meaning of the "original" idea. This contradiction—or trace, which the metaphor deconstructs—can be clearly seen in the stereotype of the cannibal. As I will elaborate, the very surplus of representations of cannibalism is underscored by the devalued usage: any signifier of death is immediately conscripted to become a representation of cannibalism. Thus skulls, coins, and gossip (as I will soon discuss) become signifiers of the act of consuming a human body.

The representation of cannibalism and eroticism within Western consumption needs to be articulated in context of a theory of value, a value that is also an overinvestment. The signifier "cannibalism" is put to use in economies of commerce, representation, and sexuality; in the value of the sign as metaphor, cannibalism is used to enforce the "savagery" of non-Western societies. Thus in a story by James Dixon entitled "A Cannibal Episode,"[12] in which cannibalism does not literally occur, the signifier overinvests in the narrative the various social, political, and moral values in excess of the narrative itself. The white mythology is usurious; it adds excessive "interest" (in the registers of mercantilism and curiosity) to an object. As I detail below, the objects related to cannibalism are classified according to a commercial value in collecting and souveniring, providing a market in which cannibalism can circulate through the imperial culture. The stereotypes are given value through their appropriation and consumption by Western audiences—narratives and pictures gain value not only through book sales and author royalties, but also through the evaluation of Western Reason as proper and truthful.

THE "FASCINATION" WITH
CANNIBALISM IN COLONIAL TEXTS

In this section, I pursue a crucial rupture in colonial claims to reason raised in an article by Joseph Pugliese entitled "Embodied Economies of Desire in Hegel's Empire of Reason." In outlining Hegel's ethnocentrism in *The Philosophy of History,* Pugliese writes that one particular economy following "colonial penetration" is "a form of unconscious cannibalism, in which an epistemic violence is visited upon the body of the other in the very processes of representation and cultural consumption" (176). Pugliese, in his reading, which stages a return of the non-Western body and unconscious to Hegel's rational West, suggests that observation and representation, particularly of the non-Western body, prepares for "colonial histories of violence without reserve" (182). As an object that circulates within various discourses of science and horror, that signifies the monstrous, the savage, and the uncivilized to a Western audience, cannibalism is a point where the power of colonial representation itself consumes the body of the non-Western other.

Through various accounts of cannibalism, I want to trace some regularities, the stories that move from haphazard guesswork to scientific fact through repetition, the objects that recur in representations of cannibalism, and the tropes of cannibal narratives. My investigation of cannibalism is limited to Australian and Aotearoa/New Zealand descriptions of these events, how they were circulated, and the utility they took in various institutions. There are obvious precursors to these representations, but the focus of this study are the forces and transformations in Europe and Australia during the colonization of the Pacific. The word "cannibalism" derives from Columbus's naming of Caribbean indigenes as "Caribs," which is translated into "cannibal"; the concept of anthropophagy, on the other hand, has a longer European history, one that dates to the ancient Greeks (Hulme, 15–17). Although Western representations of cannibalism are documented before this time, most notably early European representations of Native Americans, I am concerned with how the representations of Pacific Islanders were organized—indeed, how they became an entirely different object, a different practice, with the emergence of Australian colonialism in the Pacific. There are similarities between European representations of indigenous Caribbean cannibalism and later African and Pacific Islander cannibalism; however, the regional colonial political agenda influences the strategy of naming a group of people "cannibals." That is, the study, representation, and dissemination of Pacific Islanders as cannibals operates within specific institutions and discourses organizing relationships of power between the colonizing nations (such as Australia) and the terrain of the colonized.

The majority of studies of cannibalism foreground an alleged "fascination" by the West with the subject of cannibalism, a fascination still prevalent in contemporary studies. Indeed, this chapter fits into the genealogy of studies that reproduce Pacific cultures as the subjects of Western observation and study, and profits from the sensationalism of their racist representations. In an effort to both situate and problematize these effects, I want to elaborate on how such studies maintain this authority. In one of Australia's earliest scientific papers devoted to cannibalism, Thomas Steel delivered a lecture titled "Cannibals and Cannibalism" to the Field Naturalist Club of Victoria in 1893. His paper begins by elaborating on the interest in cannibalism:

> To most people there is a certain fascination of feeling about [cannibals and cannibalism]. However repugnant it may be to our minds, we cannot help feeling interested in a custom which we know to be so widespread amongst savage people, and which is so greatly at variance with the amenities which civilisation has developed in our own social state. Indeed, it is perhaps to this strong contrast between our own manners and customs and those of the more primitive races of mankind that the anthropological studies owe their chief attractiveness. (4)

Fascination, with its etymology in witchcraft and spells, speaks of an emotive and irrational interest in something outside society, both foreign and occult, and describes a peculiarly imperial process of power.[13] At this level, the bewitching possibility spells something of cannibalism's danger within Western systems; as if it were contagious or were to reveal something of the West's own economy of consumption, the very knowledge of cannibalism can mesmerize and overcome the Western viewer. Steel's paper stages a movement past emotive fascination by arguing that the impulsive or entrancing interest is modified into the "sensibility" of a research topic, the anthropological study. Fascination occurs here within the Enlightenment desire to know, or as Steel considers, its "attractiveness" arises from possible comparative studies between the contemporary civilized and the prior "primitive." The fascination in turn produces a discourse of rationalism in the observing West. Precisely the "fascination" of investigation that is valorized as a success of Cook's "explorations" quite easily became, as Salmond notes, an "obsession" (*Two Worlds*, 244) with cannibalism by the officers and crew of the *Endeavour*.[14] Indeed, Steel proposes to move past the occult fascination, because his study stages a civilized present and non-Western antiquity in which cannibalism signifies an anterior culture or desire observed from the "modern" position of the imperial scientist. Under this study, cannibalism becomes mythical: to employ the frequently used statements, a relic of the Stone Age (Cowan, 569), of "considerable antiquity" (Steel, 5), or a "thing of the past" (Watt, 227)—to restate Derrida, a white mythology making Europe and Australia the seat of reason.

In Peter Hulme's *Colonial Encounters*, he notes the importance of "fascination," leading him to ask, "why are there no sociological investigations of the fascination [with cannibalism]?" (81). Yet the question Hulme concludes with—were the Caribs really cannibals?—relocates the signifier "cannibalism" onto the body of the other. Underlying Hulme's reading is the racialization of cannibalism; for, unquestioned in his account, is its location in non-Western culture. However, cannibalism is prevalent in Western culture, as some recent studies have demonstrated: cannibalism has been widely reported in European cultures and was a regular occurrence in maritime disasters or failed expeditions.[15] Yet these occurrences do not initiate a similar racial and colonial politics found in the anthropological texts.

Fascination, moreover, suggests a Freudian examination, one in which cannibalism is discussed in terms of psychoanalysis. Yet to propose an unconscious desire and fear related to sex and death problematically suggests a universal consciousness for cannibalism and completely negates the force of colonialism, which was to project "cannibal horrors" onto non-Westerners. This is not to negate indigenous narratives of cannibalism, which may be comparable to Western "horror" stories, but they are quite a distinct practice, which cannot be conflated with Western narratives.[16] The use of Freudian theory to "read" cannibalism, such as Obeyesekere's "latent wish," Paul Lyon's consideration of jokes,[17] or Caleb Crain's orality,[18] frequently involves psychoanalytic concepts instead of descriptions of the colonial violence in which representations of cannibalism are occurring.

Questions of "but did *they* really do it?" quite neatly ignore the speaker's enrollment of moral civility and scientific rationalism to determine what cannibalism means. As if cannibalism were a coherent and universal practice that can be uncovered through investigation, questions of "doing it" ignore, precisely, what "it" is, and what "it" means in specific cultural contexts. These questions repeat the structure Steel proposes: that of the civilized mind and the primitive body, of investigative Westerner and occult Pacific Islander. Hence, I am neither concerned with verifying or negating the occurrence of the eating of human flesh in Pacific Island cultures nor of asserting what cannibalism could mean to Pacific Islanders; rather, I am concerned with how cannibalism circulates in imperial and colonial discourses and the strictly Western meaning it takes from these discourses.

CANNIBALISM IN AUSTRALIAN COLONIAL TEXTS

Pacific travel books and missionary tracts of the late nineteenth century read by an Australian audience commonly began with either a picture or a discussion of cannibalism that, I propose, set out at once cultural distinctions based on European concepts of "race." These distinctions were signposted by cannibalism, which provides the racial hierarchies for the reader to understand what assumptions to bring to the text. Edward Reeves, the Aotearoa/New Zealander author of *Brown Men and Women,* an account of a tour around islands of the South Pacific in 1895, opens with a discussion of cannibalism. On the very first page, the body is mentioned as a commercial object "traded away . . . to the cannibal for his gruesome feast" (1–2), and the reader is asked to remember the compatriots who have disappeared down islanders' throats (1); the topic is then promptly dropped and does not recur in the narrative. Accompanying these opening sentences is a photograph of "A Cannibal Feast in Fiji, 1869." The photograph shows a group of Pacific Islanders carrying a trussed-up body. Reeves uses photography's realist formal conventions to frame the fantastic subject within a rational discourse. One purpose of his text, Reeves states, is to fulfill the "absence of pictorial illustration" in books on the Pacific, particularly the "misleading character of engravings and woodcuts" (10). Photographs, the "most perfect form of illustration" (10), would rectify this fault. However, as Barthes suggests in *Camera Lucida,* the coherency of photography is self-referential; Barthes writes on his photographed representation, "All I look *like* is other photographs of myself" (102). Reeves's suggestion that photography is the "perfect form" suggests an equivalence between the photograph and the "real." Yet the photograph of the "cannibal feast" suggests connections with other photographs more than it does with the so-called real.

Reeves's photograph is by Thomas Andrew, an Aotearoa/New Zealand photographer who worked mainly in the Pacific Islands, and comes from a series on a "cannibal feast."[19] Andrew worked in Samoa from 1890 until the 1930s, and the majority of photographs produced from his company were studio portraits for Samoans and thus differed somewhat from souvenir photographs for tourists. However, his cannibalism series is a departure, for it appears to be marketed strictly to Australian and Aotearoa/New Zealand tourists. It is rather peculiar that the opening photograph of Reeves's text is a staged tableau and thus not representative of what he considers photography's values: representing "real current life and action . . . a faithful picture of these lovely islands and their inhabitants" (11). For a start, cannibalism's antiquity is explained by the inaccurate date of the photograph: it was taken in the 1890s, not 1869, a farcical means to antiquate cannibalism. The scene is most obviously acted out for the photographer, and hence any notion of "real current life" is spurious. The veracity of photography elides the elements that structure the view—the politics of the observer, the conventions of the medium—with an apparent "naturalism" of reality. Reeves himself hints at the possibility of manufacturing the "faithful" picture when he later writes of the actions of two colonial illustrated newspaper photographers who would " 'get up' picturesque groupings of natives and fly around . . . in a despairing effort to place effective niggers up trees [and] get in a nice bit of tree with a peep of sky in it" (198). Placing the Islanders in the tree readily gives the reader an association with the then fashionable social Darwinian belief that non-Western cultures were closer to apes and chimpanzees, and hence were not as "civilized." The supposed "reality" of the photograph surreptitiously slides into conventions of realism without announcing its departure. The very fact that cannibalism is used to introduce a travelogue in which cannibalism never occurs outlines the connection between fantasy, the photograph, and cannibalism. The reader need not believe the event is "real current life," only that it conforms to knowledges and beliefs enabling it to be taken as such.

Another crucial signifier of a culture's cannibalism, for the European, is the skull. The skull productively associates human sacrifice, cannibalism, paganism, and measurements of indigenous "nature" and intelligence through sciences such as phrenology. When Joseph Banks wants proof that the human bone he buys from a group of Maoris is from a human body (and thus proves cannibalism), he asks for them to "bring [the skulls] and we shall then be convinced that these are men" (Salmond, 245). In no way does a skull imply cannibalism, but it is remarkable the haste with which colonial observers draw this conclusion. There is a crossover here between head-hunting and cannibalism; often conflated, these quite disparate practices are similarly read by ethnographers and anthropologists in terms of a "savage" consumption. One of the earliest European pictures that associated these signifiers is John Webber's *Human Sacrifice, in a Morai, in Otaheiti* (1784), drawn for Captain James Cook's third voyage. The picture, which

Bernard Smith writes was to become "one of the best known illustrations of the century" (317), carries out what Cook suggests as the function of the illustrations of the voyage: to be "interesting to the generality of readers, as well as instructive to the sailor and the scholar. Mr. Webber was pitched upon . . . to bring home such drawings of the most memorable scenes of our transactions" (109). While the picture is of human sacrifice, the drums, skulls, oven, and trussed-up body form the basis of what were to become the regular features of cannibal feast pictures, the genre that Thomas Andrew's work is in. The proximity made between "sacrifice" and cannibalism by Western observers implies that Pacific Island law is based on "primitive" actions, whereas Western law abides by personal rights. Britain's and Australia's practice of capital punishment does not, then, possess the barbarity of indigenous law or the inappropriate forms of indigenous consumption.

The circulation of skulls can be conceived in terms of an economy because they deliver up the representation to be consumed by the Western viewer. Skulls frequently became objects of value for numerous collectors who were not necessarily anthropologists or ethnographers. The Australian filmmaker Frank Hurley was to capitalize on the interest in cannibalism in his films, and the profit was not simply revenue from the films. A diary entry, made while Hurley was traveling in New Guinea filming for his quasi-documentary *Pearls and Savages* (1921–1923), details an economy in cannibalism and skulls:

> Skulls, human bits and pieces, filled our bags while knives, axes, and fabrics, were substituted—in the cause of science! From a dim alcove I gave a yell of delight . . . treasure beyond bonanzas! What luck! Human heads stuffed, painted, and decorated. . . . I have never seen objects more ghastly and horrible, but we had raided a bank and carried off the bullion we could scarcely have been more pleased. (Bickel, 79)[20]

The transition from object to commodity is clearly enunciated in this passage. The skulls, at once signifiers of the ancient and uncivilized—they are after all, Hurley comments, from a "lost tribe [that] could have passed for bronzed Babylonian Jews" (Bickel, 80)—play a role truncated between objects of fascination and science, in which they realize a treasure equivalent to gold.[21] Hurley's popular films subscribed to an Australian "cannibal fascination," and he was to make five films on New Guinea and the Pacific: *The Lost Tribe* (n.d.), *Pearls and Savages, The Jungle Woman* (1926), *Headhunters of Unknown Papua* (1923), and the pearling film *Hound of the Deep* (1926).[22] The body parts of the dead, consumed by Hurley, thus gave the wealth for his films, like they gave Reeves the audience for his travel narratives or J. Chalmers the donations of his generous church parishioners. The Islander body, the marked and categorized body, enters an exchange system on which colonialism was to drive the market to support its imperialist ideals.

THE EMERGENCE OF ANTHROPOLOGY AND REPRESENTATIONS OF CANNIBALISM

With the introduction of ethnography and anthropology into the Pacific, new rules emerged for the observation and recording of cannibalism. Yet much of the simplistic and "horrific" inferences and speculations found in the missionary texts and travel narratives were to remain. For a start, the veracity of cannibalism relies on the colonial belief that the Islanders always lie. Rev. W. Watt, a missionary from the Presbyterian Church of New Zealand, initiates his account of cannibalism with a cautionary preamble: the "natives . . . are capable of spinning a yarn as any old salt" (226). Deeming the native informant untrustworthy, Watt is then able to make wholesale decisions about what is true and false in Islander history. He states that "we may safely then conclude, I think, that the practice is not yet totally abandoned" because "we hear every now and again of some one having been cooked and eaten" (227). Factors that prove this statement are the dubious statistic of a falling population, and "according to all accounts, human flesh was esteemed by many as a luxury" (227). These points are in abeyance of the statement that "during my residence of twenty years on the island I have never heard of anyone being eaten" (228). One advantage to the colonial agent of this logical sidestepping is the incorporation of myths, yarns, and gossip into factual narratives of the colonial agent. Once again, the mythology of cannibalism here is usurious; the colonial administrator excessively values the acquisition of too much interest as a surplus of hearsay. Sweeping statements by colonial administrators such as W. T. Pritchard demonstrate the twinned construction of horror stories and colonial reminiscences: "It is true that the practice [of cannibalism] was one of the institutions of the country, and that stories told of the deliberate eating of a fellow-man while that fellow-man was still living are facts" (371). Pritchard's verification of stories of eating the living is exemplary of the "fascination" that drives much colonial science; objects of study are often selected because of their utility in colonial strategies, yet the "purity" of the scientific study is dependent on narratives of horror that popularize and promulgate imperial discourses.

The authoritative ethnographic imprimatur is found in a study of one account of cannibalism that is considered by Western historians and anthropologists as the most gruesome. Discussed in a *Pacific Island Monthly* article by Lew Priday, "NG's Most Celebrated Cannibal Feast," the narrative states that in 1858, 317 Chinese were captured, fattened while in captivity, and eaten by Rossel Islanders of the Louisiades (a western archipelago in Papua New Guinea). Priday notes this account has been a "periodical sensation . . . ever since" (83). The Chinese were aboard a French ship transporting them to the gold fields of Victoria when it ran aground. The captain and crew left in a longboat for Noumea, from where they mounted a rescue mission with the boat *Styx*. When they returned, they found only one survivor. The veracity of the story comes from confirmation given by two highly esteemed figures in colonial administration and anthropology in two separate investigations: the lieutenant governor of Papua, J. H. P. Murray, and noted anthropologist Dr. A. C. Haddon. Murray and Haddon both consider that although they did not "obtain a clear account" (Murray, quoted in Priday, "NG's Most Celebrated Cannibal Feast," 99), they were satisfied that cannibalism had happened. The islanders themselves stated that they were not cannibals; however, this was not convincing enough to sway the assumptions of the Western investigators who relied on the discovery of some coins to confirm the massacre and digestion of the Chinese. The two authorities never broach how coins can signal digestion of human flesh, but their scholarly training was obviously an asset in reaching this conclusion.

I wish to dwell on this assumption for a moment: evidence of cannibalism in the accounts, to a certain degree, appears decided before any investigation of the event. Priday's interest in cannibalism is not solely through this story, for previously he had written a history of New Caledonia entitled *Cannibal Island*. In representing the Kanaks of New Caledonia, Priday bases their culture around cannibalism:

> Cannibalism was indulged in as much from superstition as from lack of meat, and they looked forward to their great cannibal feasts with the relish of the gormandiser. Choice morsels, such as human eyes and the breasts of nubile girl prisoners, were generally reserved for the chiefs, who also possessed more wives than the commonality. (1)

With references to sexuality and excess, Priday's description of Kanak culture is sensationalist and colonial, as indeed is the article for *Pacific Island Monthly*. The basis for Priday's article is the appendix to W. E. Armstrong's study of Rossel Island, in which Armstrong quotes extensively from a variety of texts about the event, including Haddon's and Murray's assertions. To distance his article from the "periodical sensationalism" found in most accounts, Priday refutes the claim that the Chinese laborers were penned like sheep and proposes a more "rational" version; instead, they were merely eaten. This is verified through a firsthand account of the rescue of the last surviving Chinese laborer by the French ship, the *Styx*. In giving a synopsis of the account, written in 1861 by a French investigator, V. de Rochas, Priday does not happen to mention that the single reference to cannibalism in the account comes not from the Chinese laborer, but from de Rochas himself.[23] Priday would rather rely on Haddon's introduction to Armstrong's text, stating the account is "confirmed" by the book, rather than on the ambiguous material assembled in the appendix.

At about the same time as Murray's Rossel Island report,[24] the Sydney *Sun* correspondent from New Guinea (August 15, 1911) penned an article entitled "Cannibalism: Natives of New Guinea Fondness for Babies." To substantiate claims of baby eating, the correspondent writes of Papuans as having no reverence for life and thus no fear of death. The correspondent, under the subheading "No Fear of Death," quotes from Murray:

> I do not think the average Papuan has the slightest fear of death. I have known a native when charged with murder to fall asleep within five minutes of the beginning of the trial. As a judge I have sentenced a man to death while he yawningly reminded me that he was tired of the whole legal process. (3)

There is no questioning, of course, whether Murray would eat the body of the convicted Papuan.

Haddon, similarly, already had a demonstrable colonial interest and knowledge in cannibalism. Haddon was an eminent Cambridge anthropologist and leader of the 1898–1899 Cambridge Anthropological Expedition to the Torres Straits and published widely on culture and artifacts belonging to various Pacific Island and Aboriginal peoples.[25] There appears more than an accidental interest in cannibalism for Haddon. As one of the first professional anthropologists, Haddon's success came out of a long dispute between ethnology and anthropology, in which anthropologists, under the name "The Cannibal Club," staged a split from the Ethnological Society some forty years before Haddon's arrival (Stocking, 248–62). That European study of non-Western culture can fall under the rubric of "cannibal" demonstrates a bias in the very foundation of the scientific discipline. This was not Haddon's only connection with cannibalism. According to his biographer, A. Hingston Quiggan (*Haddon the Head-Hunter*), the search for body remnants was not novel:

> Even in these early days he [Haddon] earned the title of "head-hunter" which clung to him through life, for somehow or other he acquired some human skulls. He hoped to scare his sisters with them, placing them, dimly illuminated, in a row on a shelf, turning out the light and hiding the matches. He was disappointed when the girls showed no alarm. (7)

Here, we see the English anthropologist as cannibal, using the horror of cannibal displays to frighten his sisters. Maybe the disappointment of his sisters' lack of interest led him to search for greater and more ghastly episodes. The commodification of horror is only one aspect of the economy of anthropology, which profits from the dissemination of cannibal representations and objects. Indeed, in the Cambridge Anthropological Expedition to the Torres Straits, one of the earliest, if not the first, organized anthropological fieldwork trips, Haddon used his position for commercial gain. At this point in his career, Haddon was changing his area of scholarship from zoology to anthropology, for he saw possibility in the study of "savage" people[26]; the possibility, Quiggan elaborates, was also economic: "he [Haddon] had always intended to make the most of his opportunities of seeing and learning what he could of his first 'savages'; he had also a secondary motive . . . as he hoped to recoup himself for some of the expenses of his journey by collecting 'curios' for museums" (82).

His collection of "curios" included a large number of skulls. The collection turned out to be quite profitable. Quiggan, quoting from Haddon's field notes, describes his pleasure: "They [Thursday Islanders] know, poor souls, that they have no need for these things, but they *have* need for baccy [tobacco]. . . . I really have had wonderful luck" (88). Haddon additionally collected a number of items such as string bags, stone clubs, pots, and so on, but these "ethnographic" objects were supplemented by the more sensational skulls.

The consumption and profit through collecting objects of cannibalism can be clearly seen in the importance given to the coins found on Rossel Island. For here is a connection to Derrida's notion of *usure;* the value of the coins in a particular economy is erased—they are not valuable as money—yet there is a surplus, an "acquisition of too much interest" (Derrida, 210) in that the coins verify, and this is their excessive value and interest in white mythology: an account of cannibalism. Their value is to make "savage" the Rossel Islanders and validate the learned research of Haddon and Murray. Thus, even though the signification of cannibalism has been erased—there are no bodies or accounts of the cannibal activity—a Western system of value, notably coins, can enter to inscribe an imperial economy: a value, a history, and a morality. For in these scientific histories can be seen the West's ethnocentric rationalism attempting to extricate a valorized practice of consumption—a consumption based on Western reason that denies its own complicity in the cannibalism of the bodies of the Pacific Islanders.

NOTES

1. See, for example, Arens; Obeyesekere ("British Cannibals"), Hulme; Goldman; and Root. Root's text concentrates on Western appropriation of indigenous objects and knowledges as cannibalism and not on Western representations of cannibalism, as this chapter does.

2. Chow states, "As we continue to use Chinese women's writings and lives as the 'raw material' for our research in the West, then the relationship between us as

intellectuals overseas and them 'at home' will increasingly take on a the coloration of a kind of 'master discourse/native informant' relationship" (109).

3. Originally dated January 3, 1873, the manuscript formed part of Rev. Dr. William Wyatt Gill's anthropological papers. There are two versions in English. One is translated by Stephen Savage and was published in 1911. Marjorie Crocombe notes this is a "rather free" (Crocombe and Crocombe, 33, n. 1) translation. Crocombe's translation is republished as Maretu, *Cannibals and Converts*.

4. *The Journal of Polynesian Society* was published from Wellington, Aotearoa/ New Zealand. Among Gill's numerous ethnographic publications on Polynesia are *Life in the Southern Isles; Jottings from the Pacific;* and *From Darkness to Light in Polynesia.*

5. For the alternative translation, see Maretu, *Cannibals and Converts*, 40.

6. A *Marae* is a traditional building or sacred area.

7. This is yet another translation of some of Maretu's stories by William Wyatt Gill (*Jottings from the Pacific*, 234–35).

8. Obeyesekere concludes, "The British discourse on cannibalism produced, in very complicated ways, the Maori practice of cannibalism" ("British Cannibals," 653).

9. Salmond is quoting from Beaglehole's edition of Bank's journal.

10. A stratified reading for Derrida implies that "a simultaneous critique of the model of transcendental history of philosophy and of the model of systematic structures perfectly closed over their technical and synchronic manipulation" (254–55).

11. Derrida specifically employs tropes relating to light and sun to deconstruct their authority.

12. The story is one of lost love: for a Fijian village to avoid attack a young man is sacrificed to a great chief who is unrivaled in the number of murders committed or amount of human flesh eaten. The young man's love follows him, witnesses his murder, and is sold by the chief to a white trader, whom she kills. In escaping, she swims into the ocean to rejoin her love: "On, and ever on she swam. . . . Her memory swept clean of all save her love; his image ever before her, beckoning" (267). Cannibalism is employed to emphasize the chief's inhumanity; he is both a murderer and a slave trader.

13. For the association between witchcraft and cannibalism, see Arens, 93–96, 155. For a similar discussion of fascination, see Hamilton, 57.

14. Salmond states that cannibalism was often written about in the journals of the officers and crew; she writes that Banks comments, "eating people is now always the uppermost idea in their heads" (Salmond, 252).

15. A. W. Brian Simpson, in *Cannibalism and the Common Law*, gives detailed accounts of cannibalism during the seventeenth and eighteenth centuries in maritime disasters and exploration parties who survived by consuming their dead. Included in his work are a number of popular ballads describing stories of cannibalism on the sea; for example, from "The Shipwreck of the *Essex*,"

> Then his messmates they killed him and cut off his head,
> And all from the ships crew from the body did feed,
> And at eight different times lots amongst them were drawn,
> For to keep them from starving that's the way they went on. (387)

16. Cannibal stories told by Fijian, Maori, or Hawaiian cultures are sometimes appropriated into Western histories to demonstrate an implied universal fear. See Sahlins, *Islands of History*, 86, 98, for examples of indigenous narratives on cannibalism. Sahlins's reading of these, as a Levi-Strauss structure of raw women and cooked men, is problematic.

17. Lyons proposes an unconscious desire for cannibalism displaced by jokes.

18. Crain's article focuses on connections between attraction and revulsion in both homosexuality and cannibalism in the nineteenth century. Orality is used in terms of the "first erogenous zone" (35). Additionally, a number of anthropology articles have attempted psychoanalytical readings of cannibalism, including one by Géza Róhiem that "interprets" cannibalism as a process from oral frustration, through denial of anxiety, to "boasting modesty" in which the victim becomes "a representative of the super-ego" (494–95). Róhiem also interprets a dream of a "native informant" in which he interprets the Duau man's desire to kill him in an act of confession: "He would really be in trouble if I told the Government," Róhiem comments (493).

19. For more details, see City Group.

20. Bickel states this quote is a diary entry, and a similar passage is written in Hurley, *Pearls and Savages*, 380. Nicholas Thomas, in *Entangled Objects*, discusses this section, stating that the passage was also published in the Sydney *Sun*, February 7, 1923. For details on Hurley, see Legg; Cunningham.

21. On Hegel's use of gold to describe Africa, Pugliese writes, "The signifier 'Gold' introduces the twinned elements of desire and commerce: Africa, as exotic other of Europe, is here situated in sexualized and commodified economies of desire, conquest, and exploitation" (165).

22. The film *Pearls and Savages* (1921–1923) is described as an "'educational' melodrama" (288) by John Tullock because it mixed genres of documentary and adventure. Hurley's first nondocumentary feature, *The Jungle Woman* (1926), is a love story set in Papua, with the movie advertisement stating, "Love knows no barrier of caste or colour beyond the outposts of civilisation." Because the movie dealt with interracial love, Hurley was not allowed to film in Australian territory and instead filmed in Dutch New Guinea (Irian Jaya). Also see Cohen. *Headhunters of Unknown Papua* was also titled *With the Headhunters of Papua* (1923).

23. Warren Niesluchowski translated the account for me. The Chinese laborer the *Styx* picked up could not speak French (his first words—"all dead"—were spoken in English). It appears he demonstrated the captivity and killings by acting out "the drama" in which the Chinese laborers' throats were slit and the Rossel Islanders divided up the "still palpitating bits" (197–98). However, as Rochas notes, these details were only confirmed after the Chinese laborer's story was later translated in Sydney. Member of the *Styx* found a pile of clothes and pigtails belonging to the Chinese laborers. The Rossel Islanders stated to Sir William Macgregor that the Chinese made rafts and left the Island (211), and they were not eaten. Priday dismisses this by asserting Macgregor "tried not to believe it" ("NG's Most Celebrated," 99).

24. Murray's report, quoted in Armstrong's appendix, is dated 1911 and is published in *Annual Report, Papua, 1911–12*, 19–20.

25. Haddon, in *Black, White, and Brown*, also studied Borneo.

26. Haddon, according to a footnote supplied by Quiggan, was careful of his use of the term "savage." He distinguished the noun from the verb: the noun meant "backward people," which describes non-Europeans, whereas the verb meant "acts of barbarity," a concealing "manoeuvre which promises a neutral description but does no such thing" (Quiggan, 83, n. 2).

REFERENCES

Arens, W. *The Man Eating Myth: Anthropology and Anthropophagy.* New York: University Press, 1979.

Armstrong, W. E. *Rossel Island: An Ethnographic Study.* Cambridge: Cambridge University Press, 1928.

Barthes, Roland. *Camera Lucida: Reflections on Photography.* Translated by Richard Howard Jonathon. London: Cape, 1982.

Bickel, Lennard. *In Search of Frank Hurley.* Melbourne: Macmillan, 1980.

Chalmers, J. *Work and Adventure in New Guinea.* London: Religious Tract, 1902.

Chow, Rey. *Writing Diaspora: Tactics of Intervention in Contemporary Cultural Studies.* Bloomington: Indiana University Press, 1993.

City Group. "Deconstruction in Camera: Thomas Andrew." *Photofile* 6, no. 3 (1988): 30–32.

Cohen, Hart. "Expeditions, Exoticism, and Ethnography: Film and the Pacific." *Photofile* 6, no. 3 (1988): 34–40.

Cowan, James. "The Last of the Cannibals." *Lone Hand* 5 (1909): 568–73.

Crain, Caleb. "Lovers of Human Flesh: Homosexuality and Cannibalism in Melville's Novels." *American Literature* 66, no. 1 (1994): 25–53.

Crocombe, R. G., and Marjorie Crocombe. *The Works of Ta'unga: Records of a Polynesian Traveller in the South Seas, 1833–1896.* Suva: Institute of Pacific Studies USP, 1984.

Cunningham, Stuart. "Hurley/Chauvel." *Photofile* 6, no. 3 (1988): 41–46.

Derrida, Jacques. "White Mythologies." In *Margins of Philosophy*, translated by Alan Bass, 207–73. Chicago: University of Chicago Press, 1982.

Dixon, James. "A Cannibal Episode." *Lone Hand* 1 (January 1909): 260–67.

Gill, W. W. *From Darkness to Light in Polynesia.* London, 1894.

———. *Jottings from the Pacific.* London: Religious Tract, 1885.

———. *Life in the Southern Isles; or, Scenes and Incidents in the South Pacific and New Guinea.* London, 1876.

Goldman, L., ed. *The Anthropology of Cannibalism.* London: Bergin and Garvey, 1999.

Haddon, A. C. *Black, White, and Brown.* London: Methuen, 1901.

Hamilton, Annette. "Mistaken Identities: Art, Truth and Dare in *The Good Woman of Bangkok.*" In *The Filmmaker and the Prostitute: Dennis O'Rourke's "The Good Woman of Bangkok,"* edited by Chris Berry, Annette Hamilton, and Laleen Jayamanne, 57–65. Sydney: Power Publications, Power Institute of Fine Arts, University of Sydney, 1997.

Hulme, Peter. *Colonial Encounters: Europe and the Native Caribbean, 1492–1797.* London: Routledge, 1992.

Hurley, Frank. *Pearls and Savages: Adventures in the Air, on Land and Sea in New Guinea.* New York: Putnam, 1924.

Legg, F. *Once More on My Adventure.* Sydney: Ure Smith, 1966.

Lyons, P. "From Man-Eaters to Spam-Eaters: Literary Tourism and the Discourse of Cannibalism from Herman Melville to Paul Theroux." *Arizona Quarterly* 52, no. 2 (1995): 33–62.

Maretu. *Cannibals and Converts: Radical Change in the Cook Islands.* Translated, annotated, and edited by Marjorie Tuainekore Crocombe. Suva: Institute of Pacific Studies USP, 1993.

Narokobi, Bernard. *Life and Leadership in Melanesia.* Suva: Institute of Pacific Studies USP, 1983.

Obeyesekere, Gananath. "'British Cannibals': Contemplation of an Event in the Death and Resurrection of James Cook, Explorer." *Critical Inquiry* 18 (1992): 630–54.

Priday, Lew. *Cannibal Island: The Turbulent Story of New Caledonia's Cannibal Coast.* Wellington: Reed, 1944.

———. "NG's Most Celebrated Cannibal Feast." *Pacific Island Monthly* 19, no. 10 (1959): 83, 97, 99.

Pritchard, W. T. *Polynesian Reminiscences: Or, Life in the South Pacific Islands.* 1866. Reprint, London: Dawson, 1968.

Pugliese, Joseph. "Embodied Economies of Desire in Hegel's Empire of Reason." *Social Semiotics* 4, no. 1–2 (1995): 163–83.

Quiggan, A. Hingston. *Haddon the Head-Hunter.* Cambridge: Cambridge University Press, 1942.

Reeves, Edward. *Brown Men and Women; or, The South Seas in 1895 and 1896.* London: Swan and Sonnenschien, 1898.

Róhiem, Géza. "Cannibalism in Duau, Normanby Island, D'Entrecasteaus Group, Territory of Papua." *Mankind* 4, no. 12 (1954): 487–95.

Root, Deborah. *Cannibal Culture: Art Appropriation, and the Commodification of Difference.* Boulder, Colo.: Westview Press, 1996.

Sahlins, M. *Islands of History.* Chicago: University of Chicago Press, 1985.

Salmond, A. *Two Worlds: First Meetings between Maori and Europeans, 1642–1772.* Honolulu: University of Hawai'i Press, 1991.

Savage, Stephen. "Extracts from Dr. Wyatt Gill's Papers, No. 13, Maretu." *Journal of Polynesian Society* 20 (1911): 194–96.

Simpson, A.W. Brian. *Cannibalism and the Common Law: A Victorian Yatching Tragedy.* London: Hambledon, 1994.

Smith, Bernard. *European Vision and the South Pacific.* Melbourne: Oxford University Press, 1989.

Steel, Thomas. "Cannibals and Cannibalism." *Victorian Naturalist* 10 (1894): 4–10, 26–30.

Stocking, George W., Jr. *Victorian Anthropology.* New York: Macmillan, 1987.

Thomas, Nicholas. *Entangled Objects: Exchange, Material Culture, and Colonialism in the Pacific.* Cambridge, Mass.: Harvard University Press, 1991.

Tullock, John. *Legends on Screen: The Narrative Film in Australia, 1919–29.* Sydney: Currency, 1981.

Watt, Rev. W. "Cannibalism as Practised on Tanna, New Hebrides." *Journal of Polynesian Society* 4 (1895): 226–30.

Chapter 9

Global Genocide and Biocolonialism

On the Effect of the Human Genome Diversity Project
on Targeted Indigenous Peoples/Ecocultures as
"Isolates of Historic Interest"

M. A. JAIMES GUERRERO

The purpose of this essay is to examine linkages with genetic research and the legacy of conquest and colonialism in the United States, including a eugenics movement that had its heyday at the turn of the nineteenth century and that today is inherent in what is being called "biocolonialism." In this context, the new research in genetics is shown to be a portent to a new strain of eugenics inherent in what is being called the Human Genome Diversity Project (which I refer to as the Diversity Project in this chapter), as distinct from the overall Human Genome Project. This Diversity Project targets more than seven hundred indigenous peoples and their respective cultures worldwide, as objectified subjects that these leading geneticists insensitively refer to as "isolates of historic interest" (GS Report on Second Workshop, 8–9). This chapter argues that the Diversity Project is a covert or "invisible" genocide that takes place in the context of biocolonialism linked with biopiracy, as entrepreneur enterprises for the unethical genetic patenting of indigenous knowledge, referred to as "indigenous knowledge systems"; this also includes the patenting of gene sequences from plants, animals, and humans for pharmaceutical consumerism. The terms "indigenous knowledge systems" and "intellectual property issues" are used to counter the advocacy for bioprospecting, the corporate agenda for profit-driven genetic patenting of indigenous knowledge in the commercial commodification of plants, animals, and humans in what they term "biomedical discoveries" from this reductionist mind-set.[1]

Such denigrating genomic agendas that erode further the rights of indigenous peoples and their respective cultures are countered in this chapter with the advocacy for biodiversity, meaning the recognition of the relationship between biology, including humans, and the bioregional land base and the natural environment as Nature. Inherent in this meaning is also the recognition of the reciprocal relationship between humans and other biological entities (i.e., plants, other animals, and nonhuman species), with the land as an indigenous habitat and homeland, and how that manifests in their respective land-based cultures and traditional kinship and ceremonies. This can also be philosophically interpreted as the conceptual meaning of Indigenism, to be born of a place, but which also implies to be in reciprocal relationship with that place: as a sense of beingness or identity with a sense of place and homeland.

A crucial intent of this work is also to make contextual connections to the historical treatment of Native peoples in the Americas, and particularly to focus on the American colonialist legacy of Native genocide and the bio/colonialism that followed in the aftermath of the Indian–Settler wars for U.S. empire building. This legacy has been documented by a discourse on Native genocide in the Americas,[2] and is still practiced today by way of sociopolitical hegemony and the institutionalization of racism in U.S. society. Yet a more insidious agenda, with roots in institutionalized racism, has dire portents for the future survival of indigenous peoples worldwide. The DNA blueprinting, in particular, lends itself to the commodification of indigenous peoples as natural human resources for genetic engineering and biomedical profiteering by megacorporate pharmaceutical companies. The advocates of this biomedical research prefer to use the term "bioprospecting," whereas its critics among indigenous peoples and their allies in protest call it "biocolonialism" linked with "biopiracy" (Harry, "Human Genome Diversity Project," 38–39).[3] As a Native critic of the effect of the "new sciences" of genetics and biomedicine on indigenous peoples and their respective cultures, I deem it important to make the connection between this kind of genetic determinism and potential genocide (as a biological or physical decimation of a communal people) that is linked with ethnocide (as cultural and economic erosion or decimation) as well as ecocide (as environmental erosion or decimation of an ecosystem, as a bioregional homeland for biodiversity) among land-based groups. I intend the descriptor "erosion" to be linked with genocide, ethnocide, and ecocide because this destruction can be seen as a devastating process, as well as the act of an intentional decimation of a people, their respective culture, and the natural environment that is the habitat in which they reside, the latter as a land base for their respective indigenous homeland.

The Diversity Project, therefore, is focused on the patenting of human DNA among approximately seven hundred indigenous peoples worldwide, as well as natural resources in their designated habitats (Jaimes, "Federal Indian Identification Policy").[4] A major premise of this research is that this scientific racist ideology is now manifesting and being "justified" within the genetic discourse and "scientific rationale" of what it means to be "objective" in a "pure science." As a case in point, the state of Vermont just passed legislation to sanction "DNA certification" of its mixed-blood Native population, arousing concerns on how this genetic blueprinting will be used.[5] The Biodiversity Conventions that came out of the international 1990 Rio Summit, to which the United States under the Bush Administration did not send any representatives and refused to sign, call for the input of targeted indigenous peoples regarding the bioprospecting agendas as a result of Native protest on the biopiracy of environmental natural resources. It should be noted, however, that the so-called Biodiversity Conventions are not directly connected with the Diversity Project because the notion of "humans" as commercial subjects was ruled out during the conventions. Although the biodiversity conventions and consequent indigenous peoples' responses are not in the scope of this chapter, it is important to show the movement of genetic science from indigenous plant and other nonhuman DNA sampling and collection to human subjects among indigenous peoples. I explain the organizational structure of the Human Genome Diversity Project in the following section and its intent in today's genetic research.

As part of the bigger picture, this work is also interested in how the genomic agendas can be perceived within a discourse of Native genocide in the Americas. The more comprehensive non-Native authors to write on this subject are Harvey Pearce, Reginald Horsman, and Richard Drinnon, who wrote on genocidal campaigns against American Indians in the early history of U.S. conquest and colonialism. Later, David Stannard wrote a book about an *American Holocaust* that is a more current contribution to this genocidal discourse. Native scholars have also been putting forth their treatises on the "cultural imperialism" perpetrated upon Native peoples and their cultures, and these treatises focus on more contemporary times; most notable among these is that of senior scholar Vine Deloria Jr.[6] Hence, it is my intent to link this body of writing to other forms of genocide, such as ethnocide and ecocide, among those indigenous peoples targeted by the Diversity Project.

This essay starts with an overview of the construction of the Human Genome Project and a distinct related entity, the Diversity Project, to present a case for a racialized genetics in what can be called genetic racism premised on the turn-of-the-century legacy of "scientific racism." This essay is also a call for an interdisciplinary and integrated Indigenous Global Studies as a resolution that would present the indigenous perspectives and values in both theory and practice/praxis; such a curriculum would advocate for political accountability; cultural integrity; economic self-sufficiency with environmental sustainability; and bioethics for ecological preservation and restoration of indigenous "ecocultures."

The set of questions that have been formulated from this research, as a general inquiry that poses these queries to the geneticists and others who advocate these genomic agendas, are as follows: (1) What criteria are being used by these geneticists to target these indigenous peoples and not others?

(2) What do targeted indigenous peoples gain or benefit from this genetic research? (3) What are the profit-driven enterprises behind such an agenda for commercial commodification, and in the context of the language terms (i.e., "isolates of historic interest," "genome diversity," etc.) used in the scientific language as rhetoric? (4) How does this genetic research affect indigenous peoples not targeted, as well as nonindigenous peoples? (5) What are the bioethical implications in terms of basic human rights being raised about these genomic agendas? (6) What is the prospectus for the future in regards to the long-term consequences to this genetic research and biotech enterprises? In this overall inquiry is the underlying critical query: Whose genes are these in the first place?[7]—a question Native peoples already know the answer to—in order to challenge what geneticists are determining to be "isolates of historic interest." As Tom Abate succinctly put it, regarding the most important question of the Gene Age, we should not be asking "how?" but rather "why?" ("Bioscope," *San Francisco Chronicle,* June 26, 2000, B1–B2).

AN OVERVIEW OF THE CONSTRUCTION OF THE HUMAN GENOME DIVERSITY PROJECT AS GENETIC RACISM

Here, I focus on the agenda of the Human Genome Diversity Project and its effect on targeting indigenous peoples, who are being objectified as "isolates of historic interest" by a group of leading geneticists in terms of their DNA, which these geneticists wish to sample. An overview of the Diversity Project, in its overall construction, can be linked to the historical legacy of the 1900s eugenics movement, which is relevant to the reductionist genetic mind-set that prevails in this new genomic agenda. In this vein, I criticize the way in which this genetic research is being conducted by geneticists, who are advocating a controversial and unethical plan in the pursuit of biomedical discoveries. In its organization, the Diversity Project is sponsored by private corporations that purport to be separate from the government-sponsored Human Genome Project (see chart in Friedlander, 23),[8] which is collecting DNA samples for a larger data bank from the human population at large. There is also the issue of "DNA certification," with the state of Vermont, as I noted above, to first pass legislation advocating this requirement and its implications as to who can be identified as an "American Indian" or "Native American." This racialized mind-set has its roots in "blood quantum" criteria established by the U.S. federal government since the mid-1800s to determine a policy of "federal Indian identification" for tribal and Indian "benefits," the subject of my 1990 doctoral thesis. This kind of reductionist research can also be correlated to the early racist doctrines of "scientific racism" as a science of bigotry espousing eugenics, and that referred to indigenous peoples, as well as all women, as "inferior," physically and intellectually, as a result of the size of women's skulls compared with those of northern and Western male Europeans. This scientism, as it directly related to the "inferiority" of Native populations and regardless of sex, was known as "Crania Americana" (see Gould). Today, these new genetic schemes, under the guise of "diversity," imply unethical and immoral aims by way of a duplicitous rationale for genetic research in biotechnology and biomedicine, with one of its major objectives being the patenting of data accumulated from genetic resources as "intellectual property" by geneticists and other scientists in collaboration with government and corporate sponsors.

In the current genomic scheme of the Diversity Project, indigenous peoples are being targeted worldwide for genetic research through the sampling of individual members for DNA blueprinting of a particular group; such a selection is made by the Project geneticists, who consider particular groups to be distinct genetic and cultural entities. There are scientists who claim that they are interested in the targeted group's preservation for future study, so they solicit DNA sampling and collection from human subjects among their group membership. At the same time, these same scientists do not seem concerned to address the physical demise of these peoples (as genocide), or preservation of their distinct cultures (as ethnocide) and their unique bioregional knowledge of biodiversity (as ecocide), as manifested in their respective indigenous communal ways.

A report issued by a team of geneticists, who came together briefly in the Washington, D.C., area (February 16–18, 1993), contains a summation of results conducted by a group of genetic researchers on the Diversity Project. This gathering was held on the campus of the National Institutes of Health, in Bethesda, Maryland, in which geneticists were participating in a third workshop, which came to be called the "Washington meeting." Such workshops also generated a list of approximately seven hundred indigenous groups worldwide, which was attached to their report, to be targeted subjects worldwide; approximately seventy of these are located in North America, the United States, and Canada. This document also indicated that a data bank of this genetic research was being considered for location at Los Alamos, New Mexico.[9]

Such a list raises many questions as to what groups are targeted by the participating geneticists, why, and where. The geographic breakdown for "DNA collection" among these targeted peoples, as reported by Debra Harry ("Human Genome Diversity Project," 38–39), is as follows: Africa, 165; Asia, 212; Oceania, 101; South America, 114; North America, 107; and Europe, 23 (total, 722). It is also interesting to note that most of these indigenous groups are non-European and are located in parts of Africa, Asia, and South America as well as throughout the hemispheric Americas. This could read like some kind of contest (what indigenous groups made this list, and which ones, for whatever reasons, did not?) because the criteria for inclusion on these lists are not clearly indicated or discussed. Hence, the critical question is, why are these groups targeted and not others? Some of those not targeted share cultural and political values and are in close bioregional proximity to some of those that are targeted. The geneticists who made this selection have been evasive about the answers to questions such as these; meanwhile, they skirt around the question of what criteria were established to determine this selective list in the first place.

This third workshop on the Diversity Project was formatted into three roundtable discussions that claimed to focus on "an exploration of the ethical and human-rights implications" of the Diversity Project:

> (1) The ethical concerns raised by this Project are both real and significant. Although no participant stated that those concerns are so serious that the Project should not go forward, the participants agree that careful attention must be paid in designing and executing the Project in order to minimize the risks of harm; . . . (3) the Project should be designed and executed with help from the populations to be sampled as far as feasible, although the participants realize that there will often be enormous logistical barriers to such assistance; . . . (7) Some people will almost certainly attempt to misuse the Project's data and findings in support of racist or nationalist ends. . . . Whether that misuse would have any significant consequences is unclear, but the participants believe the Project has a duty to try to minimize the effects of such misuse; . . . and finally (11) There is no reason to believe that the ethical concerns raised by this Project are insurmountable. . . . The value of this research and the urgency caused by the continuing disappearance of isolated human populations make the ethical concerns all the more important. If the Project does not proceed carefully and properly, it could spoil the last good opportunity to obtain some of this data. (GS Report on Third Workshop, 1–3)

In scrutinizing this genomic agenda, a case can be made that the overall conclusions put forth regarding the ethical and human rights implications of their genetic research focus mask a hidden agenda.

The federal government announced that it will contract out to private corporations to take over the research for the broader Human Genome Project that is sampling the U.S. population at large (*CNN News* broadcast, 1998). There is evidence that this development is setting a precedent to privatize such genome research in other countries as well, and that this will affect national citizenry among both indigenous and nonindigenous populations. Such commercially engineered entrepreneurial genomic agendas, with little or no political accountability, also raise the question of taxes: what are nationalist citizens actually paying their federal governments for in these corporate takeover times, with a globalizing "new world order" underfoot? Eugenics "experts" have already experimented with the genetic engineering of plants and animals (Shiva), which leads one to ponder what they have in store for humans. Therefore, one of the most controversial issues is around the patenting of and privatization of "indigenous knowledge systems" as "intellectual property issues."

A recent report from the Rural Advancement Foundation International (RAFI; see <http://www.rafi.org>), entitled *Phase II for Human Genome Research—Human Genetic Diversity Enters the Commercial,* warns that there are financial stakes involved in the escalating race to find and commercialize human genetic variation—a race taking place in the absence of public debate and government action. The RAFI Report notes that "the human rights abuse of research subjects has worsened and governments and intergovernmental institutions have fallen all over themselves trying to sidestep responsibility for this complex ethical and medical conundrum" (see <http://www.rafi.org/documents/phase_2.pdf>). RAFI executive director Pat Mooney is quoted as saying, "In 1993, we first warned that the collection and management of human diversity research was taking place in an almost total policy and regulatory vacuum. . . . That the vacuum still exists is cause for outrage."

RAFI as a watchdog organization has been described as "an international civil society organization headquartered in Canada, and it is dedicated to the conservation and sustainable use of biodiversity, and to the socially responsible development of technologies useful to rural society. It is also concerned with the loss of agricultural biodiversity, and the impact of intellectual property on farmers and food security" (see RAFI's mission statement at <http://www.rafi.org>). However, it is already evident that genetic research is operating under the guise of biodiversity at the expense and exploitation of Native peoples as distinct cultural and biological entities for genetic research and experimentation, and with an agenda of commercial aims and corporate monopolies. Part of this discussion is what is meant by or how these participating geneticists contextually define "culture" and "diversity," as well as the racialized implications of these targeted indigenous groups as separate biological entities.

There are growing concerns and voices of protest among many Native human rights activists, some of whom refer to this genetic sampling as the "Vampire Project" (Harry, "Human Genome Diversity Project," 38–39) because the best way to get a DNA sample is from the subject's blood. In a similar vein, I criticize the Diversity Project as part of the "global genocide" that affects indigenous peoples targeted by the Human Genome Diversity Project. Such biocolonialist schemes are often sponsored by international and transnational corporations, especially those with interest in pharmaceuticals, often with the financial backing of government-sponsored geneticists. Critically, scientists can no longer hide behind the claim of "neutrality" or assert that science is not political or elitist; this is a criticism that is referred to as scientism. Also at issue are the group or collective rights of distinct cultural entities or what are traditionally called "communal rights" (and later "tribal rights") as a result of colonialism, in contrast to individual rights of citizenry; hence, these collective or communal rights are being denied to these indigenous peoples targeted by geneticists. This is an ongoing debate that also involves whether or not indigenous peoples are considered to be "peoples" or "populations" before the United Nations (Harry, "Human Genome Diversity Project," 38–39) and other international forums. Yet megacorporations and scientific projects do make their own claims for collective rights, and in the name of the "common good"; but this actually favors profit-driven markets and other privileged domains that operate more and more transnationally and globally at the expense of accountability to the national domain and its taxpaying citizenry.

The organizational structure of the Human Genome Diversity Project is said to be different from the overall Human Genome Project, which is sampling all nation-state populations with the backing of the nationalist governments. It has been speculated that because the broader project is interested in determining human dispositions toward certain kinds of diseases, and indicated in their DNA blueprinting, that there is interest in determining the degree of environmental radiation in an individual's genetic makeup.[10] The Diversity Project workshop focused on the "ethical and human rights issues" put forward by critics and was headed by the internationally renowned geneticist, Dr. Luca Cavelli-Sforza. Ironically, this team of geneticists decided to go ahead with this research; they made only lame recommendations that researchers address ethical and human rights considerations of subjects who were not present or represented at this meeting (GS Report on Third Workshop, 1–19).

In telling terms, these geneticists used dehumanizing language to define their "human subjects"—for example, they refer to human groups as "isolates of historic interest," a term established in a report by the organizing committee of a 1992 workshop. The introduction to this document reads,

> many populations around the world, especially isolates living traditional lifestyles, will soon disappear as independent units, because of disease, economic or physical deprivation, genetic admixture, or cultural assimilation. In this report, we refer to such groups as "isolates of historic interest" because they represent groups that should be sampled before they disappear as integral units so that their role in human history can be preserved. The organizers have attempted to use terminology in this report that is as sensitive as possible in this regards. Undoubtedly, errors have been made. There is no attempt to make judgments about the inherent values of any people or populations, cultures, languages, and the like. The ethics review mechanisms of the Project will be designed to protect, to the extent that it is possible, against any such sensitivities. (GS Report on Second Workshop, 8–9)

Therefore, what is implied in this report is a eugenicist assumption that genes equal people, an assumption that threatens the self-determination for survival among these groups. Also inherent in this scientific jargon is the blatant disrespect for human life by implying that these indigenous peoples are already on their way out as soon-to-be-extinct cultural entities and therefore warrant this kind of commercial exploitation. This involves the commodification of their respective indigenous knowledge, which now includes archiving their human DNA for posterity, but with little or no intention of assisting them with their survival in the twenty-first century. Yet these indigenous peoples possess valuable knowledge—enough so that these geneticists want to patent this knowledge in their own names. Something is very wrong with this picture!

It is evident that by using such understated language, these geneticists are attempting to rationalize the neutrality of their scientific attitudes at the expense of the assumed extinction of these targeted peoples. Also indicative is their condescending concern for the consequences of their decisions as well as their inhumane attitudes toward their subjects, who seem to be viewed as experimental animals rather than people. Hence, many unanswered questions remain as to what is really behind these genomic agendas, and to what purpose they will be put in the long run once these groups have disappeared by way of physical or cultural extinction.

In these genomic workshops, however, neither indigenous peoples nor their representatives are present or have input into the important decisions being made about their physical survival. These genomic agendas are also about the posterity of these peoples' genetic makeup, once their respective cultures and they themselves have physically disappeared. The clever language of these geneticists results in a kind of duplicitous rationale, as in how they use the term "diversity" to imply their interest in "cultural diversity," but what is really genetic racism. This is what I have earlier referred to as circular reasoning or a catch-22 in regard to who or what group is monopolizing the discourse, in both theory and practice, among the so-called experts. For example, I have noted in my earlier work that "one cannot identify as an American Indian or Native American unless one has 'federal recognition.' However, one cannot have 'federal recognition' unless one is identified as an American Indian or Native American" (Jaimes, "American Racism," 41–61).

In a more recent scenario of this "reasoning," the Yuchi (Euchee) people of Oklahoma were among those targeted in the United States for DNA testing in these genomic schemes. However, their spokespersons stated that they would not cooperate unless they were granted "federal recognition," which they had been striving for. Since their petition was denied for this tribal status, this illustration points out the glaring hypocrisy of the "Diversity" agenda: this population is good enough for genetic research but not good enough to attain "federal recognition." One spokesman, Corky Allen, is quoted as saying, "Our DNA is regarded as a vital, irreplaceable part of the global heritage of humankind, yet we are denied federal acknowledgment which would give us a political standing, more clout, in the fight to keep our language, our culture." As the author of the article, R. A. Grounds, points out, "The discussion of these issues [the Yuchi's request for federal recognition] within the Yuchi context presents a microcosm of the larger controversy" (64–68). This case therefore indicates the legislative ironies and legal issues that are raised in regard to subject rights in the targeting of indigenous peoples for genetic research. Therefore, it is often stated that the Diversity Project came after the fact and in order to "counter racism" (1–19), as Cavelli-Sforza purports, with an interest in preserving the "diversity" among those indigenous peoples targeted. Such language is stated in the genomic agendas of the Diversity Project and can be perceived to be a kind of rhetorical subterfuge for obfuscation on the Diversity Project's real intent (GS Report on Third Workshop; Cavelli-Sforza, 1–19). Yet it is evident that these genomic agendas advocating "diversity" are not really as interested in the preservation of either cultural diversity or biodiversity as they are interested in racializing genetics in these profit-driven biomedical schemes as well as tracking human origins among indigenous peoples.

There is also the argument for the Diversity Project among geneticists who claim an urgent need for the research because these targeted groups are being "threatened" with extinction, which creates the need to make biomedical discoveries using these peoples—discoveries the peoples themselves will not be around to benefit from. Even if there were those who were able to survive the onslaught of hypermodernism and technology, these groups would most likely not be able to afford such biomedical discoveries as a result of patents to privatize the biotechnological products by these scientific teams of geneticists, who are themselves in collaboration with the profit-driven pharmaceutical companies with corporate interests in the monopoly of such "discoveries." The hidden agenda that is actually behind these genomic agendas is corporate greed—greed led by a team of elitist geneticists who rationalize their actions for the greater good of humanity while they pursue patents to make them even more elite and wealthy in these monopolizing biomedical schemes.

Hence, the bigger picture of these genomic agendas reveals the subterfuge and obfuscation behind their rhetoric and scientific rationales that use "biological determinism" to claim these targeted indigenous subjects are "isolates of historic interest," as "endangered species" labeled as though they were already history. Meanwhile, the scientific campaign itself is continuing the history of genocide instead of supporting the survival of indigenous peoples worldwide. There are cases in point of the actual profit motive and corporate schemes behind these genomic agendas, as in the case of the attempted (blocked by litigation) patenting of the Hagahai people in New Guinea, as well as implied in the Yuchi case in Oklahoma discussed above. In these scenarios, the U.S. scientists are in collaboration with transnational pharmaceutical corporations (e.g., the now defunct Shaman Pharmaceutical, based in San Francisco, Calif.) and others to gain a lead and an eventual monopoly in biomedical "discoveries" for biotechnology and genetic engineering. All of these credentialed individuals are considered to be among the leading "genetic experts," and several are affiliated, ironically, with the National Institutes of Health. These same individuals, as well as others, often show up in similar circles around the Diversity Project agenda. Among them, of course, is Luca Cavelli-Sforza, leading designer of the initial master plan for the Diversity Project.

Cavelli-Sforza, a lead player in the genomic agenda and touted as a liberal humanitarian, is a renowned academic and a professor emeritus of genetics at Stanford University. He presented a paper to UNESCO under the auspices of the United Nations (Geneva, Switzerland), in Paris, France, on September 21, 1994. In it, he plays up his academic position, which he uses as a fund-raising ploy in his advocacy for the implementation of the Diversity Project, here subsumed under rhetoric expressing concern for "humanity's genetic heritage":

> The Human Genome Diversity Project (HGD Project) is an international anthropology project that seeks to study the genetic richness of the entire human species. This kind of genetic information can add a unique thread to the tapestry of our knowledge of humanity. Culture, environment, history, and other factors are often more important but humanity's genetic heritage, when analyzed with recent technology, brings another type of evidence for understanding our species' past and present. The Project will deepen our understanding of this genetic richness and show both humanity's diversity and its deep and underlying unity. I have spent most of my career studying human genetic diversity, and I am the chair of the International Executive Committee of this proposed [Diversity] Project. In my talk, I will briefly discuss the Project's history, describe the Project, set out the core principles of the Project, and demonstrate how the Project will help combat the scourge of racism. (1)

The overall orientation of Cavelli-Sfroza's paper was to solicit international corporate and private support, partnerships, and funding, as well as national or federal institutional assistance, to carry on this genetic research. Cavelli-Sfroza also sought to ensure the continuation of already established funds (i.e., U.S. National Science Foundation; National Institutes of Health; Department of Energy). His paper also notes that the Diversity Project he advocates is estimated to cost its corporate sponsors a mere $3 million over a five-year period (which has proved to be an extremely optimistic estimate since the time of his report). He compared the cost to that of the overall Genome Project, which seeks to sample varied mainstream populations worldwide with federal government sponsorship—estimated to cost a whopping $30 million to the year 2003. The Diversity Project is therefore estimated to cost approximately 10 percent of the overall Genome Plan (Cavelli-Sforza, 1–19). However, UNESCO did not follow up with an endorsement for the United Nations' oversight of the Diversity Project at that time, despite his effort; it is presumed that the agency wanted more time to look into this genetic area.[11] Cavelli-Sforza has also noted, in regard to regional meetings in the Americas, that a North American committee under the leadership of Professor Kenn Weiss of Pennsylvania State University "is the only region so far to have proposed bylaws for its functioning" (1–19). A South American Committee has also been formed, as well as European regional ones and a Chinese Committee. The North American Committee has since met twice at Stanford University, in January and August of 1994 (Cavelli-Sforza, 1–19), the institution with which this notable geneticist and a leader of the Diversity Project is affiliated.

In a national Indian health board issue brief on "Genetic Research and Native Peoples," Brett Lee Smith is quoted by Brett Shelton on this issue under the category of "genetic diversity projects":

> Since indigenous populations represent a significant portion of the world's human diversity, they are also priority subjects for scientific curiosity. To a scientist, the best samples of genetic material from an indigenous population group are as genetically "pure" as possible, to ensure that the sample is "untainted" by the genes of other ethnic groups. Therefore, "full-bloods" provide the ideal samples. Further, it is better if members of a family all provide samples, across several generations and across several degrees of relations (as in biological kinship relations). (2; quotation marks inserted)

This analyst also describes two of the more prominent projects focusing on the need for diversity in human genomic samples, and he describes the Environmental Genome Project with the goal of discovering "connections between genetic susceptibility to diseases and environmental factors . . . the Project personnel claim that better intervention strategies for individuals and populations should eventually be the result" (Shelton, 2). The other project he discusses is the Human Genome Diversity Project. Both projects have the same agenda: they seek biomedical discoveries from genomic research that involves human subjects for both commercial and medical interests.

It is my contention that the promotional spin for medical intervention is not thoroughly factual because such rhetoric in the advocacy of genetic research is deliberately vague and evasive, and even contradictory in parts. Cavelli-Sforza points out one such glaring inconsistency between the Diversity Project and Shelton's statement:

> The truth is that there is no documented biological superiority of any race, however defined. Nowhere is there purity of races, except in plants and in some domestic animals that have undergone a special inbreeding process

for laboratory purposes. Even in these cases there in no absolute "purity," which is very difficult to achieve. No damage is caused in humans by racial mixture. Humans thrive by remaining individually different one from another. In fact, the concept of race can hardly be given a scientific, careful definition. (16)

Yet the "superiority" of one race over another is often correlated with social Darwinian interpretations of genetic "natural selection" and "survival of the fittest," both of which imply that the "superior" groups have a high degree of survival and live longer than more interracial, "inferior" types. I refer to this as "Darwinian economics" working in tandem with "Newtonian scientism" from the Cartesian philosophical hegemony. Also, nineteenth-century eugenicists based this notion of the "superiority" of Anglo-Saxons on what I call a "purity principle," which sometimes even advocated inbreeding among its aristocracy, despite knowledge of medical danger to the contrary. At the same time, this "white race" was contrasted with other denigrated racialized groups among "people of color," who were seen as mixed-blood mongrel types as a result of their interbreeding or exogamy in terms of their degree of miscegenation; these groups were referred to by such terms as "mulattos," "mestizos," and "metis" (Jaimes, "American Racism," 41–61; Gould, 82–90).

My work in this area is interested in the hidden agendas of these genetic research plans: what is behind the propaganda that is campaigning for huge taxpayer dollars while most people remain unaware of the implications to their lives and children in the not-so-distant future? It is, of course, expected that miraculous biomedical discoveries, likely involving what is being called "gene therapy," which has the potential to someday even reverse the aging process, will be made—but at what cost to those who act as human experimental animals for research, and at what cost to our greater humanity in terms of commercial exploitation, profit-driven privatization, and corporate monopolies? It is also necessary to comprehend such methods used in this new scientism of biotechnological genetic engineering in determining the promotional aims and intents of those engaged in these genomic campaigns. The RAFI Report discusses issues on privatization and corporate monopolies with genetic interests:

With computer-assisted DNA sequencing machines running faster and more cheaply than its originators ever imagined, researchers are now turning from the crude "generic map" of the Human Genome Project to its inevitable Phase II—the drive to plunder, patent, and privatize the commercially-important bits of variation found in individuals, indigenous peoples, disease and disability groups, and ethnically-distinct communities [referring to the Diversity Project]. "What has changed since RAFI first reported on the subject, is the intensification of research on human genetic diversity and its commercialization," notes RAFI's Director of Research, Hope

Shand[, who adds,] "The genomics companies are working hand-in-hand with the Gene Giants, and the rush is on to claim exclusive monopoly patents on even the tiniest bits and pieces of the human genome." The real money in human diversity mapping lies in identifying and patenting single nucleotide polymorphisms (SNPs or "snips") that code for specific traits including diseases. The Gene Giants are hoping to patent SNPs in order to develop diagnostic kits, monitoring instruments, and even "designer drugs" tagged to the specific DNA of wealthy customers. Hundreds of millions of dollars are being spent in the effort to find and control SNPs but the long-term profits will be in the billions and could ultimately restructure the entire health care industry. (RAFI Report)

It should be noted that the same Diversity Project players, including the geneticists who met at the Stanford workshops in 1994 and earlier, are also key participants in the broader Genome Project. It is also evident that these projects offer opportunities for scientists to personally benefit from their results, both professionally and financially. Both projects are tied in with what is called the internationally based "Human Genome Organization," as illustrated by the overall organizational chart presented in Friedlander (23). However, a critical distinction is that the Diversity Project was originally advocated for and funded by private corporations, which represent big pharmaceutical companies interested in profit-driven biomedical discoveries as well as research scientists with genetic engineering interests.

As a recent inter/transnational case in point, a RAFI communiqué (news release) notes,

Were the commercial value of human genetic diversity research ever in doubt, those misgivings were unambiguously laid to rest when Iceland sold its genetic heritage to the genomics company deCODE, who in turn hawked the human data to Hoffman LaRoche of Switzerland for US $200 million. The spectacular and controversial deal turned genomics research overnight from an obscure biotech niche industry into a mainstream commercial venture. Suddenly, almost unheard of genomics companies like Millennium (US), Genset (France), and Axys (US), are patenting diversity studies into a multi-billion-dollar commercial product strategy aided and abetted by researchers at universities and even some governments. The extension of patentability by the US Patent and Trademark Office to . . . SNPs (as the smallest unit of genetic variability) has further galvanized commercial pharmaceutical enthusiasm for the new industry. SNPs are the genetic basis upon which diversity researchers define their investigations and distinguish individuals and human populations from one another. (RAFI 2000, 2)

There is also interest (as noted earlier) in the Native origins of indigenous peoples of the Americas, which is a hotly contested arena of controversy and debate, and among Native groups themselves, as well as nonindigenous peoples. I refer to this arena as a "Native Genesis," which hypothesizes a "cradle of civilization" among the ancient Pueblo cultures of what is now the U.S. Southwest and parts of Central and Latin America. Since crucial issues over ethical and human rights considerations have surfaced, such as issues about "hereditary meritocracy," a "biological underclass," and "genetic discrimination" in the overall genomic agendas (Shattuck, 215), the U.S. government, as a leading player in these genetic campaigns, has only recently negotiated the broader Genome Project under private corporate contract, and it seems to ward off taxpayers' potential curiosity and concerns regarding its costs and objectives. This move seems to give the government less direct accountability for this national and globalizing plan with U.S. capitalism as the vehicle. It has been additionally criticized for its own interest in these profit-driven schemes, in collaboration with corporate interests and monopolies, as Big Business in biogenetic research for biomedical discoveries. Another distinction is that the national Genome Project is interested in sampling individuals for population profiles, whereas the Diversity Project is targeting indigenous peoples as distinct genetic and cultural groups; at the same time, these groups are discouraged from organizing themselves and their interests in the plan as a collective entity. It is also interesting to note that the United States places the National Center for Human Genome Research under the Department of Health and Human Services; the Diversity Project has a much wider international agenda that includes Japan, France, the United Kingdom, and others, along with the United States, where it is linked with the Department of Energy as well as an International Executive Committee (see chart in Friedlander, 23).

Protests and criticisms of the Diversity Project will certainly occur as indigenous responses, which include the Indigenous Women's Network as well as the Indigenous Environmental Network, as signers of the Declaration of Indigenous Peoples to the Western Hemisphere, which is calling for a worldwide moratorium on these genomic agendas. There is also the conservative National Congress of American Indians, which supports this call for a moratorium and which is in direct opposition to a few tribal entities that are negotiating for "shareholding" interests, which would allow them to share in whatever profit is realized from these genomic enterprises. Such significant declarations among indigenous organizations and their respective delegations to the United Nations human rights forums (mainly the "Working Group on Indigenous Populations/Peoples") are challenging what I refer to as the outcome of global genocide. Hence, what is emerging is an indigenous movement that is inter-American, international, transnational, and global, as a result of biocolonialism and biopiracy in the exploitation and commodification of indigenous peoples and their cultures worldwide. It is also a movement that had Native representatives and indigenous delegations at the confrontation with the World Trade Organization in the November–December 1999 Seattle protests—but that the media failed to find newsworthy. In this movement, Native women are key players in the leadership and activism via their indigenous organizations, among others in the inter-American and international theaters before human rights forums, as in the case of nongovernmental organizations before the United Nations Working Group on Indigenous Populations/Peoples in Geneva, Switzerland. These protests have emerged as an international and even transnational indigenous movement that challenges and counters, by advocating for indigenous biodiversity rights, these human genomic agendas in the further genocidal denigration of indigenous peoples by geneticists. Such agendas are therefore also linked to indigenous ethnocide and ecocide, as well as with the use of genetic racist language that inhumanely labels these targeted indigenous peoples as "isolates of historic interest."

To end on a bittersweet note as to the state of affairs to date, such indigenous delegation protests, in alliance with grassroots activism among those peoples targeted, have in fact been able to shed light and concerns on these human genomic agendas by advocating for more information and education about these genetic enterprises as megacorporate genomic schemes. They focus on indigenous perspectives as indigenous studies. They have even been effective in breaking up the monolithic entity known as the Human Genome Diversity Project into smaller subsets of research areas, as well as shutting down corporate pharmaceuticals, such as the San Francisco–based and ironically named Shaman Pharmaceuticals.[12] However, this has resulted in the establishment of smaller human genomic projects and agendas, which claim to address issues of human rights and genetic ethics. This remains to be seen: they continue to pursue profit-driven biomedical monopolies via patents that perpetuate their own self-interest and the exploitation of others at the immediate expense of indigenous peoples and with long-term costs to nonindigenous peoples,[13] resulting, ultimately, in a loss to future generations and to our greater humanity.

NOTES

1. "Biocolonialism and Biopiracy" was the title of a 1998 conference which focused on the Human Genome Diversity Project, held on the Flathead Indian Reservation of the Salish-Kootenai Confederated Tribes, in Polson, Montana; I was among the presenters.

2. Pearce; Horsman; Drinnon; Stannard; Ward, *Struggle for the Land* and *A Little Matter of Genocide.*

3. In a broader scope, the construction of the indigenous argument will also show a linkage with the past, especially in the context of what is termed "cultural anthropology" in the continuing objectification, commodification, and today's commercialism for the further exploitation of indigenous peoples and their cul-

tural and ecological knowledge. The latter is what I conceptualize as countering this subordinate hegemony as "ecocultures." See Harry, "Patenting of Life"; Friedlander; and Shiva.

4. My analysis of this genomic agenda culminates in an indigenous philosophical and spiritual argument on basic human and sacred rights. In earlier work, I address the related issue of "federal Indian identification" as racialized formulas that include "blood quantum" criteria to determine who is an "American Indian" and therefore "eligible for federal Indian services" ("American Racism," 41–61).

5. This legislation was cited in an e-mail memo as Internet news.

6. The non-Native authors who write on this subject are cited above; see Vine Deloria Jr.'s "Native Colonization as Cultural Imperialism" as the final statement in *Integrateducation.*

7. Inspired by two articles: Christie; and Liloqula.

8. Note the telling use of "Groups" in the title instead of "Peoples" in the chart in Friedlander (23).

9. See the cover letter by Jean Doble (to Pat Mooney, International Development Research Centre, RAFI, Ottawa, Ontario, Canada), assistant director for Morrison Institute for Population Resource Studies, at Stanford University, Palo Alto, Calif., in the GS Report on Third Workshop.

10. On the radiation connection, see the *Newsweek* magazine feature on the Human Genome Project, April 10, 2000.

11. Charles Hanley, "Genes Project Sends Drums Beating," *Cairns* (Australia) *Post,* June 14, 1996, p. 8.

12. See *Gene Hunters, Pt. 1* (ZEF Productions, Luke Holland, producer; aired February 11, 1991, Film for Channel Four [UK]; sponsored by the Ford Foundation and Television Trust for the Environment, among others) as an overview on the targeting of indigenous peoples, as "endangered species," by the Human Genome Diversity Project for biotech genetic engineering ventures and the lack of scientific ethics.

13. See *DNA Hunters: The Power over Life, Pt. 1* (Alligator Films Video Production, directed by Markku Fink, TV2, New Zealand) on specific cases of indigenous peoples being targeted by the Human Genome Diversity Project and corporate pharmaceuticals for biomedical research, as in the case of the Hagahai people in New Guinea, and the U.S. agenda, a case blocked by litigation before the World Court, to patent their human DNA.

REFERENCES

Cavelli-Sforza, Luca. "The Human Genome Diversity Project." Paper delivered September 21, 1994, to United Nations (UNESCO), Paris, France.
Christie, Jean. "Whose Property Rights, Whose Genes?" *Cultural Survival Quarterly* 20, no. 2 (1996): 34–36.
Deloria, Vine, Jr. "Education and Imperialism." *Integrateducation* 19 (1981): 58–63.
Drinnon, Richard. *Facing West: The Metaphysics of Indian-Hating and Empire Building.* New York: Schocken Books, 1990.
Friedlander, Jonathan, ed. Special issue, "Genes, People, and Property: The Furor over Genetic Research on Indigenous Groups." *Cultural Survival Quarterly* 20, no. 2 (1996).
Geneticists' Summary [GS] Report on Second Workshop. October 29–31, 1991. State College, Pa.: Pennsylvania State University.

Geneticists' Summary [GS] Report on Third Workshop. Washington meeting, May 17, 1993.

Gould, Stephen Jay. *The Mismeasure of Man.* New York: Norton Books, 1981.

Grounds, R. A. "The Yuchi Community and the Human Genome Diversity Project: Historic and Contemporary Ironies." *Cultural Survival Quarterly* 20, no. 2 (1996): 64–68.

Harry, Debra. "The Human Genome Diversity Project and Its Implications for Indigenous Peoples" [IPR Statement 6, January 1995]. *Cultural Survival Quarterly* 20, no. 2 (1996): 38–39.

———. "Patenting of Life and Its Implications for Indigenous Peoples" [IPR Info 7, January 1995]. *Cultural Survival Quarterly* 20, no. 2 (1996).

Horsman, Reginald. *Race and Manifest Destiny: The Origins of American Racial Anglo-Saxonism.* Cambridge, Mass.: Harvard University Press, 1981.

Jaimes, M. A. "American Racism: The Impact of American Indian Identity and Survival." In *Race,* edited by S. Gregory and R. Sanjek, 41–61. New Brunswick, N.J.: Rutgers University Press, 1994.

———. "Federal Indian Identification Policy: An Usurpation of Indigenous Sovereignty in North America." In *The State of Native America,* edited by M. A. Jaimes, 123–38. Boston: South End Press, 1992.

Jaimes Guerrero, M. A. "American Indian Identification/Eligibility Policy in Federal Indian Education Service Programs." Ph.D. diss., College of Education, Arizona State University, 1990.

Liloqula, Ruth. "Value of Life." *Cultural Survival Quarterly* 20, no. 2 (1996): 42–45.

Pearce, Harvey. *The Savage and Civilization: A Study of the Indian in the American Mind.* Baltimore, Md.: Johns Hopkins University Press, 1965.

Rural Advancement Foundation International Report [RAFI Report]. *Phase II for Human Genome Research—Human Genetic Diversity Enters the Commercial.* January 21, 2000. Available at: <http://www.rafi.org>. Accessed April 10, 2002.

Shattuck, Roger. *Forbidden Knowledge: From Prometheus to Pornography.* New York: St. Martin's Press, 1996.

Shelton, Brett. "National Indian Health Board Issue Briefing on Genetic Research and Native Peoples and the Human Genome Project." February 18, 1998. Unpublished paper.

Shiva, Vandana. *Biopiracy: The Plunder of Nature and Knowledge.* Cambridge, Mass.: South End Press, 1997.

Stannard, David. *American Holocaust: Columbus and the Conquest of the New World.* New York: Oxford University Press, 1992.

Ward, Churchill. *A Little Matter of Genocide.* San Francisco: City Lights, 1997.

———. *Struggle for the Land: Indigenous Resistance to Genocide, Ecocide, and Expropriation.* Monroe, Maine: Common Courage Press, 1993.

Chapter 10

Angola, Convict Leasing, and the Annulment of Freedom

The Vectors of Architectural and Discursive Violence in the U.S. "Slavery of Prison"

DENNIS CHILDS

> My recall is nearly perfect, time has faded nothing. I recall the very first kidnap, I've lived through the passage, died on the passage, lain in the unmarked, shallow graves of the millions who fertilized the Amerikan [*sic*] soil with their corpses; cotton and corn growing out of my chest, "unto the third and fourth generation," the tenth, the hundredth. My mind ranges back and forth through the uncounted generations, and I feel all that they ever felt, but double. I can't help it; there are too many things to remind me of the 23½ hours that I'm in this cell. Not ten minutes pass without a reminder. In between, I'm left to speculate on what form the reminder will take.
>
> —George Jackson, *Soledad Brother* (1970)

George Jackson's words underline what is one of the most readily identifiable limits of modern liberal discourse: its inability to deal with the vestiges of chattel slavery in "America."[1] They point out that the most salient aftershock of the "peculiar institution" of slavery is the "correctional" institution; whereas during slavery blacks were held captive on the plantation, they are now disproportionately encased and caged within the prison industrial complex.[2] Throughout this chapter, I will discuss how one particular space within this terrain of racialized incarceration symbolizes the maintenance of black unfreedom—how Angola Prison (or "The Farm," as it is commonly known), Louisiana's slave plantation turned convict lease farm turned state penitentiary, stands as a *living monument* to the timelessness of racial subjection in the United States.[3]

A Louisiana State University history professor has described Angola Prison as an "economic and sociological anachronism" (Butler and Murray Henderson, 9). Indeed, on viewing Liz Garbus and Jonathan Stack's documentary on Angola, *The Farm: Life Inside Angola Prison* (1998), one would have to agree with the prison plantation's warden in his description of the setting: "It's like a big plantation from days gone by." "America's" largest expanse of prison land covers 18,000 acres at the border of Louisiana and Mississippi; the space was given the name "Angola" during the antebellum period because many of the region's original slaves arrived from the country in Africa that now has that name. Of the nine hundred men sent to Angola in 1997, half were given life sentences, and nearly 80 percent of the new inmates were black. One of the typical "anachronistic" scenes at the penitentiary is captured in the film as George Crawford, a 22-year-old black man from one of New Orleans' projects who has just been sentenced to life without parole, is led onto the farm at 5 A.M. to begin his "payment" to society.

The young man is one of a large group of black male prisoners bent over picking one of the prison's many crops (which still include cotton) while a white guard dressed in camouflage and armed with a double-barreled shotgun sits on horseback, monitoring their every move. The main difference between this scene and the ones that took place at this very spot when Angola was widely acknowledged as a slave plantation is that the prison captives are carrying milk crates rather than burlap sacks as receptacles for the produce. The only other distinguishing aspect of this scene—a difference that is negligible at best—is that Crawford and his co-workers will get paid two cents an hour for their day of toil in the field. Overseer and officer meld with the "warping" power of the documentary footage: one warping that occurs is the aforementioned bending of time with a "postslavery" moment bearing a striking resemblance to the antebellum panoptic practice of the all-seeing overseer keeping watch over his charge; the second warping that we must recognize is that of a liberal discourse that attempts to contort the racist damage of such spectacles under the rhetorical camouflage of "correction."

I want to make perfectly clear that the object of this work has little to do with the perceived "guilt" or "innocence" of those whose narratives I will discuss (although Crawford emphatically attests to his innocence on the murder charge at the outset of *The Farm*). Currently, more than one third of "America's" black men, and 12 percent of the nation's Latino men, between the ages of 20 and 29 are either in prison, in jail, or on probation or parole (A. Davis, "From the Prison," 64), and it is equally important to note that most of these individuals are being quarantined as a result of petty drug offenses, not violent crimes. The absurdity of such statistics testifies to the vexing nature of any discussion of culpability as it relates to the targets of sustained racial profiling in the United States. The ideological assumption that rests behind the power structure's use of punishment as its most regular means of dealing with those who face racial and economic repression is that the imprisonment of black, brown, and poor people is viewed as a natural, even inevitable, fact of life. Indeed, it is partly through this arbitrary criminalization of whole segments of society that prevailing asymmetries of power are (re)solidified. The state apparatus neglects to exhibit concern for those who are raised in disempowered localities until they are deemed worthy of arrest; then, a whole ensemble of agencies that have ignored the child's social welfare for his or her entire life suddenly become highly efficient and dedicated to "public safety." Since slavery, black people as a whole have never been able to claim full ownership of the accouterments associated with "public" or "civilian" status; they are only granted such status when it comes to paying public or civil "debts" (Hartman, 24).

The narratives of George Crawford and the other black men represented in *The Farm* all speak to how Angola Prison is a salient example of what Hortense Spillers calls "America's" "mythical time" functionality in relation to black people. For Spillers, the combination of discursive and literal violence against black bodies freezes time:

> Even though the captive flesh/body has been "liberated" . . . the ruling episteme that releases the dynamics of naming and valuation, remains grounded in the originating metaphors of captivity and mutilation so that it as if *neither time nor history,* nor historiography and its topics, *shows movement,* as the human subject is "murdered" over and over again. (459, emphasis added)

The history of the state's implementation of such violent metaphors within the criminal justice system began after the Civil War, when the homology coupling "black" and "slave" shifted to an equaling damaging identification of "black" and "criminal" (A. Davis, "From the Prison"). Spillers subverts the dominant reading of U.S. history as a narrative of progress; she does so by highlighting the long-standing communion of discursive and physical torture against African "Americans"—of naming and maiming— and how the putatively freed black captive is always left invadable by a catalog of racialized ascriptions that function as "instant replays" of the original moment of captivity. In the case of Angola Prison—and in U.S. prisons in general since black "emancipation"—these replays of the originary moment of repression are brought into acute relief through an assortment of state terror techniques.

The moment that defines the negation of Crawford's identity as much as his displacement onto the prison plantation's fields is the forced removal of his family name by prison officials. Crawford's literal disappearance from familial and social interaction is figured in the disappearance of the clearest indicator of the new arrival's selfhood. The distance of the bus ride that Crawford takes from his hometown to Angola can be read as an emblem of the equaling disarming symbolic distance that stands between his old name, George Crawford, and the new "name" grafted onto his person: 375946. In his autobiography, Malcolm X alludes to the dubious effectiveness of this prison complex version of the antebellum period's practice of (dis)naming the black captive: "your number in prison became a part of you. You never heard your name, only your number. On all your clothing, every item, was your number, stenciled. *It grew stenciled on your brain*" (176; emphasis mine). Hence, the physical violence of imprisonment is compounded by the treatment of the black body as a virtual palimpsest: the inmate's selfhood is written over by the ideological ascriptions and inscriptions of the state. The prison system's stenciling of the black body then stands as a literalized example of the state's overall discursive branding of the progeny of slaves. Whereas Malcolm later tells of how he has forgotten (or more probably repressed) his number, we recognize that the replacement of "Crawford" by "375946" is unerasable inasmuch as the possibility of escape from life imprisonment is unimaginable. In fact, the only other "names" that will be associated with the one who used to be called George Crawford will be an ever-growing sequence of digits: the figures contained in the plantation's account books. And even if the "convict" somehow does reenter society at some point, this branding process will always have left its mark in the form of the ever-present criminal record.

Webster's New World Dictionary of the American Language offers this definition of "brand": "*a mark burned on the skin* with a hot iron, formerly *used to punish and identify criminals, now used on cattle to show ownership* . . . the iron thus used . . . *a mark of disgrace; stigma . . . an identifying mark or label on the products of a particular commodity;* trademark" (emphasis added). Here we see how semantics can operate in correlation with historical processes— how the definition of a particular word can offer a linguistic screening of epochal projects such as "Western" imperialism, slavery, and capitalism. And like many other segments of the dominant historical archive, definitions can be as important for what they omit as for what they include. There is no mention within the *New World Dictionary* of the fact that black slaves were modernity's most common target of literal branding—of the mark burned on the skin. But a symptomatic reading of the definition unveils how violence was committed against the African captive through a combination of literal and figurative inscriptive practice: the reference to cattle gestures toward the "chattel" (or human cattle) status of slaves; the fact that the brand is said to impart disgrace onto its object signifies how an overall devaluation of blackness was instituted through ideological, discursive, and material stigmatizations; and the manner in which the brand is said to be used in the marking of commodities registers the property status of blackness throughout "New World" history. During slavery, the black body was always treated as a commodity, as an alienable property. Also, the definition's direct reference to the branding of "criminals" symbolizes how the carceral regime propelled the commodifying and objectifying principles of racism into the postbellum period. Indeed, there is no stigma that currently has more damaging effects on the black community than that of "criminal." Capitalist/racist engines such as the prison in-dustrial complex and globalization function as matrixes of modern-day (in)human objectification (Gilmore)[4]: today's prisons and multinational factories/plantations continue to mark whole communities as natural-born unfree laborers in order to guarantee the cheapest production of assorted corporate "brands."

The diverse brandings and stencilings of the black body at Angola Prison can be considered figures for domestic and global structures of dominance. Notwithstanding the fact that The Farm offers firm testimony to Angola Prison's status as "America's" most overt specular and socioeco-nomic "throwback" to slavery, I want to consider the extent to which the racialized conjoining of discursive and architectural violence exhibited at Angola Prison is representative rather than aberrant—how when The Farm is viewed as one node within a terrain of legally sanctioned unfree labor, it exemplifies the ubiquitous anachronism that is the U.S. prison system. I use the term "architectural violence" to describe structural terror in terms of both literal and ideological architectures, and how both spheres have worked in collusion to assault the black captives of the past and present. The dimensional similarity of two of the most draconian racialized coordi-nates in history—the compartments allotted to each African aboard the slave ship, and the constricted space of the prison cell—underlines a direct spatial correlation between two putatively distinct systems of captivity. The area allotted to one black man aboard the slave ship *Brookes*—six feet by one foot four inches (Spillers, 465)—directly resembles the specifications of today's jail cells.[5] Each cell at the prison at Jackson, Michigan (the world's largest walled prison, which contains an 80 percent black male pop-ulation), for example, is six feet across and eight feet long. When one takes into account the common punitive practice of "double-celling" (M. Davis, 230)—the confining of two individuals into one compressed location—the difference between the architectonics of slavery and "freedom" is revealed to be negligible. Here we see the degree to which prison spaces are not merely empty (apolitical) vessels of social terrains: like all other topogra-phies, they bear the ideological and political imprints of the social forma-tion in which they appear (Smith). The architectural dimensions of prison cages (and plantations) not only register the relations of racial dominance that began with chattel slavery, but also are instrumental in reproducing those relations.

The very existence of topographies such as Angola Prison belies con-ventional "Western" historiographic models that would posit a stark line of demarcation between the periods of slavery and freedom. This problem-atic is exemplified in reductive forms of Marxist analysis, for instance, where race is viewed as a mere "superstructural" emission of the economic "base"—as the ideological residue of "primitive" modes of production. According to this sort of methodology, the materiality of racist practice is elided and slavery is severed from its elemental role in the development and maintenance of capitalism. An attentive analysis of the pulses of racial subjection in the United States necessitates a concentric or accumulative view of history rather than a diachronic one. It recognizes the tandem operation of so-called premodern and modern structures within the capitalist mode of production and how the asymmetrical power grids of modernity are predicated on the replay of ostensibly outdated methods of violence.[6] Such analysis considers seriously the ways in which, as Stuart Hall states, "different modes of production can be combined within the same social formation" (22).

As I have already mentioned, spatial constraint within the U.S. prison system is one of the most salient markers of this sort of temporality without necessary progress—of the state's repetitious compulsion of committing racist violence against the black body. One inmate at Jackson Prison describes his routinized experience with being encaged: "You can't move around. A lot of times I'm restless, I'll pace the floor about $2^1/_2$ steps back and forth. You can't communicate with anyone. You're just shut up and shut off" (House, 69). Another prisoner traces how this quotidian spatial circumscription induces a personal temporal distortion that is metonymic of the "time-warping" power of the postbellum carceral regime. "Nothing ever [changes] except the days. . . . For me time *has seemed to stand still.* I know that time goes but since I don't see my daughters and have *no family,* it really isn't for me anymore. I guess when I'm released, I will find it hard to really understand what . . . has changed" (House, 71, emphasis added). Two of the constitutive elements of slavery are evidenced within this anonymous testimony: abduction and kinlessness (Meillassoux). The disappearance of the inmate into the prison topography is commensurate with the loss of familial bonds and his immersion into a state of "social death."[7] Again, liberal notions of progress are exploded as the inmate conceives of time as a perpetual gyre of torture—protracted lifelessness enacted through lifelong captivity. From the convict lease system through the prison industrial complex, black men and women have been made into unfree laborers "doing time" under mythical time. Thus, the jail sentence represents an infinite revolving door—or rather, a signifying chain: if one is not physically incarcerated within Angola or Jackson Prisons, one is "(un)duly convicted" by "America's" timeless discursive chains that extend outside the prison walls.

Paradoxically, the document that acted as legal fodder for this architectural and discursive quarantining of black captive bodies was the Thirteenth Amendment (A. Davis, "From the Prison," 75–76; Shakur, 64). The opening of the amendment reads, "Neither slavery nor involuntary servitude, *except as punishment for a crime* whereof the party shall have been duly convicted, shall exist within the United States, or any place subject to their jurisdiction" (emphasis added). Here within legislation that is posited as one of the most humanitarian moments in U.S. history lies a most dubious conceit: the relegalization of slavery through the punitive apparatus (A. Davis, "From the Prison," 75). Even before the national government's practice of "noninterference," the widespread disavowal of Reconstruction, and Supreme Court decisions such as *Plessy v. Fergusen* (1896), the law lent itself directly to the South's continued marshaling of the black body. The manner in which the brain trust of the convict lease system was able to utilize this loophole within an ostensibly liberating document speaks as much to a lacuna within U.S. legal practice as it does to the manipulative powers of white southerners. Saidiya Hartman describes this breach within the law as proof positive of its "inventiveness" (199), the legal realm's mutability when it comes to preserving racist ideology and practice: "Perhaps this is best explained as the law's excess—that is, a domain secreted by the state and that secretes the state. Production and concealment operate here in tandem" (205). The racist "production" and "concealment" of the law is, then, part and parcel of the overall dissembling mechanisms of liberal discourse that rationalize racial terror through humanitarian pretenses. (I will say parenthetically that it is this same sort of rhetorical equivocation that is currently being utilized by the U.S. government, as it has resorted to the absurd public relations ploy of "humanitarian" food drops in Afghanistan in order to validate its bombing of that country's already decimated civilian population.)

As I have already suggested, the most debilitating discursive cloaking that takes place within the realm of penology is its use of the rhetoric of "correction." Angela Davis discusses how the genealogy of the U.S. "correctional facility," or the "slavery of prison" as she calls it, can be traced to Enlightenment principles of "Human" perfectibility:

> Quaker reformers played a key role in developing the US penitentiary. Indeed, the penitentiary system emerged from an abolitionist movement of sorts—a campaign to abolish medieval corporeal punishment. The campaign to replace corporeal punishment with the penitentiary and the abolitionist movement against slavery invoked similar philosophical arguments based on the Enlightenment belief in a universal humanity and in the moral perfectibility of the human being. ("From the Prison," 103)

Ideally, incarceration was to work hand in hand with rehabilitation: the prison was to be the site where the "fallen man" was to regain his rightful place within an "Enlightened" community. Even the root of the word "penitentiary"—penitence—implies that the site of punishment will be one in which the convict can regain a social status that has been temporarily negated through a wrongful act. Of course, this etymology brings to mind a major problem with both abolitionist and punitive discourse vis-à-vis the black slave and the black prisoner: inasmuch as the structural mechanisms of both time periods count(ed) all black bodies as so many "altered human factors" (Spillers, 463), the black slave and the black inmate have been racially preappointed as uncorrectable. What Althusser calls "preappointment" describes the preprogramming sector of ideology where an "individual is always-already [interpellated as] a subject, even before he is born" (176). In a manner akin to antebellum preappointment where nearly every black person was automatically tagged "slave" before and after birth—"every black child shall take on the condition of the mother"—black men, women, and children[8] in the postbellum dominant imaginary have been caught within a signifying chain of association inextricably linking them with criminality.

If, at the turn of the century, the rationale for reincarcerating the ex-slave had little or nothing to do with his or her rehabilitation, then recaptivity centered on the continued torture and objectification of the black body as the preeminent lever of the southern economy. When I use the word "economy," I am not limiting the discussion to matters of market exchange: although imprisonment during the convict lease system as with slavery had capital interests as its immediate focal point, the prison system also mimicked the plantation in terms of a broader economy of power. What I mean by this is that while the slave master's status was predicated on literal currency, he was able to accrue through the subjugation of the black captive his sense of "being in the world," which rested on the psychological and ontological currency of white supremacy.

This entanglement of economies is best evidenced by the case of a particular Angola Prison "trusty" whose experience at the plantation predates the narratives showcased in *The Farm*. The Farm has a long history of inmate trusteeship that stretches back to the early twentieth century, a practice that necessitates a total recall of the "paternalism" of the antebellum plantation. Under this system, selected inmates were forced to act as house servants for the "free families" of the prison staff. The first trusty that I will introduce was literally raised at Angola Prison during the 1940s, and from the beginning of his incarceration in this twentieth-century slave plantation, he was made the victim of repeated bodily injury, causing him to become deaf and dumb. Consequently, the only recorded name that I have found for this man is "Dummy."

The account of the torture of Dummy mediated through the recollections of JoAn Spillman, the daughter of John Spillman (a second-generation captain at Angola Prison), brings to the fore Angola Prison's positioning as a clear-cut axis between the prison of slavery and the slavery of prison.

> [Dummy] was an old black man who had been at Angola ever since he was a young boy . . . and while he was there they had beat him to the point where he couldn't talk; he was deaf and dumb. We had quite a few of the inmates working for us. Dummy was sort of a handyman for my father, and

he would meet me at the end of the road to the house when I got off the school bus. He was always there, and I had a little dog named Napoleon, and *they were constant companions.* My father was very protective of Dummy, but he loved to play tricks on him. Daddy [would] get these exploding cigars, and Dummy loved cigars. Daddy would say, *"Here Dummy,* you've done a good job today, here's a cigar," and he'd put the cigar in his mouth and start smoking, and that thing'd blow up. He couldn't say anything, but *poor thing,* you could tell he was aggravated. (Butler and Murray Henderson, 40–41, emphasis added)

This account is so replete with the ontological and ideological remainders of chattel slavery that without prior knowledge of the time that the testimony was given, it would be difficult to pin down exactly what century it belongs in. The bestowal of the name "Dummy" onto the victim of such racist violence figures the general invocation of incipience to the black community that has taken place for centuries. Within Spillman's testimony, the historical collusion of naming and maiming is unveiled through literal (dis)naming practice: the prison plantation's erasure of the captive's actual name symbolizes the overall effacement of the captive's subjectivity and his vulnerability as an object of perverse amusement. Again, this discursive branding process is akin to that of the antebellum period in which slaves were always subject to both bodily torture and the removal of kinship ties, both of which were given symbolic finality through nominative dispossession. Hortense Spillers characterizes this "grid of associations . . . that [came] to surround and signify the captive person" (461) as an interpellative phenomenology embedded in the history of black incarceration in the New World: "the metaphorical implications of naming [are] the key sources of a bitter Americanizing of African persons" (461). For blacks, the prison system represents the state's continued sentineling and revamping of this antebellum "Americanization" technique.

The alignment of blackness and atavism through ritualized (dis)naming is best exemplified in Spillman's account in the section quoted above where the family canine and trusty are spoken of as equals. Indeed, within "America's" prevailing ideological framework, blacks and animals have been made into constant companions. The perversity of this taxonomic tendency is augmented in the trusty's case by the fact that the actual animal is given the name "Napoleon." The ironic invocation of aristocratic nobility to an animal entrenches the family's attribution of incipience to Dummy. In *Our Nig'; or, Sketches from the Life of a Free Black* (1859), Harriet Wilson examines this associative morphing of blackness and animalism through her narrator's observational linkage of the black protagonist and the family dog:

Fido was the entire confidant of *Frado.* She told him her griefs as though he were human; and he sat so still, and listened so attentively, she really believed he knew her sorrows. All the leisure moments she could gain were used in teaching him some feat of dog-agility. . . . Fido was the *constant attendant* of Frado. (42, emphasis added)

The dubious irony of the novel's subtitle—*Life of a Free Black*—cannot be more evident than in this portion of Wilson's work, as again a putatively free black subject cannot shake the "constant" signifying chain classifying blackness as analogous to animalistic qualities. Although Frado's dog is not given an equivalent aristocratic appellation to that of Napoleon, he is described as humanlike to the point that Frado's humanness is subverted, as the servant must tutor the canine on dog mannerisms. This role reversal, with the black unfree laborer training a lower species, speaks directly to the perceived "untrainability" of the black prisoner, and his or her always-already exclusion from the Enlightenment contract of imprisonment.

In *Angola,* Anne Butler's autobiographical treatment (with C. Murray Henderson) of The Farm, we are given segments of the Spillman family photo album that reinforce the extent to which the captives at Angola Prison were placed at par with livestock. The youthful JoAn Spillman is shown posing with two trustees (the first of which could possibly be Dummy), Napoleon, and two of the family's horses. Both pictures attest to the reality that it was the black body as much as beasts of burden on The Farm that were defined as irrational, tamable beings; their only purpose was to cater to the financial stability and ontological security of their white masters. In *Things of Darkness,* Kim Hall discusses the extent to which such portraits offer a visual emblem of modernity as a whole; she does so by tracing this sort of rendering of the black body to the Renaissance period. Hall discusses how late-sixteenth- and seventeenth-century portraits commonly pictured aristocratic nobility along with a collage of their worldly possessions, which commonly included "exotic" properties such as family jewels, animals, and slaves. One of Hall's captions can just as easily serve as editorial comment for the Spillman family photos: "The . . . dog [mimics] the stance of the groom and the horse and thus may evoke a connection between [animals] and blacks" (236). Hall's unearthing of the Renaissance practice of visually coupling Africans and animals testifies to Michel-Rolph Trouillot's assessment of how racialized strategies of containment and concealment represent a general vector of power, an intransigent belief system that is delineated by the gaps in "Western" historical production:

> Effective silencing does not require a conspiracy, not even political consensus. Its roots are structural. . . . best described within a U.S. parlance within a liberal continuum, the narrative structures of Western historiography have not broken with the ontological order of the Renaissance. (106)

The Spillman family's interpellation of Dummy as incipient thus draws directly on what can be called modernity's racialized law of conservation:

JoAn Spillman's account is a mere avatar of a discursive and repressive model that has been centuries in the making. At a particular juncture in her narration, the traditional aspect of the family's racism is clearly underlined as she invokes the family's notion of its connection to a feudal past: "It was wonderful. I was the princess [young mistress], and my daddy and mother were the king [master] and queen [mistress of Angola Prison], and we didn't want for anything. . . . And it was like a storybook childhood" (Butler and Murray Henderson, 38–39).

One spectacle that the young JoAn was easily able to file in the Spillman family idyllic plantation storybook was that of the prison-sponsored minstrel show. Inmates confined to Camp A—what was then Angola Prison's all-black barrack—were given the "privilege" of traveling around the area immediate to the prison grounds if they donned "burnt-cork" and performed white southerners' fantasies of blackness. The practice of blackfacing at Angola can be read as a symbolic representation of the overarching structural theater, which convoluted blackness and crime—a blackfacing of criminality—which erased the subjectivity of the black convict and cosmetically disguised white culpability. In a speech commemorating the twenty-first anniversary of the end of slavery in the nation's capital, Frederick Douglass detailed how ex-slaves were not the only "criminals" wearing the mask:

> In certain parts of our country, when any white man wishes to commit a heinous offense, he wisely resorts to burnt cork and blackens his face and goes forth in the similitude of a Negro. When the deed is done, a little soap and water destroys his identity, and he goes unwipt of justice. *Some Negro* is at once suspected and brought before the victim of wrong for identification, and there is never much trouble here, for as in the eyes of many white people, *all Negroes look alike.* (quoted in A. Davis, "From the Prison," 83, emphasis added)

Inasmuch as this literalized version of the blackfacing of crime signifies what was (and is) a general escape mechanism for white criminality—a projection of guilt onto the black body—it also figures what was the inevitability of punishment for the objects of projection. Indeed, there was no miraculous "soap and water" that would allow black captives to go "unwipt of justice."

Douglass's metaphorical use of the term "whipping" in the early postbellum context gestures toward the fact that the prison regime conserved the use of this brand of punishment in an all-too-material fashion. In fact, the whip was used as the regular form of punishment at Angola, and most other southern penal institutions, well into the twentieth century. C. Murray Henderson, who was The Farm's warden from 1968 to 1975 (and who was credited with bringing a semblance of "reform" to the plantation), indicates how the time-warping functionality of the whip at Angola Prison was anything but an exception to the rule in the South. He discusses how the forms of punishment at the Louisiana State Prison during the 1940s were "probably no worse . . . than at other Southern prisons. . . . the only punishment besides solitary confinement administered at Angola was the strap." The warden makes it clear, however, that the whip was merely one mode among an entire ensemble of torture methods: "some guards seemed to stretch the definition of strap to include all sorts of weapons made of shaved-down sections of lumber, [and] pipes. . . . Improvements in this area of inmate life at Angola would be a long time coming" (Butler and Murray Henderson, 55). During the convict lease system, captives were known to resort to self-mutilation in order to circumvent the work regimen and were severely whipped after their infliction of self-torture (Fierce, 100–101). Milfred Fierce's description of the forms of bodily injury inflicted during convict leasing in Texas indicates that the array of punitive technology at Angola Prison represented one node of an entire system of violence; he describes how one inmate was forced to "whip another with a bat; another was beaten with a piece of lumber; others were whipped with 'knotted rope with bridle reins and hit over the head with a shotgun.' More barbaric whippings were conducted with a wet leather strap dragged through the sand" (101). Although the whip has finally been done away with at Angola Prison and is not used within the current manifestation of convict leasing—the prison industrial complex—the methods of physical and psychological brutality used within the U.S. prison system are as severe as ever. As with other markers of modern know-how, technological "improvements" in carceral measures usually translate into increased proficiency and efficiency in methods of corporeal rupture and panoptic control. After all, what is a more "efficient" method of deterring a captive's insurgence, the whip or the semiautomatic assault rifle?

In the same way that many slave narratives dispel the proslavery rhetoric of the happy-go-lucky, trusty slave, James Bruce's story serves to undercut the aforementioned characterization that JoAn Spillman gave of the edenic paternalism that she believed existed at Angola Prison. Bruce occupied the same role as Dummy for thirteen years within the Spillman household and was treated as the constant "whipping boy" of Rubye Spillman (JoAn's mother, earlier described as the "queen" of the prison plantation). Although Bruce performed his domestic duties for thirteen years, there was never a moment when he was free from the arbitrary physical abuse of Angola Prison's version of the plantation mistress; JoAn recounts how her mother would "hit him with a broomstick when he didn't do something she wanted" (Butler and Murray Henderson, 42). Moreover, Bruce's physical condition calls attention to the very real possibility that he sustained torture from more than one party while incarcerated at The Farm: he "walked with a limp, dragging one foot, and was said to have a steel plate in his head" (Butler and Murray Henderson, 42). But the trusty's ostensible dogged fidelity to the family (he occupied the roles of housekeeper and cook), and the fact that he was one of the prisoners who regularly painted on the smiling mask for the minstrel shows to which I alluded earlier gave JoAn the impression that the bondsman was perfectly content; for her, Bruce was "always whistling and singing; you'd have thought he was the happiest person in the world" (41).

Although Butler's text offers us a filtered account of the events leading up to Bruce's escape from Angola, what we can glean from the testimony reveals that what appeared to JoAn as the trusty's contented song and dance was a part of the traditional survival strategy to which Paul Laurence Dunbar referred in his poem "We Wear the Mask" (1896). On October 19, 1948, Bruce attempted to extricate himself from the ideological and physical blackfacing that had entrapped him for much of his adult life. Most of the testimony we are given of this day seems to fall directly under what one would consider the quotidian brand of physical burden that domestic unfree laborers have always confronted. While Mrs. Spillman prepared for an afternoon tea, Bruce busied himself with his normal house duties, preparing "noontime dinner" and later serving dinner to Captain Spillman at approximately seven in the evening. He also monitored the telephone all day, letting friends of the family such as Mrs. Robertson know that Rubye Spillman had left earlier in the day for the engagement at "Afton Villa" (42). Peculiarly, Mrs. Spillman never arrived at her afternoon tea. In fact, she was found dead at 2:30 A.M. the next morning behind the armoire in JoAn's bedroom: "Her neck had been broken by a sharp blow to the chin, which caused her death. She had also been stabbed several times with a sharp instrument like an ice pick" (Butler and Murray Henderson, 43). At some point between the time that Mrs. Spillman first spoke to Mrs. Robertson at eight in the morning the previous day and the point at which Captain Spillman came home for his break from patrolling the farm at noon, the family trusty killed his mistress and gave a performance through which he was finally able to remove the mask.

Rather than immediately running away after stabbing Captain Spillman's wife, Bruce remained at the Spillman property in order to preserve the appearance of normality. And after waiting for Spillman and JoAn to go to bed, Bruce adorned himself in the dress that Rubye was to wear to the tea party and escaped through Angola's cane fields under the cover of darkness. Ironically, Bruce had been using the prison minstrel shows as a dress rehearsal for his one-man revolt; he was renowned as one of the stars of the blackface routines for his performances in drag. One is immediately reminded of a parallel use of cross-dressing in William Craft's *Running A Thousand Miles for Freedom* (1860), in which Ellen Craft disguises herself as a white gentleman in order to shuttle herself and her husband to freedom. The contiguity of the two narratives is further crystallized if we keep in mind the fact that within the racialized legal imagination, agency gets cast as culpability: in the same way that the escape of the husband and wife from bondage in Craft's piece was considered a breach of the legal ownership of the slave by the master, Bruce's escape represented a trespassing of his status as state property. Compounding this racist equivocation in Bruce's case was the fact that the tag of sexual deviant was added to that of escaped criminal. When questioned regarding the trusty's sexual orientation, JoAn comments that he "may have been a little strange." Butler continues,

> JoAn says that even at the age of twelve, she was aware of homosexuality and sexual perversity being a part of the shadowy world of inmate camp life, "but I didn't [initially] associate that with James. We had one inmate in the house that was like that, and I knew, because he would take my ironing board and use it, my mascara and noxema, but I never did know that James was like that or anything. Come to think of it, he might have been a little prissy." (41)

Nowhere in either JoAn's testimony or Butler's commentary do we find any clear indicator of Bruce's sexual orientation. As is with the case with many antebellum slave narratives, the mediating factors of white authentication/narration and the uneven power dynamic of the social situation make any clear-cut deciphering of the incarcerated subject's actual bonds of intimacy and sexual preferences virtually impossible. Indeed, it was this very uneven economy of power that in many instances precluded slaves of the antebellum period and of the prison system from freely establishing these ties to begin with.

However, for my purposes, Bruce's actual sexual orientation is immaterial: what is clearly at issue is the degree to which the trusty's possible homosexuality is linked with abnormality and added to the nominative grid that projected guilt onto the victim of violence. As Hartman suggests, this "projecting all culpability and wrongdoing onto the enslaved" caused the incarcerated subject to be "the site on which 'crimes' of the dominant class and the state were externalized in the form of a threat" (81). In other words, it was irrelevant whether Bruce was the "sexual deviant" that he was portrayed as after his escape—irrationality was always-already inscribed onto his person. This particular branding erased both the agency that Bruce had exercised in escaping the source of his physical abuse and the pathology of the ideological system that had placed him into twentieth-century slavery in the first place. It was through this version of the signifying chain that the physical torture that resulted in Bruce needing a steel plate in his head was effaced—racialized damage was conjured into a "negligible injury" (Hartman, 81)—not just by the administers of violence at Angola Prison, but by the very Constitutional amendment that had putatively rendered such racial terror obsolete. Thus, when it was found that the escaped inmate had drowned in an attempt at crossing a rough section of the Mississippi River, the state's active role in the trusty's death was submerged along with Bruce's body.

Again, the tandem operation of typecasting the inmate as both metaphysical criminal and sexual deviant under the rubric of racialized ascriptive practice—the naming of the black captive as both criminal and a sexual monstrosity—functions in direct accord with the overall temporal suturing between the antebellum and postbellum periods to which I have been alluding throughout this chapter. We are all too familiar with the tagging of the black male as sexual threat, the black woman as lascivious Jezebel, and the marking of black sexuality in general as unspeakable—even as it is continually made to be the object of white epistemological, literary, and legal desire—not to recognize Bruce's experience as a continuance of a long-standing psychosexual tradition.

Notwithstanding the fact that Bruce's escape attempt ended in death, his actions symbolize the history of inmate rebellion at Louisiana's prison plantation—how prisoners at Angola Prison have repeatedly performed such acts of insurgency in order to resist involuntary servitude. While Bruce was forced to perform the type of domestic labor that one would associate with the house slaves of the antebellum period, most of the inmates at The Farm, especially in the early to mid-twentieth century, were (and are) subjected to the work of field slaves for at least some portion of their time served. In the summer of 1952, one such group of postbellum field captives from Camp I (another of the plantation's all-black barracks) decided to take collective action by implementing a work stoppage. In an interview with Dr. Harry Oster (available on CD), Roosevelt Charles describes how he and the other strikers decided that they were not going to spend one more day picking cotton, corn, and sugarcane in sweltering heat without being granted "higher wages" (Charles). By this, they were not demanding an increase in monetary compensation: the prisoners' virtual slave status made actual compensation an impossibility. The members of this plantation labor camp were striking in order to receive something akin to adequate food, clothing, and bedding. On the day of the strike, Charles and his fellow inmates locked themselves in their cell block rather than lining up to go out to the plantation fields. According to Charles, the warden approached the building and asked, "Now, I want to know what's the matter with my old niggers."

Some hours after he and his fellow inmates let the warden know of their demands, Charles remembers seeing a caravan of state troopers from Baton Rouge and New Orleans, local police, and Angola Prison guards approaching the building. "It looked like it was going to be an army out there," Charles states; they had "machine guns, shotguns, sawed-off shotguns, pistols and rifles too. . . . In a few minutes here come a whole truckload of baseball bats, pick-handles, hoe-handles, and all of that, and guards with them, all from Camp A" (the other all-black barrack that I mentioned above). This "army" of police officials and guards then proceeded to shoot rounds of tear gas into the cell block; and as the inmates came rushing out into the prison yard, they were met with a barrage of blows from the baseball bats. Charles, who had been fortunate enough to remain in the building with a wet towel wrapped around his head, looked out through a window and saw his fellow strikers being beaten: "Man, you ought to have been there to see how they was hitting them with them baseball bats; you would have thought they was having a ball game out there . . . it was nothing but home runs on their heads and backs." Despite the fact that the members of this makeshift prison union were severely beaten and placed into what was known as the "Dungeon"—a block of solitary cells—the rest of the prisoners of Camp I were given a multiple-course breakfast for the first time on the very day of the strike. Also, from that day on, the inmates were given clean clothing twice a week, as well as blankets and white linens on their beds. "That was something strange," Charles remembers; "we didn't know what white linens was, and [before this] didn't have blankets to keep warm by." Angola's officials understood that if they did not grant the inmates of Camp I some semblance of "humane" treatment, a full-scale rebellion would be immanent. It was through the continuance of such collective inmate action that conditions at Angola Prison have shown relative "improvement" over the years.

As much as the strike at Camp I testifies to the possibility of rebellion within topographies of social death, however, it also registers the vexed nature of agency within such localities (Hartman). One of the most insidious qualities of the state is the manner in which it is able to mutate in order to turn rebellion into a crime worthy of more intense torture—to transmute the captive's attempt at asserting human rights into the condition of possibility for more intense inhumane treatment. Narratives such as George Jackson's *Soledad Brother* (1970) and Angela Davis's *Angela Davis: An Autobiography* (1974) reveal that the modern prison uses solitary confinement as a prime method of diffusing the politicization of inmate populations.

One key aspect of modern-day Angola Prison that Garbus and Stack's film does not cover is the issue of solitary confinement at The Farm—namely, the case of the "Angola 3." In 1971, Albert Woodfox and Herman Wallace started a chapter of the Black Panther Party at Angola Prison in order to organize against the prison's segregation policy and against plantation working conditions. In 1972, Robert King Wilkerson, another Angola inmate, joined Woodfox and Herman in their efforts, thus forming the Angola 3. Woodfox and Herman were convicted of killing a white guard in 1972, and Wilkerson was convicted of murdering a fellow inmate in 1973: The Angola 3 were all given sentences of life without parole and were then placed in solitary confinement for what now amounts to nearly thirty years.[9] The cases against all three men reveal that the Angola prison administration used every means at its disposal to dissolve the political work that the Angola 3 were instituting at the plantation. Briberies, payoffs, and coercion of witnesses were all used to guarantee that these men would never be able to live among other human beings again, let alone organize a prisoners' political platform. The case against Robert King Wilkerson was finally overturned in 2001; he was freed from The Farm and is now touring within the United States and internationally to advocate for the release of Woodfox and Wallace. In Wilkerson's case, the testimony of two key witnesses was revealed to have been completely fabricated by the prison authorities: one of the inmates supplied a sworn affidavit stating that his testimony had been prepared by Angola's warden, and the other witness finally admitted to being nowhere near the murder scene. These details, along with the fact that the inmate who committed the crime confessed to have acted alone, allowed for Wilkerson's release. But the question we must ask is this: how does one ever get "released" from the effects of nearly thirty years of solitary confinement? And what about the two men who are still being made to spend their entire life in the "hole" of Louisiana's prison plantation?

The well-known tenet of U.S. jurisprudence, where one is considered innocent until proven guilty, has been nullified for the progeny of slaves. From the convict lease system through the prison industrial complex, a seemingly irrevocable badge of guilt has been grafted onto blackness; this branding, or blackfacing, of crime has preempted claims to innocence or the Enlightenment contract of penitence on the part of Africans in "America." One of the most insidious properties of this particular encoding of criminality is its use of retroactive labeling, or what I refer to as racialized preappointment. We must attend to the primary vector of naming practice within the United States: the mythical time being served by all black people stenciled as perpetual convicts.

NOTES

1. Throughout this essay, whenever I use the term "America," I use quotation marks. I do this to highlight the fact that the common attribution of this designation to one country within the Americas is an indicator of U.S. hemispherical chauvinism. For my awareness of this fact, I am indebted to Keorapetse Kgositsile.

2. The term "prison industrial complex" describes the trend within American correctional practice toward privatization. Imprisonment has now become a major capitalist venture. Now one can actually buy shares in prison-building companies such as the Corrections Corporation of America, which is represented on the American stock exchange. As Mike Davis has pointed out, a state such as California is now so invested in capitalizing on the unfree labor of inmates that it can now boast of housing the third most inmates in the world, behind two countries: the United

States and China. The most insidious aspect of the system—the fact that inmates are made into unfree laborers working for little or no pay for private companies—is also the aspect that attaches it to slavery: both systems rationalize profit motives through ideological frameworks. Included among the clientele of the companies that utilize prison labor within the current prison industrial complex are IBM, Motorola, Compaq, Texas Instruments, Honeywell, Microsoft, and Boeing (Gordon).

3. The convict lease system is the institutional apparatus that marked the ideological association of blackness and criminality. This forerunner to the prison industrial complex was openly practiced from 1865 to 1933. After the Civil War, white southerners were faced with two major problems. First, their economy had been virtually annihilated. Second, the black bodies that were the region's major labor resource had been granted formal freedom with the passage of the Thirteenth Amendment. The solution to this crisis came with the invention of an entire new set of indictable crimes, the "Black Codes," statutes that I refer to as the BWB (or "breathing while black") laws. These ordinances made punishable "offenses" such as vagrancy, breech of job contracts, absence from work, the possession of firearms, and "insulting gestures and acts." The only issue left to resolve had to do with where to house the newly invented criminal population because most of the actual prison structures had been demolished during the confrontation with the North. Ironically, this problem turned out to be the cause of an economic windfall: the reincarcerated black inmates (many of whom were ex-slaves) were leased out to private corporations. Business complexes became replacement slave plantations operating under the auspices of the law. In her essay "From the Prison of Slavery to the Slavery of Prison," Angela Davis outlines how conditions under the convict lease system exposed blacks to a brand of slavery that possibly outstripped its forerunner in its implementation of terror: "black men and women were condemned to live out the worst nightmares of what slavery might have been had the cost of purchasing slaves been low enough to justify conditions of genocide" (87). In *Slavery Revisited,* Milfred Fierce alludes to the fact that blacks comprised as much as 90 percent of the population of the lease system and how in Mississippi, for instance, the death rate of "convicts" in 1882 was 17 percent (117).

4. In "Globalisation and U.S. Prison Growth: From Military Keynesianism to Post-Keynesian Militarism," Ruth Wilson Gilmore makes the point that no discussion of the prison industrial complex can be complete without recognition of how the incorporation of imprisonment fits into the larger structure of globalization—how the "uneven" power dynamics of the United States are metonymic of global vectors of power.

5. Of course, this physical proscription is not limited to the spaces I have just mentioned: in *Blues, Ideology, and Afro-American Literature,* Houston Baker suggests how architectural subjection is a mainstay of the nation's urban enclaves: "buildings [may] best signify the existence of Africans in America" (28).

6. In *Discipline and Punish,* what is for the most part a groundbreaking foray into the genealogy and philosophical makeup of the modern prison system becomes untenable inasmuch as Foucault attempts to draw a clear distinction between premodern and modern regimes of punishment. His arguments lose weight to the degree that he focuses on the ostensible noncorporeal and nonspectacular aspects of modern punishment relative to its historical precursors. Of course, the excessively corporeal and spectacular brands of punishment waged against the black body in U.S. "modern" history, such as lynching festivals and chain gang labor, belie any such sweeping periodizations. Foucault's negligence in regard to contextualizing race is again representative of a blind spot of traditional "Western" historiographies, in which analysis of historical racism is off the conceptual radar screen.

7. Here I use the term "social death" as defined in Orlando Patterson's *Slavery and Social Death*. In his comparative study of slavery throughout world history, Patterson uses the term to indicate the paradoxical bargain faced by every slave. In the slave's initial confrontation with the master, the master forces the bondsperson either to succumb to physical death (ostensibly the only method of escaping a life of perpetual captivity), or to "choose" to maintain their physical existence, in which case they "live" under the perpetual threat of actual death according to the arbitrary whims of the enslaver. Along with the constant threat of actual death, a characteristic aspect of this "living death" is the slave's "natal alienation," his complete removal from all kinship ties. This dissolution of family ties is a constitutive aspect of the carceral regime's subjection of its captives.

8. In an interview with Avery Gordon, Angela Davis points out that during 1995, the population of black women within the nation's prison rose more than 270 percent. Although black men have historically represented a prime target of the "criminal" designation, all strata of the black community—as well as other communities of color—have been left invadable by the punitive regime. The fact that the legal apparatus does not discriminate according to sex or age was thrown into relief by the passage of Proposition 21. Under this California statute, any group of two or more children as young as fourteen can be designated a "gang." If convicted of a felony, these children "gangbangers" can now be punished within the adult court system and can be sent to the state penitentiary. The definition of a felony was drastically changed in order to increase the probability that new child "convicts" could be brought into the adult system. For example, whereas before the bill was passed one had to commit $50,000 worth of property damage to warrant a felony conviction, now a 14-year-old child can be sent to a penitentiary for committing $400 worth of damage. The targeting of women, children, and men by the prison industrial complex is a part of America's long-standing divestment of social ranks such as "child," "woman," and "man" from the black community, whose very collective "human" status has always been a subject of debate within dominant epistemic and ideological arenas.

9. For a detailed account of the history of the Angola 3, see <http://prisonactivist.org/angola/>. Accessed April 15, 2002.

REFERENCES

Althusser, Louis. "Ideological State Apparatuses (Notes towards an Investigation)." In *Lenin and Philosophy*, 127–86. New York: Monthly Review Press, 1971.
Baker, Houston. *Blues, Ideology, and Afro-American Literature: A Vernacular Theory*. Chicago: University of Chicago Press, 1984.
Butler, Anne, and C. Murray Henderson. *Angola: Louisiana State Penitentiary—A Half-Century of Reform*. Lafayette: University of Southwest Louisiana Press, 1990.
Charles, Roosevelt. "Strike at Camp I." In *Angola Prisoners' Blues*. From Arhoolie CD 419, www.arhoolie.com. Used with permission. El Cerrito, Calif.: Arhoolie Productions, 1996.
Davis, Angela. *Angela Davis: An Autobiography*. New York: International Publishers, 1974.
———. "From the Prison of Slavery to the Slavery of Prison." In *The Angela Y. Davis Reader*, edited by Joy James, 74–95. Malden, Mass.: Blackwell, 1998.
Davis, Mike. "Hell Factories in the Field: A Prison-Industrial Complex." *Nation* 260, no. 7 (1995): 27–33.

Fierce, Milfred. *Slavery Revisited: Blacks and the Convict Lease System 1865–1933*. New York: City University of New York Press, 1994.

Foucault, Michel. *Discipline and Punish: The Birth of the Prison*. New York: Vintage Books, 1979.

Gilmore, Ruth Wilson. "Globalisation and U.S. Prison Growth: From Military Keynesianism to Post-Keynesian Militarism." *Race and Class* 40, no. 1–2 (1998): 171–88.

Gordon, Avery. "Globalism and the Prison Industrial Complex: An Interview with Angela Davis." *Race and Class*, 145–52. London: Sage, 1998.

Hall, Kim. *Things of Darkness*. Ithaca, N.Y.: Cornell University Press, 1993.

Hall, Stuart. "Gramsci's Relevance for the Study of Race and Ethnicity." *Journal of Communication Inquiry* 10, no. 2 (1986): 5–27.

Hartman, Saidiya. *Scenes of Subjection: Terror, Slavery, and Self-Making in Nineteenth-Century America*. New York: Oxford University Press, 1997.

House, Gloria. *Tower and Dungeon: A Study of Place and Power in American Culture*. Detroit, Mich.: Casa de Unidad Press, 1991.

Jackson, George. *Soledad Brother: The Prison Letters of George Jackson*. New York: Bantam, 1970.

Malcolm X. *The Autobiography of Malcolm X*. As Told to Alex Haley. New York: Ballantine, 1992.

Meillassoux, Claude. *The Anthropology of Slavery: The Womb of Iron and Gold*. Chicago: University of Chicago Press, 1991.

Patterson, Orlando. *Slavery and Social Death*. Cambridge, Mass.: Harvard University Press, 1982.

Shakur, Assata. *Assata: An Autobiography*. Chicago: Zed Books, 1987.

Smith, Neil. "Contours of a Spatialized Politics: Homeless Vehicles and the Production of Geographical Scale." *Social Text* 33 (1993): 55–81.

Spillers, Hortense. "Mama's Baby, Papa's Maybe." In *Within the Circle*, edited by Mitchell Angelyn, 454–81. Durham, N.C.: Duke University Press, 1994.

Trouillot, Michel-Rolph. *Silencing the Past: Power and the Production of History*. Boston: Beacon Press, 1995.

Wilson, Harriet. *Our Nig'; or, Sketches from the Life of a Free Black*. 1859. Reprint, New York: Vintage Books, 1983.

Wynter, Sylvia. Lecture given at "The State and Soul of Jamaica" exhibition, held at University of California, Berkeley, March 31–May 31, 1993.

Chapter 11

Bernhard Goetz and the Politics of Fear

JONATHAN MARKOVITZ

On December 22, 1984, Bernhard Goetz, a 37-year-old white man riding the number 2 IRT express train in the New York City subway system, was asked for five dollars by four black men who were 18 and 19 years old. In response, Goetz shot each one of the young men. Barry Allen, Troy Canty, and James Ramseur would eventually walk out of the hospitals they were taken to. But the bullet that hit Darrell Cabey severed his spinal cord and left him paralyzed for life. As the train came to a halt (in the tunnel before the next stop), Goetz told a conductor that "they tried to rip me off," and then he jumped onto the tracks and escaped.[1] Within a day, the New York City Police department established a "Vigilante Task Force" to identify and bring in the gunman, and by Christmas Day, the story occupied central stage in the New York media. On December 31, Bernhard Goetz surrendered to the state police in Concord, New Hampshire. By then, every major newspaper in the country had started discussing developments in the Goetz case within their editorial pages, and as front-page news. Over the next three years, as the case made its way through the legal system,[2] Goetz was the subject of unceasing public scrutiny and fascination. In 1996, the case became front-page news once again as Cabey was awarded $43 million in a civil suit against Goetz. Throughout all of this time, the debate over Goetz within the mass media tended to focus on whether he was a hero who had done what most of "us" fear to do, by finally standing up to street criminals, or a dangerous vigilante who acted irresponsibly (possibly endangering "innocent" passengers) by taking the law into his own hands. There was even some concern that his actions would spawn copycats who had no regard for the law, and whose actions would therefore threaten the basis of our civilization. Occasionally, the mainstream media gave voice to people who insisted that not only was Goetz a vigilante, but his actions were the equivalent of a lynching, and the support for his actions was evidence of a racist mob mentality.

The extreme violence that Goetz used, coupled with the fact that he was white while his victims were black, quite possibly made this last explanation inevitable; the idea that Goetz's actions were the modern-day equivalent of a lynching raised troubling questions about the prevalence of racism in the United States in light of the tremendous amount of popular support that

Goetz received. When Goetz's identity was revealed, the New York Guardian Angels[3] organized a fund-raising drive for Goetz's defense and had collected more than $700 in cash donations on their first day, along with 200 phone calls asking where donations could be sent. One man even offered to pay Goetz's bail with a $50,000 cashier's check, which represented his life savings.[4] Even before Goetz turned himself in, the hotline that the police set up in order to determine his identity was immediately flooded by callers "expressing sympathy and offering to help pay his legal fees."[5]

This chapter examines the ways in which the Goetz case, which so forcefully drew the attention of a national audience to matters of "vigilante" violence and fear, has been represented and understood within a variety of settings. I argue that the case sheds important light on the often unacknowledged—and at times unintentional—ways in which the national media and legal system work to reinforce and legitimize racialized understandings of crime, and I suggest that the politics of fear constitute a crucial arena for struggles over race and justice.

GOETZ AS POPULAR HERO

The mainstream media's extensive attention to the kind of information mentioned above made it seem as though Goetz's support was simply overwhelming, and indeed, a *New York Times* editorial about Goetz's indictment claimed that "by charging him only with lesser offenses, [the grand jury] expressed what 110 percent of the American public has already expressed: support for the subway vigilante."[6] This statement was made even though less than a week earlier, the first national poll results about Goetz's actions had been released, and they showed that only "roughly half the people 'generally approved' of what Goetz did."[7] As Lillian B. Rubin notes, the poll results were consistently downplayed throughout the national media in order to further the relatively unquestioned representation of Goetz as a popular hero (146).[8] The *Washington Post* presents the support for Goetz as almost gleeful when, for example, it chides its readers by claiming, "The first reaction even among the most militantly non-violent [people who heard what he did] was, alas, 'Hooray' followed by sheepish second thoughts."[9] This quote is particularly telling because it suggests that whatever problems there are with popular support for Goetz have to do with an unproblematic acceptance of violence. Goetz's supporters are noticeably *not* chided for their thoughts about race.

Instead, Goetz's support is seen as the product of commonly shared and nonracialized fear of crime, while Goetz's actions were in turn portrayed as eminently reasonable. Part of this portrayal is intrinsic to the idea that Goetz was a "vigilante." When the New York City police set up the Vigilante Task Force to determine Goetz's identity, they were surely suggesting that Goetz had acted outside the bounds of the traditional legal system. But at the same time, they were reinforcing the view that Goetz's victims were the real criminals. Webster's dictionary (online at <http://www.m-w.com/cgi-bin/dictionary>) defines a vigilante as "a member of a volunteer committee organized to suppress and punish crime summarily (as when the processes of law appear inadequate)," or more broadly, as "a self-appointed doer of justice," and the idea that Goetz's actions were the only way to deal with street criminals who would otherwise elude the criminal justice system was absolutely taken for granted within the mainstream media. So even though Goetz was the only person on that IRT subway train who was actually accused of committing a crime (or series of crimes) that day, he is consistently presented as having taken a stance *against* crime. This is why his actions inspired a series of articles and editorials not about racial violence, but about subway muggings. When the *Times* says that "much can be done about subway crime," it is not suggesting that more needs to be done to rein in people like Goetz; instead, it is arguing for a better-organized Transit Police force that would keep "muggers and chain snatchers," as well as "graffiti, vandalism, [and people who are] harassing passengers for handouts" under control.[10] The *Times* consistently implies that Goetz's victims were the real criminals, when, for example, it asks, "why hasn't government undertaken any serious new anti-crime program," and uses this rhetorical question to explain Goetz's popularity: "No wonder the public supports the Goetz Anti-Crime and Self-Defense Act of 1984. No wonder people applaud someone taking the law into his own hands."[11] The image of Goetz as victim instead of criminal is furthered by then President Ronald Reagan's statement that it "seemed that we got overzealous about protecting the criminal's rights and forgot about the victim"[12] and Senator Alfonse D'Amato's statement that "Mr. Goetz was justified in his actions . . . [since] the issue is not Bernhard Goetz. The issue is the four men who tried to harass him. They, not Mr. Goetz, should be on trial."[13]

VICTIMS AS VILLAINS: ALLEN, CANTY, RAMSEUR, AND CABEY IN THE PRESS

In fact, there was no need to try Goetz's victims, since as far as the press was concerned, it was assumed from the start that they were guilty of something, despite the absence of formal criminal charges against them.[14] Even before Goetz's identity was determined, the press reported details about the criminal records of each of the four victims, noting that Cabey had been arrested on charges of armed robbery, while Ramseur and Canty had each served sentences for petty thievery, and Allen had pled guilty to two charges of disorderly conduct.[15] The media also continuously reported the erroneous information from police that all four of the victims were carrying sharpened screwdrivers, "dangerous weapons capable of killing," when they were shot. Even when Jimmy Breslin managed to get the police to admit that there were only two screwdrivers that were recovered, and that they were *not* sharpened, most of the press continued to refer to the sharpened screwdrivers as part of the basis for Goetz's fear. Lillian Rubin notes that a full week after the police corrected their statement, television personality Phil Donahue, "in a nationally televised program . . . suggests that the gunman was provoked by a quite comprehensible fear of the sharpened screwdrivers," despite the fact that Goetz never even claimed to have seen the two screwdrivers that *were* in his victims' possession (6–9).[16] As the case progressed, one of the victims, James Ramseur, was arrested and convicted for rape, and this fact was mentioned prominently in most of the subsequent coverage of the case.[17] If there had been any doubts about the fact that Goetz had chosen worthy victims, Ramseur's rape conviction seemed to erase them.[18]

The criminal records of Goetz's victims were thus used as a crucial part of the explanation for the public approval of Goetz's actions. And although constant references to Ramseur's rape conviction surely helped to justify the shootings by invoking age-old stereotypes of black male sexuality and bestiality, for the most part, the media argued that race was at most a peripheral issue in the case. Again, the mainstream press *did* allow space to quote people like New York City police commissioner Benjamin Ward, who argued that Goetz's actions were comparable to Klan activity:

> I have a little different definition of a vigilante. . . . I would equate—maybe it's my background—I think those fellows wearing those pointy hats and white sheets call themselves vigilantes, too. When we asked them where the black people hang out around here, they would very frequently point to the highest tree and say "Right there." (quoted in Chambers, 40)

The *Times* even included Ward's later critique of Goetz's supporters:

> I'm not surprised that you can round up a lynch mob. . . . We were always able to do that in this country. I think that the same kind of person that comes out and applauds the lynching is the first that comes out and applauds someone that shoots four kids.[19]

For the most part, however, this perspective was accorded little space within the mainstream media. When the idea that Goetz's support might be due to racism was brought up, it tended to be in letters to the editor, or toward the end of larger articles, in the inside pages of the newspapers. Instead, the more common explanation for Goetz's support had to do with a largely nonracialized and universal fear of crime.

EQUALITY OF FEAR?

The *New York Times* consistently suggested that Goetz's support came from diverse segments of the population who were fed up with, and afraid of, crime. It noted, for example, that "Many people—from Chicago to Hawaii to Canada—have responded passionately and vehemently to an event that seems to have embodied their fears and frustrations about crime in their own cities" and claimed that "citizens have responded with overwhelming appreciation for the anger that apparently motivated Mr. Goetz to shoot the youths."[20] Note that "citizens," Goetz, and "the youths" are all addressed without reference to race. In its explanation of the differences in verdicts between Goetz's criminal and civil cases, the *Times* claims that the criminal trial was conducted in a different climate: "In 1987 New York was in the middle of a drug-fueled crime wave that made *everyone* [emphasis added] feel like a potential victim."[21] Another article explains the first verdict by stating that "Mr. Goetz epitomized the frustrations of many New Yorkers about crime."[22] An editorial analyzing Goetz's actions in the context of a criminal justice system in which "your chance of arrest is 1 in 10, [and] of imprisonment one in 50" for committing a felony posed the rhetorical questions: "What to do if I think someone is going to mug me? Why do I have to surrender meekly?" and claimed that "Mr. Goetz's angry answer evoked a primal response from millions."[23]

The *Times* did not merely ignore the relevance of race; it specifically downplayed it by arguing that Goetz's support was based on a fear of crime that cut across racial lines. An article by Columbia law professor George P. Fletcher considers both of Goetz's trials and concludes that "our effort to give both sides their due weighs more heavily in these results than does racial politics." Part of his evidence for this is that "black jurors played an important role in Mr. Goetz's 1987 acquittal," and his speculation that if the "civil trial had taken place in Manhattan, instead of the Bronx [or if there had been a predominately white jury this time], my sense is that the judgment would have gone against Mr. Goetz," because "violent felonies in the subways" in 1996 were "down 50 percent compared with 1984," and so New York no longer had the same climate of fear.[24] The fact that the two black jurors helped to acquit Goetz of most counts in the criminal trial is consistently taken as evidence that Goetz's support, and his fear, were universal. This idea is echoed in the articles, which discuss the support that Goetz received from black New Yorkers. The claim that "the day of the subway shootings, it seemed there was hardly a person in New York, black or white, who couldn't relate [to] the story of a mugging inflicted on himself or a friend or family member" is typical.[25]

This image of Goetz's cross-racial support is only partially borne out by poll results. A Gallup poll conducted for Newsday in March 1985 showed that 57 percent of the respondents approved of Goetz's actions, but as Rubin notes, when the results are broken down by race, only 39 percent of nonwhites supported Goetz. Rubin notes that in early January, blacks and whites supported Goetz by roughly the same percentage (49 percent of blacks and 52 percent of whites surveyed approved of the shootings), but argues that an ABC poll conducted in March shows that "by March 1, a sharp shift was in progress, with the black approval rate dropping by 12 percent and the white rising by 5 percent: 37 percent of blacks approve compared with 57 percent of whites" (Rubin, 197). If Goetz's support had at one time cut equally across racial lines, this was clearly no longer the case. As the director of the ABC polling unit said,

> The issue is definitely no longer color-blind. Blacks now disapprove of what he did; whites now approve. Blacks think he went too far and should have been indicted for attempted murder; whites don't. There were no significant differences in attitudes along racial lines in the first poll. Now there are. (quoted in Rubin, 197)

The mainstream media found little space in which to report this change in public sentiment, and the 63 percent of blacks (and 43 percent of whites) who did not approve of Goetz's actions were marginalized and depicted as out of touch, as the image of a racial consensus dominated the print media and airwaves.

THE RACIALIZATION OF FEAR

Occasionally, the media *did* consider the possibility that race was an important factor in Goetz's support, but when the relevance of race wasn't dismissed outright, it was generally presented in a matter-of-fact way, with the implicit assumption that fear of young black men is part of common sense, no matter how unfortunate that recognition may be.[26] For example, a *New York Times* editorial, which argues emphatically that Goetz's acquittal was *not* due to racism, nonetheless suggests that it has the potential to lead to troubling racial outcomes:

> To blacks accustomed to continuing charges of police abuse, the Goetz acquittal might look like part of a pattern. . . . It's not surprising when some voices charge systemic racism. . . . Unsurprising, but also unwarranted. The New York police, under a black commissioner, are working to cope with discipline problems among rapidly recruited young officers. Judges and juries err, if at all, on the side of the defendant, whatever his race. The Goetz jurors found too much reason for doubt about the prosecutor's evidence against a white man. . . . The more immediate reason for black anxiety about the Goetz verdict is its potential for inflaming racial discrimination based on fear of crime.

Although the article expresses concern about this possibility, it nevertheless suggests that fear of crime based on race is perfectly logical:

> There is no denying that race is an element behind such fear: blacks are found to commit robbery at a rate 10 times that of whites. It is widely as-

sumed that young black males are by definition dangerous. Mr. Goetz's defense played off that assumption. He said he shot down four young blacks not because they brandished weapons or assaulted him but because of their body language. The jury had no trouble putting itself in his place.

The *Times* isn't comfortable with this situation: it notes that "accepting assumptions and stereotypes creates another class of victims" and cautions that "adopting stereotypes of fear is too easy, and too costly," but it does nothing to combat the assumed link between young black men and danger that it mentions, and so ultimately reinforces exactly the stereotypes that it warns against by implying that fear of blacks is reasonable.[27]

Thus, when the *Times* does acknowledge that race may have played a part in Goetz's actions or in the support he received, it tends to suggest that race was relevant only in a minor and fairly levelheaded manner. The logic suggests that we might still find this troubling and would want to make sure that our biases don't get the best of us, but even the most fair-minded of us would have to admit that we would have shared some of Goetz's trepidation. Attention to some of the mail surrounding the case, and to Goetz's own statements, as well as his defense team's strategies, however, shows that racism was not always nearly so subtle in the case.

A rare editorial in the *Times* acknowledges that some of the support for Goetz does indeed have something to tell "us about racial hatreds." The editorial prints various pro-Goetz letters, which are meant to demonstrate that "the Goetz affair has set powerful feelings in motion in this city. Not all of them are pretty." Among the uglier letters is one that says, "Bernhard Hugo Goetz makes me proud, P-R-O-U-D, to be a white, male American! At long last we can hold up our heads again!" Another asks,

> Why do you conceal the truth and write that merely "a lot of" the crimes in the New York subways are caused by blacks and Hispanics? You know very well that they commit virtually all of the crimes (as well as in the city generally). When are you going to use your column on our behalf and call out "Enough!" Tell them we have had enough of their cold, murderous ways.[28]

The most virulently racist letters, however, never made it into the newspapers. Shirley Cabey, Darrell Cabey's mother, showed Lillian Rubin some of the hate mail that she received after her son was shot and his identity was revealed. These are letters that say "that it's too bad her son has *only* been paralyzed, that express regret that the others will walk again, that threaten to do them violence of one kind or another." These letters include explicit racial epithets and suggest that any and all black men are legitimate targets (Rubin, 104–5).

There is some debate about the degree of Goetz's own racism, but it seems clear that his views about race are relevant in determining the basis for his actions.[29] In his videotaped confession, Goetz discusses an earlier instance where he was mugged by a black man, and he says that that man's "eyes were shiny."[30] Some of Goetz's defenders argued that statement may not have been a racial reference, but this seems implausible given what else is known about Goetz. For example, Myra Friedman, a *New York* magazine reporter and one of Goetz's neighbors, claims that Goetz told an anticrime group in their apartment building, "The only way we're going to clean up this street is to get rid of the spics and niggers" (quoted in Rubin, 182),[31] and months after the shootings, he claimed that "the society has dishonesty and lies at all levels. . . . [But] lying and dishonesty in the black community is more pronounced" (quoted in Rubin, 183).

Whatever Goetz's own views, race was clearly an important factor for his legal team. The mainstream media consistently claimed that race did not enter into Goetz's criminal trial. Indeed, the court transcripts almost never refer to anyone's race. What was said, however, may ultimately be less important than what was done. At one point in the trial, Goetz's legal team attempted to recreate the crime scene. Part of the recreation involved having four black men act as "props." The men were volunteers from the Guardian Angels, and Goetz's attorney, Barry Slotnick, had specifically asked the Angels to send black men. From a legal perspective, their race should have been irrelevant. As George P. Fletcher notes:

> There is no doubt that having four street-clad black kids standing in for the four alleged aggressors enhanced the dramatic power of this re-creation of the crime. If one were re-creating the incident on the stage, there is no doubt that one would want to cast young blacks in the roles of Canty, Allen, Ramseur, and Cabey. Authenticity demands no less. But the purpose of the demonstration was solely to clarify . . . claims about possible inferences from the established paths of the bullets. There was, therefore, no legal warrant for Slotnick's calling black youths . . . in order to illustrate points about bullets' passing through human bodies. The witness was not authorized to speak about the rational inference of danger from being surrounded by four young black toughs. But Slotnick designed the dramatic scene so that the implicit message of menace and fear would be so strong that testimony would not be needed. (129–30)

Fletcher notes that there were other moments in the trial where Slotnick relied on implicit assumptions about race:

> Indirectly and covertly, the defense played on the racial factor. Slotnick's strategy of relentlessly attacking the "gang of four," "the predators" on society, calling them "vultures" and "savages," carried undeniable racial undertones. These verbal attacks signaled a perception of the four youths as representing something more than four individuals committing an act of aggression against a defendant. That "something more" requires extrapolation from their characteristics to the class of individuals for which they

stand. There is no doubt that one of the characteristics that figures in this implicit extrapolation is their blackness. (206)

It may well be that Goetz benefited from the fact that racial biases were appealed to covertly rather than directly, since this meant that they never became the subject of open debate. It also made it easier for the media to maintain its claim that the case was about fear rather than race. But analysis of Slotnick's courtroom activities should be enough to demonstrate that the case was about fear, which was thoroughly racialized.

BLACK FEAR AFTER THE VERDICT

Perhaps the best evidence that fear is racialized comes not from Goetz's supporters but from some of his most vocal detractors. I've already noted that in March 1985, 37 percent of African Americans who were surveyed, along with 52 percent of whites, supported Goetz and presumably agreed that he acted on what they saw as a reasonable basis for fear. A very different kind of fear is hinted at when considering the kinds of hate mail received by the families of Goetz's victims. In the wake of the first grand jury's failure to indict Goetz on anything but weapons charges, and in light of the verdict in the criminal trial, it was not whites who were given new reasons to fear for their safety. Black fear of vigilante violence is allotted very little room in the mainstream media's coverage of the case (although this was a prime issue in New York's African American press), but it is occasionally discussed as a side issue or within the letters pages. An article that addresses the reactions to the verdict in Goetz's criminal trial among black politicians notes that Goetz's actions and treatment by the legal system have been a cause for concern within the black community. Then Manhattan Borough president (and future New York City mayor) David Dinkins is quoted as saying that he was "shaken and dismayed by the verdict [which is] a clear and open invitation to vigilantism," while the Black and Puerto Rican Legislative Caucus in Albany called the decision "frightening [because] it sanctions dangerous vigilante actions on the part of misguided citizens." This position was echoed by a variety of black political figures, including Wilbert Tatum, the editor in chief and chairman of the African American newspaper the *New York Amsterdam News,* who said that the verdict was "a tragic miscarriage of justice, not so much in terms of the young men [who were shot] but in terms of the fear it has engendered in all of us . . . [now that] there is no question that there is now license for an open season"; and Harriet R. Michel, the president of the New York Urban League, who said that the verdict "which allows people to act with less impunity on their own personal fears, is very anxiety-producing for black people, especially for young black men."[32]

I've taken the time to discuss black fear of racist vigilantism in light of

Goetz's acquittal partly because of how easy it might be to ignore, given the tremendous amount of ink that was spilled sympathizing with Goetz's plight and suggesting that the kind of fear that he experienced was ubiquitous. Black fear also points to the importance of collective memories of racial violence. By heightening a climate of racial terror, Goetz's actions— and their public and legal reception—can be seen as one more event on the same continuum of racial violence as lynching, at the same time as memories of lynching surely make black fear of vigilante justice after the criminal verdict both more reasonable and more potent. But the more important reason that I've discussed black fear of vigilantism here is to help establish that at least as far as violent crime is concerned, there are clear links between race and fear. Although this may seem an obvious point, it needs to be made explicitly because, as I've shown, the mainstream media consistently denies it. It was also denied within Goetz's trial, and within the courtroom, as various parties attempted to determine whether the shootings were motivated by race *or* by fear.

THE STAKES: RACE, FEAR, AND SELF-DEFENSE

For Goetz, there were high stakes associated with the clear separation of race and fear. His justification for shooting the four young men was that he was acting in self-defense. Goetz's defense hinged on the idea that his belief that he was in imminent danger was reasonable, despite the lack of more traditional evidence of this danger (there were no threats, no drawn or visible weapons, and no explicit demands for money). But it wasn't clear exactly what was meant by "reasonable," and there was a protracted dispute about the legal standard that should be used. The prosecutor for the second grand jury argued that the standard should be "whether the defendant's conduct was that of a reasonable man in the defendant's situation." In other words, if Goetz's fear and subsequent actions made sense to a "reasonable man," the self-defense claim could work. If, however, the "reasonable man" standard suggested that Goetz's fear was *not* reasonable, self-defense would not be a viable defense. The trial judge and Appellate Division argued that this standard was too exacting. The only concern should be whether Goetz's actions were reasonable to him. If his fear of imminent violence was real to him, self-defense might justify the shootings. This decision was eventually overturned by Chief Judge Sol Wachtler on the New York State Court of Appeals, who argued that the standard proposed by the lower courts "puts too much emphasis on subjective belief and not enough on reason," and that

> We cannot lightly impart to the Legislature an intent to fundamentally alter the principles of justification to allow the perpetrator of a serious crime to go free simply because that person believed his actions were reasonable and

necessary to prevent some perceived harm. To completely exonerate such an individual, no matter how aberrational or bizarre his thought patterns, would allow citizens to set their own standards for the permissible use of force. It would also allow a legally competent defendant suffering from delusions to kill or perform acts of violence contrary to fundamental principles of justice and criminal law.[33]

Wachtler's decision was praised by the *New York Times,* and for good reason.[34] The standard proposed by the lower courts would have allowed for anyone's fear, no matter how idiosyncratic, to become justification for extreme violence. Wachtler may have even had in mind the possibility that a racist fanatic could justify a shooting spree by referencing absurd racist fears. It is likely that the intent of the ruling was to rule out the possibility of racism as an excuse for extreme violence, and the ruling was certainly intended as a way to limit Goetz's defense by disallowing the possibility of a self-defense justification in the event that his fear was not reasonable.

The problem with this logic comes when we consider the systematic nature of racism and of racial fears. Of course it makes no legal sense to allow raving lunatics to go around shooting anyone they're afraid of, so Watchler was right to strike down the lower courts' standards. But racism is neither "aberrational" nor "bizarre," and its prevalence makes it virtually impossible to argue that someone who kills because he is afraid of black men is acting on the basis of irrational fears. As I noted above, the *Times* occasionally goes so far as to argue that fear of black men is perfectly rational, if unfortunate. The problem is foreshadowed in other portions of Watchler's opinion. Watchler notes that

> A determination of reasonableness with regard to the defense of justification . . . must be based on the "circumstances" facing a defendant or his "situation." Such terms encompass more than the physical movements of the potential assailant. These terms include any relevant knowledge the defendant had about that person. They also necessarily bring in the physical attributes of all persons involved, including the defendant. Furthermore, the defendant's circumstances encompass any prior experiences he had which could provide a reasonable basis for a belief that another person's intentions were to injure or rob him or that the use of deadly force was necessary under the circumstances.[35]

"Relevant knowledge" is never defined in Watchler's opinion, and no mention is made of *which* "physical attributes" should be taken into consideration, but at the very least, there is nothing in this language to preclude consideration of race. If, however, Goetz felt that he *knew* that blacks were likely to be criminals, and if this "knowledge" was bolstered by "prior experiences" (he has discussed having been mugged by a black man), then his fear becomes more reasonable. Although we might want to criticize the basis of his "knowledge" by pointing out that the majority of blacks are *not* criminals, it would be difficult to argue that there was no reasonable basis for his fear given the ubiquity of what Katheryn K. Russell calls the *"criminalblackman"* throughout the national media (3).[36] The presence of this image suggests that Goetz was surrounded by a culture that insisted that his fear *was* reasonable.

CONCLUDING REMARKS: RACE AS SELF-DEFENSE

For many observers who were critical of Goetz's actions—and of the reception that those actions received within the mass media and the legal system—the case conjures up some of the most troubling images of racist violence in national collective memory. The Goetz case marks a departure from the traditional lynching scenario (the cheering mob came *after* the shootings, no one was killed, etc.), but in important ways, it relies on and extends some of the logic that was central for the dynamics of lynching. After all, lynchings firmly established the links between fear of black men and racist terrorism that were in play in the events surrounding Goetz's criminal trial. Once again, blacks were given reason to fear vigilante violence, and the figure of the black criminal stood in for the myth of the black rapist as shootings were justified as self-defense. Collective memories of earlier racial fears certainly provided the Goetz case with an alarming kind of historical resonance.

If Watchler's goal *was* to eliminate racism as a valid defense for violence, then his decision ultimately suffers from the same conceptual problem that I've argued occurs throughout the mainstream media's coverage of the Goetz case. Consideration of race and fear as discrete categories makes it impossible to recognize the ways in which these concepts are interrelated. The question of whether Goetz's actions were based on race or fear precludes attention to the possibility that they were based on both simultaneously because fear is racialized. Near the end of his book on Goetz's criminal trial, Fletcher argues that

> The question [of] whether a reasonable person considers race in assessing the danger that four youths on the subway might represent goes to the heart of what the law demands of us. The statistically ordinary New Yorker would be more apprehensive of the "kind of people" who mugged him once, and it is difficult to expect the ordinary person in our time not to perceive race as one—just one—of the factors defining the "kind" of person who poses a danger. The law, however, may demand that we surmount racially based intuitions of danger. Though the question was not resolved in the Goetz case and there is no settled law on this issue, the standard of reasonableness may require us to be better than we really are. (206)

That may be. But perhaps the real lesson to take away from the Goetz trials is that if fear is socially constructed in a racist manner, there is a problem in allowing it legal sanction as a justification for violence. It is quite clear that we are expected to envision the "kind of people" who mugged the "statistically ordinary New Yorker" in the above example as nonwhite. The fact that the passage is not race neutral is highlighted when considering Dorothy Gilliam's challenge to "just try to imagine whether a pistol-toting black man would have had such a sweeping vindication had he shot four white teenagers" (quoted in Kennedy, 424). The notion that race can be an acceptable criterion for determining the likelihood of criminal activity is clearly, then, a one-way street in which race-neutral language masks the continuing association between black men and criminality.[37]

Cheryl I. Harris writes that before abolition in the United States, "White identity and whiteness were sources of privilege and protection; their absence meant being the object of property," and she argues that in that context, whiteness should itself be understood as a form of property, if "by 'property' one means all of a person's legal rights" (279–80). The Goetz case suggests that in the contemporary United States, whiteness continues to function as a similar type of property, except that its absence now entails being the object not of property, but of heightened suspicion by the criminal justice system and of legally sanctioned violence.[38] The legal standard of reasonableness, which requires us to be, as Fletcher says, "better than we really are," plays a crucial role in maintaining the property value of whiteness. In order to reduce what George Lipsitz refers to as "the possessive investment in whiteness" (1998), and to eliminate racism as a valid defense in criminal trials, it is imperative that we develop a better standard for self-defense that does not acknowledge the legitimacy of racially based fears, reasonable or not.

.

NOTES

1. This is the standard account of the events. See Fletcher for a detailed account of variations and disputed versions of the events in question.

2. On January 25, 1985, a grand jury refused to indict Goetz for attempted murder but did indict him for illegal weapons possession. A second grand jury *did* indict him for four counts of attempted murder, one count of reckless endangerment, four counts of assault, and four weapons charges on March 27 of that year. Some of those charges were subsequently dismissed and reinstated in a series of appeals. Finally, on June 16, 1987, Goetz was found innocent of attempted murder, assault, and reckless endangerment, but guilty of weapons possession. After appeals, Goetz ultimately served about eight and a half months in prison for weapons charges. Carol A. Roehrenbeck provides an excellent time line in her compilation of court transcripts of the lawyers' summations and charges to the jury (ix–x). See also Fletcher for an interesting analysis of the legal issues involved in the Goetz case. More recently, on April 23, 1996, Darrell Cabey, who was paralyzed by one of

Goetz's bullets, was awarded $43 million in his civil suit against Goetz. See George P. Fletcher, "Justice for All, Twice," *New York Times*, April 24, 1996, A21 +.

3. The Guardian Angels is a volunteer group devoted to preventing crime that has itself been seen in some quarters as a troubling vigilante organization.

4. Marcia Chambers, "Goetz Rejects Offers on Bail from a Stranger and Family," *New York Times*, January 5, 1985, L25. $50,000 is a remarkably small amount of money to ask for bail for a man who admits to having shot four men and fleeing the state. Recognizing this, and perhaps suspecting that the request was politically motivated by Goetz's popular support, Judge Leslie Snyder, who presided over Goetz's arraignment, said, "This is a low bail request by the people. I'm surprised. If Western Civilization has taught us anything, it is that we cannot tolerate individuals' taking law and justice into their own hands" (Marcia Chambers, "Goetz Held at Rikers I. in $50,000 Bail in Wounding of 4 Teen-Agers on IRT," *New York Times*, January 4, 1985, B1 +).

5. Suzanne Daley, "Suspect in IRT Shootings Agrees to Return to City to Face Charges," *New York Times*, January 3, 1985, A1 +.

6. "Gates, Guards, Guns and Goetz," editorial, *New York Times*, January 27, 1985, section 4, p. 20. The image of Goetz's public support was apparently not lost on Goetz. He announced his plans to run for mayor of New York City in the year 2001, saying that he would be a viable candidate. He advocated the death penalty for a criminal's first violent sexual offense; in addition, he sought vegetarian lunch options in public schools and a ban on circumcision in the city. "Questions for Bernard [*sic*] Goetz," *New York Times*, November 1, 1998, section 6, p. 25.

7. Jon Margolis, "Jumping the Gun on 'Hero' Goetz," *Chicago Tribune*, January 21, 1985, Perspective, p. 11. Margolis notes that "general approval is far from wholehearted support, much less unabashed hero-worship. The other half were either opposed or confused."

8. The exact poll results were that 45 percent approved of Goetz's actions, while slightly *more*, 46 percent, disapproved. Rubin goes on to argue that "the media fed the belief that the public was of one mind in the case [and that] this gave permission for the kind of unrestrained combination of rage and glee that was so commonly heard, while it also helped to mute the opposition voices" (146).

9. Mary McGrory, "The Vigilante Discomfits Officialdom," *Washington Post*, January 13, 1985, B1.

10. "Why Surrender on the Subway?" editorial, *New York Times*, January 4, 1985, A26.

11. "Gates, Guards, Guns and Goetz," editorial, *New York Times*, January 27, 1985, section 4, 20.

12. Mary McGrory, "The Vigilante Discomfits Officialdom," *Washington Post*, January 13, 1985, B1.

13. Alfonse D'Amato, letter, *New York Times*, February 9, 1985, A22.

14. There were no grounds for charging Goetz's victims; not even Goetz claims that they actually tried to mug him. (His claim of self-defense was based only on his fear and assumption that they *would* do this.) Nevertheless, district attorney Robert Morgenthau refused to grant any of Goetz's victims immunity before the first grand jury because of the possibility that they would be charged. Goetz's victims were thus unwilling to fully testify before the grand jury. This helps to explain the first grand jury's failure to indict Goetz for anything but illegal weapons possession. For a detailed discussion of the motivations for, and the effects of, Morgenthau's decision, see Rubin, 130–49.

15. Fletcher argues that the press focused on Goetz's victims' backgrounds immediately after the shooting because they needed stories and had no information

about Goetz himself (3–4). This claim may have some basis in fact, but it does not explain why the press continued to focus on the victims' criminal records after Goetz's identity was revealed, or why, as I discuss below, they continued to circulate false information about sharpened screwdrivers.

16. Rubin notes that Goetz's victims claimed that the screwdrivers were used for breaking into video-game machines. This is clearly not a legal use, but it is a far cry from intentionally carrying a deadly weapon.

17. See, for example, the claim that "one of the Goetz victims has now been convicted of rape; public passions about the case have been stirred once more," in "'A Reasonable Man' Named Goetz," editorial, *New York Times*, April 29, 1986, A26.

18. Rubin argues that, in general, Goetz's victims were dehumanized, while Goetz was rendered sympathetically early on: "Goetz becomes a many-faceted, complex human being; they are stereotypes. We know how tall he is, how slight his build, the color of his hair and eyes, what kind of glasses he wears, what clothes he prefers. All things that make him seem life-size, human. But the young men who were shot lie in their hospital beds, the reviled actors in this latest national morality play. We hear nothing about their physical characteristics, about the clothes they wear. . . . We have no idea whether one is better looking, more appealing than another; whether one is shy and another bold. . . . No one tells us, either, that they're all slight of build, more so than Bernie Goetz. . . . Without these facts, our imaginations are left to work overtime, as we picture four huge blacks menacing this one small, lone white man" (56).

19. Joyce Purnick, "Ward Declares Goetz Didn't Shoot in Self-Defense," *New York Times*, February 22, 1985. Ward is far from a civil rights zealot. Just weeks earlier, he took issue with a Bronx grand jury that indicted a police officer in the slaying of Eleanor Bumpurs—an elderly African American woman who was killed by a shotgun blast while the police were attempting to evict her from her apartment. The police claimed that the killing was an act of self-defense, since Bumpurs had lunged at the officer with a butcher's knife. This account is disputed by Bumpurs's daughter, who noted that Bumpurs's arthritis would have made it impossible for her to have acted this way. Bumpurs's daughter also argued that the family had not been given adequate information about the impending eviction. The case has since become one of the most widely recognized and discussed instances of racist police brutality in the nation.

20. Esther B. Fein, "Angry Citizens in Many Cities Supporting Goetz," *New York Times*, January 7, 1985, B1 +.

21. "The Goetz Verdict," editorial, *New York Times*, April 24, 1996, A20.

22. Adam Nossiter, "Race Is Dominant Theme as 2d Goetz Trial Begins," *New York Times*, April 12, 1996, B3. As the headline suggests, this article *does* suggest that race was relevant, but only in the second trial, where a predominately black jury found Goetz guilty.

23. "The Other Goetz Jury," editorial, *New York Times*, June 17, 1987, A30.

24. George P. Fletcher, "Justice for All, Twice," *New York Times*, April 24, 1996, A21 +.

25. John O'Connor, "Review/Television; Goetz Trial as Drama," *New York Times*, May 11, 1988, C26.

26. The attempt to construct "common sense" in such a way as to include the notion that there are valid reasons to fear young black men is, of course, nothing new. It goes back at least as far as lynching and stereotypes of black male bestiality and is an essential part of recent and current expansions of the criminal justice system and the growth of what Angela Y. Davis refers to as the "prison industrial

complex." Davis argues that "fear has always been an integral component of racism" and asks "whether and how the increasing fear of crime—this ideologically produced fear of crime—serves to render racism simultaneously more invisible and more virulent." Davis goes on to argue that the "figure of the 'criminal'—the racialized figure of the criminal—has come to represent the most menacing enemy of 'American society,'" and that "the prison is the perfect site for the simultaneous production and concealment of racism" (270–71).

27. "The Goetz Case in Black and White," editorial, *New York Times,* June 18, 1987, A30. Ironically, the assumption that there is a reasonable basis for fear of black men tends to surface most explicitly in articles, which are intended as correctives to racist stereotypes. For example, an article that opens with the claim that the "crude presumption—that blackness indicates criminality—haunts the trial of Bernard Goetz" goes on to note that "blacks commit robbery at a rate 10 times that of whites." The article notes that "the vast, innocent majority of blacks" suffer because of racist stereotypes, but ultimately reinforces the image of a racial divide where only whites are victims when it asks "who . . . is more disadvantaged, the innocent white subjected to crime and fear of crime, or the innocent black forced into humiliating inconvenience and heightened risk of violence from mistaken acts of self defense?" The idea that blacks might have reason to fear forms of violence that are not the result of a mistaken act of self-defense is noticeably absent here, as is the possibility that whites might, in fact, be criminals. "Fear of Blacks, Fear of Crime," editorial, *New York Times,* December 28, 1986, section 4, p. 10.

28. Sydney H. Schanberg, "The Bernhard Goetz Mailbag," *New York Times,* January 19, 1985, A21. The reference to "Hispanics" points to the fact that like blacks, Latinos are often stereotyped as criminals. As Katheryn Russell notes, "Latinos . . . are viewed as stealthy and criminal. They, however, are not perceived as posing the same kind of criminal threat as Blacks. Latinos, like Asians, tend to be viewed as involved in intraracial crimes" (xiv). Coverage of William Master's actions in California often referenced the Goetz case. Masters, a white man, confronted two young Latino men who were writing graffiti beneath a highway overpass in Los Angeles. He argued with them, then shot them. He killed 18-year-old Cesar Arce and claimed that he was acting in self-defense because his victims had threatened him with a screwdriver and threatened to rob him. The police accepted the claim of self-defense and initially refused to prosecute. Eventually, Masters, like Goetz, was convicted of weapons charges. He served a total of four days in jail and was sentenced to community service and three years of probation. His surviving victim, meanwhile, was sentenced to twenty days in jail, sixty days of graffiti removal, and three years' probation for trespassing (Efrain Hernandez Jr., "A Valley Man Who Killed Tagger Gets Probation," *Los Angeles Times,* November 9, 1998, A1). Also see Seth Mydans, "A Shooter as Vigilante, and Avenging Angel," *New York Times,* February 10, 1995, A20. That article notes that Masters was compared with Goetz, and with the main character in the film *Falling Down* (1993), which it describes as a film about "a frustrated man [who] rampages through Los Angeles exacting vigilante justice." The article does not note that other than a Nazi storekeeper and his own wife, the main character, D-Fens, directed his vigilante violence against a host of racial stereotypes. Most important for the current discussion, D-Fens is menaced by Latino gang members. When he gets his revenge by shooting one of them, the scene is played for laughs.

29. Goetz sued William Kunstler and his publishers, Carol Communications Inc., because Kunstler had claimed in his autobiography, *My Life as a Radical Lawyer* (1994), that Goetz was, among other things, a racist. The suit was dismissed because Kunstler's book was seen as clearly stating an opinion, rather than a matter

of fact, and because Goetz was a public figure. The court noted, though, that "defendants submit evidence that before the shooting, Goetz stated 'the only way we're going to clean up this street is to get rid of the spics and niggers.'" The court found this statement significant because "in New York, truth is a complete defense to an action for defamation, regardless of the harm done by the statements." In other words, Goetz couldn't sue for being called a racist if he was in fact a racist. *Goetz v. Kunstler et al.*, 164 Misc. 2d 557; 625 NYS 2d 447; 1995 NY.

30. "... You Have to Think in a Cold-Blooded Way," *New York Times*, April 30, 1987, B6.

31. This statement was ruled inadmissible in Goetz's criminal trial. Fletcher defends this decision by arguing that "if this expression of prejudice was relevant at all, it was to demonstrate racial hostility as a motive for the shooting. Allowing the prosecution to bring in evidence of Goetz's racial bias would have invited the defense to produce witness after witness to testify that Goetz had a sound attitude toward blacks. The trial would have turned into a farcical battle between character witnesses for and against the subway gunman" (204). Perhaps, but it would certainly have been possible to impose limits on the number of character witnesses each side could bring forward. In any event, the attempt to proceed as though race was simply irrelevant is at odds with nonverbal reliance on race in the courtroom that I mention below, as well as with the ways in which people throughout the city and country understood the case.

32. David E. Pitt, "Blacks See Goetz Verdict as Blow to Race Relations," *New York Times*, June 18, 1987, A1+.

33. *People v. Goetz*, 116 AD2d 316. NY 1986.

34. "If You Were Bernhard Goetz...," editorial, *New York Times*, June 9, 1986, A26.

35. *People v. Goetz*, 116 AD2d 316. NY 1986.

36. Russell claims that there are "at least four related, though distinct, components" of white fear of blacks. These include "the fear of crime, the fear of losing jobs, the fear of cultural demise, and the fear of black revolt" (125). Russell argues that "while it may be commonplace for Whites to fear Blacks, it is not necessarily reasonable," and notes that a great deal of white fear is based on sensationalistic media stories, rather than a realistic evaluation of the evidence about black crime (127). Although I agree that white fear is not *justified* by the statistics on black crime (or on job loss, cultural demise, etc.), I would argue that there is a clear rationale for racist fears that is based, as Russell notes, not on the facts, but on an understanding and acceptance of prevalent representations of black men. Thus, when I claim that racist fears are reasonable, I mean only that there is a systematically expressed logic behind them. This is a very different sense of "reason" than James Q. Wilson had in mind when he claimed that black crime is responsible for white racism. It is this sense of the term that Russell is responding to in her critique.

37. This association is powerfully borne out not only in the media, but also in the criminal justice system. As David Cole notes, "The per capita incarceration rate among blacks is seven times that among whites. African Americans make up about 12 percent of the general population, but more than half of the prison population. They serve longer sentences, have higher arrest and conviction rates, face higher bail amounts, and are more often the victims of police use of deadly force than white citizens. In 1995, one in three young black men between the ages of twenty and twenty-nine was imprisoned or on parole or probation. If incarceration rates continue their current trends, one in four young black males born today will serve time in prison during his lifetime (meaning that he will be convicted and sentenced to more than one year of incarceration). Nationally, for every one black man who

graduates from college, 100 are arrested" (4). There are a number of explanations for these statistics, including the economic devastation facing many minority neighborhoods due to deindustrialization, unemployment, and discrimination in housing, education, and hiring (see Lipsitz, 10). Added to this is a variety of systematic racial disparities within the criminal justice system itself, including, among many other things, the fact that "a predominantly white Congress has mandated prison sentences for the possession and distribution of crack cocaine one hundred times more severe than the penalties for powder cocaine. African Americans comprise more than 90 percent of those found guilty of crack cocaine crimes, but only 20 percent of those found guilty of powder cocaine crimes" (Cole, 8), and a variety of forms of what has become known as racial profiling. As Cole notes, "'Consent' searches, pretextual traffic stops, and 'quality of life' policing are all disproportionately used against black citizens" (8).

38. For an in-depth discussion of the ways in which the judicial system has legitimated racially based standards of suspicion, see Kennedy, 136–67. See also Cole, 16–62.

REFERENCES

Chambers, Marcia. "Goetz Rejects Offers on Bail from a Stranger and Family." *New York Times,* January 5, 1985, L25.

Cole, David. *No Equal Justice: Race and Class in the American Criminal Justice System.* New York: Free Press, 1999.

Davis, Angela Y. "Race and Criminalization: Black Americans and the Punishment Industry." In *The House that Race Built,* edited by Wahneema Lubiano, 264–79. New York: Vintage Books, 1998.

Fletcher, George P. *A Crime of Self-Defense: Bernhard Goetz and the Law on Trial.* New York: Free Press, 1988.

Harris, Cheryl I. "Whiteness as Property." In *Critical Race Theory: The Key Writings that Formed the Movement,* edited by Kimberly Crenshaw, Neil Gotanda, Gary Peller, and Kendall Thomas, 276–91. New York: New Press, 1999.

Kennedy, Randall. *Race, Crime, and the Law.* New York: Vintage Books, 1997.

Lipsitz, George. *The Possessive Investment in Whiteness: How White People Profit from Identity Politics.* Philadelphia: Temple University Press, 1998.

Roehrenbeck, Carol A., ed. *People vs. Goetz: The Summations and the Charges to the Jury.* Buffalo, N.Y.: William S. Hein, 1989.

Rubin, Lillian B. *Quiet Rage: Bernie Goetz in a Time of Madness.* New York: Farrar, Straus and Giroux, 1986.

Russell, Katheryn K. *The Color of Crime: Racial Hoaxes, White Fear, Black Protectionism, Police Harassment, and Other Macroaggressions.* New York: New York University Press, 1998.

Chapter 12
Pierced Tongues
Language and Violence in Carmen Boullosa's Dystopia

MARGARITA SAONA

CORDELIA. Unhappy that I am, I cannot
heave my heart into my mouth.
—William Shakespeare, *King Lear,* 1.1

An ancient Nahua ceremony is described in Carmen Boullosa's novel *Cielos de la Tierra*: young men have their tongues pierced with thorns by their fathers in a penitence ritual. One of the narrators of the novel, Hernando, a Nahua Indian educated by the Franciscan friars in the Colegio de la Santa Cruz de Santiago de Tlatelolco, recalls this with mixed feelings: his father disappeared during the Spanish invasion, and he never experienced the pain of having his tongue pierced. His father's absence allowed for the integrity of his tongue, but that absence also meant that he would never be able to occupy the social position his lineage deserved in Nahua society.

Cielos de la Tierra was published in México City in 1997, between the celebration of the five-hundred-year anniversary of the discovery of the New World—which was considered by many Mexicans the celebration of a genocide—and the end of the millennium. An apocalyptic tone dominates a novel that, according to the author, grew out of violence. The image of the tongue piercing condenses the problem I want to explore: the relationship the novel establishes between language, violence, and the entire American continent as utopia.

Hernando's text is part of a complex narrative structure. It is framed by two other narrations. Hernando's memories are translated from Latin into Spanish by a twentieth-century Mexican historian named Estela, who offers her own memories along with the translation. However, the text the reader receives has yet another intermediary: Lear, a woman from a future post-apocalyptic world called L'Atlàntide, who is transcribing Estela's and Hernando's stories into a new system for the preservation of texts. In the three stories, the dream of a perfect society manifests itself through "language reforms." The Tlatelolco School tries to integrate young Indians from prominent families into the colonial apparatus through the teaching of

Latin; the hope for a continental revolution in Latin American twentieth century was supposedly embodied by a literary Boom; and the Brave New World of L'Atlàntide portends to supersede the limitations of language through new forms of communication. Perfect societies, however, often go awry, and social projects sometimes end up oppressing the people they were supposed to liberate. The utopian imaginary realms of Tlatelolco, the Latin American revolution, and L'Atlàntide turn into dystopic symbolic orders whose violence will be inscribed in the real, in the body.

In Carmen Boullosa's narration, the Nahua tongue piercing could be easily read in Lacanian terms as the bodily inscription of the Law of the Father (Lacan, *Écrits*). According to Lacan, it is the Name of the Father, the name that is also a *"non,"* the primordial prohibition of incest and the threat of castration, which marks the entry of the child in the symbolic order. The child is forced to abandon the imaginary realm of his union with the mother to enter, simultaneously, language and the law. It is in this process that, according to Lacan, subjectivity is constructed. When Hernando recalls that the absence of his father not only spared him the pain of the thorns in his tongue but also allowed him to remain at his mother's bedside longer than any other boy, it is impossible not to make a connection between the real mutilation of the tongue and the symbolic threat of castration. With his tongue intact, Hernando was able to enjoy the closeness of his mother. However, this privilege had to be paid for. The loss of his father was accompanied by the disruption of the whole social order. Without a father, Hernando could have never taken his place among the Nahua *"principales."* And this was not only his case, but also his generation's:

> Pero si el [oficio] del padre había sido ser juez, gobernador, recabador de impuestos, sacerdote y maestro, guerrero, o propietario de grandes extensiones de tierra, que me digan qué oficio podían enseñar a sus hijos, si los jueces no eran ya jueces, ni los gobernadores los que gobernaban, ni los alcabaleros, los alcabaleros, ni los terratenientes los terratenientes, ni los sacerdotes los sacerdotes, si los que fueron dioses son ahora demonios, si todo quedó de cabeza. (122)

> But if the father's [trade] was justice, governor, tax collector, priest and teacher, soldier, or landowner, just tell me what kind of trade could these men teach their sons, if the justices were not justices anymore, and the governor did not govern, and the tax collectors were not tax collectors, or the landowners, landowners, or the priests, priests, if the gods are devils now, if everything is upside down.[1]

The violence of the Spanish invasion mutilated the same social order the mutilation of his tongue was going to reinforce. In my reading of Boullosa's account of the tongue piercing, it symbolizes the entrance of the boys into the social order through the use of language, even if that relationship was not immediate in the real practices. There are several accounts of the importance of speech in the socialization processes of Nahua society. In the *Florentine Codex,* compiled by Bernardino de Sahagún, we find that "They took great care that their son should converse fittingly with others, that his conversation should be proper" (VIII, 20) and that the fathers will be concerned with their sons' speech manners: "You are to speak very slowly, very deliberately; you are not to speak hurriedly, not to pant, not to squeak, lest it be said of you that you are a groaner, a growler, a squeaker" (VI, 22). *The Book of Chilam Balam of Chumayel* tells that among the Mayas, the chiefs of the towns would have the tips of their tongues cut off if they lacked understanding (91). The use of language and the symbolism of the tongue supported a whole social system among indigenous cultures. Hernando was spared the pain of the tongue piercing, but he will have to pay for this by experiencing the destruction of the structure that was supposed to provide him with social articulation. As an old man, Hernando feels ashamed that he once rejoiced in the integrity of his tongue:

> Estas pajillas fueron por mí tan temidas desde mi más tierna infancia, que, lo confieso (aunque grato no sea) más de una vez no lamenté la ausencia de mi padre ni la caída de los míos, sino que me felicité por ellas, cambiando así, con infantil ceguera, un reino y un padre por la ausencia de unas pequeñas pajillas cruzando mi lengua abierta. (195)

> I have been so afraid of these little twigs since my earliest childhood, that I confess (even if it is not pleasant) not only did I not regret my father's absence nor the fall of my people, but I even celebrated the loss of them, trading, with a childish blindness, a kingdom and a father for the absence of tiny twigs crossing my open tongue.

Saved from the symbolic castration at his father's hands, Hernando experiences other forms of violence, which also disrupted the bliss of the imaginary union with his mother:

> De mis primeros años, no puedo cantar los armónicos arrullos. Rorro, a la meme, riquirranes, no puedo, tintón, dame dame, dulce bien, no porque no los hubiera para mí, que mamá siempre estuvo presta para darme mimos, sino porque su bisbiseo queda enterrado por la cruel melodía que se apoderó entonces de estas tierras. Violación de asilo, cruces enlutadas por las calles, tormentos, lenguas zumbando en desmedido, ahorcamientos y descuartizamientos a mano de la justicia, lluvias de piedras sobre los respetables y sus mujeres y sus hijos, pues cuando salió Cortés se desencadenaron peleas a muerte sobre los beneficios reales y los imaginarios de estas tierras, y los indios bailamos al son de la violencia sembrada por sus pugnas. (97)

> From my first years I cannot sing the harmonic lullabies. Hush little baby, I cannot, rock a bye baby in the tree top, not because there were not any for

me, since mom was always ready to pamper me, but because its whispers remain buried by the cruel melody that overtook these lands then. Violation of asylum, mourning crosses in the streets, torments, tongues buzzing without measure, hangings and quarterings by the law, stone showers over the respectable men and their wives and children, because when Cortés left, a deadly fight broke out over the real and imaginary benefits of these lands, and we, the Indians, dance to the sound of the violence planted by their struggles.

The real and imaginary wealth of the American continent will result in the most nightmarish violence: the quest for utopia is transformed into a quest for dystopia. And the blissful utopian union between Hernando and his mother is also disrupted. Eventually, Hernando will experience the separation from his mother as castration when the Franciscan friars take him away from her to the Colegio de la Santa Cruz de Santiago de Tlatelolco. The deep sense of alienation experienced by the boy when he is cut off from his mother, his town, and his culture is turned into a metaphor of castration: "el día que me llevaron a Tlatelolco, a mí me mocharon las manos. Me las amputaron. Me las separaron del cuerpo. Quedé sin con qué rascarme la cabeza, sin con qué llevarme comida a la boca, inválido, incompleto" (143; "The day they took me to Tlatelolco, they cut off my hands. They amputated my hands. They separated them from my body. I was left with no way to scratch my head, without anything to take food into my mouth, invalid, incomplete"). The violence Hernando experienced as castration is no longer the violence of the wars of conquest, but a form of cultural violence. The Spanish institutions and the Church in particular take the place of the father and it is henceforth their laws that separate Hernando from his mother.

However, as with the Name of the Father, language is able to provide Hernando with a new subjectivity. The signifier of the tongue, which was once the site of castration, becomes at the same time the bodily organ and language, and presents itself as the possibility of rearticulation:

A falta de manos, toqué y aprendí a palpar y reconocer con la lengua. Con ella sentí y soñé el contacto con las cosas . . . y aprendí a sobrevivir con algo que me atreveré a llamar alegría, pues en la lengua aprendí también la inconciencia y el arropo, el refugio de la imaginación y la memoria. (143)

Lacking hands, I touched and learned to palpate and recognize with the tongue. With it I felt and dreamed the contact with things . . . and I learned how to survive with something I will dare to call happiness, because in the tongue I learned also unconsciousness and cuddling, the shelter for imagination and memory.

It is in the formal learning of Spanish and Latin that Hernando not only constitutes himself as a subject, but also recovers forms of pleasure he thought he had lost forever when he lost his mother. The study of grammar, of Spanish and Latin, in a way represents the structure of the law, and all the rules Hernando has to obey in the Colegio. However, they also seem to incarnate a new sensibility, a form of touch, which allows him to get in contact with the world.

In what follows, I explore the ambivalent relationship between body, language, and violence in *Cielos de la Tierra*. As the case of Hernando makes clear, Boullosa imagines violence as inscribed in the body through language, through the establishment of the law. But on the other hand, her novel assumes that no-body exists in the absence of language, which is posited as a whole universe for the subject and as such can contain the dialectical reverse of violence as well. Language represents the embodiment of the law, and of violence, but also the embodiment of pleasure. The physical and cultural violence of the Spanish Conquest of the New World disrupted an order, which had its own forms of violence (the tongue piercing is just one of the examples of physical punishment in the Nahua laws described throughout the novel). For Hernando, the sweetness of his mother tongue is reenacted in the pleasure he encounters in the learning of Latin.

In *After Exile: Writing the Latin American Diaspora*, Amy Kaminsky has argued in favor of the "embodied production of language" in an attempt to remove our notions of language from the associations with the masculine realm of the "Law of the Father" (59). She insists on the materiality of language, the fact that it is produced and perceived by the body, in order to recuperate the place of the mother in the production of language.[2] The sensual aspects of language have also been claimed by other feminists, such as Hélène Cixous in "The Laugh of the Medusa," as a way of contesting the patriarchal control of language. This, however, is itself problematic because it reinforces the association between the body and the feminine. What I read in *Cielos de la Tierra* is a use of language that would allow for the construction of complex subjectivities, male or female. While language inscribes violence, pain, and the prohibition of the law in the body, it is also a source of comfort and pleasure.

Boullosa's novel opens with two epigraphs. The first one, by Bernardo de Balbuena, reads, "Indias del mundo, cielos de la tierra" ("Indies of the world, heaven on earth") and evokes the idea of the American continent as the embodiment of utopia. The second one is a quotation from Alvaro Mutis, who is referred to throughout the novel as "a poet's poet": "Me pregunto cómo has hecho para vencer el cotidiano uso del tiempo y de la muerte" ("I wonder what you did to defeat the everyday use of time and death"). In these lines, poetry is the place of utopia, the only place where we can survive the ultimate violence. From the start, Carmen Boullosa confronts the topic of the New World as utopia with the utopia of language. The American continent, where More and others wanted to place Utopia, bears the signs of violence: it is not heaven on earth, and was not even before the violent Spanish invasion. And language is also a form of violence, a pierced tongue that forces us to conform to the law. However, it may offer the only way to "defeat the everyday use of time and death."

Dystopic narratives describe the corruption of a society once conceived as ideal. The most common examples of dystopia are George Orwell's *1984* and Aldous Huxley's *Brave New World*. A society that aspired to perfection turns out to be perfect only for the elite and becomes authoritarian. The principles that are meant to achieve the social good become forms of power that exert violence over people. For critics such as Leszek Kolakowski, utopia always leads to a form of totalitarian coercion: the search for perfection necessarily constraints diversity, and conflicts among individuals are part of human experience. In his view, utopia is always doomed because it implies the imposition of a worldview that not everybody will be able to share, and those who refuse to conform end up being forced into accepting it or becoming outcasts. For other critics, such as Krishan Kumar in *Utopia and Anti-Utopia*, contemporary antiutopia is related to the history of the twentieth century: in the past, utopia relied on its faith that reason and the progress of science would achieve a perfect society. However, in the last century, this trust has been confronted with world wars, massive unemployment, fascism, Stalinism, the nuclear threat, and the devastation of natural resources. For dystopian writers, reason and progress result in social illnesses that are worse than those they were supposed to cure. In *Cielos de la Tierra*, utopias collapse both because of specific historical factors (racism, colonial heritage, caste alliances, difference between rich and poor) and because of structures that seem to be part of any human society (the limitations of language, for example).

In Hernando's narration, the Colegio de la Santa Cruz de Santiago de Tlatelolco becomes paradise. The study of grammar presents itself as a nonviolent form of conquest:

> Ay, aquello fue el paraíso terrenal, y se perdió tan pronto . . . ! No volveré a decir lo que es verdad, que se abrió para nosotros un otro mundo. Sin herir ni llevar espada, sin arrebatar a nadie lo propio ni violentar ni sembrar la muerte, éramos nosotros, los alumnos del Colegio de la Santa Cruz de Tlatelolco, los conquistadores indios que viajaban por nuevas tierras. Ni diré lo que es cierto, que aprendimos gramática. (177)

> Oh, that was earthly paradise, and it got lost so soon . . . ! I will not say what is true, that another world opened up for us. Without hurting anyone or carrying spades, without snatching things from others, or forcing or planting death, it was we, the students of the Colegio de la Santa Cruz de Tlatelolco, the Indian conquerors traveling through new lands. Nor will I say what is true, that we learned grammar.

The pursuit of knowledge through the study of language is contrasted with the quest for land and power. When the rhetoric of the conquest is imposed upon the idea of knowledge and language, it is immediately linked to "the violence of the letter" and to the notion of "phallogocentrism."[3] However, in Hernando's case, the use of language becomes on the one hand, a source of pleasure associated with the maternal ("la inconsciencia y el arropo"), and on the other a strategy of self-defense from a subaltern position. When he is insulted because of his race or origin, he appeals to his linguistic abilities to demonstrate his superiority: "Yo no pude reprimir decir, en latín: 'Nosotros primero que nada, según es sabia costumbre, tenemos lo que usted no tiene para nosotros: un saludo'" (294; "I could not help but say in Latin: First of all, according to wise customs, we have what you don't have for us, a greeting"). Hernando defends his subject position demonstrating his proficiency; however, his subjectivity is also constructed in a different use of language, where language is associated with a sensorial nature ("aprendí a palpar y reconocer con la lengua. Con ella sentí y soñé el contacto con las cosas. En ella sentí a las hojas de los árboles y al viento que las frota" [144]; "I learned to palpate and recognize with the tongue. With it I felt and dreamed the contact with things. Through it I felt the leaves from the trees and the wind that rubs them").

The fact that Hernando compares the Colegio de la Santa Cruz de Santiago de Tlatelolco with utopia is not an apology for the Spanish conquest. The violence of the conquest and the racism of the society it produced are condemned throughout the novel. However, the Colegio de la Santa Cruz de Santiago de Tlatelolco, as projected by Bernardino de Sahagún in 1536, is regarded in *Cielos de la Tierra* as the privileged space where the coexistence of Nahuatl, Spanish, and Latin could have created a communicative bridge between two cultures. In *The Conquest of America: The Question of the Other,* Tzvetan Todorov has explained the defeat of the Aztecs in hands of the Spaniards in terms of a superiority "in the realm of interhuman communication" (97). His analysis has lately been contested: it was not only a matter of communication, but of war strategies and internal conflicts, like the one among Tlaxcalans and Mexicans (Clendinnen). Yet some of Todorov's observations about the importance of the power of language among the Aztecs, as well as his appreciation for Sahagún's project, seem pertinent at this point.

Todorov reminds us that "the association of power and language mastery is clearly marked among the Aztecs. The ruler himself is called *tlatoani,* which means, literally, 'he who possesses speech'" (79). And that is the main reason why Montezuma's refusal to engage in a linguistic exchange constituted an "admission of failure." The Aztec sovereign was supposed to be "above all a master of speech" (71). This was, nonetheless, a form of speech rooted in repetition, ritual, and a cult of the past, which was supposed to provide interpretations for the future. Confronted with the new reality of the Conquest, with people from a completely different world, their favoring of "conformity-to-order over efficacy-of-the moment" proved to be ineffectual: "Indeed, most of the Indians' communications to the Spaniards are notable for their ineffectiveness. In order to convince his visitors to leave the country, Montezuma sends gold each time: but nothing is more likely to persuade them to remain" (87). In Todorov's view, a form of communication triumphs over the other, but "this victory from which we all derive, Europeans and Americans both, delivers as well a terrible blow to our capacity to feel in harmony with the world" (97).

Fifteen years after the defeat of Tenochtitlan in 1521, the Franciscan seminary of Tlatelolco was founded. Todorov seems to share with Boullosa's Hernando the fascination for Sahagún's project:[4]

> We may muse upon this rapid development of minds: toward 1540, scarcely twenty years after the siege of México City by Cortés, the Mexican noblemen's sons are composing heroic verses in Latin! What is also remarkable is that the instruction is reciprocal: at the same time that he introduces the young Mexicans into the subtleties of Latin grammar, Sahagún himself takes advantage of this contact to perfect his knowledge of Nahuatl language and culture. (220)

After the violence of the Conquest and the imposition of one form of communication over the other, Todorov sees in Sahagún's seminary the utopian project of translation: two cultures working together to understand each other. However, this project failed because of the violent structure of domination incarnated in the colonial apparatus:

> The rapid advances of Mexican students provoke as much hostility in the surrounding society as the monks' interest in the other's culture. . . . Language has always been the companion of empire; the Spaniards fear that in losing supremacy over the former realm, they may lose it over the latter as well. (220–21)

The explicit violence of racism and discrimination, together with the inner contradictions of the colonial institutions, are recognized as the main causes for the collapse of this utopia in Boullosa's novel:

> en México había un escándalo, porque fray Mateo y Diego López y su hermano, Sancho López, secretario de la Real Audiencia, andaban diciendo que estaba muy mal que el latín nos enseñasen, que a los indios esto les podía muy mal, que hereticaríamos, que hacíamos mal uso de todo. (304)

> in México there was a scandal, because brother Mateo and Diego López and his brother, Sancho López, secretary of the Real High Court, were saying that it was wrong that they taught us Latin, that it was wrong for the Indians, that we would commit heresy, that we had a wrong use for everything.

But even if the racism of colonial institutions is going to destroy the dream, Hernando's association of the Colegio with his love for words transforms

this space into a privileged one, almost as special as the imaginary identification with his mother. Far from the concept of language as inherently
violent, word and thought not only provide subjective articulation: they
also evoke the paradise lost after the separation from the mother. For Hernando, language can incarnate the need for submission: it is the Name of
the Father, the threat of castration of the tongue piercing. But language
not only offers the possibility of articulating the self in response to the
violent discourse of the other; it also evokes the memory of the words Hernando imagines as a "mother tongue," and it is his last refuge when he
writes his memories in his old age, when all the colonial institutions are
collapsing around him.

Estela is Hernando's "tongue," to use a term frequent in colonial texts.
She is his interpreter and translator, the author of the Spanish text Lear is
going to find in a distant future. Estela is aware of the complexities of her
role as "tongue," *traduttore traditore,* and she confesses the violence she
performed on Hernando's text: "Yo lo he obligado a vivir pasajes que él de
ninguna manera habría articulado en sus palabras" (145; "I have forced
him to live passages that he would not have articulated in his words after
all"). Estela uses words to articulate experiences Hernando could not express. But for her, the text is also a refuge. To read Hernando's text and to
translate it is for Estela a retreat from the violence she experiences in everyday life: "La violencia, Hernando, se ha deslizado hasta formar parte de
una cotidianeidad que no pertenece ya a los tabloides y las páginas de los
periodiquillos sanguinolentos, sino que es ingrediente de la charla más
inmediata" (146; "Violence, Hernando, has slid down until it has become
a part of an everyday life that does not belong only to tabloids and to the
pages of little bloody newspapers anymore, but is the ingredient of the
most immediate chat"). Estela's depiction of the present is apocalyptic
(and it is filled with references to actual events in recent Mexican history:
for example, there is a specific reference to a scandal that surrounded Raúl
Salinas de Gortari, brother of the ex-president). She writes about the crime
on the streets, but also of crimes and corruption in the government: "La
violencia ejercida por bandas organizadas . . . o la violencia 'espontánea'
de muertos de hambre y desempleados, pero me temo que esta segunda
es muchísimo menor" (147; "The violence performed by organized gangs
. . . or the 'spontaneous' violence of the hungry and the unemployed, but
I fear the latter is the lesser").

When Estela explains her interest in Hernando's text, she writes about
sexual and racial discrimination in her own family and says,

> Porque soy mexicana y vivo como vivimos los mexicanos, respetuosa de un
> juego de castas azaroso e inflexible, a pesar de nuestra mencionadísima
> Revolución y de Benito Juárez y de la demagogia alabando nuestros ances-
> tros indios. Y porque, creo, nuestra historia habría sido distinta si el Colegio

de la Santa Cruz de Santiago Tlatelolco no hubiera corrido la triste suerte que tuvo. (64–65)

Because I am Mexican, and I live as we Mexicans live, respecting a random and inflexible game of castes, in spite of our well-known Revolution and of Benito Juarez and the demagogy that praises our Indian ancestors. And because I believe that our history would have been different if the Colegio de la Santa Cruz de Santiago de Tlatelolco had not had the sad fate it had.

She writes about a history of violence and discrimination in which she herself participated, even if only as a witness. For Estela, the dream of utopia was embodied by the aftermath of the Cuban Revolution during the 1960s and 1970s, and on the way the hope for a new world manifested itself in the literary Latin American Boom. However, she believes both the Revolution and the Boom failed because they could not really break with their colonial roots. In her analysis of *One Hundred Years of Solitude,* for instance, she observes how the arcadia dreamed by García Márquez excluded the Indian population. Historical violence is reenacted in the narrative, and Estela herself feels guilty because she too feels powerless to change these violent structures: "No soñé, ni yo, ni mi generación, con un sueño que borrara la estructura suicida de nuestro pasado colonial" (204–5; "I did not dream, neither I nor my generation, a dream that would erase the suicidal structure of our colonial past"). In the moment she writes, surrounded by a world that has become violent without measure, she tries to vindicate herself by resurrecting Hernando's words, even if only for herself: "Sigo con mi traducción de Hernando, y a lo que más me atrevo es a reparar lo que es ilegible en el original, y a mentir un poco aquí y otro poco allá, para hacer más posible su historia" (205; "I continue with my translation of Hernando, and I only dare to repair what is unreadable in the original and to lie a little here and a little there, to make his story plausible"). She is concerned with the text of this Indian who at some point dreamed about participating in the intellectual life of colonial society and whose dreams were shut down by discrimination, envy, and political intrigues: in Hernando's words (or, rather, Lear's version of Estela's translation of Hernando's text),

El mío devino en falso sueño, porque cuando los Colegios se incorporaron a la Universidad, al de la Santa Cruz no le fueron abiertas sus puertas. Nadie podría dudar de que éramos los mejores y más aventajados, pero eso de ser indios . . . La Universidad no aceptó al Colegio de los Indios, aunque fueran nobles. . . . a los españoles . . . no les agrada que los indios tengan alguna ventaja sobre ellos. (220)

Mine became a false dream, because when the schools were incorporated into the University, it did not open its doors to the school of Santa Cruz. Nobody could doubt that we were the best and the more advantaged, but the thing about being Indians . . . the University did not accept the School of the Indians, even if they were part of the nobility. . . . Spaniards . . . do not like that Indians would have any advantage over them.

However, in translating the text, Estela is also betraying Hernando by retouching it and "to lie a little here and a little there, to make his story plausible." Is there translation without violence? Is the subaltern story possible? And can language signify without violence?

In Lear's world, this last question will lead to the abolition of language as such. In the postapocalyptic society of L'Atlàntide, Lear is translating Estela's text with her version of Hernando's memoirs into a system of word conservation that remains unexplained. At the same time, Lear is writing a testimony of her time, precisely when a language reform is being implemented: the use of language is being restricted to certain spaces and certain circumstances and will be eventually banned from L'Atlàntide.

Lear starts by explaining that she is the only one who uses names in L'Atlàntide. The others use only codes to refer to themselves. Lear not only uses names for herself and others; she changes those names as she pleases, defying the very meaning of naming. In this case, the Law is not created by the Name. Lear's names resist the Law. Lear falls into contradictions: "El problema es que yo tengo que escapar a los nombres . . . ni modo, . . . reconozco que es risible cambiar de nombre. . . . Pero aunque indefendible, es algo que no puedo evitar" (113; "The problem is that I have to escape names . . . no way . . . I recognize that it is laughable to change names. . . . But even if it is indefensible I cannot help it"). Nevertheless, contradiction is probably unavoidable because language is the only medium one can use to forbid language.

The use of the name "Lear" for a female character is disconcerting at the beginning. However, when the reader learns that she used to call herself Cordelia before she decided to use the name "Lear," the reference to Shakespeare's *King Lear* is unavoidable. Boullosa's Lear is at the same time the father—the king who ruined his kingdom by overturning family laws and dividing his lands before his death—and the daughter who was rejected by her father because she refused to use grandiose words, exaggerating her true feelings, as her sisters did. Shakespeare's Lear wants to know: he needs his daughters' love to be articulated in words. Cordelia knows that is not possible. The Name of the Father is only the mirror image of the lost object. LeaR is only the reflection of the unreachable ReaL. There is no way of knowing the real object. Cordelia's distrust for language made her too cautious and led her to disgrace. Boullosa's Lear/Cordelia knows about the deficiencies of language, but she also knows that avoiding words might prove more dangerous. The Name of the Father cannot articulate the order that will fix the subject's identity because the very notion of "name" is being put into question.

L'Atlàntide used to be paradise: "En la última comunidad de hombres y mujeres, todos fueron iguales, nadie hizo menos al otro por razón de raza, sexo o apariencia. Nadie fue rico ni pobre, poderoso o esclavo. Se vivió en armonía, se venció la enfermedad, la vejez y la muerte" (362; "In the last community of men and women everybody was equal. Nobody made less of another because of race, sex or appearance. Nobody was rich or poor, powerful or slave. They lived in harmony; they defeated illness, old age and death"). However, as in Shakespeare's Lear, the incapacity to tolerate language's deficiencies turns the kingdom into a nightmarish world. Boullosa's Lear is the only one in her community who opposes the language reform, because she knows that any form of communication will have problems:

> El lenguaje fue manco también lo acepto ("la palabra ya, en sí, es un engaño, una trampa que encubre, disfraza y sepulta el edificio de nuestros sueños y verdades, todos señalados por el signo de lo incomunicable," escribió mi poeta), pero tenía el poder de invocar la memoria de los tiempos y las imaginaciones, y lo que fue, por la ley arbitraria de la realidad, imposible. (19–20)

> Language was maimed too. I accept that ("word is already deceit, a trap that covers, disguises, and buries the building of our dreams and truths, all of them marked by the sign of the incommunicable," my poet wrote), but it had the power to invoke the memory of time and imagination, and of what was, because of the arbitrary laws of reality, impossible.

Language is maimed, just like Hernando after being separated from his mother. But as Hernando had already discovered, language itself may provide for a substitution of the lack. In Lear's words, we understand that even if language cannot stand for the Real, it goes beyond the Law.

Initially, Lear defends language as a tool for communication. Her friend Rosete is obviously sad when he announces that his role as the messenger of the community will end, since there will be no more words to transmit. Lear tries to ask him about his sadness, and they end up having an argument. Rosete refuses to comment on his feelings, saying that words are always confusing, and Lear should not ask. Lear says there is no way to understand his feelings if he doesn't explain them. The argument itself is a demonstration of the equivocal nature of language: Lear's efforts to comfort Rosete irritate him, but it is also obvious that words are meaningful to him and that he is trying to silence what he has to say. The discussion is interrupted and repressed by an alarm that detected a vain argument and noise (90–95).

When the language reform starts to involve more drastic measures, Lear realizes that language was more than the possibility of conversation: that the universe itself, and even existence, dissolves in the absence of words. The prohibition of language becomes castration: the inhabitants of L'Atlàntide willingly submit their brains to a surgical procedure that will affect their speech faculties. Lear, who refuses to abandon language, describes in horror how the very existence of the material world collapses when there is nobody who can articulate it in words. The bodies of the former members of her community lose form and become unspeakable objects once their linguistic capacities are excised.

Lear finds the first signs of physical decay in Rosete's mouth. Since the operation, he stopped taking measures against radiation, and Lear discovers that his mouth is full of sores (290). Rosete's wounded mouth responds to an inscription of the Law that differs radically from the Nahua piercing of the tongue: in the Nahua practice, an order was supposedly reinforced. In L'Atlàntide, the prohibition of the Law cancels itself out: the only way to establish a prohibition of language is through language itself. What cannot be expressed in the Symbolic takes its effect on the Real.

Lear, the only one who resisted the language reform, witnesses the corruption of her world. Reality has ceased to be intelligible:

> Para nada hay un hilo conductor. Las cosas suceden, pero no quedan, no se fijan, no permanecen. No son completamente reales. . . . Entre los hoyos que se han ido formando en la superficie de la realidad, de la realidad de todos los miembros de mi comunidad, se ha colado toda posibilidad de interrelación. . . . La malla tensa de la realidad de que gozaron los hombres de la historia, y sobre la que emprendieron diálogos y malentendidos, así como acciones y hechos, se ha roto, se ha abierto. . . . Su reforma del lenguaje, la insistencia en el olvido, nos ha borrado. (322)

> There is not a conducting thread at all. Things happen, but they do not remain, they do not fix, do not stay. They are not completely real. . . . Between the wholes that have appeared on the surface of reality, the reality of all the members of my community, any possibility of interrelationship has slipped. . . . The tense net of reality enjoyed by the men of history, the net on which they started dialogues and misunderstandings, as well as actions and facts, is now broken, open. . . . Their language reform, with its insistence on forgetting, has erased us.

Once the ability to communicate has been lost, even mere referents disappear. Bodies start to fall apart. In a terrible scene, Lear describes how the former members of her community start tearing apart their bodies: they pull out arms that get stuck in empty trunks. There is no blood or internal organs—these are no longer organisms—just a jumble of spare parts with no sense or meaning. Not only society, but even bodies become literally dismembered. There are no-bodies left because "al romper con la lengua, se rompía con todo lo que el hombre fue o podría ser" (336; "in breaking up with language, they broke up with all that men were or could be").

Before this point, Lear's faith in language gave her hope in what "could be." Even admitting all the faults of language, she will hold on to it, as a possibility for something else. Language imposed limits to reality, but it also meant a space for creativity and for an encounter with others. When L'Atlàntide collapses in front of her eyes, Lear dreams about becoming words, turning into words, and joining Estela and Hernando in a new community:

> Salvaremos al lenguaje y a la memoria de los hombres, y un día conformaremos al puño que nos relate, y nos preguntaremos por el misterio de la muerte, por el necio sinsentido del hombre y de la mujer. Sentiremos horror, aunque nuestros cuerpos no conozcan más ni el frío ni el dolor. Un abismo estará abierto a nuestros pies. Esos serán los cielos de la Tierra. (369)

> We will save language and memory of men, and one day we will shape the fist that will tell about us, and we will ask about the mystery of death, the stupid nonsense of men and women. We will feel horror, even if our bodies do not know cold or pain anymore. An abyss will be open at our feet. This will be heaven on earth.

Lear's utopia does not imply a return to Nature, a blissful past, or the imaginary union with the mother. Her only hope is to recuperate language, in order to remember, to interpret history and to ask, even when there are no answers and when asking will mean experiencing the pain of thorns piercing her tongue. Because only through language can we articulate the world.

What is the relationship between these inscriptions of language in the body and the American continent as the site of Utopia? In juxtaposing these stories—Hernando's struggle as an Indian friar in colonial México, Estela's testimony of the pervasive violence of twentieth-century México, and the dissolution of L'Atlàntide—Boullosa puts into play a number of associations that confront five centuries of New World history with the image of a failed utopia. As Krishan Kumar reminds us, Raphael Hythloday, the narrator of Thomas More's *Utopia,* "had supposedly accompanied Amerigo Vespucci's fourth expedition" and "many of the customs of Utopia as described by Hythloday—its communism, absence of monarchy, scorn of gold and jewels—could be found in Vespucci's own account . . . of his encounters with peoples of the New World" (*Utopianism,* 1). The narrative construction of the "New World" was filled by a utopian spirit since the beginning: "there were such remarkable utopian descriptions in the accounts of their travels given by Christopher Columbus, Amerigo Vespucci, Vasco de Balboa" (52). Through Hernando's testimony, Boullosa's text not only accounts for the violent, antiutopian character of the "encuentro de dos mundos," but also for the fact that Nahua society was not utopian to begin with. The narrative construction of the American continent is in itself a form of violence performed to signify the unreachable Real of its lands, and, as Estela discovers, even in its more beautiful forms—*One Hun-*

dred Years of Solitude—it perpetuates forms of discrimination it supposedly rejects.

How can we write about Latin America at the end of the millennium? How can Boullosa write this novel? "What shall Cordelia do? Love, and be silent." Should she have measured her words as Shakespeare's Cordelia, trying to be truthful? Already in her preface, Boullosa writes about the violence that surrounds her and uses this as a form of disclaimer: violence is the real author of her novel. The discomfort we perceive in that preface will have an echo in one of the passages narrated by Lear. After examining the wounds in Rosete's mouth, Lear goes back to her books. She is horrified, but even so, she decides to take refuge in literature; she imagines that if Rosete could still speak, he would ask about her what Brontë's Catherine asks in *Wuthering Heights:* "What in the name of all that feels, has he to do with books, when I am dying?" (quoted in *Cielos de la Tierra,* 291). And there is no answer to that question. Except that without language, reality falls apart; that no-body exists outside of language; and that even within the constrictions of language, there is also place for "la inconsciencia y el arropo," unconsciousness and cuddling.

In *Cielos de la Tierra,* we see the "violence of the letter" and the signs of oppression inscribed in language once and again: the pierced tongues of the Nahua costume, the imposition of Spanish over the indigenous languages, the complicity of the Latin American literary Boom with the racial and cultural discrimination of our colonial heritage, the verbal articulation of the Law that is supposed to prohibit language itself. However, the novel also shows the inscription of violence in the body: what cannot be expressed in the Symbolic takes its effects on the Real. In the absence of language, bodies too are mutilated. Boullosa's novel brings to the fore the question of writing itself in a continent where language is complicit with oppression. But, as for Hernando, language also offers the possibility to reconfigure the self and the world. In the context of neocolonialism, globalization, or even a new world order in which indigenous and mestizo cultures are still subjugated to the violence of a hegemonic discourse that disguises the oppression of actual bodies, *Cielos de la Tierra* conceives of a language that is capable of reclaiming dissenting voices.

The American continent is not the site of utopia. There is no such place, as there are no words that would satisfy Shakespeare's Lear's will to know about his daughter's love. But Hernando, and Estela, and Boullosa's Lear teach us that we can still hang on to words when everything else seems to be falling apart, even at the price of speaking with a pierced tongue.

N O T E S

1. English translations of the novel were done in collaboration with Jeffrey Gore.

2. In her argument, the loss of the mother tongue, or its inability to communicate once the subject has been displaced, occupies a preeminent position in texts written by Latin Americans in exile. If we consider Hernando's displacement (from his town to the convent) as exile, we need to notice at the same time a nostalgia for his mother's words and the gratification he feels in the learning of new languages.

3. For some feminist critics, language participates in the patriarchal system in imposing authority principles that legitimate male power. Evelyn Fox Keller, for example, analyzes the way in which scientific language creates its object as feminine. In Teresa De Lauretis's "The Violence of Rhetoric," even the discourses of Foucault and Derrida, which are supposed to problematize the violence implicit in language, recreate a sort of sexual violence, in dealing only with "signifiers" when there is a concrete, material violence that acts on women's bodies in the realm of the real. De Lauretis also claims that a semiotic system that constructs male as active and female as passive negates women the possibility to occupy the position of subjects.

4. Boullosa mentions Todorov's work in her novel *Llanto: Novelas imposibles*, where she seems to subscribe to his thesis that Cortés won the war because he knew how to interpret the signs of the other, whereas Montezuma did not. There is no evidence that she also used Todorov regarding his observations on Sahagún's work in *Cielos de la Tierra*, but they seem to share a positive view toward this attempt of communication between cultures.

REFERENCES

Boullosa, Carmen. *Cielos de la Tierra*. México City: Alfaguara, 1997.
————. *Llanto: Novelas imposibles*. México City: Ediciones Era, 1992.
The Book of Chilam Balam of Chumayel (*Chilam Balam de Chumayel*). Norman: University of Oklahoma Press, 1967.
Cixous, Hélène. "The Laugh of the Medusa," revised 1976 version. In *New French Feminisms: An Anthology*, edited by Elaine Marks and Isabelle de Courtivron, translated by Keith Cohen and Paula Cohen, 245–64. New York: Schocken Books, 1981.
Clendinnen, Inga. "Fierce and Unnatural Cruelty: Cortés and the Conquest of Mexico." *Representations 3*, no. 33 (winter 1991): 65–100.
De Lauretis, Teresa. "The Violence of Rhetoric: Considerations on Representation and Gender." In *Technologies of Gender: Essays on Theory, Film, and Fiction*, 31–50. Bloomington: Indiana University Press, 1987.
Derrida, Jacques. *Of Grammatology*. Translated by Gayatri Chakravorty Spivak. Baltimore, Md.: Johns Hopkins University Press, 1976.
Florentine Codex. Compiled by Bernardino de Sahagún. 12 vols. Santa Fe, N.M.: Monographs of the School of American Research, 1950–1969.
Foucault, Michel. *The Archaeology of Knowledge*. Translated by A. M. Sheridan Smith. London: Tavistock Publications, 1972.
Kaminsky, Amy. *After Exile: Writing the Latin American Diaspora*. Minneapolis: University of Minnesota Press, 1999.
Keller, Evelyn Fox. "Feminism as an Analytic Tool for the Study of Science." *Academe* 69, no. 5 (September–October 1983): 15–21.
Kolakowski, Leszek. "The Death of Utopia Reconsidered." In *The Tanner Lectures on Human Values*, Vol. 4, edited by S. M. McMurrin, 229–47. Cambridge: Cambridge University Press, 1983.

Kumar, Krishan. *Utopia and Anti-Utopia in Modern Times.* Oxford: Basil Blackwell, 1987.
————. *Utopianism.* Minneapolis: University of Minnesota Press, 1991.
Lacan, Jacques. *Écrits.* Paris: Editions du Seuil, 1966.
Shakespeare, William. *King Lear.* Edited by J. S. Bratton. Bristol: Bristol Classical Press, 1987.
Todorov, Tzvetan. *The Conquest of America: The Question of the Other.* Translated by Richard Howard. New York: Harper and Row, 1984.

Part 3. Performing Race, Gender, and Sexuality

Chapter 13

Constituting Transgressive Interiorities

Nineteenth-Century Psychiatric Readings of Morally Mad Bodies

HEIDI RIMKE

> Interiority is an effect and function of a decidedly public and social discourse, the public regulation of fantasy through the surface politics of the body.
>
> —Judith Butler, *Gender Trouble* (1990)

In this chapter, I argue that historically, psychiatric efforts to regulate social transgressions were premised on a materialist conception of the soul that was "empirically" read from the body. Nineteenth-century psychiatric attempts to provide and sustain a medical doctrine of immorality, it has been argued, was advanced through a hermeneutics of the body in which the interior depth of subjects was read by means of the body's surface, structure, and movement. It claims that the social history of the psychiatric invention of the category "moral insanity" and other classifications of moral madness centered on the coconstitution of "inferiorized" bodies as recognizably immoral *and* insane.[1] This chapter implicitly relies on the notion of the fold in order to understand and critique a notion of interiority as fixed, essential, bounded, asocial, and ahistorical. As such, it provides an illustration of how social practices and technologies of the body both contribute to and are the result of the enfolding of exterior processes of social power. It argues that bourgeois psychiatrists read morally mad bodies as a social text within a cultural context preoccupied with combating what was perceived as the increasing vice in the nineteenth century. Situated within that context, the psychiatrization of morality can be understood as but one attempt to combat the problem of transgressors (the dangerous, the degenerate, the perverse), or what Jacqueline Urla and Jennifer Terry have referred to as the "biologically demonized underclasses" (2). The ways in which psychiatrists documented and represented the morally mad in relation to conceptions of classed, gendered, and racialized bodies will also be examined.

The concept of the fold suggests a way in which internality can be understood without postulating any prior interiority, and thus without recreating a particular version of the law of this interiority whose history we are seeking to subvert (Rose, 37). The "folding" back of exterior relations of power through the ascription and inscription of qualities into and on the body assisted in creating morally and socially transgressive "interiorities."[2] Rather than starting from the position that normative values and moral codes are static and unproblematically internalized into preexistent interiorities, this chapter seeks to demonstrate how psychiatry, as a positive science, contributed to the production of interiorities as recognizable through the body. Instead of presuming the a priori existence of interiorities and the meanings of bodies as prediscursive, the interiorization thesis emphasizes how the interior, as a distinct characteristic of human being, is itself a product of cultural and historical forces warred upon the body. Although I construct a direct relationship between morality and medicine, my point is not to dispel the evidence on which the "discovery" of moral madness was based, but to ask, "How can we understand its place in the scientific production of transgressive selves?" To do this, I argue for a notion of the body as a text so as to elucidate how a "hermeneutics of the body" operated in psychiatric attempts to intervene and act as a social authority of "the conduct of conduct." Such an appropriation of hermeneutics refers to those interpretive modes through which bodies are assumed to indicate or bespeak some aspect or essence of the self through manifest or internal physical characteristics, movements, constitutions, or conditions, and can be decoded and known. Interpreting "body language" or "nonverbal communication," for example, assumes that the body displays meaning intentionally or inadvertently, thus acting as a kind of "silent speaker" of inner truths, all of which presumably can be perceived and deciphered by the interpreter. Psychiatric bases of knowing the interior psychic life of subjects were to a large degree based on a hermeneutics that deduced corporeal performativity to the interior movements of the soul.

The psychiatric drive to objectify and understand the body was contingent on the desire to understand and materialize the inner psychic life of subjects. Relying on a content analysis of a selection of nineteenth-century English and American texts on moral madness, the arguments illustrate one of many ways in which psychocentric discourses can be understood as creating or inventing the self (Rimke; Rose). Rather than viewing the psyche as a transhistorical, universal, and natural object, I challenge such an objectification and interrogate psychiatry's moral regulatory underpinnings, which have historically paraded under the dubious veneer of objective "science" and which demonstrate the social forces at play in the constitution of transgressive interiorities.

The humanization of morality in nineteenth-century psychiatry entailed a shift from animistic explanation for the soul to one that began describing and explaining interior essence in scientifically plausible ways.

As an immaterial entity or monad, the soul's existence could no more be proven than the existence of God with extant theological or philosophical frameworks. Vice could no longer be explicitly and sufficiently explained as the cause and effect of the devil; to ensure scientific authority and social respectability, corrupt souls needed to be explained within the framework of pathological medicine. "It is not sufficient to ascribe immorality to the devil; that we must, if we would not leave the matter a mystery, go on to discover the cause of it in the individual" (Maudsley, *Body*, 126).

The classifications of moral insanity and moral imbecility included many degrees of severity ranging from "simple viciousness to those extremer manifestations that pass far beyond the bounds of what any one would call vice" (Maudsley, *Pathology*, 285). Evidence of the existence of the morally mad showed itself in a vast variety of forms "producing eccentricities of character of every conceivable and possible kind" (Kitching, "Lecture" [1857a], 391). Bucknill and Tuke classified homicidal mania, suicidal mania, kleptomania, erotomania, pyromania, and dipsomania as forms of moral insanity; others, such as Maudsley, Hayes, Kiernan, and Gray, further included "self-abuse" or masturbation, egocentricity and self-importance, nymphomania, and the destruction of property. As the doctrine of moral insanity was gaining increasing medical interest and popularity in the mid-1800s, its "signs and stigmata" (Carlson, 127) were also expanding.

Psychiatry deployed a scientific approach that sought to unravel the mysteries of universal individual essence and as such created a somatic science of the interior by reading the body as a interpretable text—as an assemblage of meaningful signs and symbols. The mutual constitution of corporeal meaning and psychic internality of subjects was a double movement based on both a hybridization of medical science with Christian morality, and the belief that the body—as a hypothesized container—carried a knowable interior reality. The psychomedical invention of moral insanity in the nineteenth century provides an illuminating cultural example of how the scientization of corporeal difference came to be inscribed as biological and physiological registers of pathological interiorities. As an exterior representation of abnormal, inferior, dangerous, or deranged interiorities, bodies provided a way in which to evaluate psychical constitution that, inter alia, was deduced from corporeal "natures."

READING MAD BODIES AS SOCIAL TEXT

The explanation, detection, and evidentiary proofs of vice in nineteenth-century psychiatries can be understood through the following hermeneutic modes of recognition, capture, and interpretation: (1) the moving or animated body (i.e., gestures, motions, movements, conduct); (2) a corporeal architecture such as facial characteristics (i.e., nose, face, eyes) or the internal structure (i.e., nerves) or inner organs (i.e., the brain, the bowels); (3) a corporeal morphology, or the profile and physique of the body; (4) the desiring body; and finally, (5) the infectious body (as a carrier or transmitter of vice). I consider each in turn. Specification and identification of gestures and movements of the body qualified in part of the recognition and diagnostic process. Henry Maudsley, for example, claims that some reveal their moral insanity in their gait such as "a turkey-like strut—the pride with which they are possessed; while others shuffle along in a slouching and slovenly manner. In the former we see . . . the convulsion of conceit; in the latter, the paralysis of self-respect—both equally indications of extreme degradation" ("Illustrations," 159). Another patient is recorded: "Now and then she would all of a sudden pirouette on one leg, and throw her arms about; and with a sudden impulsiveness, would not unfrequently break a pane of glass" (*Pathology*, 348–49). A "thief and vagabond" was documented as "fond of decorating himself with gaudy-coloured articles, . . . was very filthy in his habits, and seems best pleased when he has got his hands well daubed with tar" (Hayes, 542). Metaphors of dirt and filth convey a strong imagery of pollution, disorderliness, and uncleanliness, particularly in an age that increasingly focused on social and moral purity and hygiene, both physically and metaphysically.

The architecture and design of the body's structures were used to identify and explain innate temperament and the moral faculty. Another clinical case is described: "His physiognomy is strikingly that of a person of a low type of organisation; . . . he belongs evidently to that class from which so large a proportion of our convict population is derived" (Hayes, 542). Muscles were also read as highly expressive and interpretable: "their individual action betrays a particular movement of the soul" (Duchenne, 5). Benjamin Rush claimed that parts of the human body were directly connected with the human soul, thus influencing morals and appetites (19). The causes of immoral behavior were determined or localized in any part of the body. By explaining morality and passions within the framework of the body, the doctrine of moral insanity single-handedly dispensed with the idea that reason was the supreme arbiter of human being. A moral sense not only acted through the physique but were equally matters of physicality. The theory of Galenic bodily humors that acted as transparent spirituals liquids that circulated through the body explained the quality of an individual's character. Hayes refers to the "bilio-lymphatic temperament" of a 17-year-old woman who is described as "troublesome and obstinate," "quarrelsome in disposition, moody and reserved, and of idle and vicious habits" (534). Or consider the following physical description: "In appearance he was extremely ugly, one eyed, mean looking, weak, and contemptible—a most miserable frame for a blustering soul" (Landor, 542). A case study is described: "The pupils are often dilated, the breath bad, the face sallow, and the body somewhat emaciated" (Maudsley, "Illustrations," 154). And another: "Her eyes glistened brilliantly; the conjunctive was reddened; her head was hot, her extremities cold, her bowels disordered; there was a disagreeable odour of the body" (Maudsley, *Pathology*, 285). Corporeal topographies and morphologies further provided a means of mapping exterior traits to the interiority of mad subjects. The presentation of degenerative characteristics such as anomalies of the cranium, left-handedness, outstretched ears, and asymmetries of the face were criteria for establishing the presence of moral insanity (Italian Phrenetic Society, 7, 38). Rush argued for a scientific understanding that emphasized the connection between the physique and other features of the body with moral qualities. Claiming that the shape and texture of the human body influence morals, he ascribed both a "good temper . . . and benevolence to corpulency, and irascibility to sanguineous habits." Faces that "resemble each other, have same manners and dispositions" (3, 20). Similarly, Bucknill and Tuke argued that "good nature usually coexists with a sleek and fat habit of body" (182). Describing a child suffering from moral insanity, Maudsley writes: "He is thin, withered looking" and had a "deficient sensibility also to the skin" (*Pathology*, 286). Maudsley's attention to the skin is significant. Conceived as an organ of social receptivity, the skin could indicate a perverted social sensibility through the "natural" capacity of the inner nervous system or nervous fibers. The identifying symptoms included the "inability to join with other children in play or work, and the impossibility to modify their characters by discipline; they cannot feel impressions as they should naturally feel them, nor adjust themselves to their surroundings . . . ; and the motor outcomes of the perverted affections of self are accordingly of a meaningless and destructive character" (287). The "faulty" or insensitive skin was represented as a corporeal marker for an ineptitude or insensibility to the socially prescribed demands of a situation. Conceived as the outward and visible sign of the invisible and defective interior, the skin was also to be read as text. Libidinal lust, intoxicating passions, or an "excessive" sexual appetite also worked as symptoms for diagnosing the morally insane body: "Sexual desires are developed at an unusually young—in fact, sometimes at an infantine—age" (Savage, 150). In his obsession with autoerotic pleasure, Maudsley asserts that "in a great many cases of mental derangement connected with self-abuse . . . some degree of hereditary taint has co-existed" ("Illustrations," 153). Unrestrained passions and innate human concupiscence pointed to immoderate desires or coveting of sensual things "delighting in sexual excess" (Kiernan, 558). The fear of "savage sexuality" was also pathologized through a racialization of sexual inferiority as the natural result of subaltern moral, physical, and intellectual development. Rush argued that Negroes, unlike healthy or white men, had a extraordinarily strong venereal appetite (Takaki, 31). Irregular desire, lasciviousness, wandering cogitation, and "sensual appetites" (Landor, 543) were not characteristic of virtuous people, particularly morally decent women who "curb the impulses of sensuality, and restrain the ardour of passion" (Kitching, "Lecture" [1857b], 453). G. B. Duchenne went so far as to claim he had located "the muscle of lasciviousness" in the nose (17). Attention was similarly placed on women's physical temperaments, which were also rallied to designate their wantonness, promiscuity, and "uncontrollable sexual proclivities" as nymphomaniacs (Tuke, 176). Neurologists, anatomists, and phrenologists searched diligently for the organic cause of nymphomania in the brain and skull. The smallest transgressions of white middle-class feminine modesty became classified as symptomatic of disease: popular diagnoses involved identifying the fallen women by their attempts to attract men by wearing perfume, self-decoration, or talking of marriage (Groneman). Indeed, the denial of pleasurable bodily experience through a corporeal governance was seen as wholesome and honorable, a virtue most transgressors lacked.

Moral insanity was alternatively conceived as a disease transmitted from generation to generation either through a "germ" or "hereditarian dispositions." The "natural evidence" of heredity and lineage served to establish a familial history of pathology that was marshaled as evidence for a patient's current form of madness. Rush observed that moral qualities could be hereditary: "we often find virtues and vice as peculiar to families" (3). Transmission could also occur in utero: some children were saturated with moral insanity while in the womb (Savage, 150). "If he be not entirely impotent, what an outlook for any child begotten of such a degenerate stock! Has a being so degraded any right to curse a child with the inheritance of such a wretched descent? Far better that the vice and its consequences should die with him" (Maudsley, "Illustrations," 158). Psychiatric subjects were doomed by birth—not simply metaphysically, but in terms of their corporeal lineage and heritage. Even before birth, the individual was predestined not only to health and sanity or illness and insanity, but also to vice or virtue, strength or weakness. At birth, one was predisposed by "hereditary taints," "racial biology," and social circumstances to a physical constitution inextricably intertwined with the soul and moral character. Another psychiatric model proposed the idea that vice could be transmitted by a germ, causing the body to became a site of battle between good and evil, at risk of becoming potentially besieged and infected by foreign invisible matter. Poisonous emanations, and the propagation of vice and disease were conceived through an epidemic model in which the space of the body was a natural carrier of moral contagion. Treatment of moral contagion was thought to be best remedied by moral hygiene efforts based on an epidemic model: such infectious bodies needed to be confined and removed from the community and their fellow citizens. In his section on asylums for moral lunatics in *In Darkest England,* General William Booth of London's Salvation Army writes, "It is a crime against the race to allow those who are so inveterately depraved the freedom to wander abroad, *infect* their fellows, prey upon Society, and to multiply their kind" (204–5; emphasis added). Maudsley proclaimed that "a diseased element in the social organism [social body] . . . must be isolated or removed for the good of the organism" (*Pathology*, 292). "Such a course must be wiser than allowing them to go in and out amongst their fellows, carrying with them the contagion of moral leprosy, and multiplying a progeny doomed before its birth to inherit vices and diseased cravings of their unhappy parents" (Booth, 205). Narratives of vice as communicable and contaminating created an image of purity in which pristine bodies became infected by foreign bodies that could result in a dangerous outbreak of uncontrollable anti(social)-bodies such that "when they have reached a certain point access to their fellow man should be forbidden" (Booth, 205).

CLASSING, RACING, AND GENDERIZING INTERIORITIES

Elizabeth Fee argues along classical Marxist and feminist lines in "Psychology, Sexuality, and Social Control in Victorian England," claiming that moral insanity was a way from which to understand and control social deviance from the perspective of a bourgeois ideology. She argues that criminality constituted the masculine form of antisocial conduct, whereas the diagnosis of insanity was more often used in attempts to classify female deviance. Rather than offer such a dichotomy and advance the "social control thesis" or the other extreme—that moral insanity was a "neutral" category that did not rely on sociological referents, as Michael Donnelly (138) claims—the medical literature on moral insanity was shaped and informed by the intersection of explicit and implicit forms of classism, sexism, and racism. The class basis of moral insanity cannot be adequately explained by a unidimensional or unidirectional movement of the social control of one class by another: bourgeois psychiatrists did not single out the "lower" classes as primary targets on which to impose their beliefs and values; nor was the designation of moral insanity simply reserved for the middle or upper classes[3]; working or "lower"-class subjects are commonly identified in the literature. For example, D. H. Tuke, like others, includes cases on subjects from "a good position socially" and "a low social position" (178). A variety of occupations are identified throughout the clinical case studies: a magistrate, a farmer, a priest, a sailor, a "man of hard work," a surgeon, and a squire, for example (Hayes; Landor; Prichard). Diagnoses did not occur along class lines: the diagnostic criteria of moral insanity included a multiplicity of diagnostic signs and symptoms, and many were not necessarily dependent on wealth, occupation, or status.

The idea that the wealthy classes were at risk of consuming passions was not new. "Habitual luxury, and the vices of refinement" were "curses of the polished life" causing insanity in the upper ranks while "the lower orders," George Man Burrows argued, "provoke it by their excesses" (18–

19, 21). The degenerate physical and moral conditions of the laboring classes became a chief concern for medical and philanthropic ends. The "want of finer moral feelings" among the poor suggested that the inner life of the lower classes and Other races[4] was more primitive and less checked by civilized restraints, whereas the upper classes' desire for luxuries of all sorts placed them at serious moral danger. Excessive indulgence, idleness, or lack of an ascetic lifestyle were used to explain inferior interiors. Anybody could fall prey to the monstrosity of moral madness, whether single or married, young or old, male or female, and irrespective of one's occupation and class position. Certainly the psychiatrists who accepted and applied the doctrine of moral insanity were members of a bourgeois, professional class. Educated, white, and male, and in a position of producing and exercising knowledge in the social realm, such subjects need to be understood as possessing a kind of ruling subjectivity, one that was informed by both their economic and cultural capital. As "men of science," they were expected to act as expert authorities over problematic conduct and took great honor in doing so.

Discrimination, however, did occur in etiological schemes. Although moral insanity in the working classes, for example, was often explained as the result of coming from "bad stock" (Kitching, "Lecture" [1857a]; Maudsley, *Pathology*), the middle or upper classes were commonly described as having undergone a "remarkable change in character" as a result of a fever or blow to the head (Clark; Prichard). The etiologies offered for the middle and upper classes routinely removed responsibility from them for their pathology, whereas the morally insane poor were overly made responsible through metaphysical notions of "freedom," "will," and "self-restraint." Although all classes were identified, the class-specific explanatory schemes were informed by ontologized conceptions of the working classes as "filthy," "unruly," and "disorderly" or naturally predisposed to moral madness, which indirectly also served to legitimate their poorer lot in life. Moral evaluations of the life conditions and physical constitution of the nonbourgeois classes informed the construction of psychiatric interpretations of diagnostic criteria. On the basis of a fear that the middle and upper classes were also potential candidates for moral degeneration and insanity, the probability of acquiring moral insanity, more significantly, represented and demonstrated a bourgeois fear of becoming like the "Other." Cautionary advice stressed the dangers of consorting with the degenerate classes. For example, James Cowles Prichard describes a magistrate as becoming "boisterous, irascible, extravagant, and given to intoxication" as a result of associating "with people of the lowest class," as if the latter were an objective medical symptom (31).

The genderization of moral insanity involved a process of psychiatrically evaluating appearance in terms of exterior genderized traits. Bodies were scrutinized and measured against bourgeois social standards of normative masculinity and femininity, standards certainly not qualifiable as "objective" "neutral," and "rational." As a cross-gender inscription, the representations of immoral Others relied on bourgeois appraisals of masculine and feminine exteriorities that provided a grid for recognizing pathological interiorities. Whereas morally mad boys and men were often inscribed and described with traits such as "cowardly," "small," "emasculated," "solitary," or by "a want of manliness of feeling," morally insane females were described as "vulgar," "insubordinate," "indelicate," "aggressive," or "obstinate," or her habits "unwomanly and offensive" (Hayes; Landor; Maudsley, "Illustrations," *Pathology*). The feminization of males and defeminization of females was read off the body as symptomatic of moral madness. John Connolly decodes a woman "whose bold eye and prominent mouth were never, even from early infancy, employed to express any of the higher or softer sensibilities of a woman's soul" (651). Hayes refers to a teenage boy as loving his mother in the same way as a daughter might be expected to do: "There is very little manliness about him . . . he would not play cricket, and when he plays he is well padded, and avoids every ball . . . ; when skating he always pushed a chair before him; . . . the approach of a wasp or bee causes him to shrink and shriek . . . ; in any games he attempts he displays an absolute want of courage" (547).

Gendered descriptions and explanations for moral madness were routinely based on corporeal appraisals and interpretations as somehow tied to moral character. Connolly compares two morally mad women: first, one from the "propertied class," then another from "lower origins": "The raised hands, pressed together, indicate the intensity of her prominent emotions; the eyes, somewhat uplifted, but gazing on nothing; the deep corrugation of the overhanging integuments of the lower forehead, portray the painful questioning of a woman not forgetful of her former life" (651).

Yet despite her moral insanity, Connolly presents her as intelligent, lucid, and self-conscious: "Her irritable hands have traced marks of agony on her forehead; her neglected curls hang raggedly over her ears. . . . Even her large and well-developed brain seems to impress the beholder with thoughts . . . of the miserable deformation" (651). The moral evaluation of the poor women is in stark contrast to the former patient:

A different history from the preceding is plain enough. . . . Here the bloated face, that pendulous masses of cheek, the large lips uncontrolled by any voluntary expression, and to which refinement and delicacy seem never to have belonged; that heavily gazing eyes, not speculative, scarcely conscious; the disordered, uncombed, capriciously cut hair, cut with ancient scissors or chopped with impatient knife; the indolent position of the body, and the heavy resting of the coarse, unemployed, out-stretched fingers, together with the neglected dress and reckless *abandon* of the patient, all concur to declare the woman of low and degraded life, into whose mind, even before madness supervened, no thoughts except gross thoughts were wont to enter. (651)

Again, the woman from a "respectable" class position is represented as less responsible—indeed, at some level physically regretful for her transgressive state; the patient from lower class is signified as the victim of her naturally inferior disposition.

Discussions on the "primitive" and "savage" are, unsurprisingly, also located in these medical texts. The eurocentric representations of "race" moved beyond purely physical judgments and sought to articulate the physicality of inferior moral character. Commonly depicted as animalistic, "dark-skinned" races were characterized by "animal excess" and other traits not found among the "civilized." Maudsley, for example, purports that the morally insane, in regressing to "a primitive sort of feeling," denoted a stage of barbarism in which these patients "cannot help doing in the rudest form of primitive society" (*Pathology*, 99). Rush promoted the idea that uncleanliness and idleness were characteristic of "savages." Indians were considered strangers to both morality and decency and, like the natives of Hispaniola and Jamaica, would eventually be extirpated (Takaki, 29). Claiming that "primitive people" were in essence amoral because they had not progressed in the scheme of evolution, Maudsley argued that "savages" were incapable of becoming morally insane, which also meant inferiorized "races" were categorically disqualified from possessing a moral faculty: in order to be rendered morally mad, one first had to possess the potential capacity for a moral sense.

Social Darwinism and evolutionary laws were often invoked to demonstrate the superiority and purity *sui generis* of the European races and lack of morality, humanity, and civility of the "inferior" races (Ackerknecht). "We must remember that what is in startling contrast with modern civilized society may represent the normal tide-mark of a former barbarism" (Tuke, 185). Rush claimed that citizens needed to tame their appetites so as to quell the lower "animal" appetites through a strict and masterful self-governance (Takaki, 21). While a white morally insane man was conceived as "but a little higher than the brutes . . . [,] like the brutes [he] will perish everlastingly," marking "the beginning of race-degeneracy" (Maudsley, *Pathology*, 99, 102). Marshaled to denote the digression, degeneration, and demoralization of the morally insane as "brutish" and "inferior," thus echoing popular nineteenth-century eurocentric definitions of the "uncivilized," the assemblage of interiorities should also be understood as formed and informed by ethnocentric conceptions and standards of European "progress" and moral supremacy. Good moral feeling was the product of human evolution not found in uncivilized lands (Maudsley, *Pathology*, 102). However, racist conceptions and representations were not only confined to eurocentric biases; such themes also occurred along nationalist lines such that the English or Americans represented themselves as the pure ideal type. American physician James Redfield, for example, provides a sketch comparing the skull and facial physiognomy of an Irishman to that of a terrier to "prove" their striking corporeal resemblance and the natural inferiority of the Irish.

The racialization of interior dispositions was informed by visual assemblages through which different ethnicities were racially conceptualized and constructed through a hierarchalization of physical differences by means of various technologies of the body. During the nineteenth century, the notion of degeneracy was pivotal to psychiatric medicine, particularly the study of the relationship between physical variations and moral dispositions in the different "species." Relying on scientific practices and techniques of appraisal and comparison, craniologists, phrenologists, and physiognomists argued that physical measurements were "proof" of the innate inferiority of the nonwhite races. The study and measurement of external features revealed and indicated the temperament and moral faculties in which the white bourgeois scientists used themselves and their kind as the ideal type of heuristic device; bodies deviating from "the average white man" were thus used as empirical evidence to prove the inferiorities, both externally and internally, of different cultural identities. Alternatively, the nonwhite woman or "Hottentot" and "Bushwoman" was constructed as scientific oddity whose corporeal characteristics supposedly reflected animalistic sexual tendencies, and whose extruding genitalia and buttocks captured a primitive form of female sexuality in human evolution (Fausto-Sterling; Gilman).

The intersection of "race," class, and gender informed and constituted the visual terrain of moral madness that acted as a means of othering difference through a sermonizing, bourgeois vision of white civility. An alternative understanding of the normal and pathological emphasizes not "the social control of deviance" but rather *the cultural production of difference as pathology* through the practice of reading the body. The multiple locations of social and cultural positions in diagnoses of moral madness are what made the doctrine so powerful in its day: it was applicable to everyone and anyone who transgressed the limits of (Anglophone) bourgeois civility and morality. Bourgeois psychiatry constructed, problematized, and represented difference through both a global pathologization of vice while advancing tailored explanatory schemes for particular social groups. Oscillating within the specification of certain social identities, moral prescriptions and standards varied according to the social category under question. Yet the conception of physiological, cultural, and moral particularities constituted a social matrix from which to judge subjects relative to their cultural location and appearance within that grid.

PATHOLOGIZING PRESENCE AND ABSENCE

Nietzsche emphasized how the concentration on, and examination of, the pathological implies and illuminates the normal such that the construction of things occurs through an imperceptible process of othering that is an instance of the process of recognition—an extension of essence revealed through its opposite. "It is the value of all morbid states that they show us under a magnifying glass certain states that are normal—but not easily visible when normal" (29). As such, the constitution and sedimentation of the virtuous implicitly relied on the construction of transgressive interiorities as an inevitably relational process in which the movement toward locating subjects morally was multidirectional and variegated. Documentary systems located within nineteenth-century medical texts provide an example of this form of "other-recognition." But this form of recognizing the other through its other also entailed an estimation of excess, or quantitative presence. The process of quantifying objectivized and cognitized the presence (pathological), and therefore the absence of excess (normal). Similarly, the quantification of excessive absence also called into being the idea of deficiency as pathological. Processes that quantify are key in the social construction and recuperation of conduct as psychologically normal or pathological. The inability or failure to physically perform empathy and sympathy for others in one's conduct marked the presence of moral insanity. Conduct was thus understood within a social heuristic of evaluation; the performative subject needed to display the "appropriate amount" of socially prescribed behavior to avoid transgressing normative limits.

For transgressions to be forgiven or absolved, the condition of regret and shame needed to follow the transgression. An absence of interior moral sense was apparently determined by the lack of performance that was necessary in the social signification of remorse. The expression of embarrassment represented a self-conscious and conscientious being, but more importantly, it demonstrated a "performative decency," an acknowledgment of normative rules of conduct through the admission of guilt—an admission the morally decent and socially disciplined displayed. The present absence of contrition signaled a defect or paucity in the transgressor. Thus, an absence or lack was just as significant as the presence of a symptom. A patient was diagnosed by both presenting signifying symptoms and not presenting those indicative of normalcy and virtue.

Textually ordered knowledge is elaborated not simply through a hermeneutics of language and signification but significantly, in the course of practical investigation (reading the body) and documentation (representing that reading). The practice of reading the body, as an extension or expression of the soul, is a social capture, and recognizes that such an understanding of "reading" comprises the perception of the "reader" or captor. Rather than an empiricism that unveiled that which always existed, the constitution of transgressive interiorities must be understood as an empirical project coupled with the hermeneuticians' subjectivities that created it.

Against an understanding of the constitution of individuals' essential makeup as a product of governing cultural values and beliefs about the decencies of virtuous living, the construction of transgressive interiorities in nineteenth-century psychiatry was the result of an enfolding of white, male, middle–upper class judgments into the bodies of the Other—those social subjects who in one way or another transgressed the pristine dictates of bourgeois "respectability" through the appearance of difference. As an effect of a modernist normalizing power that inscribed meaning into an economy of identities, the body became the site of monstrosities or the space of difference where monstrous identities were visibly inscribed (de Courville Nicol).

The semiotic assemblage that constructed interiorities out of corporeal features hinged on practices of abstraction that isolated parts of the body in order to calculate the interiority of the soul. "Peculiar" corporeal signs were read as symbolic of inward perversion or corruption. Through a hermeneutic assessment of an "antisocial" body,[5] a condition of moral insanity was constituted and established. Psychiatrists organized their gaze in a systematic and habituated manner—rules set out by canonical conventions. The textual forms and practices of constructing clinical cases and case files are reflections and organizations of the social world—reflections constituted by an "orderly" rationalization of difference.

The body represented the visual compendium for organizing the structure of the interior and formed the model for proper or improper corporeality and performativity. As a site for the display of social and moral purity or pollution, the mad body provided a surface and structure for the recognition of difference. A somatic hermeneutics, then, provides a point of entry into the larger social and moral order, demonstrating the psychiatric imaginary's need to visibilize the invisible psychical life of subjects through corporeal captures. Medicomoral discourses must be understood as a historical pathologization not simply of individuals who challenged bourgeois culture, but also as an inferiorization of those cultural traits, physical differences, and ways of living that did not reflect white middle- and upper-class "respectability" and Weltanschauungs. The discursive production of moral pathologies should be understood not solely as a social production of psychiatric knowledge but also as *social discourse produced within a social context.* The psychomedical interpretation and capture of corrupt, unruly, disorderly—indeed, *ungovernable*—selves hinged on an exterior reading of the body as a text—as a decipherable, knowable, and (re)presentable object— which both expressed and confirmed the existence of pathological interiorities. Such a production entailed processes of enfolding cultural meanings and values into and on bodies, and such a production demonstrates how appearance and essence were unified and collapsed under the psychiatric gaze.

Psychiatry has not dealt with "pure facts," nor has it progressed teleologically as a value-free, nonmoralizing discourse about the Truth and Reality of psychic life. At its foundations, nineteenth-century psychiatry promoted the belief that the determinants of pathological interiorities were physically structured and expressed. Therefore, psychiatry did not only secure the existence of individualized psychological problems, but also bound up the physical expression of those problems in the proviso of the corporeal. This demonstrates that we cannot understand the interior as explained by physiology, socialization, internalization, or the progress of ideas alone, but rather as the product of scientific practices designed to provide a narrative of the visible body, pointing to the invisible depth of its interiority. The "sick soul" or "abnormal psyche" of the morally insane's body acted as an imprisoning effect because the soul was calculated as an "interior" capture that produced an exterior regulatory psychography. The emergence of moral insanity as a forerunner to contemporary psychopathology and personality disorders was produced by a materialist medicine of the soul that relied on a hermeneutics as the means to read, articulate, and identify the internal unruliness of socially transgressive bodies.

N O T E S

I thank Arturo Aldama, Bruce Curtis, Valerie de Courville Nicol, Barry Edginton, Joe Hermer, Alan Hunt, and Steve Meszlenyi for comments and suggestions. The preparation of this chapter was made possible by the Social Sciences and Humanities Research Council of Canada.

1. The locution of the word "moral" in nineteenth-century medicine had a triple meaning. First, it was used to refer to the emotional, psychical, and soulful life of an individual. Second, the term "moral" was concerned with ethical or proper conduct and deportment of citizens. And third, it referred to the inherent sociality of the self; moral beings were in essence social such that individuals were understood as intrinsically constituted through bound and nonnegotiable social relations and ties.

2. Such a position moves beyond the internalization thesis (cf. Gilman), which assumes the metaphysical existence of the interior that becomes socialized through consciousness.

3. Unlike Alan Hunt, who argues that the moral regulation of masturbation was initially concerned with the bourgeois family, my research suggests that by the mid-nineteenth century, the population of medicomoral subjects was considerably more extensive and went beyond a preoccupation with the sexual refinement and conduct of middle- and upper-class teenage boys.

4. I intentionally use the term "race" to reflect nineteenth-century ontologi-

zations of different "species," as well as the fluctuation between both biological and cultural forms of racism.

5. By the 1860s, the term "antisocial" was being applied to patients viewed as morally dangerous.

REFERENCES

Ackerknecht, Erwin H. *A Short History of Psychiatry.* Translated by Sula Wolff. New York: Hafner, 1968.

Booth, William. *In Darkest England.* London: Salvation Army, 1890.

Bucknill, John C., and Daniel H. Tuke. *A Manual of Psychological Medicine.* Philadelphia: Blanchard and Lea, 1858.

Burrows, George Man. *Commentaries on the Causes, Forms, Symptoms, and Treatment, Moral and Medical, of Insanity.* London: Underwood, 1828.

Carlson, Eric T. "Medicine and Degeneration: Theory and Praxis." In *Degeneration: The Dark Side of Progress,* edited by Sander L. Gilman, 121–44. New York: Columbia University Press, 1985.

Clark, Daniel. *Mental Diseases: A Synopsis of Twelve Lectures.* Toronto: William Briggs, 1895.

Connolly, John. "Physiognomy of Insanity: Insanity Supervening on Habits of Intemperance." *Medical Times and Gazette,* December 25, 1858, pp. 651–53.

de Courville Nicol, Valerie. "Monstrous Overflowing: A Gothic Counter-Production of Modernity." *Space and Culture—The Journal* 1 (1997): 67–82.

Donnelly, Michael. *Managing the Mind: Medical Psychology in Early 19th-Century Britain.* London: Tavistock, 1983.

Duchenne, G. B. *The Mechanism of Human Facial Expression.* Edited and translated by R. A. Cuthbertson. 1862. Reprint, Cambridge: Cambridge University Press, 1990.

Fausto-Sterling, Anne. "Gender, Race, and Nation: The Comparative Anatomy of 'Hottentot' Women in Europe, 1815–1817." In *Deviant Bodies,* edited by Jennifer Terry and Jacqueline Urla, 19–48. Bloomington: Indiana University Press, 1995.

Fee, Elizabeth. "Psychology, Sexuality, and Social Control in Victorian England." *Social Science Quarterly* 58, no. 4 (March 1978): 546–632.

Gairdner, W. T. "A Case of Moral Insanity or Dipsomania." *Journal of Mental Science* 8 (1863): 590–93.

Gilman, Sander L. *Difference and Pathology: Stereotypes of Sexuality, Race, and Madness.* Ithaca, N.Y.: Cornell University Press, 1985.

Gray, John Perdue. *Insanity, and Its Relations to Medicine.* Utica, N.Y.: Roberts, 1871.

Groneman, Carol. "Nymphomania: The Historical Construction of Female Sexuality." In *Deviant Bodies,* edited by Jennifer Terry and Jacqueline Urla, 219–49. Bloomington: Indiana University Press, 1995.

Hayes, Stanley. "Clinical Cases Illustrative of Moral Imbecility and Insanity." *Journal of Mental Science* 10 (1864): 533–49.

Hunt, Alan. "The Great Masturbation Panic and the Discourses of Moral Regulation in Nineteenth and Early Twentieth Century Britain." *Journal of the History of Sexuality* 8, no. 4 (1998): 575–615.

Italian Phrenetic Society. "Moral Insanity." *Alienist and Neurologist,* 1888, pp. 1–41.

Kiernan, James. "Moral Insanity—What Is It?" *Journal of Nervous and Mental Disease* 11, no. 4 (1884): 549–75.

Kitching, John. "Lecture on Moral Insanity, Part 1." *British Medical Journal* (1857a): 389–91.

———. "Lecture on Moral Insanity, Part 2." *British Medical Journal* (1857b): 453–56.

Landor, H. "Cases of Moral Insanity." *British Medical Journal*, June 26, 1857, p. 27.

Maudsley, Henry. "Illustrations of a Variety of Insanity." *Journal of Mental Science* 14 (1868): 149–62.

———. *Body and Will.* New York: Appleton, 1873.

———. *The Pathology of Mind.* 3rd ed. London: Macmillan, 1886.

Nietzsche, Friedrich. *The Will to Power.* Translated by W. Kaufman and R. Hollingdale. 1901. Reprint, New York: Vintage Books, 1968.

Prichard, James Cowles. *A Treatise on Insanity.* London: Merchant, 1835.

Redfield, James. *Comparative Physiognomy.* New York: Redfield, 1852.

Rimke, Heidi. "Governing Citizens through Self-Help Literature." *Cultural Studies* 14, no. 1 (2000): 61–79.

Rose, Nikolas. *Inventing Ourselves: Psychology, Power and Personhood.* Cambridge: Cambridge University Press, 1996.

Rush, Benjamin. *An Inquiry into the Influence of Physical Causes upon the Moral Faculty.* Philadelphia: Barrington and Haswell, 1839.

Savage, George. "Moral Insanity." *Journal of Mental Science*, July 27, 1881, pp. 118, 147–54.

Takaki, Ron T. *Iron Cages: Race and Culture in Nineteenth Century America.* New York: Knopf, 1979.

Tuke, D. H. "Moral or Emotional Insanity." *Journal of Mental Science* (1885), 174–91.

Urla, Jacqueline, and Jennifer Terry. "Introduction: Mapping Embodied Deviance." In *Deviant Bodies,* edited by Jennifer Terry and Jacqueline Urla, 1–18. Bloomington: Indiana University Press, 1995.

Chapter 14

When Electrolysis Proxies for the Existential

A Somewhat Sordid Meditation on What Might Occur if Frantz Fanon, Rosario Castellanos, Jacques Derrida, Gayatri Chakravorty Spivak, and Sandra Cisneros Asked Rita Hayworth Her Name

WILLIAM ANTHONY NERICCIO/
GUILLERMO NERICCIO GARCÍA[1]

ELECTROLYSIS PRIMER

> No art can possibly comfort HER then, even though art is credited with many things, especially an ability to offer solace. Sometimes, of course, art creates the suffering in the first place.
> —Elfriede Jelinek, *The Piano Teacher*

Ever since Gayatri Chakravorty Spivak's English-language edition of Jacques Derrida's *Of Grammatology* appeared in 1976, critical inquiry in philosophy, literature, and the arts has been in a tizzy about the category of the name. All right, perhaps names have never been that out of vogue among the so-called intelligentsia, but Derrida via Spivak certainly did hand us a novel rhetorical armature we have yet to trade in or throw out. In this vein, the pages that follow can be read as a donation to a hermeneutic vault called "name theory," examining how different writers deploy the category of the name in their writing while also, and not incidentally, touching on the nature of stereotypes. What are "stereotypes" but the ready *names* we apply to S/subjects with differences somehow beyond the scope of our understanding or our experience?

One might be moved at the utterance of Derrida's overalluded-to name to remark at this point, "So what?"; I agree.

For that reason, our discussion moves rather quickly from the theoretical to the particular, scrutinizing two particular names, one particular person: Rita Hayworth—born into this world as Margarita Carmen Cansino (or "Marguerita," depending on your sources). In the process of reviewing "Hayworth's" evolution, we will begin to attune ourselves to the particular and peculiar phenomena that are engaged when we consider the relationship of names to people and words to subjects. One important phenomenon is "violence," to the psyche, *por supuesto*, and to the body as well. Without giving too much away here at the outset, I do think it obvious enough to note and important enough to underscore that a simple inquiry into the history of names shows an undeniable connection to those histories that concern themselves with violence. And we need not trot in Siggy Freud here in our endnotes to submit that the psychic repercussions of name changes can have an uncanny effect on the psyche at the level of the unconscious. The story of Rita Hayworth will teach us this and more. That her literal body changed (hair follicles are, after all, a noteworthy feature of our lovely corpus) alongside her name makes her case all the more curious. But I am getting ahead of myself, and I need to introduce our other guests and guides.

To retell the story of Rita Hayworth, I have brought together extracts from Frantz Fanon's *Black Skin, White Masks,* Rosario Castellanos's "Woman and Her Image," Jacques Derrida's *Limited Inc.,* Gayatri Chakravorty Spivak's "Who Claims Alterity?", and Sandra Cisneros's *The House on Mango Street* so as to provide points of entry (some mutually exclusive) for our reexamination of the life of Rita Hayworth. Our psychiatrist from Martinique, word-wizard diva from México, philosophical deity from France, postcolonial theorist from India, and Chicana eccentric from Chicago (although of late, Cisneros has been cross-dressing as a *Tejana*) all have generously agreed, through the magic of citation, to assist us on our quest.

With friends like these, one might imagine that the success of our exegetic enterprise is a given, but I wouldn't be too sure about that! Allow me to confess that the last thing I want to do is to restore dignity, personhood, and wholeness to Margarita Carmen Cansino. My theoretical pointwoman, the late Mexican dramatist/novelist/poet/theorist/ambassador (!) Rosario Castellanos cured me of that urge in "Woman and Her Image." Here one finds a disturbing, if sobering, warning to critics seduced by the romantic *jouissance* of their own righteousness: "Let us not allow ourselves to fall into the old trap of trying to change by a syllogism or magic spell, the mutilated man—who according to St. Thomas is a woman—into a whole man" (243). Justly chided, firmly repositioned, we are freed: establishing the *whole woman* must not be our object. Moving from the theoretical delicacies of México to a perhaps more familiar offering from France, we find Castellanos's censure echoed years later in the words of cyberquotable French maven Jean Baudrillard in *Simulations,* where the prince of simulacra urges us to avoid "retrospective hallucinations." Baudrillard: "It is always the aim of ideological analysis to restore the objective process; it is always a false problem to want to restore the truth beneath the simulacrum" ("Precession," 22, 48). As "TRUTH" is not our issue, nor *my* specialty, I will leave "truth," or its absence, the aporia of the indeterminate, for Paul de Man's acolytes to debate.[2]

In any event, to restore the objective woman Margarita Carmen Cansino would not heal the body of a dead woman—healing Rita Hayworth is beyond the scope of a piece of critical film theory, no matter the verbosity and good intentions of this or that theoretical pundit. In the end, a monomaniacal focus on alienation (the retrieval of the tortured star's alienated body) would merely reproduce the most annoying academic fetish, that we can via prose recuperate and restore alienated Subjects—Spivak, quite rightly, calls them "subject-effects." It is at moments such as these that Fanon's declaration that "intellectual alienation is a creation of middle class society" (224) cautions those hoping to effect change from the ivory tower. We "institutionally placed cultural workers"—the long if accurate names the eccentric Bengali intellectual Spivak conjured (280) for us— should not overestimate the effect of our textual labor.

After all, can a commentary on a movie ever hope to affect with the force of the movie itself? Of course not. Many of you reading these words would just as soon plunk down $100 for drinks and dinner with Madonna, Bernardo Bertolucci, Spike Lee, or Robert de Niro than a free twenty minutes with Cynthia Chase or Jürgen Habermas, no offense intended. So this is no time for hubris. Especially when even our best-intended actions (such as, say, multiculturalism's embrace of all things diasporic or even recent Chicana/o paeans to the transnational) may be, as Spivak suggests, in and of themselves suspect: "Heterogeneity is an elusive and ambivalent resource (except in Metropolitan 'parliamentary' or academic space) as the recent past . . . [has] shown" (Spivak, 280). So we will show some caution and continually attempt to underestimate the importance of these proceedings as we, *estilo* Michael Taussig, run away from High Theory, while preserving its haughty suspicion of the obvious (Taussig, 7).

None of this means that I will avoid passing judgment on the weave of texts, of media (film, film fanzines, film reviews, and film theory) informing "Rita Hayworth." I have noted that some forays in critical theory have led to erudite if disappointing intrigue where critical caginess devolves willy-nilly into borderline wishy-washiness. Sample, for example, a *position* statement by the redoubtable and usually quite excellent Richard Dyer in his gyno-noir piece on Charles Vidor's Hayworth vehicle, *Gilda:* "I am not aiming to produce a definitive reading, nor yet a 'counter-reading' in the spirit of [citing Eco] 'semiotic guerrilla warfare.' Rather, *I am interested in indicating some of the readings that the film makes possible"* (93, emphasis added). Now, I am a big fan of Dyer, and yet even I can't stomach this kind of hedging, although I will certainly try to get away with murder, as would any theory-pocked writer. In a sense, this is my way of warning you that your time in these pages will be a bit more *vulgar*—in the best, most Gramsci-doused sense of the term. For ultimately, each frame in the *text* of a given piece of cinema can be subjected to an infinite number of readings—recorded images are the epitome of what our aforementioned nineteenth-century Viennese cigar-smoking entrepreneur Freud called *overdeterminacy* in his dissection of the *dreamwork*.

Seeking to avoid this attractive, if only momentarily satisfying, open-endedness, this reading of the life and times of Rita "Hayworth" aspires to a somewhat less cagey statement of position: *Rita Cansino got screwed both figuratively and literally, and the way this screwing "functions" speaks eloquently to ethnicity and gender as lived and living categories;* further, it sheds light on the way these categories have been utterly tainted by motion picture technologies in the twentieth century.[3]

Other Rita chroniclers have taken a somewhat different tack than Dyer with regard to the late Hollywood legend, and they are anything but inconsistent. Pity us readers and visual aficionados of Rita Hayworth as we endure the repeated droning of her commentators and biographers. Like some drugged-out chorus chained to a merry-go-round, they speak time and again to the tragedy of Hayworth's "love goddess" life, the tragedy of the fallen princess. All this schmaltzy shedding of tears masks all the while more crucial, less tasteful issues. For instance, I find it more profitable to see Rita Hayworth as a proto–Richard Rodriguez, a proto–Michael Jackson (*dig* that new *cara*, damn!), or as a proto–Clarence Thomas—that is, as tortured and homogenized ethnic-esque types, endlessly prowling the hallways of celebrity in search of solace for their wounded souls—souls scarred by ethnic, gender, and sexual warfare.

Although many (Kobal; Ringgold; Morella and Epstein; Leaming; et al.) have documented Rita Cansino's transformation into femme fatale, love goddess, alcoholic, senile, Alzheimer's victim Rita Hayworth, few have probed the cultural artifacts that remain from this grand *metastrophe,* few have poked through the traces in order to understand the significance of this deevolution in the cultural legacy of the United States.

A STAR IS FORM[ED]

> So we don't have another dame with big boobs on the [studio] lot. So what?. . . We'll make one.
> —Harry Cohn, Columbia Pictures studio chief[4]

Of all stars, why Rita Hayworth?

For at least two reasons. While many think they know about this Hollywood "glamour girl," few have inquired into the sordid processes that brought about her metamorphosis from an incestuously violated Latina vaudevillian by the name of Margarita Carmen Cansino to Tinseltown celebrity, Rita Hayworth. Her name change, at Columbia Pictures mogul Harry Cohn's suggestion ("Cansino was too . . . well . . . Spanish-sounding" [Morella and Epstein, 36]), was only the start of her material translation from one mode of being to another, her de*latina*zation—an event that makes concrete and "brown" Fanon's lament that "what is often called the black soul is a white man's *artifact*" (14, emphasis added). Latino/a souls are just as susceptible to this *artifacture*. For it was not *just* a name change Ms. Cansino endured. As we will shortly witness, Hayworth/Cansino suffered months of painful electrolysis on her hairline so as to assure her "attractiveness"—to ensure she would not look like a "Spanish dancer" ([*sic*]; Southern Californian gringo patois for "damned Messican").

The second reason for discussing Rita Hayworth is to bring various interlocutors of critical theory back down to earth. What is more basic to *estadounidenses*[5] than cinema? Too often, theory languishes in the airy heights of reverie and pretension—this especially in the hands of secondary commentators seduced into replicating jargon they neither relish nor understand. You only have to call to mind the watered-down, mutated versions of Derrida's deconstruction stalking the halls of academe in the United States. Pity poor Derrida as his slippery anticoncepts (deconstruction, *différance, pharmakon*, hymen, *marge*, supplement, etc.) enter the commodifying context of corporate culture USA, the academy included. Urban African American and Latino/a rap artists from the metropoles must have shared Jacques's sentiments when they saw the pudgy ultrawhite Pillsbury Dough Boy rapping in prime-time television commercials. Something has definitely been lost (silenced?) in the translation.

So as to avoid diluting any of the theoretical sophistication we have come to expect of our cultural commentators while at the same time opening up the field of play to a greater range of players, I have assembled an unlikely grouping of commentators—unwitting agents, really—and will bring their voices to bear on Rita Hayworth's name change.

As we consider the violence perpetrated on the body and the psyche of Margarita Carmen Cansino, we are reminded how the dynamics of cinema and the dynamics of self increasingly overlap in twentieth-century Western mass culture. We see again how the legendary silver screen *disseminates* particular versions of ethnicity and gender to its passive spectators, to *la cultura estadounidense*.[6] Before we congratulate ourselves on the New World Order, or guzzle champagne as we triumph the success (aesthetic?) of Multiculturalism, we ought to bother to recall along with my much-cited theory diva/ docent that when "we 'remake history' only through [the] limited notion of power as collective validation, we might allow ourselves to become instruments of the crisis-management of the old institutions, the old politics"

(Spivak, 270)—in other words, status quo conservative flunkies in the guise of intellectual progressives. We will have to be diligent about this, and even then the outcome is uncertain.

What can be forwarded for the moment is the following: this comparative analysis, linking avatars of cultural critique with a manufactured Hollywood goddess, reveals a bitter, alienating matrix where Cansino becomes Hayworth, where Latina becomes *latinesque,* and where, curiously enough, victim becomes both worshipped deity and commodified fetish object.

Daddy Dearest

Two citations prepare us for the story of Rita Hayworth, the story of how a fractured self goes on to become a superstar. They are recent revelations and come from the pen of Rita's (that's what I'll call her for now) latest biographer, Barbara Leaming, a good writer with a penchant for armchair psychiatry. The revelation concerns young Rita Cansino's introduction to the world and to the world of sex. We begin with Leaming quoting Eduardo Cansino, Rita's father, and a statement attributed him on the birth of his child: "I had wanted a boy . . . what could I do with a girl?" (8). Unfortunately for Rita, Eduardo came up with a startling answer to his own question some fifteen years later, an answer Rita only revealed to "her second husband Orson Welles." Save for Leaming, no other biographer or commentator has even hinted at it. *"What could I do with a girl?"* Leaming answers the father's question directly: "during this period her father . . . repeatedly engaged in sexual relations with her" (17). This is the key (shades of Freud's "Dora" and Nabokov's Lolita/Dolores) to the puzzle of Hayworth's emotional volatility for Leaming—and her greatest contribution, if accurate, to Hayworth archaeology. The urge to read Rita as victim may well overwhelm us before we reach the end of the story, but there is much more left to see and tell.

HAIRCUTS

"Screwed" (the verbal keynote I used above to characterize actions taken at Rita's expense deployed) is a "saturated" term with references to tools, sexual practices, and acts of injustice bouncing about its semantic domain. We shall have to look about for better, more precise terms.

Again, and especially with regard to Rita Hayworth, Rosario Castellanos's words come to mind.[7] Listing a gaggle of male philosophers, scientists, and know-it-alls from centuries previous, Castellanos relents and allows the terms of one Moebius to serve as emblem for Western intellectual attitudes toward women: "Moebius found women physiologically retarded" (242). Castellanos's essay establishes that this *retardation* is not a "natural" state but the work of dominant cultural elements on what we can call quite literally the woman's *body politic.* When we need further illus-

BEFORE

FIGURE 14.1.
Portrait of Rita Hayworth in the
1930s. Taken at Columbia
Pictures, the studio that
groomed her and launched her
to stardom. *Used with the permission
of Underwood & Underwood/CORBIS.
© 1939 Underwood & Underwood/
CORBIS.*

tration of this retardation (manipulation, amputation, decapitation—call
it what you will), the life of Rita Hayworth provides painfully eloquent testimony.

Take the problem of Rita Hayworth's hairline.

Yes, hairline.

It boggles the imagination the degree to which the placement of hair-
bearing follicles on the forehead of a young actress affected the course of
film history in the United States. As we will see in the next section, the
bloodline and cultural lineage of Rita Cansino led to quite a debate early
in her career: was she Mexican, was she Spanish, or was she (Orson Welles's
favorite designation for her) a Gypsy?

But it was her hairline that initially drew the most attention and labor.
This was no small issue for Rita's early handlers (Ed Judson, her first husband; Winfield Sheehan, the man who *discovered* her [shades of Cortez,
Colón et al.] in a Tijuana nightclub; and Harry Cohn, the studio boss at
Columbia), and it was resolved with the electrically charged pincers of a
Hollywood electrologist. These digitized reproductions of Cansino/Hay-
worth publicity glossies capture the dimensions of Rita's *offensive-for-some*
hairline for posterity and her transformation into a more semiotically palat-
able Hollywood commodity (Figures 14.1 and 14.2).

As our eyes drift from the photo and back to the page, we might want
to recall how Rita began her show business career as her father's dance
partner in nightclubs (some posh, some not) in northern México and

AFTER

FIGURE 14.2.
Portrait of Rita Hayworth. 1952. *Used with the permission of Bettmann/CORBIS.* © *1952 Bettman/CORBIS.*

southern California. There, apparently, her father had accentuated her "Latina" looks—too much so, it appears, for her future boss, the formidable Mr. Cohn at Columbia Pictures. For that reason, it was suggested, then decided, by the studio that Rita needed a haircut and tint.

Now there is nothing particularly objectifying, "amputating," or alienating about getting a haircut, but Rita's was of a special nature. Ed Judson, Rita's aforementioned first husband, and Helen Hunt, Rita's *hairmaster* at Columbia, conspired to "Americanize" Rita by arranging to have electrolysis performed on her forehead—this apparently would serve to *demexicanize* the *mestiza* features of Rita Cansino (Kobal, 76). John Kobal, citing extensively from a letter by hair-*commandante* Hunt, details the particulars of the process: "I worked with the electrologist, drawing lines on a still picture showing the line we wanted . . . *this lasted another year until the work was finished*" (emphasis added). Hunt continues her narrative with great energy and excitement (somewhere Pygmalion and Gepetto share a martini, grinning as one wonders whether it is a woman or the raw materials of a taxidermist being discussed): "achieving a new design for Rita's forehead entailed a long and very painful process. Each hair had to be removed individually, then the follicle deadened with a charge of electricity" (77). In the creation of the movie star, in the transformation of Margarita Carmen Cansino to Rita Hayworth, we witness an example, in the flesh, of Baudrillard's speculation on simulation, where "simulation is the generation by models of a real without origin or reality: a hyperreal . . . the product of an irradiating synthesis of combinatory models in a hyperspace without atmosphere" (23). In this instance, the "real without origin" may well be the "American" implicit in Kobal's term "Americanize." Post–*Happy Days* Ron Howard notwithstanding, What, after all, is particularly "American" about a large forehead? One would be hard pressed to discover the origin of this aesthetic/cosmetic ideal, though I am sure SS clinical archives would provide a host of ever-so-useful guides.

Needless to say, Rita wasn't thrilled with the year-long ordeal, and according to Leaming, she "desperately wanted to avoid the agonizing treatments" (41). But she needed this electricity-charged regime as part of her transmutation from *Mexicanesque* dancing girl/incest victim to American Hollywood Star—so "American" her image graced the first atomic bomb (she wasn't too thrilled about this *honor* either).

Curiously or predictably (your pick), Cansino/Hayworth's biographers often reenact the roles of her hair-plucking handlers. Kobal, writing on critical disregard of her early films, notes that in "these little known films . . . her work is usually written off because of her hairline" (65)—critics as well as studio bosses, husbands, and hairstylists seem to find something wrong with the young actress's hairdo. Pity the "pure" Mexican starlet looking for jobs in Lalaland with the wrong acreage of forehead. Some years after Cansino's *erasive* encounters with these hairkeepers from hell, Frantz Fanon chronicled the psychological fractures accompanying similar processes in *Black Skin, White Masks,* where, describing the "inferiority complex of the black man," he notes the "internalization—or, better, the epidermalization—of . . . inferiority" (11). Altering the terms but not the spirit of Fanon's findings so as to better understand the trials of Rita Hayworth, we might speak of a "defollicization," a dehairing, of difference that blanches perceived defects. The physical operation is different; the psychological result is the same.

Rita's hairline, her hair in general, was not just an issue of taste with regard to fashionable and unfashionable ethnic traits; it was, of course, a matter of money—Capital and ethnicity have always shared structurally significant positions in that transparent matrix called ideology. Rita, after all, was an investment of great consequence for Columbia Pictures—as Leaming so pithily puts it, "it wasn't just hair, it was a studio asset, a valuable piece of property" (135). No shock, then, to read of Columbia Pictures president Harry Cohn's howling reaction to Orson Welles's cutting and tinting of Rita's hair for her role in *The Lady from Shanghai* some years later. Cohn: "Oh my God! What has that bastard done" (Ringgold, 171).

The studio was to make much of Rita's transformation, and many were led to believe that "like some latter day Athena, Rita had sprung fully formed from the head of a Zeus-like Harry Cohn" (Kobal, 59). This is objectification in its vulgar form, and it is good for spectators and critical theorists alike to see it as such. Cohn, Hunt, Judson, and others are players in a horrific drama: "the antithesis of Pygmalion, man does not aspire, by means of beauty, to convert a statue into a living being, but rather a living being into a statue" (Castellanos, 239)—a mass-reproducible statue, moreover, consumed with no little profit accruing to the sculptor. These are not, let me repeat, hard-to-understand concepts of high theory. Rita's ne'er-do-well first husband, the inimitable "pimp" (as Welles called the dastardly Ed Judson), appreciated the investment his "sculpting" of Rita represented. When confronted with Rita's reasonable request for separation, he threatened to "toss acid in her face," and in doing so, he hoped to destroy the product he felt he had helped fabricate (Leaming, 64).

Watching Rita's films again recently in preparation for this investigation, I was brought back time and again to Castellanos's excellent description of the way patriarchy retards collectively and individually the psyches and the bodies of figures named woman: "In the course of history . . . woman has been a myth . . . and the cumulative mythmaking process manages to conceal its inventions with such opaque density, insert them so deep in the recesses of consciousness and at such remote strata of the past, that it obstructs straightforward observation of the object, or a direct knowledge of the being that has been replaced and usurped" (236). Castellanos's words here provide a spur of sorts, for if woman is myth and cinema is the site extraordinaire of twentieth-century Western myth production, then the body of events shaping the intriguing story of Rita Cansino Welles Hayworth Judson et al. may well provide us with a working model so as to better define a late twentieth-century paradigm shift: a move from the inwardly introspective (the existential) to the outwardly spectatorial (the ocular)—an ocular economy of the self by and large determined by advances in image technology. An elaboration of this odd mestizo semio(n)tics, where the semiotic and the ontologic frolic beneath the sheets, will have to await a later venue, as we have but touched the surface of Rita Hayworth.

The result of Hayworth's hairline renewal, her "subject-effect" manipulation, was that she began to internalize the divide between her living and her cinematic self. So it is that Leaming speaks of "the familiar 'Rita Hayworth' mask Rita was apt to wear" (100). Shifra Haran, Welles's secretary and later Hayworth's assistant, confides that "Miss Hayworth herself said she was two people . . . the star on the screen and the person" (122). Here, we might with some benefit imagine ourselves on a terrain much like that Argentine seer Jorge Luis Borges surveyed in the oft-cited poem "Borges and I." Borges writing on "Borges" describes how "it's to the other man, to Borges, that things happen" (278). Rita's saucy paraphrase? "Men go to bed with Gilda, but wake up with me" (122).[8]

Borges and Hayworth share an analogous space, and an unhappy one at that. Somehow, involvement with the production of narrative and the mass distribution of the same creates a special sort of alienation as *celebrity* (outside recognition/adoration) barges its way onto the scene. Rita's long-time friend, the *make-up artist* (almost *too* appropriate!) Bob Schiffer, de-scribes the degree to which she internalized the desires of her artist/keepers: "[Rita] reflected what the men wanted. Unfortunately, that's the way she thought it should be" (Leaming, 39). In short, as Madonna sings in "Vogue,"[9] she "gave good face," but which one it was, and whose it was to give, remain items ripe for additional inquiry.

¿Spic?

We began with the apparently inessential—haircuts. We learned quite shortly that hair was a central issue with Rita Hayworth. Now we move to a more obviously charged arena. Anyone the least bit politically erect under-stands that *ethnicity* in cultural studies is a category with few peers, and given the politico/cultural history of this country, this ought not come as a surprise.

It goes without saying, but I'll say it anyway, that the question of Rita's hairline was really a question of ethnicity. Having danced in México and thus being Mexican-identified, Rita Hayworth was too Latina for her inves-tor/handler Harry Cohn—how could he pour money when, in his own words, "Latin [*sic*] types are out" (Leaming, 34)? It was not only the gen-eral public, apparently, that feared the specter of Cansino's "Latin[a]" visage gracing the contours of the silver screen; critics (surprised at Hay-worth's meteoric rise) also harbored latent Latina-phobic tendencies. In this regard, Gene Ringgold speaks condescendingly of "the creation of Rita Hayworth from *the unlikely foundation* of one Marguerita [*sic*] Carmen Cansino" (11, emphasis added). Not only critics are to blame. Fanzines and popular rags contemporary with the *electrolyzed statuette* did their bit to play up the unlikely rise of Rita Hayworth–born–Cansino. These sources depict her as the pièce de résistance of a "Hollywood know-how that could transform just another dirty-faced Mexican kid into an all-American dream" (Kobal, 50).

And before electrolysis, "she certainly looked Mexican," with most maintaining that "the Mexican look was good for the [Tijuana dance] act" with her father (Morella and Epstein, 21). The critics and biographers all make some mention of her apparent *Mexicanicity,* with even Leaming chim-ing in that Cansino "passed for a Mexican" (26).

Rita's breeding becomes a topic for extended discussion and conjecture in many of these biographies—Joe Morella and Edward Z. Epstein are particularly scrupulous, evincing a dedication that would have made Joseph Mengele proud. Readers of *Rita: The Life of Rita Hayworth* know from the first sentence of the book that Cansino's parents were "well-bred": Volga Haworth, the mother, had stalwart, upstanding Pilgrims and Irish-born luminaries *stocking* her lineal closet, whereas Eduardo, equally "well-bred," was the son of entertainers from Madrid (13–14). Other biographers are not quite so sure of this purity of lineage, with Leaming casting doubts on Eduardo's claim to a gloried bloodline: "Although in America Eduardo liked to claim his father was descended from the Moorish kings of Granada, in Spain, others called [his father Antonio Cansino, nicknamed Padre] a Gypsy" (2).[10]

I'll conclude these notes on Rita Hayworth's ethnicity by following up on this last piece of Leamingian speculation: not everyone was sure that Cansino was indeed Latina—or even Spanish, for that matter. Conjecture abounds that she was, in fact, part or all Gypsy. So it is that Hermes Pan, Rita's choreographer, whispers to Leaming that "she always reminded me of a Gypsy" (55); Jack Cole, yet another choreographer, echoes these sentiments, concluding, "she was just a dancing Gypsy girl who would have been very happy working in a chorus happily married" (Kobal, 183). Biographer Leaming herself seems moved by the testimony attributing a "dark Gypsy pessimism" to the young star (81). Leaming's views seem particularly informed by her close friendship with Hayworth's second husband, Orson Welles, and it is worth noting that she came to Rita via Welles, having first written a biography of the "mighty Orson." Welles, never short of words on any topic, speaks endlessly of Rita's "Gypsy blood" (80). When moved to describe Rita's growing neuroses during the course of their marriage, Welles moves to familiar ground, offering up the following confession: "I wasn't smart enough to know [she] was neurotic. I just thought it was Gypsy and I said, 'This is that Gypsy kick and I've got to cure her of that'" (85). I'll end this catalogue of Gypsy-centered commentaries with friend Ann Miller's description of an older, more volatile Rita Hayworth, a woman who reflects the psychological impact *statuification* (to adapt Castellanos's statement above) had on the star. Miller: "[Rita] was really . . . a dual personality . . . [she] was a very shy person. But when she drank, *out came this spittin' Gypsy*" (Leaming, 334; emphasis added). In the end, husbands, lovers, secretaries, hairdressers, fans, and critics alike all seem to have focused their energies ferreting out the ethnicity of this particular star.

NAME[S]

But where do we go from here? To what use can we put this mildly entertaining, certainly disturbing, information about a star from yesteryear? What is our context? Our aim? One of the things I want to do is unravel the fabric binding ethnicity, celebrity, and show business, and I want to do this in that rarified, well-armored quadrant called *theory,* with specific emphasis on what more and more people call cultural studies.

This is serious business, but the last thing I want to be is too serious. So many self-proclaimed theoryheads (those comfortable using the word "deconstruction" in mixed company) are all too serious. This is somewhat puzzling. All one has to do is read Derrida's *Limited Inc.* to understand the very real seriousness of taking yourself too seriously.

This is why my focus, while ostensibly that of ethnicity and manipulated bodies politic, also uses materials with which the reprehensibly conservative Mary Hart of *Entertainment Tonight* fame would herself be comfortable. For while the masses are not comfortable with the verbose, *highfalutin* armaments of poststructural critical theory, they are for the most part at home with movies. VCR and DVD sales and video rental receipts provide material testimony in support of this position.

So how will we now use Rita Hayworth? We will begin by talking about her name—and, perhaps, using the history of her particular manipulation so as to found the lexicon that would unpack the political and existential issues at stake in her renaming. This is not a simple task, but also, it is not at all hopeless, as, returning to the pages of Derrida's *Limited Inc.,* I have found a statement which prepares us for the job at hand: "The structure of the area in which we are operating here calls for a strategy that is complex and tortuous, involuted and *full of artifice:* For example, *exploiting the target against itself by discovering it at times to be the 'basis' of an operation directed against it; or even 'discovering in it' the cryptic reserve of something utterly different"* (55, emphasis added). If we allow a figurative gloss of these words and apply it to what has preceded, we find a summary or echo here of "Rita." Derrida describes Hayworth's body, her psyche, and yes, her utility—for in the end, even cultural commentators are mercenary, wedded to a class Spivak calls "functionary-intelligentsia" (Spivak, who claims alterity, 274). For in Cansino's story, in the play enacted on her body, one does find a "cryptic reserve of something utterly *different,*" a semantic residue with which to mildly assault the culture industry which did her damage even as it profited gloriously from its actions.

Given that we are about to discuss the renaming of Margarita Carmen Cansino, it is no little accident that I have prefaced these proceedings with Derrida's *Limited Inc.*—a delicious diatribe that shows just how *real* a Subject's investment in his or her signature really can be. In this instructive text, Jacques, the European/North African guru mestizo, the Algerian Jew living the dialectic Memmi captured in *The Colonizer and the Colonized,* plays Virgil to our Dante: "no signature is possible without recourse at least implicitly to the law, the test of authentication is part of the very structure of the signature" (133). That is, we can discover in the various events surrounding the renaming of Rita Cansino and the alteration of her signature/self laws governing the manufacture of the relative value of various individuals and communities in the United States of America (circa 1940–1950)—especially with regard to the relative value of Latina and Latino citizen/Subjects. These processes continue into the present, as the post-script appended below succinctly attests.

So what *is* the history of Rita's name? At birth, October 17, 1918, she was named Margarita Carmen Cansino. Later, when she *passed for/served as* father Eduardo's wife in Tijuana nightclubs, she was billed as "Marguerite Cansino," perhaps so as to add an "exotic" Frenchiness to the name—anyone publishing in critical theory knows the value of a Gallic accent. Later, Twentieth Century Fox production chief Winfield Sheehan discovered Rita in one of those aforementioned nightspots and shortened her name.

Morella and Epstein recreate this scene: "the next step [for Rita] was a new identity. Margarita Cansino is too long a name for the marquees, decreed Sheehan . . . [so] *Rita Cansino was born*" (25, emphasis added).

But they were not done with her yet. Despite the fact Rita's new name fit on the marquees of film houses across the country, there was still room for improvement. Enter Columbia bossman Harry Cohn. Cohn had a ready eye on the bottom line (not to mention the marshaled desires of his Columbia motion picture consumers) and was not at all content with Rita's new name. Leaming provides a somewhat timid play-by-play in these lines glossed above: "Cohn declared that she really ought to change her name. Cansino was too . . . well . . . Spanish-sounding" (36).

Morella and Epstein's version of the event seems more representative of Cohn's *wit*—Cohn: "She sounds too Mexican" (25). It is at this very moment that soon-to-be-ex-husband (he of the tossed acid) Ed Judson pipes in something to the effect of "how about her mother's maiden name, Haworth." Cohn grumbles, says add the "y" so the spelling will match the pronunciation—don't want to confuse the ticket-buyer—and the now-familiar refrain appears, again slightly altered: "*Rita Hayworth was born*" (34, emphasis added).

Having reviewed the history, it is useful to return now to the theoretical informant who penned *Limited Inc.* Derrida's skewering of John Searle is one of the more eloquent public spankings of an intellectual colleague to be seen since the Encyclopaedists drew quill-and-ink swords. Throughout the piece, Derrida defends himself from Searle's would-be assaults on the French philosopher's reading of J. L. Austin. One of Derrida's wittier moves, critically devastating at the same time, is to rename Searle as Sarl, an acronym for *Société à responsabilité limitée*. When Derrida intones at one point how he "hope[s] that the bearers of proper names will not be wounded by this technical or scientific device" (36), he is only too well aware of the rhetorical, personal, and intellectual violence he is perpetrating, calling into question not only the unity of his adversary's attack, but also the stability of the person masquerading under the copyright "© John R. Searle."

This is a terrain not circumscribed to brilliant French innovators or to theorists in general—not for nothing have novelists labored in the past and in the present to expose the intersect of identity, ethnicity, and names. Chicana/o artists, living within the borderline of culturally diverse origins, are among those contemporary artists who most eloquently speak to the problem of names—as such, they add texture to our tour of all things "RITA."

Sandra Cisneros is only the most recent, and perhaps most eloquent, chronicler of this connection. So it is that *The House on Mango Street* monumentalizes, in an apparently minor incident, the hit-and-run death of "Geraldo no last name" (65), an undocumented worker killed after a night of dancing—the lack of a proper name underscores the pathos of this unidentified, unacknowledged victim who perishes between territories, between cultures. Cisneros's narrator, Esperanza, a gifted young writer guiding us through her development as a young artist in urban Chicago, captures the kind of traps, the kind of limitations figured by an imposed name—especially when that name is "Latina"-laced. I will cite Cisneros's prose at length from the chapter tellingly entitled "My Name":

> In English, my name means hope. In Spanish, it means too many letters. It means sadness, it means waiting. . . . *I would like to baptize myself under a new name, a name more like the real me, the one nobody sees.* Esperanza as Lisandra or Maritza or Zeze the X. Yes. Something like Zeze the X will do. (11, emphasis added)

Here, Esperanza dreams of changing her own name—it is not shortened for a marquee by an other. Note, in addition, that Esperanza has not diminished her Latina identity; she has, if anything, accentuated its exotic eccentricity as she tries to reimagine herself as "Zeze the X."[11]

Hayworth, too, learned in her lifetime to overcome the manipulations to which she had been subject early in her career. Sensitive to the significance of names in christening corporations, and taking advantage of recent film successes such as *Gilda,* Hayworth began (late in 1946) to renegotiate her contract with Cohn at Columbia, demanding from then on a share of the studio's profits. The name of the corporation she founded was "Beckworth," an amalgam of her daughter's name "Becky Welles" with that of her proper name, "Margarita Cansino Haworth" (Leaming, 127). As was alluded to above, Haworth (without the "y" but pronounced the same) was Rita's mother Volga's family name.

Co-escritores

Cisneros, Derrida, Fanon, Spivak, Castellanos, and Hayworth have shown the degree to which one's everyday life, one's everyday self-perception, and one's ethnic community may be affected by the intrigues of something we still naively call "show business" or the "entertainment industry"— Adorno, following on the findings of Benjamin, knew what he was talking about when he called it a "culture industry." In his meditation on the signature, Derrida, especially, shows the way to link the efforts of those of us who work in cultural studies with the "objects" under our observation. For in a very real sense, any of us who work to reveal the traces of Cansino's legacy are cosigners on Rita's odyssey. Derrida had uncovered a similar conspiracy in his tête-à-tête with Searle/Sarl. "What a complicated signature" (*Limited Inc.*, 31) Derrida says, as he determines the identities of the "investors" silenced and masked by the apparent unity of the corporately endorsed signature "© 1977 John R. Searle." Derrida cleverly suggests, however, that this signature includes those individuals Searle thanks for prior consultations on the merits of his writing in the first footnote of his "Reply to Derrida"—a footnote which is appended, curiously enough, to the title, the "head" of his article: these include one "D. Searle, and H. Dreyfus." Things really get tricky when Derrida confesses his own close personal and intellectual association with H. Dreyfus—meaning, implicitly at least, that Derrida is a coinvestor of sorts in Searle's (Sarl's) critical piece which allegedly attacks Jacques Derrida—talk about a "complicated signature."[12] In the same way, we (those of us with some investment in all things Rita) may be seen to cosign the textual space, the textual artifacts— cinematic or otherwise—bequeathed by her person. I have wagered the consequences and taken the somewhat precious move of illicitly appending her signature to this essay.

Short Subjects

Before I bring this extended not-so-sordid meditation (several, actually) to a close, I would like to share some brief tidbits à la Siskel (R.I.P.) and Ebert about a few of Rita's films; also included are suggestions for future critical inquiries. It being in the nature of journals produced by professor types to share topics for further inquiry, and with fatigue of this project rapidly settling in, I thought it best to open *Ritarchaeology* to the scholarly and not-so-scholarly masses. Unless otherwise attributed, factual information is culled from sources cited above (Ringgold; Morella and Epstein; Leaming; Kobal); I bear responsibility for any unattributed interpretations.

Dante's Inferno
1935, Twentieth Century Fox

Harry Lachman directed this collage of a film that marries old footage (mostly sensational nude writhings and tortuous gyrations in a splendid, sensual hell) from the first version of the film (Fox 1924) to a new storyline featuring Spencer Tracy and Claire Trevor. Tracy called it "one of the worst pictures ever made." Rita's father, the aforementioned incestuously bent

Eduardo, was the choreographer for the feature, and thus 17-year-old Rita Cansino (still Cansino) made her attributed screen debut[13] as a dancer on the doomed cruise ship/"inferno" named *Paradise*. Noteworthy are the representations of duplicity, of masking, which wind their way through the film—in retrospect, these augur Cansino's own lifelong problems with her own masks, literal and figural. The most memorable image of the film? Spencer Tracy as Jim Carter (carny *cum* venture capitalist *cum* swindler) shadowed by a leering, grotesque gargoyle. The juxtaposition of the evil Carter and his statuesque twin is remarkable. The hell sequences are kind of hot also—tumescent screen aficionados will have a ball voyeuristically touring the body-strewn landscapes from the 1920s—a terrain at least as dense as the one Peter Greenaway rendered in *Prospero's Books* (1991; Channel Four Films, Cámera One, et al.), his version of Shakespeare's *The Tempest*, with fewer penises, of course.

Human Cargo
Twentieth Century Fox, 1936

Allan Dwan is on board this time as director of this B movie about the United States and its borders. Rita Cansino plays an illicit border crosser by the name of Carmen Zoro—talk about an *overdetermined* name; unfortunately, she does not stay on the screen too long: "Rita dies before the climax, an illegal alien blackmailed by a smuggling ring" (Ringgold, 68). I have not been able to track down a print of this film (reader *ayuda me*), but given its storyline, I believe it might be read to some advantage with Orson Welles's bordertown classic *Touch of Evil* (Universal Pictures, 1958).

Gilda
Columbia Pictures, 1946

It all comes together here, a movie if there ever was one that symbolizes Hayworth as statue, as cinematic simulacrum. All that Gilda presents is fake (or apparently so) in this masterpiece of film noir: her name, her looks, her hairline, and, last, in her grand would-be striptease musical number "Put the Blame on Mame," her voice—Hayworth's voice was dubbed. Directed by Charles Vidor and produced by Virginia Van Upp, *Gilda* was *the* 1946 postwar megahit—before there were J-Lo and Britney Spears, before there was Madonna, before there was Bardot, before there was Monroe, there was Hayworth. Rita is Gilda, Glenn Ford is Johnny Farrell, and George Macready is Ballin Mundson. Set in postwar Buenos Aires, the film traces a homo/heteroerotic ménage à quatre between Ballin, Johnny, Gilda, and, in a touch that would have made Sigmund Freud bulge, Jacques Lacan fidget, and Jane Gallop smile, a concealed sword hidden in a cane. Johnny, commenting on the gender of this remarkable protagonist/cane, waxes eloquently: "it's a her . . . because it looks like one thing and right in front of your eyes it becomes another thing," which paraphrases Rita's life quite nicely, albeit with an ironic twist.

Other memorable lines of note from the film:

- Johnny to his bossman/savior Ballin: "I belong to the boss."
- Ballin on Gilda: "She was born the night she met me."
- Gilda to Johnny: "Good evening, Mr. Farrell, you're looking very beautiful."
- Last, Gilda, on the arm of recent pick-up, to Johnny: "If I had been a ranch . . . they would have named me the bar nothing."

The Lady from Shanghai
Columbia Pictures, 1947

Rita Hayworth plays Elsa Bannister in this film directed by Orson Welles. The most useful scene with regard to our ongoing inquest appears at the film's climax where Elsa, her husband (Everett Sloane as inert and deliciously lascivious Arthur Bannister), and Welles (as Michael O'Hara) square off in a mirrored room at an amusement park. This gallery of images, reflections, and distortions figurally reinforces the plot of the film, filled as it is with deception, infidelity, and noirish intrigue. The scene concludes with a ménage à shoot-out with Arthur, Elsa, and a score of mirrors ending up shattered on the floor—Welles as O'Hara lives to close the movie. This stunning conclusion can be read with great effect alongside Castellanos's challenge to women, that "the feat of *becoming what one is . . .* demands . . . above all the rejection of those false images that false mirrors offer woman in the enclosed gallery where her life takes place" (244). Unfortunately, Welles's film would seem to suggest that potentially self-validating moves like these (destroying false mirrors) lead to destruction for strong, singular women who dare to buck the system. *Fin.*

Follicular Denouement
"Can you even dye my eyes to match my gown?"[14]

This review of the life and times of Rita Hayworth reminds us of a lesson Fanon taught with regard to Afro-Caribbean subjects and that I have appropriated here for what I have been calling the Latina body politic. Writing in *Black Skin, White Masks,* Fanon tells of the need "to teach the negro not to be the slave of their archetypes" (34). Rita's corpus teaches us to do much the same thing, and in many ways, her offering up of wisdom was at the price of her own happiness; the same may be said to a certain extent in the case of Fanon.

"I came into the world imbued with the will to find a meaning in things, my spirit filled with the desire to attain to the source of the world, and then I found I was an object in the midst of other objects" (109), Fanon writes, and his words capture the pain—the real pain—that ethnic manipulation, ethnic obfuscation perpetrates on collectivities and individual bodies, individual selves. Castellanos chronicles the risks of resisting this process as she speaks in a related fashion of women in relation to men: "the victor—who plants his heel on the cervix of the vanquished enemy—feels in each heartbeat a threat . . . in every move, an attempt to revolt" (237). The threat of an ethnically indeterminate woman or (worse) an ethnically determined "Mexican" woman was observed to clearly endanger the profit potential of various studios, bosses, and handlers. This perceived threat, this subtle knowledge of and reinforcement of mainstream U.S. attitudes vis-à-vis Latinos/as, led directly to the transformation of the Brooklyn, New York–born Margarita Carmen Cansino into the tempestuous West Coast simulacrum, Rita Hayworth.[15]

In her later years, Hayworth, a victim of alcoholism and Alzheimer's disease, became more and more detached from the world around her, although she continued to make occasional, often scandalous and outrageous, public appearances. Even these finally stopped as Cansino's waking world became less and less tethered to material, concrete realities.

Hayworth's life ends with the kind of irony humanists and poststructuralists alike love and cherish: the sculpted simulacrum ends her life in a fictional space. Timothy Carlson, writing Rita's obituary for the *Los Angeles Herald Exam,* described this simulated living space to his readership on May 16, 1987, the day after Hayworth died: "In 1981 [Hayworth's daughter] Princess Yasmin Khan was given permanent control of her mother's estate and was provided round the clock nurses. Yasmin duplicated [Rita's] Manhattan apartment with the furnishings of Hayworth's Hollywood home so she would not realize she had been moved from the city where she had reigned" ("'Love Goddess' Rita Hayworth Dead at 68," *Los Angeles Herald Examiner,* May 16, 1987, n.p.). Carlson describes here a simulated space with a surprisingly sensual, reassuringly spiritual and altruistic aura.

For Hayworth (née Cansino), all is not as it was when it began. This time, a simulacrum was created to give her soul some peace, to give her tortured personage a break—some needed, loving distraction before the film on the reel broke off for the last time and the lights went up in the house.

1991 POSTSCRIPT: RITA'S STORY HAS NOT ENDED

A few days before I missed the original deadline for the first incarnation of this essay, I ran across the following item in the San Diego County edition of the *Los Angeles Times.* The byline was by Robert Epstein under the title "Latino Actor writes Open Letter to Hollywood—Is It All in a Name?" (July 25, 1991, F4, F9). Epstein tells the story of one Gary Cervantes who "paid $1200 for a full-page advertisement in . . . *Daily Variety* to tell casting agents, directors, producers and story editors that the person known as

Carlos Cervantes for the past nine years and one hundred roles was no more. It will be Gary Cervantes again. Carlos is no more." There are some memorable lines in the piece, especially resonant in the wake of our Rita revelations. "I was," "Gary" confesses, "a Mexican *Leave It to Beaver.*" Epstein finishes the clause for the chameleon/actor, "but there were few roles for Beaver Cleaver Cervantes and when he tried for Latino roles, he was told he didn't look 'Mexican enough.'"

Gary/Carlos ends his ad with the following sign-off: "I am reminded daily by Hollywood that I am Latino, and I am labeled Hispanic out of convenience. But I am an American." [signed] Gary Cervantes.

1995 POSTSCRIPT TO THE POSTSCRIPT

Like anyone these days, I rent motion pictures at the corner video outlet. And there I chanced on "American" Gary Cervantes's latest motion picture role—Gary, formerly Carlos, plays the swarthy Latino Rolex thief who obliterates pale Steve Martin's leg with a gunshot in Lawrence Kasden's otherwise moving *Grand Canyon* (Twentieth Century Fox, 1991).

At least they let him grow his hair out for the role.

2002 POSTGRAPHIC TO THE POSTSCRIPT TO THE POSTSCRIPT

I am at the heralded and boisterous *House of Blues* at Mandalay Bay in Las Vegas with a friend on the guest list for a Cinco de Mayo celebration and I am introduced by a mutual friend to Brooke, a former Oakland Raiderette cheerleader, current Miller Lite Girl, and would-be celebrity. After food and drinks, I am privy to the sad tale of Olga Morales, now Brooke of Brooke.com and SimplyBrooke.com. Brooke (aka Olga) tells of young teenager Olga Morales growing up in Agoura Hills, California, who had fallen hard for a cute Anglo teenager in the neighborhood. Upon hearing the name "Olga," said SoCal hunk broke into laughter—the why of this reaction is left to students of Henri Bergson's *Laughter,* readers of Freud's *Wit and Its Relation to the Unconscious,* and patient researchers of Southern California anti-Mexican sentiments. The short of it was that this sensitive and beautiful young model, winner of the Miss Hawaiian Tropic Pageant at the age of 17, changed her name to Brooke, forever.

Somewhere in her celluloid Alzheimer's-fed simulacrum, Rita Cansino laughs, cries, or screams.

NOTES

1. Had I been born a mile or so south of the old Mercy Hospital (Laredo, Texas) in Nuevo Laredo, Tamaulipas, my name would be different: not "William,"

FIGURE 14.3.
The Existential Guillotine. Guillermo Nericcio García, © 2002 digital mixed media.
Used by permission of the artist.

but "Guillermo"; not "Nericcio," but "Nericcio García," following the practice in most Latin American families where the family name of the mother follows the last name of the father. (The next time you are in a bookstore, check where they stock Gabriel García Márquez; I am not saying the proprietors are barbarians if you find his oeuvre listed under Márquez, but they do need some cultural retooling—then again, said stocking practice may also be viewed positively as a bit of gyno-driven resistance to *the name of the father, chapeau Irigaray*.) But to return, the peculiarities of my Laredo/Nuevo Laredo border space suggest the degree to which naming, geography, and bicultural *territorialization* mark the self that lives within that border, supplementing somewhat Deleuze and Guattari's overcited, mouthful of a concept. Postscript (March 2002): When *Romance Language Annual* (Purdue Monographs, winter 1992) published an earlier version of this essay, they removed my second name, written in Spanish. And while I am forever in debt to those generous *gente* at Purdue, especially Anthony Tamburri, that decision, that matronymic "scalping," is not without significance, given the discussion that now follows.

2. One ought not allow my saucy tone to throw them here. Alleged Nazi fetish-ism notwithstanding, I was as moved as any other theorist of my generation by the theoretical contributions of Paul de Man. But as I argue below with regard to Der-rida and the Pillsbury Dough Boy, something definitely happens as ideas move from the mouth of the "priest" to the soul of the writing "acolyte." On another topic, fans of de Man mournful of his current leperlike infamy should patiently wait a decade or so. The 1990s recuperation of Richard Nixon ("Nixon" logo T-shirts were all the rage in Southern California) and Henry Kissinger (the noted Nobel Prize–winning genocidist) shows just how forgetful and forgiving the collec-tive unconscious of a given Western state can be.

3. I have grappled elsewhere more extensively with the effect of technology on discursive and semiotic media in "Artif(r)acture."

4. As quoted in a moving reminiscence by John Lahr, son of Burt "The Cow-ardly Lion" Lahr ("The Voodoo of Glamour," *New Yorker* 70, no. 5, March 21, 1994, p. 113).

5. *Estadounidenses:* Unitedstatesians. I have discussed the problem of the term "American" in more detail in "Autobiographies at *la frontera*" and again more recently in "Of Mestizos and Half-Breeds."

6. For more, much more on this, see William Anthony Nericcio, "Autopsy of a Rat."

7. Had she remained alive and writing, it's frightening to think (exhilarating may be the better term) how the course of American (in the best sense said *palabra* can be used) intellectual history might have been changed. Castellanos is every bit as theoretically adept as Irigaray and Kristeva, surveying in the 1960s terrain similar to that of the French dynamic duo. She also had an eccentric and delicious wit. The irony of her death (she was electrocuted while turning on a lamp after taking a shower) is just one of those ugly events you have to get used to on this damned chaotic planet.

8. With her penchant for self-portrait, Frida Kahlo represents a similar if dis-tinct case; I wrestle with this in "A Decidedly 'Mexican' and 'American' Semi-[er]otic Transference."

9. From *Songs Inspired by the Film "Dick Tracy"* (Epic, 1990).

10. I do not have space here to pursue a discussion of Spanish attitudes with regard to ethnic bodies named Moor, North African, Jewish, and the like, although the topic relates directly to the foregoing discussion. Needless to say, Leaming's statement is ripe for forensic inquiry. Some works which do address these issues, both recent and dated, include Syed Ameer Ali's *A Short History of the Saracens;* Lee Anne Durham Seminario's *The History of the Blacks, the Jews, and the Moors in Spain;* and E. William Monter's *Frontiers of Heresy.* Also of use is Perry and Cruz, eds., *Cul-tural Encounters.*

11. Renato Rosaldo pursues a comparable line of argument in *Culture and Truth,* 161–67.

12. In a bit of gossip *chisme*-queen Liz Smith might have passed over, Searle was so annoyed by Derrida's critical response to his writings that he refused Northwest-ern University permission to reprint his essay, "Reiterating the Differences: A Reply to Derrida," in their book collecting the pertinent documents of the debate. Searle, darling apparently of some editor at the *New York Times Book Review,* where his bitter anti-Derridian darts often appear, continues to harass Derrida to this day.

13. Cansino had already appeared in U.S. short features and Mexican films.

14. Judy Garland as Dorothy in Victor Fleming's *The Wizard of Oz* (Metro-Gold-wyn-Mayer, 1939) sings these lines while in a salon being dolled up in anticipation of meeting Oz in the Emerald City.

15. Given my efforts in this essay, it seems prudent to add that Hayworth was not always already a victim; indeed, she profited personally if only temporarily from these transactions. She also had a Hell of a life.

REFERENCES

Adorno, Theodor. *The Culture Industry: Selected Essays on Mass Culture*. London: Routledge, 1991.

Ameer Ali, Syed. *A Short History of the Saracens; Being a Concise Account of the Rise and Decline of the Saracenic Power and of the Economic, Social and Intellectual Development of the Arab Nation from the Earliest Times to the Destruction of Bagdad, and the Expulsion of the Moors from Spain*. London: Macmillan, 1924.

Baudrillard, Jean. "The Precession of Simulacra." In *Simulations*, translated by Paul Foss, Paul Patton, and Philip Beitchman, 1–79. New York: Semiotext(e), 1983.

Borges, Jorge Luis. "Borges and I." In *The Borges Reader*, edited by Emir Rodriguez Monegal and Alastair Reid, 278–79. New York: Vintage Contemporaries, 1981.

Castellanos, Rosario. "Woman and Her Image." In *A Rosario Castellanos Reader*, edited by Maureen Ahern, 236–44. Austin: University of Texas Press, 1988.

Cisneros, Sandra. *The House on Mango Street*. 1986. Reprint, New York: 1989.

Derrida, Jacques. *Limited Inc*. Translated by Sam Weber. Evanston, Ill.: Northwestern University Press, 1988.

———. *Of Grammatology*. Translated by Gayatri Chakravorty Spivak. Baltimore, Md.: Johns Hopkins University Press, 1976.

Durham Seminario, Lee Anne. *The History of the Blacks, the Jews, and the Moors in Spain*. Madrid: Playor, 1975.

Dyer, Richard. "Resistance through Charisma: Rita Hayworth and Gilda." In *Women in Film Noir*, edited by E. Ann Kaplan, 91–99. London: British Film Institute, 1980.

Fanon, Frantz. *Black Skin, White Mask*. Translated by Charles Lam Markmann. New York: Grove Press, 1967

Kobal, John. *Rita Hayworth: The Time, the Place and the Woman*. New York: Norton, 1978.

Leaming, Barbara. *If This Was Happiness: A Biography of Rita Hayworth*. New York: Viking, 1989.

Monter, E. William. *Frontiers of Heresy: The Spanish Inquisition from the Basque Lands to Sicily*. Cambridge: Cambridge University Press, 1990.

Morella, Joe, and Edward Z. Epstein. *Rita: The Life of Rita Hayworth*. New York: Delacorte Press, 1983.

Nericcio, William Anthony. "Artif(r)acture: Virulent Pictures, Graphic Narrative and the Ideology of the Visual." *Mosaic: A Journal for the Interdisciplinary Study of Literature* 28, no. 4 (December 1995): 79–109.

———. "Autobiographies at *la frontera*: The Quest for Mexican-American Narrative." *Americas Review: A Review of Hispanic Literature and Art of the USA* 16, no. 3–4 (fall–winter 1988): 165–87.

———. "Autopsy of a Rat: Odd, Sundry Parables of Freddy Lopez, Speedy Gonzales, and Other Chicano/Latino Marionettes Prancing about Our First World Visual Emporium." *Camera Obscura* 37 (January 1996): 189–237.

———. "A Decidedly 'Mexican' and 'American' Semi[er]otic Transference: Frida Kahlo in the Eyes of Gilbert Hernandez." *Latina/o Popular Culture*, edited by

Mary Romero and Michelle Habell-Pallán, 188–207. New York: New York University Press, 2002.

———. "Of Mestizos and Half-Breeds: Orson Welles's *Touch of Evil.*" In *Chicano Cinema: Representation and Resistance,* edited by Chon Noriega, 47–58. Minneapolis: University of Minnesota Press, 1992.

Perry, Mary Elizabeth, and Anne J. Cruz, eds. *Cultural Encounters: The Impact of the Inquisition in Spain and the New World.* Berkeley: University of California Press, 1991.

Ringgold, Gene. *The Films of Rita Hayworth: The Legend and Career of a Love Goddess.* Secaucus, N.J.: Citadel Press, 1974.

Rosaldo, Renato. *Culture and Truth.* Boston: Beacon Press, 1989.

Searle, John. "Reiterating the Differences: A Reply to Derrida." *Glyph* 2 (1977): 198–209.

Spivak, Gayatri Chakravorty. "Who Claims Alterity?" In *Remaking History,* edited by Barbara Kruger and Fred Mariana, 269–92. Seattle: Bay Press Dia Art Foundation, 1989.

Taussig, Michael. *The Nervous System.* New York: Routledge, 1992.

Chapter 15

Double Cross

Transmasculinity and
Asian American Gendering in
Trappings of Transhood

SEL J. WAHNG

Trappings of Transhood (1997), directed by Christopher Lee and Elise Hur-witz, is a documentary that starts out with a rockin' drumbeat and Chea Vincent Villanueva stating, "I like to fuck. . . . I like a nice blow job too, but I do like to fuck." At first this seems to set the tone of transmasculinity, and hence masculinity, as simple outward phallocentric projection. How-ever, I will demonstrate through an analysis of *Trappings* that many fun-damental assumptions around masculinity—and race—are disrupted, complexified, and reorganized in new and provocative ways. This happens particularly through the representation of bodies of color in Lee's videos.

Lee, as filmmaker and sometimes as subject of his transvideos, is a San Francisco–based artist and part of what I would call "old guard" Genera-tion X (since Generation X, by now, encompasses some thirty years). He was born in the mid-1960s, and this places him currently in his mid-30s. As a former butch-identified lesbian, now FTM (female-to-male transsexual), it is his positioning as a biracial Asian American Generation Xer that in-forms and inflects his shaping of the particular transmasculine vision in his transvideos. Lee's videos can be characterized by distinctly transmasculine qualities of self-reflexivity, embodiment, recoding, and performativity—concepts that will be explicated and analyzed in this chapter. His videos also serve as examples of an increasingly complex cultural and racial land-scape, where multiple articulations of FTM identities, practices, experi-ences, and bodies are the norm rather than the exceptions.

THE TRANSMASCULINE LANDSCAPE

The 1990s witnessed a burgeoning politicized transsexual and transgender movement, one never apparent before in the history of the United States. (This movement had also not existed in any modern nation-states until the 1990s.) The phenomenon of this new movement was discussed even in the mainstream U.S. press. For instance, John Cloud wrote an article for *Time .com* entitled "Trans across America," in which he noted that "'transgenders' were emerging as the newest group to demand equality" (1). Cloud relates that transsexuals first "burst on the [U.S.] scene" in the 1950s with the public disclosure of former GI Christine Jorgensen's sex change from male to female (1). He also notes that although Stonewall was actually initiated by MTF (male-to-female) transgendered people, such as Sylvia Rivera, this fact had traditionally been obscured or elided within U.S. gay and lesbian history (1).

The transgendered political movement had seen some "remarkable successes" built by "gender noncomformists." This new movement started in the early 1990s, when transsexual and transgendered people formed grassroots political groups that picketed the American Psychiatric Association (2). At the time of the publication of Cloud's article in 1998, Cloud wrote that one state, Minnesota, and several cities, including San Francisco, Seattle, and Evanston, Illinois, had passed laws protecting transsexuals and transgendered people from job and housing discrimination. Lawyers with the Transgender Law Conference had also helped pass statutes in at least seventeen states allowing transsexuals to change the sex designation on their birth certificate (3).

In the August 10–17, 2000, issue of the *Boston Phoenix,* Dorie Clark published an article entitled "Transgender Activism: Can the Nascent Transgender Community Resolve the Age-Old Battles between the Sexes?" Clark's article was a more in-depth analysis of the contemporary transgender community, partly due to Clark's extensive research and knowledge of transgender identities and practices. Although only a scant two years had passed since Cloud's article, the transgender community had been able to exponentially increase its political currency and cultural viability within this short span of time. The transgender community itself had also diversified internally, with clearer articulations of different and divergent transgender identities and practices, a point I will return to when I discuss Lee's videos.

Clark touches on this, first stating that there is no consensus on how to define the term "transgender," since this term had been applied to not only transsexuals—individuals who take hormones, undergo surgery, or both—but also includes other identities, such as drag queens or women who "pass" as men without any hormones or surgery (2). Clark also writes that the contemporary trans movement coalesced in the early to mid-1990s and cites FTM Leslie Feinberg's fictionalized memoir *Stone Butch Blues* and MTF Kate Bornstein's treatise *Gender Outlaw: On Men, Women, and the Rest of Us* as two groundbreaking books that helped unite this movement (3). Clark quotes Nancy Nangeroni, host of the radio program *Gender Talk,* who states that the Internet and online accessibility has greatly facilitated the organization and networking potential of a nascent transgender community. The accessibility of new technologies brought together "radical activists" with those who are just seeking greater comfort with themselves as transsexuals and transgendered people in day-to-day life (2).

Clark's article is indicative of some of the current strains and growing pains of the contemporary transgender movement, which is characterized by Nangeroni as "moving into an adolescence where the movement has won a certain degree of respectability" (4). One of these current trends is summed up by MTF Stacey Montgomery, who declares, "We're not going to assimilate to society. . . . Society will assimilate to us. . . . Whether it's being intersexed or transgressive in terms of how one dresses, I think society is going to be more culturally relaxed" (4).

As part of this "cultural relaxation," Clark cites MTF Penni Ashe Matz, who observes that increasingly, there are transgendered people who are less interested in blending in and becoming invisible. Matz states, "I would have to put myself in that category . . . I've personally developed a philosophy and I'm seeing it in other transgender people—I want to pass, but not too well" (4). Clark then elaborates that those transgendered people who prefer to blend in with one gender or the other may be very different, politically and philosophically, from those who want to shake up the gender duality. As an example of the latter, Clark cites "lo-ho" transsexuals— those who are taking low doses of hormones such as testosterone or estrogen—in order to create deliberately androgynous bodies (4–5). Thus, Clark's article starts to map out the contemporary transgender landscape at the end of the 1990s, in which an array of various and incommensurable transgender identities circulate within the same movement.

This diversity has also been reflected in the proliferation of FTM cultural productions since 1990. For instance, FTM literature, such as the *FTM Newsletter,* and FTM communities, such as those organized around the True Spirit conferences, sponsored by American Boyz,[1] not only circulate the terms "lo-ho," but also "no-ho" (FTMs who don't take any testosterone), "non-op" (FTMs who opt not to have surgery), and other kinds of liminal gender identities.[2]

For those FTMs who do take hormones, FTM communities have also been able to accommodate the experimentation with radically diverse hormonal therapies. For instance, FTMs have not only experimented with varying *dosages* of testosterone, but also with different *types* of testosterone (for example, testosterone cypionate, testosterone enanthate, testosterone propionate, and testosterone decanoate); various modalities of testosterone supplementation (such as injection, the testosterone patch, and testosterone replacement gel); and different types of androgens and antiestrogenic agents (such as nandrolone, trenbolone, methenolone, clomiphene, aminoglutethimide, anastrozole, tamoxifen, and orally administered androgens). Sometimes the different hormones listed above are mixed together, according to personal preference, into what are termed "hormonal cock-tails" (Raverdyke, 4–6).

It is from this contemporary transmasculine context, then, that Christopher Lee's *Trappings of Transhood* emerged. *Trappings* was filmed during the mid-1990s and had its first theatrical release in 1997, traveling within the lesbian, gay, bisexual, and transgender film festival circuit internationally. In showcasing divergent views on identity and masculinity, often operating through contradictory responses by the interviewed subjects, *Trappings* reflects diverse FTM transgender practices.

It is relevant to note that among these ten transmasculine subjects in Lee's video, none identify as a white heterosexual man. Six of these subjects identify as people of color, including a Eurasian Filipino/white American, a Panamanian American, a Latino Cuban/Venezuelan American, a Eurasian Chinese/white American, an African American expatriate living in Britain, and a Pakistani British. Of the four white subjects, one identifies as a gay man, two are involved in homogenderal couplings, and the last self-identifies as a "boydyke." In this video, Lee and Hurwitz construct a finely calibrated landscape of a transmasculinity made up of heterosexual FTMs, queer-identified FTMs, gay male FTMs, transfags, and transbutches, although none of these terms is mutually exclusive.

FTMS, DIVERSITY, AND MASCULINE HOMOGENDERALITY

In *Trappings,* the concept of masculine homogenderal couplings is especially compelling. Much has been written about the concept of compulsory heterosexuality in queer studies and theory, such as in Judith Butler's works *Gender Trouble* and *Bodies That Matter*. However, in queer theory, compulsory heterosexuality has been viewed as an institutionalized symbolic "law" that governs *genetic* male and female bodies. The particular institutionalized pressures for transsexuals to also conform to compulsory heterosexuality have rarely been discussed in queer theory and in lesbian and gay studies. In some ways, the law of compulsory heterosexuality has historically been even greater for transsexual bodies than genetically sexed bodies. This is because it has been only within the last ten years or so that public discourse has been able to acknowledge and conceive of a *transsexual* body that is also *homosexual.* Historically, only heterosexual transsexuals have been recognized.[3]

Part of the logic that accompanies resistance to the transsexual lesbian or gay man is the refusal to acknowledge sexuality beyond *one* axis. In this case, the choice of homosexuality versus heterosexuality is only deemed relevant for *genetic* bodies, and transsexual bodies are conveniently elided. Thus, according to this logic, a person who was born a genetic female, for

FIGURE 15.1.
The directors of *Trappings of Transhood* and festival directors of Tranny Fest:
Transgender and Transgenre Film, Video, and Culture Festival. *From left to right:*
Elise Hurwitz, Al Austin, and Christopher Lee. *Photo: Christopher Lee.*

instance, and is attracted to males *must* be heterosexual. This kind of limited erotic system cannot take into account that perhaps a genetic female
identifies as a gay man, and so desires men *as a gay man*—and does not
desire men as a heterosexual woman. This limited logic has been reflected
in both medical literature and popular culture.

In the essay "Trans(Homo)Sexuality?" doctor and scientist Vernon A.
Rosario II states that a heterohegemonic logic is in place within the institutions of U.S. sexology in regards to transsexualism. Thus, Rosario cites Robert Stoller, for instance, who suggests that the FTM had been raised by a
feminine and depressed mother and a masculine and distant father who
had not sufficiently supported the mother psychologically. The FTM child,
as a daughter, was encouraged to play the role of the husband substitute
for the mother, in order to comfort the mother and gain the mother's
inadequate affection. Once the daughter reached puberty, she would seek
out another female who would support the transsexual's illusion of possessing a penis, which would defend both girls against any acknowledgment of
a lesbian attachment, so that homosexuality could be denied. Thus, according to Stoller, and other sexologists, such as Vamik D. Volkan, As'ad Masri,

Charles W. Socraides, and Karen Horney, the FTM transsexual strives for an idealized heterosexuality, and thus *must* desire a feminine female, because the FTM (delusionally) sees himself as male (Rosario, 38–39).[4]

In the heterohegemonic logic, then, the stigma of transsexualism is weighed against the stigma of homosexuality. An FTM transsexual can gain the normalcy of heterosexuality at the cost of his biological breasts and genitals by becoming a heterosexual male. However, a queer-identified FTM transsexual is considered to be striving for double stigmatization, as transsexual and homosexual, which is considered a "dysfunctional goal" by these sexologists (Rosario, 40).[5]

Thus, the institutionalized recognition of the queer-identified, or homosexual, transsexual is historically groundbreaking.[6] Rosario scrutinized how transgenderism has been described in relation to homosexuality and heterosexuality in both the revised third edition and the fourth edition of the *Diagnostic and Statistical Manual of Mental Disorders* (DSM-III-R, 1987, and DSM-IV, 1994, American Psychiatric Association). In the DSM-III-R, the classification of "transsexualism" was divided into "homosexual" and "heterosexual" subtypes. However, sexual orientation was based on one's *birth sex,* so that an FTM who was attracted to women would be deemed a *female homosexual* transsexual,[7] whereas an FTM attracted to men would be considered a *female heterosexual* transsexual. These diagnoses were especially confusing since a female *homosexual* transsexual—that is, an FTM who desires women—would actually identify himself as a *heterosexual* transman. And an FTM who desires men, a female *heterosexual* transsexual, would self-identify as either a *gay* man or *queer*-identified FTM.[8]

The DSM-IV superseded the classification of "transsexualism" with the diagnosis of "Gender Identity Disorder,"[9] which includes the subtyping specifier of "Sexually Attracted to Females" or "Sexually Attracted to Males." The DSM-IV notes that virtually all those born female as their birth sex receive the specifier of "Sexually Attracted to Females," although it does acknowledge that there are "exceptional" cases of "females" who are "Sexually Attracted to Males."[10]

As shown by the changes between the DSM-III-R and DSM-IV, Rosario writes that "sex" and "gender" are *historically* contingent (37, italics in original). However, Rosario elaborates beyond the DSM by stating that he does not want to attach qualifiers such as "true" or "biological" to any sex or gender terms. He also does not want to restrict the designation of "transsexual" to only those seeking sex-reassignment surgery. Rosario's definition of transsexuality moves away from "objective," ontological typology to a broad, existential distinction that is far more independent of "scientific" gender definitions and psychosurgical interventions. He terms this a "subject-centered" approach, in which transsexual and transgendered subjects are able to define what the terms "transsexual" and "transgender" mean for themselves (37). Rosario's observations have also been reflected in transsexual and transgender communities from the 1990s to the present. Most FTM communities now stress self-definition, rather than medical definitions and diagnosis, as the most important part of transsexual or transgender identification.[11]

If the 1960s ushered in the concept of *homogenderal* genetic gay male and lesbian couplings, then the decade of the 1990s reflects an exponentially more complex time. The 1990s has not only brought the introduction of transsexuality as a viable identity, but also witnessed the growth of the transgender movement into a cohesive political and cultural force. The transgender movement has demonstrated a great capacity to accommodate diversity within its communities, so that a seemingly infinite number of different transgender and transsexual identities have been defined and articulated. An FTM involved in a masculine homogenderal coupling—either with a genetically male gay man, another FTM, a butch lesbian, or some other masculine-identified body—is not considered odd or exceptional in most contemporary FTM communities. In fact, many FTMs do not restrict their sexual orientation to the homosexual/heterosexual binary, but also may identify as bisexual, polysexual, or pansexual (Fifth Annual True Spirit Conference program, 2001).

Trappings is situated within these greater transgender movements, utilizing what Rosario calls the "subject-centered approach." This allows the transgendered subjects to define their own identities, along with revealing a vast array of diverse FTM life experiences and approaches. In *Trappings,* there is no "central" FTM identity that emerges with other FTM "exceptions" relegated to the margins. All the FTM identities share the center, sometimes intersecting with each other in interesting ways. Thus, it becomes clear how U.S. medicosurgical views on transgenderism, sexuality, and identity are often lagging behind actual identities and practices emerging and flourishing in grassroots communities and day-to-day life.

At least five of the ten subjects participate in some form of masculine homogenderality in *Trappings.* The second shot in the introduction to this video has Euroamerican Shadow Morton emphatically stating that he identifies as a gay man. In a combined interview, African British Zach Nataf states his attraction to large penises, and Del LaGrace, a Euroamerican expatriate residing in England, speaks of his unusual partnerships— involved with a "boydyke" girlfriend and also married to a gay man with whom he has had sexual relations. Cuban Venezuelan American Kory Damon Martin discusses his prior relationship to another Latino FTM, one of Mexican descent. And Euroamerican Zak Sinclair speaks of his emerging transfag identity, his attraction to another transfag within a gay male bar, and his desire to "bed [his] first fagmeat." Upon further reflection, Sinclair wonders how his passing as a white gay man will also be a problematic site of recognition for him.

Lee and Hurwitz employ specific editing strategies in order to demonstrate the spectrum of FTM diversity embodied by their subjects. The editing style is rhythmic, interspersed with montages of rapid-paced jump cuts. Indeed, subjective and topical continuity are achieved through the association of ideas implicit in connected shots (Giannetti, 135).[12] In *Trappings*, then, short shots of interviewees are edited together throughout the entire documentary, with the topics of conversation weaving together into a rich fabric. Each interviewee is filmed in conventional head-and-shoulder medium shots usually centered within the camera frame, interspersed with some close-ups and classical cutting. This convention provides the necessary clarity and focus for the subjects to articulate their thoughts and feelings. Various topics are covered, such as family, kinship structures, sexual partners, FTM and lesbian communities, testosterone, racial and ethnic identifications, and the concept of gender identities and the gender continuum.

The most poignant moments are at the points of direct contradiction. Here, one interviewee will juxtapose and contrast another point of view, achieved through the montage style of editing. Rather than negating each other's experiences and statements, these points of contradiction add additional layers of depth and diversity to the transmasculine experience. For instance, during the section on race and ethnicity, Damon Martin speaks of his experience as a Latino within the predominantly white city of Seattle. He states that he does not know many transgendered people of color. This shot directly cuts to Filipino American Villanueva asserting that he *does* know many transgender people of color, but they pass as (genetic) men or women on the street and do not necessarily want any recognition as "transgendered."

During the section focusing on families of origin, Morton talks about how his family approves of his FTM choice. This segues to Yosenio Lewis explaining how he is accepted on a conditional basis, as only a female family member—that of sister, daughter, and niece within his Panamanian American family. Damon Martin, who experienced strained family ties by moving from Cuba to the United States, attests that his FTM status has completely severed all relations with his Cuban family.

In the beginning of the video, Nataf confesses his long-standing fascination with penises, even when he was a lesbian. He then affirms his present-day attraction to "big cocks" and discusses his sexual interactions with bisexual men. This is contradicted by Damon Martin's narrative, midway through the video, in which he states that he does not particularly like penises, and cherishes his vagina and clitoris. He also states that his dating experiences with (genetic) gay men have been negative. All these examples reveal that no single FTM experience—concerning family, racial identity, sexuality, transition, or gender identity—dominates the video's construction. Instead, a multivocal articulation of diversity is expressed, particularized to each individual's experience.

Trappings, however, does not entirely consist of interview sequences. What gives it true visual and ideological flavor are the sequences of rapid-paced montages, usually accompanied by punk and rock music. This music is recorded by well-known independent-label queer and transgendered musicians and injected with healthy doses of humor. In the first rapid-paced montage, shots are edited together graphically accompanied in parallel sound by the punk song "Transie Chaser" by the Transisters. A close-up of a photo in which Sinclair is in female drag, with his partner in sailor drag, is juxtaposed with Nataf revealing his breast removal surgery incisions, Del LaGrace flexing his tattooed biceps, followed by a close-up of an anonymous male crotch covered in denim, a pan of feminine attire and shots of garter belts worn by various individuals, including a dog!

The second rapid-paced montage highlights shots of Euroamerican Dorian making jerking off movements, then placing his/her entire fist within his/her mouth,[13] thereby effectively penetrating himself, which is then followed by shots of a "gender-fluid" individual[14] in S/M fagboy gear, fondling his/her dick, and posing in leather vest and pants, with both dick and breasts showing. The song "Faggot Man" by Alyssa Izen accompanies this sequence.

"Wrong Bathroom" by hardcore punk dyke band Tribe 8 provides the soundtrack for the third graphic montage, in which train tracks are juxtaposed with Pakistani British Stephen James Siddique, in jest, pretending to *go back* into the closet, close-up crotch shots of male Star Trek dolls, close-ups of Tonka toy trucks, boy scout uniforms, a trannyboy (FTM) in female drag (which I term "double cross-dressing") dancing behind a scrim, a group photo shot of transmasculine subjects groping each other, female and male bathroom symbols, and Dorian "terrorizing" his cat with his dildo. This sequence ends with a close-up of a half-eaten plum.

All the shots in the montage sequences are either tightly framed close-ups or looser medium shots, but there are never any long shots. The visual rhythm of watching tight frames with somewhat looser frames creates a visual tension that contributes to the heightened excitement of the erotic and sexual possibilities of these masculinities.

Partially taking its cue from gay male culture, graphic relationships of gendered textures are also represented. Feminine signifiers such as garter belts, lipstick, and erotic dancing are shown with the actual visual representations of FTMs in feminine drag. This creates a depth and texture of interwoven feminine signifiers within a field of masculinity and masculine signifiers. These feminine signifiers do not negate or cancel out the masculinities represented but perform as self-reflexive extensions of FTM masculinities, as opposed to the "other" for the FTM "self." The abundant close-up shots and attention to gendered details create an intimacy that maps out the profusion of gendered capital that exists within the FTM landscape.

Many FTMs have elaborated on the expansion of both their personal gender repertoire and their views on gender during and after transition. The particularized attention to detail of both feminine and masculine signifiers represented in *Trappings,* then, is also associated with the augmentation and diversification of gender capital.[15]

REORGANIZED LOGIC/VULNERABILITY OF TIME

One example of this diversification of gender capital are the several allusions to "double cross-dressing," which is the practice of FTMs dressing up in feminine attire. This is indicated in both the advertisement for *Trappings* and within *Trappings* itself. If we could map out this performance it would look something like this:

$$F \quad T \quad M \quad T \quad DQ \quad T \quad M \quad T \ldots$$

in which each particular gender articulation (female to male to drag queen to male to . . .) could be read as what Eve Kosofsky Sedgwick calls "provisional meaning-consolidation[s]." She elaborates further, stating,

> if it has been chosen with some luck and some *self-knowledge,* many new paths and itineraries evidently become visible—paths that seem radically contingent only in the sense that *their existence could never have been guessed from the place from which one began* . . . they appear as necessary—that is, as much a part of the landscape of the *grounded and real—*as anything could be. (238, emphasis added)

The mapping of this particular trajectory, then, can be seen as articulations of self-knowledge.

In *Trappings,* the provisional meaning-consolidations of double cross-dressing invoke sites of revisitations that are repeated visually throughout the video. Yet each repetition, each visual representation, is read differently, interrogating and excavating another shift in meaning. A second reading, then, could be as follows:

$$F^1 \quad T \quad M^1 \quad T \quad dq \quad T \quad m^2 \quad T \ldots$$

where F^1 and M^1 are construed as originary sites of access to femininity through femaleness, and masculinity through maleness, in the particular spatiotemporal section I am looking at represented by the double cross-dressing example.[16] The crossing from "drag queen" to m^2 allows for another site of excavation, in which the "2" designates a new situated territory of masculinity not previously touched or known in the first crossing over to M^1. The designation of drag queen shifts from capital letters to lowercase letters to further elucidate this as a newly excavated site that has happened from a double cross—as opposed to signifying this as a stable identification which capitalization may imply.

And yet even this could be unpacked further. Another cross-examination, another crossing of this particular gender text, reveals yet another trajectory:

$$F^1 \quad T \quad M^1 \quad T \quad f^2 \quad T \quad m^2 \quad T \ldots$$

In this case, the primary female-to-male sites lead into secondary revisitations of femininity as second order (through drag queenness) and masculinity as second order, which can lead into tertiary sites, etc., depending on the repetitions of this practice and/or the relevance of these meaning-consolidations. And yet secondary (or tertiary, for that matter) does not mean "subsidiary" or "second place," or even necessarily derivative of the "primary" gender articulations, much as a double cross is not somehow "less than" a primary cross.

I would like to offer that these revisitations are extensions and elaborations from the primary sites but not false replications or the "bad copy." I question whether the emphasis on "primary" or "originary" as the only real or authentic site of articulation—whereas secondary, tertiary, and subsequent revisitations or extensions are construed as bastardized or false replications of the former—is actually a distinctly Western Enlightenment formulaic concept.

Because of the editing style in *Trappings,* the rhythmic montage of these visual representations is to happen fairly close in time to each other. There are also graphic relationships that support this practice, such as the feminine signifiers of garter belts, lipstick, and erotic dancing—not necessarily in direct relation to transmasculinity per se—along with the actual visual representations of trannyboys in drag, that create a depth and texture of interwoven feminine meaning-consolidations within a field of masculinity and masculine meaning-consolidations.

Thus, if we could take the visual crossings of this particular text in a rhythmic way, it would look like this:

$$F \quad T \quad M \quad T \quad DQ \quad T \quad M \quad T \ldots$$
$$F^1 \quad T \quad M^1 \quad T \quad dq \quad T \quad m^2 \quad T \ldots$$
$$F^1 \quad T \quad M^1 \quad T \quad f^2 \quad T \quad m^2 \quad T \ldots$$

These provisional meaning-consolidations construct a visual field through their repetitions. The "T"s—these crossings—syncopate between these gender articulations. The nuances that are uncovered by repeating, by revisiting, are subtle and varied enough to be exciting in their differences.

The spaces that exist in between each crossing and gender articulation are not even, regulated spaces. There can be variations in distance, time, speed of travel, and extensions of gender expression that cannot be fully expressed in this diagram. And yet the "T"s form a continuity of breaks, crosses, and contingencies. This is a social ground of variable masculinities in which provisional meaning-consolidations occur and variable spaces surround and embrace each gender term and each crossing, while also being punctuated and disturbed by the terms. A constant exchange of movement happens between spaces and crossing, between spaces and articulations, within this social field.

This is not about gender play as mere pleasure (or frivolity) but rather is of the order of heightened tension, in which the Derridean notion of the "postponement of satisfaction, the abandonment of a number of possibilities and the temporary toleration of unpleasure (or nonclosure)" is a step on the long indirect road to *jouissance* (19). In *The Postmodern Condition,* Jean-François Lyotard states that uncertainty and unknown outcomes increase as accuracy increases (56). In applying this to the mapping of double cross-dressing, then, the apparently unstable resignifications and disruptions of any kind of gender and sex determinism directly link not only to more accurate and precise gender articulations, but more accurate and precise masculinities.

Indeed, Lyotard refutes the positivist "philosophy" of efficiency and stresses that *legitimacy* comes from "counterexamples . . . the unintelligible . . . paradox . . . new rules in the games of reasoning" (54). Echoing Derrida's concept of the long, indirect road to *jouissance,* then, a lag time is a key component in this legitimation—a time of the unintelligible, the paradox. This lag time can thus be seen as a vulnerability in time, before and after, and sometimes during, an articulation—not exactly the crossing or the spaces, but not entirely separate from these either. Perhaps the vulnerability in time has to do with the intricate exchanges between the two. Thus, we can see how this project is also a strategic one, a spatiotemporal ground of accurate and precise masculinities not only composed of articulations, crossings, spaces, and exchanges, but also of particular vulnerabilities in time.

Gender potentials of transmasculinities also carry definitive political overtones. For instance, in "The Theoretical Subject(s) of *This Bridge Called My Back* and Anglo-American Feminism," Norma Alarcón explicates that (Anglo-American) feminism may have problematized gender relations to a certain degree but has not disturbed the actual *logic of identification*—through which the subject of knowledge and her *complicity* with the notion of consciousness as synthetic unificatory power, the center point of organization that links together representations in a certain narrow and deterministic way, remains intact: "As a result, some Anglo-American feminist subjects of consciousness have tended to become a parody of the masculine subject of consciousness, thus revealing their ethnocentric liberal underpinnings" (357).

If the logic of identification with this particular mode of consciousness can then be extended to the transmasculine project, what are the political and social ramifications? Indeed, the transmasculine subject is not necessarily a "parody" of the masculine subject of consciousness but may have direct access to what Jean Bethke Elshtain describes as the "Western masculine" terms of "raw power, brute force, martial discipline, law and order" (Alarcón 357, 358). One performance of such would be that of simple outward projection—projection onto another(s), a crossover that is informed by, and reestablishes, specific and certain power relations.

In one humorous moment in *Trappings*, Sinclair realizes that for him to identify as a transfag is problematic because he will be passing as a *white* gay man, with, one assumes, the attendant complicated negotiations of racial and gender power disparities. The play of double cross exceeds the narrow realms of "gender territory" and really points to prior and current acts of power within many histories, including racial, ethnic, and class discourses. Alarcón cites Sandra Harding in that "there are suggestions in the literature of Native Americans, Africans, and Asians that what [Anglo-American] feminists call feminine versus masculine personalities, ontologies, ethics, epistemologies, and world views may be what these other liberation movements call Non-Western versus Western personalities and world views" (358).

JeeYeun Lee reiterates similar concerns in "Why Suzie Wong Is Not a Lesbian: Asian and Asian American Lesbian and Bisexual Women and Femme/Butch/Gender Identities." It is of utmost significance that the "illogical" masculine practices exhibited in *Trappings* not be conflated with "retrogressive" femininity or feminizations, since this reduction would serve to reify the Euroamerican logic of masculine identification. JeeYeun Lee states that "our gender identities do not resonate solely in the context of compulsory heterosexuality: they are also affected by histories and practices of racialization and ethnocentrism and differences in cultural standards . . . what it means to be masculine or feminine are influenced not only by dominant U.S. norms but also by [Asian American] perceptions of various Asian cultural standards of gender" (117).

Thus, when gender evaluations are made according to white American hegemonic norms—ethnic histories and cultural differences are distorted, elided, or erased—then queer, colored gender identifications, performances, and play are constantly misinterpreted or reinterpreted. For instance, one butch-identified Asian American woman states that within Cantonese heterosexual roles, the men are softer[17] and more family-oriented than the white Western heterosexual masculine role: "It's just not the same" (124). Relationships to gender identities—including gender play (such as double cross-dressing)—point to the intersections of sex, appearance, anatomy, sexuality, race, culture, and economic systems (115).

However, it is equally significant that the transmasculine project discussed in this chapter goes beyond that of "Western" versus "non-Western" cultural differentiations. I believe that what is being proposed are actually valences of new strains of masculinities that offer strategic wide-spread ramifications. These, then, are alternatives whose complex sedimentary layerings of meanings unravel in and through the vulnerability of time.

The transmasculine project of double cross follows what, in this historical moment, may appear as an *illogics* of masculine identification—that is, not only repeatedly crossing over boundaries that separate two or more categories, but also concerned with the continual linkage of outward projection to inward reception, the performance of gender potentials to masculine interiorities, the constant rhythmic turning back—self-reflexive circuitries. This shifts the cast of masculinity, and other associated terms, such as *mastery,* from that of a decidedly limited "Western" Enlightenment or Euroamerican subject of consciousness. Thus, transmasculinity can start to be related to masculinities of color in cogent and relevant ways, such that even, say, a white gay FTM who subscribes to this *illogic,* then, is intrinsically linked to particular value systems that also inform masculinities of color. The variable masculine spatiotemporal social ground, intrinsically connected to accuracy, vulnerability, and legitimacy, can be extremely generative not only of gender and sexuality but also of new relationships to national, racial, and cultural values and legacies.

In the essay "Tribes within Nations," Martin Thom elucidates the differences between the political ideologies of Ernest Renan and Emile Durkheim. Renan proposes that the imprint of an invading force becomes the mold or imprint of the actual resulting nation or culture, the invasion or conquest characterized by "harshness and arrogance" (30). Durkheim, on the other hand, proposes that nation and community are held together as a consequence of a complicated mesh of *internal relations.* He rejects the "metaphysics of invasion," in which national identity is based on the legacy of memories between conquerors and conquered, and instead stresses a community based on the composition of individuals as the factors of social life. His concept of "social tissue," originally proposed by Schaeffle, is concerned with the shared origins, traditions, and value systems of individuals; "the collective consciousness is above all composed of clear ideas" (37–38).

Durkheim's concepts of social tissue and clear consciousness provide some interesting insights to how a variable masculine social ground can be a viable intervention—and indeed a generative force—for new cultures, races, nations. Indeed, this project is about more accurate and precise meaning-consolidations and intricate and complex *internal* relativities among gender articulations, vulnerabilities, time, exchanges, and crossings. This is also a project of clear ideas producing individual and collective masculine "consciousness." Durkheim states that his model of social tissue is concerned with the ideal links and values that do or do not bind together members of a community: "Yet they are interwoven in a thousand different ways. They cross in the heart of each individual" (cited in Thom, 37).

However, the variable masculine social ground differs from Durkheim's proposal in a fundamental way. Thom equates Renan's philosophy with that of an "obscure consciousness" as generating force, in which "dynasties" were founded through barbaric and unconscious epochs, where "humanity lives in those mysterious shadows which found respect" (30). Thom deems this as "irrationalist" and contrasts this to Durkheim's concepts of "rational" movements based in clarity. This is obviously a connection that seeks to stabilize the Enlightenment tradition of linking the rational-logical-clarity value system, and it is this very system that the transmasculine project not only disrupts and questions but also *reorganizes*.

I argue that the variable social ground carefully begins to separate clarity from logic and the rational, as also a definitive postcolonial move. The linkage of clarity to the *illogics of masculine identification* is an extension of both Alarcón's critique of the rationalist logic of masculine identification and Rosario's discussion of the limits of the heterohegemonic logic in U.S. sexology. It is inherently synchronous with postcolonial, poststructuralist, and transgender endeavors. According to María Fernández, "Postcolonial studies has been concerned primarily with European imperialism and its effects: the construction of *European master discourses,* resistance, identity, representation, agency, gender and migration, among other issues" (59, emphasis added). If part of postcoloniality's project is to excavate and clarify the perceived obscurantist effects resulting from conquest, invasion, colonization, war, and exploitation, then this focus is aligned with the focus inherent in these complex gender articulations, for both are concerned with vulnerabilities in space and time.

Therefore, both Renan's and Durkheim's theories can be bridged in that the obscurant consciousness of prior violence, harshness, and arrogance can cross over into new meanings. For instance, recognition of violence previously introjected within the Enlightenment project points to obscurant sites of incompatibility, incommensurability, and nonclosure. And yet the widespread rigidification of gender and sexual orientations that have permeated many races, nations, and cultures points to *deeper* layers of obscurant histories. Feudalist and religious-based inequitable economic systematic violence, and conquest, intraracial and intraethnic, have also contributed to gliches in gender and sexual potentials and identities.[18] However, through focus, care, and attention to the sites of obscurantism, and through the cultivation of a "surplus"[19] necessary for the continual sustenance of such focus, other kinds of clarity emerge, perhaps ones that could not have been predicted or known before—another kind of illogic.

It would be simplistic to understand variable masculinities as only those of "racial or cultural differences." The illogics of this project are spatiotemporal responses and impulses that emerge from specific collective experiences of colonization and economic exploitation. This social ground is *informed* by these prior discourses but not *determined* by them.

The collective consciousness of a new culture, nation, or race does not necessitate that every individual must have the same experiences.[20] Indeed, Durkheim states,

> Society is not a simple collection of individuals, it is a being which has preceded those of whom it is composed and which will survive them, which acts upon them more than they act upon it, which has its own life, its own consciousness and its own destiny. (cited in Thom, 36)

This collective cultural consciousness, therefore, is one that is informed by fundamental tenets of postcolonial and racialized reorganization around a system of illogics in which *clarity* facilitates the creation of masculinities, genders, and identities not necessarily known or recognized before, yet is somehow dependent on the recognition of the effects from a layered obscurantist "metaphysics of invasion."

With this masculine social ground, then, what kinds of new nations, cultures, races, and identities are generated? It is interesting to correlate Lyotard's description of the positivism of efficiency and productivity to colonialism's program of racial and economic exploitation as a way to increase productivity of goods and capital. This positivist philosophy of efficiency, then, can be seen as a colonial imprint that seeks to mark and stabilize an Enlightenment logic of racial, gender, and sexual identifications with an investment in the foreclosure of time for sake of "efficiency." The Derridean transmasculine paradigm considers the abandonment of a number of possibilities, the movement into a number of different provisional meaning-consolidations, the long indirect road, and the circulation of *jouissance*. Finally, it is about the nonclosure, disclosure, and vulnerability of time—in which time is revealed as that of exposure to crossings, to unintelligibility, to paradox—and time's own inherent instability. By making these connections, we can see how Enlightenment discourse has oftentimes located racialized peoples, queer subjects, and women within the "murky" realms of madness and the irrational—oftentimes conveniently deposited onto the site of the "feminine"—with the attendant conclusions around barbarism and/or primitivism.

Although these correlations have been critiqued, deconstructed, and unpacked in numerous other scholarly enterprises, I think it is crucial that the most delicate and minute associations around logic and time also be examined. I assert that any interventions around race, sexuality, culture, nation, or history cannot effectively be considered without these more subtle distinctions and interpolations.

PASSING/SEDIMENTATION

How can spatial and temporal interventions be employed in discussing racialized identity, especially Asian American racialization? Lee is a mixed-race Asian American, so how does this aspect of his identity, and the Asian American body in general, figure within the past and current U.S. masculine symbolic? What connection can an examination of Asian American identity make, if any, to transmasculinity?

Lisa Lowe attributes an "enormous widening of the definitions of 'Asian American'" to the 1965 Immigration and Nationality Act, which abolished former national-origin quotas and exclusions (7). Since this was also the time of increasing awareness and criticism regarding the United States in the Vietnam War, a paradox was established—on one hand, "Asians" were scripted as bodies of victimization, frozen in a traumatized past, and on the other hand, the bodies of Asian immigrants were experiencing an unprecedented flow and *directed* movement into the United States. As Lowe states, the "return of the repressed" is the repressed history of U.S. imperialism and neocolonialism in Asia borne out in the "return" of immigrants to the imperial center (16).

Because of this paradox, and the numbers of Asian immigration after 1965, Lowe maps how the Asian American has come to figure as the perpetual immigrant, employed as flexible "variable capital" according to U.S. economic needs and the "transraceable" subject par excellence within the period of modernity—sometimes white, sometimes not, sometimes black, sometimes neither—according to the capricious dictates of the times (16). I would also like to argue that it is not mere coincidence that the Asian American body, scripted as "yellow," resonates closely to the linguistic figuration of the mulatto as "high yellow," which has historically been another site of transraceable anxiety.

Judith Butler, in *Bodies That Matter*, investigates the mulatta in Nella Larsen's *Passing*. Clare's crossing of the color line between black and white enacts nonclosure, since it is not that she crosses the color line once and stays put—as Irene does within a racialized bourgeois context—but crosses back and forth over this line, exposing it as permeable. What kinds of masculinities, or gender identities, then, could emerge and revolve around Clare's performances of racial nonclosures? Clare traces different trajectories of racial difference and privilege each time, in the crossing back—*retraversée*—through the mirror that subtends all speculation, which Luce Irigaray terms the "elsewhere" of "feminine" pleasure. This *retraversée* is an eroticism structured by repetition and displacement, penetration, and exposure (46, 167–78).

In *Are We Not Men?*, Phillip Brian Harper discusses the "fundamental femininity" of the mulatta/o, in which even a *nonhomosexual* male mulatto is demarcated by a feminine identification (108–13, 115–17). In examining the novel *Passing,* Harper links Clare's crossings as indicative of a feminine "instability" that is viewed as essentially sinister because of the fathomless interiority of its enigmatic nature (114). Thus, the term "yellow" points to a femininity that is fundamentally unstable and profoundly interior.

As Clare crosses back and forth over the color line, Lee also performs a similar crossing back and forth over the gender line, double movements, double trajectories, both in the rapid-paced montage sequences of *Trappings* and in other transvideos such as *Christopher Chronicles I* (1996) and his FTM/FTM porn videos *Sex Flesh in Blood* (1999) and *Alley of the Trannyboys* (1998).[21] However, unlike Clare in *Passing,* Lee's travels are not dictated by the fluctuating circumstances of his environment. Lee enacts gender performances that are strategically deployed with skill and mastery of both craft and subject matter. This strategic deployment arises out of Lee's knowledge of the contours of his own self and various FTM communities.[22]

In the graphically edited montage sequences, both female and male body parts are revealed and then sometimes concealed; repeated phallic and "boy" images are sometimes displaced by feminine fetish objects, such as lipstick and garter belts. The repetitions and displacements do not serve to cancel out or undermine the masculine identities and presence in the video, but rather aim to construct new meanings and images of masculinity, thus broadening and widening the scope of possibilities. If feminine iconography and signifiers, especially in racialized contexts, can be read as signs of vulnerability and disclosure, then the crossing over—the *revisitations*—to those sites serve as acts of complex sedimentary layerings within the tropes of masculinity.

It is often much too easy to collapse any kind of new gender (and for that matter, racial) articulations into the domain of the "feminine"—in which femininity serves as the catchall for gender and racial performances that do not fit within hegemonic masculine gender norms. As a way to avert any actual threats to this order, potentially disruptive identities, such as the racially passing mulatta, are reduced to "inoffensive frivolity" (Harper, 118). I would like to consider, then, what could happen if the third term of the mulatto (or a third sex, or transsex) was not conveniently collapsed into the "enigma" of a feminine space but was allowed to remain as a point of precise tension—a precise tension revealed through particular surface textures.

The visual tension that would arise from this disjunctive gender identity also correlates to the visually disjunctive experience of Lee's mixed-race heritage. Many mixed-race Asian Americans have articulated the concept of intimate familial relations that have been built on the premise and through the experience of visual disjunction. That is, the child is not seamlessly racially mirrored by either parent. However, many mixed-race Asian Americans, including Lee, have attested to the profound linkages that are formed within family that does not, and cannot, assume visual and racial-ized seamlessness.[23]

However, in traditional Asian American studies and discourse, "opposi-tional resistance" to white U.S. hegemony has often been "figured" as the full-blooded Asian American body, raised within biological family. This full-blooded body claims an anachronistic mythic belief in an Asian agency through a "legacy" of full-blooded ancestors in their past (as a "corrective" to the actual role of Asian Americans as flexible variable capital). This mythic belief, then, presupposes a "racial harmony" formed through the regeneration of visually similar racialized bodies. However, how would Asian American identity shift, complicate, and deepen through the funda-mental reorganization of *racial* identity that is based on the premise of *visual disjunction*, in which visual disjunction is actually the basis of a knowl-edge of self, an intimacy between family members, and thus, a site of racial identity? Lee himself has articulated how his embodiment and experiences as a mixed-race Asian American have informed his ability to inhabit and relate to different FTM identities and practices.[24]

In the beginning of this essay, I stated that in *Trappings* multiple FTM identities are the norm, rather than the exceptions. Thus, I end with the question of how multiple Asian American identities, including mixed-race identities, can also become the norm of Asian American discourse, rather than the exceptions. This accommodation of mixed-race identities in Asian American discourse must also contend with the actual experiences of dif-ferent (inter)racialized embodiments and familial arrangements. And Asian American agency cannot afford to continue in its belief of a full-blooded racialized and visual symmetry of race, but must instead find a new and complex agency through more particularized excavations of self, history, and nation.

In conclusion, the historical trajectories of transsexual movements and identities have profound relevance for the conception of race and ethnic-ity. In order for new cultural identities to emerge, a critique and disman-tling of certain internalized logics around identity must occur. A reorganization around an illogics of identity must also include the map-ping of what has been previously considered a feminized "enigmatic interi-ority" and the accommodation of double crosses into multiple, visually disjunct, gendered, and racialized sites of embodiments.

NOTES

1. American Boyz is the largest FTM organization in North America, with affil-iates in twenty-three states and provinces. It was started by mixed-race Native Ameri-can Gary Bowen in 1995, with an intention to specifically focus on the needs and

issues of queer-identified FTMs, while also accommodating FTMs of other sexual persuasions. American Boyz annually sponsors the True Spirit conference.

2. For instance, for the Fifth Annual True Spirit Conference held in Washington, D.C., in February 2001, the workshops and demographic and community questionnaire included these gender identity categories: Androgyne, Drag King, Feminist, Leatherperson/S/M, Male (genetic), Third-gender, Transman, Tomboy, Butch, F2M/FTM, Genderbender, MTM, Questioning, Transgendered, Transwoman, Cross Dresser, Female (genetic), Intersexual, M2F/MTF, SOFFA (an acronym that stands for Significant Others, Friends, Family, and Allies), Transsexual, Refuse to be Labeled, Liminal Gendered, and, of course, a space for "Other." The categories for sexual orientation and preferences included Bisexual, Lesbian, Gay, Poly, Heterosexual, Refuse to be Labeled, and "Other." For both these questions, participants were allowed to check all categories that applied to them, thus encouraging multiple responses from any given respondent that would, it was hoped, reflect more finely calibrated demarcations of their identity (Fifth Annual True Spirit Conference program, 2001).

3. In order to look at how compulsory heterosexuality has historically functioned as symbolic law for transsexual bodies, consider two MTF autobiographies that Patrick Califia-Rice has written about in *Sex Changes: The Politics of Transgenderism*. Califia-Rice states that Christine Jorgensen "never rocks the social sex-role boat" (28). In her autobiography, *Christine Jorgensen: A Personal Autobiography*, Jorgensen sees herself as "nature's mistake" and different than the corrupt and willful sexual minorities (read "gay and lesbian people"). Jorgensen surrounds herself with "normal" men and women, and Califia-Rice notes that other transsexuals are rarely mentioned. Jorgensen passes perfectly as a woman in her flawless and tasteful wardrobe and feminine jewelry. Of course, Jorgensen's sexual orientation as a heterosexual woman is imperative as part of her sex change (28).

As contrast, Califia-Rice also discusses MTF Jan Morris's autobiography *Conundrum*. Morris successfully lived as an adult man before her sex change to a woman. As a man, she met her "soul mate," Elizabeth, with whom she had five children, three boys and two girls. Morris describes her relationship to Elizabeth as "one particular love of an intensity so different from all the rest, on a plane of experience so mysterious, and of a texture so rich . . . so absolute was our empathy" (quoted in Califia-Rice, 33). Yet after her transition, Morris is careful to characterize her relationship to her wife as an asexual one (37). Califia-Rice notes that Morris does not want the added marginalized status of being a lesbian along with the stigmatized identity of transsexual. Morris apparently is never involved with anyone else after transition, since she perceives all the men she is attracted to as inaccessible in one way or another (37). After the transition, Morris and her wife decided to alter their relationship; they become "sisters-in-law," and Morris becomes an adoring and interfering aunt in the raising of her children (35).

Califia-Rice writes that health care professionals, as gatekeepers, allowed some transsexuals to receive sex changes and denied others who wanted sex changes if the latter did not fit the medical profession's criteria of "true transsexuals." These decisions by the medical institutions had a huge effect on the way transsexuals viewed themselves, as well as the way they presented themselves to each other and to the public (48). Therefore, Morris, who distinctly states a strong emotional and physical connection to her wife, is unable to conceive of herself continuing these ties after her transition—that is, to identify herself as an MTF lesbian—and instead becomes one of those "kind, busy, unmarried [women] of a certain age" (37).

4. Rosario also cites several psychiatrists who confusedly exclaim that if a "woman" has "normal" attractions to men, why would she want to become male

in order to be homosexual (39–40)? Thus, in 1987, Ray Blanchard, Leonard Clemmensen, and Betty Steiner decided to exclude the one FTM gay man in their study and statistical analysis of seventy-two gender-dysphoric females, entitled "Heterosexual and Homosexual Gender Dysphoria." They state, "We do not mention this very unusual case further" (cited in Rosario, 39). This bias was also reflected in mainstream U.S. culture, even within the 1990s. Rosario cites two sources—Amy Bloom, in the *New Yorker* in 1994, and Lou Sullivan, in his book *Information for the Female to Male Cross Dresser and Transsexual*—that indicate that FTM attractions for other men were deemed contradictory to the diagnosis of transsexualism itself (Rosario, 39).

5. Ki Namaste also asserts the medicosurgical institution's primacy on heterosexuality. Thus, she writes that transsexuals often have to lie and invent personal histories in order to validate a heterosexualized narrative of masculine or feminine development. Thus, FTMs, for instance, are expected to speak about their lives as little boys and to conceive of themselves as heterosexuals, since she warns that psychiatric institutions often cannot acknowledge FTM gay men or MTF lesbians (197).

6. Rosario points out that it wasn't until 1983 that the first FTM with sexual attractions to homosexual men was described in clinical literature. This was in psychoanalyst and psychotherapist Leslie Lothstein's monograph *Female-to-Male Transsexualism* (Rosario, 39). Although Lothstein mentions an FTM gay man in his study, other researchers have been resistant to this conception into the 1990s. Jay Prosser finds Lothstein problematic because Lothstein suggests that the transsexual subject's autobiographical account of himself must also be corroborated with biographies produced by significant others in order to detect the inauthentic transsexual from the authentic one (110–11, 246).

7. To complicate matters even more, Rosario examines the term "transhomosexuality," coined by Dorothy Clare in 1984, in which individuals express a strong penchant for, attraction to, or idealization of homosexual persons of the opposite sex. Thus, Rosario states that according to the DSM-III-R and Clary's classification, an FTM who both identifies as a gay man and desires gay men would have been described as a "female heterosexual transhomosexual transsexual." That is a mouthful!

8. These diagnoses, now deemed archaic, conflate homosexuality with transsexuality in regards to the "female homosexual transsexual" or the "male homosexual transsexual," in which transsexuality is placed as the "extreme" form of homosexuality. Thus, a heterosexual transman—that is, an FTM who is attracted to women—would be considered the extreme form of a cross-dressing lesbian (transvestite) who desires women. Rosario also points out that how transsexuality, transvestism, and homosexuality have either been imbricated together in academic scholarship, so that transsexuality is confused with cross-dressing (Marjorie Garber), or else vilified as an antifeminist plot of the patriarchy (Janice Raymond, H. S. Rubin). For many scholars of gay and lesbian studies, transsexuality has simply been overlooked so that, for instance, the "invert" has been embraced as the Victorian ancestor of homosexuality instead of transsexuality (George Chauncey, David Halperin, Esther Newton). Yet there is evidence that the invert was actually the predecessor of the transsexual. Gert Hekma, for instance, notes that nineteenth-century sexological research actually equated "sexual inversion" with gender inversion—not sexual orientation—and that this sexual inversion was understood as the "third sex" (Rosario, 42).

9. The psychiatric criteria for the diagnosis of Gender Identity Disorder are basically twofold: first, "strong and persistent cross-gender identification," or "the

desire to be, or the insistence that one is of the other sex"; and second, gender dysphoria, or "persistent discomfort about one's assigned sex or a sense of inappropriateness in the gender role of that sex," *specifically* a "preoccupation with getting rid of primary or secondary sex characteristics (e.g. request for hormones, surgery, or other procedures to physically alter sexual characteristics to simulate the other sex" (DSM-IV, as cited in Rosario, 37; emphasis added). Rosario observes that these definitions are extraordinary because one of the diagnostic criteria is the demand for medicosurgical intervention. Rosario gives an analogy that the condition of "appendicitis" could be diagnosed *only* if the lower right quadrant abdominal pain in a patient was accompanied by the patient's insistent demand to have an appendectomy (37).

10. These "exceptional" cases may not be so exceptional, especially because seven years have elapsed since the publication of the DSM-IV. Some researchers associated with the Tom Waddell Clinic in San Francisco have noted that gay male and queer-identified FTMs (that is, the diagnosis of Gender Identity Disorder, Sexually Attracted to Males) actually represent the *majority* of FTMs in that city, and that heterosexual FTMs (Gender Identity Disorder, Sexually Attracted to Females) are the minority.

11. However, it is important to note that those transsexuals and transgendered people who choose hormonal supplementation, often termed "hormonal replacement therapy," with or without surgical intervention, must still keep current with the trends in medicosurgical institutions in order to know how to situate themselves within these systems for adequate health care and medical services.

12. As a point of contrast, in another transmasculine documentary, *You Don't Know Dick: Courageous Hearts of Transsexual Men* (directed by Candace Schermerhorn and Bestor Cram; 1997), portraiture is created by a staid camera placement on each transmasculine subject, interspersed with classical cutting of shots from their day-to-day life. Each FTM is allotted a certain amount of time before moving on to the next interviewee, in linear, "logical" sequence.

13. Since Dorian does not necessarily identify as transgendered, but rather as a "boydyke," the choice of exact pronoun is open to question.

14. As described by Christopher Lee, e-mail correspondence, January 28, 2000.

15. E-mail correspondence with Lee, February 18, 2001.

16. This is clearly not to say that those born female are feminine. However, it is generally understood that those born female most likely have had direct access, or even coercion, toward femininity. Also, my use of "male" is contingent on self-definition and nothing else.

17. I would have to argue, however, that the definitions of "hard" and "soft" would definitely have to be interrogated further in this context.

18. An example of intraracial systematic violence is the course of Japanese imperialism and invasion into other Asian countries during the first half of the twentieth century, which culminated in the Pacific War. An estimated 30 million Asians died during the course of Japanese imperialism and the Pacific War (Park, 107).

19. In terms of this discussion, I propose that testosterone supplementation literally performs as a physiological and psychological surplus.

20. I would also like to assert that a collectivity based on a "shared" experience around post- or neocoloniality does not mean that this collective consciousness is automatically "postcolonial." Indeed, there are many such collectives and cultures that still inherently subscribe to Western Enlightenment values, which need to be problematized

21. Both *Alley of the Trannyboys* and *Sex Flesh in Blood* are produced and edited by J. Zapata.

22. E-mail correspondence with Lee, February 18, 2001.

23. This is discussed in *Christopher Chronicles I.* Also see the Asian American magazine *Oriental Whatever,* vol. 2, no. 2, edited by Dan Wu and Wei Ming Dariotis, and "GenerAsians: Transgressive Sexuality and Transformations of Identity," a dissertation by Wei Ming Dariotis. Familial intimacy based on visual disjunction must also include transnational Asian American adoptees. South Korea had been the single largest source of transnational adoptees to the United States from 1953 to 1988. Recently, there has been a trend for U.S. couples to adopt baby girls from mainland China. These Asian American adoptees have overwhelmingly been adopted by non-Asian families, usually Euroamerican families. See narratives in *Association for Korean Adoptees* newsletters.

24. E-mail correspondence with Lee, February 18, 2001.

REFERENCES

Alarcón, Norma. "The Theoretical Subject(s) of *This Bridge Called My Back* and Anglo-American Feminism." In *Making Face, Making Soul: Creative and Critical Perspectives by Feminists of Color,* edited by Gloria Anzaldúa, 356–69. San Francisco: Aunt Lute, 1990.

Association for Korean Adoptees Newsletter. 1995–present.

Bornstein, Kate. *Gender Outlaw: On Men, Women, and the Rest of Us.* New York: Routledge, 1994.

Butler, Judith. *Bodies That Matter: On the Discursive Limits of "Sex."* New York: Routledge, 1993.

Califia-Rice, Patrick. *Sex Changes: The Politics of Transgenderism.* San Francisco: Cleis Press, 1997.

Clark, Dorie. "Transgender Activism: Can the Nascent Transgender Community Resolve the Age-Old Battles between the Sexes?" *Boston Phoenix,* August 10–17, 2000, pp. 1–6. Available at: <http://www.bostonphoenix.com/archive/features/00/08/101transgender.html>. Accessed September 30, 2001.

Cloud, John. "Trans across America: Watch out, Pat Buchanan: Ridiculed for Years, 'Transgenders' Are Emerging as the Newest Group to Demand Equality." *Time.com,* July 20, 1998, 1–4. Available at: <http://www.time.com/time/magazine/1998/dom980720>. Accessed September 30, 2001.

Dariotis, Wei Ming. "GenerAsians: Transgressive Sexuality and Transformations of Identity." Ph.D. dissertation, University of California, Santa Barbara, 2000.

———. "Hapa Road Trip." *Oriental Whatever* 2, no. 2 (fall 2000), 16.

Dariotis, Wei Ming, and Dan Wu. "Hapa Patrol." *Oriental Whatever* 2, no. 2 (fall 2000), 18–21.

Derrida, Jacques. *Margins of Philosophy.* Translated by Alan Bass. Chicago: University of Chicago Press, 1982.

Feinberg, Leslie. *Stone Butch Blues.* Ithaca, N.Y.: Firebrand, 1993.

Fernández, María. "Postcolonial Media Theory." *Art Journal* 58, no. 3 (fall 1999): 59–73.

Fifth Annual True Spirit Conference: Celebrating Human Diversity (conference program). Washington, D.C.: American Boyz, 2001.

Giannetti, Louis. *Understanding Movies.* 7th ed. Englewood Cliffs, N.J.: Prentice Hall, 1996.

Harper, Phillip Brian. *Are We Not Men? Masculine Anxiety and the Problem of African American Identity.* New York: Oxford University Press, 1996.

Lee, JeeYeun. "Why Suzie Wong Is Not a Lesbian: Asian and Asian American Lesbian and Bisexual Women and Femme/Butch/Gender Identities." In *Queer Studies: A Lesbian, Gay, Bisexual, and Transgender Anthology,* edited by Brett Beemyn and Mickey Eliason, 113–32. New York: New York University Press, 1996.

Lowe, Lisa. *Immigrant Acts: On Asian American Cultural Politics.* Durham, N.C.: Duke University Press, 1996.

Lyotard, Jean-François. *The Postmodern Condition: A Report on Knowledge.* Translated by Geoff Bennington and Brian Massumi. Minneapolis: University of Minnesota Press, 1984.

Namaste, Ki. "'Tragic Misreadings': Queer Theory's Erasure of Transgender Subjectivity." In *Queer Studies: A Lesbian, Gay, Bisexual, and Transgender Anthology,* edited by Brett Beemyn and Mickey Eliason, 183–203. New York: New York University Press, 1996.

Park, Won Soon. "Japanese Reparations and the 'Comfort Women' Question." *Positions: East Asia Cultures Critique* no. 1 (1997): 107–34. (Special issue, *The Comfort Women: Colonialism, War, and Sex*)

Prosser, Jay. *Second Skins: The Body Narratives of Transsexuality.* New York: Columbia University Press, 1998.

Raverdyke. "How Much Is Too Much? Double Your Pleasure, Double Your Fun, Double Your Dosage of Synthetic Testosterone Esters Delivered Via Intramuscular Injection with Single-Use Needles and Syringes." In *Trans-Health.com,* 2001. Available at: <www.trans-health.com/Iss2Vol1/double.htm>. Accessed October 15, 2001.

Rosario II, Vernon A. "Trans(Homo)Sexuality? Double Inversion, Psychiatric Confusion, and Hetero-Hegemony." In *Queer Studies: A Lesbian, Gay, Bisexual, and Transgender Anthology,* edited by Brett Beemyn and Mickey Eliason, 35–51. New York: New York University Press, 1996.

Sedgwick, Eve Kosofsky. "A Response to C. Jacob Hale." *Social Text,* no. 52–53 (1997): 237–39.

Thom, Martin. "Tribes within Nations: The Ancient Germans and the History of Modern France." In *Nation and Narration,* edited by Homi K. Bhabha, 23–43. New York: Routledge, 1990.

Chapter 16

Teumsae-eso

Korean American Women between
Feminism and Nationalism

ELAINE H. KIM

Cultural geographer Bernard Nietschmann lists North and South Korea as among the world's very few actual "nation-states," which he describes as distinct from either nations ("geographically bounded territories of a common people") or the state ("a centralized political system . . . that uses civilian and military bureaucracy to enforce one set of institutions, laws, and sometimes language and religion within its claimed boundaries. . . . regardless of the presence of nations" [1]). According to Nietschmann, the noninterchangeable nation-state, then, is "a common people with a common historical territory that is governed by an internationally recognized central political system" (1).

Powerful Korean state nationalisms, both South and North, expect Koreans within as well as beyond state boundaries to identify with them. Korean American women are continually called upon by the Korean nation-state to "be Korean," embraced and rejected in turns. The visiting Korean American is harshly berated by a South Korean taxi driver for not being fluent enough in Korean because he imagines her as solely and exclusively "Korean" and views her broken Korean language as a betrayal of the nation-state. Her shame at not being fluent emerges from a similar, if not the same, viewpoint. If she visits North Korea, she will probably be enjoined to somehow serve the fatherland abroad "as a Korean" after she departs. The Korean American struggles to master the language and tries to serve the fatherland, in some part because she wants to avoid the heartbreak of rejection that Theresa Hak Kyung Cha represents in *DICTEE*:

> You return and you are not one of them, they treat you with indifference. All the time you understand what they are saying. But the papers give you away. Every ten feet. They ask you identity. They comment on your ability and inability to speak. Whether you are telling the truth or not about your nationality. They say you look other than you say. As if you didn't know who you were. You say who you are, but you begin to doubt. . . . Not a single word allowed to utter until the last station, they ask to check the baggage.

You open your mouth half way. Near tears, nearly saying, I know you I know you. I have waited to see you for this long. They check each article, question you on foreign articles, then dismiss you. (57–58)

Cha's work is marked by concomitant invoking of and calling into question Korean national identity and "tradition."

"Being Korean" is ultimately not possible for the Korean American feminist, who must in some sense let go of Korea. At least she must let go of Korean state nationalism, which checks the baggage, looks at the papers, adjudging the appearances and "realities" of identity, and requires acceptance of female marginality and subordination. At the same time, she must defend herself against the material violence occasioned by racial and sexual discrimination, political and economic inequality in the United States, and the psychic violence of both abjection and homogenization into conceptual invisibility by the U.S. racialized state.

Certainly Korean and Korean American women have had to grapple continually with androcentrism and sexism within dissident South Korean movements for social change. The labor movement in South Korea was sparked by women textile workers, who comprised almost 90 percent of the textile work force that jump-started South Korean modernization from the 1970s onward. When they began to organize, male goons were hired by company bosses to terrorize the women workers, some of whom were killed or badly injured. Male thugs of similar class backgrounds were hired to rub human excrement into the women's hair and mouths. Even today, when much South Korean effort has gone into writing revisionist histories of those dark days of martial law, when criticizing a government policy could result in arrest and even execution, the pivotal role of women workers in building what ultimately became the world's most spectacular labor movement is far from being fully recognized. Instead, they are bypassed and sidelined because *minjung* nationalism agrees with the state that only men can be the real subjects of history. Thus Pak Kwang-su's moving film *Chŏn T'ae-il* (*A Single Spark*, 1995), which revisits the Peace Market textile factories in 1970, centers on the male worker who immolated himself to bring attention to the plight of the mostly female factory workers. Chon T'ae-il must "save" the young female bodies that need menstrual leave and bathroom breaks. Delicate, pretty, innocent, sweet, and utterly without agency, they are deserving of his strategizing, his help, and his ultimate sacrifice.

Korean American progressive social movements have also been built around belief in the ultimate importance of male political and social centrality, and Korean American women have historically found themselves serving food, being subject to sexual harassment, objectified as sexual conquests, and sometimes becoming victims of physical violence by men even within these movements. Thus the putatively progressive Korean American male leadership all too often reinforces rather than challenges South Korean state-promulgated gender norms and values, which emerge from the blend of "old" Korean neo-Confucianism and "new" militarized masculinity.

Korean American feminists have understandably been attracted to pan–Asian American progressive women's organizations, such as the Asian Women's Shelter (AWS) and Asian Immigrant Women Advocates (AIWA), just to name two San Francisco Bay–area organizations. AWS serves women who are victims of domestic violence; AIWA serves superexploited Asian immigrant women workers. The effectiveness of these organizations lies in part in their ability to forge networks and alliances across ethnicities and language groups as well as even social classes while deploying what can be termed "female styles of organizing." This might mean that in place of conventional hierarchical decision-making processes, rank-and-file opinions and input are solicited and utilized. AWS pays special attention to the children of battered women. AIWA meetings include family members and feature child care because the women organizers understand, as many Korean American male organizers do not, that the women's paid jobs, unpaid household labor, and participation in organizing efforts cannot be easily separated. In AIWA, lines of affinity between immigrant women workers and college women are reinforced not only through consumer boycott strategies but also in workplace literacy programs in which college women teach English to immigrant women workers while themselves learning firsthand about labor exploitation, anti-immigrant policies and sentiments, and gender and race inequality. But what Helen Heran Jun, in her brilliant essay "Contingent Nationalisms," calls the "woman's touch" in community organizing is best seen in the ways AIWA and AWS negotiate their interstitial positions by calling in turn upon the resources of the labor and women's movements on the one hand and of the ethnic communities on the other, sometimes strategically leveraging these arenas off against each other with a kind of lithe flexibility that neither those movements nor those communities themselves possess. This interstitiality that is the basis of the danger of Korean American women's conceptual erasure is also the place from which ever-more heterogeneous and mixed strategies of resistance to domination and exploitation can emerge.

Aihwa Ong has argued that we must modify sweeping generalizations about East and Southeast Asian "patriarchy" as being solely responsible for the construction of unequal industrial relations in Asia. The "dialectic of gender and capital," Ong asserts, tends to "intensify, decompose, and recompose existing gender hierarchies" (71). Thus, far from *destroying* traditional patriarchies, capitalism *rearticulates* them so that oppressions overlap. At the same time, Ong notes, new patterns of "flexible accumulation" that emerged after the worldwide recession of the early 1970s have resulted in "mixed production systems" in countries such as industrializing

South Korea, where high-tech labor in free trade zones coexists with work in family firms, home work, and subcontracting—all controlled by industrial capital. These mixed production systems can be located any- and everywhere, including within the American heartland, where the largest beef packing plant in the world hires thousands of nonunionized immigrant Asian and Mexican workers in low-paying, dangerous jobs, housing them in trailer parks separated from others who previously inhabited these small southwest Kansas towns "in the middle of nowhere." The immigrant workers have never heard of Wyatt Earp, Truman Capote, or *The Wizard of Oz*. The fabled cornfields have been converted into odiferous feedlots that stretch as far as the eye can see. America is not what we are used to thinking it is, and analyses based on the core–periphery dyad should go the way of the pet rock.[1]

The Korean American woman may focus on what she shares with women workers in both South and North Korea under global capitalism and U.S. military occupation. She may trace her affinities with the Korean woman worker who, like her, is spatially and temporally distanced from the imperial center—*there* in what Laura Hyun Yi Kang has described as "extraterrestrial" free trade zones, military bases, and forbidden territories, and *here* in racial ethnic labor markets (412). The convergence of Korean and Korean American feminisms becomes visible when we focus on the relationship between immigration and the global restructuring of capitalism that is at the root of present-day exploitation of both Korean and Korean American women, whether as factory workers or housewives, as peddlers or prostitutes,[2] whether as beef packers, garment workers, or small business operators.

To give up Korea without being abandoned to other oppressions, Korean American women might build an emancipatory but not atavistic or sentimental Korean American feminist nationalism that creates space for rearticulations of Korean and Korean American female subjectivity and community. This particular nationalism would exist in the kind of opposition to state nationalisms that David Lloyd suggests in "Nationalisms against the State." Korean American feminist nationalism goes against both Korean and U.S. state nationalisms when joining the effort on behalf of the mostly female pico Korea workers, who came to New York in 1989 to protest the sudden closing of the subsidiary of a New York–based company that ceased operations and left South Korea without paying the workers when they started to organize. Korean American feminist nationalism would also oppose Korean and U.S. state nationalisms when supporting the Mexican *maquiladora* workers now striking the South Korea–based Han Young plant in Tijuana.

Korean American feminist nationalism might employ mixed strategies, differently applicable in differing situations, calling into question and subjecting to rearticulation and carnivalization what have been traditionally viewed as fixed and clear-cut boundaries between congealed entities— Korea and the United States, workers and consumers, material and psychic needs, social structures and cultural representations, and perhaps even resistance and complicity.

So far, male-centered dissident movements have not much explored the possibilities of women's cultural struggles, not just over wages and benefits but also for dignity and respect. The heroic South Korean women of the Dong-Il Textile workers strike of the mid-1970s said they wanted to recover their human rights. In the early 1980s, Korean immigrant hotel maids in San Francisco struck for "respectful treatment." As one Korean immigrant room cleaner said, she wanted to learn English so that she could say to her supervisor, "You don't have to yell." She explained, "Why can't she just talk to me about how she wants the work done instead of screaming 'Look at that! Look at that!' "[3]

Robin D. G. Kelley and others have suggested that we pay closer attention to what Raymond Williams has called "structure[s] of feeling" that are a crucial part of social dynamics, so that we can consider how, through the development of new notions of self and community, everyday attitudes and practices might lead us to not only resist but also challenge structures of exploitation and oppression in diverse and perhaps new ways.

In recent years, Korean American women writers and artists have been attempting to create alternative spaces for memory, performances of identity, and social critique by addressing both material conditions and "structures of feeling" in work about Korean immigrant women as well as about women in South Korea. In textual and visual or cinematic work by Korean women scholars and filmmakers in the United States, one of the most frequent subjects is the Korean female sex worker, especially the prostitutes who work around U.S. military bases in South Korea and, after immigration, in this country. Examples include Katharine Moon's book about the implications and politics of camptown prostitution in South Korea, *Sex Among Allies;* Ji-Yeon Yuh's writings on comfort women and work in progress on Korean military brides living in the United States; Hyun Sook Kim's writings on comfort women and on military prostitution, as well as specifically on Kum Yi Yoon, a bar hostess murdered and mutilated by a U.S. serviceman who was finally tried by a South Korean court after months of Korean citizen demonstrations; and on Chong Sun France, the former "bar girl" who immigrated to the United States and was convicted of killing her child after a television fell over on him while she worked at a nearby nightclub; Hyunah Yang's essays on Korean military comfort women; Chungmi Kim's play about comfort women, *Hanako,* premiered in Los Angeles at the East West Players Theater in Los Angeles on April 25, 1999; Dai Sil Kim-Gibson's film *Silence Broken: Korean Comfort Woman,* as well as sections of a book based on extensive interviews of surviving Korean comfort women; and a special issue of the journal *Positions: East Asia Cultures*

Critique entitled *Comfort Women: Colonialism, War, and Sex* (1999) edited by Chungmoo Choi with contributions from Korean and Korean American as well as Japanese and Japanese American writers and artists; Nora Okja Keller's novel *Comfort Woman*, about a Korean woman who escapes from military sexual slavery under the Japanese, marries an American missionary, and lives with her mixed-race daughter in Honolulu; Hye Jung Park and J. T. Takagi's *The Women Outside* (1996), a video documentary on women living and working near U.S. military bases in South Korea; Diana Lee and Grace Lee's *Camp Arirang* (1996), a video on the same subject; and visual artwork by Yong Soon Min that references military prostitution[4] and sex tourism.

Why Korean American women's fascination with this topic? Is it because it is sensational and attention-getting at a time when so many stories compete so fiercely for public attention? Is it because it's relatively easy, since oppression of prostitutes is less complex and less ambiguous than the exploitation of, say, Korean immigrant women electronics assemblers or hotel room cleaners, some of whom hail from the South Korean middle classes and know very well the difference between MIT and Cal Tech as destinations for their sons? Is it because we are locked into a kind of puritanical thinking that separates the "good" girls from the "bad" so that we still have trouble considering sex work as legitimate labor? Or is it about the creation of political and social agency for one class at the expense of another, as women racialized in the West as Koreans are positioned to "give voice to" and represent the subaltern who cannot speak?

In her groundbreaking essay "Si(gh)ting Asian/American Women as Transnational Labor," Laura Hyun Yi Kang rightly connects South Korean industrial workers with sex workers in her discussion of what she calls their "intense corporeality" within the context of United States, European, and Japanese political and economic domination of South Korea. She goes on to suggest that emphasis on Asian women sex workers, and particularly focus that makes use of visual images of these women's bodies, are disturbing because they "uncritically [uncover and expose] the denuded . . . body [putting it] on display" (429), instead of focusing on the political and economic conditions that interpellate Asian women as exploited industrial or sex workers. Invoking Rey Chow and Fredric Jameson, Kang suggests that in view of the differential power relations in visualization and imaging, "uncovering" and "exposing" the Korean prostitute can be thought of as an unnecessary act of aggression, invasion, and exploitation, much like pornography, that could divert attention from the roots of these women's oppression.

Gayatri Chakravorty Spivak notwithstanding, perhaps Korean American women can rethink the old core–periphery relationship between the so-called bourgeois woman-of-color intellectual residing in the West and the so-called subaltern woman still "stuck" in the "third world." Just as it may not be useful to think solely in terms of class consciousness leading to class struggle leading to structural change along a linear trajectory, Korean American and Korean women's identities may overlap in many places, making it difficult to place one as the sovereign and opportunistic voyeur and the other as idealized or victimized and completely without agency.

Korean patriarchy values above all else male lineage and female chastity to preserve that lineage. Abducted and raped women have no legitimate place in the hierarchy. "It does not matter how the vase was broken," according to a Korean adage. Prostitutes, especially those who fraternize with foreigners (*yang saekssi,* or "Western miss"), and mixed-race children (*ainoko, chapjong, t'wigi,* Japanese, Sino-Korean, and Korean vernacular words for "mongrel breed") of these relationships are outside the realm of Korean patriarchal legitimacy. Comfort women have been unrepresentable except as the nation to be avenged by Korean patriarchal nationalism.

Korean American feminist fascination with Korean military prostitution may be rooted in the desire to challenge conventional sexual moralism as well as the narrative of fidelity to the fatherland and to identify instead with the women derided as *yangkongju* (Western princess) or *yanggalbo* (whore of the West) and viewed as traitors to the nation, even when poverty and gender discrimination afford them few other viable options, and even as they support their more highly valued brothers with their earnings and bring needed foreign exchange into the fatherland.

Korean American women may be interested in comfort women and sex workers because as Asian women living in the United States, they too are marginalized and suspect as possible traitors to the Korean nation, and because they too feel subject to the processes of racialization and sexual objectification. Focusing on prostitution works against both gendered Korean nationalism, which based its modernization efforts from the 1960s onward on the creation of an entire class of oppressed female industrial and sex service workers, and against racialized U.S. nationalism, which forcibly distances both the Korean and the Korean American woman as alien Others. Perhaps the Korean American women are turning their attention to the overlooked residues of history, the fragmented, sidelined elements that disrupt the totalizing narratives of South Korean and U.S. nationalism. Perhaps they focus on Korean comfort women and sex workers in an attempt to create space for the inscription of subjugated knowledges and haunting unarticulated histories swept aside as just so much inconsequential litter by the official "winners of history." Perhaps it is their interstitial location between two powerful patriarchal nationalist discourses that allows these Korean American women writers and artists to recognize themselves in those sisters across the waves.

Hye Jung Park, the New York–based codirector of the documentary *The Women Outside,* admits that she was motivated by her own contradictory feelings about her mother's relationships with U.S. servicemen, something she had been ashamed of and had never admitted to other Koreans and Korean Americans before she began to understand the political context. *The Women Outside* is the Korean American visual text that can be said to most "display" the bodies of Korean sex workers, three of whom are interviewed at some length on film. The camera zooms in on their tears as they recall the psychological and physical abuse they suffered at the hands of their estranged American husbands. One woman is interviewed holding a mirror and seated, her legs wide apart as she applies face powder and eye makeup. The camera follows various women soliciting and keeping company with U.S. servicemen in diverse locales near the military bases. The film certainly represents sex work as strategic labor for economic survival. *The Women Outside* might be criticized for attributing the analyses to scholars and case workers and the "feelings" to the prostitutes, and for not doing more to "uncover" and "expose" Korean procurers and American johns. But the visualization of the women's bodies does not displace discussions of the political and economic conditions out of which these "lived experiences" emerge and through which we can better understand and analyze. Park and Takagi trace some of the women's family histories, exploring how a significant part of contemporary South Korean prostitution was formed in the nexus of Korean patriarchy and U.S. military occupation and cultural colonization, within the context of the economic consequences of colonization and war. Moreover, the film carries some of the stories of Korean women married to American military men to the United States, where what is "uncovered" and "exposed" is the racial discrimination and injustices they encounter in America as working-class immigrant women of color.

Some have criticized Nora Okja Keller's 1997 novel *Comfort Woman* because they feel it misrepresents Korean military sexual slavery by fictionalizing it. But I invoke *Comfort Woman* here for the ways it connects Korean and Korean American women by establishing the centrality and subjectivity of the raped Korean mother and the molested Korean American daughter. As lower-class females, the one a raped World War II military prostitute and the other a mixed-race incest victim, they are both "illegitimate." The two women exist in excess of patriarchy, state nationalisms, and their cultures. Keller represents the raped and abused woman as someone who becomes a subject through rape rather than being merely subjected to its violation.

The comfort women in the novel reclaim their selfhood through the language of the body. Forbidden to speak in the comfort stations, they learn to communicate with each other by humming or with their bodies— their eyes, their posture, the tilt of their heads. Before she leaves Korea, Soon Hyo ingests Korean riverbank mud so that Korea will always be part of her. She drinks tea made with American soil when she is pregnant and rubs American earth across her nipples so that her baby will "taste America" with her mother's milk. *Comfort Woman* is about female lineages across national boundaries.[5] Soon Hyo struggles to protect Beccah from what she thinks of as "the poison of male eyes and male breath" by showing her that her body is "hers to name in her own mind, before language dissects her to pieces that can be swallowed and digested by others not herself" (22). Years later, when Beccah is a teenager, she experiences the ways in which language used by men robs a woman of her body by naming it as detestable or desirable. Soon Hyo wants Beccah to have her own subjectivity and her own body, which are more than the nation spaces of Korea and the America contained within the lines on world maps, and which allow for letting go of patriarchal postcolonial Korea and making her own body her "home." Thus she passes the embodiment of her female experience of Korean history to her American daughter.

In "Cooking American, Eating Korean: Food in the Lives of Korean Military Brides," Ji-Yeon Yuh focuses on the intersections of the body, race, gender, class, and nation not through the Korean woman's sexuality but through her relationship to Korean and American food habits and eating practices. Having spent more than three years meeting and interviewing Korean military brides in the United States to explore their encounters with American culture through their experiences of food and eating, Yuh finds out about their shopping for standard brands in chain grocery stores; about their learning to cook food that is called "American" but might in fact be ethnic Jewish, African American, Italian, and so forth; about their trying to incorporate altered Korean dishes into so-called American meals or to serve some Korean food "American" style; about their longing almost to the point of starvation for the Korean food that signifies home and identity; and about their experiences of this longing as a powerful daily reminder of their difference as they find themselves seeking out other Koreans to share meals with or having to eat Korean food alone because their American husbands, in-laws, and children reject it. Yuh is able to show concretely how power inequities—in terms of gender, race, and culture—are expressed in food choice, production, and consumption within the women's families. But what is particularly exciting about Yuh's project is the absence of hierarchy between herself as researcher-writer and the women she meets.

It is clear that as a researcher-writer, Yuh has the background to frame, organize, analyze, interpret, and conjecture about the "larger significance" of what the women told her. Indeed, like her interview subjects, she knows from everyday life experience about certain kinds of domination and discrimination. Like them, she has already tested the possibilities and limits of "biculturalism" in inequality. As a Korean American woman, she also knows about the power dynamics in American gender politics. But she can speak *beside* instead of only *about*—or, as Kobena Mercer and others have said, *from* instead of *for*—the women she interviews because she too yearns for and loves to talk about Korean food. She can share meals with her interviewees, who might ask her how her mother prepares a certain dish or who exclaim, "It's more than just fun to talk about this, don't you think?" According to Yuh, this particular woman notes "that she has lived in the United States for so long that it seems like home [but] at times like this, cooking and eating Korean food with another Korean woman, even a stranger like myself, gave her an indescribable feeling. 'Maybe something like drinking water after being thirsty for a really long time. . . .'"

I like to think that the Korean American feminist writer's and film-maker's "woman's touch" does not push the reluctant Korean female body onto a stage lit up for pornography and commodification but instead reaches for the lines of affinity that might link us in a mutual struggle to understand and struggle against our respective experiences of colonization, racialization, and gender oppression.

NOTES

1. Recent Korean American writing points to gaping distances between positionalities. Europe, Africa, and Asia were named by the ancient Greeks to identify the landmasses bordering the Aegean Sea. Although the idea of these three continents has since become hegemonic, Martin W. Lewis and Karen E. Wigen point out that from a geographical standpoint, Europe is merely "a peninsula of the Eurasian land mass, which hardly justifies continental status." According to them, "It would be just as logical to call the Indian peninsula one continent while labeling the entire remainder of Eurasia—from Portugal to Korea—another."

2. Many South Korean bar girls and masseuses move in and out of various forms of self-employment.

3. *Dust and Threads* (training film), directed by Louise Lo and produced by Asian Women of California in 1986 for AIWA.

4. In *Remembering Jungshindae* (1992), the body of the military prostitute is recalled by the empty dress Min has fashioned by stretching starch-stiffened fabric over a wooden armature and then laying on paint, modeling paste, gravel, dirt, and charcoal bits to give the rigid structure a textured surface, all expressing the severity of the comfort woman's history. The dress is elegiac black, not a traditional color for a Korean dress, and a wire mesh screen is placed at the opening of the neck so that the red light of the acetate seems to glow from inside. Also, gashes in the skirt emit red light like fire or bloody wounds. The Korean script translates, "Your story will not be forgotten."

5. In *Comfort Woman,* Keller celebrates female lineages and networks by repeatedly acknowledging her debt, in terms of themes, images, and language, to other Asian American women writers who came before her: Maxine Hong Kingston, Theresa Hak Kyung Cha, Cathy Song, and Joy Kogawa.

REFERENCES

Cha, Theresa Hak Kyung. *DICTEE*. New York: Tanam Press, 1982.
Choi, Chungmoo, ed. Special issue, "The Comfort Women: Colonialism, War, and Sex." *Positions: East Asia Cultures Critique* 5, no. 1 (spring 1997).

Jun, Helen Heran. "Contingent Nationalisms: Renegotiating Borders in Korean and Korean American Women's Oppositional Struggles." *New Formations, New Questions: Asian American Studies,* edited by Elaine H. Kim and Lisa Lowe. Special issue of *Positions: East Asia Cultures Critique* 5, no. 2 (fall 1997): 325–55.

Kang, Laura Hyun Yi. "Si(gh)ting Asian/American Women as Transnational Labor." *New Formations, New Questions: Asian American Studies,* edited by Elaine H. Kim and Lisa Lowe. Special issue of *Positions: East Asia Cultures Critique* 5, no. 2 (fall 1997): 403–37.

Keller, Nora Okja. *Comfort Woman.* New York: Viking, 1997.

Kelley, Robin D. G. *Race Rebels: Culture, Politics, and the Black Working Class.* New York: Free Press, 1994.

Lewis, Martin W., and Kären Wigen. *The Myth of Continents: A Critique of Metageography.* Berkeley: University of California Press, 1997.

Lloyd, David. "Nationalisms against the State." In *The Politics of Culture in the Shadow of Capital,* edited by Lisa Lowe and David Lloyd, 173–97. Durham, N.C.: Duke University Press, 1997.

Moon, Katharine. *Sex among Allies: Military Prostitution in U.S.–Korea Relations.* New York: Columbia University Press, 1997.

Nietschmann, Bernard. "Miniaturization and Indigenous Peoples: The Third World War." *Cultural Survival Quarterly* 11, no. 3 (1987): 1–15.

Ong, Aihwa. "The Gender and Labor Politics of Postmodernity." *Annual Review of Anthropology* 20 (1991): 279–309.

Park, Hye Jung. Remarks at the Articulations of Korean Women conference, Berkeley, Calif., April 15, 1994.

Yuh, Ji-Yeon. "Cooking American, Eating Korean: Food in the Lives of Korean Military Brides." Philadelphia: Balch Faculty Forum, 1998.

Chapter 17

Mapuche Shamanic Bodies and the Chilean State

Polemic Gendered Representations and Indigenous Responses

ANA MARIELLA BACIGALUPO

In southern Chile, Mapuche shamans, known as machi, mount their cinnamon-tree altars and pound their painted drums to propitiate ancestral spirits, Catholic saints, and national figures who help them divine and heal. Machi are women or men who wear heavy silver jewelry, elegant black shawls, and multicolored scarves and ribbons in order to seduce the spirits, flatter them with stories of power, and beg them for healing knowledge. Once the spirits arrive, machi assume masculine, feminine, and cogender identities—moving between masculine and feminine gender polarities or combining them—for the purpose of healing. Machi become masculine to exorcise illness by drawing on the help of ancestral warriors, Chilean generals, or Jesus. They become feminine to reintegrate patients into their communities by embodying Old Moon Woman, the morning star, and the Virgin Mary. This ability to move between genders also enables machi to embody the four aspects of the deity Ngünechen (male and female, young and old) in order to "become divine," create new worlds, and transform sickness into health and unhappiness into well-being. However, in everyday contexts, machi respond to the heterosexual normative gender models of Chilean society by reinventing themselves as celibate Catholic priests and nuns, heterosexual doctors and nurses, or mother moon priestesses.

Gender is one of the metaphors machi use to mark boundaries and connections between local and national ideologies, link ordinary worlds with spiritual realities, and facilitate health and healing. Gender is also a primary way of signifying relationships of power and difference (Scott, 42). Machi bodies, gendered performances, and their gendered representations become sites for local conflicts and expressions of identity and difference between Mapuche and the Chilean state—the places where power, hierarchy, and healing are played out.

The redemocratization of Chile in 1990, after sixteen years of military dictatorship under General Augusto Pinochet,[1] and the passing of the Indigenous Law in 1993 brought indigenous issues to the political forefront and saw the development of many Mapuche organizations and movements. Since 1990, the Chilean democratic governments have used Mapuche shamans to distance themselves from Pinochet's military dictatorship in legitimizing presidential discourses about pluralism, while machi use these public appearances to gain popularity. These "democratic" presidential gestures toward machi, however, have not changed national gendered ideologies of ethnicity and power where machi are constructed as exotic traditional folk practitioners, earth mothers, witches, and sexual deviants. Nor have they recognized Mapuche claims to cultural rights, territory, or political autonomy.[2] Rather, the new democratic governments perpetuate the political and economic structures instituted by General Pinochet, while instituting new forms of power and reaping the legitimacy gained from democracy.[3] Democratic president Eduardo Frei's political manipulation of the Mapuche machi captures this process.

Machi Maria Angela smiled straight at the camera and beat on her shamanic drum as she posed for photographers beside President Frei when he took office in 1994. She had been invited to the presidential palace along with several other machi from competing schools of practice. The president said his invitation was a gesture toward "maintaining the ancestral culture of the Mapuche indigenous people in order to create a truly democratic Chile" (*La Nacion,* August 6, 1999). Journalists flocked around Frei after his speech, and a couple asked the male Mapuche community chiefs how they viewed the encounter. But the machi, who were women or partially cross-dressed men, were never interviewed. When the Mapuche leaders spoke, the machi legitimized them by beating their drums in the background. Frei's government violated the indigenous law of 1993 by supporting the expansion of the forestry industry and approving the building of a highway and a hydroelectric dam on Mapuche land in the name of national development. When Mapuche movements arose in protest, Frei imposed martial law and had them arrested.

National ethnic and gendered stereotypes of machi as feminine, antimodern and apolitical have little to do with their actual practices. Machi reify and challenge a series of national representations about Mapuche women, shamans, and indigenous people. On December 21, 1997, I rode on a bus with a group of Mapuche activists to a *weichan nguillatun,* or collective warring ritual, held in the community of Lukutunmapu. We passed through several communities whose forests have been depleted by a private firm, Forestal Mininico. A 42-year-old female machi named Tegualda presided at the ritual. Tegualda masculinized herself in ritual by assuming the role of traditional male orator and performing spiritual warfare. She propitiated ancestral spirits and the Mapuche deity Ngünechen to battle against forestry companies who were exploiting their land and against President Frei who supported them. Tegualda beat her drum over her head and demanded that the participants echo her cry, "*Marichiweu*" ("We will win ten times over") while Mapuche chiefs strategized on how to gain cultural rights and territorial and political autonomy. Tegualda defied national gendered stereotypes about machi and resignified traditional rituals and gave them political meanings. Nevertheless, the Chilean journalist who was present ignored Tegualda and her rituals, focusing instead on the political activities of Mapuche men.

In this chapter, I explore the role gender and ethnicity in signifying relationships of power and difference between machi, the Chilean nation-state, and Mapuche discourses of assimilation and resistance. I demonstrate that machi negotiate various gendered ideologies in their identities and practices. I argue that gendered representations establish differential distributions of power and become implicated in the conception and construction of power itself. I explore how Chilean national gender ideologies and Mapuche resistance movements use machi as emblems of the traditional. Weaving together ethnographic research conducted with twelve machi between 1994 and 2000 with reports by the Chilean media, I analyze the contradictory roles ethnicity and gender play in machi representations, their political implications, and the various pragmatic responses by machi. I argue that machi cannot be conceived either as having unlimited power and agency or as merely adapting to the existence of competing gendered ideologies and representations. Rather, machi pragmatically negotiate various gendered concepts of power for their own ends.

CHILEAN MODERNITIES AND TRADITIONAL EXOTICISMS: MACHI THROUGH DOMINANT GENDERED LENSES

More than a million people self-identify as Mapuche, 80 percent of whom live in urban areas. Half the Mapuche populations of Chile live in the capital, Santiago. Nevertheless, the Chilean state views the Mapuche as a rural and "uncivilized" people for political purposes. The Chilean state constructs itself as the Europe of South America, the emblem of the modern dynamic center: the nonindigenous, the masculine, the urban, the heterosexual, the civilized and developed.

The Chilean state has subjugated the Mapuche through military action and violence, claiming it has done so in order to protect and civilize them and solve their problems.[4] Chilean state paternalism was used historically in order to justify the colonization of the Mapuche leading to the military occupation of the Araucanian region and establishment of the reservation system (1830–1884); colonization, assimilation, and redistribution of Mapuche lands and their integration into the state (1884–1929); and suppression of their indigenous rights under military dictatorship (1973–1990).[5] The Mapuche reinforced their identity as separate from that of

Chileans and created resistance movements during the democratic governments (1990–2001). Nevertheless, the neoliberal expansion in the 1990s
exacerbated the image of a masculine civilized state. The current Chilean
state views itself in the role of a democratic father struggling to bring economic progress to the "feminine" and "puerile" and rural Mapuche. Ro-
manticized dominant discourses about the bravery of ancient Mapuche
warriors obscure the discrimination and racism to which the Mapuche continue to be subjected. The Mapuche and their territories are viewed as
"underdeveloped."

The Chilean government has labeled the Mapuche as effeminate marginals outside the modern masculine Chilean state, while erasing their demands for autonomy by claiming that they are Chilean citizens. Knowledge
and power in Chile are decentered, diverse, and nonbinary (in a classical
Foucauldian sense), although it is the knowledge of the governing elite
that is expressed in authoritative discourses. The interests of the dominant
Chilean classes are legitimized through the workings of what Gramsci calls
hegemony—dominant meanings and values permeate the whole of society
without appearing to be imposed.

Theorists of nationalism have often used maleness and femaleness to
distinguish between outsiders and insiders. In the same way that man and
woman are defined reciprocally (although never symmetrically), national
identity is determined on the basis of what it is (presumably) not. With
historical regularity, men tend to stand for national agents who determine
the fate of nations in a metonymic relation to the nation as a whole. In
contrast, women function only symbolically or metaphorically to mark the
boundaries of nations, to conserve tradition, and to serve as passive vessels
for male national agency (Schein, 107; Williams, 6, 12).

Female machi illustrate the way in which the Mapuche have been conceptualized by the Chilean state. National discourses construct machi as
emblems of the stigmatized margin of society: the traditional ethnic poor,
the feminine, the rural, the sexually deviant, the mystical, and the backward. Machi drumming and singing over a patient's body to heal him or
her, entering trance states to communicate with spirits and the divine, and
their use of herbal medicine and massages are considered excessively sensual, feminine, and superstitious by many Chileans. By associating masculinity with neoliberalism, the Chilean state constructs machi as traditional
and opposed to the project of modernization. Like the Chinese Miao
women studied by Schein, machi are viewed as feminized minorities within
the state who become oppositional objects in a colonizing process.

Although the knowledges of machi are no longer denied, they are still
constructed as superstitious, unscientific, and inferior to those of the Chilean intellectual elite. Chilean professionals especially establish a distance
between the machi and the public world of urban learned men, modernization, and politics. Mapuche machi, much like the Korean shamans studied

by Laurel Kendall ("Who Speaks"), are still perceived by the majority discourse as exotic remnants of past folklore that must remain unchanged in order to be authentic. They are often represented and objectified as icons of Mapuche tradition, depicted on postcards and tourist brochures as national symbols of the "true" Chile. Chilean politicians use this image of the traditional machi to gain the support and votes of indigenous sympathizers, while Mapuche leaders draw on this same image in order to legitimize their political discourse. But the flesh-and-blood machi and their gendered identities remain muted artifacts in the production of the nation's history.

Majority discourses feminize machi in different ways. In some instances, Chilean national notions perpetrate the association between domesticity, reproduction, womanhood, and lack of political power. Female machi are often viewed as apolitical fertile earth mothers who perform private healing rituals and therefore as nonthreatening to the masculine state. At other times, machi are viewed as threatening and powerful. Male machi are often constructed as effeminate homosexuals who threaten the masculinity of Chilean men. The collective fertility rituals of female machi are viewed as having political implications, and machi are often arrested or beaten by the police during their public ritual performances. Female machi are sometimes viewed as sexual deviants and perverse witches who are dangerous to Chilean citizens. *El Mercurio*, a conservative newspaper, took this latter approach in an article entitled "The Sacrificed Boy," in which the mother of a Mapuche boy sacrificed by a female machi forty-one years ago was interviewed:

> In Isla Huapi a machi ordered a boy to be killed and thrown to the sea to placate the fury of a sea earthquake in 1960. The mother of the boy lives on the island today and still cries the awful sacrifice of her son. . . . Could the sea wave have produced so much panic as to alter the collective consciousness and light the spark of irrationality to kill a 5-year-old and throw him into the sea to calm the waters? How did machi Luisa Maria Namuncura perturb the senses of the child's family to make them blindly obey her? . . . the worst of this barbaric crime was that when they killed the boy, the sea had been calm for hours. (August 15, 2001)

A commission of anthropologists in 1960 came to the conclusion that the sacrifice was a cultural practice and the machi was freed from any criminal responsibilities. The ex-mayor of Puerto Saavedra explained the event as the "backwardness of the Mapuche forty years ago" and claimed that the sacrifice was produced by their "crude religious beliefs." Anthropologist Aldo Vidal posed that the Mapuche viewed disastrous natural events as divine punishments where they needed to make sacrifice in order to reestablish balance (Arturo Zuñiga, *El Mercurio*, August 15, 2001). *El Mercurio*'s rendition of the only machi to ever perform a human sacrifice perpetrates the image of female machi as exotic, savage, and irrational. Machi are also construed as evil and nonmaternal and as able to manipulate people's minds. Although the anthropologists tried to contextualize the event by explaining it in terms of cultural practice, they did not highlight the uniqueness of the event or the fact that it was criticized by many Mapuche, machi and nonmachi alike. The article homogenized Mapuche culture as barbaric and deviant, ready to sacrifice its own children.

The democratic Chilean state claims that it supports local indigenous voices on their own terms, but in fact, the basic configurations of power that relate the state to Mapuche machi remain unchanged. The state's racial discrimination against the Mapuche and its homophobic attitudes have affected machi practice. Machi bodies are often viewed as "Other" in Chilean majority discourses, and patriarchal gender hierarchies and the heterosexual models subsume their discourses, healing technologies, and modes of representation. The Chilean state has rejected Mapuche polygamy and the gender-bending practices of Mapuche machi as symbols of Mapuche "barbarism." These state representations reflect what Renato Rosaldo has called "imperialist nostalgia," where the dominant class mourns for the loss of what has been destroyed through "progress" (68–87). Machi are cherished because of their exotic value but are stigmatized and subordinated in national gender/status/sexuality hierarchies. These national images of machi become dominant because they are widely disseminated throughout Chilean society.

Traditional machi practice has been viewed as an impediment for the Mapuche to become modern Chilean citizens throughout the twentieth century. Anthropologists constructed female machi as bastions of the past and custodians of tradition (Titiev; Faron; Stuchlik; Degarrod), and both church and state see machi as resisting acculturation and thus as a threat to modern Chilean society. These gendered and ethnic constructions of shamans are fairly common. Anthropologists have portrayed female and feminized shamans around the world in terms of deprivation from male dominant state apparatuses. Female possession is seen as peripheral (Lewis) and resisting the power of men (Lambek; Boddy), and female shamanism is often depicted as the product of women's motherhood and fertility (Sered; Glass-Coffin). Lewis[6] and V. Basilov have proposed that women or low-status men who are discredited and marginalized by state bureaucracies and institutional religions become shamans to compensate for their peripheral social status or sexual deprivation (Spiro; Obeyesekere). Machi, however, have been women or feminized men at least since the sixteenth century, predating the Chilean state and institutionalized Catholicism by three centuries. Most machi today are Catholic, like the Chilean majority. Thus, the Chilean state and institutionalized Catholicism do not play a decisive role in the initial feminization of machi or in their gendered practices, but they do control the way in which they are perceived and represented in national discourses.

The Chilean national goal throughout the twentieth century was to educate and convert machi to Catholicism and in doing so eradicate "deviant" sexualities and "uncivilized" healing practices, and integrate them as citizens into hegemonic national identity. Religious, economic, and social interests motivated the efforts of political and cultural integration of the Mapuche into the Chilean state. The state's "civilizing" and integrating project was carried out through education and Christian evangelization, mainly through Capuchin missionaries who have been working in the Araucanian region since 1848. The Chilean church did not officially separate from the state until 1926 (Noggler; Bengoa, *Historia del pueblo*, 343; Foerster and Montecino; Degarrod).

The Capuchins provided basic education to the Mapuche but discouraged higher education. They claimed that nature was the best educator for the Mapuche and that they should become agriculturists. Father Jerónimo de Amberga claimed that love of the land was the most important element in the making of loyal Chilean citizens. Mapuche men received elementary education and incorporated nationalistic, patriotic, male-centered values during their military service, which became obligatory in 1916.

Capuchin missionaries educated Mapuche women in order to eradicate polygyny, replace extended families with nuclear families, and incorporate them into national gender models of womanhood and motherhood. Chilean women were often seen as biological and cultural reproducers of the nation's people through childbearing and the teaching of national traditions and Catholic values. The nation-state viewed Mapuche women as the custodians of Mapuche tradition and believed that by evangelizing women, they would create Christian families and "civilized citizens" (Noggler; Casanova). In fact, in 1926, the Catholic Church stated that the way to eradicate all Mapuche rituals and shamanic practices was by "civilizing Mapuche women."[7] These national gendered perspectives about the Mapuche and machi were accentuated during General Pinochet's military regime.

The Chilean state under current President Ricardo Lagos has shown more willingness than the Frei (1994–2000) administration to incorporate diversity as a value in programs and policies. His government, however, views Mapuche claims as issues of cultural identity, ignoring their demands for cultural and collective rights. Like other democratic presidents, Lagos uses machi as apolitical symbols of traditional culture in opposition to the modernizing project of the nation. Lagos created a commission for indigenous people that included indigenous leaders, representatives of the logging industry and the churches, and his Social Democratic government.[8] He approved sixteen measures in response to the report issued by the national Working Groups for Indigenous Peoples and an Interministerial

Working Group for the Incorporation of Indigenous Peoples. Nevertheless, the state is still reticent in dealing with the more substantive claims for territory, autonomy, or collective political representation. Such demands challenge the state's interconnected goals in the economic (strengthening Chile's position in the global market) and ideological (maintaining a unitary Chilean national identity) spheres (Richards).

During his election campaign, Lagos invited Mapuche community heads and machi on stage while a choir sang in the Mapuche language, Mapudungun. When he was elected president in March 2000, he sent a minister, Alejandra Krauss, to the southern city of Temuco, where she danced with machi in a collective ritual in a rural community to show that indigenous issues were an important item on the new government's political agenda. President Frei claimed to respect Mapuche traditions, but he considered machi healing practice illegal because it threatened Western medicine. His minister of health decreed that the state would regulate the commercialization and sale of traditional medicinal plants, which machi protested vehemently. Minister Krauss now promised a group of machi that the ministry of health would give them credentials that recognized their therapeutic role and would reforest the land with the medicinal plants they need in order to heal.[9]

Meanwhile, the Lagos government proceeded with the construction of a bypass and hydroelectric dam on Mapuche lands approved by the Frei administration but without Mapuche authorization. Lagos also allowed forestry companies to work land taken from indigenous communities. One Mapuche leader stated "the arrests, searches and trials express the Chilean government's repression of the Mapuche in order to protect the powerful." The Chilean government only responds favorably to Mapuche demands and identities that fit into the paradigm of national modern development, Chilean citizenship, and national gender ideologies. The democratic governments erase ethnic and class differences, framing Mapuche demands in terms of socioeconomic problems and the discrimination against machi in terms of national gender inequalities.[10] Mapuche leaders criticize Lagos for not recognizing the autonomy of Mapuche territories and not establishing mechanisms to ensure Mapuche political participation.[11]

EMBLEMS OF DIFFERENCE:
MAPUCHE POLITIZATION OF MACHI

Mapuche discourses sometimes replicate Chilean national ideologies of gender, ethnicity, and power for their own ends. At other times, they resist majority discourses. In contrast to the Chilean state, contemporary Mapuche movements see culture as highly politicized and use discourses about Mapuche tradition and machi gender identities and practices as emblems of difference for political mobilization.

Dominant sex-based notions of gender, the association of femininity and motherhood, and the rejection of effeminate male machi have been gradually incorporated into Mapuche gender ideologies. This occurred as land fertility became a major concern for the Mapuche relegated to small, eroded plots of land on reservations, and collective *nguillatun* rituals were performed, primarily to ask deities for bountiful crops and fertile animals. The idea that female machi, who can give birth from their bodies, are more effective in ensuring land fertility became generalized throughout the twentieth century. Although female machi today are considered to be both masculine spiritual warriors and powerful feminine women, it is their female bodies that give them authority over the fertility of the land. As machi practice has become increasingly associated with domesticity, land fertility, and women's work, some Mapuche have also begun to reject male machi who wear women's clothes. Female machi also hold credibility as healers in the realm of spirits, illness, and witchcraft. The Mapuche believe that female machi are less invested in the male ancestral spirits of competing patrilineages within a community than are male machi. Therefore, they are better suited to be spiritual representatives of the body politic. Female machi have begun to invoke the pan-Mapuche deity Ngünechen on behalf of a much larger ritual community beyond the patrilineage (Bacigalupo, "El Rol Sacerdotal"; "Rise").

The switch to predominantly female machi was gradual, but it produced a permanent shift in the way Mapuche conceived of gender and spirituality. Chilean perceptions of spiritual and political power as contrasting ways of viewing the world had a major effect on the way machi perceived their roles and gender identities. By the beginning of the twentieth century, the spiritual power of machi was seen as conflicting with the political power of male chiefs within Mapuche communities. Male machi's legitimacy as spiritual intermediaries was threatened by the imposition of Chilean ideals of male roles as political and public. Machi spiritual power, associated with femininity, is now independent from political power and is passed down through the female line, often through a maternal grandmother. When machi lost their political power, female machi's spiritual power and bodies alone accorded them status and prestige in other realms of Mapuche society, something that is much more difficult for male machi to accomplish. In addition, by constructing healing as "domestic women's work," machi reinforce national associations between domesticity/womanhood and lack of political power.

The increasing feminization of machi practice has also had political implications for the Mapuche, situating them in relation to national gendered polarizations of tradition and modernity, spirituality, and politics. Modernity and tradition are not dichotomous, but articulated in diverse ways where cultural production is always hybrid (García Canclini). Mapuche responses to gendered national discourses, however, have often been heavily polarized. Here, I outline two extreme Mapuche positions: those who adopt national notions of socioeconomic and cultural modernity,[12] and those who support an ideal fundamentalist return to "uncontaminated" rural traditions.

The Mapuche developmental model proposes the modernization of the Mapuche and their respectful integration into the Chilean state. Mapuche organizations created by urban Mapuche leaders in the early twentieth century incorporated these national perspectives. Federación Araucana emphasized the importance of tradition and cultural identity; Union Araucana negated ancestral culture and argued for assimilation and modernization; Sociedad Caupolicán took an intermediary position, which argued for the gradual incorporation of national values into Mapuche culture (Foerster and Montecino; Degarrod). These organizations incorporated national gender ideologies where women were considered weak and more easily associated with witchcraft, and emphasized the obedience of wife to husband.[13] Union Araucana and Sociedad Caupolicán opposed the machi practice, petitioning the government to end collective *nguillatun* rituals and the practice of Mapuche shamanism. José Alonqueo from Union Araucana claimed that women were deceitful creatures who went to machi to learn how to manipulate poisons and weaken men. Some Mapuche chiefs also abided by national norms viewing machi as "ignorant women" who deceived people and asked the government to prohibit machi practice (Foerster and Montencino; Painevilu, in Guevara).

In contrast, the Mapuche fundamentalist approach, what José Bengoa calls the "nativistic approach" (*Historia de un Conflicto*, 122–27), is antimodern and proposes a return to a time of origins and a rescue of a "traditional and authentic" Mapuche rural culture. These critics of modernity have argued that national plans of socioeconomic development are detrimental to the Mapuche and have created sociopolitical movements that draw on traditional culture to resist economic modernity. Land tenure, territoriality, and tradition have remained central to Mapuche politics, creating serious identity problems for the predominantly urban Mapuche and disregarding the changing dynamics of Mapuche culture. Mapuche sociologist and historian José Ancan criticizes this fundamentalist perspective used by Mapuche resistance movements because it hails the rural community as a timeless, uncontaminated, and exclusive refuge of the "real Mapuche," glosses over the complexities of contemporary ethnicity, and leads to internal discrimination, rupture, and self-denial.

Mapuche resistance movements' understanding of the traditional and its relationship to machi practice are both similar to and different from those of the Chilean state and Mapuche developmentalists. Like them, Mapuche fundamentalists view machi practice as an essentially feminine occupation associated with tradition. But they view tradition as the basis for the development of cultural rights and political sovereignty and have politicized the image of traditional feminine machi to legitimize their resistance movements against the Chilean state.[14] In this context, female machi have become emblems of traditional cultural knowledge and spiritual intermediaries who have the ability to mobilize spirits and divine forces to support Mapuche communities and defend their interests.

Chilean majority discourse often depicts machi women who legitimize Mapuche resistance movements as rural women "who wander beyond the home making trouble," "who do not know their place" and get involved in "political movements they know nothing about." Nevertheless, machi and Mapuche women sometimes do assume political positions and participate in instances of negotiation with the Chilean state,[15] and machi sometimes aspire to political positions. When the king of Spain visited Chile in 1990, machi Jorge presented himself as the representative of Mapuche culture, and machi Victor was one of the candidates for mayor of Carahue.[16]

MACHI PRAGMATIC NEGOTIATIONS OF GENDERED DISCOURSES

The Chilean state has marginalized machi because of their Mapuche ethnicity, their shifting gendered identities, and their spiritual healing practices. Machi, however, are neither idealized victors nor passive victims of oppression. They are active agents and self-reflective subjects. I argue that Mapuche individuals do not become machi because they are socially deprived or marginalized from state bureaucracies, as Lewis and Basilov would have it, but rather because they are legitimized by local Mapuche processes: spiritual callings, shamanic training, initiation, and prestige gained through ritual performance. Although machi have been objectified, represented, and constructed as passive retainers of culture by both national and Mapuche public political discourse, in practice, machi are powerful spiritual intermediaries and active agents in their communities. Machi pragmatic healing practices reinterpret and contest national images and draw on prestigious national professions in order to legitimize themselves. Machi play on national gendered discourses about traditional culture and present themselves as apolitical in order to avoid persecution. But their complex hybrid healing practices use the symbols of the dominant majority and often have political implications. Machi have power and agency, but they are also adapting to the existence of competing gendered and ethnic ideologies and representations.

National and Mapuche fundamentalist discourses lead to misperceptions of machi, ignoring their complex, hybrid, syncretic healing practices and their use of images from modernity.[17] Machi often argue that the Mapuche should ignore national ideologies, participate in rituals, and attend to the *admapu,* or customary laws (Dillehay), although their practices are increasingly hybrid. Machi juggle diverse religious and healing epistemologies and incorporate and resignify the knowledge and symbols of Catholicism and the national medical and political systems into their spiritual practice using outside cultural influences for the purpose of dynamic self-definition. Machi flourish in areas near urban centers, treating Mapuche spiritual illnesses produced by maladjustment, discrimination, and poverty. They treat non-Mapuche clients for stress, insomnia, and minor ailments treated with herbal medicine, and find lost people. Machi often have offices in the city where they see their urban patients. They travel frequently to Chilean and even Argentine cities to exorcise houses and bring patients luck in love, money, and work (Bacigalupo, *La Voz del Kultrun*), and they occasionally perform for tourists.[18]

Machi are aware of the different ways in which the discourses of tradition and modernity can be used. They make flexible responses to the world as they know it, yet play to their customer's sense of the traditional.[19] This became apparent to me one winter evening in July 1995, when machi Maria, her family, and I were watching a soap opera on an old black-and-white TV plugged into a car battery. When a truck driven by Chileans came up the driveway, everyone jumped up. Maria's brother hid the television set and the car battery.[20] Her sister helped her put on her machi scarf, while her mother went outside to greet the visitors. Maria explained later that because Chileans had a mental picture of what it meant to be a machi, if they saw her watching TV or speaking Spanish instead of Mapudungun, they would question her authenticity and her power to heal.

Machi pragmatic responses to the heavily polarized context of Mapuche relations to the Chilean nation-state are varied and complex. Machi are aware of how traditional culture has become commodified. They exploit their image as traditional practitioners, parody and transform the roles the state assigns them, and increase their prestige by serving as a legitimizing factor in local and national politics. Some participate actively in local Mapuche movements that protest against the Chilean government; others try to gain power through their ties to state rulers and participate in presidential campaigns. Machi negotiate conflicts between Mapuche communities and celebrate the restitution of Mapuche communal lands.[21] They sanction a number of intercultural educational and health interventions in the Araucanian region.[22] Machi participated in the Mapuche movements that protested the construction of a bypass through Mapuche lands. But when the construction proceeded and disturbed several ancient Mapuche burial sites in Licanco, two machi from the area prayed for the rest of the ancient souls and asked the local spiritual forces to be benevolent to the Licanco community and to those working on the construction of the bypass.[23] Shamanism is not a "desiccated and insipid category" (Geertz), but a widespread "historically situated and culturally mediated social practice" (Atkinson) that interacts with national contexts (Taussig; Joralemon; Balzer; Tsing; Kendall, "Who Speaks").

Like most Mapuche, machi see the representatives of the Chilean state as masculine and use the diverse possibilities that Chilean politicians and political parties can offer them for their own purposes. The Mapuche see General Pinochet as a hypermasculine figure of military power, and machi use this image according to their individual epistemologies. Machi Sergio and machi Jorge support Pinochet and associate his military prowess with that of ancient Mapuche warriors and machi newfound masculinities. When machi Jorge was detained on the road for drunkenness, he threatened the police, saying that General Pinochet would punish them if he was not released immediately. Machi Sergio performed his military service in Chile, supported Pinochet's right-wing military regime, and was an honorary guest at ceremonies in Villarica when Pinochet visited the region.[24] Machi Ana takes a pragmatic approach and uses the images of the Spanish king and Pinochet creatively in her healing rituals in order to exorcise evil spirits from her patients' bodies. Other machi perform collective rituals in honor of Mapuche assassinated during Pinochet's regime and associate the dictator with evil spirits.[25] Chile's democratic presidents have not made it into machi's spiritual imagery, but some machi do support their governments. Machi's support of Mapuche resistance movements is not without consequences. Those who perform shamanic rituals aimed at obtaining the support of ancestral spirits in recovering Mapuche lands are often arrested and beaten by the police. In fact, one of the demands made by Mapuche leaders to the current government's commission for indigenous people is that machi be allowed to heal and perform rituals without fear of violence or arrest.[26]

Mapuche and machi do not just reproduce the hegemonic gender ideologies of the Chilean state internally by regendering those elements of culture that are criticized by dominant ideology, as Lydia Degarrod claims. Machi juggle various gendered systems of knowledge and identities according to their intentions, who is present, and in which context. In their ritual healing practices, machi perform masculine, feminine, and cogender identities that challenge national perceptions of gender as permanent and associated with sex. In their everyday performances, however, machi often reiterate the national system of gender hierarchy and the alignment of women and feminized men with rural traditions. Machi spirituality is increasingly associated with femininity, fertility, and abundance. Machi gender identities are constructed both in relation to their special cogender identities defined by spirits as well as national notions of gender and heterosexuality.

Although machi are viewed as increasingly feminine by Mapuche and non-Mapuche (Bacigalupo, "Mapuche Women's Empowerment"), in practice, machi continue to perform masculine and feminine gender roles in rituals, expand their practice by incorporating male ritual functions, and have drawn on national gendered discourses for their own ends. As the local political power held by Mapuche men wanes and they gain prestige as external intermediaries with the Chilean state, female machi have taken over local male political functions as ritual orators in the performance of collective rituals and have become important in both maintaining cultural ethos and implementing change within the communities (Bacigalupo, "El Rol Sacerdotal"; "Rise"). Mapuche and Chilean imaginations create different gender boundaries that machi reinforce and cross in order to connect different worlds, heal, and legitimize themselves or their communities. The expectations of machi and the judgments about them are varied and complex because Mapuche and non-Mapuche individuals are reflexively considering machi shifting gender identities and interpreting their actions from different contested gender ideologies

Mapuche see machi as people with special gender identities different from that of women and men but also view them in terms of dominant notions of sexuality. Machi same-sex relationships are usually more acceptable for machi than for ordinary Mapuche women and men, as long as they are with nonmachi. But machi themselves never assume homosexual identities. Homosexuality is a negative label imposed by others, and machi self-identify as heterosexual or celibate, regardless of the sexual acts they perform. Increasing homophobia against men, both from outside and within Mapuche communities, has produced a growing rejection of male machi who are "feminine," thus undermining their prestige. Social pressure leads male machi to display femininity solely in ritual contexts and to subtly differentiate their clothing from that of women, aiming for similarity rather than complete identification. Through ritual dress, gestures, and voice, they become feminine enough to access spiritual power while at the same time adapting to a heterosexual binary model. Most male machi assume the social identity of men that is acceptable in heterosexual Chilean society. They often refer to themselves as doctors or "machi priests," although they shift genders during rituals. They draw on majority-gendered discourses of power by associating themselves with national male positions of prestige while retaining their status as traditional Mapuche practitioners.

Forty-seven-year-old machi Sergio assumes the gender identity of a "celibate Catholic priest." He identifies himself with a prestigious male national religious figure who is neither heavily masculinized nor sexualized. Sergio refers to himself as a "Mapuche priest," and not a machi moon priestess, when he officiates in collective fertility rituals. He dresses in traditional men's clothing when riding the bus or at home, although he wears silver bracelets and a woman's scarf around his neck to distinguish himself from other men. During healing rituals, he wears a woman's shawl, several blue or purple scarves tied around his head and neck, or feathers and a blue blouse. Blue and purple are associated with female power, knowledge, and fertility.

Machi Jorge assumes the gender identity of a male "spiritual doctor" and is also a registered nurse. He renews his machi powers on Christmas Day and calls himself the "second Jesus Christ." Jorge is 48 years old. He wears blue, red, or purple scarves, feathers, and silver jewelry during healing rituals and a male poncho on an everyday basis. Jorge was once married and has fathered a child. Now he has sexual intercourse with both men and women. Machi Pamela claims that Jorge's anatomical sex and sexuality change with the moon. Like the Chilean majority, she sees anatomical sex as a guiding metaphor for sexuality, but she also ascribes to Mapuche shifting genders and sexualities. "When the moon is growing Jorge has a penis, when it is waning he has a vagina. He sleeps with women. He sleeps with men. We never know when he is working with evil spirits and when he is healing." Jorge's shifting sex and sexuality are considered a sign of witchcraft because he is believed to seduce people and take their power.

Discourses about gender are central to the way in which power and difference articulate. Although the image of the female machi stands for the feminine in their daily lives, female machi like Tegualda are considered masculine transgressors who never conform completely to the role of women on account of their spiritual powers. In contrast, homophobia within Mapuche communities has severely limited the gendered representations of male machi and controls the way in which they are perceived and represented outside the community. There is enormous pressure for machi to assume permanent social gender identities and roles that are acceptable within a heterosexual context. Those machi who are perceived as effeminate, and those who like Jorge do not ascribe to this heterosexual model, are associated with witchcraft. However, those male machi who, like Sergio, dispel national images of male machi as effeminate homosexuals by reinventing themselves in public roles as "celibate Catholic priests" or "spiritual doctors" and distinguishing themselves from machi moon priestesses, are also experiencing a resurgence. Within the constraints of these various gendered discourses, the machi decide how they are going to relate to these representations, when and in what context they will use them to their advantage, and when they will create alternative ones.

By participating in the gendered and sexual discourses of the state, machi challenge representations of them as marginal tradition-bearers and sexual deviants. They strive for a less marginal position where they can negotiate the prestige and status associated with ideologies of gender propriety and sexual containment. Ironically, by assuming positions as celibate priests, mother moon priestesses, and nuns, machi simultaneously reiterate the prestige accorded to heterosexuality and the naturalness of sex and gender, the very system that stigmatizes their ritual gender bending.

In this essay, I have argued that although national gendered ideologies use machi as emblems of the marginal, feminine, and apolitical to assert their positional superiority as modern and masculine, in practice, machi pragmatically negotiate notions of gender, tradition, and modernity, and their actions clearly have political implications. The artificial dichotomy of the feminine/spiritual as opposed to the masculine/political and national discourses of effeminacy and homosexuality are used as a tool for domination to mold machi and Mapuche to state-defined masculinities. The fact that the trope of the feminine is used to signify motherhood, domesticity, marginality, tradition, witchcraft, deviance, and backwardness reinforces the idea that femininity remains unquestioned in Chilean national discourses as the subordinate abject in a hierarchical social ordering.[27]

The Mapuche are often complicit with modernizing dynamics and national gender and ethnic discourses, appropriating them for their own ends. The concept of tradition has been positively resignified by the Mapuche and has become the central element in defining cultural rights and in the struggle for political and territorial sovereignty. Heavily stigmatizing national labels of homosexuality, witchcraft, and sexism, however, have also been incorporated by the Mapuche to police internal boundaries of deviance and tradition.

National and Mapuche discourses conflict and are resisted, appropriated, and transformed by machi cultural practices. Machi encourage representations of themselves as traditional apolitical figures to legitimize the spiritual practice within and outside the community—and to protect themselves from prosecution while they incorporate and deploy dominant symbols of power and perform rituals that have political implications. As a result, in their own communities, machi are construed both as custodians of tradition and as creators of new worlds.

Mapuche resistance movements use female machi as symbols of political autonomy while Chilean politicians use machi to demonstrate their willingness to engage in a dialogue with the Mapuche. Machi also gain recognition, popularity, and prestige by these associations. They are consciously involved in politics and use their political associations with various political figures and movements pragmatically for their own ends.

When female machi were stripped of their formal political power by the Chilean state and regendered as feminine and spiritual, they responded in two ways. First, they played on national essentialist images of fertile rural mothers whose bodies effect fertility and gain power as emblems of Mapuche identity while drawing on national symbols of power. By privileging femininity to access spiritual power while at the same time embodying symbols of institutional power such as Pinochet and the Virgin Mary, machi reverse the social order of dominant society and challenge male dominance. Machi pragmatically use majority depictions of themselves as "marginals" to the state for their own ends and also transgress them as "special" gender-bending women who reverse metropolitan gender hierarchies. Second, machi have expanded traditional Mapuche notions about the relationship between femininity, spirituality, and power. Because homophobia targets male machi in a way that female machi do not experience, female machi have incorporated male political functions as ritual orators in collective *nguillatun* rituals and have begun performing a contemporary version of male machi spiritual warfare. Female machi have become "warrior machi" and draw on ancestral warriors to combat forestry companies who have taken their land, and draw on traditional knowledge to rally for cultural rights and political autonomy from the state. In healing rituals, they kill evil *wekufe* spirits that threaten the bodies of their patients or their communities.

The feminization of machi practice has not eliminated male machi. In fact, male cogenderism and the adoption of Catholicism have given rise to unprecedented contemporary spiritual masculinities. The Chilean majority, and some Mapuche too, stigmatize cross-gender performances as "deviant," but male machi still need to become feminine to be possessed by spirits. Male machi faced with this predicament struggle for legitimacy and participate in majority-gendered discourses of power by associating themselves with national male positions of prestige while retaining their status as traditional Mapuche practitioners. Male machi distance themselves from the practice of female machi by constructing themselves as "celibate Catholic priests" and "spiritual doctors" to try to dispel the majority images of them as effeminate homosexuals or witches and to legitimize themselves in a national context. Male machi remind city folk that they are Catholic while claiming that priesthood has always been a traditional Mapuche gender role. After all, the Catholic priest is the only national male personage who acts as an intermediary with the divine and who holds authority, yet wears skirts and has a sexuality distinct from that of the ordinary family man.

To what degree, then, and in what way are machi subjects or objects of their own gendered and sexualized history? Machi do appropriate, transform, and subvert gender and sexual ideologies and representations as they draw power from various ordinary and spiritual realities in order to survive in contemporary Chile. Yet machi do not act on their own accord. Machi gendered identities and sexualities are not restricted to the intention of machi themselves but are rhetorical and tactical responses to Chilean national and Mapuche discourses of authority for effects of a practical sort. Larger systems also determine the conditions within which machi live, and actions become meaningful. Machi gendered actions and words are constructed according to majority discourses, manipulated by national and political discourses, and distorted by the media. Meaning is not located solely in the agency of individual subjects but in the way the subjects' words and actions are constrained by local and dominant gendered imageries and the interpretations of others.

The agency of machi lies in their intensely pragmatic and political approach to the use of various gendered identities and sexualities and in deciding which of these are contextually acceptable or more appropriate. Machi practice demonstrates that culture is produced dynamically by individuals who engage in different cultural tropes to support and subvert power relations. The emergence of cultural change in machi practice has been heavily politicized; it is contextual and tied up with changing local and national structures of male power and prestige. Machi perform what Matthew Gutmann called "transformative consciousness" (260–61). They draw on widely accepted gendered ideologies of tradition and modernity and transform them according to context, allowing the emergence of cultural change. In shifting the frame of reference from tradition and modernity to healing practice, or in using dominant gender ideologies in their own terms, machi challenge dominant representations of themselves and acquire new meaning. Power lies not only with those who impose gendered structures but also with those who creatively transform them—making and remaking worlds according to multiple gender ideologies and sexualities.

NOTES

1. General Augusto Pinochet, who was in power between 1973 and 1990, was under arrest in London in 1999 facing possible extradition to Spain to stand trial on charges of gross human rights violations, including torture and genocide. Pinochet was not extradited to Spain, has now lost his legal immunity as a senator in Chile, and has not been tried in Chile because of his health.

2. José Mariman notes that there have been four different Mapuche proposals for political autonomy and self-determination since the redemocratization of Chile in 1989: assimilation, indigenism, fundamentalism, and confrontation. Curivil notes that the Chilean claim that the Mapuche are the "real Chileans" neutralizes their project of being legally recognized as an autonomous people.

3. This is a classic maneuver of the sort described by Althusser—a shift from repressive state apparatuses (military terror under Pinochet) to ideological state apparatuses. In their effort to "modernize" Chile, the current government continues to use many of the policies instituted by Pinochet in order to bring Chile in line with U.S.-based capitalism. A recent example is the Chilean government's opting out of the South American economic union in favor of negotiating with the United States for partnership in NAFTA (*New York Times*, December 3, 2000).

4. This image of a paternal state combines Mapuche notions of patrilineality and patrilocality with colonizing paternal images: that of the masculine Spanish conquistador and his hunger for honors, titles, and social recognition; that of the mestizo landowner, who becomes feudal lord and father through sexual and social exploitation (Bengoa, *Historia de un Conflicto*); and that of the modern neoliberal office man.

5. Chilean historian Sergio Villalobos claims that the indigenous people are "less evolved," whereas the Chilean and Spanish nations are "highly evolved" (*El Mercuris*, May 14, 2000, p. 6). Humanity and history are made, he states, when Chilean and Spanish nations oppress and assimilate the ethnic minorities.

6. According to Lewis, men perform as the central figures in "main morality possession religions," whereas women and downtrodden men are said to perform in "amoral, peripheral possession cults" (1981).

7. This statement appeared in *Diario Austral*, March 22, 1926, and is cited by Foerster and Montecino; and by Degarrod.

8. *El Metropolitano*, March 17, 2000.

9. "Visita a IX Region: Ministra Krauss Bailo en Torno a un Rehue," *Diario El Mercurio*, March 30, 2000, and "Ministra Krauss Confía en Otorgar 150 Mil Hectáreas a Mapuches," *Diario el Mercurio*, March 31, 2000.

10. Patricia Richards demonstrates how the Chile National Service for Women (SERNAM) reflects this policy.

11. "Lideres Mapuches Cuestionan 16 Medidas," *Diario La Tercera*, June 2, 2000.

12. Ximena Valdés and Kathya Araujo differentiate between this socioeconomic and cultural modernity in Chile and propose that there can be many different modernities.

13. José Alonqueo in *El Araucano*, no. 14 (1927).

14. Under current president Lagos, Mapuche protesters kidnapped a judge and a minister, set fire to logging trucks, and took over farms in Mapuche territories ("Lagos y su Conflicto Mas Grave," *Diarios La Frontera*, April 2, 2000).

15. Three indigenous women form part of the commission for indigenous people created by President Lagos. Isolda Reuque and Beatriz Painequeo, both Mapuche women, are leaders of indigenous communities.

16. "98 Mapuches Postulan en 54 Comunas Sureñas," *Diario El Mercurio*, October 29, 2000.

17. Numerous ethnographic accounts give testimony to the ways in which shamans are affected by contacts between peoples, struggles for territory, the growth and collapse of empires, the imposed view of colonialism (Vitebsky), and the dynamic religious and healing practices that result from this (Kendall, *Shamans;* Taussig; Thomas and Humphrey; Tsing).

18. "Una Machi y una Mexicana Fueron las Sorpresas del Unplugged de La Ley," *Diario Austral,* June 30, 2001.

19. A similar process occurs among shamans from Malaysia (Laderman) and Korea (Kendall, "Who Speaks").

20. This image recalls the Gary Larson cartoon of "natives" stowing the TV and VCR as figures in pith helmets come up the path, with the statement "Anthropologists! Anthropologists!"

21. "Entregan fundo a communidad mapuche Antonio ñirripil," *Diario Austral*, April 7, 2001; "Convocan a nguillatun para restablecer confianzas," *Diario Austral*, April 19, 2001.

22. These include inaugurating the Diego Portales University and the Liceo "Kingdom of Sweden," evaluating intercultural education programs, and expressing gratitude for the installment of intercultural health hospitals in Makewe and Nueva Imperial. See "Universidad Diego Portales amplía inversion," *Diario Austral*, December 21, 2000; "Proyectan un hospital intercultural," *Diario Austral*, January 19, 2001; "Una puerta hacia la educación intercultural," *Diario Austral*, June 1, 2001; "Autoridades inauguran obras en liceo de Puerto Saavedra," *Diario Austral*, March 15, 2001; "Gobierno de cara a la comunidad," *Diario Austral*, March 21,

2001; "Rogativas y Palín por nuevo hospital intercultural," *Diario Austral,* January 17, 2001.

23. "En EEUU analizarán osamentas de Licanco," *Diario Austral,* April 17, 2001.

24. Machi Sergio stated: "When Chile almost went to war with Argentina and there were trenches and tunnels here down south, I was ready to volunteer to fight for my General Pinochet and our country Chile." Sergio believed Pinochet upheld Mapuche tradition, while the return to democracy under a civilian government has seen the birth of numerous native rights groups that he says are not very representative: "We, the Mapuche, have progressed a little because of this, but we still will never be in agreement about the land which was taken away from us. We will never approve completely of any government, but of the Chilean presidents, Pinochet was the best. Some Mapuche are not so bright and allow themselves to be manipulated by the socialists."

25. See, for example, the video *Nguillatun, Rogativa Mapuche* made by ICTUS-Grupo Pasos in 1992.

26. On June 2, 2000, the Mapuche International Link in Bristol, England, posted an electronic message asking supporters of indigenous groups to join social organizations in Germany in protest against the visit of President Lagos to Berlin. The message stated that the repressive laws and state apparatus of Pinochet's 1973–1990 military dictatorship remained intact in democratic Chile and continued to be used against the Mapuche. One case cited as evidence is the beating by police of several machi during their performance in a *nguillatun.* In their effort to "modernize" Chile, the current Chilean government also continues to use many of the policies instituted by Pinochet in order to bring Chile more into line with U.S.-based capitalism. An example is the Chilean government's opting out of the South American economic union in favor of negotiating with the United States for partnership in NAFTA (*New York Times,* December 3, 2000).

27. Louisa Schein observes a similar phenomenon among the feminized Miao in China.

REFERENCES

Amberga, Jerónimo de. "Estado Intelectual, Moral y Económico del Araucano." *Revista Chilena de Historia y Geografía,* 1913.
Ancan, José. "Urban Mapuches: Reflections on a Modern Reality in Chile." *Abya-Yala News* 10, no. 3 (1997): 1–3.
Atkinson, Jane. "Shamanisms Today." *Annual Review of Anthropology* 21 (1992): 307–30.
Bacigalupo, Ana Mariella. "El Rol Sacerdotal de la Machi en los Valles Centrales de la Araucanía." In *Modernización o Sabiduría en Tierra Mapuche?,* edited by Cristián Parker and Ricardo Salas, 51–98. Santiago, Chile: Ediciones San Pablo, 1995.
———. "Mapuche Women's Empowerment as Shaman/Healers." *Annual Review of Women in World Religions* 4 (1996): 57–129.
———. "The Rise of the Mapuche Moon Priestess in Southern Chile." *Annual Review of Women in World Religions* 6 (2001): 208–59.
———. *La Voz del Kultrun en la Modernidad: Tradición y Cambio en la Terapeútica de Siete Machi.* Santiago, Chile: Editorial Universidad Católica, 2001.
Balzer, M. "Changing Images of the Shaman: Folklore and Politics in Sakha Republic (Yakutia)." *Shaman* 4, no. 1–2 (1996): 5–16.

Basilov, V. "Chosen by the Spirits." In *Shamanism: Soviet Studies of Traditional Religion in Siberia and Central Asia,* edited by M. Balzer, 3–48. Armonk, N.Y.: M. E. Sharpe, 1990.

Bengoa, José. *Historia del pueblo Mapuche Siglo XIX y XX.* Santiago, Chile: Ediciones Sur, 1985.

———. *Historia de un Conflicto: El Estado y los Mapuches en el Siglo XX.* Santiago, Chile: Editorial Planeta, 1999.

Boddy, Janice. *Wombs and Alien Spirits: Women, Men and the Zar Cult in Northern Sudan.* Madison: University of Wisconsin Press, 1989.

Casanova, Holdenis. "Presencia Franciscana en la Araucanía: Las Misiones del Colegio de Propaganda Fide de Chillan." In *Misioneros en Araucanía,* edited by Jorge Pinto, Holdenis Casanova, Sergio Uribe, and Mauro Matthei, 121–98. Temuco: Ediciones de la Universidad de la Frontera, 1991.

Curivil, Ramon. "Identidad Mapuche." Document posted on Nuke Mapu Web site. 1997.

Degarrod, Lydia. "Female Shamanism and the Mapuche Transformation into Christian Chilean Farmers." *Religion* 28 (1998): 339–50.

Dillehay, Tom. "La Influencia Política de los Chamanes Mapuches." In *Revista de Ciencias Sociales y Humanas* 2, no. 2, 141–57. CUHSO. Temuco: Universidad Católica de Chile, 1985.

Faron, Louis. *Hawks of the Sun: Mapuche Morality and Its Ritual Attributes.* Pittsburgh, Pa.: University of Pittsburgh Press, 1964.

Foerster, Rolf, and Sonia Montecino. *Organizaciones, Líderes y Contiendas Mapuches (1900–1970).* Santiago, Chile: Centro de Estudios de la Mujer, 1988.

Foucault, Michel. *Power/Knowledge: Selected Interviews and Other Writings.* Edited by Colin Gordon. New York: Pantheon Books, 1980.

García Canclini, Nestor. *Las Culturas Híbridas. Estrategias Para Entrar y Salir de la Modernidad.* México City: Editorial Grijalbo, 1990.

Geertz, Clifford. *The Interpretation of Cultures.* New York: Basic Books, 1973.

Glass-Coffin, Bonnie. *The Gift of Life: Female Spirituality and Healing in Northern Peru.* Albuquerque: University of New Mexico Press, 1998.

Gramsci, Antonio. *Selections from the Prison Notebooks.* Edited by Quentin Hoare and Geoffrey N. Smith. New York: International Publishers, 1971.

Guevara, Tomás. *Folklore Araucana.* Santiago: Imprenta Barcelona, 1917.

Gutmann, Matthew. *The Meanings of Macho: Being a Man in Mexico City.* Berkeley: University of California Press, 1996.

Joralemon, D. "The Selling of the Shaman and the Problem of Informant Legitimacy." *Journal of Anthropological Research* 46, no. 2 (1990): 105–17.

Kendall, Laurel. *Shamans, Housewives and Other Restless Spirits: Women in Korean Ritual Life.* Honolulu: University of Hawai'i Press, 1985.

———. "Who Speaks for Korean Shamans When Shamans Speak of the Nation?" In *Making Majorities: Constituting the Nation in Japan, Korea, China, Malaysia, Fiji, Turkey and the United States,* edited by Dru C. Gladney, 53–72. Stanford, Calif.: Stanford University Press, 1998.

Laderman, Carol. "The Limits of Magic." *American Anthropologist* 2 (1997): 333–41.

Lambek, Michael. *Human Spirits: A Cultural Account of Trance in Mayotte.* Cambridge: Cambridge University Press, 1981.

Lewis, I. M. *Ecstatic Religion: An Anthropological Study of Spirit Possession and Shamanism.* Baltimore: Penguin, 1971.

Mariman, José. "Movimiento Mapuche y Propuestas de Autonómica en la Década Post-Dictadora." Document posted on Nuke Mapu Web site. 1997.

Noggler, Albert. *Cuatrocientos Años de Mision Entre los Araucanos.* Padre Las Casas: Editorial San Francisco, 1972.

Obeyesekere, G. *Medusa's Hair: An Essay on Personal Symbols and Religious Experience.* Chicago: University of Chicago Press, 1981.

Richards, Patricia. "Expanding Notions of Women's Citizenship? The Representation of Mapuche and Pobladora Women in Chile's Servicio Nacional de la Mujer." Paper presented at the 23rd International Congress, Latin American Studies Association, Washington, D.C., September 6–8, 2001.

Rosaldo, Renato. *Culture and Truth: The Remaking of Social Analysis.* Boston: Beacon Press, 1989.

Schein, Louisa. *Minority Rules: The Miao and the Feminine in China's Cultural Politics.* Durham, N.C.: Duke University Press, 2000.

Scott, Joan. *Gender and the Politics of History.* New York: Columbia University Press, 1999.

Sered, Susan. *Priestess Mother, Sacred Sister: Religions Dominated by Women.* New York: Oxford University Press, 1994.

Spiro, M. *Burmese Supernaturalism: A Study in the Explanation and Reduction of Suffering.* Englewood Cliffs, N.J.: Prentice-Hall, 1967.

Stuchlik, Milan. *Life on a Half Share.* London: Hurst, 1976.

Taussig, M. *Shamanism, Colonialism, and the Wild Man: A Study in Terror and Healing.* Chicago: University of Chicago Press, 1987.

Thomas, Nicholas, and Caroline Humphrey. *Shamanism, History and the State.* Ann Arbor: University of Michigan Press, 1994.

Titiev, Mischa. *Araucanian Culture in Transition.* Ann Arbor: University of Michigan Press, 1951.

Tsing, Anna Lowenhaupt. *In the Realm of the Diamond Queen.* Princeton, N.J.: Princeton University Press, 1993.

Valdés, Ximena, and Kathya Araujo. *Vida Privada: Modernización Agraria y Modernidad.* Santiago, Chile: CEDEM, 1999.

Vitebsky, Piers. *The Shaman: Voyages of the Soul, Trance, Ecstasy, and Healing from Siberia to the Amazon.* London: Little, Brown, 1995.

Williams, Brackette. "Introduction: Mannish Women and Gender after the Act." In *Women Out of Place: The Gender of Agency and the Race of Nationality,* 1–33. New York: Routledge, 1996.

Part 4. Understanding "Trauma": The Psychic Effects of Material Violence

Chapter 18

Re/membering the Body

Latina Testimonies of Social and Family Violence

YVETTE FLORES-ORTIZ

> The body speaks in languages left unread. The body encodes the
> *agravios,* the assaults that sometimes lead to numbness and alien-
> ation, to depression and despair, to a desire for an endless night
> of sleep. Our stories document how women's bodies are dismem-
> bered by the ravages of institutionalized racism, by the patriarchal
> structures that accord privilege on the basis of gender and class, by
> the sexism and heterosexism that forbids love and silences desire.
> —Yvette Flores-Ortiz, introduction to *The Body Remembers*
> (2001)

THE BODY REMEMBERS

As an academic clinical psychologist, I engage in intellectual inquiry regarding the etiologies of social and family violence (Bauer; Flores-Ortiz et
al.; Flores-Ortiz, "Mujer," "Broken Covenant," "Fostering Accountability,"
"Injustice," "Migración"). As a practicing psychologist, I engage in *el artey-
ciencia* (the art and science) of psychotherapy with women and men victimized by social and family injustice (Flores-Ortiz, "Injustice," "Migración").
In this chapter and in other writings (Flores-Ortiz, unpublished), I argue
that the body, both metaphorically and factually, is often the site where
women's oppression is recorded. Theoretical formulations grounded in
Western psychology have done little to inform the practice of psychology
with dominated groups (Flores-Ortiz, "Injustice"). Thus, a more extensive
analysis of women's experience informed by feminists of color and cultural
studies scholars is required in order to fully understand how Latinas'
agency and mental health can be compromised by violence.

Moreover, although feminist psychologists argue for the inclusion of a
gender (and sometimes class) analysis in understanding the mental health
challenges of women of color, few have directly addressed the necessity
to understand the position of Latinas as subjugated others. Furthermore,
although writings grounded in Western psychology address the effect of
violence on women's psyches (Herman), most dichotomize the body and
the mind, thus relegating the physical sequelae of oppression to "psychoso-

matics."[1] In so doing, rather than promoting a holistic understanding of women's psychology, most theories further pathologize Latinas or suggest that they lack the "psychological mindedness," meaning intellectual capabilities, to experience more sophisticated disorders such as depression. The artificial mind/body split, which is a legacy of Western psychology, obscures the complex ways in which experiences of violence assault the entire *self* of women. In fact, exposure to the multiple types of violence Latinas routinely endure does affect the psyche, the body, and the soul. Through an analysis of the language of Latinas' narratives, I hope to demonstrate in this chapter how social and familial injustice is encoded in the body, resulting in what Western psychology labels depression, dissociation, and anxiety.

SOURCES OF THE NARRATIVES

This chapter is based on information obtained in a study of three hundred Latina/o college students and community residents who participated in a combined-methodology investigation of the psychological effect of exposure to violence (Flores-Ortiz, unpublished). Specifically, we examined how social and family injustice influence the formation of narratives about the self and perceived agency.

Methodology

All the participants completed a survey. In addition, five male and five female focus groups were conducted. The survey documented the extent of social and family violence that participants experienced; the focus groups investigated the effect of those experiences on the respondents' sense of self and perceived agency in greater depth.

In this chapter, the narratives generated by women participants are analyzed through a feminist social justice lens (Flores-Ortiz, "Fostering Accountability"). The audiotapes of the focus groups were transcribed. A qualitative thematic analysis was then conducted. Specifically, themes were identified where the body emerged as a symbol of the *agravios* (assaults).

General Findings

One hundred seventy-five women completed the survey. The majority of the women were of Mexican descent; thirteen were of Central American origin. The average age of the women was 21 years. Ninety-five percent of the women sampled indicated their families were of working-class background. The rest were middle class. A total of 130 of the women were college students; 27 were community residents with less than a high school education whose average age was 30.

Eighty-five percent of the women disclosed personal experiences of physical violence in their childhood home, where the father or mother was the perpetrator. One hundred women reported witnessing at least one incident of domestic violence between their parents. Fifty women reported being abused by a family member. Of these, twenty were sexual violations. Among the sexually abused women, the age when the abuse began ranged from 4 to 18 years. Nearly 14 percent of the sample experienced abuse before the age of 9. While growing up, the women reported having been exposed frequently to community or social violence (witnessing violence among peers or neighbors; witnessing incidents of police brutality). Twenty of the community residents reported experiences of violence in their marriages, and over half of the college students reported at least one incident of violence in their intimate relationships. One hundred twenty-nine of the women reported verbal or physical attacks because of their race, and eighty-five women reported incidents of sexual harassment.

It must be noted that college students are generally perceived as a resilient and privileged population. Certainly, very few Latinas attend college (Flores-Ortiz, "Injustice"). Although the degree of exposure to family and social violence among college students is unknown, the extent of violence these women had endured or witnessed was extremely high. The only large-scale epidemiological study of family violence in the United States that included Latinos was conducted over a decade ago (Straus and Gelles). That investigation did find higher rates of intrafamily violence among Latinos than among European Americans. However, without accurate data, it is difficult to contextualize the findings of my study. Nevertheless, these findings do suggest that Latinas in higher education are no less likely than working-class women to come from abusive families or communities.

Sequelae of Violence

The college students were asked to describe how experiences with any type of violence had affected them. Their responses can be subsumed under two categories: psychological and academic correlates of exposure to violence, as follows:

Psychological	*Academic*
Hyperalertness	Low academic attainment
Depression	Poor concentration
Low self-esteem	Memory lapses
Anxiety	Lack of assertiveness
Worries	Hypersensitivity
Poor concentration	Trouble finishing tasks
Difficulty trusting	Early drop-outs
Difficulty forming intimate bonds	Apparent lack of interest
Difficulty with intimacy and sexuality	Reduced motivation

Most focus group participants, when asked how they experienced the effect of violence at the time it happened and over time, responded in terms of the body:

> I know I am depressed because I can't stop crying. I feel tightness in my chest; I can't breathe. It's like my body remembers certain things, even though I don't want to remember, and then I try to give a name to it. Oh yes, I say to myself, this is depression. What is my body remembering? Well, all the times he came into my room late at night, sat on the side of the bed, then climbed on top of me. His body would be heavy on my chest. I could not breathe. At first I was scared, then I would just close my eyes and fly away. I don't consciously want to remember the rest. But my body does. When I am in class sometimes it happens, I am trying to concentrate, and *boom*, the tightness comes and then I am out of the room. I don't know where I go, but I come back and half the lecture is over and I have no idea what the professor said. How can I remember what my instructor says when I am not even present in the room, except in body? (Maria, aged 22)[2]

In her narrative, Maria describes the process of dissociation that occurs during sexual or physical abuse. A psychological strategy to copy with such profound violence is for the mind and body to separate. The conscious mind attempts to erase what is happening, but the body encodes it. The experiences can be repressed for many years. Often it is not until the individual feels safe that she can begin to remember what previously occurred. Typically, the memories return as flashbacks or disjointed images (Flores Ortiz, "Broken Covenant"). As Herman and others have indicated, sexual and physical violence often results in what is known in psychology as post-traumatic stress disorder. In fact, the psychological correlates of violence the women participants outlined are consistent with the symptoms of post-traumatic stress disorder.

LATINA NARRATIVES

Violence in all its forms attacks the *self*. Women described themselves as suffering from low self-esteem, difficulty trusting others, especially men, and attacks on the self. Among the college students and community residents, one consistent effect of verbal and emotional abuse was low self-esteem. One college student stated,

> I doubt the good qualities people seem to point out about me. I basically have a low self-esteem about my appearance, my abilities. I think it happened over time. He used to call me *gorda, fea, vieja, mensa* [fat, ugly, old, dumb]. He used to tell me Mexican women were not as fine as the white girls were. I would wonder, then why is he with me? I think I started to feel he was doing me a favor. After all, yeah, if you look at the women on TV, yes, they are taller and thinner and clearly lighter-skinned than I am. So,

yeah, he must be right. It took me a while to realize that he was being abusive. But part of me still believes what he said to be true. (Sofia, age 21)

Another woman stated,

I struggle with low self-esteem because as a child I was told I was nobody—in fact, worthless. It started at home, with my dad calling me "white girl" because I am light-skinned, but continued at school where I was called beaner, greaser, stuff like that by the other kids. The teachers always referred to me as the Mexican kid. I eventually got tired of telling them I was Salvadoreña. (Juana, age 30)

In Sofia's case, her boyfriend's attacks on her appearance resonated with media images reflecting a standard of beauty irrelevant to (and unattainable for) many Latinas. The man she loved repudiated her appearance, and she did not see anyone who affirmed her worth in the media. Sofia suffered multiple erasures, which targeted her body and racial identity. Both Sofia and Juana described the pain of enduring such erasures over time.

Physical abuse, sometimes viewed by respondents as discipline, also affected the women's self-esteem:

When I was a little girl, my father's solution to all his children's problems was to hit us and that was the end of it. Nothing said. If you had a problem with it [being hit], you would just be hit again. We were never spanked, just hit with whatever my dad had in his hand at the time, such as a shoe, stick, or belt. Yes, I felt bad. I never felt safe because I could not predict when the attack would happen. I felt stupid, like I should know how to avoid the attacks, but I never seemed to know how. (Rosa, age 22)

I remember one time seeing a cooking show, and then I thought, oh my gosh, that's what mom hit us with, a wooden spoon, a spatula, a frying pan. These things were not used for cooking, they were used to hit us . . . well, because we were bad and she was frustrated. I understand. But it wasn't 'til that moment that I had really thought about her hitting us kids. (Elena, age 22)

Both Rosa and Elena came to view the childhood physical abuse they experienced as normal. Furthermore, they attempted to discern their father's and mother's moods, leading to hypervigilance and chronic worrying. These ways of coping continued into adulthood.

Women victimized by violence often internalize blame for the abuse and "punish" themselves for the injustices suffered. When women are made to feel culpable for their own victimization, they may attack what they perceive to be the culprit: the physical attribute that called attention to themselves. This reaction is particularly common where the body has been the site of the abuse. These attacks on the self can take the form of self-denigration or hatred, with attempts to alter appearance to look more or less "ethnic," eating disorders, substance abuse, self-mutilation, a myriad of physical maladies (e.g., colitis, gastritis, eczema), depression, high-risk behaviors (including sexual acting out), and the ultimate assault on the self: suicide.

A number of respondents described incidents of sexual and racial harassment, which were viewed as inescapable, everyday experiences leading to attacks on the self:

> *Ay señora,* you can't walk down the street in México without being harassed.
> My mother used to tell me I should accept the compliments and ignore the rest. She used to say that someday men would no longer *piropearme.*[3] But here [in the United States] it is different. Here you are invisible, nobody notices you. Maybe it is because after having kids, I got fat. So nobody wants to look at me. (Eleanor, age 35)

> Well, here [in the United States], I feel women may have more rights, but if you are Latina, you still can't stop this stuff from happening. My boss was coming at me with compliments, or so he claimed when I confronted him. He used to call me *"chiquita"* and tell me how beautiful my long black hair is. I told him he made me feel uncomfortable. So he acted all innocent and said I must be a feminist. What a fool. Yes, I was angry, but what could I do? I need the job. I just try to ignore him until I can find another job. But the one thing I did was cut my hair. (Daniela, age 22)

Daniela experienced both sexual and ethnic harassment. Her boss used a term often ascribed to Latinas. *Chiquita* is a coded term, as it generally refers to "Chiquita bananas," a brand name of the United Fruit Company, which occupied many regions of the continent and which was sometimes used to refer to Latinas in the region. An implication of the term is that the women were as much the property of the company as the bananas they cultivated. It is a term intended to objectify and put women in their place. Having grown up in Central America, Daniela understood the use of the word and how it positioned her relative to her Anglo boss. So she cut off her long black hair, the object of his desire.

A consequence of sexual violence is eating disorders (Herman; Chamorro and Flores-Ortiz; Flores-Ortiz, "Broken Covenant"):

> I wanted to be invisible. He used to tell me that I made him do these things he did to me. He said I was a tease, I made him lose control. I was 7, but I loved him. He was my daddy. So I stopped eating. I was always thin. As I got older and my breasts began to grow, he would tell me that my breasts made him crazy, that he could not stop himself. I did not want to have breasts. I wanted to look like a boy. (Jenny, age 23)

The most long-term effect of physical, sexual, psychological, verbal, and emotional violence, whether perpetrated by strangers or intimates, is lack of trust. Most of the women who participated in the survey and focus groups felt insecure with men because primarily men perpetrated the violence they experienced. One woman stated,

> Well, I think I've become very unattached, especially to guys. I have become very hard minded. Men are just like *bluh,* I don't trust them and there's nothing they can say to make me believe them. I have closed my heart to them. (Alicia, age 24)

> I am always on the defensive prepared for attack whether it be verbally or physically. . . . It has been an ongoing process [trusting again]. It's like adrenaline is always rushing through my veins. I tend to feel all revved up. I feel like the few instances where I was attacked verbally or physically have made me shut myself down around people I just met. I don't open up easily and I can't trust easily for fear of someone turning on me. I trust no one and find it hard to get along with males. (Josefina, age 26)

> What has affected me is being raped and being physically abused by an ex-boyfriend. That has changed the way I see men. It traumatized me for a while; I am kinda over it now. I have been through counseling for a long time and I have dealt with it and moved on. It took me three years to realize it. I blocked it out of my head and I was 20 before I realized what happened to me and I didn't tell no one and how come I didn't stop it. I had trained myself to think that I wanted it. That I wanted to have sex with him and I knew I didn't. I knew that he physically abused me because that was obvious. The physical and mental abuse, that was obvious, but the sexual abuse, I just kinda told myself, "you wanted it, that's not rape." Three years later, I said yeah, it was rape. I am fine now, I think. I think that was the most traumatizing experience. (Margarita, age 23)

> If you cannot trust your own father, who can you trust? (Alicia, age 25)

Ultimately, experiences with violence affect the entire self and can be manifested somatically and psychologically. The long-term sequelae, however, may compromise not only the physical and psychological health of those affected by injustice but may compromise the spirit as well:

> Who are we if not the sum total of our pain and victimization? (Luisa, age 35)

> I feel at times like the walking dead. I don't believe in god. How could a god, whether Christian or something else, allow little children to be hurt by those who are supposed to care for them? My body will walk this earth until I die, but my spirit left a long time ago. (Tina, age 35)

> The spark of life grows ever dimmer. I was once a vibrant child, a happy little girl. Then her assaults began, the verbal beatings, the humiliation, the physical punishment. I could feel myself shrinking. I may be over 50 years of age, but a hurt little girl lives inside me. She is the only part of me that

is alive. *Se me fué el espíritu desde hace tiempo* [my spirit left me a long time ago]. (Olga, age 55)

FINDING MEANING

Healing from violence can be a long and arduous path. Social and family violence results in feelings of victimization. Healing entails transforming trauma into recovery—shifting from feeling victimized to feeling like a survivor. Central to this journey is healing the spirit, reconnecting the body and the mind and regaining a sense of agency. Most victims of violence, however, need to find meaning in their experiences of violation. Women also seek explanations for the behavior of the perpetrator. If he or she is a family member, women tend to seek explanations and create narratives that exonerate the abuser.

Women who participated in this study and were victimized within the family generated narratives based on three general themes: woman as treacherous Malinche, man as "*descontrolado*" (out of control), and woman as protector and nurturer of men. These stories reflect internalized dominant stories of disempowerment (Flores-Ortiz, "Injustice"), which obscure the political roots of injustice.

The knowledge and stories families and communities negotiate and engage in, in order to give meaning to their experiences, in turn shape the lives and relationships of people (Aboriginal Health Council of South Australia). I argue that Latinas' social position within U.S. culture and the gender relations of men and women within ethnically dominated societies tend to produce narratives of conquest and disempowerment (Flores-Ortiz, "Injustice"; "Migración") that create scripts for negotiating injustice. Specifically, the experiences of marginality, dislocation, and repudiation experienced at the social level are replicated in the family. Over time, women come to feel responsible for the social and family violence they endure, as well as for the behavior of the men and women who are violent. This burden of unearned responsibility results in self-blame and the myriad psychological sequelae described by the participants of the study. Latina college students frequently explained their victimization in terms of the oppression of their men relying on cultural symbols and scripts:

> I knew I was a Malinche. I knew it was my fault. How could a father, a brother, hurt a child this way? I had to be doing something to provoke them. (Flores-Ortiz, "Broken Covenant," 62)

In this narrative, an incest survivor assumes responsibility for her victimization and decides to protect the perpetrators, whom she knows will be treated differently by the justice system. A central organizing theme in her narrative is treachery. She did not want to be a *traidora*, so she betrayed herself by remaining silent. The use of the symbol of Malinche, Cortez's interpreter, lover, and presumed collaborator in the conquest of México, racializes and situates the narrator as one of the countless women, who according to Mexican history and popular culture, have betrayed her race. In so doing, she seems to absolve the perpetrators of responsibility.

Latino families must negotiate survival within a context of race and class discrimination (Hurtado). Women in these families are often called upon to understand, anticipate, and absolve the behaviors of men leading to narratives that suggest men are often the victims of *descontrol* (loss of control):

> We were unruly kids, you know, there were so many of us. We lived in a small apartment. Mom had to keep us all in check, clean the house and make do with very little. Dad was tired, you know, he worked really hard. So he would come home and have a couple of beers to relax. Now I understand that when you are really wound up and start to relax you can actually feel all the stress and oppression of the day-to-day life. So sometimes one of us would make a lot of noise or whatever, and he would lose it. He would yell, scream, call us names, hit us. If my mom got in the way, to protect us, she would get hit. So once it started, we would just let him beat us—better than have mom get hurt. I used to carry a lot of anger inside, but now I understand he couldn't help himself. He would just lose control because of everything he went through. Mom would tell us we had to be forgiving because he was weak and could not control himself. (Ana, age 24)

The notion of men as weak and out of control was manifested in narratives that positioned women as nurturers and protectors of men. I have named this "the *pobrecito* syndrome": *pobrecito* means "poor little one," which may be an endearing term used by women to refer to men as they explain or excuse men's foibles. The *pobrecito* syndrome is evident here as women recollect the excuses made for men's inappropriate behavior:

> I think sometimes his seeing me just set him off. I don't know why, to this day I don't know why, but like he was not like that with my sister . . . , but with me he was always harder and there were times when he'd come home from work and my mom would tell me, "why don't you just go to your room or leave or something, 'cause I don't think your Dad needs to see you right now." It is better now 'cause I don't live there anymore, but it also hurt that my mom didn't protect me, just his feelings. We were supposed to protect his feelings, no matter how much I hurt. (Julia, age 20)

> My mother would say, *hay pobrecito,* he works so hard, he needs to unwind. This was the explanation for his drinking, his yelling, his womanizing, his coming in late, his beating her and me. I am so full of rage because I could never complain. Then I feel guilty because, yeah, it's true, he worked hard and I know how Chicanos are treated, so yeah he was a *pobrecito.* . . . It is really fu— up. (Sonia, age 22)

Latinas victimized by family violence must negotiate cultural scripts that mandate family loyalty, which can result in a culture of silence that protects the men at the expense of the women's mental and physical health. Ultimately, everyone is compromised. The man is not afforded the help he needs; women explode in frustration and rage, hurting themselves and sometimes their children; male children learn aggression as a social script, and female children may learn to suppress feelings of rage, potentially leading to disempowerment and depression.

THE PATH TO HEALING

Moving from dominant stories about one's life to preferred stories is like making a journey from one identity to another.
—"Reclaiming Our Stories," Aboriginal Health Council of
South Australia (1995)

Healing from legacies and experiences of injustice requires a journey from victim to survivor. This path requires an active engagement with the realities of oppression and a questioning or deconstructing of one's internalized "isms." This process is largely cognitive. However, to reconnect the body and the mind, the heart and the soul, injustices must be named and culpability externalized (Aboriginal Health Council of South Australia; Flores-Ortiz, "Injustice"; "Migración").

In other writings (Flores-Ortiz, "Injustice," "Introduction," unpublished), I have argued that to counter the internalization of injustice and oppression, and to heal the body and the spirit, a liberatory psychotherapy must be developed that foregrounds the social roots of intrafamily injustice. I recommend psychotherapies that are feminist, justice-based, and amenable to the incorporation of body work (that is, massage therapies, dance, or any type of exercise) and spiritual guidance for those in the process of recovery. Furthermore, healing from social and family injustice is not only a family but also a community task. Women need the support of other women and a nurturing family (whether consanguineous or fictive). Giving testimony, as the participants in this study did, often is a first step in the path to healing:[4]

The reason I came (to the focus groups) is basically because I have been a victim of violence, not so much around me but that I have been directly affected. I think that it is a big issue in the Chicano/Latino community. . . . That's why I figure that I should talk about it with people. . . . I need to let a lot of males know that this does happen. Women do get raped, women do get abused, and as much as you think that happens to everyone else except your mom and your sister, it does. They need to know that it does happen. And it happens by all men. That's why I am here. (Elena, age 22)

Well, I am here because I was—my father physically abused my mother. And that has really affected me, the way I perceive men and all that, because I was small and the thing is that, the issue is like kinda held in, only the family knows, like nobody ever talks about it. So I want to let people know that it does happen, that it is going on, it goes on and it, just hopefully I can help to reach out to the community. (Josefina, age 21)

Giving testimony on behalf of other women and children victimized by family violence begins a process of healing for the women and the community. Through the process of reconnecting to body, heart, and soul, women begin to hold accountable the men and women who injured them. In so doing, survivors hold the community and social structures that oppress and propitiate victimization accountable as well. This may be central to reclaiming one's agency and feeling more whole:[5]

I am far more than the paintings I give birth to out of my pain. I don't want to be remembered as an incested woman, a survivor of family violence. I want to be remembered for the totality of my being, for everything I have done, not for what was done to me. (Becky, age 29)

I finally inhabit my body. I feel the beating of my heart, I know what I am thinking in the moment, I can translate my emotions, and I have conquered fear. I can say I am no longer afraid to love, to make love, to be touched. But more importantly, while I cannot recover the innocence he robbed, I got back my soul. (Teresa, age 29)

Joyfulness, playfulness, aliveness have replaced depression, dissociation, and despair. Pretty cool, huh? (Olivia, age 21)

Transformative healing experiences can ultimately lead to rescripting cultural narratives. A critical analysis of the structures and systems that oppress and the ways in which families replicate social injustice and cause suffering among family members can provide compassion and understanding for the perpetrators. However, their behaviors cannot be exonerated without accountability and restitution. Breaking the patterns of violence within and outside the family is a way to exonerate historical injustices and promote hope for future generations. Finding wholeness through healing experiences reintegrates the body, heart, and soul. Remembering the body is often the first step.

NOTES

1. "Psychosomatics" is the physical manifestation of psychological distress; psychosomatic illnesses do not have an identifiable physical cause. These disorders are

currently named "somatoform" in the most recent *Diagnostic and Statistical Manual of the American Psychiatric Association* (DSM IV).

2. The names provided are pseudonyms. All participants selected a name by which they would be identified in order to maintain the confidentiality of their responses.

3. *Piropear* is the practice of paying unsolicited compliments to women. These can range from statements about appearance and beauty to sexual innuendo and vulgar propositions. This is a long-standing cultural practice in the Americas.

4. This is controversial, however, because in the same way that family violence can produce devastating psychological sequelae for survivors, giving testimony as a research participant can be experienced as exploitative. How, then, can researchers justify collecting these stories? How can research participants and researchers alike be protected from retraumatization? I argue that liberatory research practices can have a healing effect on individuals victimized by the family and the society. In fact, "Giving Voice" to injustice can transform dominant stories of victimization into preferred stories of survival, resilience, and agency. In our study, the research assistants were trained extensively on interview techniques and received weekly supervision. Weekly debriefings were held to allow researchers to express and process their own experiences. As one research assistant says, "I would hear their stories and remember my own. I would cry for them and for me. But these stories must be told, because that is what makes our Raza so strong, that we can survive so much horror, and still succeed." In addition, referrals to mental health professionals were made available for students and community members who participated in the study.

5. These women described their current feelings and their healing process. All three had received psychotherapy from feminist Latina psychologists. They had also participated in healing rituals that were part of their cultural traditions. Two had had extensive body work performed as well.

REFERENCES

Aboriginal Health Council of South Australia. "Reclaiming Our Lives." Australia: Dulwich Centre Newsletter, 1995.

Bauer, H., M. Rodriguez, S. Skupinski-Quiroga, and Y. Flores-Ortiz. "Barriers to Health Care for Abused Latina and Asian Immigrant Women." *Journal of Health Care for the Poor and the Underserved* 11, no. 1 (2000): 33–44.

Chamorro, R., and Y. Flores-Ortiz. "Acculturation and Disordered Eating Patterns among Mexican American Women." *International Journal of Eating Disorders* 28, no. 1, 125–29, July 2000.

Flores-Ortiz, Y. "The Broken Covenant: Incest in Latino Families." *Voces: A Journal of Chicana/Latina Studies* 1, no. 1 (1997): 48–70.

———. "Fostering Accountability: A Reconstructive Dialogue with a Couple with a History of Violence." In *101 Interventions in Family Therapy,* edited by T. Nelson and T. Trepper, 389–96. New York: Haworth Press, 1998.

———. "Injustice in the Family." In *Family Therapy with Hispanics,* edited by M. Flores and G. Carey, 251–63. Boston: Allyn and Bacon, 1999.

———. "Introduction to *The Body Remembers.*" In *Telling to Live: Latina Feminist Testimonios,* edited by the Latina Feminist Research Collective, 63. Durham, N.C.: Duke University Press, 2001.

———. "Migración, Identidad y Violencia/Migration, Identity and Violence." In

Breaking Barriers: Diversity in Clinical Practice, edited by M. Mock, L. Hill, and D. Tucker, 46–59. California: California State Psychological Association, 1999.

——. "La Mujer y La Violencia: A Culturally Based Model for the Understanding and Treatment of Domestic Violence in Chicana/Latina Communities." In *Chicana Critical Issues,* edited by N. Alarcon et al., 169–82. Berkeley: Third Woman Press, 1993.

——. "Social and Family Violence in the Lives of Latino College Students." Unpublished manuscript.

Flores Ortiz, Y., M. Esteban, and R. Carrillo. "La Violencia en la Familia: Un Modelo. Contextual de Terapia Intergeneracional." *Revista Interamericana de Psicología* 28, no. 2 (1994): 235–50.

Herman, J. *Trauma and Recovery.* New York: Basic Books, 1992.

Hurtado, A. "Variations, Combinations, and Evolutions." In *Understanding Latino Families: Scholarship, Policy, and Practice,* edited by Ruth Zambrano, 40–61. Thousand Oaks, Calif.: Sage, 1995.

Straus, M. A., and R. J. Gelles. *Physical Violence in American Families: Risk Factors and Adaptations to Violence in 8,145 Families.* New Brunswick, N.J.: Transaction, 1990.

Chapter 19

Sita's War and the Body Politic

Violence and Abuse in the Lives of South Asian Women

SUNITA PEACOCK

Statistics show that among the large number of immigrants in the United States, 2.8 percent are Asians. The 1990 census further reveals that of the 2.8 percent Asian immigrants, 1 million are South Asians. This group includes people from India, Bangladesh, Pakistan, Nepal, and Sri Lanka, and in this group, the incidence of domestic violence is on the rise (20 to 25 percent). Unfortunately, the percentages are inaccurate because a large number of cases go unreported "owing to underutilization of existing social and health services" (Hasnat, 146). Other barriers include issues of immigration status, language problems, and existing cultural norms within South Asian societies that play an important role in women not reporting violence and abuse in their lives. By use of information about the problems of domestic violence in South Asian communities, and specifically Indian communities, I will attempt to discuss and link such violence to neocolonial issues among immigrants, especially women, in Western hegemonic societies. In discussing the subordination and violence perpetrated on women and the space they occupy in an abusive household, I will draw parallels between the space women have occupied during nationalist/colonialist struggles and the master/slave dichotomy between the colonizer and the colonized.

First, in order to examine the violence in the domestic sphere of immigrant families in Western societies, one has to understand the link between power and violence, because when one examines abusive situations and attempts to understand domestic violence, one notes the dominance of the abuser in a household situation. Second, to further understand power and subjection, it is profitable to elaborate on Foucauldian, Hegelian, and Althusserian definitions of the power of subjection and subordination. Third, I will use these definitions along with theories from feminist and cultural theorists, such as Judith Butler and Partha Chatterjee, to draw parallels between the abuse women experience in violent situations and the abuse that colonized nations have experienced under the yoke of the colonizer.

One of Foucault's definitions of power may be paraphrased as follows: "power" forms the subject, which could make the subject dependent on the power. In turn, the power weakens the subject or the dependent (Foucault in Butler, *Psychic Life*, 2). In Foucault's estimation, "subjection" allows the person who is subjected to become "subordinated," as well as to become the subject. In the case of the immigrant woman in an abusive situation, subordination is rampant. To understand the reasons behind this subordination or subjection, one has to look at some specific religious and cultural myths—myths that become realities in Indian (South Asian) immigrant homes.[1] The example at hand looks at a particular religious text from ancient Indian or Vedic scriptures. The text is the *Manu Samhita*, or *The Treatises of Manu*. This particular text was written by an eighth-century social theorist and was later codified into religious law (*Laws of Manu*, 100). One particular law about marriage states that "of the eight forms of marriages, the demonic (rakshasa) form is one. 'Rakshasa' marriage involves raping a woman, thereby making her one's own" (100). Another law about marriage articulates women as the property of men (fathers, husbands, sons) at different stages in their lives. When the woman becomes property, the right to rape becomes a "permissible action" (Mazumdar, 135).

In the case of the woman who is abused, we see a formation of a subject because of the external power of the abuser and power that is given to the abuser because of religious, cultural, and societal norms, to say the least. According to the feminist theorist Judith Butler, when an external power exerts pressure on the subject, it can subordinate it and also "assume a psychic form that constitutes the subject's self-identity" (*Psychic Life*, 4–5). Conversely, Butler argues that the subject needs more explanation about its formation (4). To understand the formulation of the abused subject, then, one must verify the situation of the abused immigrant woman.

There are several problems that South Asian immigrant women encounter in Western hegemonic societies. Some of these barriers include their status as immigrants, their problems with language, their deep-rooted belief systems from their natal culture, and their lack of knowledge of the services available for their abusive situations. Many South Asian immigrants are not legal residents of the United States; because of their illegal status, many work illegally in grocery and fast-food stores, making minimum wage without any benefits. The lives of these immigrants are filled with fear and drudgery. There are also many South Asian immigrants who have to rely on family members who have smuggled them into the country, and thus speaking out about their domestic problems would cause familial constraints. These familial constraints also cause cultural constraints, giving the abused a false sense of loyalty in a negative situation. Many immigrant women are in a foreign or Western country for the first time. They have probably been brought from a remote part of India or another South Asian country and do not speak the language of their new home. It is because of such inadequacies in their lives that cases of abuse go unreported.

To better understand the reasons for some of the problems that South

Asian immigrants face in their new country of residence, one needs to look at the demographic concentration of these immigrants in the United States. Two groups of South Asian immigrants reside in the United States. The first group arrived during the early twentieth century (1890s to 1950s), and the second group arrived in the 1970s. I will concentrate on the second group because violence in the second group seems more common. One reason for the increase of violence in these South Asian communities could be due to some of the reasons listed below.

First, the complexity and diversity of South Asian groups have increased since the 1970s. When the first wave of immigrants arrived in the early twentieth century, many of them came mainly from the Punjab region of India and settled in Canada and the northwestern regions of the United States (Seattle and Oregon in general). These early immigrants worked in the lumber industry and also in the agricultural areas of northern California. Second, the newer group (from the 1970s onward) of South Asians comes not only from India, but Pakistan, Bangladesh, Sri Lanka, and Nepal. So now there are "many kinds of Hindus, Muslims, Buddhists, Christians, Sikhs and Parsis," which then leads to the "importance of caste and community," especially "for purposes of marriage" (Leonard, 70). Third, 70 percent of the South Asian immigrants are concentrated in the major metropolitan areas of New York, California, New Jersey, Pennsylvania, Michigan, Illinois, and Ohio (Bhardwaj and Rao in Leonard, 70), and because of such an influx of South Asian immigrants, the laws for immigration have become stricter. In 1986, the Immigration Reform and Control Act was passed, and the Special Agricultural Worker clause was passed to legalize Indian, Pakistani, and especially Bangladeshi workers in agriculture. Between the years 1990 and 2000, the Immigration Reform and Control Act was phased out, thus making it harder to hire immigrants in agricultural professions, which leads to a constant influx of illegal immigration (70). Thus, the census cannot account for a large number of illegal immigrants in the United States, and because of illegal immigration, there is a "continuous socioeconomic decline in the South Asian communities" (82).

Many South Asian immigrants come into the United States through Canada and México. They come as tourists and then "overstay" (Leonard, 82). Added to this illegal entrance into the United States are the jobs that most of these illegal immigrants scramble for: they seek employment as dishwashers in restaurants, truck loaders, convenience-store clerks, and other casual labor (82). To acquire legal immigrant status, the first thing that is commonly done is to marry a legal resident of the United States— "In fact, the matrimonial advertisements in the ethnic press often indicate preferences for spouses who have green cards or are U.S. citizens" (80). And again, because of a large influx of South Asian immigrants, there are higher levels of unemployment. "As of 1988, U.S.-born South Asians (along with U.S.-born Filipinos) had much higher levels of unemployment (7.6% Indians) than did other Asian Americans and non-Hispanic whites, and only 35% of them had completed more than sixteen years of schooling" (82). A recent study also shows that in California, Oregon, and Washington, just over 10 percent of the South Asian Indian population is living below the poverty line. California has the highest percentages of South Asian Indians living below the poverty line (14 percent; the national level is 9 percent). One reason for this increase in poverty among South Asian immigrants is that many of them are not coming as professionals: "The initial post-1965 Asian Indian immigration featured professionals and their families, but since the mid-1970s, more immigrants have been starting small businesses or investing in such businesses as a part-time sideline" (82).

Thus, one can see from some of the reasons listed above about immigration problems why there could be an increase of violence and spousal abuse in such communities. Then again, one does not want to make excuses for violence and abuse.[2] When discussing the South Asian/Indian community, one needs to understand the intermingling of these similar, yet on rare occasions different, communities. There are a couple of reasons for the intermingling of the culture of India and the people from the neighboring countries of Bangladesh, Pakistan, Nepal, and Sri Lanka. One reason is that historically when Islam, Buddhism, and Christianity were introduced to India, many Hindus from the lower castes converted to escape the fundamental Hindu religious practices, especially the caste system. So "Hindu rituals have endured" even outside the Hindu/Indian culture. "Furthermore, Hinduism is not contained within India only. Nepal, Bangladesh, Sri Lanka and Pakistan, all have substantial Hindu populations, as do other Pacific Rim countries" (Mazumdar, 131). The second reason for the deep cultural connections between various South Asian groups is because as immigrants, South Asians as a whole tend to live in close proximity to each other in a foreign country because of similar cultural traditions, especially if they are in the dominant country illegally.

Aside from the imposition of laws because of immigration or a lack of support by the dominant government because of illegality issues, another aspect of the increase of spousal abuse in South Asian communities is a lack of fluency in the dominant language. Because the victims are not being able to communicate to social workers in English, and because they are not comfortable in a culture that is willing to help women in abusive situations, numerous cases of spousal abuse go unreported. Unfortunately, programs started by South Asian women, such as Sakhi, still cannot penetrate the silences embedded in the language of these abused women.

In their joint collaboration about abused women in the Indian community of New York, S. D. Dasgupta and S. Warrier note that Indian/South Asian women want to embody steadfast devotion to their husbands in the footsteps of the Indian goddesses of Sita, Savitri, and Sati. Unfortunately, this steadfast devotion leads to the woman being silenced. Thus, to preserve family and religious traditions, the women want to present "an unblemished image" of their family life to their community. For example, in Pakistani society, "the code of honor and shame has been a central issue in community dynamics. A family's honor is linked to the purity of its women, which means not only that the woman must retain her virginity before marriage and be faithful after but also that she ensure that no hint of scandal be cast upon the family through rumor" (Hasnat, 141). Similar traditions are seen in Hinduism, which is the predominant religion of India and Nepal as embodied in the silent devotion of Hindu goddesses, such as Sita and Parvati.

Dasgupta and Warrier also note that when some of these abused women have been confronted about their abuse, they have refused to speak of "sexual abuse" (237). There is an "uncomfortability with language" when mentioning issues of sexuality. Because of language, Dasgupta and Warrier feel that the area of sexuality "effectively silences women who are not just abused with their marriage or partnership relations, but are victims of assault by strangers or intra-family relationships" (238–39). This idea is further elaborated by L. Kelly, who agrees with the issue of silence playing a significant role in the language of abuse. Kelly believes that all women who are abused and who are violated are prevented from fully "participating in society" (Kelly in Moane, 140). Silence permeates their language as the sexual climate in the abusive situation escalates. Cultural attitudes also play a role in maintaining silence in the language of the abused subject.

Some negative cultural attitudes within Indian/South Asian communities are embedded within the institution of marriage. Marriages may be arranged in such communities, as evidenced by the matrimonial advertisements in South Asian newspapers published in the United States. Once a woman is married to a man, whom she may barely know, he has proprietorship over her. The woman becomes the property of the man and then essentially follows the function of a "breeder" (Mazumdar, 135). The role of the woman is that of a domestic to perform the duties of a wife, which are linked to the duties of the goddess to the god. In Hindu mythology and religion, the goddesses such as Sita, Savitri, and Sati venerate their husbands as gods. In Islamic society (Pakistan, Bangladesh) as well, men are the protectors of women and providers for their family. Additionally, Islamic law states that the only way to provide and care for women is to segregate them (Hasnat, 142). Thus, both Hindu and Muslim cultures create subordinated positions for women. This subordination and steadfast devotion to one's husband and family is another reason for silence in the language of the South Asian women.

As social and feminist theorists have noticed, the story of subjection of women is universal. Foucault postulates that in subjection "the simultaneous subordination and forming of the subject emerges without a passionate attachment to those on whom he or she is fundamentally dependent" and that even if the passion is "negative" in the psychoanalytic sense, there is subordination (Foucault in Butler, 7). According to Foucault, to become a subject, one has to subordinate himself or herself. In turn, Butler's reply to Foucault's postulation of subordination and subjection is that "no individual becomes a subject without first becoming subjected or undergoing subjectivation. This is because the agency of the subject appears to be an effect of its subordination" (12), making the theory of subjection ambivalent and circular. This ambivalence and circularity penetrate the very language of the abused, causing her to become ambivalent about the abuse.

Subsequently, the South Asian woman becomes the subject of abuse that she herself permits because of the silence bestowed on her by her culture and language, allowing herself to be "vanquished" by the abuser. In her examination of the complex relationship between aggression and love, Melanie Klein declares that there is always a "desire to vanquish what one loves." In an abusive situation, many times the abuser will apologize profusely after committing the crime of abuse. The abused, on the other hand, is "already lost" and becomes "eligible for a certain kind of vanquishing" (Klein in Butler, *Psychic Life*, 26). In other words, the dominant party or abuser has established a "regulatory power" that maintains the subject in subordination (29). The subject here, the South Asian woman, allows the dominant party to subjugate her—not because she thinks it is her fault, but because it is her fate. Once again, one sees the culture-specific concepts that move into the realm of abuse.

In a recorded interview with a middle-aged South Asian woman with two grown children who was and is continuously abused by her husband, her reply to the abuse is, "I don't think it was my fault at all. This is my fate. I just thought that this was part of my life. You know, no one's life is perfect. There is one thing or another in everyone's life. And I just look at this [domestic violence] as something that I had to tolerate" (Hasnat, 151). The abused woman's tolerance for abuse gives her abuser exploitative power, and she in turn lives in a situation where, in the Lacanian sense, the boundaries of subjectivity "[pervade] the interiority of the subject" (Butler, *Psychic Life*, 89).

But every aspect of Hindu and Islamic culture does not accentuate the subservient attitude of women. In these cultures, there is the provision of role models for women that are powerful and dynamic. So why is it that women still hide themselves behind the destructive elements of abuse? For example, in Hindu religion and philosophy, the concept of "Shakti," or femininity in control of her own sexuality, is a "pervasive image that is widely accepted in Indian society. . . . Indian history is also redolent with courageous and active women leaders" (Mazumdar, 143). In Islam, the Koran advocates "gender equality, justice and education for women. . . .

The Prophet Mohammed made women integral to his plan for Muslim education and learning when he declared: 'Acquisition of knowledge is obligatory for every Muslim, male or female'" (Hasnat, 143). In all probability, an important reason for such inequities is the bombardment of culturally based practices that are in the forefront of South Asian communities. What the women from these South Asian communities need to distinguish are the two separate roles created for them, one created by religion and philosophy, and one created through "cultural practices" (Hasnat, 143).

Such cultural practices dominate all spheres of a woman's life, regardless of her ethnic background. bell hooks urges fellow black women who are abused to shift their focus from "a framework of victimization to one of accountability" (83). hooks believes that domestic abuse faced by black women when they "allow" men to impregnate them without the benefit of marriage or money happens when social and cultural issues are confused with personal and sexual issues (84). South Asian women face the same dilemma when their culture makes them reticent about abuse in their lives. The norms (societal, communal, and family) imposed on them by their society keeps them in abusive situations. The effect of these factors are illustrated in a conversation with a woman called Munni whose account of her conjugal life reads as follows: "When I got married, my father said to my husband, 'my respect and honor is in your hands. Please take care of my daughter.' From then on he was my husband. It was my job to take care of him. For my family honor, family respect, and to [maintain] this respect, we have to put up with it [violence]" (Hasnat, 153). There is no mention of the religious teachings of Shakti or the strength that women have to have in order to leave the situation. The abuse revolves around cultural norms.

The conflict between the abused and cultural norms results in a specific definition of spousal abuse that becomes problematic. Physical abuse can include rape, battery, sexual assault, kicking, pushing, choking, and even murder. Abuse is not established overnight, but "it is often perpetrated in a sustained way over a long period of time," causing bodily harm and mental damage as well. Sadly, such abuse is common in intimate relationships between men and women (Moane, 40). Further, when a system of violence has been established, both the oppressor and the oppressed are submerged in it: "The oppressor develops a focus on possessing and controlling, leading to dehumanization and objectification of the oppressed, which in turn generates more violence." On the other hand, the oppressed feels an "ambivalent attraction of horizontal violence, and a split or dual consciousness in the oppressed" (Freire, 82). This diagrammatic representation of the oppressor or abuser and the oppressed or abused parallels the psychological discourse of the colonizer and colonized.

When examining Hegelian theories of the master/slave dichotomy, one notices a similar pattern (oppressor/oppressed, colonizer/colonized) in which both the master and the slave have a dependency toward each other. D. Mannoni prescribes the theory of dependence in a colonial situation when he analyzes the relationship between the Malagasies in Madagascar and their French colonizers. Mannoni discusses the colonialist theory of the dependency complex of the black man. According to Mannoni, the Malagasies feel safe when they are "securely held by the traditional bonds of dependence" and feel inferior when "the bonds of dependence are somewhat threatened" (40). Mannoni's argument is similar to that of Rousseau and Hegel, who confirm that there are two groups of people in this world: the master and the slave. To put it in Hegelian terms, "the master is willing to negate his 'animal' life in order to affirm his 'human' life" (Lauer, 7), and the slave does just the opposite. As soon as the latter gives up his humanity, he becomes dependent on the master. He is not unhappy with this change because as Rousseau would posit, "a dependent person would give up his freedom for tranquillity" (137). Mannoni furthers Rousseau's argument by explaining how the Malagasies' dependent nature is a "key to the psychology of the 'backward peoples'" (40). Their dependency stagnates their civilization and it "elucidates what seems to us [the colonizer] at first sight, incomprehensible in the psychological reaction of that mentality" (40).

Frantz Fanon discusses how, in his theory of violence, "The colonizer first initiates the violent situation by changing the image of the native into a brute. The colonizer has the native undergo physical, cultural, and psychic changes in his/her personality" (36). In fact, Mannoni's colonial discourse hides the violence behind the mask of his so-called dependency theory. The colonized *appears* to be dependent because of the violence inflicted on her if she does not adhere to the rules established by the colonizer. Accordingly, a dual consciousness is created in the psyche of the colonized, which is similar to the dual consciousness of the abused or oppressed subject. This duality emerges further into a dialectic of trauma in the conflict between naming experience and reality—speaking out and keeping silent. In both—the abused and the colonized (i.e., political)—there is an ambivalence in the relationship with the dominant and the subordinate group. This relationship is derivative of both "love and hate, admiration and contempt, attraction and repulsion" (Moane, 84).

To further understand the parallels between the dependent colonized subject and the dependent abused woman, one can retrospectively examine the situation of the colonized subject. In all situations of colonial domination, the subject was at first economically dependent on the colonizer. A similar ideology works in the lives of women in abusive situations: "Fear, the threat of further violence, the shame and stigma attached, and economic dependency are among the factors which prevent a woman from disclosing experiences of violence" (Moane, 40). Because of domination over an extensive time period, the mechanisms of control become more pervasive and subtle, "focusing on control of economic, political, and symbolic systems." In turn, "these mechanisms become institutionalized and shrouded by ideology such that it becomes difficult for both the dominants and the subordinates to recognize them" (Freire, 32).

One would think that the woman and the colonized part company when nationalistic discourse appears when the colonizer is supposedly ousted. Social theorist Partha Chatterjee discusses the main tenets of nationalistic discourse, which is a male ideology and in which the female is involved only because the male directs or assigns a role to her. In nationalistic discourse, the woman's issues are submerged, making this discourse fundamentally incompatible with feminism (Davis, 160). Chatterjee's elaborate discussion on colonialism and nationalism reveals how Indian nationalism against British colonization embodies the idea of the submersion of women's issues in the language of nationalism. At first, when Indian nationalism against British colonization began from the mid-nineteenth century to the early twentieth century, women were encouraged to join the nationalist movement. But then the language of the nationalist discourse changed, with the ideal woman becoming the guardian of nationalism in the home. According to Chatterjee in *Nationalism*, there was a virtual disappearance of women from the nationalist program when the ideology of nationalism distorted the definition of true "Indian-ness," which it was committed to defend as "a private spiritual realm located in the home and represented by women." M. Jacqui Alexander and Chandra T. Mohanty describe this negation of women from the nationalist scene in India by agreeing with Chatterjee's premise of the private and hidden sphere of women and by stating that women's bodies are disciplined "within specifically nationalist discourses, as guardians of culture and respectability" (xxiii).

During the nationalist movement in India against the British, women were regarded as the keepers of the spiritual and traditional identity of India. In fact, Chatterjee's article "Colonialism, Nationalism, and Colonialized Women" shows how several nineteenth-century Bengali writers, such as Michael M. Dutt (1824–1873) and Amritlal Bose (1853–1929), ridiculed Indian women who tried to imitate their Western counterparts. For example, "new items of clothing such as the blouse, petticoat and shoes, the reading of novels, and the use of Western cosmetics and jewelry" were seen as vulgar (625). Thus, to maintain the traditions of Indian culture within the home was the Indian woman's duty, and any deviance from the norm was considered to be a violation of what society expected from the woman. So just as the colonizer delegated a space for the colonized, so the Indian nationalist, while fighting against the colonizer, delegated a place for the Indian woman. Similarly, parallels can be drawn between the discourse of the colonizer, the discourse of the nationalist, and the discourse of the abuser in a violent domestic situation. The abused immigrant woman is disciplined into becoming the *guardian of culture* in a situation where she is dependent on the oppressor. The South Asian woman who remains in a violent situation is dependent because of a complex and contradictory history of immigration of residents of third world countries to the United States.

Anannya Bhattacharjee drives this point home by stating how domestic violence in the heterosexual and patriarchal home can involve physical, emotional, and sexual abuse.

> A woman can be denied food, money, adequate clothing, shelter. . . . She can be forced to live in isolation by her abuser, who can lock her up or instruct her not to answer the phone, thus denying her access to other community members. Isolation is one of the most severe forms of abuse in the home by a man against a woman, contributing to a battered woman's perception that her condition is uncommon and shameful. It is one of the primary ways in which a man makes sure that the woman's voice is never heard and that she remains *dependent* on him in every way. (Bhattacharjee in Leonard, 314; emphasis added)

One major reason for this dependence is immigration laws that require spouse-based sponsorship in the United States. South Asian immigrant women usually fall under the category of people who are sponsored by their husbands. It is common in South Asian immigrant communities for the men to first seek employment in the United States before they bring their wives into the country: "It is common for single men first to come to the U.S. on employment-based visas and later marry a woman from South Asia, or for married men to come here on employment-based visas accompanied by their wives." In both cases, the woman is dependent on the man's sponsorship in order to obtain her legal immigration status through spouse-based visas (Leonard, 314). The woman remains dependent on her husband for two years because she has conditional residency status first. After two years, her spouse has to sponsor her to give her permanent residency. The spouse, if he is an abuser, can sometimes withhold sponsoring his wife, making the abused woman even more dependent on her oppressor, because without permanent residency, she becomes an "undocumented" person (Leonard, 314–15). Even though to alleviate such situations Congress passed the Violence against Woman Act to help immigrant women, senators from various states have expressed their concern of a "misuse" of the rights that these South Asian immigrant women would have. The Act would help the woman to self-petition for permanent residency. Unfortunately, concern expressed by the dominant culture has stopped abused women from exercising their rights. At any rate, most cases of spousal abuse are undocumented because of the dependency, either economic or cultural, of the abused spouse on her abuser. As I mentioned above, many of the women who are abused in immigrant South Asian communities will not self-petition because of language, cultural, economic, and societal constraints. Thus, the question of "misuse" does not even come into play.

Similar to the Hegelian master/slave dependency discourse and the postcolonial nationalistic discourse, the discourse of the abuser/abused has reached a stage of dependency because immigration laws have "privatized" the role of the abused woman by not allowing her to become a "legal resident of the national community" (Leonard, 317). The colonizer has bound the colonized. The nationalist subjected the woman to a private place, thus barring her from the "national community." The abuser and his culture, as seen earlier in the essay, have barred the woman from seeking help. In Althusserian terms, the external, dominant power has thus successfully been able to impose its power on a subject, to subordinate the subject, and to have her identify with her subordination (Althusser in Butler, *Psychic Life,* 7). Althusser further notes that the subordination of the subject is through language, and the subject "accepts subordination through speech as the inculcation of the conscience has already taken place" (Althusser in Butler, 8). The abused woman, privatized in her enclosed area of abuse, remains in the situation because she has accepted the subordination imposed on her through her abuser and her culture.

On a recent visit to India, I was able to interview the founder and organizer of Swayam, an organization that helps women who are subjected to violence in their lives, whether spousal or parental. I include the work that Swayam performs in Calcutta (one of the foremost cities of India) to show that some of the abuse faced by Indian/South Asian women begins in their home countries. In my interview with Anuradha Kapoor, the founder and organizer of Swayam, I sought parallels with the Indian women who face abuse in their own country and the Indian women who face abuse outside their country to prove that much of the abuse faced by South Asian immigrant women emerges from extended cultural baggage. I posed four main questions to Kapoor: (1) Are the women who come to Swayam for help from all the social stratas of Indian society? (2) What are the three most common reasons for the women not leaving the abusive situation? (3) Do you think Swayam is able to address abusive situations effectively, and if so, what is its rate of success? If not, what needs to be addressed? (4) What makes the abused woman come to Swayam eventually? What is it in the abusive situation that triggers the woman to finally seek help? I felt these four questions were generic enough to be used in all situations of abuse, whether they were in the United States or in a South Asian country. The answers that I received helped me understand and assess the reasons for some of the major problems that South Asian women face in abusive situations outside their home countries.

To begin the dialogue, I first must give a definition of Swayam and its commitment to abused women. According to a pamphlet entitled *Swayam,* the meaning of the word "Swayam" is "oneself," and the organization was created to "provide holistic support to women facing violence in their lives. . . . To question and try to change established norms and values that have deemed violence against women acceptable." Swayam's work is thus to help the abused woman change the *established norms and values* within Indian and other South Asian societies that *deem violence acceptable*—a deep-seated cultural problem that South Asian women face despite their departure from their home country.

Further, the questions I asked Kapoor helped me understand how a specific culture can permeate and destroy lives on a regular basis. So when one is looking at a culture-based problem, the answer to the first question I asked, "Are the women who come to Swayam for help from all the social stratas of Indian society?", is yes: abuse is a widespread phenomenon that affects women from all socioeconomic circles in Indian society. Kapoor's answer to the second question—What are the three most common reasons for the women not leaving the abusive situation?—was as follows: The women had no place to go, and the social stigma in Indian society of a woman leaving her husband and family was too great for the woman to successfully destroy the cycle of abuse. The importance of societal acceptance or rejection is crucial in understanding the insurmountable barriers that are placed in the lives of women who are abused in such societies.

Even though we are living in a world that has advanced technologically in the past hundred years, human society still has a long, arduous journey to face, especially in its treatment of women. In particular, South Asian societies still place much importance on marriage, family, and the specific roles of men and women. One of the main reasons for rampant violence against women in such societies is that it is considered *acceptable*. Of course, there are several reasons for such acceptance, some of which Kapoor stated: In such societies, men are considered superior to women because they are the breadwinners and the decision makers in most, if not all, situations in the home and family. Thus, the woman is considered to be the man's property. Once she is his property, he is the one who is "expected to be worldly-wise and a woman's place is supposed to be her home" (*Swayam—Annual Report*). So if the woman acts in a fashion that the man thinks is deviant, he has the right to abuse her, and if she tries to get help or leave the situation, she is unlikely to receive family or societal support. Also, in most South Asian countries, the woman is economically dependent on her husband; even if she belongs to a wealthy family, she is still dependent on her husband for her wealth. Because of the specific hierarchical positions that men and women occupy in society, women do not leave the privatized space set up for them in the home. Violence in such situations thus "serves the function of maintaining the status quo in the social order and is used to control and subjugate women in every possible way. It is the result of an unequal societal structure where men dominate and women are conditioned to accept a secondary position" (*Swayam—Annual Report*).

The answer to the third question (Do you think Swayam is able to address abusive situations effectively, and if so, what is its rate of success? If not, what needs to be addressed?) is a difficult one to put down on paper. This question is difficult because what the organization may consider to be success, the abused woman—or even a person reading about violence among woman—may not see as success. According to Kapoor, the first step is making a woman aware that she is living in a situation where she is abused; the rate of success varies from woman to woman. The final question (What makes the abused woman come to Swayam eventually? What is it in the abusive situation that triggers the woman to finally seek help?), which addresses the time frame between the moment the woman finds herself in an abusive situation and the moment when she seeks help from Swayam, was answered as follows: According to Kapoor, the women who were experiencing violence in their lives for the most part came for help only after they had no options and left the violent situation. This is a frightening notion because one sees how drastic the abuse has to get in order for the woman to leave. On the other hand, according to Kapoor during my interview with her, each woman has her own perception of the cycle of abuse.

In many abusive scenarios, the women take the blame for the abuse inflicted on them. In an abusive situation, every day is not a bad day, and there is a strong emotional tie between the abused and the abuser. Although this particular theory is worldwide and transcends all societies, it gains particular importance, in my opinion, in the lives of South Asian women because of the cultural importance of the woman's place in the home and the stigma placed on her if she leaves her husband because of violence in their relationship.

In conclusion, the abuse and violence faced by South Asian immigrant women is a problem that is ongoing despite the strides made by social organizations within and outside the United States. As discussed in this chapter, one crucial question that has to be discussed continuously is how these women can transcend the barriers placed in their path by their traditional cultures. It is a culture that tells them that because of religious, social, and economic reasons, they cannot leave the abusive situation. One light at the end of the tunnel of the cycle of abuse is that more and more abused South Asian women have been made aware of their predicament. I can only hope that with the help of social organizations, the percentages of women leaving violent situations will increase.

NOTES

1. I use the terms "South Asian" and "Indian" interchangeably because the social, cultural, religious, and economic aspects of all the countries neighboring

the Indian subcontinent are fairly similar. For example, Hinduism, Islam, and Christianity are religions that are present in all the South Asian countries of India, Bangladesh, Pakistan, Nepal, and Sri Lanka.

2. There is a strong connection between all South Asians. India is a multiethnic, multireligious country, and even though the South Asians in the United States come from Bangladesh, Nepal, and Pakistan, the Hindu/Indian culture is part of the culture of these other South Asian communities.

REFERENCES

Alexander, M. Jacqui, and Chandra T. Mohanty. *Feminist Genealogies, Colonial Legacies, Democratic Futures.* New York: Routledge, 1997.

Butler, Judith. *The Psychic Life of Power: Theories in Subjection.* Stanford, Calif.: Stanford University Press, 1997.

Chatterjee, Partha. "Colonialism, Nationalism, and Colonialized Women: The Contest in India." *American Ethnologist* (summer 1989): 622–33.

———. *Nationalism and Sexuality.* New York: Routledge, 1992.

Dasgupta, S. D., and S. Warrier. "In the Footsteps of Arundhati: Asian Indian Women's Experience of Domestic Violence in the United States." *Violence against Women* 2 (1996): 238–59.

Davis, Charlotte Aull. "Nationalism, Discourse and Practice." In *Practicing Feminism: Identity, Difference and Power,* edited by Nickie Charles and Felicia Hughes-Freeland, 156–77. London: Routledge, 1996.

Fanon, Frantz. *The Wretched of the Earth.* Translated and edited by Constance Farrington. New York: Grove Press, 1963.

Freire, Paulo. *Pedagogy of the Oppressed.* New York: Continuum Press, 1996.

Hasnat, S. "Lifting the Veil of Secrecy: Domestic Violence against South Asian Women in the United States." In *A Patchwork Shawl: Chronicles of South Asian Women in America,* edited by Shamita Das Dasgupta, 145–59. New Brunswick, N.J.: Rutgers University Press, 1998.

hooks, bell. *Killing Rage: Ending Racism.* New York: Holt, 1995.

Kapoor, Anuradha. Interview with author, June 18, 2000, Calcutta, India.

Lauer, Quentin. *A Reading of Hegel's "Phenomenology of Spirit."* New York: Fordham University Press, 1982.

Laws of Manu. Translated and edited by G. Buhler. New York: Dover, 1969.

Leonard, Isaksen Karen. *The South Asian Americans.* Westport, Conn.: Greenwood Press, 1997.

Mannoni, D. *Prospero and Caliban: The Psychology of Colonization.* New York: Praeger, 1964.

Mazumdar, Rinita. "Marital Rape." In *A Patchwork Shawl: Chronicles of South Asian Women in America,* edited by Shamita Das Dasgupta, 130–40. New Brunswick, N.J.: Rutgers University Press, 1998.

Moane, Geraldine. *Gender and Colonialism: A Psychological Analysis of Oppression and Liberation.* London: Macmillan, 1999.

Rousseau, Jean-Jacques. *On the Social Contract and Discourses.* Edited and translated by Donald A. Cress. Reprint, Indianapolis, Ind.: Hackett, 1983.

Swayam—Annual Reports, 1995–1997. Calcutta, India: Swayam Press, 2000. Avail-

374 / Sunita Peacock

able from Swayam, Il Balu Hakkak Lane, Calcutta, 70077, India (phone: 280 3429).

Swayam: Women against Violence (pamphlet). Calcutta, India: Swayam Press, 2000. Available from Swayam, Il Balu Hakkak Lane, Calcutta, 70077, India (phone: 280 3429).

Chapter 20

Arturo Ripstein's *El lugar sin límites* and the Hell of Heteronormativity

DAVID WILLIAM FOSTER

> No es la conducta erótica con otro varón lo que hace al individuo
> "homosexual" según este discurso [vigente en México], sino el
> gusto de hacerlo, el hecho de que se busque y encuentre placer.
> —Guillermo Núñez Noriega, *Sexo entre varones*

It is a generally accepted principle in queer studies that no adequate definition of heterosexuality would be possible without the category of the
"homosexual" (Dollimore; Katz). In conformance with basic principles of
semiotics, no sign can exist without defining what it is not, and what it is
not is as important as what it is. In the distinctive feature analysis that is
crucial to semiotics, the interplay of negative and positive valences is what
comprises the unique unit that is any specific sign. In semiotics, no one
sign is dominant, and all are held together in a structure by the interrelationship of their contrasting valences. Some valences, or combinations of
some valences, may be statistically more frequent than others, and some
valences can only combine with each other in specific ways; furthermore,
some valences may be statistically more pertinent than others.

In a social semiotic, however, valences acquire ideological charges, and
thus some valences may in fact be more dominant than others. Ideology, it
would seem, can work to problematize the combinations of valences, and
it is not always clear that valences that emerge as hegemonic and those that
are kept in a position of subalternity conform necessarily to a metatheory
of semiotic possibilities. Nor is it always clear that, metatheoretically, there
is a stable coherence regarding the conformation of the signs of a social
semiotic (see Greimas for a model of sociosemiotic analysis).

This is particularly evident in the case of the social sign of "heterosexuality" and its associated sign of "homosexuality." Although the heteronormative patriarchy proposes a fully coherent and transparent sign of
heterosexuality and matches it with an implied fully coherent and transparent sign of homosexuality, it is far from evident that there is any reliable
stability as to what these two terms mean. I am not referring to the way in

which meaning for these terms might vary widely with respect to historical context—that is, that they are not universal signifiers, even though they are often proposed, by both heteronormativists and gay activists, to be precisely that. Rather, within the coordinates of any one specifically identifiable society, there may be considerable confusion as to what these terms can possibly signify. It is both a question of their mutual interdependence and the inherent instability of distributed meaning between one and another, such that, unlike elementary signs such as "male" and "female" (which, to be sure, are not without their own problems of analysis), heterosexual and homosexual are engaged in a constant process of redistributed valences that renders them highly suspect as signs of meaning, leaving them more as opaque symbols—rallying cries, if you will—rather than units of meaning that can be analyzed.

Queer studies is fundamentally dedicated to charting the implications of what I have just sketched out, and two of the axioms that drive such a field of studies are as follows: first, homosexuality cannot be viewed as deviance from or a degradation of heterosexuality; the two terms (in reality, two clusters of terms) only make sense when viewed as converses of each other; and second, the principles on which a division of meaning between the two is constructed (i.e., the way in which their respective differentiated valences are proposed) reveal a considerable degree of squishiness, such that they can only be useful in a social discourse untroubled by bad faith and oblivious to incoherences of meaning. That internal contradictions or incoherence may indeed be a circumstance affecting all of the macrosignifiers of social meaning, such as race, class, gender, or ethnicity, is what has led queer studies to be interested in larger issues concerning the construction of social meaning rather than just that of sexual preference (Warner, in his introduction to *Fear of a Queer Planet,* explores the queer studies interest in sociosemiotic incoherence of heteronormativity). It is for this reason that Richard Dyer, in a work on "whiteness" and why it is an unmarked category of Western cultural production, can relate the marked/unmarked binary to an array of such categories in our society that queer studies proposes to interrogate:

> The man/woman binarism is a sexist production. Each consists of two terms, the first of which is unmarked and unproblematized it designates "the category to which everyone is assumed to belong" (unless someone is specifically marked as different). . . . The marked (or queer) term ultimately functions not as a means of denominating a real or determinate class of persons but as a means of delimiting and defining by negative and opposition the unmarked term. . . . Heterosexuality . . . *depends* on homosexuality to lend it substance, and to enable it to acquire by default its status *as* a default, as a *lack of difference* or an *absence of abnormality.* (44)

The problem with Dyer's formulation, as accurate as it may be both in reference to the interrogation of the homologies of binarisms that informs queer studies and to the way in which heteronormative patriarchal thought cannot do without those binarisms, is that it fails to take the next step of questioning the coherence of the logic of such thought. The category of the dreaded Other that patriarchal thought finds so necessary to hold firmly to its own carefully delimited sphere of sociosemiotic meaning—a dreaded Other that postcolonial thought reinscribes as, first, the legitimated Other, then as a fully independent category of sociosemiotic meaning—is virtually a grab bag of any and every sign that exceeds such a delimited sphere. This is particularly obvious in the case of a concept such as "homosexual," because with each use of the term, it is necessary to attempt to clarify what is meant by it; the only stable meaning inherent to it is something like "not convincing as a transparent straight"; what always remains squishy is how the individual is not convincing.

As such, it cannot simply be an easily perceivable binary of "this" and, if not "this," then "that": that is, it is more than the valence markings of plus or minus that underpin semiotic analysis on its most basic of levels, as in the case of structural or generative phonology. Rather, the categories that lie on either side of the binary divide must constantly be strategically constructed, because it is not always self-evident what is "white," what is "male," what is "straight" (at least not in the way in which it is self-evident what is voiced or unvoiced in phonology—and then, even so, this is not a binary that is all that irreducibly self-evident). And it is in this strategic construction wherein the limits between what lies on each side of the binary divide, between what lies inside or outside of the category that is privileged as the norm or the normal, where incoherences, ambiguities, internal contradictions, and, quite simply, absurdities of meaning, can be perceived to occur. Daily life in a society may be a parallel activity whereby such strategic constructions are constantly taking place, while at the same time the members of that society are engaging in a tacit agreement to ignore the lapses that occur in such constructions that might not resist too close an interrogation of the logical bases of those same constructions. Yet when the binary discourse breaks down and when deadly violence is the consequence of that breakdown, it becomes necessary to interrogate those constructions without turning a blind eye to their fundamental incoherences.

Arturo Ripstein's 1978 film, *El lugar sin límites* (released in English as *Place without Limits*), based on a novel of the same title by José Donoso, is just such a site of interrogation.[1] Ripstein tells the story of La Manuela, a transvestite prostitute killed by one of her preferred customers for having gone too far in insinuating a questioning of his masculinity as regards his preference for men cross-dressed as women over supposedly real women. Ripstein pursues the incoherence of the construction of heterosexuality in terms of three separate narrative strands (concerning the codes of masculinity in the film, see Mora). The first narrative concerns the circumstances of La Manuela's death at the hands of Pancho, and why, after seeming to find in La Manuela a subtle agent of sexual satisfaction, Pancho now feels compelled to kill her. The second narrative concerns the circumstances of how La Manuela, together with her colleague La Japonesa, have come to be the owners of the brothel where the action of the film takes place and how they come to be the parents of La Japonesita, now a woman in her 20s. The third narrative involves the role of Don Alejo, the local bigwig, and the circumstances that surround his being both La Manuela's and La Japonesa's sponsor and, in an extended sense, La Japonesita's godfather, and yet how he is able to be a nonparticipant bystander in La Manuela's death, despite the inevitability of the chain of events that get set into motion and that he might have been able to halt (although Urbistondo does not speak of the patriarchy in feminist/queer terms, his seeing of Alejo as a metaphor of god captures the essence of his social role).

La Manuela, as she is played by Roberto Cobo (whose first major role was as El Jaibo in Luis Buñuel's 1950 *Los olvidados* and whose career has since involved transvestism in various ways), is pretty much a stereotype of a brothel worker (Cobo makes a cameo appearance as a mature Tijuana madame in Alejandro Springall's 1997 *Santitos*). Notably unattractive physically and now around 50 (but quickly approaching 60), La Manuela seeks to portray a fiery flamenco dancer, a red mantilla her distinctive trademark. Part of the entertainment at the brothel she and La Japonesa have long inhabited, and which their daughter, La Japonesita, administers, is the frequent abuse of Manuela, perhaps as much out of resentment for the circumstances of her birth (more on which below) as for any homophobia she may experience.

The space of the brothel, after all, is generally conceived of as a privileged arena of patriarchal heterosexuality, inasmuch as it is organized around women whose role is to provide sexual services to men. If it could be argued, as campaigns of public decency often do, that brothels are a threat to the patriarchal family, the response is that, quite the contrary, they afford a beneficial sexual outlet to men. These men may be those who occupy positions of power whose supposedly concomitant sex prowess makes it convenient for them to seek with prostitutes a frequency of sexual contact and a range of sexual practices so that their respectable wives are left to the tranquil administration of the home and the family. Moreover, the brothel provides a public space in which, within the closed circle of men as worldly figures of patriarchal agency, the customers confirm in the presence of each other, if not directly, then at least metonymically, their heteronormative sexual identity and performativity (metonymically in the sense that consorting with prostitutes and engaging in the various rites of seduction are metonyms of the subsequent, if customarily invisible, sexual compliance with a proper masculinity).

Brothels also play an important social role for men who are socially inferior to those who are the preferred customers and who are even likely to be the owners of said establishments. This is so because, although it is expected that these other men will also be fulfilling their patriarchal responsibilities with women of their own class, it is assumed that they, too, as proper men, are possessed of a sexuality in excess of what they can legitimately satisfy with their legal wives: whores pick up where the sexual responsibilities of decent women leave off. Because it is inconvenient for society for these men—whose sexuality may, because of their class origins, be lawless in a way not assumed for highly placed men—to be engaged in random sexuality with women in general, and even perhaps with the daughters of the powerful (who would likely consider it rape punishable by death), prostitutes provide the necessary escape valve. In large cities, there is a social categorization of brothels, but in Latin American small towns, brothels are often frequented by men of all social classes, which may not thus make them the most democratic institution in town, but which may rather provide yet one more realm for the display of class privilege: there can be little doubt as to who gets the pick of the women, who can demand what of the women (and pay for it), and who can determine the parameters of sociability within the highly charged social microcosm of the brothel (concerning brothel life in México, one might begin with González Rodríguez).

It would appear from the foregoing that the space of the brothel is a carefully and strictly regulated realm for the enforcement of heteronormativity, and along with it, other controlling structures of the patriarchy, such as social hierarchy between men and the rigid disjunction between men as sexually served by women construed as sexual servers; concomitantly, women who administer brothels are enforcers of these circumstances. Yet homoeroticism appears in the space of the brothel in three ways. First, it appears as the hidden ingredient in all forms of homosociality (this is a point Sedgwick makes repeatedly in her groundbreaking work). While homosociality enforces heteronormativity via the pacts that are forged and maintained between men for purposes of masculine social control (with the clear understanding that those pacts could not adequately function, at least not in what we understand to be the ground zero of Western patriarchy, if they were perturbed by the existence of sexual desire among men), the line between homosociality and homoeroticism is potentially unstable, such that there are ample opportunities to suspect that sexual desire may indeed circulate among men bound by a pact of homosociality, which explains those nagging doubts about locker-room antics, fraternity hazing, bar room buddyism, and the beau geste of brothers in arms (or in sports; see Pronger; with regard to homoeroticism and Latin American soccer, see Sebreli).

This sort of latent homoeroticism that is the hidden face of homosociality—hidden because it can never be acknowledged and therefore never acted upon—is not unreasonably accompanied by the presence in the brothel of men who have to one degree or another recognized consciously their own same-sex desires, such that what they are able to witness in the brothel, if not obtain there, is a display of male sexuality that may satisfy in one way or another their own desire. Whether these men also engage the services of prostitutes as functioning bisexuals or self-enforcing heterosexuals, or whether the time they spend with the women is only for the purposes of "talking," they can usually feel confident that they will not be compromised because many a prostitute is relieved to take a man's money and not have to do much for it other than talk with him. In both of these senses, homoeroticism is present as the never-absent dimension of all sexuality, both to the extent that absolute heterosexuality is probably not much of a human fact, which is why heterosexism makes so much of its privilege, and the way in which homoeroticism, no matter how denounced, can never adequately be banished from even the most strictly enforced social realm: even if you round all of "them" up and shoot them, you still have no way of knowing if you have really ever gotten all of them.

The second instance of homoeroticism in the brothel concerns the relationships between brothel personnel, which occur along a number of axes of power and involve madams, prostitutes, and female staff. These are all lesbian relationships in one configuration or another: male staff may be involved in heterosexual relations, or wish to be involved in heterosexual relations, but there is less cultural production and commentary to this effect (one can think of the unrequited love toward the prostitute Santa harbored by the blind piano player of the house where she works in Federico Gambao's 1903 novel *Santa*). Because lesbianism is defined in ways that are radically different from those of a female-marked version of gay male sexuality, it may not always be readily apparent to the male scrutiny of relationships between women, a scrutiny that is likely to insist on genital sex as the confirming sign of same-sex sexuality. Yet the way in which the brothel, despite inevitable feuds, rivalries, and jealousies between its occupants, is a female homosocial space both evinces the same sort of segueing between heterosexuality and homoeroticism characteristic of male homosociality and promotes lesbian relationships when viewed from the perspective of Adrienne Rich's lesbian continuum and the proposition that, far more than being defined by genital sexuality, lesbianism is primarily present whenever women define their lived experience in terms of other women.

The way in which the brothel figures in many texts, albeit it in enormously deficient ways, as a lesbian commune, and the way in which, despite forces brought to bear to divide them (i.e., the way in which feuds, rivalries, and jealousies may be promoted as forms of controlling the women), women sense the need to band together against their exploiter (and always remembering that madams are agents of brothel owners and the system of exploitation in general) promote the sort of sisterhood that can be read as a form of lesbianism.[2]

Finally, the third way in which homoeroticism is present in the brothel concerns the extent to which a brothel may actually cater to self-sex preferences by having one or more male prostitutes available or by tolerating sexual contact between the male clients and male employees, probably typically young boys who serve, literally, as factotums.

All of these elements may not be present in the universe of Ripstein's film, but they are part of the brothel culture the film evokes because the film takes place entirely within the confines of La Japonesa's and La Manuela's house. But the real issue, with regard to *El lugar sin límites*, is how the realm of the brothel defies the heteronormative principles on which the foregoing discussion continues to be based, assuming as it does that there is a difference between what is systematically maintained between men and women, between the straight and the queer.[3] This is, however, not true in the universe of the film because of the way in which La Manuela is a female impostor. La Manuela, to be sure, considers herself to be a woman and wishes for everyone to maintain her alignment with the feminine. However, there can be little doubt that it is common knowledge that La Manuela is a cross-dressed man and that the attention she garners is for her condition as a cross-dresser. Cross-dressing does not in and of itself constitute an example of same-sex preference, although it is unquestionably queer to the extent that it disrupts the controlling principles of heteronormativity that require no blending of sexual identity (Garber). However, when cross-dressing accompanies a sense of the individual's having been mistakenly gendered—that one is, in fact, a woman trapped in a man's body or vice versa, and that one's goal is to be reconstituted as belonging to the sex other than the one to which one has been assigned—then it is likely that although the gender binary is disrupted by the concept of incorrect sexual assignment and its manifestation in cross-dressing (complete surgical and pharmacological transgendering not being an option available to someone of La Manuela's world), this queering is going to involve same-sex preference—if not from the point of view of the person doing the cross-dressing (who clings to the conviction that the other sex is really involved), then from the point of view of the person desiring the cross-dressed body because what is being desired is a body that does not adhere to the severe categorizations of the heteronormative binary.

It is often claimed that the desire of a "real" man for a cross-dressed woman (that is, for a man cross-dressed as a woman) is inexplicable: if such a man wants a woman, there are plenty of "real" women available (for a sociological analysis of transvestite prostitution in México, see Prieur). Let us leave aside for the moment whether such "real" women are so readily available, especially in the social universe of Ripstein's film, as we bear in mind that houses of prostitution exist in large measure because women are not always so readily available and that, indeed, one version of the patriarchy is to ensure that women are never available for sex outside matrimony.

But to what degree are there men whose desire is for women who are in reality men cross-dressed as women? That is, their desire is precisely for a body that in some complex way suspends the heteronormative binary by constructing a calculus of desire that involves the fetish of both the male and the female, as opposed to the fetish of the categorical same sex (i.e., gay or lesbian) or the fetish of the categorical opposite sex (i.e., the straight). (My discussion here is inspired by Judith Butler's widely cited theorizing of the performance of sexual identity, *Gender Trouble*.) Such queer desire constitutes the center of the plot of Ripstein's film, both its existence and the impossibility of calling attention to its existence. That is, La Manuela sees in Pancho a suitable client; perhaps as a woman rather than as a prostitute, she may even entertain a measure of sexual desire for him. La Manuela engages in a game of seduction of Pancho, as she dances flamenco for him, wrapped in her trademark red mantilla: the suggestion of the appropriateness of the relationship between the two of them is that Pancho's truck is also fire-engine red, like La Manuela's mantilla. Throughout the sexually charged sequence of La Manuela's dance, Pancho cannot take his eyes off of La Manuela, which only encourages her in her stratagem of seduction.

However, the tension comes to a head when La Manuela makes a direct play for Pancho, and the latter's brother-in-law begins to tease Pancho about preferring the attentions of a transvestite fag. There is, so the narrative logic of the film would have us believe, no option available to Pancho but to kill La Manuela, and her death both affirms his masculinity (in the sense that it is an appropriate revenge for La Manuela's apparent assumption that Pancho would find her to be a desirable sexual partner) and removes permanently from his world someone who might continue to display to his world the possibility that Pancho might find La Manuela to be a desirable sexual partner. It is important to note that the way in which Pancho displays transgressively that La Manuela is a desirable sexual partner is not in having sexual relations with La Manuela or in penetrating her, but in allowing himself to be kissed by her. This explicit marker of romantic love is what makes Pancho a target of ridicule.

These two reasons are adequate within the macho logic that drive Pancho in his retaliatory rage, although we don't know to what extent it is the consequence of homosexual panic at actually finding La Manuela sexually desirable and to what extent it is propelled by the need to confirm to his peers that he is a "real" man who needs to avail himself of the services of someone like La Manuela (Palaversich places Donoso's novel in the context of Latin American sexuality and heternormative violence and discusses homosexual panic in the novel, which Ripstein transfers intact to the film). But his murderous rage leads one to wonder if more is involved. What would the attraction be to an apparently straight man of another man cross-dressed as a woman? Or, more specifically, what fetishes provoke sexual desire for the former in the sexual theater being described here? How does a straight man make sexual use of another man cross-dressed as a woman?

Although these questions might seem to be answered rather straightforwardly on the basis of sexual practices customarily attributed to the passive role in standard erotic enactments, it is interesting to note that in some research done on transvestite prostitution, there emerges the claim that male clients frequently insist on playing the so-called passive role, while the transvestite prostitute is to play the so-called active role in such standard erotic enactments (concerning this dynamic, see Schifter). Thus, not only is someone like Pancho possibly identifiable as a "real" man who prefers the company of transvestites, but furthermore, he may be one of those clients who wishes the transvestite to play the active role of the "real" man. Ripstein's film does not insinuate such a dynamic, but it is important to understand the social semiotic his film is tapping into. In the arena of sexuality, everything is possible, yet only certain things may be acknowledged publicly: there are desires that one cannot acknowledge to exist and that one cannot acknowledge to practice or to wish to practice; moreover, one cannot tolerate having attributed to him (because we are here speaking of the need for the male to defend his masculinist privilege by not allowing any detraction from his masculinity out of fear of losing that privilege) desires and practices that belong to the realm of the unacknowledgeable.

There is certainly no hint in the film that Pancho might wish to play the passive partner in any sexual relations with La Manuela, just as it is not completely clear initially that he is even attracted to La Manuela at all, although he does become visibly excited when she dances flamenco for him, and despite the attributions of his companions. Yet the details of La Manuela's relationship with La Japonesa certainly demonstrate that La Japonesita is not incapable of penetrative sexual activity; more on this below. But what can be confirmed from what is explicitly displayed in the film is that although La Manuela may view herself to be a woman and therefore unable to be engaged in same-sex desire in her approach to Pancho, Pancho and his companion know very well that La Manuela is what is conventionally called a man and that, therefore, sex with her would transgress the heteronormative paradigm. There is an important aside to be made here: Gonzalo Vega, who plays the part of Pancho, has long been a heartthrob of women in México for his work in film and television; presumably, he has also been a heartthrob of gay males. Yet it is fairly common knowledge that Gonzalo Vega is gay, although this is not publicly acknowledged to be so. Because it is inevitable that spectators in the know will read his part in terms of Vega's personal life, this may always be so in cultural production, but it seems to be especially so in the case of film and television, which is why historically, actors and actresses have so jealously controlled information about their personal lives. As in the case of the now paradigmatic closeted Hollywood actor, Rock Hudson, the "real-life" gayness of the body playing Pancho cannot help but afford some pathetic rhetorical highlights to the homosexual panic and homophobic rage that lead him to murder La Manuela (see Ehrenstein regarding the relationship between the sexuality of movie stars and the roles they play).

Where all of this becomes incoherent is the way in which the La Manuela–Pancho formula both maintains heteronormativity and queers it. This is so because as has been stated, La Manuela would appear to sustain a conventional female–male binary in her seduction of Pancho. Yet Pancho's reaction, the reaction of his companion, and his eventual killing of La Manuela are all based on the understanding that La Manuela is a man posing as a woman and is therefore implicitly challenging the validity of the rigid binary divide. The fact that the film sees none of this as fantastic, that the audience is asked to see what happens as completely logical, if pathetically unfortunate, that Pancho kills someone for creating an insinuation that he is less than a "real" man, is only possible because of the incoherence at the heart of heteronormativity whereby the rigid gender binary and queer transgressions, along with fatal violence because of the latter and in order to maintain forms, would seem to be integral parts of the world as it is supposed to be.

The second crucial incoherence in *El lugar sin límites* is perhaps what could be called outrageous in Ripstein's film and the Donoso novel on which it is based (see Foster, 87–93): the way in which La Manuela and La Japonesa successfully meet the challenge made to them by Don Alejo, the town's primary power figure, to have sex with each other: they successfully engage in sex under his gaze, and he deeds the brothel to La Japonesa; later in time, it is the child of that single sex act, La Japonesita, who, at the time of the narrative, is engaged in administering the brothel. Don Alejo's cruel challenge could be read as a transitory decision to impose heteronormativity on the inhabitants of his brothel—that is, to straighten out La Manuela, as well as La Japonesa, who is untroubled by the former's self-attributed female identity. Although he is successful in getting La Manuela to perform "like a man," at least for this once, Don Alejo is unaware that he is only serving to further queer La Manuela, who performs the penetrative role, but as a woman. In fact, in order to encourage her, La Japonesa tells La Manuela, "Piensa que yo soy la macha y tú la hembrita" ("Just think I'm the man and you're the woman"). Moreover, in making the bet with Don Alejo in order to obtain the deed to the brothel, La Japonesa tells him, "No es el primer maricón que puede engendrar, sólo hay que meterle un dedo por allá para que funcione" ("He isn't the first fag to have a child. All you have to do is stick a finger up there and he'll perform fine"). That is, La Japonesa encourages La Manuela in the latter's penetrative role by suggesting that she fantasize that she is in fact being penetrated by La Japonesa.

Yet she also reinscribes La Manuela for Don Alejo into a masculine penetrative role, while at the same time suggesting that he (La Manuela) will be aroused enough to penetrate by virtue of having been penetrated by her, a woman, in the way in which, as common knowledge would have it, gay men are used sexually by other men. The fact that heterosexual sex may in fact involve the arousal of the man by the woman in this fashion is not part of that common knowledge because it would serve to suggest that all men, straight or queer, are aroused by anal penetration, which would in turn constitute a double defiance of the logic of the rigid gender binary: women don't penetrate and men are not penetrated. Thus, Don Alejo's challenge is both a reinscription of heteronormative logic (a man and a woman having procreative sex together, confirmed eloquently by the fact that La Japonesa and La Manuela do, in fact, have a child as the result of this event) and a further queering of it (La Japonesa and La Manuela can only have straight sex through a gender role reversal that involves an act customarily thought to be a paradigm of gay sexuality). The fact that La Japonesa is played by Lucha Villa comes into play here: Villa is a woman who, although not identified as gay in the way Gonzalo Vega is, is someone whose imposing body is also associated with unconventional sexual roles, to the extent that she often appears less to be a conventionally feminine woman and more a cross-dressing man.

The third element of incoherence in the film involves Don Alejo's non-reaction to the murder of La Manuela. It is not that Don Alejo should come to the defense of La Manuela as a human being—but, after all, La Manuela is an integral part of the town's economy. Don Alejo may have deeded ownership of the brothel to La Manuela and La Japonesa, but it is clear throughout the film that as the major power broker in town, he has a vested interest in its functioning. However, Don Alejo also has a vested interest in the power of the patriarchy, which means that he has little choice but to invest in the proper functioning of the system of compulsory sexuality, both in its public face (bourgeois decency) and its hidden one (the brothel as an essentially legitimate escape valve for that system).

To put it differently, Don Alejo, although he could well hold Pancho to an accounting for the loss of chattel, has little choice but to collaborate with the system of heteronormativity because a large measure of his real power derives from the symbolic power of the established sexual system, which is why brothels are so integral a part of the power structure and so often a point of congregation of the powerful, as can be seen over and over again in Latin American cultural production (e.g., María Luisa Bemberg's superb and final film, with Marcelo Mastroiani, *De eso no se habla,* 1993).[4] In this sense, then, Don Alejo is trapped between conflicting interests or between conflicting compelling needs, and his response is a look of bewilderment as he contemplates La Manuela's twisted body (Pancho kills her by running her down with his truck and then punching and kicking her to death, the red of his truck merging with the red of La Manuela's mantilla and her blood). Interestingly enough, Ripstein follows through on his use of principal actors, because the public personas of Roberto Cobo and Gonzalo Vega as gay men underscore the horror of being obliged to collaborate with murder as an acceptable way of enforcing the patriarchy—not just in punishing deviance, but in confirming a particular code of sexuality that at the same time demands deviancy in order to effect that confirmation. If violence without recourse is the lot of La Manuela, whose alleged deviancy and the murder it brings with it constitute a historical necessity, then she cannot escape witnessing violence without recourse. By extension, it is the spectator's lot to reduplicate Don Alejo's gaze. It is another matter whether spectators will accept the legitimacy of Pancho's revenge or understand how hellish the system of heternormative sexuality is that is being defended—but of which Ripstein's film offers such an eloquently staged critique.

NOTES

This essay is part of a monograph on queer issues in Latin American filmmaking, under contract with the University of Texas Press.

1. The Spanish phrase "*lugar sin límites*" is a metaphor for hell.

2. Arturo Ripstein is unquestionably one of México's top five current filmmakers. For an overview of this career, see "Retrospective."

3. Reference may be made to Jorge Ibargüengoitia's quasidocumentary novel *Las muertas* (1986), which turns on lesbian rivalries leading to murder in a small-town Mexican brothel of the sort evoked in Ripstein's film.

4. Pérez Turrent relates *El lugar sin límites* to brothel-based Mexican films but recognizes its significant difference from treatments of female prostitutes (*las ficheras*) (108).

REFERENCES

Butler, Judith. *Gender Trouble: Feminism and the Subversion of Identity*. New York: Routledge, 1990.

Dollimore, Jonathan. *Sexual Dissidence: Augustine to Wilde, Freud to Foucault*. Oxford: Clarendon Press, 1991.

Donoso, José. *El lugar sin límites*. México: J. Mortiz, 1966.

Dyer, Richard. *White*. London: Routledge, 1997.

Ehrenstein, David. *Open Secret: Gay Hollywood, 1928–1998*. New York: Morrow, 1998.

Foster, David William. *Gay and Lesbian Themes in Latin American Writing.* Austin: University of Texas Press, 1991.

Garber, Marjorie. *Vested Interests: Cross-Dressing and Cultural Anxiety.* New York: Routledge, 1992.

González Rodríguez, Sergio. *Los bajos fondos.* México, D.F.: Cal y Canto, 1990.

Greimas, Algirdas Julien. *The Social Sciences: A Semiotic View.* Foreword by Paolo Fabbri and Paul Perron. Translated by Paul Perron and Frank H. Collins. Minneapolis: University of Minnesota Press, 1990.

Katz, Jonathan Ned. *The Invention of Heterosexuality.* Foreword by Gore Vidal. Afterword by Lisa Duggan. New York: Dutton, 1995.

Mora, Sergio de la. "Fascinating Machismo: Toward an Unmasking of Heterosexual Masculinity in Arturo Ripstein's *El lugar sin límites.*" *Journal of Film and Video* 44, no. 3–4 (1992–1993): 83–104.

Núñez Noriega, Guillermo. *Sexo entre varones: Poder y resistencia en el campo sexual.* 2nd ed. México, D.F.: Coordinación de Humanidades, Programa Universitario de Estudios de Género, Instituto de Investigaciones Sociales, 1999.

Palaversich, Diana. "Caught in the Act: Social Stigma, Homosexual Panic and Violence in Latin American Writing." *Chasqui: Revista de literatura latinoamericana* 28, no. 2 (1999): 60–75.

Pérez Turrent, Tomás. "Crises and Renovations (1965–91)." In *Mexican Cinema,* edited by Paulo Antonio Paranaguá and translated by Ana M. López, 94–115. London: British Film Institute, 1995.

Prieur, Annick. *Mema's House, Mexico City: On Transvestites, Queers, and Machos.* Chicago: University of Chicago Press, 1997.

Pronger, Brian. *The Arena of Masculinity: Sports, Homosexuality, and the Meaning of Sex.* London: GMP, 1990.

"Retrospective: The Films of Arturo Ripstein and Jaime Humberto Hermosillo." In *The Mexican Cinema Project,* edited by Chon A. Noriega and Steven Ricci, 59–65. Los Angeles: UCLA Film and Television Archive, 1994.

Rich, Adrienne. "Compulsory Heterosexuality and Lesbian Existence." In *The Lesbian and Gay Studies Reader,* edited by Henry Abelove, Michèle Aina Barale, and David M. Halperin, 227–54. New York: Routledge, 1993.

Schifter, Jacobo. *Lila's House: Male Prostitution in Latin America.* New York: Harrington Park Press/Haworth Press, 1998.

Sebreli, Juan José. *Fútbol y masas.* Rev. ed. titled *La era del fútbol.* Buenos Aires: Editorial Sudamericana, 1998.

Sedgwick, Eve Kosofsky. *Between Men: English Literature and Male Homosocial Desire.* New York: Columbia University Press, 1985.

Urbistondo, Vicente. "La metáfora Alejo/Dios en *El lugar sin límites.*" *Texto crítico* 7, no. 22–23 (1981): 280–91.

Warner, Michael, ed. *Fear of a Queer Planet: Queer Politics and Social Theory.* Minneapolis: University of Minnesota Press, 1994.

Chapter 21

Medicalizing Human Rights and Domesticating Violence in Postdictatorship Market-States

LESSIE JO FRAZIER

Since the formal end of the cold war, transitions from authoritarian states to less authoritarian states have come to be framed by policy makers and analysts under the rubric of "reconciliation" understood as the healing of national bodies fractured by internal conflict and brutalized by state violence. My own intervention in the study of the reformation of nation-states begins with my fieldwork on the gendered politics of the therapeutic project by the Chilean postdictatorship government (1990s–present) to treat and then reintegrate survivors of state violence (Frazier, "Memory"; Frazier and Scarpaci, "Mental Health"). The mental health services of the Chilean postdictatorship state inadvertently feminized their patients in the context of larger efforts to contain the ramifications of state terror, and by the second civilian presidency, the entire mental health system was gendered through the privileging of the female and the child as nonpolitical victims, leaving intact the gendered politics of the military regime in which the military disciplined and domesticated the unruly national body through a process of depoliticization.

In this chapter, I argue that the gendered medicalization of human rights in the Chilean transition to democracy is part of a hegemonic project for constraining possibilities for political agency and furthermore reflects structures of political culture fostered under military rule. By not interrogating these structures instantiated during the period of state terror, postdictatorship societies cannot dismantle the legacies of authoritarian rule, including the ongoing subterranean power of military sectors and their backers. One of these legacies has been the widespread absorption of the militaries' rhetoric of antipolitics, expressed through the metaphor of the diseased national body such that being political is pathological. If being a political actor is bad, then what hope is there for building viable democracies where people can exercise citizenship, especially in societies in which the tortured and torturers share the same streets? Civilian governments' policies that pretend that this is not an issue—or at best hope to avoid it or diffuse the question by promoting "reconciliation"—underestimate the power of that prior moment to continue to shape political and social dynamics, including the perpetuation of violence.

STATE VIOLENCE AND THE NATIONAL BODY

South American military regimes of the 1970s and 1980s justified their brutal dictatorships with a rhetoric imbued with metaphors of the body; military metaphors of disease depicted bodies, contaminated by political ideology, attacking the integrity of the national body defended only by the blood of its soldiers:

> In our reflections, we must remember our dead, because the blood shed here has no price; it is because, of the memory of this loss that we will never accept anything which will ruin or pervert the military victory or make us forget the clear and tremendous cost. (Loveman and Davies, 203)

In this 1980 speech, Argentine General Leopoldo Galtieri summoned the specter of the soldier martyred for *his* nation, a largely mythological figure of sacrifice, given the minimal scale of the opposition by armed guerrilla movements. The general conveyed a specifically gendered sense of ownership and gaze onto the nation, a totalizing masculinist gaze. The mythical blood spilled "here" demarcated the space of the nation, displacing from the nation the bodies of the disappeared and tortured civilians (Frazier, "Subverted Memories"); such delimiting of who belongs and who doesn't, usually through gendered and racialized categories, has been central to the process of nation-making (Pratt). Though he seemingly speaks of soldiers' bodies, in effect, what the general promises never to forget is a reign of state terror under military rule in Argentina lasting from 1976 until 1983, and in Chile, from 1973 until 1990.

Military regimes operated under the rubric of National Security Doctrine, a cold war strategy to fight communist subversion and to assert order within the space of the nation that proscribed the kidnapping, detention, torture, exile, execution, and disappearance of thousands of citizens, often youth, union leaders, and most other organized sectors of society. Under this doctrine, anyone involved in politics became suspect, and political practice was cast as inherently dangerous—or as in the passage above, perverting—to the nation. Militaries claimed to defend the nation as its apolitical guardians who followed National Security Doctrine in a spatially organized process of identifying, locating, and eradicating those it defined as the national enemy; and thus, the doctrine became a blueprint to carve up national landscapes—the national body instantiated in territory—into administrative police-state units as they restructured national economies around neoliberal, free-market principles, inscribing in the memory of both the subjugated and the supportive populace a particular landscape of state terror glorifying militarism, the nation, and the authoritarian state (Frazier and Scarpaci, "State Terror"; Frazier, "Forging Democracy"). Paramilitary and military personnel were anointed the new vanguards of the homeland and were indoctrinated into the role of torturer. The act of torture instantiated a cult of masculinity, and security personnel who refused to torture were themselves interrogated about their (homo)sexuality and allegiance to the fatherland (Graziano; Feitlowitz); military regimes engaged and maintained a specific construction of the relationship between heterosexual masculinity and violence undergirding the primacy of patrimony wherein the promise of security of the house and security of the nation were mutually constituted.

Under National Security Doctrine, the military saw the nation-state as an organism vulnerable to contamination by subversive forces depicted as diseased bodies, as Argentine foreign minister Admiral Cesar Guzetti elaborated in August 1976:

> When the social body of the country has been contaminated by a disease that corrodes its entrails, it forms antibodies. These antibodies cannot be considered in the same way as microbes. As the government controls and destroys the guerrilla, the action of the antibody will disappear, as is already happening. It is only a natural reaction to a sick body. (LCIHR, 3–4)

The nation as body, the military as antibody, and the guerrilla as a diseased, monstrous body: these comprised the organizing metaphors of National Security Doctrine[1]; purging the subversive disease from the national body became the overriding task, worth the cost of civilian lives. Former vicar of the Argentine Army Monseñor Victorio Bonamin's method for healing the national body is revealing: "When blood spills there is redemption; God is redeeming, through the Argentine Army, the Argentine nation" (Gregory and Timerman, 70). Both the contaminated and the innocent blood of the nation would be let to cleanse the body of the nation. Through the flow of national blood, redemption would reach across the *patria* (fatherland), the national patrimony encompassing the feminized space of the motherland as culture, affect, and social reproduction, together with more masculine realms of political institutions, economic resources, and the frontiers to be defended from encroachment. Thus, the *patria* served as a place encompassing state and civil society, *la plaza mayor* (the town square) and *la casa* (the home) in which this nationalist redemption took place.

State terror transcended public/private dichotomies; yet at the same time it allowed the domestic to seem like a refuge from repression, and from political conflict more generally. To think about the domestication of state violence, Chile's mode of transition to democracy provides a particularly interesting case in that the inadvertent gendering of reparations projects reinforced the intertwined dynamic of domestic violence and state terror. Politicians leading the constrained transitions to civilian rule in the late 1980s and 1990s tread a narrow path between the human rights movements' outrage and desire to prosecute abuses and the militaries' ongoing ability to forcefully forestall and circumvent such attempts. Negotiating these conflicting interests to forge a space for civil society, civilian leaders tried to reinscribe boundaries of public and private by circumscribing past conflict under the rubric of so-called political violence. Like the yellow tape around a crime scene, civilian politicians defined the temporal and spatial limits of political violence and human rights in an effort to contain and bring to an end the era of state terror.

DOMESTIC BODIES IN TRANSITIONS
TO FREE-MARKET DEMOCRACY

The central problem in Chile over the last decade since the end of formal military rule has been the inability to address human rights violations of the past (in terms of reparations or prosecutions of perpetrators), especially the problem of *survivors* of torture, detention, and internal and external exile (except for the health program, state reparations policies overwhelmingly privileged the immediate families of people who had been killed, and the civilian government's official "Truth and Reconciliation" report only documented cases ending in death). This is why the shift in the state health reparations program away from human rights issues to intrafamilial violence is so disturbing. The premise was that after a certain amount of time, those affected most directly by state violence should "get over it" and reintegrate into society. This is the obvious problem with the policy shift, but there are deeper, more disturbing implications. Feminist movements have taught us that "the personal is political," but here we have an example of bringing in something defined as "domestic" as a way of depoliticizing issues defined as "political." After feminism, we have to explore the linkages between these forms of violence as they are *all* "political."

Chile's transition from military to civilian rule began in the early 1980s, when the worldwide recession undermined the legitimacy of the military regime's neoliberal economic policies of privatization, incentives for foreign investment in the export sector, and the reduction of government social programs. In the midst of the recession, numerous social movements began to stage large-scale public demonstrations against the military. Leading this movement were shantytown associations, collective soup kitchens, human rights groups, and other organizations in which a large proportion of militants and leaders were women; among these groups were feminist organizations, such as Mujeres Por La Vida (Women for Life), who explicitly articulated the need for democracy both "on the street and in the home" (Franco, 48–65; Matear, 84–100; Pratt, 21–33). The military had

attempted to formalize its rule with a new Constitution stipulating a plebiscite to choose between civilian or military rule by the end of the decade;
however, through this 1989 plebiscite and subsequent presidential election, approximately 60 percent of Chileans managed to vote the military
and its most vehement supporters out of power, and civilian rule resumed
in 1990.

In order to mark the transition from military to civilian rule, the new
civilian government established a commission to undertake a very limited
investigation of human rights abuses under military rule. Because the investigations were limited to cases resulting in death, the full extent of torture
was never fully documented. The Commission of Truth and Reconciliation
made a number of recommendations to the civilian government to facilitate its objective of historical closure, including recommendations for reparations to victims of state violence. Most of these reparations were directed
toward the immediate families of those who had died, although some housing and small business loan programs were extended to ex–political prisoners and those returning from exile. The most far-reaching and fiscally
significant reparations project was the establishment of a Mental Health
and Human Rights program that extended comprehensive health care,
with an emphasis on psychosocial services, to families of the executed and
disappeared, returned exiles, and ex–political prisoners.

The mental health reparations program grew out of two decades of
work by mental health care professionals in using psychosocial therapy for
human rights victims as a form of political activism. The Mental Health
and Human Rights Movement in Latin America crafted a type of political
psychology that refused to pathologize the troubles of those damaged by
human rights abuses (understood as a collectivity) and instead insisted that
it was the social, political, and economic structures that generated state
violence that required dismantling (Caro Hollander). The institutionalization of this movement by the new civilian government changed its political
emphasis, and in fact caused deep divisions between those professionals
who decided to work with the civilian government and those who questioned the government program's organizing presuppositions. Reviewing
the state's mental health program's published reports and interviewing
program officials, health care professionals, social workers, and patients
made it clear to me that although the program was designed in a spirit of
advocacy for those abused by the state, ultimately, it was intended as a
temporary measure to help reintegrate human rights victims into a re-
emerging civil society, and thus complemented the notion of a transition
to democracy as a defined, liminal spatiotemporal configuration between
the time of the military dictatorship and a period termed democracy. In
this liminal space, state psychiatrists, psychologists, and social workers
would delimit and resolve individual and familial memories of state violence. Political leaders argued that the delicacy of Chile's shift from mili-

tary to civilian rule limited their ability to bring military officials to justice because while the military had retired from complete control of the government (except for military-designated senators for life, pro-military judges packed in the courts, and government lower-level administrative and clerical staff), the military's institutional structure remained completely intact, with the former dictator as supreme commander.[2] The civilian state's pragmatist politics meant that one of its most significant efforts to address the legacies of the past worked through a health program directed at taming the memories of those most directly scarred by that history of state violence. Still, this program provided vital—although limited by scarce resources—health services to that sector of society in a context of the commodification of health care and the nearly total privatization of state health services (and thus unaffordability of health care) begun under the military and intensified by the civilian government (Paley).

In 1994, presidential elections and the peaceful transition from the first civilian presidency to a second prompted the state's declaration of a completed transition to democracy in Chile (though later retracted); consequent with this official policy that transition from military dictatorship to civilian democracy was complete, the Mental Health and Human Rights Program was incorporated into the Ministry of Health, as the Mental Health and Violence Program, whose main emphasis was domestic violence against children, women, and the elderly, was defined as apolitical. Relegating issues of political violence to the past, the civilian government also refused, at that point, to recognize ongoing human rights abuses in Chile, especially in the area of police violence against political protesters, common criminals, and especially drug-related offenders, as well as ongoing legacies of state terror. State policy shifted from a project of treating subordinate memory as pathology to the erasure of those memories as anachronistic. Moreover, the shift in the program's emphasis entailed the domestication of human rights and violence, thus relocating human rights from the realm of the political and public to seeing violence as a product of culturally and socially backward dysfunctional (i.e., anomalous) individuals in the domestic sphere, or of cultural and social backwardness.

The undercurrents in the initial mental health and human rights program had already resulted in an inadvertent gendering of program politics, a pattern more overtly exacerbated in the program's shift in emphasis to intrafamilial violence. The domestic violence program was oriented around the treatment and advocacy of so-called victims defined as nonmasculine: subject to abuse, nonadult (children and the elderly), and feminine, and thus worthy of state intervention. This feminization of the state's clientele extended the implicit gendering of the prior mental health and human rights program that had worked primarily through patterns of treatment. Because men generally were more reticent to engage in psychotherapy, there was an overrepresentation of women who actually used the full range of resources (although, in practice, little systematic therapy seems to have been conducted as a result of limited resources). The men tended to only go for regular medical care, and men were much more likely to protest the paternalistic structuring of health care delivery relations. Many men resented the underlying assumptions that the program's staff knew the answers and that the patients were the problem, as well as the refusal by some staff members to believe men's stories of torture and to refuse to see any connections between torture and current physical problems. The program staff, according to my interviews and to the projects' official report, also experienced a disproportionately high turnover of male professionals (Domínguez et al.); they seemed less willing to tolerate the stressful working conditions and the relative lack of infrastructural support from the central government. In thinking about the implications of this implicit gendering of the program for its shift to an emphasis on domestic violence, I base the following discussion of the program on a key text, the program's 1998 technical manual, because I am interested, for the purposes of this chapter, in the ways in which state actors have framed the problem of violence and human rights during the crucial first decade after military rule (Ministerio de Salud, 1998). How programs actually work in practice is another matter, as we saw in the case of its predecessor, the mental health and human rights program; for purposes of focusing on the politics of memory in periods of democratization, I am focusing on this articulation of state policy to understand the first decade of civilian rule when the civilian government formulated crucial strategies for a political transition from military rule.[3]

To the program officers' credit, the manual revealed that they were clearly aware of the need to think about women's rights as human rights and the state's responsibility to protect human rights (30), undoubtedly also related to trends in international funding for public health and social services projects as "women's rights as human rights"; this was an important theme for international organizations in the 1990s. For example, they discussed the problem of obligatory or coerced maternity (58–59), they openly confronted the abuse of power in the home, and furthermore, the program recognized women as agents of their own lives (70, 75) and used gender—which they defined as culture plus biology (19; a term against which right-wing senators had launched a political diatribe a few years earlier)—as a way of thinking about relations of power: "Violent conduct is understood as an effective form of 'control over the other'"(30). While the program represented an enormous step in state policies toward women and the family, I see two crucial limiting elements in this framework.

First, in the manual, there was almost no use of the term "men" to specify the predominant agents of intrafamilial violence, let alone "patriarchy" as an operative concept. As in the sentence quoted above, discussion of violent actions was generally phrased in the passive voice, refusing to specify the perpetrator. Similarly, the discussion of coerced maternity skirted the issue of patriarchal investment in women's bodies as instruments of reproduction. One of the program's concrete strategies for "promoting healthy family relations" was to provide information to the public about the benefits of a more "flexible distribution of the roles associated with the genders" (46), but such a strategy promises to have little impact if it never confronts men's investment in not flexibly redistributing gender roles (note the prevalence of neoliberal vocabulary). While the manual noted the "gradual democratization of the family" as a component of the current social structure, it did not espouse the democratization of family dynamics as an ultimate goal; rather, it was noted as a stress factor that results in violence (20). Although the program's explanation of its mission points to men's abuse of power as the problem, it never questioned their right to that power, implying that the alternative to abusing power was the benevolent exercise of that power. Without confronting men's stake in unequal gender definitions, it is understandable that almost all of the program's interventions were still directed toward the "victim," rather than challenging power directly. In this strategy, the program to treat the mental health problems resulting from "domestic" violence replicated the politics of its "political" violence predecessor.

On a more profound level, and my second major concern with the program's framework, the two phases of the program also similarly expressed a relatively depoliticized understanding of the politics of violence. The analysis of intrafamilial violence located this violence in the realm of "cultural beliefs" (30), echoing the state's recent project of "cultural modernization" and the early twentieth-century rhetoric of the "social question" (e.g., alcohol and other vices) as the source of social conflict (as opposed to class exploitation). When describing the factors contributing to stress in today's families, the program noted increasing "external pressures" and "growing instability" without specifying the political and economic changes that had created these conditions. Although correctly pointing to the stresses of poverty for children, women, and the elderly (39), the program neglected to mention that these conditions hold for a great percentage of Chilean families, and by leaving this observation at the level of general phenomena, the state naturalized poverty (46) and its concomitant layers of brutality. For example, in blaming cultural ignorance, the program made public education a core component of its strategy (42). What is left out of this call for education is the context of the collapse of Chile's education system with privatizations begun under the military and continued under civilian rule. Grounded in modernist compartmentalizations of human life, violence was displaced from the realm of political economy and relocated to the realms of society and culture, divisions overlapping the gendered distinction between public and private. In sum, domestic violence, in the state's conception, was thoroughly domestic.

Attempting to foreground the domestic, international activists have worked to ensure that universalistic discussions of human rights address the particular problems of subordinate groups such as women and children as political problems; however, this discourse is vulnerable to readings from the opposite direction—in other words, using subjects from the domestic sphere to depoliticize questions of violence and human rights. In spite of the limitations of the mental health and human rights program, it had constituted an important effort; the civilian government virtually abandoned a program that explicitly recognized human rights abuses under military rule and that, albeit in a patronizing manner from the point of view of many patients, created a certain official space for those most directly affected by military rule. In its place, the state positioned itself paternalistically as advocate and protector of sectors of society perceived as vulnerable and "voiceless."[4]

In the neoliberal restructuring of Chile around the logic of the market, debates about state policies toward the domestic/the family may have been more about the commodification of patrimony and the concomitant redefinition of the relationship between state patriarchy and the prerogatives of the local patriarch than about the interests of patriarchy's most subordinate sectors: women, children, and the elderly. To illustrate this process of redefinition, I conclude this section with an example of recent legislative action. In 1998, I attended a session of the Chilean Congress with a number of women's organizations because on that day, there was to appear on the legislative docket a bill to increase the penalties against women who had abortions, and women's groups wanted to form a presence in the chamber to protest the measure. The abortion bill actually never came up that day; however, ironically, the most important legislation tackled that day was a bill to remove the oldest piece of social legislation in Chile: the law distinguishing legitimate from illegitimate children.[5] The debate ranged from opinions offered by senators of the ruling coalition parties to senators from the promilitary parties; even Senator for Life Augusto Pinochet spoke, his feeble voice nearly drowned out by cries of indignation from the women observing from the gallery. The general insisted that without a law to regulate inheritance based on legitimacy, the family and thus the nation would be endangered. The only senator to bring the concerns of women and children to the table and to point to the problem of negligent patriarchs (Hurtig) was conservative Evelyn Mattai, daughter of a prominent military officer, who pointed to the rampant neglect of children and the need for more responsible fathers. What the rest of the Congress debated, in effect, across ostensibly political lines, was the relationship of social laws defining legitimacy to the problem of national patrimony understood as the regulation of the inheritance of private property.[6] When the former dictator defended the nineteenth-century law as a safeguard of national security, he further underlined the link in military logic between

National Security Doctrine and patriarchy—in other words, locating national patrimony in the domestic. Thus, those who favored abrogating the law in this congressional debate were deregulating inheritance and thus pushing neoliberal logics far beyond the point that the military had been willing to pursue them, to subsume the domestic as national patrimony within the space of the Market.

During the military dictatorship, feminist activists in Chile had argued that authoritarianism in the public sphere was linked to that of the private. For example, the group Mujeres Por La Vida took to the streets, demanding democracy in the street and in the home. Among these activists, there grew a recognition of the connection between military rule and the struggle over patrimony, a recognition drawing on the work of fellow Chilean feminist Julieta Kirkwood, who developed a theory of domestic authoritarianism in which she insightfully pointed to the ways in which the ideologies of the left, center, and right confined women to the sphere of the "domestic private" and reduced the "feminine problem" to "the dispute over the defense of the family (Chilean or proletarian) and left without mention all that this engendered and perpetuated: hierarchical interior nets, disciplining, rigid, and authoritarian" (121). Under the military, this feature of Chilean political culture was used to the military's advantage; Kirkwood argued that in order to impose its authoritarianism, the military not only called on the power of the armed forces, but also the brutal "underlying authoritarianism in civil society," resulting in the "total imposition of a patrimonialist State" (117, 119). For Kirkwood, then, authoritarianism and its violent methods could not be understood without a gendered theory of politics. Kirkwood saw the domestic and the public as mutually constituting realms and realized that fighting an authoritarian state requires the dismantling of authoritarian structures across those spaces. I argue that this work has not taken place in Chile's regime transition from military to civilian rule, and the dominant narrow definition of democracy has limited the range of possibilities for political subjectivity and the ability to recognize the political nature of violence in Chile today.

THE LEGACIES OF STATE VIOLENCE

> Reconciliation constitutes a difficult beginning of an era of maturity and responsibility realistically assumed by everyone. The scars represent not only a painful memory, but also the foundation of a strong democracy, of a united and free people, a people which learned that subversion and terrorism constitute the inexorable death of liberty.
>
> —Argentine military junta

The Argentine and Chilean states' shifts from military to civilian rule shared the rhetoric of reconciliation as "healing," a means adopted by civilian leaders for coping with the political challenges posed by collective memories of state violence. These cases have become templates for regime transitions in other parts of the world, such as Africa and Eastern Europe. Reconciliation as healing has been a trope adopted not only by civilian political leaders, but also by military leaders, as the quote above by the Argentine military junta demonstrates. Healing metaphors inadvertently perpetuated the military narrative of the nation as a body subject to intervention; from this perspective, reconciliation became the suturing together of the national body on which the rhetorical "scars" served as a reminder of the "liberating" necessity of the violence of military rule, a justification often invoked to defend the greater good of (particularly in the Chilean case) economic neoliberal restructuring. The militaries (as in the quote above), then, rightly implicated "everyone" in this project. The relevant transition, the restructuring of the Argentine and Chilean economies around a market ethic, already had happened well before redemocratization, and thus patrimony, as construed in the patriarchal intervention of the military, had already been safeguarded.

The South American militaries' rhetoric of their own agency as apolitical melded handily with discourses of "the end of history" in the post–cold war era more generally (Moulian, 22). We see the power of this valorization of the apolitical and demonization of political actors in recent public assaults on activists, most notably Rigoberta Menchu, for being "political" actors rather than appropriately "innocent" victims of human rights abuses. Unfortunately, human rights movements have often implicitly echoed this rhetoric in their defense of prisoners of conscience as privileged over those implicated in or advocating the use of force (classically defined as politics by other means). As a consequence, those actors defined as having been political, and especially those whose scarred bodies mark their prior involvement, operate within an increasingly constrained public space.

The Chilean case, in particular, has become a paradigmatic and precedent-setting one for the pursuit of justice in the aftermath of state terror. The efforts of a Spanish judge to extradite General Pinochet from England (where he had traveled for minor surgery) on charges of crimes against humanity opened up new possibilities in the international politics of justice. The British House of Lords ruled that, indeed, General Pinochet could be extradited to Spain for trial for the crime of torture, and the testimony of torture survivors was critical for this verdict. The Chilean (civilian) state sent government officials to argue against this decision in the name of national sovereignty. In the end, the general was not extradited on grounds of ill health and was returned to Chile with the agreement that the Chilean judicial system would pursue these human rights crimes. However, subsequent judicial investigations in Chile have not dealt with cases of torture, but rather with disappearances (the covert seizing of people whose existence is thereafter denied and whose bodies have never been recovered), legally interpreted as kidnapping, and with illegal executions. Simultaneous civil cases have sought reparations from the Chilean state for families of the executed and the disappeared. Although torture had constituted the central grounds for the pursuit of justice in Britain, by and large, cases of torture survivors have been silenced in the Chilean public discourse on justice by the civilian state, the military, and human rights lawyers.

Much of my fieldwork in Chile during the first decade after military rule focused on ex–political prisoners as they contended with the shifting of the democratizing state's reparation health program from so-called political violence to so-called domestic violence. In March 2001, I accompanied an ex–political prisoner, Miguel Rojas, to the public hospital emergency room three days in a row, where he claimed his right to health care as a reparations program beneficiary. As a nurse attempted to draw blood, making two unsuccessful punctures in his arm, Miguel explained that she would have more luck getting the needle in if she switched to his other side as that arm had suffered multiple fractures as a result of torture sessions. As she jabbed the needle under his skin, she said, "Well, you must have been political [hence interrogated for a reason]. What party were you in?" Today, to claim agency as a political actor is to be labeled pathologically suspect, a scarred body subject to emasculating penetration by the state. Human rights discourses that insist on redeeming political activists—cast by the military as diseased bodies—as passive victims perpetuate the same rhetoric operationalized by military regimes.

Yet the ramifications of politics of the postdictatorship civilian government extend further than this. Under the transition to a neoliberal market-oriented economy, the state's role became that of the rational, dispassionate technocrat (as in the figure of the doctor), whose job it has been to manage the privatization of much of the two key components of the national body, the state sector and civil society (cf. Somers), and to ensure that what is left of both sectors functions efficiently and apolitically in the interests of the market. This is the role of the market-state. In the case I have presented here, the state attempted to domesticate former political activists through a medical program that privileged "feminine" and "child" patients (the families of the disappeared) and then shifted altogether to a focus on so-called domestic or intrafamilial violence where, again, the privileged patients were "feminine" and "children." In this project of domesticating the national body for the market, the state counted on a cultural understanding of the domestic or private sphere as apolitical such that it could symbolically domesticate the vestiges of Chile's formerly vibrant political culture of activism. In this project, the civilian government functionaries have radically underestimated the legacies of state violence in structuring all sectors of Chilean society, especially the most intimate ones.

In August 2000, I attended a meeting of a chapter of the Chilean Human Rights Commission in northern Chile whose members included ex–political prisoners, families of the executed and the disappeared, and activists who have struggled for years to dislodge the military dictatorship and to pressure the civilian state for justice and reparations. A group of parents of young girls from the city's satellite shantytown had asked to speak to the commission about the refusal of government officials—the civilian administrators and militarized police officials—to fully investigate the disappearance of their daughters, seven adolescent girls. State officials had asserted that the girls had run off with their boyfriends and had probably ended up as prostitutes in the capital. Police officials even claimed to have evidence that several of the parents had abused their own daughters and had, in effect, driven them into a life of crime. As I listened to the parents' accounts, I was struck at how closely they paralleled the experiences of the families of the disappeared during the dictatorship, who had been similarly told by military and justice officials that their children were delinquents who had escaped to another country or that their husbands had run off with other women. Finally, in November 2001, the girls' bodies were discovered in a mass grave that symbolically replicated the infamous mass grave of political prisoners uncovered in the region in 1990, the first year of civilian rule. The serial killer, identified by a victim who managed to survive and escape, had killed a number of young women before killing this group of girls. Although the bodies of the earlier victims had been discovered, the cases had never been investigated properly because the dead were poor young women whose sexual honor could be questioned by incredulous police officials, a number of whom themselves had been implicated in the state violence of the dictatorship. Had these first murders been fully investigated as serious crimes, the young women in the mass grave might have lived.

Cold war military dictatorships mobilized metaphors of the body to articulate National Security Doctrine as the need to excise disease, in the form of cancerous subversives, from the national body—disease that festered not only in explicitly political public sectors, but even in domestic spaces. In this way state terror had penetrated all sectors of society. If Chile's transition from military to civilian rule followed and deepened a transition to a neoliberal, market-oriented political economy, the domestication of human rights through a state medical reparations project that feminized its patients was taken to its ultimate logic when the state as doctor switched the emphasis of the entire "mental health and violence" program from so-called political violence to domestic violence, using the idea of the apolitical domestic/family body to depoliticize the political/national body. Medicine, as a rational and technical intervention, and especially psychology, became a substitute for political action, specifically the pursuit of justice and broad reparations. This state policy ignored the ongoing legacies of state violence and the insights of Chile's long-active and vibrant feminist movement, which had long ago made the logical connection between authoritarian state structures and domestic structures. This failure on the part of civilian officials meant that not only did the state attempt to silence former activists such as the ex–political prisoners, but it also failed to recognize the political nature of violence against women. The failure to recognize has entailed a failure to act and, as in the cases of the murders of young women and the humiliation of ex–political prisoners, has perpetuated the violence.

NOTES

For comments, I thank Arturo Aldama, Jeanne Barker-Nunn, Deborah Cohen, Janise Hurtig, and Margaret Power; and for funding, the University of Michigan, the University of South Carolina, Fulbright, and the Wenner-Gren Foundation for Anthropological Research. This chapter is a revised version of material that appears in "Gendering the Space of Death: Memory, Democratization, and the Domestic," forthcoming.

1. Providing a historical context for my case, Benigno Trigo makes the compelling argument that over the course of the nineteenth and twentieth centuries, Latin American intellectuals argued that the region was constituted by a "normative state of crisis" both gendered and racialized and called for the governing of difference by that same class; "conversely, the object of government would be the bodies, populations, and collectivities identified both as different and as in crisis" (124–25).

2. Ariel Dorfman portrays the terrible intimacy between a woman survivor and her torturer, and, although rejecting vengeance, refuses to resolve conflicting memories of state violence in the paradigm of forgiveness.

3. By 2000, the Ministry of Health had begun to disarticulate the so-called political and domestic components of the program, due in large part to the increased demand for services by the "political" clients and their mobilization in a national federation of program beneficiaries.

4. On the infantilizing paradigm for late-modern citizenship, see Berlant; on market-citizenship in Chile, see Schild.

5. Some senators noted during the legislative debate that it was odd to penalize illegitimate children when key founders of the Chilean nation-state, especially Bernardo O'Higgins, were themselves illegitimate; see Montecino on the foundling in Chilean national identity.

6. Nineteenth-century liberal efforts to loosen strictures of gender-differentiated inheritance were not based on notions of greater equity, but rather on the need to relocate more resources to the realm of the market (Arrom).

REFERENCES

Arrom, Silvia. "Changes in Family Law in the Nineteenth Century: The Civil Codes of 1870 and 1884." *Journal of Family History* (fall 1985): 305–17.

Berlant, Lauren. "America, 'Fat,' the Fetus." In *Gendered Agents: Women and Institutional Knowledge,* edited by Paul A. Boyle and Silvestra Mariniello, 192–244. Durham, N.C.: Duke University Press, 1998.

Caro Hollander, Nancy. *Liberation Psychology.* New Brunswick, N.J.: Rutgers University Press, 1997.

Domínguez V., Rosario, et al. *Salud y derechos humanos: Una experiencia desde el sistema público de Chileno 1991–1993.* Santiago, Chile: Programa de Reparación y Atención Integral de Salud y Derechos Humanos, Ministerio de Salud, 1994.

Dorfman, Ariel. *Death and the Maiden.* New York: Penguin, 1991.

Feitlowitz, Marguerite. *A Lexicon of Terror: Argentina and the Legacies of Torture.* Oxford: Oxford University Press, 1998.

Franco, Jean. "Going Public: Reinhabiting the Private." In *Critical Passions,* edited by Mary Louise Pratt and Kathleen Newman, 48–65. Durham, N.C.: Duke University Press, 1999.

Frazier, Lessie Jo. "Forging Democracy and Locality." In *Gender's Place: Feminist Anthropologies of Latin America,* edited by Rosario Montoya, Janise Hurtig, and Lessie Jo Frazier. New York: Palgrave Press. Forthcoming.

———. "Memory and State Violence in Chile: A Historical Ethnography of Tarapacá, 1890–1995." Ph.D. dissertation, University of Michigan, 1998.

———. "'Subverted Memories': Countermourning as Political Action in Chile." In *Acts of Memory,* edited by Mieke Bal, Jonathan Crewe, and Leo Spitzer, 105–19. Hanover, N.H.: University of New England Press, 1999.

Frazier, Lessie Jo, and Joseph Scarpaci. "Mental Health and Human Rights: Landscapes of State Violence and the Struggle to Reclaim Community—A Case Study of Iquique, Chile." In *Putting Health into Place,* edited by Robin Kearn and Wil Gesler, 53–74. Syracuse N.Y.: Syracuse University Press, 1998.

———. "State Terror: Ideology, Protest, and the Gendering of Landscapes in the Southern Cone." *Progress in Human Geography* (winter 1992): 1–21.

Graziano, Frank. *Divine Violence: Spectacle, Psychosexuality, and Radical Christianity in the Argentine "Dirty War."* Boulder, Colo.: Westview, 1992.

Gregory, Steven, and Daniel Timerman. "Rituals of the Modern State: The Case of Torture in Argentina." *Dialectical Anthropology* 11 (1986): 63–72.

Hurtig, Janise. "Gender Lessons: Schooling and the Reproduction of Patriarchy in a Venezuelan Town." Ph.D. dissertation, University of Michigan, 1998.

Kirkwood, Julieta. *Feminarios.* Edited by Sonia Montecino. Santiago, Chile: Ediciones Documentales, 1987.

Lawyers Committee for International Human Rights [LCIHR]. *Violations of Human Rights in Argentina: 1976–1979.* Geneva: Report by the LCIHR to the United Nations Commission on Human Rights, 1979.

Loveman, Brian, and Thomas M. Davies Jr., eds. *The Politics of Antipolitics: The Military in Latin America.* Lincoln: University of Nebraska Press, 1989.

Matear, Ann. "'Desde la protesta a la propuesta': The Institutionalization of the Women's Movement in Chile." In *Gender Politics in Latin America: Debates in Theory and Practice,* edited by Elizabeth Dore, 84–100. New York: Monthly Review Press, 1997.

Ministerio de Salud. *Manual de apoyo técnico para las acciones de salud en violencia intrafamiliar.* Santiago, Chile: Publicaciones de Salud Mental, 1998.

Montecino, Sonia. *Madres y huachos.* Santiago, Chile: Cuarto Propio, 1991.

Moulian, Tomás. "A Time of Forgetting: The Myths of the Chilean Transition." *NACLA: Report on the Americas* 22, no. 2 (September–October 1998): 16–22.

Paley, Julia. *Marketing Democracy.* Berkeley: University of California Press, 2000.

Pratt, Mary Louise. "Overwriting Pinochet: Undoing the Culture of Fear in Chile."

In *The Places of History: Regionalism Revisited in Latin America,* edited by Doris Sommer, 21–33. Durham, N.C.: Duke University Press, 1999.

Schild, Verónica. "Neo-Liberalism's New Gendered Market Citizens: The 'Civilizing' Dimension of Social Programmes in Chile." *Citizenship Studies* 4, no. 3 (2000): 275–305.

Somers, Margaret R. "The Privatization of Citizenship: How to Unthink a Knowledge Culture." In *Beyond the Cultural Turn: New Directions in the Study of Society and Culture,* edited by Victoria E. Bonnell and Lynn Hunt, 121–61. Berkeley: University of California Press, 1999.

Trigo, Benigno. *Subjects of Crisis: Race and Gender as Disease in Latin America.* Hanover, N.H.: Wesleyan Press/University Press of New England, 2000.

Chapter 22

Las Super Madres de Latino America

Transforming Motherhood and Houseskirts by Challenging Violence in Juárez, México, Argentina, and El Salvador

CYNTHIA L. BEJARANO

This chapter explores the transformation of gendered citizenship into forms of resistance by Latina mothers of "disappeared" young women in Juárez, México, while comparatively describing this situation with activist "motherist" groups in Argentina and El Salvador. The mothers collectively acted to empower and enact their agency, which transferred these *madres* (mothers) from the private sphere of citizenship as mothers and house-wives to the very visible role of activist mothers in the public sphere. Activist mothers who have previously been researched and who are discussed throughout this chapter include the highly publicized Madres de la Plaza de Mayo in Argentina and the motherist group CoMadres in El Salvador.[1] Less, if anything, has been written on the mothers of female *maquiladora* workers whose daughters have been tortured and killed in Juárez, and who have organized to demand some acknowledgment of their daughters' deaths from local authorities.

My motivation for writing about Latina mother activism is twofold. First, I am a *fronteriza*, a woman raised on the U.S.–Mexican border near Juárez who is both directly and indirectly affected by this border violence as a young Latina/Chicana/Mexicana committed to social justice and change; second, I am concerned with the violent and oppressive social, cultural, and economic abuses and constraints imposed on the subaltern communities I come from, especially against Latina/Mexican women, young and old. It is for these reasons that I have engaged in this research and triangulated these three countries and motherist groups to give evidence of the violence taking place against women in Latin American countries, and more closely, on the U.S.–Mexican borderlands as a result of the transnational nature of this area and the obsession on both sides of the border with globalization, competition, and the quintessential border talk of NAFTA, *maquiladoras*, and similar destabilizing and nonsymmetrical border practices negatively affecting marginalized "brown people" on the border. As Arturo Aldama explains, "Market driven simulacrums celebrate the transnational movements of capitalist investment and development as the alchemy of globalization, and mask and ignore the further stratification, disempowerment, hyper-exploitation, and increasing abject poverty of subaltern communities, peoples (especially women and children), and bodies who produce harvest and assemble goods consumed on the global market" (56).

As a Chicana feminist, I see these communities as an extension of myself and wanted to expose the underbelly of "the new era of globalization and progress" veiled in the *maquiladora* industry, which is acted out— unintentionally or not—through the exploitation and killings of young brown women, while highlighting the "organic" leadership powers emanating from subaltern/colonial (shantytown) communities through the mothers of these disappeared young women. The racialized, sexualized, and gendered practices along the borderlands within and around the global economy and the production of *maquiladoras* prompted me to investigate these social and cultural diseases through the discourse of empowered Latina mothers.[2]

I will begin this discussion first by presenting what I describe as state and police violence practiced within these three countries against its citizens. I will then include a discussion of how mothers have penetrated the public sphere by transforming maternal citizenship into a mechanism of empowerment against state violence, then follow with a description of the mothers' resistance, politicization, and mobilization against the violence in Argentina, El Salvador, and México, through mother-focused organizations. I will close with a description of the successes of these mothers in transforming Latina motherhood through the appropriation of maternal images, ideologies, and seemingly nonsubversive icons to combat state control and violence.

STATE CONTROL, VIOLENCE, AND DISAPPEARANCE

Latin American countries are notorious for their military coups. They are carried out through campaigns of violence, terror, and control imposed on citizens believed to be subversive or merely disposable bodies.[3] More than 100,000 people have been killed in Argentina, El Salvador, and México during the last three decades, a majority of whom were young adults.[4] Approximately thirty thousand Argentineans were killed between 1976 and 1983 during the "dirty war"[5]; more than eighty thousand Salvadorans died and seven thousand more were disappeared during the U.S.-backed civil war between 1979 and 1992; and more than 200 young women have been killed from 1993 to the present in Juárez by faceless predators who have raped, tortured, and killed young women (see Taylor, *Disappearing Acts;* Stephen; and my interview with Judith Galarza). Unofficial numbers claim 270 murdered and 450 disappeared women since 1993. About 90 have similar traces of serial killings. Others have not been investigated. Numbers vary according to government or activist groups. The majority of these people were given the status of *desaparecido* (disappeared person), meaning they could not be physically found.[6]

Disappearances include the abduction and kidnapping of men, women, and children who are electrocuted with cattle prods, starved, and physically and mentally tortured. The list of torture methods goes on and on. Oftentimes, *desaparecidos* had their faces and bodies burned and destroyed, their skulls crushed, and their fingertips removed in order to make identification of the bodies virtually impossible (Carlson). The torturers—paramilitary and police officers, and government officials—hid their identities, often by blindfolding the people they kidnapped or by placing hoods over their heads, part of the psychological torture and attempt to disconnect the individual from the outside world that ensued after their abduction (Gordon; Carlson). The state accused students, teachers, professors, labor union organizers, and simply poor people of being dissidents, giving the state a "legitimate" reason to remove these people from their homes, families, and workplaces. This struggle against the state and the elite that maneuvered it took place in both Argentina and El Salvador; a different situation unfolded in Juárez, México.

In seven years, young women have fallen prey to a person or a group of people who have kidnapped them from the streets of Juárez; tortured, raped, and killed them; and buried them in shallow desert graves on the outskirts of the city limits. They were all roughly between the ages of 10 and their late 20s, and they were typically petite with dark skin and long, dark hair.[7] Their only supposed crime was vulnerability. They had no protection or accompaniment walking to and from work (usually from *maquiladoras*) or school.[8] Nonetheless, much like the *desaparecidos* from Argentina and El Salvador, they have often been portrayed as "deviants." They were accused of being women from the streets who were involved in prostitution and drug trafficking. In defense of the *maquiladoras*, Robert Urrea, president of AMAC (Association of Maquiladoras, A.C.), a *maquiladora* trade organization that represents American factories in Juárez, accusingly stated, "Where were these young ladies where they were last seen last? Were they drinking? Were they partying? Were they on a dark street? Or were they in front of their plant when they went home?" ("Silent Screams in Juárez," *20/20*, January 20, 1999). The blame is often placed on the young women: their scruples and integrity as respectful young ladies are questioned, reinforcing the ways in which women living outside of culturally prescribed roles are blamed for the violence they receive.

The *maquiladora* industry, however, remains untainted, their "popular" names preserved and protected, even though they continue to deplete the lives of these young women, pushing them to perform at superhuman capacities to produce goods for a gargantuan consumer society. Devon G. Peña, an activist and scholar researching worker struggles and resistance in

Juárez *maquiladoras*, interviewed an *obrera* (worker) who explained, "You ask if my life is a struggle. You would do better to ask why the struggle is my life" (6). This struggle to survive has traversed the walls of the *maquiladoras*, even penetrating the buses and vans that transport these young women to and from work.

Local officials and police have concluded that a group of men working for *maquiladoras* as bus drivers abducted, raped, and killed several of these young women. Some family members and advocates, however, believe that the local police and officials could be somehow conspiring in these atrocities as well or could be failing to answer the families' demands for further investigations. Guillermina Flores Gonzalez, the sister of one of the disappeared women and cofounder of Voces Sin Echo (Voices without Echo), explained,

> We got together with Laza de Servicios Humanos [Human Services] to protest the disappearances at the international bridge. However, nothing has been done. The authorities do not listen. We go to them and they don't throw us out because there are many of us, but then, they don't do anything to help us either. Everything remains the same; women continue disappearing. (Flores Gonzalez interview)

Several of the young women have been found with their faces and skulls crushed in an attempt to make identification difficult. Some were found with bite marks all over their bodies, particularly on their breasts, which were nearly bitten off or burned, among other things ("Silent Screams in Juárez," *20/20*, January 20, 1999; "La Ciudad de Muerte," *Aquí y Ahora con Theresa Rodriguez*, February 19, 1999). Zillah Eisenstein exclaims, "The physicality of the body becomes a horribly powerful resource for those who wish to conquer, violate, humiliate, and shame" (33).

All of the *desaparecidos*, whether they were from Argentina, El Salvador, or México, have one thing in common—they were horrifically killed and are no longer physically present to have their voices heard. Their countries were ruled by violent governments who kept their citizens in poverty and in conditions of oppression that guaranteed their submission. The haunting of their children's lives led the *madres* to challenge and question the actions of state governments and its soldiers, policemen, and collaborating citizens. With much anger and ammunition in the form of questions upon questions, the *madres* went to police stations and military offices inquiring about their children, as did the mothers in Juárez, who pleaded in front of police stations, wanting to know who killed their children. Jan Jindy Pettman asks,

> Does violence demonstrate the boundaries of belonging, as well as who "owns" the territory? This threat to security—which the State, charged with the physical protection of its citizens, seems so often unwilling or unable to

guarantee—clearly jeopardizes different people's enjoyment of citizen rights, to participation and to safety and security. (17)

Mothers walked the streets with posters and banners, hand in hand, demanding to know what had happened to their children. It was in this manner that they penetrated the public sphere and transformed prior gendered notions of citizenship into the evolution of maternal citizenship.

PENETRATING THE PUBLIC WHILE TRANSFORMING MATERNAL CITIZENSHIP

My life is over yet you've taken up my claim. I live not. Just the same you'll find in all you try that I live on my friends. My hand in yours held high when you shout so do I to make my dream come true. And for as long as you stand firm I will not die.
—*Aquí y Ahora con Theresa Rodríquez*, February 19, 1999

There are many different faces of motherhood. The face of the "good" mother is, as B. Wearing explains, "always available to her children, she spends time with them, guides, supports, encourages and corrects as well as love[s] and care[s] for them physically. . . . A 'good' mother is unselfish, she puts her children's needs before her own" (quoted in Kline, 119–20). Nevertheless, when Latina mothers speak and act from this position with the intentions of being a "good" mother, they are often insulted and criticized for their activities and politicization. In a loving and caring manner, they showed their support for their children by taking on their struggles against the states in Argentina and El Salvador with the hope of making political and economic changes in their countries, long after their children had disappeared. The mothers in Juárez also demonstrated their love by making local officials respond to their pleas for acknowledgment of their daughters' disappearances and their requests for investigations.

Unfortunately, these mothers were viewed as part of the problem, a "good" mother who had turned "bad," deviant mothers who raised subversive children against state control and ideologies. A. I. Griffith and D. E. Smith state, "The focus of the dominant ideology of motherhood, and the related expectation that individual mothers will take full responsibility for their children, means that when there is a problem with a child, the individual mother's mothering practices are subjected to critical scrutiny" (quoted in Kline, 124). Another common face that these mothers wore was that of *mater dolorosa*, the mother of sorrows (Ruddick; Taylor, "Making a Spectacle"). They wore pain and agony on their faces and bodies as a result of the loss of their children, which drew advocates to their cause and worldwide attention to them. The *mater dolorosas* "elicit the sympathies that mourning tends to elicit but in a context in which passive or sentimental witness becomes difficult. This dissonance is most politicized when the representatives of suffering are disobedient to their own state or social powers" (Ruddick, 216). These grieving mothers held their motherist group and supporters together through their loss and pain, igniting their strength to become the protectors of their children's memory.[9] "The role of mother was attractive, not because it was 'natural,' but because it was viable and practical. It offered the women a certain legitimacy and authority in a society that values mothers almost to the exclusion of all other women" (Taylor, "Making a Spectacle," 193). The images of good/bad mothers, protectors of life and truth, and sorrowful mothers who had their hearts in their hands and the specter of their children's voices in their own, are some of the many faces that characterize *las madres de los desaparecidos*. These images of motherhood became ways of questioning their place within the public sphere as mothers and gendered citizens.

Gender roles have traditionally been dictated by a patriarchal system of gendered oppression placed mostly on women: "Ideologies associated with 'domestic labor,' 'the family,' and the distinction between the 'private' and the 'public' are both racialized and gendered" (Bakan and Stasiulis, 40). Roles were defined and socially constructed for men and women, and the polity of life and action were not within the roles that women, especially mothers, could select from. Their traits as "good" mothers and protectors of their children went only so far as the parameters of playgrounds and the streets of their neighborhoods, but never against the ubiquitous state and its assassins. They are now, however, acting and engaging their maternal citizenship in the public sphere as a collective of activist mothers. "Women have fought, sometimes fiercely, under the banner of motherhood and in the name of protecting the 'female' domains of family, household, kindred, and community from a broad spectrum of political loyalties and ideologies" (Scheper-Hughes, 231). *Las madres* are now contesting the state in the name of maternal citizenship.

Although mothers were considered citizens before their activism in the political arena, they were "silent" citizens, expected to remain passive about larger political issues. "Women, like the poor of every country . . . are often invited to participate as ratifiers. However, their full participation, as representatives of the people, is not desired. The exclusion is deliberate" (Stiehm, 54). These women became masters of organizing and gaining publicity throughout the world with tactics that were unlike the displaced mother that was envisioned to be entering the threshold of the public sphere. *Las madres* cloaked themselves in the vernacular and genre of the political world. Sallie Westwood and Sarah Radcliffe state, "Women in Latin America have confronted repressive state machineries as mothers seeking missing children who have 'disappeared' . . . in doing so they lay claim to their part in the nation and to their rights as citizens using the

language of the state by reclaiming and thereby transforming it into a series of demands" (16). Their demands were presented through collectives
of mothers organizing under the auspices of motherist-based groups.

MOTHERIST GROUPS IN ARGENTINA,
EL SALVADOR, AND MÉXICO

State power and its assassins in Argentina, El Salvador, and México were
eventually placed in the spotlight and accused of the deaths of several
young visionary people, political and nonpolitical alike. The question commonly asked was, what role did the state have in securing and protecting
its people? In fact, as Judith Stiehm asked, " 'Who guards the Guardians?'
Some have suggested God or natural morality, but most modern political
thinkers have (with one explanation or another) opted for 'the community' whose members are said to enjoy some semblance of equal rights and
equal power" (62). *Las madres* became these guardians of the state, questioning the state and posing accusations against it through their very public
confrontations, beginning with the well-known Madres de la Plaza de Mayo
in Argentina.

Las Madres de la Plaza de Mayo organized in Argentina as a result of
the military coup that had its reign of terror from 1976 to 1983 and that
killed people for their political beliefs. The mothers of these "subversives,"
who could be kidnapped from their homes without a moment's notice,
would rush to police stations and local officials' offices, but would leave
with little or no information on their children's whereabouts. As a result,
the mothers began to organize, realizing that they were not alone but
rather a group of mothers confronting the same nightmare. Las Madres de
la Plaza de Mayo was organized by fourteen mothers who had their children, even grandchildren, disappeared, plucked from their beds in the
middle of the night and never seen again. The group has grown to several
hundred members and thousands of advocates. To this day, they can be
seen marching in the Plaza de Mayo in Buenos Aires every Thursday afternoon at 3:30 P.M. (Bouvard). Tragically, however, twelve mothers were disappeared, including the founder of Las Madres, Azucena de Vicenti
(Taylor, *Disappearing Acts*). Las Madres seemed to mobilize the maternal
citizenship of other Latina mothers and served as a model to urge other
mothers whose children had been killed to unite and make their states
culpable for the deaths of their children. One of these was El Salvador's
motherist group, CoMadres.[10]

The Committee of Mothers and Relatives of the Political Prisoners, Disappeared, and Assassinated in El Salvador "Monseñor Romero" (CoMadres) is an organization created under the auspice of the Archdiocese of
Monseñor Romero in 1977 by the mothers and wives of people who were
considered to be "guerillas" and dissidents in El Salvador during the civil

war between 1979 and 1992 (Stephen). CoMadres first began with a group of nine women who were searching the morgues, military barracks, jails, and the body dumps in 1975 for their children (Schirmer). The main difference between these *madres* and those from Argentina was that these women were mostly *campesinas* (peasant women; rural workers), as opposed to middle-class workers like the majority of mothers in Argentina (cf. Stephen). One aspect of the CoMadres, which includes a unique recruitment of mothers unlike the Madres de la Plaza de Mayo, is the inclusion of mothers of soldiers who have been forced to join the Salvadoran army. The army made routine forced recruitments of very young men. If they refused to join the army, they were called "guerillas" and assassinated (Schirmer). Young people were killed for their political views or because they were poor and unable to hide from the military.

As a group, the CoMadres seem to have had many more personal attacks from the military than did the Madres de la Plaza de Mayo, but both groups were brutally scrutinized and violated by their state governments. Today, there are 550 members, with 50 full-time CoMadres working in their offices (Schirmer). Their focus is beginning to concentrate on the violations of women, something that the groups in Juárez are vigorously investigating.

Voces Sin Echo is an organization founded by the mother of a slain *maquiladora* worker with the help of another mother and daughter whose daughter/sister was tortured, raped, and killed as she left her job at a *maquiladora* for home. The organization began in 1998 with eight other families whose daughters, sisters, and mothers were also killed. The second group is El Comité Independiente de Chihuaha Pro Defensa de Derechos Humanos (CICH; The Chihuahaun Independent Committee of the Defense for Human Rights), which is also in Juárez and was established in 1983. It is also part of a national and worldwide human rights organization.[11]

Like Voces Sin Echo, CICH is a nonprofit organization that has no political or religious ties with local political parties or churches. Both organizations' members come from diverse political and religious backgrounds, but share a poor, lower-class standing and lack social or political clout. The CICH voices grievances against all human rights violations in Juárez, including police brutality, inhumane conditions for the *obreras/os*, poor living conditions for people in *colonias* (shantytowns), indigenous racism and discrimination, and violence against women. They included on their agenda the defense of these disappeared young women and have made these killings their highest priority.

Voces Sin Echo solely addresses the disappearances and killings of the young women and demands that the state take a more aggressive stance in finding the murderers of these women. Although these two organizations are not motherist groups per se, *las madres* are the most visible and devoted members of these two organizations. Some of them are the mothers of the more than two hundred young women who have been killed within the past seven years. Voces Sin Echo is the most recently established of the groups I discuss. Before April 26, 1998, at 3:30 P.M., there had been no need to organize against local officials, the police, and the murderers of their children. This date marks the disappearance of Guillermina Gonzalez Flores's sister, Sagrario, who was disappeared, raped, tortured, killed, and then buried in the desert mesa approximately half a mile from her home in the Colonia de Anapra in Juárez.

The bodies were left in locations in the outskirts of Juárez. Many of these young women were *maquiladora* workers. In December 1999, a 13-year-old *maquiladora* worker who escaped with her life positively identified a *maquiladora* bus driver as one of the rapists and murderers of several *maquiladora* female workers.[12] Although women's bodies continue to be found, police have virtually ended their investigations.[13]

The mothers and other family members of the victims have called for a full-fledged war against the local officials and police of Juárez. When I asked Paula Flores Bonilla, mother of Sagrario Gonzalez Flores, and her daughter, Guillermina, if they were afraid of the police and local officials, Guillermina said, "Not really; they haven't scared us or done anything to us to keep us quiet." Paula quickly added, "The name of our organization says it all!", meaning that their voices are never heard and are without echo. The police fail to listen to their pleas for help.

Las madres are fighting a struggle infused with class oppression. The disappearances, however, remain blanketed as random acts of violence or as a group of mindless men who are doing the killing. Judith Galarza from CICH adamantly states,

> In Chiapas, it is a political struggle, and over here [Juárez], it seems like it is not political, but it is. It is the same thing with the police, the mayor, the politicians—they are criminals, and we have the same objectives with them like the struggles in Guerrero, Oaxaca, and Chiapas. This is a way to subdue the people, a way of scaring women from going out into the streets . . . a dirty war. . . . This did not begin in 1993, but it began in the industry of the *maquiladoras.* (interview with Galarza)

The families and mothers recognize the underlying political agenda and attack against the masses of poor people in Juárez by the state and are fighting back.

STRATEGIES OF MOBILIZATION AND "NON"-SUBVERSIVE ICONS

> You chose white because you refuse to mourn. Your scarves illuminate . . . your pañuelos carry the wisdom of the household, of

two hands becoming twelve . . . wherever the politicians and their
henchmen gather, you stand before them, your white scarves a
mirror before their averted faces.
                                        —Marguerite Guzman Bouvard

The ingenious abilities of the mothers of Argentina, El Salvador, and
México to think creatively about the strategies that they would take to enter
the public sphere enabled the mothers to transform their homes, neighborhoods, and other social spaces into physical locations of change, sym-
bolizing their motherist activism. These spaces located close to their homes
were not the only spaces that were utilized for their activities. The performance stage of the public sphere became a space—a social and political
space at that—that provided the opportunity for *las madres* of Argentina, El
Salvador, and Juárez to display their multiple motherly faces in defiance of
injustice. It became a forum in which the categorically female/private
sphere was identified and addressed.

Las Madres carved out this space for itself within the public sphere and
blurred the lines of gendered discourses of citizenship and gendered public politicization that dictated their private spaces for so long. Public spaces
and what was identified as an apolitical space, the home and the mother/
housewife, became the catalysts for social and political change and generated innovative thinking and powerful imageries of mothers as weapons
against the state. "Action by motherist groups is predicated upon overcoming the private/public divide as it impresses upon women's lives. Thus,
they have brought mothers in their domestic clothes to the center of the
public stage, symbolically protesting in the squares" (Westwood and Radcliffe, 19).

Public spaces were transformed into locations of resistance. The mothers' voices filled these spaces as they used every means possible to draw
attention to their cause. "Sites can thus become the centre for political
action by the 'simple' presence of bodies in different sites" (Westwood
and Radcliffe, 22). Nonetheless, violence almost always followed a march,
protest, sit-in, or rally. For example, in 1987, the Madres de la Plaza de
Mayo marched, protesting a Mass of Reconciliation for members of the
armed forces to be followed by a military parade. Consequently, they were
attacked with chains and clubs by security forces, and while demonstrating
at the Plaza weeks later, they were attacked by mounted police with night-
sticks (Bouvard). They remained, however, strong and fearless, even
though their lives were always in jeopardy. Hebe de Bonafini, the leader of
the mothers, explained "Fear is a prison without bars . . . it is the worst jail
because it doesn't let you think" (Bouvard, 249). As the mothers moved to
public spaces and displayed their "private selves" in these spaces, the police interpreted this move as acts of disobedience and attempted to stomp
out this display of defiance. The same situation was found in El Salvador.

After marches and protests, warnings were made to the CoMadres that were conspicuously displayed in public spaces by right-wing forces. Some of the CoMadres and their advocates were eventually disappeared from their homes and were captured, tortured, raped, and sometimes released. The number of membership of the CoMadres reached 700 at one point, and of this large number, approximately 48 CoMadres were captured, raped, and tortured, three of whom are still disappeared and five of whom were assassinated (Stephen). CoMadre Alicia elaborated on this situation, saying, "The death squads captured a compañera [friend], Maria Ophelia Lopez. She was detained, tortured and raped. She was tied down by her hands and feet and burned with cigarettes. Every time they showed her a photo of a different comadre and asked if she knew them, when she replied no, they would torture her" (Schirmer, 41).

The practice of raping *las madres* was common in both El Salvador and Argentina. It was a strategy regularly used in wars to taint the women who were considered deviant and disobedient. They had lost their status as "good" mothers and were viewed as the "subversive whore." "The body's power—its intimacy, its creativity against systems of power, its physical dignity and integrity—is also its vulnerability. We can feel our body as we can feel nothing else. . . . The vulnerability inside our strength is why rape is so brutalizing" (Eisenstein, 33). The act of raping *las madres* has yet to extend to the mothers in Juárez, but the violations against women's bodies were visibly displayed on their daughters' cadavers as they were found strangled, raped, tortured, and burned. And still the cause behind these blatant killings goes unexplained. *Las madres*, however, continue to demand justice.

Charles Bowden, an author and journalist who worked with photojournalists from Juárez, documented their pictures in his book *Juárez: The Laboratory of Our Future*. The book displays powerful images of the surplus of violence and poverty plaguing Juárez. One picture captures seven mothers standing in front of a local government office, holding a banner with their daughters' names on it; all were *maquiladora* workers. The banner reads, "Los Familiares de las Señoritas: Elizabeth Castro, Silvia E. Rivera, Olga A. Carrillo, Adriana Torres, Angelica Marques Demandamos Justicia" ("The families of the young ladies: Elizabeth Castro, Silvia E. Rivera, Olga A. Carrillo, Adriana Torres, Angelica Marques demand justice") (68).

The mothers involved in Voces Sin Echo and CICH march, protest, and make banners and signs with their daughters' names on them. They also conduct sweeps at least twice a month or more of the deserts for young women's bodies and have pressured the police to establish a small station in their headquarters where information may be collected on the disappearances. Judith Galarza mentioned that the pictures of the young women that were hung in the police walls, which were placed by their organization, are always torn off the walls when they return to the station the following day. They now take shifts to stand guard at the station (interview with Galarza).

The mothers of the murdered young women are now seen walking the streets of Juárez in protest, demanding answers. Although these mothers do not belong to a motherist group per se, they are the most visible protestors within human rights and women's organizations in México. Like the mothers in Argentina and El Salvador, the police, officials, and even the *maquiladora* industry in Juárez try to blame the mothers for having raised *muchachas de la calle* (girls from the streets). The blame is shifted from the state and its conditions of social and economic poverty to the mother. The women's mothers are told that their daughters had *una doble vida* (a double life) and were involved in drug trafficking or prostitution, that they frequented bars, or that they ran off with their boyfriends.[14] Once again, this is a common measure of control used by officials to deflect any responsibility from themselves for the victims' disappearances and deaths.[15]

The victims' families are poor, so their grievances are of no concern to the local officials and police, who simply place the blame on these mothers, on the disappeared girls themselves, or on other suspects. Juárez police want to find men they have already imprisoned to be culpable so they do not have to continue searching for the killer or killers. However, they have failed to serve the families and mothers, who remain convinced that people in power, perhaps the police themselves, are pulling the strings of these rapists and murderers, who are possibly only the foot soldiers of a larger, elitist organization that is killing young, beautiful Mexican women for a profit.[16]

Women stepped up their organizing activities and even held protests during the time of local elections, when candidates were making promises of bringing the murderers of their young daughters to justice in Juárez. Public demonstrations such as these were successful for the mothers in all three countries because they gained the exposure needed through the images of mourning and protective mothers and as *buscadoras* (searchers) of their children seeking public support. Voces Sin Echo even painted pink crosses on lightposts throughout downtown Juárez in remembrance of the slain girls (Figure 22.1). Adriana Candia explained that they did not receive permission per se to do this, but they were not stopped by officials from doing so. Lampposts with indelible black crosses now line the streets of Juárez. Consequently, these images of motherhood were performed through the unconventional means of using household and humble attire in their public pleas for justice.

Common materials found within their homes were politically revolutionized. The use of visual aids and home memoirs were removed from the sanctity of the home and displayed in public stages. "Women's bodies and the artifacts of attachment are brought into public spaces where they were

FIGURE 22.1.
Black crosses on pink
background painted on
lampposts throughout downtown, Juárez, México, by the
motherist group Voces Sin
Echo. *Photograph by the author.*

never meant to be" (Ruddick, 216). The trademark of Las Madres de la
Plaza de Mayo is the kerchiefs they wear around their heads with the names
of their children and the dates of their disappearances. Sarah Ruddick
states,

> As kerchiefs they wore diapers embroidered with the names of many disap-
> peared children. They walked with photographs of their own children
> around their necks. These photographs belonged in a common family
> room or bedroom. Tokens of childhood, they were meant to capture events
> and stages of lives of children meant to live. Now these records of life are
> suffused with terror and policies of death. (216)

Like the mothers in Argentina, the CoMadres also transcended the
image of motherhood and *la madre mater dolorosa* by wearing black dresses
that signified affliction and white scarves representing peace, an idea they
emulated from a motherist group in 1922 (Schirmer). The CoMadres also
used photos and banners of their loved ones with strong messages against
state-sponsored violence as did Las Madres in Argentina.

These local and household tools of activism became the signature forms of action of *las madres* throughout Latin America. The photographs of the mothers' disappeared children were exhibited around their necks, grasped in their hands, and on posters and newspapers viewed throughout the world. The eerie quality of seeing what once was but is no more haunted and tormented people; the images traveled home with those who viewed them. It was an instrumental vehicle in the mobilization of others in support of the mothers. Avery Gordon describes the photos as follows:

> The mothers transformed the docile portrait or, in the case of the photocopies, the disembodied mechanical reproduction of a bodily organ into a public punctum. The prickly detail that triggers the presence of the blind field, these photographs have specific reference: They have been here once. They should be here now. Where are they? And they personified the missing person, the figure around which the banal and the singular power of the state to repress converged. (109)

These photos captured the youthfulness and innocence of several of the young *desaparecidos* who were fighting for a "better" and more "just" Argentina and El Salvador. The photos also captured the beauty of young Mexican women from Juárez in their *quinceñera* dresses (worn for fifteenth-birthday celebrations, marking their entry into womanhood), or their school uniforms, posing with groups of friends, or even holding their own young children.

The mothers' humble dress attire, photos, and even candles have been doubly powerful strategies because they come from the inner sanctum of the home. When combined with the use of a kerchief worn by the mothers over their heads or a banner with the names and faces of their children, the effect is insurmountable. "Women sought in their protests to celebrate life in the face of death through the use of photos, candles and songs which insist that the collective memory cannot be censored" (Westwood and Radcliffe, 19).

This celebration of life was also exhibited through the production of altars. Home altars were extensions of the mother's devotion to the *desaparecidos* in order to keep their memories alive. Kay Turner explains women's uses of altars:

> A woman's personal altar evokes her particular—her intimate—relationship to the divine, human, and natural realms. There she assembles a highly condensed, symbolic model of connection by bringing together sacred images and ritual objects, pictures, mementos, natural materials, and decorative effects which represent different realms of meaning and experience—heaven and earth, family and deities, nature and culture, Self and Other. (27)

Although it is uncertain whether these mothers all paid homage to their children's memories through altars, it is apparent that personal belongings

FIGURE 22.2.
Altar to Sagrario Gonzalez
Flores in her home.
Photograph by the author.

and objects reflective of home altars were used during their public performance of resistance against the state (Figure 22.2).[17]

I was fortunate enough to view a home altar built for a disappeared
daughter by a grieving family in Juárez. In the Colonia de Anapra in Juárez,
Sagrario Gonzalez Flores's family has an altar placed in the corner of their
living room. A large 16- by 20-inch picture of Sagrario hangs in her family's
humble living room. A small altar in the corner of the room is placed in
memory of Sagrario. A pink, lacy wall plaque giving tribute to a daughter
hangs over the altar. Sitting on a small table covered by a handwoven lace
tablecloth (known as a *mantel*) are two crucifixes, a Valentine memento
and card, a stuffed animal of the cartoon character Tweety Bird, a lit white
candle, and artificial flowers—daisies, carnations, and roses—resting in two
vases, which cradle a framed picture of Sagrario. Their private and remote
home, located in a shantytown in the middle of the desert, was transformed
into a political arena when people all over the world witnessed the state of
trauma and horror experienced by this family through media accounts. A

mother and daughter changed the face of citizenship and space when they invited outsiders into their half-constructed cinder block home, where chickens wandered in and out of the front door as they pleased. The sacred altar to Sagrario was given life through Voces Sin Echo, the organization that Sagrario's sister and mother were involved in that transformed them into mother-and-daughter activists.

Las madres covered the walls of their homes with seemingly nonsubversive icons, and in essence became "living altars" to their children. "The active altar comprises a language of materials, a way of speaking through objects and a setting for actual communication. . . . As well as a place for effecting transformative communication, the altar is also a place where such communication becomes effective" (Turner, 38). As active, living altars, they transformed themselves into breathing representations of their children through the objects and icons that they took from their homes into the streets of their countries, and were a powerful reminder of the lives and people that their children were. Their memories were communicated to the world through their very bodies and icons that subverted the oppression and authority imposed by state governments. Elizabeth Grosz describes the body as "a writing surface on which messages can be inscribed" (in Eisenstein, 34).

These images of mothers as living altars were often conveyed via technology and were immortalized in the public eye through the media. Media outlets were vehicles through which the mothers in Argentina, El Salvador, and more recently Juárez received international support and exposure. According to Michael Gurevitch, Mark R. Levy, and Itzhak Roeh,

> It seems plausible to assume that the opportunity afforded to television viewers around the world to become witnesses to major events in far-away places, often "live," as these events unfold, is likely to have major shaping influences on the cognitive maps of the world that these viewers carry in their heads. (214)

It is ironic, yet noteworthy, how the presence of middle-aged and elderly women were represented via technology around the world, which helped to advance their goals of exposing the underbelly of state violence and control in their countries.[18]

The medium of television has in essence been viewed as an extension and "an apparatus of justice" (Karpin, 123). Videos and news segments immortalized these mothers through television and proved to be a productive and effective means of transporting mass information about the disappearances of thousands of people. As Isabel Karpin explains, the media mobilizes people to support *las madres:*

> TV both transmits daily experience and is a part of it. In doing so it works to blur the edges of the private and public worlds. The separation of these

>

two sectors through the ideology of patriarchy is systematically undermined by mass-communications technology. In this way we can read TV as a mode of resistance. (127)

Just as the image of the *mater dolorosa* was utilized by the Madres de la Plaza de Mayo and las CoMadres, so is the image of the mourning mother used in Juárez. The U.S. news show *20/20* dedicated a segment entitled "Silent Screams in Juárez" to the killings in Juárez, as did the Latino-based news show, *Aquí y Ahora con Theresa Rodriguez,* in a segment called "La Ciudad de Muerte," both of which highlighted the image of the *mater dolorosa* through Paula Flores Bonilla, Sagrario's mother, who was shown walking through the *campo santo* (cemetery), carrying flowers to her daughter's grave as she cried and threw herself over the simple cross marker.

On the *20/20* segment, Paula said, "They [police] didn't let me see my daughter. I only saw her in a plastic bag. That's why I still cannot accept that my daughter is dead. I never even saw her body." Commenting on her other daughters, she explained, "We have more daughters, and they work at the factories. I'm always worrying that they're in danger. I watch them leave, and I don't know if they will return." Irma Perez, another mother who was interviewed on *Aquí y Ahora con Theresa Rodriguez,* said that her daughter's bones were delivered to her in a bag and was told that they were unable to adequately test the bones of her daughter to guarantee her identity because the bones had badly deteriorated (Rodriquez 1999). Like many other mothers in Juárez, the police also told Irma that her daughter had probably run away from home with her boyfriend, that she was leading a double life, or both.

Worldwide media has also spoken to members of CICH such as Judith Galarza, the spokesperson for the group. Like Guillermina from Voces Sin Echo, Judith has spoken to several media outfits throughout the world from an attorney's office in Juárez. These groups are gaining exposure and momentum from the international media, which has increased the amount of attention the world has given to these killings.[19] It remains unclear how many other motherist groups or human rights organizations are in the Juárez area. These groups have been sought out by global technology, as were the Madres de la Plaza de Mayo and the CoMadres, who have received support throughout the world.

Las Madres in Argentina used another media outlet—newspapers. They further broke the code of silence about the *desaparecidos* by publishing a full-page ad in *La Prensa* (a popular Argentinean newspaper), "listing the names and political identification numbers of 237 'mothers of the disappeared.' The *madres* pitted their maternal authority against the military's abuses of power. They also created a newspaper simply entitled 'Las Madres de la Plaza de Mayo'" (Bouvard). The mothers received several death threats and had their offices ransacked and documents and awards destroyed (Bouvard; Carlson). Like the *madres* in Argentina, the CoMadres also received death threats after publishing information in newspapers about the state's atrocities and had their offices ransacked (Schirmer).

The mothers throughout the three countries have united—not only as the homemakers whose primary concern in life was the raising of their children, but also as the activist mothers who demand justice in their disappeared children's names. At the root of all this violence and the millions of deaths are poverty and the state's control of power, wealth, land, and natural resources, as well as the state's obsession with becoming an active member in the global economy. These young people and mothers are killed because the state does not receive any reprimands and because they are blinded by their desire for power and control over their citizens and by their fixation on global competitiveness—which materializes through civil wars, nation building, and promoting patriarchy and hypernationalist identities.

Latinas are expected to display their citizenship as mothers and wives, knowing and accepting that their place is within the home. When it came to their children, however, they invoked the qualities of "good/bad" mother, protector of life and truth and the *mater dolorosa*—the many different faces of motherhood they hid behind their houseskirts. The mothers threw off the gendered standards of citizenship that had been imposed on them and transformed their private homes, neighborhoods, and ascribed roles as mothers into motherist tools against state power and oppression by exposing their atrocities to the world. Their children's disappearances and untimely deaths shifted the gender dynamics and forms of citizenship exercised by these mothers into making them maternal citizens, protectors of their children's "good" names, and pursuers of justice. "Women who act as women in public spaces transform the passions of attachment and loss into political action, transform the woman of sorrow from icon to agent" (Ruddick, 217).

They developed new tools of resistance through objects, photos, and icons that accompanied them on their travels of mobilization and resistance and that became the most visible agents of justice and social change. They liberated themselves and their children by becoming living altars, demonstrating against violations and abuses of power by state governments and their assassins. In horror, the world watched through mass media technology the hardships they confronted while simultaneously remaining captivated by their strengths as activist mothers, as super-*madres*. "We are fighting for liberation, to live in freedom, and that is a revolutionary act. The day in which there will be no more hunger, that justice will be done, that the murderers will be in jail, then we will have accomplished a revolution. To transform a system is always revolutionary" (Bouvard, 195).

POSTSCRIPT

In summer 2001, Voces Sin Echo formally disbanded as a result of an assortment of conflicts, complications, and the lack of social support from Ciudad Juárez. At this time, there is no group specifically dedicated to investigating the deaths of more than two hundred fifty young women. Human rights and women's groups estimate the number of disappeared and murdered women at well over three hundred. On November 6, 2001, eight bodies were found in a central location in the city of Juárez, buried a hundred feet from one another. A week later, another body of a young woman was discovered in a separate location. The disappearances and violence against women seem to have no end. Theories continuously circulate regarding the agents of these atrocities—suspects include bus drivers, serial killers, and police—but there are no concrete answers to who is killing the women, only that young women's mutilated bodies are constantly being discovered.

I am a cofounder, along with Greg Bloom and an online border news service editor, of an advocacy group called Amigos de las Mujeres de Juárez, which is working to reunite other families to form an organization where Voces Sin Echo left off. Our group began in October 2001, and we have been working with eight families of the murdered women in Juárez.

NOTES

I extend my thanks and admiration to Arturo Aldama for his insight, mentorship, and persistence during the development and growth of this chapter. Also, thanks to Jolan Hsieh, my colleague and friend, who inserted the pictures in this text. Most importantly, I thank the families and activists in Juárez I spoke with. My sincerest *gracias* go to the many people who assisted me with this project with their sharing of personal experiences, hardships, and knowledge. *Un mil gracias* to Julian Cardona, photojournalist and activist, whose work is displayed in Charles Bowden's *Juárez: The Laboratory of Our Future* and who assisted me in my travels to Juárez to conduct interviews; Judith Galarza, organizer of El Comite Independiente de Chihuahua Pro Defense de Derechos Humanos in Juárez; Guillermina Gonzalez Flores and Paula Flores Bonilla, the sister and mother of Sagrario Gonzalez Flores, who helped to establish Voces Sin Echo; Ester Cano Chavez, activist and founder of the first women's shelter, Casa Amiga, in Juárez; Vicki Caraveo, human rights activist and leader in Juárez; Alicia Partnoy, *una desaparecida que tuvo aparicíon con vida* and an academic scholar, who engaged with me in a short but inspirational and informative conversation during a guest lecture at Arizona State University; to Santos, a Salvadoran *desaparecido* who shared his story of torture and whose life was spared only because a Salvadoran death squad threw his body in a dump, believing he was already dead; and finally, to *mis amigas queridas,* Adriana Candia, Isabel Velasquez, and Guadalupe de la Mora, three of seven authors of the book *El Silencio que la Voz de Todas Quiebran,* for their contributions and their *recuerdos* of the young *maquila-*

dora women who were killed. Special thanks to Adriana for driving me around Juárez and tolerating the harsh treatment of INS agents toward us.

1. In this essay, I do not mean to privilege one motherist group over another. However, the mothers in these three countries will offer a better understanding of Latina mother activism prompted by their children's disappearances. For more on other Latina motherist groups, see Alvarado. Alvarado speaks of a "Mother's Club" she joined sponsored by the Catholic Church to fight for land reform and the disavowal of the Church when the women appeared to become too "political." Alicia Partnoy's *You Can't Drown the Fire* includes short stories and poetry by mothers who lost their children to state violence and by other women forced into exile from their home countries. Mary Pardo's work on the Los Angeles motherist group— Mothers of East Los Angeles—offers still another understanding of grassroots politics among Latina mothers in the United States.

2. I conducted interviews in Juárez, México, with a photojournalist/activist covering the killing of these *maquiladora* workers in Juárez; human rights activists; founders of organizations that were established to help the families of the slain young women; the mother and daughter of a *maquiladora* worker who was raped and killed; and other writers/scholars/journalists who committed their time to researching these atrocities. I coupled these interviews and day trips to Juárez with a secondary analysis of readings on motherist groups in El Salvador and Argentina to offer a comparative overview of these forms of activism and resistance to better understand this phenomena plaguing Latin/a America. I also had conversations with two *desaparecidos* from Argentina and El Salvador who were kidnapped, imprisoned, and tortured.

3. One can understand that the globalized economy, with its strength and inception into the world in the late 1960s and early 1970s, is responsible for further debilitating thousands of people struggling for economic reform and social change in Argentina, El Salvador, and México. Alicia Partnoy, a *desaparecida* from Argentina, a human rights activist, and a professor in the United States, explains in the preface of *You Can't Drown the Fire,* "Desperate oligarchies and multinational corporations resorted to their local military to curtail the social transformations that jeopardized their interests" (13). Diana Taylor states, "The crisis [dirty war] resulted from Argentina's entry into the global economic market; thus it is very much a product of a broader agenda, indeed 'our' imaginary and 'our' global economic system" (*Disappearing Acts,* xi). For further discussion of globalized economic efforts on the border, see Peña; and Cravey.

4. This number does not include those who have been killed in other Latin American countries, or people being killed as a result of the current civil war in Chiapas, México, and other southern Mexican states (e.g., Oaxaca, Guerrero).

5. The concept of the "dirty war" was used to describe the undisclosed civil war being conducted by the Argentine army and right-wing groups against the poor and left-wing supporters of reform. It was meant by junta leaders of the army— generals in charge of the thousands of murders against Argentineans—to characterize Argentineans who disagreed with the military coup as being "dissidents" and conspiring against the state government. They were portrayed as subversives working to undermine the military coup in 1976. The dirty war was expected to thwart subversive tactics by common people (the poor, activists, students, and left-wing groups and innocent people) whom leaders of the military forces accused of instilling chaos, communist ideologies, and antinationalist sentiments in others (Bouvard). They were accused of wanting to strip the country of its "harmony and unity" (23). The "dirty war" was portrayed as a "holy war," a religious crusade to save the country of radical thought (23). The ultimate goal was to instill in all people, by

force and persuasion, the desire to uphold a conservative national identity and a patriarchal ideology.

In another sense, the term "dirty war" was also used in critiques of the military and police as a civil war acted out on innocent people. This term is used by people writing of the carnage that the state government, the leaders of the military coup, police, and death squads wreaked on the innocent people of Argentina. Human rights activists, writers, and victims' families of this dirty war have reclaimed the name to denounce the acts of violence from 1976 to 1983 and thereafter.

6. Grace Paley offers this definition of a *desaparecido*: "'The disappeared' refers to people who have been kidnapped by government security forces or death squads and whose whereabouts, and very survival, remain unknown to family members, friends or co-workers" (23).

7. Most of the young people disappeared in Argentina and El Salvador were also young, ranging from approximately 16 to 35 years of age (Gordon; Stephen).

8. *Maquiladoras* are offshore production factories found throughout the northern border region of México and the United States. These companies sprouted in northern México after the Border Industrialization Program in 1965, which provided incentives to U.S. corporations who were interested in relocating their plants on the border (Cravey, 98).

9. I use the term "motherist groups" to describe grassroots activist groups whose members are almost exclusively mothers. I first learned of this term in Sarah Ruddick's "Woman of Peace." I do not know, however, whether this was a term she coined.

10. Interestingly, this Spanish term is used between the mother and godmother of a child and is also a term of endearment between close female friends. The acronym may have also implied a sense of these mothers caring for one another and the shared loss of their children, as if they were all godmothers of one another's children.

11. Family members, fathers, sisters, and children also work in these organizations; however, they do not evoke the same dedication and drive as *las madres* do.

12. Official statistics on the number of women killed in Juárez remain ambiguous. Human rights organizations and women's organizations have reported numbers higher than those reported by local officials and the police. The official statistics of the missing women are laden with errors and contradictions. Police investigations failed to take the proper precautions to ensure the security of much of the evidence found at the crime scenes. According to *El Silencio que la Voz de Todas Quiebran,* from 1993 to 1998, at the very least, 137 women had been violently killed. These numbers include all women: *maquiladoras,* domestic abuse victims, prostitutes, drug traffickers, commercial workers, homemakers, students, and other women whose identities and occupations were not revealed or were not known. Only 62 percent of 137 victims were identified since 1988. Out of these 137, only 41 of the victims' occupations were identifiable. Sixteen worked in *maquiladoras* and two in a shoe shop; seven were *bares* (worked in bars), four were prostitutes, six were students, eight were homemakers, and five worked commercially. Many of these women were workers, students, and mothers. Many of the unidentified women could have been *maquiladora* worker because their occupation was not always identified. The killings continue without much investigation.

Seventy-four percent of women were wearing pants when their bodies were found, debunking the accusations from authorities and police that the women were dressed provocatively and "asked for trouble." Women's bodies continue to be found. The most recent body (as of summer 2000) was found July 8, 2000, in a canal near the México–New Mexico–Texas border. The victim was between 20 and

25 years old. A previous victim was found half-buried in a shallow grave in Juárez. She was 18 years old and was found wearing only her blouse. Police remain convinced that the murderers of these young women have been captured, but they are unable to offer an explanation for the continuing murders.

13. Several theories have circulated in the past seven years, ranging from a gang of men who kill women in retaliation for having higher rates of employment, to a sole serial killer who likes to witness young Mexican women raped or rapes them himself. Other theories, which some of these victims' families seem to give credence to, are that wealthy officials and the Juárez police are somehow involved. Judith Galarza states, "I don't believe in the perfect crime," implying that the police were not investigating these cases aggressively enough. Police say that they do not have enough evidence to follow through with these young women's cases. Because of this response from the police and local officials, the families feel that the representatives of the state are somehow involved. In this sense, they are being punished by the state for being poor and having to work in dangerous environments.

Having grown up on the borderlands near Juárez, Chihuahua, and El Paso, Texas, it is commonplace to hear of corrupt police in Juárez who prey on tourists, Juarenses (people from Juárez), and young people on both sides of the border for money. Stories of *mordidas* on the border are abundant. The word literally means "bites," but in this context, it refers to police asking for money from people who are in police custody, or simply intimidating people by threatening to take them to jail. Mexican police are known for having corrupt policing practices. Alfredo Quijano, editor of the Cuidad Juárez edition of the Monterrey daily newspaper, *El Norte*, explains, "Everyone in Juárez knows the police work for the drug traffickers and that they kidnap and kill people . . . but government authorities haven't done anything about it" (Molly Moore, "On the Border, Juárez Is a City of Contrasts," *Washington Post* foreign service, December 5, 1999, A41).

14. See my interviews with Galarza and Gonzalez Flores. For further references, see Debbie Nathan.

15. Debbie Nathan writes about "*la doble vida*" and "*las dos vías*" in "Work, Sex, and Danger in Ciudad Juárez." Police and even the mayor of Juárez made public statements such as, "Do you know where your daughter is tonight?", implying that their daughters were *muchachas de la calle* (women from the streets, or prostitutes) by night and factory workers by day. The phrase "*las dos vías*" is a Mexican euphemism describing a woman sexually penetrated both vaginally and anally (Nathan, 25). Nathan includes the case of Alma Chavira Farel, who was strangled and raped in 1993, through *las dos vías* (25). She makes a comparison between the two phrases and indicates that a relationship exists between the "sexualized violence against women" in Juárez (26) and the *maquiladora* development in the area, which has caused changes within the economic and social roles of Mexican women on the border.

16. In her interview with me, Judith Galarza states, "This is enough [police saying they cannot find the murderers], it is people, well, we don't know who they are and if they are rich or if they have some connection with the police, but what bothers us is that they start to investigate the families. For instance, in the case of a recent victim of a child, they [the police] wanted to blame the grandfather and stepfather, but they had been looking for the young girl also. They [the police] may know people involved in the killings, and now, they manipulate information and blame the families."

The mothers are continuing their fight for the truth and will persist in their accusations against the local officials and police, who are in essence the henchmen of the state. I think that it will be only a matter of time until the mothers in Juárez will begin receiving threats and subtle forms of violence or harassment, such as threatening letters or hang-up phone calls. I fear that the violence will come full circle across the border, as it did to other motherist groups in Latin America. On the other hand, this could very well have already happened. Judith Galarza mentioned during our interview that she has been arrested and thrown in jail several times in Juárez for her activism, but her organization and other activists maintain strong ties with the media, who report on their imprisonment. The publicity provides an avenue of release from jail.

17. Through photographs and documentaries I have seen on Las Madres de la Plaza de Mayo, CoMadres, and women whose daughters have disappeared in México, I have noted that photos, personal belongings, and candles are erected in the home in memory of the disappeared, providing a sacred space for the loved ones who are no longer with the family.

18. Although these strategies provided valuable and extensive exposure for *las madres* and their plight, they could also be used against them by the military and police in order to portray them as crazy and unstable, or as a form of inappropriate policing of their children (Gordon). For every mechanism of exposure, there are consequences to that mechanism: "We can only speculate what 'scratches' were left on the minds of viewers around the world" (Gurevitch et al., 214, citing Issaacs). *Las madres* may be perceived unflatteringly as *locas* (crazy), or as annoying the media with their personal stories: "People who witness suffering may respond with sympathy and help, but they may also turn away out of indifference, fear, or disgust, or worse, be strangely excited by the spectacle" (Ruddick, 216). Nevertheless, *las madres* in all three countries began a movement that encouraged other Latina motherist groups like theirs to take action against any state-based or non-state-based entities held accountable for any disappearances of people.

19. After pressure from international organizations, including the United States, state police in Juárez, along with three FBI profilers, are investigating the murders of 180 women; there seems to be a pattern for 143 of them ("FBI to Help Investigate Women's Murders in Juárez," *Las Cruces Sun News*, February 2, 1999, A4). This ended in 1999, and the FBI only concluded that there might be more than one serial killer. Presently (as of April 23, 2002), the public, families, and advocates have pleaded for the FBI to again become involved, but the Chihuahua state police and governor refuse their assistance.

REFERENCES

Aldama, Arturo. *Disrupting Savagism: Intersecting Chicana/o, Mexicana/o, and Native American Struggles for Representation.* Durham, N.C.: Duke University Press, 2001.
Alvarado, Elvia. *Don't Be Afraid Gringo: A Honduran Woman Speaks from the Heart: The Story of Elvia Alvarado.* 1987. Reprint, New York: Perennial Library, 1989.
Bakan, Abigail B., and Daiva Stasiulis. "Foreign Domestic Worker Policy in Canada and the Social Boundaries of Modern Citizenship." In *Not One of the Family: Foreign Domestic Workers in Canada*, 29–52. Toronto: University of Toronto Press, 1997.
Bouvard, Marguerite Guzman. *Revolutionizing Motherhood: The Mothers of the Plaza de Mayo.* Wilmington, Del.: Scholarly Resources, 1994.
Bowden, Charles. *Juárez: The Laboratory of Our Future.* New York: Aperture, 1998.

Candia, Adriana, Patricia Cabrera, Josefina Martinez, Isabel Velasquez, Rohey Benitez, Guadalupe de la Mora, and Ramona Ortiz. *El Silencio que la Voz de Todas Quiebran.* Chihuahua, México: Ediciones del AZAR A.C., 1999.

Carlson, Eric Stener. *I Remember Julia: Voices of the Disappeared.* Philadelphia: Temple University Press, 1996.

Cravey, Altha J. *Women and Work in Mexico's Maquiladoras.* Lanham, Md.: Rowman and Littlefield, 1998.

Eisenstein, Zillah. *Hatreds: Racialized and Sexualized Conflicts in the 21st Century.* New York: Routledge, 1996.

Flores Gonzalez, Guillermina. Interview with author, October 25, 1998, Juárez, Chihuahua, México.

Galarza, Judith. Interview with author, January 8, 1999, Juárez, Chihuahua, México.

Gordon, Avery. *Ghostly Matters: Haunting and the Sociological Imagination.* Minneapolis: University of Minnesota Press, 1997.

Gurevitch, Michael, Mark R. Levy, and Itzhak Roeh. "The Global Newsroom: Convergences and Diversities in the Globalization of Television News." In *Community and Citizenship: Journalism and the Public Sphere in the New Media Age,* edited by Peter Dahlgren and Colin Sparks, 195–216. New York: Routledge, 1991.

Karpin, Isabel. *Pop Justice: TV, Motherhood, and the Law.* New York: Oxford University Press, 1997.

Kline, Marlee. "Complicating the Ideology of Motherhood: Child Welfare Law and First Nation Women." In *Mothers in Law: Feminist Theory and the Legal Regulation of Motherhood,* edited by Martha A. Fineman and Isabel Karpin, 118–41. New York: Columbia University Press, 1995.

Nathan, Debbie. "Work, Sex, and Danger in Cuidad Juárez." *NACLA Report on the Americas: Contested Terrain—the U.S.–Mexico Border* 33, no. 3 (1999): 24–30.

Paley, Grace. *A Dream Compels Us: Voices of Salvadoran Women.* Boston, Mass.: South End Press, 1989.

Pardo, Mary. "Mexican American Women Grassroots Community Activists: Mothers of East Los Angeles." *Frontiers* 11, no. 10 (1990): 1–7.

Partnoy, Alicia. *You Can't Drown the Fire: Latin American Women Writing in Exile.* Pittsburgh: Cleis, 1988.

Peña, Devon G. *The Terror of the Machine: Technology, Work, Gender, and Ecology on the U.S.–Mexico Border.* Austin: Center for Mexican American Studies, University of Texas at Austin, 1997.

Pettman, Jan Jindy. "Second-Class Citizens? Nationalism, Identity and Difference in Australia." In *Gender, Politics and Citizenship in the 1990's,* edited by Barbara Sullivan and Gillian Whitehouse, 2–24. Sydney: University of New South Wales Press, 1996.

Rodriguez, Theresa. Interview with author, 1999.

Ruddick, Sarah. "'Woman of Peace': A Feminist Construction." In *The Women and the War Reader,* edited by Lois Ann Lorentzen and Jennifer Turpin, 213–26. New York: New York University Press, 1998.

Scheper-Hughes, Nancy. "Maternal Thinking and the Politics of War." In *The Women and the War Reader,* edited by Lois Ann Lorentzen and Jennifer Turpin, 227–33. New York: New York University Press, 1998.

Schirmer, Jennifer. "The Seeking of Truth and the Gendering of Consciousness: The CoMadres of El Salvador and the Conavigua Widows of Guatemala." In *Viva: Women and Popular Protest in Latin America,* edited by Sarah Radcliffe and Sallie Westwood, 30–64. New York: Routledge, 1993.

Stephen, Lynn. *Women and Social Movements in Latin American Power from Below.* Austin: University of Texas Press, 1997.

Stiehm, Judith. "Women and Citizenship: Mobilisation, Participation, Representation." In *Women, Power, and Political Systems,* edited by Margherita Rendel, 50–65. New York: St. Martin's Press, 1981.

Taylor, Diana. *Disappearing Acts: Spectacles of Gender and Nationalism in Argentina's "Dirty War."* Durham, N.C.: Duke University Press, 1997.

———. "Making a Spectacle: The Mothers of the Plaza de Mayo." In *The Politics of Motherhood: Activist Voices from Left to Right,* edited by Alexis Jetter, Annelise Orleck, and Diana Taylor, 182–97. Hanover, N.H.: University Press of New England, 1997.

Turner, Kay. *Beautiful Necessity: The Area and Meaning of Women's Altars.* New York: Thames and Hudson, 1999.

Westwood, Sallie, and Sarah Radcliffe. "Gender, Racism, and the Politics of Identities in Latin America." In *Viva: Women and Popular Protest in Latin America,* edited by Sarah Radcliffe and Sallie Westwood, 1–29. New York: Routledge, 1993.

CONTRIBUTORS

ARTURO J. ALDAMA is Associate Professor of Cultural and Literary Studies in the Department of Chicana/o Studies at Arizona State University. He is author of *Disrupting Savagism: Intersecting Chicana/o, Mexican Immigrant, and Native American Struggles for Representation* and coeditor, with Naomi Quiñonez, of *Decolonial Voices: Chicana and Chicano Cultural Studies in the 21st Century* (Indiana University Press).

ALFRED ARTEAGA is a poet and professor in the Department of Ethnic Studies at the University of California, Berkeley. His numerous publications include *Chicano Poetics: Heterotexts and Hybridities; An Other Tongue; Red;* and PEN award winner *House with the Blue Bed.*

ANA MARIELLA BACIGALUPO is Assistant Professor of Anthropology at State University of New York at Buffalo and San Simon Guggenheim Fellow at the Program of Latin American Studies at Princeton. She has written extensively on Mapuche shamans, religious beliefs, healing practices, and gender ideologies. Her most recent book is *La Voz del Kultrun en la Modernidad: Tradición y Cambio en la Terapéutica de Siete Machi Mapuche* (2001).

CYNTHIA L. BEJARANO is a native of southern New Mexico and the El Paso–Juárez border. She is Assistant Professor of Criminal Justice at New Mexico State University. Her publications and research interests focus on border violence and race, class, and gender issues and Latino youths' border identities in the Southwest.

DENNIS CHILDS is working on his doctorate in the Department of English at the University of California, Berkeley. His research interests include African American cultural studies in the nineteenth century and the present, radical prison literature, and Diaspora studies. His dissertation deals with how criminality is racialized in the U.S. context.

YVETTE FLORES-ORTIZ is an associate professor in the Chicana/o Studies Program at the University of California, Irvine. She has published considerably on Latina mental health issues and is the author of *Barriers to Perinatal Substance Abuse Services: Latina Outreach and Assessment Campaign Project, Research Findings and Strategic Report.*

DAVID WILLIAM FOSTER is Regents' Professor of Spanish, Humanities, and Women's Studies at Arizona State University. He is the author of more than forty academic books, and his research interests focus on urban culture in Latin America, with emphasis on issues of gender construction and sexual identity. He has written extensively on Argentine narrative and theater and has held teaching appointments in Argentina, Brazil, Chile, and Uruguay. His most recent publications include *Sexual Textualities: Essays on Queer/ing Latin American Writing* and *Buenos Aires: Perspectives on the City and Cultural Production.* He is also the editor of *Spanish Writers on Gay and Lesbian Themes: A Bio-Critical Sourcebook* and *Chicano/Latino Homoerotic Identities* and *Gender and Society in Contemporary Brazilian Cinema.*

LESSIE JO FRAZIER is Assistant Professor of History at the University of South Carolina, with an emphasis in Latin American Studies. She is the coeditor of the forthcoming *Gender's Place: Feminist Anthropologies of Latin America* and the author of the forthcoming *Salt in the Sand: Memory and Violence in the Postcolonial Nation-State,* as well as numerous articles on gender in Latin America.

ELIZABETH GROSZ is Julian Park Chair in Humanities at State University of New York at Buffalo and Visiting Professor at Harvard University. She is the author of numerous books on feminist theory, psychoanalysis, and philosophy. Her most recent is *Architecture from the Outside: Essays on Virtual and Real Space.*

MIKE HAYES is a lecturer in the School of Applied Communication, RMIT University. He teaches and conducts research in the area of Asian media, and he has published articles on aspects of colonialism in the Pacific. Before joining RMIT, Dr. Hayes lectured at Mahidol University and Kasetsart Univerity in Thailand in the areas of Human Rights and Australian Studies.

ANIKÓ IMRE received her Ph.D. from the Department of English at the University of Washington. Her publications are in Eastern European feminist film studies, and her research interests are in comparative feminist and postcolonial theories of representation in literature and film.

M. A. JAIMES GUERRERO is Associate Professor in the Women's Studies Department at San Francisco State University, California, where she also teaches American Indian Studies in the College of Ethnic Studies. She is also author, activist, novelist, and poet. Her best-known work is as the editor and contributor to the award-winning seminal text *The State of Native America* (1992). Jaimes Guerrero is also well published in academic journals in the arenas of both feminist/womanist and American Indian publications.

ELAINE H. KIM is Professor of Asian American Studies and Associate Dean of the Graduate Division at the University of California, Berkeley. She is the author of numerous books in Asian American literary, cultural, and visual studies. Her most recent works include *Fresh Talk/Daring Gazes: Issues in Asian American Visual Art; Dangerous Women: Gender and Korean Nationalism;* and *Making More Waves: New Writing by Asian American Women.*

JONATHAN MARKOVITZ is a lecturer in the Department of Sociology at the University of California, San Diego, where he received his Ph.D. in 1999. He is author of *Legacies of Lynching: Collective Memory, Metaphor, and Racial Formation* (forthcoming) and has published articles on race relations in the United States, collective memory, film, gender, and popular culture. His current research project involves an investigation of racially based self-defense claims in criminal trials.

WILLIAM ANTHONY NERICCIO (or Guillermo Nericcio García) is Associate Professor of English and Comparative Literature at San Diego State University, where he specializes in cultural studies, film theory, and Chicana/o literature. He is presently completing work on two books, one an edited collection of essays, *Bordered Sexualities: Bodies on the Verge of a Nation,* the other *Portraits and Signatures: An Alphabet of Archaeologically Tainted Hypotheses Concerning Fin de Siècle Latina/o Artifacts.*

LEILA NETI is a Ph.D. student in English with an emphasis in critical theory at the University of California, Irvine. Her research interests include postmodern British literature, with particular emphasis on South Asian immigrant writing; postcolonial studies; critical theory; and gender studies.

SUNITA PEACOCK is an assistant professor in the Department of English at Slippery Rock University. Her research and publication interests are in South Asian and British postcolonial and U.S. multicultural literary and feminist studies. Her doctoral dissertation focused on Indian gender identity formations in Anita Desai.

CATHERINE RAISSIGUIER teaches women's studies at the University of Cincinnati. Her research and intellectual interests include feminist theory, gender and immigration, women's education, and sexual politics. She is author of *Becoming Women/Becoming Workers: Identity Formation in a French High School* and is currently working on a book manuscript entitled *Gender, Migration, and the French Republic: The Case of the Sans-Papiers.*

HEIDI RIMKE is a doctoral student in the Department of Sociology and Anthropology at Carleton University, Ottawa, Canada. She has published in the areas of cultural studies, the history of psychiatry, and political sociology. Ms. Rimke is currently completing her dissertation on the social history of the doctrine of moral insanity.

YAMUNA SANGARASIVAM teaches in the Department of Sociology and Anthropology at Colgate University in Hamilton, New York. Her research interests include globalism, nationalism, and activism. She is interested in understanding the connections between the cultural politics of transnational social movements and the transformative experiences of Tamils coping with the dislocation of self and community in the context of the Tamil nationalist struggle in Sri Lanka. Her second research goal is guided by her interest in engaging her interdisciplinary training in musicology and dance to understand the creating of identity in relation to constructions of race, class, gender, and sexuality as these social categories intersect with the experiences of colonialism and violence.

MARGARITA SAONA is an assistant professor in the Department of Spanish and Portuguese at the University of Illinois in Chicago. Born in Lima, Peru, she received her Ph.D. in Latin American Literature at Columbia University in 1998. Her scholarly and creative writing publications are in contemporary Latin American literary and gender studies.

ROLANDO B. TOLENTINO is an associate professor at the Department of Film and Audiovisual Communication, University of the Philippines. He is author of *National/Transnational: Subject Formation and Media in and on the Philippines* and editor of *Geopolitics of the Visible: Essays on Philippine Film Cultures*. He is a member of the Congress of Teachers and Educators for Nationalism and Democracy and is an associate for fiction of the University of the Philippines Creative Writing Center.

SEL J. WAHNG is completing her doctorate in Performance Studies for the Tisch School of Arts at New York University. She has served as the managing editor and gallery coordinator for *GLQ: A Journal of Lesbian and Gay Studies*. Her research and publication interests include queer Asian Pacific American studies, women's studies, and film and performance studies.

INDEX

Page numbers for illustrations are in italics.